FALLOUT

FALLOUT

The Inside Story of America's Failure
to Disarm North Korea

JOEL S. WIT

Yale
UNIVERSITY PRESS

New Haven and London

Yale University Press books may be purchased in quantity
for educational, business, or promotional use. For information,
please email sales.press@yale.edu (U.S. office) or
sales@yaleup.co.uk (U.K. office).

Set in Janson type by Westchester Publishing Services.
Printed in the United States of America.

Library of Congress Control Number: 2025938553
ISBN 978-0-300-27877-4 (hardcover)

A catalogue record for this book is available
from the British Library.

Authorized Representative in the EU: Easy Access
System Europe, Mustamäe tee 50, 10621 Tallinn, Estonia,
gpsr.requests@easproject.com

10 9 8 7 6 5 4 3 2 1

MIX
Paper | Supporting
responsible forestry
FSC® C008955
FSC
www.fsc.org

For Madge

Contents

Preface

"The past is never dead. It's not even the past."

IN THE SPRING OF 1999, I was held hostage at a remote North Korean army base near the mountainous border with China. As the State Department official in charge of implementing a landmark deal reached by President Clinton to end North Korea's nuclear weapons program, I was leading a team inspecting a site that some American spy agencies believed was a secret illegal facility. The controversy had threatened to plunge the Korean Peninsula into crisis.[1]

North Korean soldiers armed with fixed bayonets—their faces pressed against the windows—surrounded the room. While I argued with the base commander, an army colonel who had been training for years to fight Americans, my team worried that they were about to be shot. It was understandable.

Months earlier, our spies had become suspicious that North Korea was building a secret underground facility to produce nuclear weapons at a place called Kumchang-ri. The mysterious site seemed to confirm the American intelligence community's skepticism about President Clinton's deal, which was based on the premise that peaceful talks could end North Korea's threatening weapons program. A front-page story in the *New York Times* in August 1998 suggesting Kumchang-ri was a hidden atomic bomb site ignited a political firestorm.[2] Weeks later, North Korea tested a missile that flew over Japan—a chilling reminder of the threat it posed to our allies, to our soldiers in the region, and to the United States.[3]

President Clinton turned to Dr. William Perry to defuse the mounting controversy.[4] Perry, a former secretary of defense, was respected by

Democrats, Republicans, and even the North Koreans. No matter what he concluded, Washington officials still had to see the site to clear up the mystery. Uncertainty would only fuel Clinton's opponents.

I was asked to lead the Kumchang-ri inspection team because of my experience working with the North Koreans and helping to negotiate the 1994 nuclear agreement. That deal ended a crisis that began in early 1993 when North Korea announced it would withdraw from the global treaty stopping the spread of nuclear weapons, the Nuclear Non-Proliferation Treaty. The confrontation escalated to the brink of a second Korean War by spring 1994 before a negotiated settlement succeeded that fall.

Called the Agreed Framework, the Clinton deal required North Korea to give up its decades-old nuclear weapons program. U.S. intelligence agencies believed North Korea could build up to one hundred bombs by the end of the decade—a stockpile that would have rivaled China's arsenal at the time.[5] In return, the energy-starved North Koreans would receive two multibillion-dollar nuclear power reactors and fuel oil to help modernize their struggling economy.

The 1994 agreement was attacked by critics at home as appeasement, but it was a win-win proposition for both countries. For the United States, the deal headed off Pyongyang's dangerous nuclear program and started to bring down the curtain on the Cold War in Northeast Asia. For North Korea, the deal held out the prospect of better ties with the United States and economic benefits. The recent collapse of the Soviet Union and China's new initiative to cozy up to its rival, South Korea, had left the North vulnerable.

Negotiations were tough, but nothing compared to the Rubik's Cube of implementation. Building two multibillion-dollar nuclear reactors in an underdeveloped country like North Korea, sending millions of dollars' worth of fuel oil, and dispatching Americans to help ship their bomb-making material out of the country was hard. Doing this work with our allies—South Korea and Japan—was harder still.

On top of that, Republicans in Congress wouldn't fund the agreement, unimpressed that President Clinton had stopped a threatening nuclear program and averted a second Korean War. We had to seek other resources. As the official in charge of implementation, I was one of many embarrassed diplomats who scurried around the world to find money, sometimes in the most unlikely places.

During one trip, for instance, I found myself in the living room of a Scottish castle, except the room wasn't in Scotland. It was in the oil-rich

Southeast Asian sultanate of Brunei. Evidently, the royal family had a soft spot for the Scots Guards regiment stationed there when the country was a British protectorate. Woody Allen's observation that "showing up is 80 percent of success" was right.[6] The sultan could care less about Korea, but he still contributed $400,000 to the cause, perhaps because of his good relations with the United States.

The most interesting part of my job was working with North Korean diplomats, bureaucrats, scientists, and technicians. Some apparatchiks steeped in authoritarian ideology couldn't stomach a new relationship with their archenemy. Many, however, were pragmatic; though proud of North Korea's achievements, they also believed an agreement with the United States would give them a promising path into the future. One elderly Soviet-trained engineer complained to me that South Korea had benefited from its partnership with the United States while his country was stuck with the Russians.

Since the cheating allegation threatened the survival of the Clinton accord, I understood the importance of the Kumchang-ri mission as well as the risks. We didn't want to repeat the harrowing experiences of UN inspectors sent to Iraq after the first Gulf War. The Iraqis had shot at them and even held them hostage. No one expected that to happen to our team, but it did.

My first challenge was recruiting the right people. I brought a U.S. Army lieutenant colonel on board who had verified arms control agreements with the Soviet Union. There was no shortage of volunteers for the rest of the team, especially analysts from the intelligence community anxious to get a firsthand look at the country they had studied for so long. However, they also threatened to create problems with the North Koreans, who were hypersensitive to anything that smacked of spying.

The moment our team hit the ground in Pyongyang, our escorts became suspicious. The State Department's standard operating procedure to conceal identities by issuing new diplomatic passports fell flat. "Why are all of the team's passports completely new except yours?" a smiling North Korean Foreign Ministry colleague asked me when we arrived. He wasn't fooled but said no more.

A second challenge was to avoid disputes that could lead to dangerous confrontations. I had negotiated an agreement with the Foreign Ministry at a guesthouse outside Pyongyang weeks before our team arrived. The deal laid out what our team would see, do, and record, as well as the kinds of equipment we could bring with us.

Nevertheless, once we started our inspection, I was dragged out of bed one night by our escorts, who had received an angry call from soldiers at Kumchang-ri accusing us of espionage. They suspected that a beeping noise coming from our locker at the site was a hidden transmitter sending information back to the United States. In fact, one of the batteries in the equipment had died. We replaced it the next day and the beeping stopped.

A third challenge was knowing what to look for. The suspicious site was underground and therefore revealed little to our spy satellites. Intelligence agencies had to analyze telltale signs like the volume of dirt piles next to excavated tunnels, which might indicate the size of the underground area.

For Pentagon analysts who believed the North Koreans were cheating, this information was key. Before our team left for Asia, they presented their best guess, unveiling a plastic replica of the mountain at Kumchang-ri. The briefer lifted a detachable peak to reveal a cavern complete with a nuclear reactor ready to produce bomb-making material. Impressive, to be sure, but a fantasy.

Once our group finished its preparations, we flew to Japan and then to Pyongyang aboard a U.S. Air Force cargo plane. We drove to our hotel in a rickety yellow school bus accompanied by a police escort with flashing red lights.

I was surprised by the display, since the North Koreans were allergic to even the hint of an inspection, which they saw as an infringement on their sovereignty. I remarked to an escort that this was anything but low profile. "Maybe we should put a sign on the bus that says this isn't an American inspection team," he responded. We both laughed.

Our team stayed in a tourist resort north of the Kumchang-ri site, spending the next three days riding in our yellow school bus back and forth over thirty kilometers of dirt back roads. The inspection site was a sprawling army base in a mountainous part of the country honeycombed with military bases and defense plants.

Our days were busy. We suited up in coveralls in a wooden building near the entrance to the underground passage, spent mornings moving through dimly lit caverns and narrow tunnels gathering information, and returned to headquarters for a lunch of Meals-Ready-to-Eat. We spelunked some more in the afternoons, then loaded back into the bus for the return journey to the resort.

The North Korean military was unhappy with Americans crawling all over their base. Each day, we were offloaded from our bus at a checkpoint manned by machine gun–toting soldiers to present our credentials while passing between German shepherd guard dogs. By the end of the inspection, the barking dogs were wagging their tails, happy to see our familiar faces. Once through the gates, we were greeted with the intimidating spectacle of hundreds of soldiers doing their morning exercises in unison.

Despite their unhappiness, the North Korean soldiers opened a kiosk near our headquarters, stocking it with Western soft drinks, snacks, and candy for sale. They evidently had a pragmatic streak hidden beneath the layers of training and decades of hostility.

Everything went well until our last day at the base. Just as our team was about to break for lunch, the North Koreans caught one of us—a desk-bound intelligence analyst—sketching ramshackle wooden barracks. It was a stupid mistake. We weren't allowed to examine anything that wasn't underground, and the United States didn't care about the barracks anyway. The inspection was cut short, and our team was hustled into a conference room.

An angry colonel, the base commander, berated us for hours until our Foreign Ministry escorts stepped in. We agreed that all the team's notebooks, which could have included more hidden violations placing us in even greater jeopardy, would be left behind in a secure equipment locker. It didn't matter. We had all the data we needed. Later, the North Korean government sent the U.S. government an invoice for storage, which we naturally refused to pay.

As our group left Kumchang-ri for the last time, a loudspeaker truck blaring anti-American propaganda followed our yellow school bus to the gate. I turned to one of our Foreign Ministry escorts and asked, "Are they going to follow us to our hotel?" It was thirty kilometers away. "Do you want them to?" he replied with a smile. The answer was obvious.

Our team concluded there was no hidden nuclear facility nor had there ever been one at Kumchang-ri.[7] The inspection was followed by Secretary Perry's visit to Pyongyang, a session between President Clinton and North Korea's second-in-command in the Oval Office, and an unprecedented meeting between Secretary of State Madeleine Albright and Kim Jong Il. Hopes for a Clinton-Kim summit ended with George W. Bush's election. Peacebuilding on the Korean Peninsula was over for the moment.

The inspection at Kumchang-ri was my last experience as a government official. After a break, I returned to the State Department in 2001. John Bolton, a Bush administration official and later Trump's national security advisor, was engaged in a campaign that would destroy the 1994 deal. Demoted because of my association with the agreement, I left government soon afterwards.

As the North Korean nuclear threat has grown to crisis proportions in the last two decades, I have stayed in touch with Pyongyang's government officials, meeting them regularly in Europe, Asia, and North Korea. We continued to exchange ideas on improving relations between our two countries. The results were relayed to the Bush, Obama, and Trump administrations.

Sadly, we have found no solution and the stakes have become much higher. In 2017, many Americans feared the United States was on the brink of a nuclear war as President Trump and the young North Korean dictator, Kim Jong Un, armed with a small arsenal of nuclear weapons and missiles, traded threats. Today, North Korea can inflict devastation on major American cities, killing hundreds of thousands and possibly millions of people in thirty minutes, a far cry from 1994 when it didn't even have a single nuclear weapon.

How did a small, isolated, backward country with a half-starved population become an existential threat to the United States? Some would argue it has been hell-bent on building nuclear weapons all along, a legacy of the Korean War and American nuclear threats to obliterate the North.

My experience, however, tells me otherwise. True, the North Koreans see those weapons as the ultimate guarantor of their survival. But they also have been willing to give them up in return for better relations with the United States despite decades of hostile relations between the two countries.

Several excellent books have chronicled this situation. *The Two Koreas: A Contemporary History*, by Don Oberdorfer, a *Washington Post* foreign correspondent, and Robert Carlin, our country's most experienced North Korea expert, remains the gold standard. My book *Going Critical: The First North Korean Nuclear Crisis*, written with Robert Gallucci and Dan Poneman, is the best firsthand account of the Clinton administration's confrontation with North Korea. *Meltdown: The Inside Story of the North Korean Nuclear Crisis*, by Mike Chinoy, a respected CNN correspondent, details how the Bush administration tried to recover from its fatal mistake of jettisoning the 1994 agreement.[8]

Simply put, these books describe American miscalculations, misunderstandings, and myths. Brilliant as those Republican and Democratic decision-makers and opinion shapers were, few U.S. officials had experience dealing with Asia and almost none with North Korea. Their preconceived notions about that country have consistently bedeviled their ability to formulate effective policies toward Pyongyang up to the present day. As William Faulkner once observed, "The past is not dead. It's not even past."[9]

Washington doesn't have a monopoly on blame. Pyongyang has had trouble switching gears from Cold War confrontation to accommodation with the United States, puzzling over whether to depend on its nuclear weapons for survival or to reach peace with a long-time enemy. As a small country struggling with the world's greatest power, North Korea has engaged in provocative behavior intended to convince Washington to take it seriously. But its behavior has only made a difficult situation worse.

Six American presidents have tried with little success to halt Pyongyang's march toward weapons of mass destruction (WMD). Two presidents, Barack Obama and Donald Trump, bear special responsibility since the greatest threat emerged during their time in office. Today, because of their failure, Kim Jong Un's nuclear-armed missiles can reach millions of Americans in thirty minutes.

Fallout is the inside story of how the United States, especially under those two presidents, tried and failed to stop North Korea from building nuclear-tipped missiles capable of destroying American cities. I have written this book in the hope that revealing the inside story of Washington's decades-old failed policy will serve as a cautionary tale for the future. Understanding that failure is also important since the current trajectory of the United States is a collision course with Pyongyang. Another Korean War might well involve the exchange of nuclear weapons.

One last point: Readers of this book may wonder why it says so little about decades of human rights violations in North Korea. Those violations have been on the minds of every U.S. government official I have known. Their priority, however, has been to grapple with the threat to our country's security. I agree with their conclusion that the path to dealing with North Korea's human rights violations begins with winding down the WMD confrontation and improving relations. That is why I focus on this central issue.

Fallout draws on my nearly thirty years of talking to North Koreans as well as with American and other government officials, and over three hundred interviews conducted in Washington, Beijing, and Seoul. Memoirs, books, the media, and official publications also form part of my research. Nevertheless, as the author, I accept responsibility for any errors of omission or commission.

Acknowledgments

THIS PROJECT WOULD NOT have been possible without the help of three friends. Warrant Lenhart, who passed away before I finished this manuscript, my oldest and dearest friend, always had an encouraging word, urging me to finish my work. Penelope Kim and Sharon Squassoni saw me through multiple drafts of the manuscript, and offered encouragement and helpful comments along the way. Jenny Town, my colleague for fifteen years, provided invaluable support as I juggled my work obligations with finishing this book. Natalia Slavney has been indispensable since day one, organizing my research and supervising the many interns who assisted me. Rosa DeBerry King assisted me during the arduous process of preparing the final draft of my manuscript.

While my interns are too numerous to name, I want to single out Joanne Lee, William Kim, Corie Wieland, Sam Crosby, and Madison Philips for special thanks. Henry Kan and Samantha Pitz, my assistants at Johns Hopkins University, also provided invaluable help. Finally, I would like to acknowledge the generous financial support provided by the Pacific Century Institute throughout this project.

FALLOUT

CHAPTER ONE

"How silly do you think we are?"

TEN DAYS AFTER DONALD JOHN TRUMP was elected the forty-fifth president of the United States, Choe Son Hui boarded a flight from Pyongyang to Beijing. She and her aides were on their way to Geneva to meet me and a group of former American government officials.

Choe was anything but a cardboard Communist bureaucrat. A member of North Korea's elite, she was rumored to be the child of a top official's extramarital affair, perhaps even Kim Il Sung himself. Choe's adoptive stepfather was a member of the dictator's inner circle and later became his son's prime minister. She regularly attended private ruling-family events and had known Kim Jong Un since he was a child.

Educated at home, and in Beijing, Vienna, and Malta, Choe was bright, combative, and self-assured. She was respected by Pyongyang's leg breakers and tough guys. Her stepfather's friends in the security services and his role in marshaling resources for North Korea's first nuclear test in 2006 probably helped. So did the fact that she reportedly drank whiskey and smoked like a man.

While North Korean women from elite families tended to become housewives or hostesses, Choe married, had a son, divorced, and embarked on a career in the Foreign Ministry. She began as an English interpreter—she was also fluent in Chinese and Russian—working with former president Jimmy Carter when he met Kim Il Sung in 1994, former president Bill

Clinton when he met Kim Jong Il in 2009, and Dennis Rodman when he met Kim Jong Un in 2014.

Choe was also as close as any North Korean could get to being an expert on the United States, with an intellectual and personal interest in American politics, society, and popular culture. She had participated in every negotiation with Washington over the past two decades. Her rise up the ranks was assured. She would later become North Korea's foreign minister.[1]

Despite all her credentials, Choe knew what it was like to be a woman in a man's world. Months before our November 2016 Geneva session, she proudly announced over dinner in Berlin that her two-woman team had just won the Foreign Ministry's table tennis tournament. They were the first female champions in history.[2]

I had known Choe since the 1990s when we interacted officially, and then I continued to meet with her in a series of unofficial dialogues. Her self-confidence and inflexible exterior masked a wicked sense of humor and surprising flexibility.[3]

We were all in Geneva for what was called a Track 2 meeting. These sessions with private experts were most useful when two governments weren't talking to each other. The theory was that informed citizens—free to speak their minds—were better at problem solving than handcuffed bureaucrats.[4] The most famous success was the Oslo Accords between Israel and the Palestinian Liberation Organization that began as unofficial talks brokered by a Norwegian scholar.[5]

Our Track 2 sessions allowed experts to explore how to end the nuclear standoff and exchange information on what was going on in their countries. Smart American administrations used these sessions to relay messages and to stage their own "chance encounters" with North Korean officials. Talks also served as a training ground for a Who's Who of North Koreans including Choe.

Success required following a recipe: Americans had to know how to talk to North Koreans—a skill acquired through experience—but also understand the intricacies of everything from nuclear weapons to economic sanctions, and report back to the government. North Koreans likewise needed experience with Americans, had to be involved in making policy, and had to feel secure enough to brainstorm. The final ingredient was secrecy. What happened in the talks stayed in the talks.

Switzerland was a perfect venue. Given its long history of neutrality, it was one of the four nations chosen to monitor the 1953 cease-fire ending the Korean War. Switzerland also had a history of discreetly educating the children of foreign leaders, including Kim Jong Il's sons and daughter. The 1994 Clinton nuclear deal had been negotiated in Geneva.

Choe came to town with three objectives. She wanted to learn more about President-elect Trump. She wanted to explore how to avoid a brewing confrontation with the United States after a year of missile tests and her country's largest-ever nuclear detonation. Most of all, Choe came prepared to extend an olive branch to Donald Trump.[6]

Like everyone else, the North Koreans had expected another Clinton presidency. They had followed Hillary Clinton's career, first as the wife of a president interested in ending the confrontation with Pyongyang, then as Senator Clinton. Choe had read and asked me about *It Takes a Village*, the senator's book on her vision for America's children, published soon after Clinton started her run for president in 2007. Choe was disappointed when I said I hadn't seen it.

The North Koreans, however, were wary of another President Clinton. As a presidential candidate, Hillary Clinton had adopted a politically expedient position condemning North Korea. Geneva provided an opportunity to learn just how tough since some of the American participants might turn up in her administration.

After her surprise defeat, the Foreign Ministry's experts stayed up all night at their headquarters off Pyongyang's Kim Il Sung Square. They had to explain to their leaders how Donald Trump had won the election—and what that meant for their country.

Explaining his victory was easy compared to explaining his foreign policy. Businessman Trump had said in 1999 he would "negotiate like crazy" with North Korea.[7] Candidate Trump welcomed a meeting with Kim Jong Un while chomping a McDonald's burger and fries on his jet in 2016; however, his pronouncements were confusingly laced with both disdain and admiration for the "28-year-old wack job" who was a "pretty smart cookie."[8]

If the North Korean Foreign Ministry hadn't already studied the New York real estate mogul's book, *The Art of the Deal*, it became required reading after he was elected. The North Koreans probably also had compiled every statement Trump made about their country and every other foreign policy issue facing the United States.

His election may have been the chance Kim Jong Un was waiting for. North Korean leaders had been hinting they might pivot away from their weapons of mass destruction (WMD) program to focus on economic development. That could happen only if talks with the United States helped reduce tensions. Trump's trash-talking Obama, whom they disliked, and bragging about his willingness to hold a hamburger summit, seemed an opportunity.

The North Koreans at the United Nations phoned me just before I left for Geneva to ask if I could bring a Trump advisor. It was too late to switch team members, and none of us knew who they were, anyway.

Our delegation met with Choe and four of her colleagues in a downtown business hotel across from the train station about a mile from Lake Geneva. She had been spotted by reporters staking out the Beijing airport. Journalists hovered near our hotel hoping to get a word with her, so we posted a guard near our meeting room to keep them at bay.

Typically, talks began with condemnations of the United States and settled into brainstorming. This time, Choe cut to the chase. What were Trump's views on China, Russia, South Korea, and, most of all, her country? How long would it take to come up with a policy? Her questions implied that North Korea might adopt a "wait and see" attitude. The door might squeak open to restart official talks.

Choe's attempt to glean inside information from us was predictable, but we were just as in the dark as she was. Still, our group emphasized that the atmosphere in Washington was very bad after a year of North Korean nuclear tests and a raft of missile launches. Donald Trump was an "empty vessel," so we urged her to give him breathing room to figure out his policy.

Transitions between American presidents had always been tricky. North Korea exercised restraint when President Bush took over in 2001, hoping he would continue Bill Clinton's engagement policy. But he didn't. When President Obama took over from Bush in 2009, a North Korean rocket launch and nuclear test—meant to demonstrate strength after a weakened Kim Jong Il had had a stroke the previous summer—brought diplomacy to a halt. We wanted to avoid a repeat performance.

As always, Choe's irrepressible personality was on display. During a coffee break, she offered advice on how to deal with her country. "If I were an American, I would open a McDonald's in Pyongyang to expose the young people to American culture," she suggested.

On the second day, Choe extended her olive branch to President-elect Trump. North Korea wanted to reopen official contacts with the United States. They had been severed the previous summer after the Obama administration sanctioned Kim Jong Un for violating his people's human rights.

However, Choe cautioned, "Don't insist on preconditions to start negotiations." For much of Obama's second term, the North Koreans had had
to show they were serious about giving up their bomb-building program,
a process called denuclearization, before talks even began. But they refused,
fearing that any concessions would be seen as a sign of weakness. While
the White House eventually dropped the notion, the North Koreans suspected Trump might reinstate it.

She smiled and said, "We will not run out of the room if denuclearization comes up." Pyongyang had publicly reaffirmed that it was willing to
give up its arsenal. Turning the corner away from the dismal relationship,
however, would require careful choreography.

Choe warned that a glide path back to diplomacy would be upset by a
military exercise planned by the United States and South Korea in early
2017. The North Koreans had always been angered about what they saw
as threatening drills. They still felt that way, especially since the previous
year's exercise practiced how to kill Kim Jong Un.

"How silly do you think we are?" Choe admonished us. She suspected
the exercise was designed by South Korea to provoke a war. North Korea's
response would be "very tough," Choe warned. We understood she meant
more missile tests or another nuclear blast, triggering an escalation of tensions and scuttling any chance for renewed talks. What happened next
was on Donald Trump.

A week before we met in Geneva, Barack Hussein Obama Jr. sat down
with President-elect Trump thousands of miles away in the Oval Office.
No one had foreseen Trump's victory, or that his staff would be completely
unprepared for the handoff. Michael Flynn, the president-elect's designated
national security advisor, didn't meet Susan Rice, his counterpart under
Obama, until a month after the election.[9]

When Rice and Flynn did meet, she singled out Pyongyang as a serious threat to the United States. But the former general hadn't given much
thought to North Korea beyond fantasizing that Kim Jong Un was part of
a "global alliance of jihadis, communists and garden-variety tyrants." He
was more interested in wiping out ISIS—the Middle East terrorist group—
and fighting an economic war with China.[10]

Kathleen "K. T." McFarland, a Republican foreign policy hand slated
to be Flynn's deputy, did understand that North Korea could confront the
new administration with a "defining national security crisis" before most
of her colleagues "knew where their offices were or how to turn on their
computers."[11] Nonetheless, Trump's disorganized team, overwhelmed by

the flood of problems it would face, turned down a White House offer to think through how it might respond in a crisis.[12]

Once Trump was elected, President Obama personally took on the job of making sure he understood that North Korea should be his top priority. Obama had mastered the ins and outs of the danger. After one rambling, disjointed Situation Room session, the president sifted the important points out of a confusing conversation, earning him the nickname "the note-taker" from his amazed staff.[13]

Obama knew he would have to hammer his point home. Unlike Hillary Clinton, Trump wasn't a seasoned foreign policy hand. He had a short attention span, didn't know that Korea had been divided into two countries, and wasn't interested in detail. The president-elect had to understand that Pyongyang's nuclear weapons could devastate American cities during his watch.

Most observers expected the Oval Office meeting to be a disaster. There was bad blood between the two men. Moreover, as a *New York Times* columnist wrote, "Obama is everything that Trump is not: intellectual, articulate, adroit, contemplative and cool. He also happens to be a Black man."[14]

Still, the ninety-minute session appeared amicable although Trump was Trump. Aside from the president-elect fixating on how he and Obama could draw large crowds while Hillary couldn't, Trump seemed open to preserving much of what Obama had done. But once in office, the new president did all he could to roll back everything his predecessor had accomplished.[15]

Obama was perhaps too successful in warning Trump that Kim Jong Un was about to cross a technological Rubicon. His nuclear-tipped missiles would soon be able to reach American cities.

He often told his advisors, in fact, that the danger was so serious a future president might have to attack North Korea first if it threatened the United States with nuclear annihilation. Obama had ordered the Pentagon to figure out how to destroy all of Pyongyang's missiles in preparation for that day, but its plan still fell short of achieving his objective.[16]

The session ended on a high note. Despite Trump's verbal bobbing and weaving, President Obama briefed reporters that they had had "an excellent conversation."[17] The two men were all smiles when their chat ended, but the hunched-over Trump sounded somber and avoided eye contact. He seemed "humbled," "a little dazed," and "a little freaked out," according to one observer.[18]

President Barack Obama meets with President-elect Donald Trump
in the Oval Office of the White House, November 10, 2016.
Official White House photo by Pete Souza.

Obama's warning about North Korea reverberated in statement after statement by Donald Trump over the next four years. His claim that the "Obama-Biden policy" had left him with a mess was true. The president had focused on other foreign challenges, only realizing too late that a dark horse, North Korea, had come stealthily from behind and crossed the finish line first.[19]

Trump falsely claimed Obama was about to start a war with North Korea. However, the president had done what any responsible leader would do when the threat to American cities emerged: he ordered the Pentagon to devise a plan that would wipe out Kim's weapons before he could launch them.[20] Obama wasn't about to attack North Korea—he just wanted his successor to be prepared.[21]

Moreover, Obama wasn't the first president to mull over a first strike. In 1994, Bill Clinton had considered destroying a reactor before it could produce material for Pyongyang's first nuclear weapon.[22] For Obama, however, the stakes were much higher, since North Korea's nuclear arsenal now could devastate South Korea, Japan, and American cities.

Trump's claim that Obama had tried but failed to meet Kim Jong Un was "horseshit," Susan Rice recalled. It turned out that Obama's 2008 campaign promise to reach out to rogue state leaders didn't apply to North Korea.[23] The president came to view North Korea as a crime family, not a country. A summit with the family's boss was out of the question.[24]

Obama's Oval Office warning had an effect. Trump vented about North Korea two weeks later during a short phone call with Tsai Ing-wen. The first Taiwanese leader to speak directly to a president-elect since 1979, she had other pressing topics on her mind. One expert later remarked, "What Tsai Ing-wen knows about North Korea could fill a thimble."[25]

Kim Jong Un's appearance for his annual New Year's address only fanned Trump's flames. As images of factories, farms, athletes, and missile tests flashed on a video screen, the young dictator claimed that North Korea had "entered the final stage of preparation for the test launch of intercontinental ballistic missiles."[26]

Donald Trump tweeted "It won't happen" forty-three hours later.[27] The president-elect requested a secret intelligence briefing.[28] K. T. Mc-Farland asked a senior Pentagon official, "What are we going to do about it?" He filled her in on the plan to attack North Korea.[29]

Trump vented again days after his January 20 inauguration—this time in his first meeting with a foreign leader. The last thing on British prime minister Theresa May's mind was North Korea.[30]

Trump was obsessed. He asked his advisors the same question over and over again: How did past presidents let a country that still considered itself at war with the United States develop nuclear-armed missiles able to annihilate American cities?[31]

CHAPTER TWO

"The world around us
is changing."

W ILLIAM "BILL" TAYLOR HAD a visitor. It was June 1992, 7:00 A.M. on a Sunday. The American dressed quickly and walked to the front door of his Pyongyang villa.

"Dr. Taylor, I have some bad news. The meetings scheduled for you to talk to our high-level officials have been cancelled," announced a North Korean outfitted in the uniform of the Central Committee.

Then he smiled and continued, "But I have some good news. The Great Leader will meet you this morning."[1]

Taylor was an unlikely guest, with a history of staunch anti-Communism and a distinguished Army career. He had adopted a new mission, however, of avoiding confrontation with North Korea.

Taylor wasn't the first American to meet Kim Il Sung, revered in North Korea as the Great Leader, but reviled in the West as the dictator who had unleashed the bloody Korean War from 1950 to 1953. Kim's hostile relationship with the United States, spanning four decades and eight American presidents, had been punctuated by periodic acts of violence, especially against South Koreans, on and off the peninsula.

No American had been allowed into the country, let alone to meet the Great Leader, for years. That changed in 1972 on Kim's sixtieth birthday when three American journalists were granted interviews with him.

Wearing an "immaculate gray suit," he was described by one as a "big, impressive man with a mobile face and a quick chuckle."[2]

Kim's charm offensive was intended to encourage the Americans to remove troops protecting their South Korean ally as the United States struggled in Vietnam. North Korea even took out full-page ads in the *New York Times*, displaying them in Pyongyang as a sign of American respect for the Great Leader.

It was 1980 before Kim met another American, Stephen Solarz, a congressperson from Brooklyn. Solarz remembered that Kim droned on for hours since "he wasn't used to being interrupted or being asked questions." Avuncular and smiling, he was nonetheless an absolute dictator. Whenever Kim queried one of his ministers, they stood up, snapped to attention, and barked an answer.[3]

Under Republican presidents, the United States began to drop barriers when President Reagan relaxed restrictions on contacts and allowed humanitarian assistance. President Bush followed his lead. Citizens from both Koreas even enjoyed a July Fourth barbeque at the Palo Alto, California, home of Dr. William Perry, later President Clinton's secretary of defense.[4]

In fact, Republicans were just the Americans the North Koreans wanted to meet after George H. W. Bush was elected president. Before Taylor arrived in Pyongyang, the Great Leader had received a Republican lobbying group that included Douglas MacArthur II, President Eisenhower's ambassador to Japan and the nephew of the general who had devastated Kim's country during the Korean War.[5]

Despite the loosening of some restrictions, American spy satellites spotted a just-completed nuclear reactor and a plant under construction spanning two football fields—both intended to produce bomb-making material—at a facility near the city of Yongbyon.

Kim Il Sung told Solarz, who had returned to Pyongyang in 1991, that "we do not have and will not produce nuclear weapons." When the skeptical U.S. representative replied, "The proof is in the pudding," the Great Leader offered to open his facilities to international inspections.[6]

That same year, Pyongyang responded positively to President Bush's announcement that the United States would withdraw nuclear weapons around the world, including one hundred in South Korea. The two Koreas signed a nonaggression pact and pledged not to produce nuclear material for bombs. In early January 1992, after Bush offered to cancel an upcoming military exercise with South Korea, American officials were set to meet the North Koreans for the first time in decades.

The talks, held on the top floor of the U.S. Mission to the United Nations (USUN), proved uninspiring, although it was significant that they took place at all. Led by Arnold "Arnie" Kantor, the third-ranking State Department official, who quipped he wasn't even on his own short list for his job, the American script was based on the "good doggie, bad doggie principle." North Korea could enjoy a better relationship with the United States only after it stopped building nuclear weapons.[7]

Tall, charming, and polished, Kim Yong Sun, the North Korean negotiator, was a hardliner who had once been sent to work in a coal mine for teaching colleagues how to dance. He arrived in a limousine that reminded one American of a high school prom ride.[8]

Aside from suggesting the United States and North Korea ally against Japan, Kim's script was also uninspiring except for one nugget. U.S. troops could remain on the peninsula even if the two Koreas were reunified. The offer was a surprise since North Korea had been trying to end the alliance for years.[9]

Bill Taylor's June 1992 meeting with Kim Il Sung took place a few months later at the Kumsusan Palace of the Sun, a 115,000-square-foot building surrounded by a moat and located in northeast Pyongyang. Taylor and a colleague were joined by the portly Great Leader soon after they arrived.[10]

Like any eighty-year-old, Kim had good and bad days. That day, he moved vigorously and firmly shook his visitors' hands. His mind was crystal clear, his memory and speech precise, his reasoning logical, and his health apparently excellent. Kim admitted, however, that he had started to hand off responsibilities to his son, whom he saw often and talked to every day.[11]

Sitting with his visitors around an eight-foot-long table, Kim proposed, "We should have high-level US-DPRK [Democratic People's Republic of Korea] talks," hinting he wanted to meet top American officials. That was the only way to achieve denuclearization of the Korean Peninsula. The issues involved were too complicated for bureaucrats to solve.[12]

"The world around us is changing," the aging dictator lamented. The Soviet Bloc's collapse had created hardships for his country. He was proud of what North Korea had achieved but admitted, "We have a lot to do. We need help." The Great Leader quickly added, however, "We never want assistance, we will be on equal footing."[13]

Kim Il Sung knew his country had to change. He was faced with a troubled economy and mounting isolation. Not only had the Soviet Bloc collapsed; China, his other major ally, was reaching out to his rival, an economically dynamic South Korea.

Kim's thinking reflected a new goal for diplomacy with the United States that had recently been formulated by his Foreign Ministry. The idea was to compel Washington to abandon its "hostile policy" to offset the loss of his nearby communist patrons. The only way to achieve his objective was to place North Korea's nuclear weapons program on the diplomatic auction block.[14]

Hours of back-and-forth with Taylor ended when the smiling Great Leader returned to his main message: "We do need high-level talks between the United States, North Korea and South Korea to discuss the differences between our country and South Korea because some relate to U.S. policy."[15]

Over a lunch of soup and crab meat, Kim regaled the two Americans and their families—especially Taylor's young son—with tales of wild boar hunts. "You do not want to get close to a wild boar," Kim advised them. His biggest kill weighed 568 pounds. When lunch was over, the dictator shook hands with the ladies and kissed and hugged the boy.[16]

Bill Taylor didn't know it, but his meeting with Kim Il Sung took place on the eve of the first of three hinge points in history, all of which marked North Korea's path to building a nuclear arsenal that led straight to Donald Trump's doorstep.

An "extremely peculiar nation"

The United States and North Korea reached the first hinge point after the promising start in 1992 morphed into a crisis in 1993. International inspections at Yongbyon indicated that the North might have secretly produced more material for a bomb than everyone expected. When the inspectors demanded Pyongyang come clean, North Korea became the first country ever to announce its intention to withdraw from the global treaty banning nuclear weapons.

The "extremely peculiar nation"—a phrase coined by a Japanese admiral—had taken two completely contradictory steps. However, North Korea likely didn't want to be hamstrung by sanctions and inspections like Saddam Hussein's Iraq after the 1990 Gulf War.[17] Clearing the political chessboard could open the way for North Korea to arm itself with the ultimate weapon, to strengthen its bargaining position, or both.[18] Still, Kim

Il Sung's son was condemned as "the closest thing to Dr. Strangelove the nuclear age has seen."[19]

The threat to withdraw from the treaty initiated a roller-coaster ride lasting eighteen months that brought the two countries to the brink of war.[20]

Talks convened once more at the USUN in June 1993 just before Pyongyang's withdrawal took effect. Robert Gallucci, a twenty-year State Department veteran who had spent his career trying to solve seemingly unsolvable nuclear challenges, led the American team. Kang Sok Ju, a top advisor to the Great Leader, led the North's delegation. Known for his coarseness and bluster, he once exclaimed, "Do you think we can take off our pants?" after rejecting inspections.[21]

The meeting was strange for both delegations. When the North Koreans were greeted at John F. Kennedy Airport by security officers with guns, Kang asked, "Are we under arrest?"[22] Americans couldn't help thinking they were negotiating with cult members, as they sat across from grown men wearing lapel pins featuring Kim Il Sung's face.

Tough talk gave way to a last-minute deal. The North Koreans suspended their withdrawal after the two countries agreed to a statement that mirrored bromides in the UN Charter like "mutual respect for each other's sovereignty." Repeating the words didn't cost Washington anything, but the symbolism meant a lot to the North Koreans.[23]

While the negotiations began a productive partnership between Gallucci and Kang, a lasting solution to the confrontation eluded them for more than a year. Then, North Korea notified the United States in April 1994—four days before Kim Il Sung's eighty-second and last birthday—that it had decided to produce plutonium, the key ingredient for nuclear weapons. A second Korean War seemed inevitable.[24]

The United States braced itself for the worst case.[25] General Gary Luck, the commander of U.S. Forces Korea (USFK), assured President Clinton that he could reach the Yalu in six months, but warned him it would cost "a million and a trillion": one million dead and one trillion dollars spent. "No one told me that before," the president replied.[26]

I helped prepare UN sanctions to choke off North Korea's trade, including millions of dollars in remittances from sympathizers in Japan. Given its veto on the UN Security Council, Chinese support was indispensable, but by no means guaranteed. In early June 1994, however, Beijing told Pyongyang's ambassador that it would not stop sanctions unless the North showed "greater flexibility."[27]

By June, six out of ten Americans believed that vital interests were at stake in Korea, but the public seemed unaware of the crisis.[28] General Luck's staff kept a close eye on his black Labrador Retriever, Bud, assuming the dog would be evacuated if war was imminent.[29]

With tensions mounting, Jimmy Carter, a former nuclear submariner and president turned global peacemaker, decided to accept a North Korean invitation to visit Pyongyang. Clinton approved his trip despite misgivings that the strong-willed ex-president would be hard to control.

Carter and his wife left Plains, Georgia, for Atlanta and boarded a plane for Seoul. Two days later, they walked across the DMZ (Demilitarized Zone), sipped tea with a waiting North Korean vice foreign minister, then hopped into a Mercedes en route to Pyongyang.[30]

His first session with an intransigent foreign minister proved so distressing that Carter decided to dispatch an aide to the DMZ with a message for Clinton: The president should agree to talks or North Korea might move to a wartime footing. But Carter also decided not to send the message until he talked to Kim Il Sung.[31]

The two men met the next morning at the sprawling Kumsusan Palace. Their rapport was instant. Kim agreed to avoid an immediate clash by allowing inspectors to stay so they could verify that the Yongbyon reactor wasn't producing plutonium. He also proposed a swap: Kim would dismantle his nuclear program in exchange for new reactors to produce electricity for his economy.

The Great Leader's heart was still set on a summit. Perhaps "he and Clinton could sign the agreement in Pyongyang?" Kim asked. But he knew that would be difficult and suggested Carter "come in his place."[32]

Just as the former president was finishing up in Pyongyang, the sitting president and his advisors were meeting in the West Wing. They had reviewed plans to attack the Yongbyon nuclear plants before they could begin producing plutonium. They also reviewed options for a military buildup—including sending fifty thousand more troops to Korea. Either move would put the United States on a path to war.[33]

Clinton's steward interrupted them. Jimmy Carter was on the line from Pyongyang. The president began to move his chair away from the table, but Carter wanted to speak to Gallucci, who sheepishly left the room to take the call.

He told the American envoy that Kim Il Sung was willing to let the inspectors stay in place. What did Gallucci think about returning to talks and putting off sanctions in return, a move that would upend Washington's policy?

Almost as an afterthought, Carter mentioned he planned to go on CNN—a news team had accompanied him—to announce a deal and "help calm hysteria." The fact that CNN was there demonstrated the former president was determined to hand Washington and Pyongyang a fait accompli.

"You told him not to go on CNN, didn't you?" Tony Lake, Clinton's national security advisor, asked Gallucci. "No, I didn't," Gallucci replied. Lake and others glared. Carter wouldn't have listened if he had told him. The former president also refused to let Kang edit his remarks. Instead, he invited the North Korean to accompany him on CNN, but Kang declined.

Carter's message seemed critical of the United States and tolerant of North Korea. But Clinton calmly recalled that President Kennedy had received two letters—one conciliatory and the other harsh—from Khrushchev during the Cuban Missile Crisis. "The best approach diplomatically and psychologically" was to view Carter's interview in a favorable light and put the burden on North Korea to contradict that interpretation.[34]

An angry phone call from Lake to Carter and another session with Kim during a river cruise did the trick. Carter nailed down an agreement paving the way for Kang and Gallucci to meet in Geneva. His intervention had avoided a devastating conflict, but the White House appeared to have lost control of American foreign policy. Still, Carter was called on once again that fall and helped negotiate an agreement that averted a U.S. invasion of Haiti.[35]

The two countries were tested again when Kim Il Sung died just as negotiations began in early July. The North Koreans quickly reengaged after President Clinton expressed sympathy to the North Korean people and Gallucci signed the condolence book at Pyongyang's Geneva mission. North Korea wanted a deal.[36]

Picking up on Kim Il Sung's idea, Gallucci proposed that North Korea be provided with two modern reactors to power its economy in return for ending its nuclear weapons program. Kang agreed, although he didn't like the American plan for South Korea and Japan to provide the bulk of financing and technology. North Korea's objective was to strengthen ties with the United States, not its allies.[37]

Gallucci's solution was to establish the Korean Peninsula Energy Development Organization (KEDO), Northeast Asia's first multilateral organization. Tasked with building the two reactors and shipping heavy fuel oil to North Korea, KEDO would be led by the United States. While Kang reluctantly agreed, he warned that the South Koreans would use the reactors as a "Horse of Troy" to create problems. His classical allusion puzzled colleagues.[38]

Gallucci also pledged that President Clinton would send a letter to Kim Jong Il reaffirming the reactors would be delivered.[39] A shaking Kang later accepted the first formal communication ever from the president of the United States at the signing ceremony. Still, he was concerned the letter on White House stationery didn't include Clinton's title.

Finally, one issue remained: inspections to clear up whether North Korea had secretly produced plutonium—the accusation that had started the crisis.[40] While Gallucci wanted them to happen before the reactors were built, Kang insisted he would "never submit." They compromised. Inspections would not happen up front, but they would happen after construction of the reactors had begun. That way, the North Koreans would know the United States was serious.[41]

President Clinton praised the agreement as "good for the United States, good for our allies, and good for the world." It stopped North Korea's bomb program in return for energy assistance.[42] The North Koreans hailed the deal as their "biggest diplomatic victory."[43] A *New York Times* headline, "Clinton Approves Plan to Give Aid to North Koreans," however, focused on the aid side of the equation, suggesting that he had appeased Pyongyang.[44]

The North Koreans halted their nuclear program as promised. All the facilities at Yongbyon were shut down. International inspectors arrived to make sure the North Koreans honored the deal. American technicians arrived and prepared to ship out thousands of reactor fuel rods containing nuclear material for five bombs. KEDO geared up to build two new reactors. Oil deliveries began.

While Washington moved on to more pressing foreign policy problems, the Clinton administration reached another hinge point during its second term in office. With his nuclear deal on the verge of collapse, Bill Clinton had to turn his attention to North Korea once more.

No Decision Yet

I arrived at the Yongbyon nuclear installation in January 1997 for my first visit to North Korea. On the way, my driver collided with a giant ox pulling a cart. The dizzy animal recovered and lumbered away, its cart bouncing behind. We sustained minor damage.

The sprawling installation had been home to the largest American presence in North Korea since the war ended. Department of Energy technicians had stored thousands of fuel rods containing bomb-making plutonium. When I returned in August, all that was left was to arrange for the rods to be shipped out of the country.

Still, the Clinton nuclear deal appeared adrift. Construction of the two new reactors had just begun and was way behind schedule. Pyongyang had threatened to unfreeze its nuclear program and trigger a vicious cycle leading to another crisis.

Soon after the Kumchang-ri story broke in summer 1998, North Korea launched a satellite, demonstrating technologies that could be used on missiles to attack the United States. It appeared to be the first time a North Korean rocket had flown as far as Japan.[45] But a reevaluation of an earlier test concluded that this rocket had also passed overhead. North Korea was closer to developing a weapon that could reach North America than anyone had suspected.[46]

On top of all that, American spies discovered in 1998 that North Korea appeared to be violating the Clinton nuclear agreement. Egged on by Dr. A. Q. Khan, the father of Pakistan's bomb, Prime Minister Benazir Bhutto signed a deal with Kim Il Sung in 1993. She pledged to help him produce enriched uranium to build nuclear bombs in return for help in building missiles. The Pakistani scientist's dream came true in 1994 when North Koreans began visiting his research center.[47]

Faced with mounting opposition to his engagement policy, Clinton called in Bill Perry, his former secretary of defense. He worked closely with Wendy Sherman, a confidante of Secretary of State Madeleine Albright, to reevaluate the president's diplomacy. They even engaged in "serious wishful thinking" to revise the 1994 deal by substituting less complicated conventional energy plants for the promised nuclear plants.[48]

In the end, the Perry review both endorsed the deal and concluded that Clinton should double down on engagement. The more North Korea became invested in better relations with Washington, the easier it would be to address problems like missiles and the secret enriched uranium program.[49]

Perry and Sherman then embarked on an effort to sell the review's conclusions to the North Koreans. They visited Pyongyang in May 1999 after our successful inspection of the suspected nuclear bomb site at Kumchang-ri. Kang Sok Ju listened and asked questions during ten hours of meetings but was noncommittal.[50] The two envoys were convinced

Secretary of Defense William S. Cohen meets with National Defense
Commission First Vice Chairman Jo Myong Rok in the Pentagon
on Oct. 11, 2000. U.S. Department of Defense photo by Helene C. Stikkel.

their mission was a failure, but Steve Bosworth, then ambassador in Seoul,
persuaded them to wait and see.[51]

The months ahead put any doubts to rest. Pyongyang announced a
moratorium on rocket tests. In return, Washington lifted some economic
sanctions. The North Koreans also proposed sending a high-level envoy
to Washington, although nothing happened until after the first-ever summit between the two Korean leaders in June 2000.

Then, a surprising series of events brought the United States and
North Korea to the brink of their first summit. Less than a month be-
fore the November election for president, Vice Marshal Jo Myong Rok,
North Korea's second most powerful man, met Bill Clinton in the Oval
Office.

The intelligence community had warned Clinton that Jo was too brainwashed for a normal conversation, but the president discovered he was
urbane and well informed.[52] The seventy-two-year-old Jo reminded one
Korean American diplomat of a regular grandfather.[53]

The vice marshal, in full dress uniform with rows of medals on his
chest, shook like a leaf and handed Clinton a letter from Kim Jong Il, who

was willing to stop his missile program if the president would visit Pyong-yang next week. When Clinton responded, "This is a good letter," Jo pleaded for the president to make the trip. But Secretary Albright informed him, "That's not what presidents do." She would visit instead, hopefully to pave Clinton's way.

At the end of his visit, President Clinton and Jo inked a historic doc-ument, signaling that the two countries were ready to follow Perry's pre-scription for the future. Kang Sok Ju told Sherman that Kim Jong Il was prepared to take a number of positive steps, including limiting his missiles, accepting the stationing of American troops on the peninsula, and estab-lishing diplomatic relations with the United States.[54]

The joint document also included a crowbar to pry the Pakistani–North Korean connection apart. Nicknamed "Iron Butt" by his colleagues because he could listen to the North Koreans for hours, Ambassador Charles Kartman had slipped in a line about "the desire for greater trans-parency" in implementing the 1994 accord.[55] The North Koreans knew that meant they had to cut the Pakistani tie if they wanted diplomacy to continue.[56]

Eleven days after the Oval Office session, Albright traveled to Pyong-yang. It was the first time an American secretary of state met a North Ko-rean leader. The South Korean media had portrayed him for years as a dissipated, degenerate "Playboy Madman."[57] Kim admitted he "catches up on the latest films and quipped he usually agrees with Oscar nominations." But he was very polite and a good listener. She later remarked, "This guy is not a nutcase."[58]

Kim would later complain to the Russians that she interrogated him like a prosecutor. Still, he was determined to put his best foot forward.[59] One American official recalled that "he did his best to be charming."[60]

The North Korean leader went further than just being charming. When Albright told him she couldn't arrange a summit without a "satis-factory agreement on missiles," he said "yes" to almost all her requests. He agreed to stop exports, missile production, and the deployment of threat-ening new weapons. Kim was also open to other countries launching his satellites, in effect shutting down his space program.[61]

Kim even stage-managed a propaganda spectacle attended by two hundred thousand ordinary North Koreans to make his point. When a human card section flashed tens of thousands of placards displaying the missile launched in August, he remarked to Albright, "That was our first missile launch—and our last."[62]

The secretary was stunned on the last day of meetings when the dictator answered most of her technical questions himself. Key issues remained, however, especially how to verify a missile deal.

Kim agreed to Albright's proposal that experts meet in Malaysia the next week to thrash out the details; however, after Kang Sok Ju was informed at dinner that evening, he exclaimed, "What? I don't have the staff!" The decision would come back to haunt Kim and Albright.[63]

The secretary left Pyongyang optimistic about the future. The two countries appeared on the verge of an agreement that would end the potential threat posed by North Korea's WMD and transform relations. The door seemed open to an unprecedented summit.[64]

Kim Jong Il must have been satisfied. He was on the verge of accomplishing his father's dreams: a summit with the American leader that would end tensions and allow him to fix his ailing economy. As Kim told Albright, "If there's no confrontation, there's no significance to weapons."[65]

With less than two weeks left before the American election and three months before a new president took office, there was no room for error.[66] Wendy Sherman even asked Kang for his fax number to speed communications.[67]

She hoped to travel to Pyongyang to propose a summit date, probably for just after Clinton's mid-December trip to Ireland.[68] The White House had already started to figure out how to fly a large delegation to North Korea.

But the Kuala Lumpur meeting, set for the first week in November, proved to be a bust. Robert Einhorn, the American negotiator, told the North Koreans that Kim Jong Il hadn't addressed all the important issues.

Their shocked negotiator, whom the Americans called "Dr. No," was enraged. "How in the world did you translate that?" the Americans asked their interpreter. All Dr. No could do was keep repeating that everything would be resolved if President Clinton met his leader.[69]

Washington found the outcome alarming.[70] Meeting with his aides, Sandy Berger, the national security advisor, shook his head. There was no way he was going to send President Clinton to Pyongyang unless a deal was sewn up.[71]

Secretary Albright compounded the error when she convened a bipartisan group of experts to secure support for Clinton's trip. Even though she told them that Kim wasn't a "nutcase" and a presidential visit could clinch a deal, the majority, especially the Republicans, were opposed.[72] "Consulting them was crazy," a State Department aide recalled. Soon afterwards, leaks to the media fed an increasingly negative narrative.[73]

Sherman was still primed to leave for Pyongyang. But the undecided election between Vice President Al Gore and George W. Bush meant she had to wait until a final call on who would be president. Sherman even carried winter clothing on a trip to Africa just in case. Pestered by the press, she sported a sign tied with a ribbon around her neck at a reception, with the words "No Decision Yet."[74]

While Bush was declared the winner in mid-December and Republicans had been skeptical about Clinton's diplomacy, Colin Powell's appointment as secretary of state seemed to offer hope. The secretary-designate, who everyone thought would be the dominant voice on foreign policy in the new administration, signaled in meetings with Sherman, Albright, Berger, and Clinton that he would carry on where they had left off.

The president still wanted to go to Pyongyang. But despite three failed Middle East summits that year, Yasser Arafat, the Palestinian leader, "with tears in his eyes," pleaded with him, "If we don't do this now, it would be five, ten, fifteen years, maybe longer before the chance comes again."[75]

With one month left Clinton finally gave in. Berger, supported by John Podesta, the White House chief of staff, argued that it made more sense to let Bush wrap up a missile deal and manage a Republican Congress. On December 28, the president announced the North Korea trip was off.[76]

Clinton's pivot to the Middle East proved to be a failure, however, when the Palestinian leader subsequently balked at reaching an accord. Nonetheless, Arafat praised him as a "great man" in their last conversation, to which Clinton replied, "I am not a great man. I am a failure and you have made me one."

Should President Clinton have gone to North Korea? His aides thought it was too risky. Some State Department officials believed the North Koreans wouldn't allow him to come away empty-handed. If he had gone, a summit could have not just transformed U.S.-North Korean relations, but also ended, once and for all, the Cold War confrontation in Northeast Asia. Clinton thought, "I made the right decision." Years later, however, he admitted that in agreeing to Arafat's request and canceling his trip to North Korea, he may have "fatally damaged two different peace plans."[77]

The North Koreans also miscalculated. The Americans had been ready to move forward since September 1999, when Pyongyang had first said it would send an envoy to Washington. Yet, Marshal Jo didn't show up in Washington until October 2000, after Kim's first summit with the South Korean leader and just before the November election.[78]

"I believe that Kim Jong Il was ready in 2000 to complete a deal over his missile program," but "unfortunately, my country was not ready," Sherman recalled.[79]

Even though there was no summit, Pyongyang seemed poised to continue engagement. Sherman received a New Year's card from Kang, an encouraging sign. Moreover, Kim Jong Il's mid-January visit to Beijing and praise for China's economic opening also seemed positive.[80] Peaceful relations with Washington would be essential if he embarked on modernizing his own economy.

"Dyslexic, dysfunctional and schizophrenic"

Colin Powell, the "most trusted man in America," was poised to pick up where Clinton left off with North Korea.[81] But hawks fought him every step of the way. Vice President Richard Cheney argued, "We don't negotiate with evil. We end it."[82] Condoleezza Rice, the national security advisor, called the 1994 agreement a bribe. President Bush, pointing his finger in the air, informed Bob Woodward, "Either you believe in freedom . . . or you don't."[83]

The new administration's decision-making was a mess. The Bush team conducted two competing policy reviews—one chaired by a State Department official who supported engagement and another by a White House aide who thought the 1994 deal was the "the worst piece of diplomatic trash ever conceived."[84]

The split reflected significant personality and policy conflicts between Secretary of State Powell and the hawkish Vice President Cheney, seconded by Secretary of Defense Rumsfeld.

New appointees, including the vice president's aide nicknamed "Cheney's pit bull," shouted down anyone who disagreed. Chuck Kartman was forced to retire. Jack Pritchard, a retired army colonel who replaced him, was forced to change his title, "Special Envoy for Four Party Talks." It smacked of appeasement.[85]

The hawks, however, didn't have an alternative to diplomacy with North Korea. Dealing with Saddam Hussein came first. Moreover, Cheney questioned whether anyone could step into Kim Jong Il's shoes. One government wag pointed out, "We already have a North Korean government-in-exile. It's called South Korea."[86]

Normally an occasion to showcase unity, the March 2001 summit between Bush and South Korean president Kim Dae-jung, an ardent supporter of engagement, proved to be a disaster. Bush challenged Kim and referred to the Nobel Prize winner as "this man" during a press conference. It also proved to be a rude awaking for Powell, who was forced to issue a retraction by Bush after he contradicted the president on engagement.[87]

The Kim-Bush encounter proved to be a rude awaking for Kim Jong Il. He repeatedly mentioned the Bush policy review during five hours of talks with the Swedish prime minister. Kim didn't criticize the new administration despite its "provocative rhetoric," in the interest of preserving what had been achieved already.[88]

When the South Korean foreign minister visited three months later in June, the White House concocted a statement that was "dyslexic, dysfunctional and schizophrenic," according to one U.S. official.[89] The proposal demanded discussions on everything but the kitchen sink, including WMD, conventional weapons, and humanitarian concerns. Even Condi Rice recalled that we were without a workable policy."[90]

The Bush administration hit rock bottom in January 2002 when the president denounced the "Axis of Evil," including North Korea, in his State of the Union speech. Bob Carlin exclaimed, "Holy shit!," startling passengers in the Seoul airport. Powell, however, told an aide, "It's just the speech writers. We can deal with it."[91]

When Bush arrived in Seoul a few weeks later, all hell broke loose. He intended to use the inflammatory phrase in a speech again, but President Kim excoriated him. This time, Kim prevailed. While Bush called North Korea a "prison," he also offered to talk with Pyongyang about "steps that would lead to a better future."[92]

Powell quickly took advantage of what appeared to be an opening. He dispatched Jack Pritchard to the North's UN mission to reinforce the message. The North Koreans were ready to meet, but the White House then ordered Pritchard not to reply. He later compared the administration to the "Keystone Cops," the bumbling policemen of silent films.[93]

By late spring 2002, after almost eighteen months in office, Condi Rice had had enough. Seconded by the national security advisor, Powell won a raucous debate, after which Bush approved sending an envoy to Pyongyang. "I really want to help the North Korean people and so I want to have a bold approach to this," the president instructed. The secretary came up with a hodgepodge of demands from WMD to human rights.[94]

But Powell's plan was upended by reports about Pyongyang's growing uranium enrichment program. A July trip to North Korea by his envoy,

Jim Kelly, was postponed, ostensibly because of a naval clash between the two Koreas. In fact, it was because of a CIA warning that "the North was seeking centrifuge-related materials in large quantities."[95]

Still, Powell pushed ahead after the North expressed regret for the clash. He met Pyongyang's foreign minister at a multilateral summit in Asia, provoking "howls" of indignation from the hawks who hadn't been informed ahead of time. Powell told him that Kelly's trip was back on although he alluded to a "problem," the uranium enrichment program. The secretary gave the impression that everything was going to be fine. It wasn't.

Shortly afterwards, the CIA informed the president that North Korea was building an enrichment facility that could be completed by the mid-2000s and produce material for one or two bombs per year. John Bolton, Cheney's ideological ally and spy at State, burst into Powell's office, exclaiming, "See! Cheating! We've got to blow it open."[96]

The secretary, however, was cautious. Powell would later confront a similar problem and plow ahead, falsely claiming Saddam Hussein had WMD in his watershed UN speech. Rich Armitage, Powell's deputy, remembered the evidence on North Korea was "nowhere near as certain" as it was on Iraq.[97]

As secretary of state, Powell had to consider other challenges. First, America's allies, South Korea and Japan, had based their policies on the foundation provided by the 1994 deal. Japanese prime minister Junichiro Koizumi had even just held his first summit with Kim Jong Il. Second, Powell wanted to avoid another crisis given the imminent invasion of Iraq.

His solution was to tell the North Koreans that the United States was willing to build better relations—but only if cheating stopped. Cheney, however, convinced Bush to send an envoy with an ultimatum: Stop the cheating—or else. Powell was furious.[98]

He was right. Jim Kelly's early October mission proved to be a disaster. Kim Kye Gwan, Kang's second in command at the foreign ministry, frowned; his face was flushed, and his lips were pursed as Kelly presented the ultimatum. As the two delegations lounged outside the meeting room during a break, Kim suddenly emerged and ran down the hallway, probably to report to Kang Sok Ju.[99]

When the talks reconvened, the North Korean negotiator hinted at major concessions. Of course, Kim denied that Pyongyang was cheating, claiming it was the hawks' fabrication, but he opened the door to accelerating intrusive inspections to ensure North Korea wasn't hiding anything. Nonetheless, Kelly's instructions were to accept nothing less than capitulation. He couldn't bite then, or over an awkward dinner hosted by Kim that evening.[100]

Kang Sok Ju loudly denounced the United States the next day in a session with Kelly. His monologue lasted fifty-three minutes out of a fifty-five-minute meeting. Coming from an all-night session with the "relevant government departments" before reporting to Kim Jong Il, he didn't admit to having an enrichment program. He did say North Korea had a right to build nuclear weapons and had "something even more powerful" than that.[101]

The stunned Americans sent a message back to Washington that read, "North Koreans Defiantly Admit HEU [Highly Enriched Uranium] Program." A top Powell aide "looked and looked at the transcript" for any admission by Kang of guilt, however, and "didn't see it." The North Koreans later told the Chinese that Kang had meant "the great unity and strength of the Korean people."[102]

Like Kim Kye Gwan, Kang also seemed to be proposing an "Agreed Framework plus." He may have been angry, but when it was time to leave, Kang was polite, even nice, exactly his behavior in the 1994 talks when he wanted negotiations to continue.[103]

Days later, Kang handed a private group of Americans visiting Pyongyang a letter from Kim Jong Il to Bush offering to negotiate. Powell was interested. However, Stephen Hadley, Rice's deputy, pronounced, "We don't reward bad behavior."[104]

November 14 was the moment of truth. The KEDO Executive Board—the United States, South Korea, and Japan—voted to stop oil deliveries. A confrontation broke out afterwards between the frustrated KEDO staff and the Americans, who were only following orders and had fought off the hawks' attempts to make a tough condemnation tougher.[105]

The 1994 deal collapsed three weeks later after the last oil shipment was delivered. Equipment monitoring the nuclear freeze was disconnected. By February 2003, international inspectors had been expelled, North Korea had withdrawn from the treaty banning the spread of nuclear weapons, and Pyongyang had started to produce plutonium. One American official remembered thinking that the collapse "would play itself out over maybe a year, not in weeks or a few months."[106]

Caught flat footed, Bush and his advisors thought first to pressure Pyongyang, but UN sanctions were "for Iraq," Jim Kelly told the French. A military strike was too risky with thousands of North Korean artillery tubes trained on millions of civilians in Seoul. Besides, the United States was already involved in Afghanistan and about to invade Iraq. The administration's last resort was to pretend the crisis wasn't really a crisis. But that was hard to do with North Korea relaunching a WMD program that had to be stopped.[107]

Once again Powell tried to build momentum behind diplomacy. He sent his State Department aides to meet the North Koreans at the UN without informing other U.S. officials. The secretary also convinced Bush to return to talks, this time including China since Beijing had influence with Pyongyang.

But once again, Powell was stymied by the hawks. The April 2003 Beijing talks between the United States, North Korea, and China collapsed after Bush was convinced by Cheney that Jim Kelly, the negotiator, should present another ultimatum. The North Koreans didn't help matters when their negotiator threatened to send their nuclear technology to other interested countries.

When talks resumed in August, this time also including Russia, South Korea, and Japan, Cheney convinced Bush one more time that Kelly should present another ultimatum. The session ended, however, before he could do that.[108]

In the meantime, Pyongyang's WMD program accelerated. Material for five bombs was produced. Preparations began for another nuclear test. In January, the North Koreans showed visiting Americans glass jars containing ingredients for a bomb, and plausibly claimed they had "produced nuclear weapons."[109]

Ironically, when Rice replaced Powell after President Bush's reelection in 2004, Washington's policy veered to the opposite extreme. Rice had a "heart-to-heart" with Bush and argued in favor of a step-by-step negotiation, the same approach Powell had supported. "Maybe we'd have to put up with him [Kim Jong Il] for a while," said the president, relenting.[110]

After jettisoning the 1994 agreement, Bush and Rice traveled the same road over the next four years as had Clinton and Kim Dae-jung. They also empowered a new negotiator, Ambassador Christopher Hill, who was "fearless and argumentative." On one occasion, Hill sold an idea to Rice that was approved by the president twenty minutes later. The new envoy was lucky that the hawks had been weakened by the mess in Iraq.[111]

Kim Jong Il also clung to the hope that negotiations might succeed. Despite more pronouncements about its growing nuclear prowess and an early 2005 threat to suspend participation in the multilateral talks, the North Korean dictator informed a South Korean envoy he was prepared

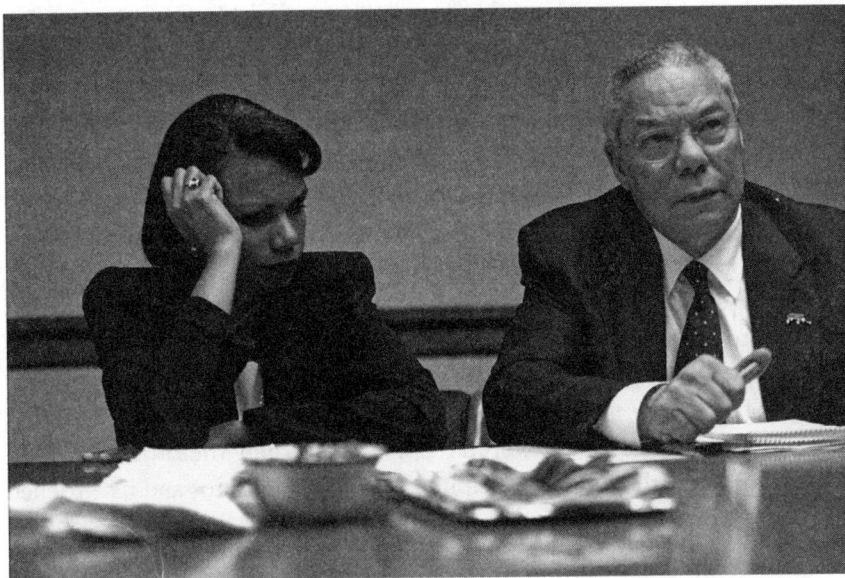

Secretary of State Colin Powell and National Security Advisor Condoleezza Rice
in the President's Emergency Operations Center (PEOC) following the
September 11 attacks on the World Trade Center, September 11, 2001.
Photo from the National Archives and Records Administration.

to resume negotiations if his country was "respected and recognized." The
Americans had to be willing to meet alone with the North Koreans, not
just with other countries in the room, as the hawks had insisted. That pro-
hibition gradually broke down.[112]

Washington's newfound dedication to diplomacy led to an agreement
in September 2005 by the six parties in Beijing. The deal featured a renewed North Korean commitment to denuclearize, but there was no requirement for Pyongyang to halt its nuclear program.[113] It was a pale
shadow of the 1994 agreement.

On top of that, Rice and Hill made two serious mistakes. She ordered
him to back away from their pledge to provide the North with new reactors "at an appropriate time." And Hill approved new sanctions just as the
deal was wrapped up. An incredulous Wu Dawei, the Chinese envoy, asked
him, "What are you doing?" Talks collapsed and only resumed eighteen
months later after Hill found a way to reverse the sanctions.[114]

The hawks thought they were about to make a comeback when North
Korea launched its first missile in six years on July 4, 2006, and three months

later exploded its first nuclear device. Hill even considered resigning. Instead, Rice decided to double down on talks, concerned that Bush's foreign policy was teetering on the brink of failure.[115]

Engagement peaked. The New York Philharmonic opened a February 2008 concert in Pyongyang with a rendition of "The Star-Spangled Banner," a stunning development. There was even talk that Rice, an accomplished pianist, might attend, propelling relations forward just as Madeleine Albright had done in 2000. But in the end, she declined.[116]

In June 2008, the world watched as a new agreement reached early that year led to the disabling of Yongbyon's plutonium production plants. The blast brought down the Yongbyon reactor's cooling tower, sending plumes of smoke in the air, and leaving a crater filled with twisted metal.[117]

The hawks, however, weren't done yet. When the administration learned that North Korea was helping Syria build a reactor and its enriched uranium program was advancing, Cheney demanded Pyongyang agree to more verification. Rice gave in, knowing she was moving the negotiating goalposts. Predictably, the North stopped disabling its nuclear facilities and began restoring them.[118]

Everything positive came to a screeching halt when Kim Jong Il suffered a stroke in August 2008. No one in North Korea knew whether he would even survive. Nonetheless, no one would counter orders he had given for a tough response to the new American demands.

Chris Hill attempted to salvage diplomacy at the end of 2008 but came up short. He managed to cobble together a verbal commitment for more verification during a trip to Pyongyang.

But Rice and Cheney wanted it in writing. When Hill proposed to record the commitment in a letter to the Chinese chairman of the Beijing talks, that still wasn't good enough. It had to be a document issued by the six parties. When the North Koreans refused, oil shipments, part of the deal that led to dismantling Yongbyon, were stopped. The diplomatic clock had run out.[119]

Rice claimed years later that the Bush administration couldn't be blamed for "what North Korea had done."[120] The president echoed her assessment. Neither mentioned that Washington would have been much better off if they had not recklessly ditched the 1994 nuclear deal.[121]

Jack Pritchard, Powell's special envoy, had it right when he observed, "The United States is less safe now than it was in 2001." By the time Barack Obama became the forty-fourth president of the United States, North Korea's WMD were unchecked.[122]

CHAPTER THREE

"John Bolton was right?"

S TEPHEN BOSWORTH LANDED AT John F. Kennedy Airport in New York City after a twelve-hour flight from South Korea. The former diplomat, now private citizen, had also spent two days in Pyongyang. He turned on his cell phone and found a message. Hillary Clinton, the new secretary of state, wanted to talk to him.[1]

Senator Barack Obama's rival for the Democratic presidential nomination, she had been confirmed on January 21, 2009, a few weeks earlier. Clinton had accepted President Obama's offer only if she could name her own staff. Just as she had promised during a primary debate, the new secretary had set about appointing an all-star team of envoys to tackle the world's toughest diplomatic challenges.

"It's more like jazz," Clinton told National Public Radio. "You have got people who are great individuals and ensemble players."[2] When it came to North Korea, "Everybody knew Bosworth had the bona fides to do the job," a close Clinton aide remembered.[3]

Stephen Bosworth had been a diplomat most of his professional life. Like Shimon Peres, who remarked, "You don't make peace with friends," he believed talking was better than not talking.[4] Calm, patient, and intelligent, Bosworth seemed straight out of central casting for a diplomat, tall with a deep voice and white hair. A colleague once reminded him, "You are just a guy from the Midwest!" They both laughed.[5]

Born in Grand Rapids, Michigan, raised on a small farm, and educated in a one-room schoolhouse, he had attended Dartmouth, a small New

Ambassador Stephen Bosworth (R) pictured with Joel Wit (L) and Ambassador
Robert Gallucci (M) during the twentieth anniversary of the Agreed Framework
conference hosted by the US-Korea Institute at the Johns Hopkins School
of Advanced International Studies (SAIS) on October 20, 2014.
Photo from US-Korea Institute at SAIS/*38 North*.

England Ivy League college. Bosworth was accepted by Harvard Law
School but joined the Foreign Service instead. "I was broke," he recalled,
and Harvard "didn't pay a salary."[6]

Bosworth rose through the diplomatic ranks swiftly, becoming an ambassador before he was forty. For a quarter century, he confronted anti-
American riots in Panama, coped with the twilight of the fascist dictator
Franco's rule in Spain, and organized oil-importing states to counter the
1973 Arab embargo. His greatest achievement was to engineer Filipino
dictator Ferdinand Marcos's ouster, ushering in a democratic government.

In 1994, Bosworth was coaxed by his former State Department colleagues into taking charge of KEDO. He worked with hostile North Koreans and harnessed KEDO's South Korean and Japanese staff, whose
countries had a long history of antipathy toward each other.

After Bosworth hired him, one American thanked the former diplo-mat over lunch at the midwesterner's favorite deli. Bosworth didn't look up from his corned beef sandwich. He smiled and replied evenly, "Not a lot of people wanted your job."[7]

In just three years, Bosworth transformed KEDO from a skeleton crew with a small rented office into a vibrant organization, occupying two floors in a Manhattan high-rise. His success was reflected in his staff's esteem. They arrived one morning to a meeting sporting lapel pins with his im-age, just like the North Koreans' pins featuring Kim Jong Il. When Bos-worth started the session, he spotted the badges, paused, smiled, and resumed talking.[8]

The North Koreans also came to respect him, and he them. Bosworth made an impression from the get-go. He and his wife held a reception for a visiting delegation and KEDO's staff at their Central Park West apart-ment. The gathering lasted well into the night. The North Koreans sent his widow a touching tribute after he passed away in 2016.[9]

In 1998, Bosworth became Bill Clinton's ambassador in Seoul and then a dean at Tufts University after George W. Bush was elected. Colin Pow-ell reassured him that the new president would engage the North. But the catastrophic March 2001 summit with Kim Dae-jung, a man he deeply ad-mired, turned Bosworth into a vocal critic of the Bush administration.

Hillary Clinton's decision to hire the veteran diplomat came as a com-plete surprise, at least to him. He had to think long and hard. North Korea had conducted a nuclear test in 2006, and no one knew if Kim Jong Il would fully recover from his stroke in 2008. The Six Party Talks had collapsed later that year.

Moreover, Bosworth's two days in Pyongyang hadn't been encourag-ing. The moment he arrived, the Western press reported that American spy satellites had spotted a long cylindrical object believed to be a rocket on a train headed for a launch site. If a satellite was fired into space using similar technologies to missiles that could attack American cities, any chance for diplomacy would be over.[10]

Bosworth was a three-time visitor to Pyongyang, a city that reminded him of what it "would've been like living in George Orwell's *1984*." Pro-foundly gray, its dreariness was magnified in February. With tempera-tures hovering around thirty degrees Fahrenheit, the massive, unheated Soviet-style granite government buildings amplified the cold. The members of his delegation wore overcoats and gloves for most of their meetings.[11]

The Americans were treated to a litany of complaints about the Bush administration. Kim Kye Gwan and Choe Son Hui also laid out an ambitious negotiating agenda, including resurrecting the Clinton-era nuclear reactors junked by Bush. "We are taking good care of your project," Kim told Bosworth, who had started construction as KEDO's director.[12]

He warned the North Koreans they had to be patient since it might take months for the new administration to come up with a policy. Kim responded, "We have nothing to do but wait while this dish is cooking to taste." However, in private, he admitted to Bosworth that North Korea was preparing to launch a rocket.[13]

"You want to force us to be your friend, but President Obama cannot shake your hand if your fist is clenched," the disappointed American responded. Bosworth predicted Washington would condemn the launch. Kim shrugged; the military was in charge. Swamped by reporters when he arrived in Beijing afterwards, Bosworth tried to put a positive spin on his meetings.[14]

If he wasn't reluctant already, his two days in Pyongyang made him even more hesitant to give up his deanship at Tufts for the uncertain future of diplomacy with North Korea. As *Time* magazine wryly noted, "It's every diplomat's dream come true: the opportunity to negotiate with a famously erratic dictator in command of an oppressive nuclear-armed regime that was once a charter member of the Axis of Evil."[15]

Steve Bosworth carefully weighed the risks, but he also loved a challenge. He thought Barack Obama and Hillary Clinton shared his belief in the power of diplomacy, so he decided to take the job.

There Had to Be a Way to Negotiate

Dinner with Barack Obama at Tony Lake's house became a regular affair after the Illinois senator took office in January 2005. Bill Clinton's national security advisor had first met Obama three years earlier when the future president was still a state legislator considering a run for the United States Senate.[16]

While Obama had been a part-time lawyer, professor, and state legislator, he had also immersed himself in foreign policy, consulting former government officials like Lake. As a critic of Bush's war to stop Saddam Hussein's WMD programs, the former Illinois state senator had given some thought to the subject of the April dinner: preventing the spread of destructive weapons.

Much of the evening was devoted to what Secretary of State Madeleine Albright had called "one of the great challenges of our time": how to deal with countries like Iraq, Iran, and North Korea that threatened the Western-led international order. As Clinton's advisor, Lake advocated "a strategy to neutralize, contain, and through selective pressure, perhaps eventually transform these backlash states into constructive members of the international community." George W. Bush went further after 9/11 and pushed for regime change, an argument central to his Axis of Evil speech and the case for the 2003 Iraq War.[17]

North Korea was the poster child for rogue states. Pyongyang had fought a war with the United States, was ruled by a dictator, had committed acts of terrorism, and was building WMD. Although President Clinton had relied on pressure, he had also reached a nuclear deal. Less patient with diplomacy, confident in coercive power, and uncomfortable with agreements suggesting moral equivalency with North Korea, Republicans saw Clinton as an appeaser.

For Obama, pressure to stop potential proliferators—by economic sanctions and even military force—was fair game. In September 2004, Senate candidate Obama even suggested the United States might one day launch surgical strikes against Iran or Pakistan to keep extremists from getting the bomb.

However, the Senate candidate told a Chicago audience in 2004, he would not support "a dumb war, a rush to war, a war not based on reason but on passion, not on principle but on politics." Other steps, including diplomacy, should come first.[18]

Diplomacy was the main topic that evening at Tony Lake's home. Negotiations between Iran and the European Union (EU) were in the offing. The Bush administration wasn't interested. Senator Obama believed the United States had to participate to stop the threat, if only to head off military action by Israel.

When discussion turned to North Korea's more advanced WMD program, one expert argued that "we can't do it through negotiations." He believed that the example of South Africa, which had voluntarily relinquished its nuclear weapons, offered some hope that North Korea might do the same. But the apartheid government had only destroyed its stockpile when it was about to fall. The North Koreans, on the other hand, would go down fighting.

Still, Obama argued there had to be a way to negotiate, even though there had been no talks in Beijing for more than a year and North Korea had just announced it had manufactured nuclear weapons.[19]

Diplomacy with dictators was already an issue in presidential campaigns. In 2004, Democratic senator John Kerry argued that Bush's lack of commitment to diplomacy had let "a nuclear nightmare develop" in North Korea far more dangerous than Iraq. During the 2008 campaign, Republican nominee John McCain would call Senator Clinton out because of her husband's diplomacy. She responded, "History is clear that nothing the Bush administration has done has stopped North Korea."[20]

Obama would struggle throughout his short U.S. Senate career and two terms as president to be idealistic and pragmatic. He wasn't interested in a foreign policy "driven by ideology and politics" but rather one "based on a realistic assessment of the sobering facts on the ground." Those impulses would shape his diplomacy with dictators, as would his foreign policy philosophy, which Obama later succinctly summed up as "Don't do stupid shit."[21]

The senator hedged his bets after North Korea's 2006 nuclear test. When asked by Tim Russert, the host of NBC's *Meet the Press*, "Would you have direct negotiations between the president of the United States and Kim Jong Il?" Obama dodged the question.[22]

However, once he entered the 2008 presidential campaign, the Illinois senator's slogan, "Change We Can Believe In," meant anything but business as usual. A disregard for diplomacy "led Hillary and the rest—not to mention the mainstream press—to follow George W. Bush into war," Obama observed. He was not content with sclerotic talks between bureaucrats. He wanted to be a leader like John F. Kennedy, willing to deploy the prestige of his office if that would yield progress.[23]

His new tack became clear during the fourth Democratic debate held in July 2007 at the Citadel, a military college and bastion of conservatism located just northwest of Charleston, South Carolina. That summer, Senator Clinton held a large lead in national public opinion polls over Obama, although the race in the upcoming Iowa primary would be close.[24]

Sixty minutes into the debate, which made novel use of YouTube videos from ordinary Americans, diplomacy with dictators took center stage. Stephen Sorta from California asked, "Would you be willing to meet separately without precondition during the first year of your administration in Washington, or anywhere else, with the leaders of Iran, Syria, Venezuela, Cuba and North Korea in order to bridge the gap that divides our countries?"[25]

"I would," Obama responded. "The notion that somehow not talking to countries is punishment to them—which has been the guiding diplomatic principle of this administration—is ridiculous."

He wrapped himself in a bipartisan mantle, and added, "Ronald Reagan and Democratic presidents like JFK constantly spoke to the Soviet Union at a time when Ronald Reagan called them an evil empire . . . to find areas where we could potentially move forward."[26]

Obama didn't just ad lib his answer, at least when it came to North Korea. His Asia team had tagged the Republicans as vulnerable because the problem had become much worse on their watch. The question was, what would he do differently? Obama's answer checked the right box.[27]

Hillary Clinton disagreed. She wouldn't promise to meet the leaders of those countries during her first year in office. The president could be used for "propaganda purposes" or "to make a bad situation worse" if their intentions were unknown. Clinton also attacked the Bush administration for turning diplomacy into a "bad word," promised a "very vigorous diplomatic effort," and unveiled her idea of "high-level presidential envoys" to prepare the way.

The two candidates' dueling answers touched on a fundamental shared criticism of President Bush. Both painted the Republican incumbent as missing chances to resolve disputes through diplomacy because he saw the world as divided between good and evil. However, they also hinted at a larger campaign issue: who was best qualified to run American foreign policy.

The debate ignited a war of words. Clinton kept up her attack the next day. "I thought that was irresponsible and, frankly, naïve," she told the Iowa-based *Quad City Times*. Obama responded in an interview with the same newspaper, "I didn't say these guys were going to come over for a cup of coffee some afternoon."[28]

When Madeleine Albright chimed in, supporting Clinton the day after the debate, Denis McDonough, Obama's foreign policy coordinator, asked him, "Didn't she go to North Korea?"

Obama leaned forward and put his whole body into his answer. "Right," he said. "It. Is. Not. A. Reward. To. Talk. To. Folks." He told Ben Rhodes, his speechwriter, to "double down on this."[29]

The candidate's staff found a clever way to double down while walking back "a fairly bold statement to something a little less bold," according to one advisor.[30] In a speech a month later, Obama repeated President Kennedy's famous dictum, "Let us never negotiate out of fear, but let us never fear to negotiate." But he also promised to "do the careful preparation that's needed." The performance was shrewd politics—stronger rhetoric with a touch of pragmatism.[31]

Still, Obama seemed willing to consider bold initiatives, including the possibility that Americans and North Koreans could work together to dismantle Pyongyang's nuclear program. He had supported a cooperative approach with Moscow to stop Russian WMD from falling into the wrong hands after the Soviet Union collapsed. Applying the same template to North Korea was intriguing.

In fall 2007, the Illinois senator met a congressional aide just back from Pyongyang. The North Koreans had told him a year earlier they weren't interested in cooperation; however, times had changed. The trip was highlighted in a *New York Times* editorial as "an encouraging new sign that the government may be thinking about the end game."[32]

Obama asked the staffer how it would work in North Korea. He explained that an American firm would be hired to eliminate the nuclear program at Yongbyon with the help of the North Korean scientists who built the facility. Dismantling their life's work would be easier if the United States helped convert the installation into a peaceful research center so the North Koreans could have jobs.[33] One Democratic advisor asked, "Is it smart politics. . . . Is it smart policy?" In the end, the idea was rejected as too risky for Obama's campaign.[34]

The proposal didn't die there, however. The North Koreans expressed an interest during a visit to Yongbyon by Siegfried "Sig" Hecker, the former director of the Los Alamos Nuclear Laboratory, me, and Keith Luse, an aide to Senator Richard Lugar, in early 2008. Then, a year later, I worked with the National Security Council to develop a plan for converting Yongbyon to conduct peaceful research. The effort was aborted once Pyongyang launched a satellite in April 2009.

Nor did the debate about diplomacy with dictators go away. Although the 2008 presidential campaign was mostly about domestic issues and the mounting financial crisis, Obama's views on diplomacy offered a stark contrast to those of John McCain. The Republican candidate, a former Navy pilot and prisoner of war, was enamored with military strikes. He wanted to return to an ideology-driven approach toward North Korea.

During their first debate in September 2008, watched by fifty-two million Americans, McCain called Obama out for "legitimizing" dictators' illegal behavior, and asserted that there had to be preconditions for meeting them. The Democratic candidate managed again to be idealist and realist, responding he would "meet with anybody . . . if I think it is going to keep America safe," but also adding a pragmatic note that "preparations were important."[35]

The proliferation battle lines had shifted away by then from North Korea to the danger of a nuclear-armed Iran. While its WMD programs weren't as advanced, the specter of another Holocaust seemed real as President Mahmoud Ahmadinejad, known for anti-America, anti-Israel rhetoric, made its denial part of his foreign policy.

North Korea was still on Obama's mind, however. He argued that McCain's fixation on attacking Iran rather than talking to its leaders would only allow Teheran to build more bombs. Since Iran's nuclear program was at the same stage of development as North Korea's in the early 1990s, Obama was intrigued by the possibility that Clinton's 1994 agreement could serve as a model to keep nuclear weapons out of Teheran's hands.[36]

George W. Bush's mistakes in dealing with Pyongyang were fast becoming a cautionary tale for candidate Obama. For President-elect Obama, heading off Iran was an opportunity. North Korea was fading in his rearview mirror.

"Even despots could be forgiven."

Frank Jannuzi boarded an early morning train in Baltimore for New York City the day after Barack Obama was elected the forty-fourth president of the United States. He had been invited to attend a Track 2 meeting, organized by a private organization and quietly supported by Chris Hill at State. Since this was the first postelection encounter with North Korean officials, Jannuzi's mission was to gauge Pyongyang's reaction to Obama's victory.[37]

A former State Department intelligence analyst, Jannuzi had worked for Joe Biden in the Senate and joined the Obama campaign after his boss dropped out of the presidential race. An advocate of engagement—he had supported Obama's forward-leaning response at the Citadel—Jannuzi was slated to be part of the transition team.

It wasn't unreasonable to assume Kim Jong Il had breathed a sigh of relief when Obama beat John McCain. When an American escort told the North Koreans, who were disembarking at Newark International Airport on Election Day, that Obama was winning, they replied, "Don't say that! You will put a jinx on it."[38]

The five-hour meeting in midtown Manhattan was populated by establishment foreign policy experts and headlined by Henry Kissinger, who first dealt with North Korea in 1969 when it shot down an American spy plane. President Nixon and Kissinger considered, but rejected, a military response that could have sparked a second Korean War. As a private citizen, the former national security advisor came to believe that diplomacy was the only way to end North Korea's nuclear program.

Kissinger's biggest concern was the American relationship with China he had worked so hard to nurture. If the two powers could not find a way to solve the nuclear challenge together, he believed Washington would blame Beijing, Pyongyang's main benefactor. That could upset the "smooth passing of the baton" in relations from Bush to Obama, the central topic of Kissinger's meeting one month later with the Chinese leader's top foreign policy advisor, Dai Bingguo.[39]

The North Koreans admired Kissinger even though he had considered bombing them. They viewed him as the grandmaster of power politics, which their country had practiced for decades, maneuvering between two communist giants, the Soviet Union and China.

There was even talk at the New York meeting of a second "Perry process"—sending Kissinger, a McCain advisor, and Bill Perry, an Obama supporter, to meet Kim Jong Il. A mission to Pyongyang that advanced the cause of denuclearization would be a crowning achievement in Kissinger's brilliant but controversial career.[40]

Speaker after speaker echoed the grandmaster's opening argument. The financial crisis facing the United States meant Obama would have to set clear foreign policy priorities. Negotiations could become untenable if the North Koreans procrastinated.

Jannuzi cautioned participants that "the plate is full," so it was important to deliver this issue in good shape. He also reminded the North Koreans about what Obama had said during the campaign. But they needed to give him a chance to get settled in his new job.[41]

The North Koreans' response fell short of Jannuzi's expectations. After they unleashed a litany of complaints about the Bush administration, the most they could manage was a cryptic comment: "We are ready, no matter what the policy is." The North Koreans weren't belligerent. They were just keeping their options open. A disappointed Jannuzi returned to Washington.[42]

The Obama transition team's main task was to set the president's agenda for the first one hundred days. That space was packed in 2008. The president-elect had to overcome fears that the United States was heading into another Great Depression after a financial crisis had rocked the country. On the foreign policy front, Obama had to follow through on his campaign promises to withdraw American troops from Iraq, fight the war in Afghanistan, reinvigorate the Middle East peace process, and stop Iran's nuclear program.

North Korea still had a chance to make the cut although Jannuzi had a tough job ahead of him, especially after the less-than-encouraging New York encounter. Moreover, North Korea in 2009 was less willing to trade its nuclear security blanket for American promises than in 1994 when Bill Clinton struck his nuclear deal. But Jannuzi's skeptical transition bosses were open to diplomacy if it would hold Pyongyang's feet to the fire, and then they would see what happened.

While the situation on the peninsula seemed calm for the moment, Jannuzi believed a diplomatic offensive was the only way to stop North Korea from becoming a greater threat. He came down squarely on one side of a debate that had plagued American policymakers for years: was time on Washington's or Pyongyang's side?

One camp, with little or no experience dealing with North Koreans, believed that the United States could wait them out. Pyongyang would eventually collapse under the weight of its political, economic, and social contradictions, ending the nuclear danger. Washington could dial up the pressure, forcing the North Koreans to make a deal, or even accelerating the regime's collapse.

The other camp, which had firsthand experience with North Korea like Jannuzi, believed it would never unilaterally capitulate. Pyongyang had withstood an American pounding during the Korean War and weathered the 1990s famine, which may have claimed as many as one million lives. The North's nuclear negotiators often boasted time was on their side.[43] The collapse of the 1994 deal in 2004, which gave their country breathing room to build a nuclear arsenal, had proved them right.

The day after the November election, three-star admiral Mike McConnell, director of national intelligence, tilted the policy scales against engagers.[44] Briefing Obama in the FBI's Chicago office, he told the president-elect that the "loony" North Koreans' arsenal was growing. Negotiations were a waste of time. They would talk, lie, escalate, threaten to walk away, and then try to renegotiate.[45]

Intelligence analysts hit the same negative note in a briefing for Obama's transition team. They focused on North Korea's secret uranium enrichment program, which, the briefer emphasized, violated the 1994 deal. There was no mention of the massive plutonium production program gutted by the agreement. The bottom line: diplomacy was a waste of time.[46]

Jannuzi had heard it all before. The message, however, was a revelation for other members of the team. "I was struck by the clarity of the evidence because just reading the media, it hadn't been clear to me," one recalled. Another remembered the briefing confirmed diplomacy was a dead end.

Susan Rice, soon to be named Obama's ambassador to the UN, also attended. She was fond of saying "don't trust, and verify," a wordplay on Ronald Reagan's famous pronouncement, "trust but verify." Tongue in cheek, Rice remarked afterwards, "So John Bolton was right?" Engagement seemed a big risk at best, and a waste of time at worst.[47]

Then, the North Koreans tipped the scales further against engagers. The multilateral Beijing talks collapsed after they refused to record new verification commitments made to Chris Hill. "Verification, verification, verification" became the focus of Bush transition briefings, according to one official, with the theme that they were cheaters.[48]

The question still remained: how could the new administration stop the growing threat? Trying to wait out the North Koreans had created the problem in the first place. Engagement preserved a chance for success, while not guaranteeing it. Obama's advisors didn't discard diplomacy, but no one wanted to put him in an untenable position.

Jannuzi's last attempt to spark talks failed. He proposed inviting the North Koreans to the National Prayer Breakfast, a yearly event held in early February and hosted by the president. However, the outgoing administration refused to grant visas for them to come from North Korea or permission to travel from New York. After the Obama team backed away from Jannuzi's proposal, he returned to Capitol Hill.[49]

In his January 2009 inaugural address, dedicated to a new beginning at home and abroad, Barack Obama declared, "America would extend a hand if you are willing to unclench yours." The *Guardian* noted, "Even despots could be forgiven."[50] When it came to North Korea, however, Obama's advisors assumed that time was on their side. Pyongyang had other ideas.

"You have no idea how bad things are going to get."

Despite the Citadel debate blowup, Hillary Clinton was more interested in diplomacy with North Korea than Barack Obama. But she had to tread carefully. Clinton had to avoid guilt by association with what Republicans called her husband's "appeasement policy." As "the secretary who knew too much," Clinton understood risks and moved cautiously, according to an aide. Finally, tensions with the White House still lingered from the Democratic primary rivalry.[51]

The secretary was also surrounded by skeptics. Kurt Campbell, her top Asia expert, was more interested in bonding with friends, especially conservatives in South Korea and Japan who opposed diplomacy, than in talking to enemies. James Steinberg, her deputy, focused on wooing China to leverage the North. Chris Hill, held over at State before moving to Iraq as ambassador, was hopeful. But one aide thought he proved the adage "Optimism is to diplomats what courage is to soldiers."[52]

Clinton made the most of the paper-filled binders produced during the transition to bring her up to speed. "We were shocked, pleasantly surprised and deeply impressed that she had read all the North Korea stuff," one official remembered.[53] Moreover, "she was so cogent in integrating it with the rest of her global strategy."

The new secretary of state was convinced Bush had made a mistake when he ripped up her husband's nuclear deal. During a trip to Asia soon after she was confirmed, Clinton engaged in a debate with a Fox News correspondent, blaming Bush's decision to withdraw from the 1994 agreement for its failure.

Hillary Clinton may have wanted to hit the ground running, but the Obama White House didn't. Chris Hill forwarded a message to Jeff Bader, the president's Asia advisor, for the "people of North Korea." It read, "We look forward to negotiating; we have mutual respect."

The message would have been quickly approved by the Bush White House. But Bader told an unhappy Hill he had no intention of "barging into the Oval Office" to get Obama to give the go-ahead on his first day in office.[54]

By the time Steve Bosworth got off the plane at New York's John F. Kennedy Airport, Secretary Clinton had watched intelligence reports pile up, warning that Pyongyang was going to launch a long-range rocket. Hill was allowed to send a message through the "New York channel," Pyongyang's mission to the United Nations, urging the North Koreans to exercise restraint. All he got back was a polite response indicating that it had been received.[55]

Bosworth's time in Pyongyang made his tough decision—whether to accept Clinton's job offer—tougher. Talking to the North Koreans had always been a stop-and-go proposition. However, there was one lesson he had learned from his life as a diplomat: talking had to continue, even if it wasn't successful at first. It wasn't a confession of weakness or of failure. It was just reality.

Since there could be a lot of downtime in the new job, why not work part time to start? Plus, he would have full-time help from Sung Kim, who had been Hill's right-hand man.

Bosworth's decision was derided in the press, but the new envoy did everything he could in the months ahead to steer policy in the right direction. He commuted from Boston to Washington, traveled overseas, and stayed in constant contact by telephone or secure video link from a nearby air force base.[56]

Secretary Clinton was on the same wavelength as her new envoy. "She was convinced that, almost by definition, diplomacy with North Korea was episodic," a close aide recalled. Bosworth often visited her office on short notice, short-circuiting the normal procedure for seeing the secretary of state. Whenever the subject of North Korea came up, Clinton invariably asked her advisors, "What does Steve think?"[57]

Bosworth's role as Clinton's envoy had a downside, however. He felt like "some sort of foreign body in the bloodstream of the administration" because he had been her choice. The new envoy would only see President Obama alone once during his two years on the job, when they took a photo together after he was appointed.[58]

Still, the soft-spoken diplomat seemed better suited to navigate the bureaucratic shoals than other members of Clinton's team. Unlike Richard Holbrooke, a Clinton envoy with a big, assertive personality, Bosworth was subtle. "He was the voice of experience," an Obama advisor recalled. "His position led one towards greater engagement with the North ... although that was not an overt or clear agenda on his part."[59]

As Secretary Clinton's trip to Asia on February 15 grew closer, so did Pyongyang's satellite launch. New intelligence reports indicated that a train carrying a long-range rocket had reached Musudan-ri, the site of past launches. Spy satellites showed personnel assembling the 105-foot-long rocket.[60]

On the eve of her departure, Clinton sought to woo and warn Pyongyang in her first major speech, delivered at the Asia Society in New York. The Obama administration wanted to build a peaceful relationship, but only if the North was willing to give up its nuclear weapons. The State Department passed a second private message to the North Koreans asking them not to test their rocket. There was no response.[61]

The secretary flew to Tokyo on Kim Jong Il's sixty-seventh birthday. Pyongyang's media denied reports that it intended to launch a rocket while she was en route. The North Koreans also defended their right to launch satellites even though there was no definitive word whether that was about to happen or not.[62]

Right from the start, resigned to not to engage in "diplo-speak," Clinton managed to get in hot water with the White House and the North Koreans. Her press briefing during a stop in Alaska resulted in a *New York Times* headline that gave the impression she would take a softer line toward Pyongyang than the president. Clinton's staff scolded the reporters. In Seoul, she angered the North Koreans with a warning that uncertainty over the succession in Pyongyang could lead to instability, and an increased threat.[63]

Clinton's global renown counted for a lot, however, especially given the coming storm with Pyongyang. In Tokyo, she met the emperor and empress and won over Japanese diplomats who felt Chris Hill had ignored them. In Seoul, Clinton bonded with President Lee Myung-bak. A proalliance conservative, he impressed her with his rags-to-riches story, affable style, and pragmatic but obstinate views on North Korea.[64]

Her stop in Beijing confirmed a bad situation was about to get worse. Chris Hill had already relayed a "tell North Korea not to test" message to Wu Dawei, China's nuclear negotiator. He urged Hill to get back to talks no matter the outcome. A senior Chinese official who had just met Kim Jong Il reported that he wanted to talk, but that he also wanted to launch a rocket as a show of strength.

However, Clinton "only gave it a junior college try," according to one aide. She didn't spend much time on North Korea given the laundry list of political, security, and economic issues that had to be discussed with China's top leaders.[65]

All in all, the secretary's trip had no effect on the North Koreans. They didn't respond to her repeated warnings not to launch a satellite. Nor did they have anything to say about her offer to normalize relations if Pyongyang denuclearized.[66]

Soon after Clinton returned home, Pyongyang announced that "full scale preparations" had begun for a launch. In Pyongyang for a Track 2 meeting at the end of February, a group of American citizens was informed by a Foreign Ministry official, "You have no idea how bad things are going to get."[67]

It was left to Steve Bosworth to make a last-ditch attempt to head off the launch. The newly sworn-in envoy traveled to the region on March 2, carrying a letter from Obama to Kim Jong Il telling him that the president would have no problem with engagement. There was one catch, however: Bosworth would only deliver the letter if the North Koreans promised not to test the rocket before, during, or immediately after he stopped in Pyongyang.[68]

"I don't at this point have plans to travel to North Korea on this trip," Bosworth informed reporters as he patiently made the rounds in Tokyo, Beijing, and Seoul. Danny Russel, a Foreign Service officer newly named to the White House staff, hand-carried a letter that was never delivered. A veteran of the 1994 nuclear talks, Russel would play a key role in forging Obama's North Korea policy.[69]

Pyongyang announced the launch window, between April 4 and 8, soon after the two diplomats returned home. Its move was intended to show-case it was acting as a responsible global citizen. With the launch date in hand, international organizations could issue safety guidelines for ships and aircraft in the vicinity. For good measure, the North Koreans also joined two global space treaties to promote "international confidence."[70]

Pyongyang escalated its threats in a secret message to Washington, warning it would take more steps to bolster its WMD programs. Those steps would include holding a nuclear test, developing an ICBM capable of reaching the United States, and enriching uranium that could be used to build more bombs. Eventually made public, the warnings would even-tually come true.[71]

North Korea's unrelenting WMD march was seen as a slap in Obama's face. White House meetings "sounded a lot like what I heard from Dick Cheney and his staff," one official recalled.

The president instructed his staff to come up with a "policy to break the cycle of provocation, extortion and reward" that had been going on for fifteen years. Looking back, one White House aide concluded, "I wouldn't say the people in the administration followed through on Obama's meta-physical guidance."[72]

Robert Gates, a Bush holdover as secretary of defense, had his own prescription: don't pay "for the same horse three times." His former boss had lifted sanctions even after North Korea detonated its first nuclear blast. Gates's turn of phrase became an Obama bumper sticker, along with an-other slogan, no "talks for talks' sake."[73]

A new policy, "strategic patience," emerged, formulated and driven by the National Security Council's Asia experts. One colleague recalled, "Danny Russel believed in strategic patience, and North Korea's behavior reinforced his position." An odd impatience permeated strategic patience: a refusal to accept Pyongyang as it was, and a refusal to take action to change it. A South Korean official commented, "Strategic patience was an attitude, not a policy."[74]

The North Korean rocket lifted off on April 5, ten weeks after President Obama took office. American warships poised off the peninsula's coast were ready to shoot the rocket down if it threatened the United States. The admiral in charge of American forces in the Pacific even held a press conference to highlight that capability, angering Obama and prompting Gates to reprimand him.[75]

Luckily, the launch failed. A North Korean general later told visitors that if the American ships had fired their interceptors, his air force was ready to attack them. A malfunction causing the rocket to veer off course and to head for U.S. territory or Japan could have started the second Korean War.[76]

Diplomacy wasn't the only casualty of the failed launch. Hillary Clinton's commitment to engagement faded. She later explained that State tried to get things going, but there was no support from the White House or the Pentagon.

Steve Bosworth was left isolated. "You could see the steam coming out of his ears whenever he discussed strategic patience," according to a colleague. The veteran diplomat kept trying to reignite talks after the dust settled; however, seven months would pass before he succeeded.[77]

CHAPTER FOUR

"Rules must be binding.
Violations must be punished.
Words must mean something."

THE AMERICAN PRESS BILLED President Barack Obama's first trip abroad in spring 2009 as his world debut. A Europe fixated on Obama's star power watched his every move. He did not disappoint. The one-week visit began with the president and Michelle Obama meeting Queen Elizabeth II, followed by an economic summit in London, a North Atlantic Treaty Organization (NATO) summit in Strasbourg, a summit with the European Union (EU) in Prague, a stop in Turkey, and a surprise trip to Iraq.

World leaders jostled to be seen with him. Campaign-style town hall sessions connected him with average people. Launching "a utopian vision for ridding the world of nuclear weapons" during his stop in Prague promised to be Obama's boldest initiative. North Korea, however, threatened to disrupt his plan.

Just hours before he was to appear before a packed crowd in Prague's Hradcany Square, the North Koreans fired their rocket across the Sea of Japan, arcing over the territory of America's close ally. The rocket stayed on course, shedding stages along the way, and finally crashing into the Pacific Ocean after it failed to boost a satellite into orbit.

Within minutes of the launch, the Obama team assembled in a secure, cramped hotel room designated as the makeshift SCIF (sensitive compartmented information facility). It was 4:30 A.M. in Prague. David Axelrod, the president's political advisor, threw on a T-shirt and sweatpants and hurried to the meeting. He hadn't even thought to comb his disheveled hair, which stood up. A perfectly groomed Obama joked, "Axe, I see you decided to dress up as Kim Jong Il for the occasion," referring to the dictator's bizarre hairstyle.[1]

Despite Hillary Clinton's campaign's attempt to brand Obama as unprepared for the "It's 3:00 A.M. and the telephone rings" crisis, he seemed unfazed. Blue tarp-covered walls prevented video surveillance and a constant mix of pop songs played in the background to block eavesdropping.

Obama wryly remarked, "Being president isn't as glamorous as they make it sound." He listened to briefers, heard from his military advisors, and conferred with Secretary Clinton on the phone.[2]

Nothing about the launch was a surprise. The North Koreans had announced they would test between April 4 and 8. After spotting technicians at the Musudan-ri launch site fueling the rocket two days before the president arrived in Prague, American intelligence agencies had warned that liftoff was imminent.

Nonetheless, Obama's advisors believed the timing before his disarmament speech was a deliberate swipe at him. Ben Rhodes, his speechwriter, recalled, "It was sobering to think that our decision to schedule a speech on nuclear weapons could have set in motion a series of decisions in Pyongyang that led to a missile being fired into the sea."[3]

Rhodes was wrong. Bad weather had delayed the launch for a day or two. Moreover, it was unlikely that the North Koreans were waiting to disrupt a disarmament speech that they may not have even known was about to happen.

The president was convinced, however, that North Korea was trying to capitalize on his initiative to get into the conversation. Obama posed two questions: How much would spotlighting their actions give them what they wanted? What was the right balance between responding publicly, and not letting the North Koreans hijack what he was trying to accomplish?

"I'm going to get some sleep," he said, and turning to Rhodes, continued, "You'd better add something on this." After Obama left, Rhodes and Obama's nuclear advisor, Gary Samore, inserted a few lines into the speech calling out the North Koreans.[4]

Hours later, Barack Obama, with the first lady at his side, mounted a stage set against the backdrop of the Prague Castle for his first major foreign policy pronouncement. He launched a series of proposals embedded in his lofty vision of a nuclear-free world in front of a cheering crowd of thousands. Obama also made it clear that the United States would not let Pyongyang dictate its actions: "Rules must be binding. Violations must be punished. Words must mean something."[5]

North Korea's test turned out to be a gift for Obama to deliver an object lesson on how international norms mattered. He accomplished his task in three short sentences. Headlines focused on Obama's utopian vision for the future, not Pyongyang's provocation. But North Korea had been put on notice. Its actions would have consequences.

The real challenge remained how to show the North Koreans they were on a "fool's errand," according to a White House staffer. Responding to Obama's call for action, the UN Security Council convened in New York City that afternoon to debate punishing Pyongyang.

American administrations had been down this road before. A Bush holdover remembered that there is always this "how-dare-they moment" the first time there is a provocation.[6] Reality would set in during the months ahead. The Obama administration would learn that punishing North Korea for its rule-breaking behavior was easier said than done.

"An older man feeling as though he were in his twenties"

Spring 2009 was a busy time for the geriatric godfathers of North Korea's Manhattan Project. Like the World War II crash effort by the United States to build nuclear weapons, the North Korean program revolved around a general, a nuclear physicist, and a captain of the defense industry. They had toiled for years for the moment their work would finally pay off.[7]

The general, O Kuk Ryol, a lifelong friend of Kim Jong Il, had led the military's drive to build WMD since the 1980s. O had helped the Egyptians fight Israel in the 1973 Yom Kippur War as a young pilot. By spring 2009, the slender seventy-nine-year-old, a meticulous planner with thinning hair and tinted spectacles, had emerged as one of the most powerful men in North Korea. An anomaly in Pyongyang's partying elite, the general was a fitness fanatic who walked several miles a day and didn't drink.[8]

A founding father of North Korea's bomb program, Dr. So Sang Kuk, the physicist, trained in East Germany and the Soviet Union. Dr. So was the author of over forty books with dull academic titles and once appeared on television pontificating about uranium ore deposits. After becoming Kim Jong Il's tutor, the grateful dictator rewarded So with a large American van. The physicist supervised Pyongyang's less-than-successful 2006 nuclear blast, then went into semiretirement, only to return to work in spring 2009.[9]

An orphan of the war with Japan, General Jon Pyong Ho, the captain of industry, was cared for by Kim Il Sung's wife, who affectionately called him "kid comrade." She taught Jon to shoot a gun and encouraged him to study technology. He went on to graduate from Moscow State University and made munitions during the Korean War. The general was eventually promoted to run WMD factories and orchestrated a network that smuggled technology from abroad. The eighty-three-year-old was still on the job in spring 2009.[10]

The three men presided over a military-industrial complex staffed by thousands of scientists, engineers, technicians, and workers determined to develop WMD. The bomb program alone may have employed up to three thousand engineers and fifteen thousand personnel working at as many as 150 facilities. Compared to the programs in the United States and the Soviet Union it was small, but very large for a country of twenty-five million people.[11]

Once the Clinton nuclear deal collapsed in 2002, O, So, and Jon redoubled their efforts. But what good was having nuclear weapons if the enemy didn't know they existed? In 2004, North Korean scientists showed Sig Hecker, the former head of the Los Alamos lab, bomb-making material to demonstrate they were on the job. Hecker pointed out they hadn't proven that the bombs would explode, and that the missiles wouldn't crash. Any self-respecting technician knew it would take more tests to show they worked.[12]

The trio's big break came in late 2005 when Kim Jong Il gave the go-ahead after diplomacy with the Bush administration collapsed. On July 4, 2006, General Jon supervised the launch of a rocket big enough to reach Alaska, but it exploded just forty-two seconds into flight. Then, he supervised North Korea's first nuclear blast three months later, but it fizzled. The testing window closed as diplomacy heated up again, but that was fine. It would take time to iron out the kinks in the aging trio's weapons.[13]

By 2008, Pyongyang's technicians had done more than just correct past mistakes. They had completed an improved bomb design and maybe a new one as well. They had corrected the flaws in their rocket, and more modern ones—some able to reach the United States—were coming down the pike. Testing would help ensure that they worked.[14]

A sudden stroke in August 2008 brought Kim Jong Il to the brink of death. He "suffered physical and psychological trauma," a South Korean official recalled. Kim probably didn't know that stroke victims had less than a 50 percent chance of survival beyond five years, and that over half became disabled. But he certainly had an inkling about his mortality.[15]

The normally micromanaging Kim became a nine-to-five dictator. For most of his life, a typical day had started with reading documents and holding meetings in the late morning. Following that, a public appearance, dinner with his family or officials, watching a movie, going to a concert, or playing games; then, more work into the early morning, four hours of sleep, and onsite visits at dawn. Now, aides consolidated reports, presented him with short summaries, and were given greater autonomy to make decisions.[16]

The stricken dictator may have still harbored hopes that diplomacy could transform relations with the United States, but his near-death experience meant Washington would have to wait. Choosing a successor, manufacturing a cult of personality, and building support from the North Korean elite, the military, and the public became his most important tasks— even his obsession.

Two of his three sons from two marriages were unlikely to succeed. It was unclear whether Kim Jong Nam had ever been a candidate. But his eldest son was out of the running by 2001 after he tried to use a forged passport to visit Tokyo Disneyland and was arrested.

The middle son, Kim Jong Chol, was spotted in 2006 dressed in a T-shirt and a leather jacket in Germany stalking his guitar idol, Eric Clapton. He was a nice guy who his father thought had the "warm heart of a girl," according to the family's Japanese sushi chef.[17]

That left Kim Jong Un, the youngest son. While South Korea's spies weren't even sure what his name was at first, the elder Kim believed Jong Un resembled him "in every way." By 2006, the year his brother was traipsing around Germany, the twenty-one-year-old, educated as a boy in Switzerland, had finished a stint at Kim Il Sung University, North Korea's most prestigious academic institution. He had been appointed to the same job Kim Jong Il had held when he embarked on his career.

Still, Jong Un was far behind the same succession course the elder Kim had navigated. He had had decades to learn the ruling ropes before Kim Il Sung died in 1994. Jong Un might have at most five years, but there were no guarantees his father would even last that long. The North Korean dictator sometimes seemed fine, but often appeared weak and distracted, riding in a customized golf cart during countless on-the-spot inspections.

The elder Kim accelerated the transition, anointing Jong Un as his successor at a private family gathering just as Obama was inaugurated in January 2009. A regency council was appointed to spearhead the handover, headed by Jang Song Thaek, the ambitious husband of Kim Jong Il's sister. The largest shakeup in his military's history followed, including the appointment of "a Dick-Cheney-like figure," General O. Pyongyang released headshots, prompting Fox News to smirk that they looked like the FBI's "most wanted posters."[18]

To cap it off, Kim Kyong Hui, the leader's sister, reappeared. She had been at the center of power since the 1970s, but vanished because she had a drinking problem. That spring, his sister was prominently displayed in public sporting an olive jumpsuit, gray coat, and sunglasses: a female version of Kim Jong Il. As she was almost always at his side until he died two years later, observers speculated she was there to hear Kim's final wishes, just in case.[19]

Finally, Kim Jong Un was moved gingerly into the limelight. "I ask that you be loyal to him and help him in the way you have been loyal to me and to the Fatherly Leader (Kim Il Sung)," his father announced during a visit to a school near a family compound.[20] By the end of the year, Jong Un had inspected military units, supervised apartment construction, begun reading reports on party officials' activities, and started to renovate a residence in the capital.

While North Korea's media would claim he was "an older man feeling as though he were in his twenties," speculating about how long Kim Jong Il would live became a favorite pastime.[21] Foreigners scrupulously studied him to see if he was healthy or not. Regardless of the ruthless reality of the regime, he was a known commodity. His death would usher in an era of uncertainty for neighbors, the United States, and the global community.

The leadership transition raised immediate questions for Washington. The adage "Better the devil you know than the devil you don't" seemed a good reason to engage Kim Jong Il. However, a North Korea focused on its own housekeeping might not respond. Steve Bosworth thought it was worth a try. But Kim's stroke reinforced the view in Washington that time was on its side. A weakened Pyongyang would have to stop its bad behavior. Patience would pay off.

The pending transition also raised questions about North Korea's future that would eventually plague the Obama administration. Could an inexperienced, Swiss-educated twenty-six-year-old take power? Would

Kim become a North Korean Gorbachev, ushering in dramatic change? Or would the elders and his uncle turn on him? Would stability or chaos follow Kim Jong Il's death? The answers had important implications for Washington's geostrategic position in Northeast Asia.

Leaving those uncertainties aside, the accelerating leadership transition was another chance for the WMD geriatric trio to resume testing. North Korea's top priority became projecting an image of strength lest foreign adversaries think they could take advantage of Kim's stroke. What better way to do that than to launch a rocket or detonate a nuclear blast? Of course, testing would also help develop new weapons.

The April 2009 rocket launch failed but was an improvement over the 2006 test. Two stages seemed to work while the third one didn't. Kim Jong Il appeared in photos posing with test personnel. Kim Jong Un was also there. So was General Jon. Pictures released later showed him behaving deferentially toward the young designated successor.[22]

Then came a successful nuclear blast on May 25 after a UN statement condemning North Korea's rocket launch. Estimates of its yield varied, but it was a big improvement over the 2006 fizzle. Dr. So wasn't present, although he was still in charge of the technical aspects of the nuclear program. He and Jon presumably were involved in the preparations.

North Korea's nuclear stockpile also grew. By August, Pyongyang had turned a batch of spent fuel rods at Yongbyon into enough plutonium to build at least one, maybe two, more bombs. Pyongyang even informed the United Nations in September that its uranium enrichment program had entered "the completion phase."[23]

Spring 2009 was the elderly trio's last hurrah. The mysterious Dr. So retired, only reappearing one more time in 2012 when he was awarded a prestigious medal. General Jon, the captain of defense industry, left government in 2011 and passed away. General O, the military commander, lingered on although, like the real Dick Cheney, his influence faded. A new generation was poised to take their place.

"Squeeze Kim Jong Il by the balls until he cries"

Rahm Emanuel, the new White House chief of staff, was angry. Legendary for his relentless "take no prisoners" approach to politics, he had raised funds for Chicago mayor Richard Daley, advised Bill Clinton, and become the fourth-ranking Democrat in the House of Representatives. "Rahmbo,"

Emanuel's nickname, shouted out enemies' names after Clinton was elected in 1992, stabbed a table with a steak knife, and pronounced each one dead.[24]

Obama's chief of staff knew nothing about North Koreans but a lot about punishing opponents. After Pyongyang's spring 2009 tests, he ordered two White House aides to "squeeze Kim Jong Il by the balls until he cries." During another meeting, Emanuel told Stuart Levey, Treasury's sanctions czar, to "turn up the pressure and not to take crap from people who said otherwise."[25]

Levey was no stranger to inflicting economic pain. The driving force behind shock-treatment sanctions administered to the North Koreans in 2005, the Harvard-trained lawyer's name struck fear into bankers around the world.

President Bush had unleashed him on Iran. The press compared "Stuart Levey's War" to *Charlie Wilson's War*, the movie about a Texas congressman's one-man campaign to kick the Soviets out of Afghanistan. The Iranians complained bitterly about him. The North Koreans hated him.[26]

The Obama team was skeptical at first but warmed to keeping Republican Levey on board. "I'm not making this phone call because Tim Geithner wants you. I consulted other people," the new treasury secretary admitted to him. Emanuel and Tom Donilon, soon to be the deputy national security advisor, also phoned Levey, one of only two Bush appointees held over. Bob Gates was the other. Levey hesitated but accepted the offer. He loved his work.[27]

Part of his job was to educate the new team on the big changes that had taken place since 9/11. The USA Patriot Act allowed the government to bar banks from doing business with institutions allegedly involved in illicit businesses. One civil servant recalled, "The first year or so, the Obama folks did a whole lot of catch-up on how the new sanctions worked and what we could do with them." They were surprised by how powerful a tool sanctions had become.[28]

Levey wasn't bashful either. He wanted to be the star of the show. The sanctions czar often clashed with Chris Hill, another big personality, who was fixated on the power of diplomacy. The State Department's negotiator believed "he had the Nobel Peace Prize in his hand and Stuart Levey took it away from him by doing Banco Delta Asia sanctions during the Beijing nuclear talks," according to one official. Levey believed the more pressure, the better. He thought his sanctions helped Hill get deals.[29]

The clash between the two men on how to meld sanctions and engagement into a strategy of coercive diplomacy was a fundamental challenge facing every administration. Former secretary of state George Shultz once observed, "Negotiations are a euphemism for capitulation if the shadow of power is not cast across the negotiating table." However, figuring out when to start relieving pressure and switching gears to talking was tricky.[30]

The topic was up for discussion again in spring 2009. The State Department had circulated draft sanctions to the Security Council before the April missile launch. Eight days later, Susan Rice, the new U.S. ambassador to the UN, reached an agreement that "tightened the sanctions screws a bit," according to the British representative.[31] While critics called it a "wrist slap," Secretary Clinton told a close aide that "the statement looks good to me."[32]

President Obama called Pyongyang's WMD programs a "grave threat to peace and security" at a Memorial Day tribute after North Korea upped the ante with its first nuclear blast in three years.[33] The Security Council was scheduled to discuss how to punish Pyongyang at 4:00 P.M. that afternoon.

However, a harsh reality set in as Obama met in the Situation Room with his advisors. Levey and his Treasury "sanctionistas" wanted to squeeze Kim just as Emanuel advocated.

Danny Russel, the new White House Korea expert, had a different approach. While he helped negotiate the 1994 nuclear deal, he had developed a moral revulsion for North Korea.

Smart, subtle, and self-contained, Russel sat in the back at meetings, but he spoke up. Obama also liked to call on backbenchers since he thought they "probably knew more intel about the situation than their bosses." Over time, the president and Denis McDonough came to rely on Russel for advice on how to deal with Pyongyang.[34]

The White House expert had also been subjected to Emanuel's rant. But he cautioned that the administration had to be careful not to "humiliate, crush or give Pyongyang no way to walk things back." More than once, he had to beat back drastic proposals floated by Treasury and the intelligence community.

Russel believed that pain inflicted gradually would bring North Korea to its senses and lead to talks. His prescription was more in line with Obama's instincts, to be deliberate and deliberative, testing every proposition every step of the way.

Russel recognized another reality: "To really squeeze North Korea, you had to go after the Chinese, since they were Pyongyang's economic lifeline," one official observed.[35] However, Obama wanted to avoid the downturn in relations with Beijing that often accompanied presidential transitions. His priority, fixing the global financial crisis, required cooperation from the world's second largest economy.

Pushing China to punish North Korea was not out of the question, however. Beijing had been trying to cooperate with the Americans while not driving "Kim Jong Il mad," according to one diplomat.[36] The Chinese had warned the North not to launch a rocket, but it did; warned the Americans to negotiate, but they didn't; and blocked a strong UN response to the launch, but Pyongyang still detonated a nuclear blast. China's vice foreign minister complained North Korea was acting like a "spoiled child" trying to get attention.[37]

While discussions on sanctions began at the UN, Washington dispatched James Steinberg, the new deputy secretary of state, to nudge the Chinese. An advisor to Bill Clinton and an Obama favorite, Steinberg thought the two countries could work together to restrain Pyongyang. His threats, calibrated for cooperation on other issues, had little impact.[38]

The Chinese were more concerned with Stuart Levey, who was a member of Steinberg's delegation. Levey had formulated the sanctions against a Macao-based bank that had threatened to hit Beijing where it hurt: in its pocketbook. The Chinese must have asked themselves, "What did he have up his sleeve this time?" one official recalled. The State Department stoked speculation, issuing a statement that the United States was looking at "other ways" to pressure North Korea.[39]

Steinberg's mission didn't change the Kabuki dance in New York. In one heated session with the Russians and Chinese who opposed tough sanctions, Susan Rice ripped a photograph of John Bolton, Bush's despised UN ambassador, off a conference room wall, banged it on the table, and exclaimed, "We can either do this the nice way or the hard way."[40]

She claimed that the new sanctions—including restrictions on North Korean arms exports and provisions for stopping ships carrying banned materials—were part of the toughest regime on the books for any country. But skeptics noted that weapons tests followed by sanctions had become an "all-too-familiar pattern." Rice herself spotlighted the Achilles' heel of the resolution: "We're going to focus on ensuring that implementation is fully achieved by us and others so that the bite is felt."[41]

Treasury issued new restrictions aimed at a few of Pyongyang's banks and companies as well as a warning to the international financial community to beware of North Korean firms. The UN chimed in again, for the first time blacklisting five North Koreans involved in its WMD programs, although none were likely to leave their country anyway. All these measures still fell short of really squeezing Pyongyang.

Action shifted to the Pacific Ocean. A North Korean rust bucket suspected of carrying arms suddenly turned back after it was tracked by a U.S. Navy vessel.[42] In August, the Indian navy searched a North Korean ship bound for Burma after chasing it for six hours. An inspection of the vessel found nothing except sugar.[43]

With sanctions taking center stage, Secretary Clinton appointed a new czar. Soft-spoken and quietly funny, Philip Goldberg had seen firsthand how sanctions helped convince Serbian president Slobodan Milošević to negotiate the Bosnia Peace Accords.

Clinton told him that she and the president wanted to send a strong message to North Korea and the Chinese, who needed to do more to punish Pyongyang. She even baited the hook, hinting that the job would help prepare Goldberg for the more prestigious position he really wanted: to run State's intelligence bureau.

Goldberg's appointment was also intended to send a message to Stuart Levey. Clinton was unhappy with Treasury leading the charge. She was ordered by the White House to include Levey on a trip, but he had to book a commercial flight after finding out her plane was full.[44] Some officials thought Levey struck too much fear into the hearts of bankers and bureaucrats. Folding in the mild-mannered Goldberg would help soften the blows.[45]

While the White House wanted the two men to work hand in glove, they traveled separately to China after the UN sanctions were passed. Goldberg's plea that the Chinese interdict suspicious ships and airplanes on their way from Pyongyang to Teheran fell flat.[46]

On the other hand, Levey, on a short leash held by a White House aide, cowed the bureaucrats and bankers. Three Hong Kong firms closed accounts linked to illicit trade based on information he provided.[47]

The American sanctions drive petered out despite the initial burst of activity. Washington switched to focus on Iran once a tentative nuclear deal reached in October 2009 collapsed. Obama unleashed Levey, who tightened the financial squeeze on Iran's economy.[48] After Goldberg moved on to the job he really wanted at State, his successor was engulfed in the burgeoning campaign against Teheran.

Inflicting pain on North Korea grew harder. Pyongyang still ranked as the administration's third-highest priority behind Iran and terrorist organizations. But as one official remembered, "It was Iran twenty-four hours a day, seven days a week."[49]

Washington's sanctions drive suffered from a sine wave of attention. "Two things would bring the wave up; the prospect of a nuclear test or anything indicating the North was moving closer to building an ICBM [intercontinental ballistic missile]," one official observed.[50] Otherwise, the multitude of agencies responsible for sanctions, anxious to take credit for capturing a boxful of bolts, pursued their own uncoordinated operations.

The results were disappointing even when decision-makers paid attention to punishing Pyongyang. The Deputies Small Group, a handful of officials who ran North Korea policy, knew little about sanctions. They sometimes instructed enforcers to take actions that would have resulted in "jail time or a congressional hearing." In contrast, the sanctions bureaucracy was intimately involved in Iran policymaking.[51]

Without the backing of senior officials, American sanctions enforcers had a difficult job. Pyongyang's smuggling rings were much smaller than Iran's networks, so the information needed to start the sanctions ball rolling was often classified. The intelligence community was inclined to block release to avoid compromising secret sources, an inclination that might have been overcome if North Korea had been a priority.[52]

Making progress overseas became more daunting. The Chinese had to be dragged kicking and screaming into enforcement. They would issue denials, convince vulnerable companies to behave themselves, and find others to sanction that didn't need access to the U.S. financial system. Beijing would even mount operations to shut down American sources of information on smugglers.[53]

Washington's performance at the UN—the epicenter for the sanctions drive—also came up short. On one occasion, a UN request to check out a smuggler's bogus American passport was denied by State after eighteen months. The department wanted to maintain the lawbreaker's privacy! Other countries provided information on illicit activities, but "we just got long dog-and-pony shows" in Washington, a UN official complained.[54]

The picture wasn't all bad. Arms trade networks were shut down—the North's expanding ties with Myanmar were a case in point—costing Pyongyang hundreds of millions of dollars. Even more important, the North couldn't use those ties in the future to "deliver twenty-kiloton weapons to ISIS," one official observed.[55]

As President Obama's first term came to an end, the frustrated sanctions bureaucracy tried to be proactive. "We wanted to be aggressive, we really wanted to go after procurement networks, we wanted to name and shame," one sanctions enforcer recalled. But their plan just languished and died.[56]

In the end, the Obama administration didn't squeeze Kim Jong Il "by the balls until he cried." We "squeezed [him] by the elbow," a State Department official admitted.[57] According to Jeff Bader, "no one expected sanctions would induce North Korea to suddenly change course." The goal was to "concentrate the minds of the North Korean leadership."[58] But even then, "We underestimated their pain threshold," another official observed.[59]

The Obama administration gradually tightened sanctions, but the North Koreans' decades of smuggling experience were paying off. They weren't standing still.

North Korea Inc.

Yun Ho Jin suspected he was being watched. The North Korean diplomat lived with his family on the top floor of a Vienna apartment building. He was responsible for Pyongyang's relationship with the International Atomic Energy Agency (IAEA), the global watchdog charged with ensuring that countries weren't building nuclear weapons.

It was ironic that Yun was the son-in-law of a member of Pyongyang's geriatric trio and North Korea's top nuclear smuggler. According to a co-worker who defected, he was "famous in the field of procurement as a hustler."[60]

North Korea's third generation of smugglers had been at work for decades by the time Obama became president. Their operations eventually became "North Korea Inc.," a system of regime-operated state trading companies that procured both licit and illicit goods.[61]

North Korea Inc. was rooted in the complicated Korea-Japan relationship. In the late 1950s, descendants of Korean migrants to Japan as well as laborers conscripted during World War II sent technology to Pyongyang, especially missile guidance systems.[62]

A generation later, Europe became Pyongyang's destination of choice for illicit technology. Operations were run out of its embassy in Vienna and mission in East Berlin. The North was also poised to launch a clandestine collection effort in Southeast Asia for microelectronics and computers, and in China as it gained greater access to U.S.-origin goods and technology.[63]

North Korea's reach even extended to the United States. In 1985, Pyongyang's Berlin attachés worked with two Malibu-based brothers who tricked an arms manufacturer into sending eighty-seven military helicopters to North Korea. Twenty-five years later, the helicopters buzzed overhead at a parade attended by Kim Jong Un.[64]

Europe was like the Wild West, prompting the CIA to warn about the "growing proliferation danger." Information was freely available on technologies intended for civilian use, such as nuclear reactors to produce power, that could also help build nuclear bombs.

Despite global export controls, technologies produced by western European firms were also available on the "gray market." Governments intent on earning money looked the other way. Pyongyang's eastern European allies may have also helped, including shipping Western technology back to North Korea.[65]

While the CIA pegged nuclear wannabes like Pakistan, South Africa, and Iraq as Europe's main gray market customers, North Korean trade delegations from East Berlin crisscrossed the subcontinent. They shopped for technology while also "picking up chocolates" to bring home, an American diplomat recalled.[66]

Concrete proof of these activities literally emerged in the 1980s. Observers noted the similarities between the nuclear reactor under construction at Yongbyon and British and French models built in the 1950s. The North Koreans may have gotten much of the information from a French encyclopedia. A factory for separating bomb-making plutonium from the reactor's spent fuel rods turned out to be a Belgian multinational design from the 1960s. Evidently, the North Koreans had acquired the blueprints.[67]

Yun showed up in Vienna in 1985, just before the confrontation with the United States. When Hans Blix, the former Swedish foreign minister in charge of the IAEA, toured Yongbyon in 1992, the ubiquitous Yun could be seen in the background. He informed the media that North Korea had "neither the intention nor the capability" to build a nuclear weapon; however, Pyongyang was doing just that.[68]

The amiable Yun often strolled through the IAEA's halls chatting with secretaries and plying diplomats. He quizzed Fred McGoldrick, based at Washington's mission, about American history and foreign policy over coffee at the five-star Hilton Hotel in downtown Vienna. After McGoldrick turned down Yun's request to meet State Department experts, he never saw the diplomatic smuggler again.[69]

The North Korean had better luck with less savvy diplomats and bureaucrats. The agency was a treasure trove of information, including drawings of civilian nuclear facilities around the world. "He would often come to ask if we could show him the materials we had," an official recalled.

If that wasn't enough, Yun attended seminars on peaceful technologies that bomb builders could pervert. He developed a network of Europeans happy to sell him anything for a price. Yun wasn't alone. There were "probably more intelligence officers roaming the hallways than actual scientists," a long-time CIA agent recalled.[70]

As Yun grew bolder, other spies got wise to him. While he had used German and Swiss trading companies that contacted suppliers to disguise his activities, intelligence agencies began to intercept his telegrams to European friends.

He was watched. The passports of one North Korean trade delegation Yun organized mysteriously went missing as they slept during an overnight train ride from Vienna to Frankfurt. The operation had the hallmarks of Western agents trying to thwart a technology-buying mission.[71]

Yun suddenly vanished from Vienna in 1997, only to reappear soon afterwards in China. No longer a smuggler in diplomat's clothing, he reinvented himself. He became the director of the Nam Chon Gang Corporation based in Beijing and Dandong, the Chinese province across the Yalu River from North Korea.[72]

By then, North Korea Inc. had become a global enterprise, with China as a key node. Access to Western technology had grown exponentially as globalization gained momentum and foreign companies set up shop. Moreover, the collapse of the Soviet Bloc, where North Korean smugglers could roam relatively free, had accelerated their focus on China. Pyongyang's vast network extended even beyond Asia.[73]

Once in China, Yun came up with a bold plan to help North Korea produce highly enriched uranium (HEU), a key ingredient in nuclear bombs. He had already dabbled with acquiring the technology in the 1980s. Yun planned to capitalize on his European contacts to buy specialized aluminum tubes used to build machines called centrifuges, which produced HEU for bombs.

First, he sent harmless orders to a small German firm, Optronic, to earn its trust. They also earned its president, Hans Werner Truppel, $1.5 million. Then, Yun ordered the tubes, supplied by a British company, to be sent to China, ostensibly for a civilian aircraft's fuel tank.

However, the German go-between made the mistake of informing the authorities after he purchased the tubes. Though Trade Ministry officials denied the export request, Truppel shipped the tubes anyway. The French cargo vessel carrying them, *Ville de Virgo*, was interdicted in Egypt's Alexandria port and the illegal cargo was removed.[74]

While Truppel went to prison, Yun disappeared. Even if he was found in China, he almost certainly still carried a diplomatic passport and could claim immunity. Moreover, the authorities would probably have shielded him. Hot on his trail later, the U.S. embassy asked the Chinese to "keep an eye" on Yun. But they denied that he or his company were operating in their country.[75]

Yun was also implicated in one of Washington's worst nightmares: a plot to arm Syria with nuclear weapons, posing an existential threat to Israel. After his company opened a Damascus branch, intelligence agencies tracked employees and technology, including goods Yun had purchased in Central Europe, to Syria. Construction of a nuclear reactor that looked just like Yongbyon began in 2001, but abruptly ended six years later when it was destroyed by Israeli aircraft.[76]

By the time Obama became president, the heyday of smugglers like Yun Ho Jin was ending. Ironically, the surprise American restrictions imposed on Banco Delta Asia in 2005 had demonstrated that North Korea's illegal activities were vulnerable to sanctions against banks. "Once that happens to you, you don't let it happen again," one official observed. The new mousetrap had spawned a better mouse.[77]

October 2009 became a milestone in the development of North Korea Inc. Even though the North had conducted a satellite launch and a nuclear test months earlier, Chinese premier Wen Jiabao went ahead and signed a raft of commercial agreements during a visit to Pyongyang, signaling it was all right to do business with North Korea. Illicit operations, under the cover of benign trade, shifted to China where they would be less exposed to scrutiny and still have access to gray market technologies for bombs and missiles.[78]

A new generation of smugglers emerged: educated members of Pyongyang's elite who lived and learned to do business in China. Like post-Medellín narcotrafficking cartels who minimized risks by outsourcing operations, the new generation worked through savvy, well-paid Chinese brokers. They, in turn, signed contracts with local suppliers and even with Western firms to gain access to more advanced products.[79]

New branches in Hong Kong worked with North Korea Inc.'s banks and companies, making it easier to use mainland intermediaries. Those relationships also allowed Pyongyang to develop ties with locals in Southeast Asia.[80]

The autonomy of the new generation was striking. They tucked away money for their own rainy days. Their children attended the best international schools and were guaranteed a place at prestigious Kim Il Sung University.

When Kim Jong Un took over in 2012, the expats were ordered to send their children home for "summer reeducation." In the past, they would have complied. This time, they didn't want to disrupt school activities. Pyongyang dropped the matter.[81]

North Korea Inc.'s activities remained shrouded in mystery for years. A former U.S. sanctions enforcer recalled, "You never knew what percentage of any country's network you were seeing." The information on North Korea was "sparser" than that on Iran.[82]

The veil gradually lifted, however. An American think-tank study concluded that North Korea Inc. demonstrated "a deep understanding of how the systems of international trade, finance and transportation work" and "how to nest their illicit operations within them."[83]

The Liaoning Hongxiang Group, run by a forty-something Chinese businesswoman who started out as a shopping-mall worker, was a case in point. Liaoning had twenty front companies in places like Anguilla, the British Virgin Islands, Hong Kong, the Seychelles, and Wales, designed to hide ties to Pyongyang's WMD programs. She and her siblings also owned Hong Kong firms that managed cargo ships shuttling between China and North Korea.[84]

The North Korea Inc. of 2009 had come a long way since Yun Ho Jin's heyday. The slow-motion Obama sanctions strategy was doomed to fail in a globalized system where smugglers remained one step ahead of enforcers.

One expert later observed that every UN sanction resolution was labeled the strongest one ever passed. Yet, "What we have found is that the DPRK's missile tests have increased, its nuclear tests have increased." North Korea Inc. was doing its job.[85]

The seventy-year-old Yun had already faded from view when he was sanctioned for the third and last time in 2013. His firm also disappeared, reincarnated as the Namhung Trading Company. While the name changed, the losing game remained the same. The UN ultimately blacklisted Yun's successor for smuggling nuclear technology.[86]

CHAPTER FIVE

"Please, please, please, we're sorry, we're foreigners."

S AINT PATRICK'S DAY, 2009, three weeks before Pyongyang's satellite launch, began before sunrise for Laura Ling, Euna Lee, and Mitch Koss. The three American journalists left their hotel in the city of Tumen in northeast China, directly across the river from North Korea. From her room, Ling could see the twinkling lights of a distant North Korean village.[1]

Working for a San Francisco–based online news outlet cofounded by former vice president Al Gore, the three Americans had been filming a documentary about human trafficking. Tumen, a small city of 136,000 people in the province of Jilin, hosted the largest population of North Korean exiles and refugees in China. It was a way station for the underground railroad operated by Christian activists who helped thousands flee desperate conditions in the North. The unlucky ones were captured by the Chinese police and returned to their country.[2]

They had been listening to the harrowing stories of women who had left North Korea for a better life, only to find themselves ensnared in the Chinese sex industry. Their destination that March morning, the last day of filming, was an isolated, uninhabited stretch of riverbank where defectors crossed into China.[3]

The three journalists had been warned that the border was dangerous, but Ling and Koss were no strangers to danger. In her last job, Ling had

63

covered Mexico's drug war in the streets of Juarez, a city with a higher death rate than Baghdad. Koss had dodged mortar shells in Afghanistan, escaped the wrath of a drunken, gun-toting bodyguard in Cambodia, and ventured into blood-soaked Algeria. Only Euna Lee, a young wife, mother, and film editor whose ambition was to be a voice for the voiceless, was on her first overseas assignment.[4]

Accompanied by a guide wearing a borrowed Chinese policeman's coat, the three Americans arrived at the frozen river, about sixty yards wide with brown branches and brush on each side, at 5:00 A.M. in the numbing cold. They started to film the escape route as the sun peeked through the fog a few hours later. The guide motioned to follow him onto the ice all the way to the North Korean riverbank near some thatch-roofed huts, safe houses for the refugees.[5]

"My heart began to pound," Lee recalled. They remained for only a minute on the North Korean side of the river. It was a minute they would regret. A nervous Ling knew they had to leave. The two turned around and headed back across the ice. They heard yelling.[6]

"Run!" Koss shouted. "Run! Soldiers!" Two uniformed North Koreans with rifles pointed in the air were running toward them. The journalists made it to the Chinese shore. But the North Koreans crossed the ice and grabbed Lee and Ling, who was hobbled by a numbed foot after falling through the ice earlier. Koss and their guide escaped.[7]

"Please, please, please, we're sorry, we're foreigners," Ling called out in English. The soldiers didn't understand a word she said. The two women were dragged back into North Korea, held for two nights at border posts with thin stained mattresses and no electricity, then moved to jail cells in Pyongyang.[8]

Ling and Lee had become unwitting participants in the unfolding struggle between North Korea and the United States. The fact that they were foreigners may have made grabbing them more attractive. A North Korean defector later told the U.S. embassy in Seoul that Pyongyang's intelligence agents had circulated a "wanted list" detailing bounties they were willing to pay for foreign journalists operating on the border. The Americans suspected that their guide, a smuggler himself, had set them up.[9]

Charged by the highest court in North Korea with "committing hostilities against the Korean nation and illegal entry," Ling and Lee were convicted in early June after five minutes of deliberation by a judge. They were sentenced to twelve years of "reform" in a labor camp, the first Americans to receive such a harsh judgment. Lee was relieved they didn't get a death sentence.[10]

The timing could not have been worse for the Obama administration trying to counter North Korea's rocket and nuclear tests with sanctions. Media headlines spotlighted Pyongyang's latest outrage. Secretary of State Clinton called the charges "baseless."[11]

Events seemed to be propelling the United States and North Korea toward a confrontation. Paradoxically, the detention of Ling and Lee presented the White House with perhaps the most important opportunity it would have during Obama's time in office to stop Pyongyang's nuclear weapons program. His administration failed to capitalize on it.

"Let the Big Dog Run"

Nine years had passed since Bill Clinton decided not to go to Pyongyang. When news of Ling and Lee's detention hit Washington, the last thing anyone wanted to do was to send a former president to retrieve them.[12] Besides, Clinton was busy, earning tens of millions of dollars making speeches, writing books, promoting humanitarian causes through his foundation, and campaigning for Democrats.[13]

Jeff Bader and Danny Russel briefed Obama, Vice President Biden, and Rahm Emanuel after the Irish prime minister had presented the president with a bowl of shamrocks. They were angry at the North Koreans for seizing Ling and Lee. But they were also angry at "American innocents abroad who stumble into such situations as if they were in downtown Los Angeles and expect to be saved."[14]

Bader and Russel opposed acquiescing to what they expected to be North Korean blackmail. They related Pyongyang's history of seizing Americans and releasing them to high-level visitors. They predicted the pattern would repeat itself once Ling and Lee were convicted. Shaking his head at what the North Koreans had done, Obama asked to be kept informed.[15]

There were two immediate tasks. Washington had to ensure the two journalists weren't mistreated. They weren't tortured, although there were daily interrogations. Ling fell into a deep depression, refused to eat, and huddled in a dark corner of her room. Since there were no American diplomats in Pyongyang, Washington worked through the Swedish ambassador, who visited her. Ling "cherished each second" with him.[16]

The second task was to keep the families informed. A State Department task force monitored developments and stayed in touch with weekly conference calls, as did Kurt Campbell, Secretary Clinton's Asia advisor.[17]

The top priority, however, was to get Ling and Lee released. The only way to do that was to talk to the North Koreans, a tricky business in the middle of the mounting WMD crisis and Washington's drive to impose sanctions. Moreover, Pyongyang's UN mission, the main channel of communication, had become little better than a mailbox. The State Department passed messages but rarely received productive responses.

The other option was what Denis McDonough, the president's aide, sarcastically called the "goon channel." American and North Korean spies had dabbled in diplomacy, at least dating back to 2002 when Carl Ford, Secretary Powell's intelligence aide, arranged a meeting with North Korean operatives in Europe. He got sick at the last minute, however, and the session was cancelled.[18]

President Obama was a firm believer in keeping communication open with enemies. He had already launched secret contacts with Iran in a bid to stop its nuclear weapons program. In the case of North Korea, Obama wanted to "maintain some degree of ownership" to avoid "a repeat of Jimmy Carter," an aide observed, recalling Carter's 1994 meeting with Kim Il Sung that may have headed off a second Korean War. But it remained etched in the minds of Americans that President Clinton had unwisely rented his foreign policy to a private citizen.[19]

The spy channel was ideal. The White House ran it, only a few people knew about it, and the North Korean "goons" were the ones holding the journalists. Some U.S. officials thought the channel was a direct line to Kim Jong Il since the security services were closer to him than the Foreign Ministry. But no one knew for sure.

While delicate talks required skills that weren't part of an average spy's training, the White House could call on Joseph DeTrani, a CIA veteran who had also been an envoy to the Beijing Six Party Talks. Nicknamed "Broadway Joe," the outgoing DeTrani had the right temperament, skills, and background for the job.

Arranging a goon channel encounter was surprisingly straightforward. American intelligence officials had the phone number of the North Korean secret police. A call was made. Sometimes they answered, sometimes they didn't, especially when they were unhappy with the United States. This time someone did. Speaking mostly English and a little Chinese, the spies agreed to meet in Singapore.[20]

American and North Korean intelligence agents sat down in a Singapore hotel three weeks after Ling and Lee were detained. The session was shrouded in secrecy. One American's wife tried to reach her husband, but the front desk told her there was no one there by that name. He had been registered under an alias.[21]

A mysterious "Mr. X" was slated to oversee the North Korean delegation. He had earned his nickname during talks with the Japanese to arrange their prime minister's groundbreaking 2002 summit with Kim Jong Il. Ryu Kyung, to use his real name, was a rising star who had been promoted to the rank of general as well as vice minister in charge of the secret police.[22]

"The Young General," as his subordinates called him, was in his fifties, well dressed, confident, ambitious, and articulate. He had lived abroad, spoke some French, didn't smoke, and wanted to be North Korea's first ambassador in Washington. Ryu later boasted that his relationship with Kim Jong Il, the only man who could release Ling and Lee, was closer than that of father and son.[23]

The talks got off to an inauspicious start. The North Koreans had launched their satellite just a few hours before the meeting. Then, the Young General didn't show up, leaving three nervous subordinates who had never encountered an American before in a room with them.[24]

The Americans urged the North Koreans to release Ling and Lee so the two countries could play ball again. They responded the two had violated their territory. They never said they would release them, but never said they wouldn't.[25]

A second session was set up for late May. In the meantime, Al Gore had met Secretary Clinton, and offered to retrieve Ling and Lee himself. After all, he was the chairman of the company where they worked. The former vice president, presidential candidate, and Nobel Prize winner seemed ideal for the job. The Americans proposed a Gore visit and even included his former foreign policy advisor in their delegation.

Two days of talks still went nowhere. While Ryu showed up, he was unimpressed with the prospect of Al Gore coming to his country. The Young General protested that he couldn't go back to Pyongyang with disappointing news, but the talks ended without agreement. Weeks went by without any communication.[26]

Just as Jeff Bader predicted, once Ling and Lee's trial ended in early June, the North Koreans signaled they didn't want to keep them anymore. They didn't want just any American to retrieve them, however. Ryu wanted someone who could jump-start diplomacy: Bill Clinton, the only president who had reached a deal with North Korea, and who, not so coincidently, was married to Obama's chief diplomat.[27]

The White House deliberated endlessly. Memories of the acrimonious 2008 Democratic primaries prompted concerns about "a former president overshadowing the current president in the early months of his administration," according to one official. No one wanted Clinton, an instinctive dealmaker, to become a new channel of communication with North Korea's leader.[28]

Tom Donilon, the deputy national security advisor; Denny Blair, Obama's intelligence chief; and the White House Asia experts argued against "paying ransom." Jeff Bader pointed out that the North Koreans would treat a Clinton trip as a state visit with "cheering, dancing girls with ribbons, massive publicity and a banquet." Obama would be embarrassed, and Kim's regime would be bolstered. The president agreed.[29]

Secretary Clinton wasn't keen either about sending her husband to North Korea, but concluded, "We have to just suck it up and do it!" according to an aide. Ling's sister was a prominent journalist. If word got out that the two Americans were stranded because Obama had refused to send Bill Clinton, "there would be hell to pay."[30]

The secretary took her own steps to secure their release. She publicly apologized to the North Koreans in early July for the two journalists' behavior, tacitly admitting they had illegally crossed the border. But she backtracked two weeks later, calling the North Koreans "attention seeking . . . unruly teenagers." Ling's sister worried that the ensuing exchange of insults would stall her release.[31]

Flying home from the Thai resort town where she had made her ill-advised remarks, Secretary Clinton called Jeff Bader into her cabin. Even though some of her advisors were worried, she told him it was time for her husband to go to Pyongyang. The trip could be a private humanitarian mission, not one to negotiate a nuclear deal. That would help avoid another "Jimmy Carter" while also limiting any political fallout.[32]

Clinton and her top deputy, Jim Steinberg, made the same argument during government deliberations after she returned to Washington. This time, Gates and Jim Jones, the national security advisor, supported her. After the secretary made the pitch to the president during their weekly meeting in the Oval Office and Al Gore called him, Obama signed off on the trip.[33]

Still, no one was going to send a former president of the United States to Pyongyang and hope for the best. The trip had to be choreographed. It had to be short, no more than twenty-four hours, with no press, no large banquet, and no welcoming ceremony. The North Koreans had to promise the journalists would be released. Clinton's safety had to be guaranteed. Some officials thought the North Koreans might even try to snatch him.[34]

While the American spies nailed down the details with General Ryu, McDonough asked DeTrani during a cabinet meeting, "Do you believe those goons?" DeTrani replied that he had the Young General's word. The snickering only subsided after Secretary Clinton said that was fine with her. Just in case, DeTrani phoned the North Koreans every hour after the former president arrived in Pyongyang to check on him.[35]

"Should I go or not go? It's a close call," Bill Clinton asked two administration officials at his first briefing. "What do you guys think?" He had already agreed to go, but, aware of White House concerns, he was subtly saying, "Don't worry, I am not going to make a spectacle of myself."[36] Clinton was like the Pied Piper enlisting skeptics in his off-the-cliff mission.

His second briefing, held at the Clintons' brick Georgian-style Washington mansion on August 1, was interrupted for lunch when the secretary of state carted in sandwich wraps from a local supermarket. Clinton listened as a raft of officials told him, "Stick to administration policy, don't engage the North Koreans except to retrieve the two reporters, channel your inner Dick Cheney, don't smile for cameras, and don't go to public events that could be used for propaganda."[37]

The former president and Steve Bosworth discussed what he should and shouldn't do in Pyongyang as they lounged around a snack table during a break. Bosworth agreed that appearances were important, but coaching Clinton not to smile was going too far.

Even more important, the American envoy thought that hog-tying him to recite boilerplate talking points would be a big mistake. A rare meeting with the charismatic former president and a few well-placed words with North Korea's leader could break the diplomatic logjam.[38]

If there was anyone who could follow marching orders and still generate forward movement, it was Bill Clinton. "No one was able to put themselves in the shoes of the North Koreans the way he was," an advisor recalled.

Clinton believed Kim wanted a better life for his people but was reluctant to give up his weapons. That might mean the end of his regime. Kim had to be coaxed forward, not forced to admit he was a "bad boy for having nuclear weapons."[39]

A few days later, Bill Clinton boarded a Hollywood producer's Boeing 737 aircraft for a long flight that ended as the plane taxied down the

Pyongyang Airport runway. An expressionless Clinton—he had practiced not smiling with his wife and daughter—walked down the stairs. He was greeted by senior officials. Choe Son Hui acted as interpreter. After he accepted a bouquet of flowers from a smiling young girl, Clinton climbed into a black limousine for the short drive to Pyongyang.[40]

While the former president was driven to his guesthouse, the delegation had to "endure Act One of the drama." They met with the chief prosecutor, who recited the women's transgressions. Then they rejoined Clinton for a session with the president of the Supreme National Assembly, who wanted to revive the Six Party Talks.[41]

Ling and Lee had been anxiously waiting for an hour at the Koryo Hotel. "Someone from the United States is here to see you," a guard told them before they were whisked from jail. They were still not sure if they were going home.

The two journalists had been prompted by the North Koreans weeks earlier when allowed to make phone calls home to suggest sending Clinton. Ling and Lee didn't know what happened afterwards.

Finally, as they were led down a long corridor lined with men in dark suits wearing clear earphones, the double doors in front of them swung open. There stood an emotional Bill Clinton, who embraced the two reporters. "I knew you would come for us," Laura said. Their captivity was over.[42]

Clinton still had to meet Kim Jong Il. One hundred kinds of flowers were in bloom on the manicured grounds of the Paekwawon State Guest House, the site of Kim's previous meetings with two South Korean presidents, a Japanese prime minister, and Secretary Albright. Clinton had hoped Kim Jong Un would attend, but just his father appeared, flanked by Kang Sok Ju, who negotiated the 1994 deal, and Kim Kye Gwan, his nuclear envoy.[43]

The North Korean leader spoke as if Clinton was a long-lost friend. He recalled that his father had told him that Clinton was "tough in private but not disrespectful in public."[44] After his father died in 1994, Kim recalled, "You were the first one to reach out to me," demonstrating that the former president was a leader of "etiquette, confidence and loyalty."[45] Later in the conversation, Kim even invited him back for a leisurely visit in the future.

Once he finished singing Clinton's praises, Kim noted that relations between the two countries "were at their worst." But Ling and Lee would be granted amnesty because he had come to North Korea. Kim's remarks, however, went beyond kind words. He hinted at wanting better relations with the United States—and a deal with Barack Obama.

The North Korean dictator lamented the collapse of Clinton's 1994 nuclear agreement. "The United States would have had a new friend in Northeast Asia in a complex world" if it had been implemented. The former president recalled that he wasn't so sure, "but as Hemingway wrote at the end of *The Sun Also Rises*, 'Isn't it pretty to think so?'"[46]

Instead, relations "had gone back to square one" under Bush, especially after North Korea was included in the "Axis of Evil" speech. Kim was also unhappy with Obama. Still, he didn't want to see Washington as a "sworn eternal enemy," an indication that better relations were possible.

It wasn't just a grand notion. Kim offered to stop rocket tests just as he had when Clinton was president. North Korea had halted launches for six years starting in 1999, slowing the development of its weapons. His move led to the flurry of high-level visits between Washington and Pyongyang that almost culminated in a summit.

The proposal, coming on the heels of the April satellite launch, was unexpected. A few weeks after Clinton left, Kim sent another signal, altering Pyongyang's mass public gymnastics performance to "fit American tastes." He cut out the rocket launch portion of the program.

It was not clear if Kim Jong Il was open to repeating the past test moratorium that covered missile tests and satellite launches. No one quizzed him on his idea. Nor did the Obama administration follow up.[47]

The North Korean dictator was hoping for a positive response, but Clinton the dealmaker stuck to platitudes: how Obama had never endorsed George Bush's Axis of Evil speech and how the president wanted peaceful relations with all countries. Kim had heard it all before.[48]

However, Bill Clinton still knew how to connect with his audience, even a North Korean dictator. Confiding in Kim, the former president regretted that he hadn't visited Pyongyang in 2000. He also heaped praise on Marshal Jo, the emissary who had met Clinton in the Oval Office.[49]

Clinton tried to paint "the best picture" he could "without crossing the line into direct negotiations." President Obama wanted him to "tell Kim personally" that he appreciated the release of the two women. At one point Clinton remarked that Obama "would help things work for the DPRK if it gave him a chance."[50]

Clinton did try to smooth the way to negotiations and encouraged Kim to jump a potential barrier to talks. He nudged him to invite Steve Bosworth to Pyongyang.

The former president also observed that "there was more than one way to skin a cat." North Korea wanted to meet one on one with the United States, but Washington wanted its allies to participate. Kim promised to think about doing both.[51]

The North Korean leader attempted to spark nuclear talks throughout the encounter. He even changed his country's formal positions "two or three times" despite notecards written by his aides telling him what to say. When Kang pushed his boss to stick to his script and Kim brushed him off, the two got into a scrap.[52]

Some delegation members thought it was a "good cop, bad cop" routine, but John Podesta believed Kim was genuine. The former White House chief of staff, trusted by Obama and Clinton, was present because everyone understood that former presidents sometimes did what they wanted. Podesta was more likely than the other Americans to shut Clinton down if he began to ad lib.[53]

The discussions ended with the real reason why Kim wanted to meet Clinton—not to relive the past or to free Ling and Lee. He asked Bill Clinton to tell Barack Obama what they had talked about, to tell him that "he thought he could do business with this guy," one American recalled. The North Korean leader knew that nobody could deliver his message better than Bill Clinton.[54]

A lavish, two-hour multicourse banquet followed. One American delegation member thought, "So much for a UN ban enacted while President Bush was in office on the import of 'luxury' goods to North Korea." Kim, however, ate very little, just some soup and fish heads, a popular delicacy in Asia.[55]

Much of the meal was taken up by small talk. Kim had "purchased" tickets to take Clinton to a mass performance attended by tens of thousands of people, just as he had done with Secretary Albright. He politely pretended not to hear the invitation even though the North Korean leader repeated it two more times. Standing behind Podesta, Kim Kye Gwan demanded an answer.[56]

The former White House chief of staff leaned over and whispered to the North Korean leader, "We're tired. It's been a long day. It wouldn't be appropriate since this is a humanitarian mission." Podesta added, "Next time we come, we will go." He and Kim winked and nodded at each other. "I've already sold the tickets back anyway," the dictator told his staff.[57]

Dinner with Kim Jong Il also gave the Americans a rare opportunity to size up his health, especially since the ex-president's doctor was present.

The intelligence community thought Kim had one foot in the grave. Clinton, however, left Pyongyang convinced he was in better health than most people had expected. An American even put his hands on Kim's forearm at one point, and thought it was strong with no deterioration.[58]

Ling and Lee boarded Clinton's Boeing 737 aircraft the next morning, greeted at the door by a now-smiling former president, who waved good-bye to the North Koreans. Twelve hours later, they landed in Burbank, California, and were met by their ecstatic families, Al Gore, and a media mob. The White House had planned for Clinton to remain on the aircraft, but he followed the two as they deplaned. Almost four and a half months had passed since Ling and Lee had been detained. They were finally home.[59]

"Michelle and I are so happy that this day has come," Obama told them on a phone call. The president informed the press that he was "extraordinarily relieved" but avoided any comment on what their release meant for the future. His aides denied that Clinton had carried a message for Kim or that the trip had anything to do with the nuclear stalemate.[60]

A few days later, Clinton and Obama met at the White House. Clinton thought the North Koreans might be ready to talk. A top aide told Obama's advisors, "This guy is not crazy. He clearly wants a different relationship."[61]

Clinton found Kim Jong Il to be firm, logical, and knowledgeable about world affairs. He was not an Asian version of Gaddafi. The Americans had learned, but evidently forgotten, the same lesson after Secretary Albright's sessions with Kim almost a decade earlier.[62]

Bill Clinton's White House briefing "humanized the North Koreans in a way that I didn't understand before," according to an Obama advisor. Kim's aides interrupted, even tried to correct him, a serious transgression in Asia let alone in a communist dictatorship. The story of Kim joking about buying and selling mass games tickets reinforced that impression.[63]

Clinton, the dealmaker, was more explicit during a session with his wife's advisors at their Washington home. Blending description with prescription, he observed there was a deal to be had. The secret was, "You know what you won't do and do everything else. You just have to keep trying," he told a Harvard audience years later.[64]

Bill Clinton's trip had been a success. He had retrieved Ling and Lee, avoided embarrassment, did his best to nudge Kim Jong Il back to nuclear talks, and reinvigorated his public persona. "Let the Big Dog Run," columnist Maureen Dowd wrote, praising him.[65]

Responding to President Clinton's request, the North Koreans invited Steve Bosworth to Pyongyang. However, Kim's offer to stop rocket tests somehow fell through the policy cracks. No American official could recall it.

The North Korean leader's feeler didn't reappear until two years after Bosworth visited Pyongyang in late 2009. In those two years, North Korea's WMD programs advanced, the United States and the two Koreas were brought to the brink of another Korean War, and Kim Jong Il's life slowly ebbed away.

"How could change come so quickly? I feel like I am dreaming."

Two weeks after Bill Clinton visited Pyongyang, a frail eighty-three-year-old Kim Dae-jung died with his family and aides at his bedside. A passionate champion of democracy and human rights at a time when his country was ruled by a repressive military regime, he had been compared to Nelson Mandela.[66]

Kim Dae-jung's greatest legacy was his groundbreaking "Sunshine Policy." Guided by Aesop's fable about the superiority of persuasion over force, he promoted reconciliation with North Korea without demanding concessions. The historic first summit between the two Koreas in 2000, with the two leaders embracing on the tarmac of the Pyongyang Airport, won him the Nobel Peace Prize.

Three months before he died, the seriously ill Kim handed Bill Clinton a memo for the ex-president's wife. The Nobel Prize winner pleaded "for President Obama and Secretary Clinton to make bold proposals to North Korea . . . rather than keeping North Korean issues on the back burner."

In June, the wheelchair-bound former leader delivered a speech defiantly defending the Sunshine Policy. In July, just before he was hospitalized, a feeble Kim remarked, "How could change come so quickly? I feel like I am dreaming." His legacy was in ruins.[67]

Lee Myung-bak was to blame. Elected president eighteen months earlier, he was known as "the Bulldozer" in South Korea for his ambitious building projects as mayor of Seoul. The former business executive's rags-to-riches story had been made into two television series. South Koreans elected Lee on the strength of his plan to make Korea the world's seventh-largest economy.

The Bulldozer also had a plan that reversed Kim Dae-jung's unconditional Sunshine Policy. Called "Vision 3000," his proposal would invest tens of billions of dollars in the North if it would give up its nuclear weapons. He argued, "When it was warm, [the North] should have taken its coat off, but it didn't."

Lee's plan was both a good deed and good politics. A devout Christian committed to helping the poor, he wanted to lift the North Koreans out of poverty. It was no coincidence that $3,000 was the magic average income experts thought would turn a dictatorship into a democracy. If his plan paved the way for reunification, Lee would go down in history as Korea's greatest leader, greater than the Nobel Peace Prize–winning Kim.[68]

However, accomplishing his objective would require deft diplomacy, starting with the United States. Pyongyang had only deigned to discuss giving up its nuclear weapons with the superpower that threatened its survival. President Lee, however, wanted to take "the lead in security and the North's nuclear discussions," he wrote in his memoirs.[69]

He was well suited for the job. A staunch supporter of the alliance, Lee was a welcome contrast to his predecessor. President Roh Moo-hyun once proclaimed, "What's wrong with being anti-American?" This prompted Secretary of Defense Robert Gates to remark he was "probably a little crazy."[70]

Lee was also a consummate salesman. He seemed spontaneous, hugging world leaders and exchanging cheek kisses with Australian prime minister Julia Gillard. That was not typical behavior for sixty-seven-year-old Korean men trained to act with formality. His spontaneity reflected meticulous planning, however. Lee went over every detail with his staff before sessions with foreign leaders.[71]

The Bulldozer built close relationships with two American presidents. Both devout Christians, Lee and George W. Bush discussed their common faith in private, prayed together, and plotted how to help the downtrodden North Koreans. "President Lee, you are going to make me cry," Bush told him when they said their last good-bye.[72]

Obama's election in November 2008 seemed to present a problem, but the Bulldozer began to build bridges right away. He didn't want to repeat the mistakes of Kim Young-sam, the last conservative president, who had been at odds with Bill Clinton, the last Democrat in office. Lee phoned Obama, congratulated him, and expressed sadness that his grandmother had died before he was elected.[73]

President Barack Obama meets with President Lee Myung-bak of the Republic
of Korea in the Oval Office of the White House on June 16, 2009.
Official White House photo by Pete Souza.

The president-elect assured Lee that he had met many Korean Americans growing up in Hawaii. "Bulgogi and kimchi" were some of his
"favorite dishes." A strong alliance was essential. So was his personal relationship with Lee and "close cooperation" on North Korea.[74]

Lee meticulously planned what he would say and do at their first face-
to-face meeting, a London economic summit just before the April 2009
satellite launch. Photographs of the young, seemingly deferential American leader whispering into the older man's ear conjured up an image of
closeness.

In public, the two leaders agreed on the need for a "stern, united response" to Pyongyang. In private, they agreed to work closely together.
Choosing his words carefully and referring to tabs in a huge binder, Obama
was a man after Lee's meticulous heart.[75]

The White House rolled out the red carpet for their second encounter after the May 2009 nuclear test. Lee argued that the Clinton
nuclear deal had been the start of paying the North for its "inappropriate behavior." Obama agreed, saying, "This pattern has to stop." Coincidentally, the two leaders appeared wearing the same navy blue suits and

light blue ties, prompting reporters to nickname them "the ROKUS brothers."[76]

President Obama's November visit to Seoul, their third summit that year, sealed their friendship. A tired Obama was touched at the end of a long trip by Lee's heart-rending story of how education had lifted him and his country out of poverty.[77] The American would often cite Korea as an example of what hard work could do. Obama "is talking about education again," a smiling Lee would tell aides after reading the press reports.[78]

In the first blush of the man-crush, the Bulldozer could do no wrong. However, as time went by, first impressions "diminished as we got to know him better," a White House official observed. The Americans realized President Lee had his own agenda even when it came to North Korea.

Lee's second challenge was North Korea. Relations had plummeted. His Vision 3000 plan both reversed course on providing unconditional assistance and appeared to be a not-so-subtle way of getting rid of the North Korean regime. After a soldier shot a South Korean tourist at a mountain resort located in the North, relations entered a deep freeze.

A thaw began a year later after Clinton's August 2009 visit to Pyongyang. Kim Jong Il agreed during a relaxed lunch with the South Korean, who ran the resort, to resume reunions of families separated by the war and to allow visits by tourists.[79] "No one would have been more pleased than Kim Dae-jung," *The Economist* observed.[80] The Nobel Prize winner had died a week earlier.

Kim would have been even more pleased with what happened next. President Lee approved a North Korean request to send a delegation to his funeral. Kim Ki Nam and Kim Yang Gon, two confidants of the North Korean leader, flew to Seoul and settled into the downtown Seoul Hilton Hotel.

Dressed in black suits and ties, the two envoys placed a wreath from their boss in front of Kim Dae-jung's portrait hanging in the parliament building. Politicians lined up to shake their hands. It had all the makings of a propaganda ploy intended to show Pyongyang's support for a president whose policies were the opposite of Lee's.

That changed when the two sent word that they wanted to meet Lee's top North Korea expert. A slim, balding, soft-spoken professor with a doctorate from UCLA, Hyun In-taek was the brains behind Vision 3000.

The conservative Hyun thought President Lee had Kim Jong Il over a barrel. Pyongyang's economy was in trouble; it was suffering from serious food shortages and Kim was in the midst of a leadership transition. North Korea had no choice but to reengage in diplomacy.[81]

Hyun slipped past reporters in the hotel lobby to join the two North Koreans in their suite. Over two hours he explained Lee's idea—that everything, including denuclearization, should be on the table—in the first candid conversation between the two Koreas in almost two years.

"Can we trust your proposal?" the North Koreans asked. Despite months of trashing Vision 3000, they were still thinking, measuring, and hesitating rather than completely rejecting it.[82]

Kim Yang Gon exploded a bombshell as the meeting ended. "I want to see your president right away," he informed Hyun. Time was short. Their plane was almost ready to leave for home. A startled Hyun promised to deliver the message to Lee immediately, but they would have to wait for an answer.[83]

After racing to the president's residence, the professorial Hyun told Lee that this moment was important for him. Kim Jong Il may have decided to see for himself whether Lee's plan was serious or not. While some advisors urged the Bulldozer to meet the North Korean envoys right away, he didn't want to seem anxious. Lee decided to wait until the next day.[84]

Hyun rushed back to the Hilton for a late-night dinner with the North Koreans. He gave them the good news. Tomorrow they would see the president. The two men seemed relieved. They had probably reported to Kim Jong Il and been told to wait. The two Kims could have faced trouble back home if they didn't successfully carry out his order.[85]

The North Korean envoys arrived at the presidential complex the next morning. Built in the traditional Korean style, the striking roof of the Blue House was covered with 150,000 blue tiles, which shimmered against the backdrop of mountains to the north.

President Lee, anxious to achieve a breakthrough but not appear too eager, had meticulously choreographed the session to be held in an ornate reception room. It would look more like an audience than an official meeting. Still, Lee wanted to make sure the North Koreans were not slighted. He had the chairs arranged so that he appeared to be presiding, his way of saying, "You are my guests, but we aren't the same rank," according to a close aide.[86]

After President Lee welcomed the North Koreans, Kim Ki Nam stood up and read aloud from a letter: "I courteously extend a warm greeting to you from our Dear Chairman of the National Defense Commission, Kim

Jong Il." He then bowed his head and added, "Our Dear Leader really wants to see you, Mr. President." Hyun had been right, although there was a catch. The North Koreans wanted Lee to provide the aid his predecessors had promised before a meeting took place.[87]

The Bulldozer explained his Vision 3000 initiative. He was willing to talk about assistance if discussions included denuclearization, but cooperation would be limited until then. Kim Ki Nam promised Lee, "I will deliver your words precisely as they are." As the thirty-minute meeting ended, the president patted the bureaucrat on the shoulder and urged him to "do his best" to deliver his response.[88]

The next day, President Lee sounded a cautious public note: "We cannot have such summits as in the past." A newspaper proclaimed, a "paradigm shift" away from the Sunshine Policy of unconditional aid to North Korea. Departing for Pyongyang, Kim Ki Nam told a throng of reporters, "We are returning in a positive mood."[89]

Lee's Blue House encounter seemed to pave the way to another summit. His enthusiastic advisors decided that "if North Korea really wants to solve the nuclear issue, we can provide them with a lot of aid," one recalled.[90] While they still had to work out the details, the budget included hundreds of millions of dollars for cooperation.

Hyun pondered flying off to a session with the North Koreans. He studied Henry Kissinger's secret trip to China that laid the groundwork for President Nixon's historic 1971 meeting with Chairman Mao. But Hyun couldn't figure out how to avoid the press that was watching him closely. He had to stay put.[91]

Instead, President Lee decided to send someone no one would be watching, someone he could trust—a former aide and member of South Korea's legislature soon to become his minister of labor. Yim Tae-hee's biggest weakness, however, was that he had no experience dealing with North Koreans. "Teach him," President Lee ordered Hyun.[92]

Exactly what happened in Yim's negotiations with the North Koreans has been lost in recriminations. After talks in Beijing and Singapore, they apparently came close to, or reached, an agreement to hold a summit.[93]

Accounts disagree on why the deal collapsed. Some sources say the North Koreans asked for too much compensation—almost $600 million in food assistance—in return for the release of a few abducted South Koreans and others held as prisoners of war. President Lee didn't want to be tarred and feathered with the charge that he had not only bought a summit but had done so in return for only symbolic gestures.

North Korea's nuclear weapons were a bigger sticking point. The South Koreans told the North in secret messages that they could give them all the things they were thinking about, but only if they took a half step on the nuclear front. The North Koreans claimed, however, that only Kim Jong Il could discuss WMD. Since Lee wouldn't meet Kim without some assurances, the talks collapsed.[94]

Hyun thought the fall 2009 meetings, faulty as they were, would continue in the New Year. Kim Jong Il's January 2010 New Year's editorial seconded the notion, proclaiming North Korea's "unshakeable" intention to improve relations. Hyun anticipated a turning point in the talks. He was right. The door to a summit would open again.[95]

"Only the United States can bring the east wind."

Steve Bosworth hadn't met a single North Korean in his eleven months as Obama's envoy. Soon after Bill Clinton left North Korea, however, a message arrived in Washington inviting the American envoy to Pyongyang just as Clinton had requested.

Bosworth had to figure out how to restart talks and make progress. On bilateral versus multilateral talks, he had a plan: meet with the North Koreans alone before resuming multilateral discussions, and then negotiate with them to their hearts' content on the sidelines.

Convincing them to reaffirm their earlier pledge in the 2005 Beijing Joint Statement to abandon their nuclear weapons program was harder. But Washington would not "indulge North Korea's dream of validation as a self-proclaimed nuclear power," Jeff Bader told a think-tank audience.[96]

Bosworth had to make sure his demands got through to Kim Jong Il, who had the last word in Pyongyang. American officials often wondered whether his diplomats told their boss the unadulterated truth or sugar-coated their reports. Bosworth needed to meet Kang Sok Ju, Kim's right-hand man.

The American envoy also needed China's support. Beijing's influence in Pyongyang had reached a high point by fall 2009 with Prime Minister Wen Jiabao's successful visit and his meeting with Kim Jong Il in early October.

"Only the United States can bring the east wind," Chinese negotiator Wu Dawei told the Americans. He was alluding to a movie about two out-matched states that defeated a superior opponent with fire when the wind shifted direction from west to east.

Wu was convinced by his own recent trip to Pyongyang that Kim Jong Il knew his days were numbered and wanted to talk. The Chinese followed up with visits by senior officials to Pyongyang who told the North Koreans they "sincerely hoped" they would return to nuclear talks soon.[97]

Convincing the South Koreans was much harder, since they thought time was on their side. All through the summer, Seoul telegraphed Washington that the North Koreans faced a degraded economy, food shortages, and a shortage of foreign currency. A failed attempt by Kim Jong Il to revalue his currency that fall—intended to transfer funds to his treasury and tighten control over an emerging middle class—made matters worse.[98]

The Blue House also had its own hidden agenda: to pursue secret talks with North Korea. The South Koreans hadn't told the Americans all the details, surprising some White House officials. But the North Koreans filled in the gaps communicating with Washington through their UN mission. Bosworth finally agreed to visit Seoul before and after his Pyongyang mission to show that the two allies were joined at the hip.[99]

It was clear "they are in an 'ain't gonna let nothing turn me around' mood," two Stanford University experts informed Sung Kim, Bosworth's deputy, after a September visit to Pyongyang. The two carried back to Washington a North Korean proposal to resume joint missions to retrieve the remains of American soldiers killed or missing during the Korean War. Secretary Gates supported the idea, but the White House wanted to stay focused on denuclearization.[100]

In late October, the last obstacles were cleared. Choe Sun Hui and her boss, Ri Gun, met Sung Kim and agreed to the Americans' conditions at Track 2 meetings in New York and San Diego. Bosworth would also meet "senior officials" although they didn't commit to a session with Kang. That wasn't unusual, since visitors seldom knew who they would see until they arrived.[101]

Four weeks later, Steve Bosworth and a small delegation boarded a military transport south of Seoul for the short flight to Pyongyang. The *New York Times* announced the beginning of "a new phase in United States diplomacy towards North Korea." Bosworth's job was to "change North Korea's position that they will not give up their nuclear weapons through engagement and persuasion."[102]

First visits to Pyongyang for most Americans who hadn't been there before were eye opening. Countryside paths with shepherds herding goats quickly gave way to empty city streets and rows of Stalinist-style buildings, remnants of Soviet influence that also existed in Berlin and Beijing.[103]

They were housed in the same guesthouse where Bill Clinton had met Kim Jong Il; one American described it as "early Ceausescu," after the executed Romanian dictator known for monumental building projects. Bosworth was lodged in a suite, the others in smaller quarters. There were no locks on the doors.[104]

Most of the Americans understood they were being monitored by microphones and cameras, but the delegation's interpreter didn't. "If I had known, I would have changed with the lights off," she exclaimed later.[105]

Even Bosworth was caught off guard when he used the Bulgarian version of Kim Il Sung's memoirs in his room as a coaster for a coffee cup. His North Korean minders panicked when they found the missing volume. Other foreigners had gone to jail for what was viewed as a blatant sign of disrespect. Fortunately, nothing more came of the incident.[106]

Fourteen hours of meetings at the foreign ministry and guesthouse stretched out over two days. During downtime, the Americans played pool at the guesthouse and strolled through the garden smoking cigars. They also visited an unheated gallery filled with kitschy paintings of flowers and landscapes.[107]

Bosworth delivered his message in his usual low-key, straightforward style: "We are willing to assist the DPRK's economic development in order to improve the lives of the people of North Korea and to normalize relations, but that willingness is dependent on your abandoning nuclear weapons." North Korea had to reaffirm the 2005 pledge made in the Beijing talks to denuclearize.[108]

Reassuring, optimistic, and positive, Bosworth picked up on Kim Jong Il's comment to Bill Clinton that he didn't view the Americans as sworn enemies. President Obama's policy was "not one of hostility," Bosworth told Kim Kye Gwan, the North's chief negotiator. The United States had no intention to attack North Korea or to change the regime, staples of its suspicions about Washington.[109]

The American diplomat was also optimistic about denuclearization, saying, "If we proceed on a clear timeline of concrete and irreversible steps, we can make swift progress on a comprehensive and definitive resolution of the issues between us." He believed that could be accomplished through "bilateral discussions and with key regional stakeholders."[110]

As for the still-unscheduled meeting with Kang, Bosworth came with a baited hook: a letter from President Obama for him to pass to Kim Jong Il.

A "dumbed down" version of the message he would have delivered in spring 2009, its gist was "Try me, there is something to be done here," a

White House aide recalled.[111] The letter did the trick. The next day, Bosworth was informed he would see Kang later that afternoon.

The two men had first met thirteen years earlier in a high-ceilinged room of the Supreme People's Assembly when Bosworth was head of KEDO, implementing the Clinton nuclear deal. This time, he hoped to have more than a short polite chat.

A session with Kang was essential but risky. His legendary histrionics had made a bad situation worse in 2002 when he tore into Jim Kelly, the Bush envoy who accused the North Koreans of cheating on the 1994 deal. Clinton-era negotiators avoided afternoon sessions with Kang since they knew he grew irritable and impatient as the day wore on.

An older, less robust Kang appeared at the appointed time wearing a huge gold watch. He swaggered into the same conference room where he had met Bosworth before. Described by one American as pompous, arrogant, and gangster-like, Kang was seen by even the understated Bosworth as a "little Napoleon-type." This time, however, he delivered a toned-down performance.[112]

Kang liked President Obama's inaugural gesture to reach out to countries like North Korea. He liked Obama's Prague objective of achieving a "nuclear-free world," which echoed Kim Il Sung's vision for a nuclear-free Korea. Kang also liked the 2005 Beijing statement that laid out a vision for denuclearization and how to resolve differences between the United States and North Korea.

However, he didn't like America's "hostile policy," North Korea's catch-all phrase for decades of tension. In Kang's vision of the future, the United States would sign a peace treaty first to end its hostility before his country gave up the nuclear weapons developed to defend itself.

"If I go back to Washington with that, I will be out of a job," Bosworth responded. Kang's demand was exactly the opposite of what he wanted and what the 2005 agreement said. North Korea had to denuclearize before a peace treaty was signed.[113]

Kang's presentation was sprinkled with colorful language, such as ending hostility meant lifting the "sanctions cap." One American pictured a woeful child sitting with a dunce cap in a corner. Kang and Kim Kye Gwan even complained that the Italians had refused to sell their country yachts.[114]

Still, the North Koreans admitted it would be enough if Ambassador Goldberg, State's sanctions czar, stopped trying to convince other countries to implement restrictions. "If you return to the Six Party Talks, we will take his credit card away so he will not be able to travel," Bosworth joked.[115]

There were other more serious problems, however. The North Koreans insisted their uranium enrichment program—Pyongyang had admitted its existence in September—was exempt from negotiations since it had started after the 2005 pledge. Both untrue and unacceptable, such an assertion would have allowed North Korea to keep enriching uranium and building weapons.

They also insisted that Pyongyang would keep launching satellites—also unacceptable. More launches would violate global sanctions, not to mention help develop missiles able to reach the United States. Neither the Americans nor the North Koreans brought up Kim Jong Il's offer to Bill Clinton and what it might have meant.

The Americans came away from the meeting with different interpretations, as was often the case. One skeptic thought Kang had no interest in talks. "This was the Obama administration. Bosworth was not John Bolton."[116] Another American saw Kang's rhetoric as "what you would expect." The fact he had met with them meant "we were moving up the food chain."[117]

Kim Kye Gwan told Bosworth before he left for the airport that, despite their differences, North Korea was ready to rejoin talks. "We should make haste slowly. With enough preparation we will be able to make up for lost time." He looked forward to hearing soon about next steps.

Bosworth was cautious. He told the press that his talks had been "generally positive." More talks were necessary. Pyongyang sent a secret message to Washington through its UN mission that it was ready to meet again.[118]

Still, "people saw what they wanted to see," one delegation member recalled. Danny Russel's first visit to Pyongyang reinforced his skepticism about diplomacy, as did the contrast between ordinary citizens' poverty and the elite's extravagant lifestyle.

Garden strolls during breaks revolved around "Danny trying to keep the screws on Steve" and stopping him from having more lengthy discussions, one delegation member recalled. A White House aide remembered that Russel was "sent to make sure Bosworth spoke the correct lines." After the envoy returned home, Susan Rice told him at a Christmas party that Obama's policy wasn't going to change.[119]

Cabinet members and bureaucrats endlessly raked over the dying embers of Bosworth's mission, fed by White House suspicions. One skeptic characterized his attitude as "I've got a hammer, and everything looks like a nail." The frustrated veteran diplomat even reached out to friends in Congress to see if they could urge the White House to hurry up.[120]

Washington finally invited Kim Kye Gwan to visit New York four months after Bosworth returned to Washington. Just thirty-five hours later, however, an explosion near the stern of a South Korean corvette broke the ship in half and killed forty-six sailors. As evidence mounted that the North Koreans were the culprits, what had appeared to be a diplomatic opening morphed into a witch's brew of confrontation. Korea seemed on the brink of a second devastating war.

CHAPTER SIX

"If Wi worried, we worried."

T HE YELLOW SEA, A semienclosed, oval-shaped body of water
stretching six hundred miles north to south and over four hundred miles east to west, had been a dangerous flashpoint since
the end of the Korean War.[1]
General Mark Clark, commanding United Nations Forces, drew a
maritime line in 1953 called the Northern Limit Line, or NLL, that in-
corporated South Korea's five coastal islets under UN control near the
North Korean coast. The line was never discussed with Pyongyang, blocked
its access to rich fishing grounds, and had "no legal basis in international
law." But the South embraced it as a de facto boundary. When the North
claimed what Seoul thought were its waters, the Yellow Sea became a
spawning ground for bloody conflicts.[2]
On the night of March 26, 2010, a small South Korean naval corvette,
the *Cheonan*, was patrolling its regular route near the NLL looking for
enemy submarines. Fleet command had warned that a North Korean submarine and its support vessels had disappeared a few days earlier from a
naval base to the northwest, near Pyongyang. But this evening there was
no sign of trouble.[3]
Choi Won-il, the commanding officer, left the bridge at 9:05 P.M. to
check emails in his cabin. At 9:22 P.M., an explosion shattered the normal
hum of operations. The 1,200-ton, 289-foot-long vessel shot up in the air,
then listed right as it took on water. The power was out, but survivors heard
the loud screeching of steel frames shorn apart. Choi struggled to escape

his cabin, water up to his neck. Emerging, he realized the stern of the ship was gone.[4]

The crew used their cell phones to relay the ship's distress to the Second Fleet watch officer. Choi gathered survivors and assessed the damage. Over half the vessel sank beneath the surface of the Yellow Sea in just twenty minutes. U.S. and South Korean rescue ships and aircraft arrived within an hour.[5]

No one could survive more than a few hours in the frigid seas. Fifty-eight sailors were picked up. Forty bodies were recovered once floating cranes raised the stern close to the site of the sinking. Six were never found.[6]

Speculation raged about what had happened. The crew thought "war had broken out," and that a North Korean torpedo or mine had sunk the ship.[7] A nearby South Korean patrol boat had fired warning shots at an unidentified object heading north. It was only a flock of birds.[8] Others thought the ship had hit a reef or run aground. Experts blamed faulty maintenance. Some survivors claimed the vessel was in poor shape.

President Lee's advisors concluded within hours that a North Korean torpedo was responsible and that he should retaliate. However, the Bulldozer reacted cautiously. Information was incomplete. His priority was to recover the sailors and the wreckage and "to ascertain the cause."[9]

Washington was likewise cautious.[10] Asked whether North Korea was at fault, the State Department warned, "Let's not jump to any conclusions here."[11] A U.S. military commander later recalled, "I don't believe anyone thought it had been sunk by North Korea."[12] The president sent condolences and Washington pledged to support its ally.

American investigators arrived in mid-April to view the wreckage. Rear Admiral Thomas Eccles, a submarine expert with three engineering degrees from the Massachusetts Institute of Technology, surmised that a torpedo had sunk the *Cheonan.* President Lee seconded his conclusion in a phone call to Obama.[13]

International investigators confirmed a month later that the *Cheonan* had been sunk by a torpedo, although not by a direct hit. The weapon had exploded underwater near the vessel, generating a shock wave called a "bubble jet" that caused the ship to break apart. They had marshaled an array of evidence, including parts of a North Korean torpedo recovered by a dredging ship at the site of the explosion.[14]

No one knew exactly why Pyongyang would sink the *Cheonan.* It could have been payback for past bloody clashes in the West Sea, the result of tensions, especially during President Lee's tenure, over the disputed area.

The sinking may have bolstered the military's support for the leadership transition underway. Whatever the case, Kim Jong Il appears to have disappeared for a month "until the regime was confident it could weather international outrage," according to one expert.[15]

Still, the investigative team's finding was engulfed in controversy and alternative theories by other governments, experts, and conspiracy mongers. Missteps by the South Korean military, such as displaying an incorrect schematic of the North Korean torpedo during a televised briefing, fed the frenzy. Less than a third of the public believed the conclusion.[16]

Nevertheless, Lee and Obama were convinced. They agreed to conduct a naval exercise off the peninsula's east coast to send a message of solidarity to North Korea. The South Korean president also stopped almost all trade with Pyongyang, and Obama imposed new sanctions.

China, however, was concerned about aggravating tensions, and blocked their attempts to secure international restrictions. Obama "really leaned into" emphasizing the attack was a serious problem in a meeting with President Hu Jintao.[17] President Lee warned the Chinese prime minister that "you run the risk of spoiling the child if you are always permissive." Both pleas fell on deaf ears.[18]

Steve Bosworth still wanted to meet Kim Kye Gwan in New York to throw the weight of American diplomacy behind its ally. The Clinton administration had coaxed North Korea to apologize in 1996 after one of its submarines ran aground and a team sent ashore killed South Koreans.

However, Jeff Bader, the White House's top Asia expert, believed a meeting would not only "send a message of indulgence of North Korea's bad behavior," but would also be "badly received in the South."[19] With Seoul's support, he killed the idea.[20]

Instead, the Blue House used the crisis to advance its own agenda: to allow President Lee to take the lead in nuclear diplomacy. It insisted that North Korea would have to talk denuclearization with Seoul before any discussions with Washington. The demand was a showstopper since Pyongyang hadn't held nuclear talks with South Korea in almost two decades.[21]

Wi Sung-lac, South Korea's experienced nuclear negotiator, was worried. "If Wi worried, we worried," one American official recalled. His concerns turned out to be well founded.[22] The next twelve months was a roller-coaster ride as the peninsula veered from the brink of a second Korean War to the prospect of President Lee meeting Kim Jong Il.

"Going to Disneyland and not knowing
what rides you are going to go on"

The home of the anticommunist Hoover Institution, Stanford University also had the unlikely distinction of long-standing links to North Korea's communist dictatorship. John Wilson Lewis, a China expert and dedicated teacher, was responsible. From helping Henry Kissinger shape President Nixon's opening to China to participating in anti–Vietnam War teach-ins, Lewis bridged the divide between the establishment and activists. He bluntly told Kissinger that Nixon's 1971 invasion of Laos was a big mistake.[23]

Lewis believed that better relations between people could lead to better relations between countries. He was a young naval cadet at UCLA when the Korean War started. His interest in North Korea led him to visit Pyongyang in 1986. Lewis reciprocated by inviting North Koreans to Stanford.[24]

Colleagues had warm memories of him connecting with North Koreans. On one occasion, Lewis belted out a folk song, "Hallelujah, I'm a Bum," in his rich baritone voice after dinner with them. Another time, he discussed crops with a North Korean farmer as the rest of his delegation stood in the freezing cold.[25]

John Lewis tirelessly connected people. He invited a young Russia expert, Condoleezza Rice, who later became secretary of state, to come to Stanford. Lewis also recruited Siegfried "Sig" Hecker, a nuclear scientist who had never thought about visiting North Korea, to join his team.[26]

Born in Poland, raised in Austria, and educated in Cleveland, Hecker spent most of his career at the Los Alamos National Laboratory, the birthplace of America's nuclear bomb. When the Soviet Union seemed on the verge of collapse, he collaborated with Russian scientists to stop their weapons from falling into the wrong hands: terrorists and rogue states. Making the world a safer place guided his work at Stanford with Russian, Chinese, and North Korean scientists.[27]

After their first trip to North Korea in 2004, Hecker and Lewis returned six times over the next six years. The former lab director's expertise proved as invaluable as his ability to bond with foreign scientists. Separated by decades of hostility, they were still part of a global nuclear fraternity. Hecker amazed colleagues when he bantered with the North Koreans about the history of the American bomb. They knew all about it.[28]

Robert Carlin, a career intelligence analyst who had participated in every major Clinton negotiation with North Korea, was another Lewis recruit. He was impressed with the Stanford professor who "had actually met, talked with, and observed the North Koreans." Lewis brought him to Stanford when Carlin left government in 2006.[29]

Over the next decade, the activist professor, the scientist dedicated to making the world safer, and the veteran intelligence analyst traveled to North Korea trying to cut the nuclear Gordian knot. The *Cheonan's* sinking may have put a damper on Steve Bosworth's diplomacy, but the trio visited North Korea in November 2010.

Lewis once said that traveling to North Korea was like "going to Disneyland and not knowing what rides you are going to go on."[30] However, this trip was different. A think tank had published disturbing commercial satellite photos of construction at Yongbyon before they left. The North Koreans weren't rebuilding the reactor cooling tower that had been razed as part of Chris Hill's 2007 agreement. They were up to something mysterious.[31]

A second piece of the puzzle fell into place when the three Americans transited Beijing on their way to Pyongyang. Jack Pritchard, the former Clinton White House staffer and Colin Powell's North Korea envoy, had visited the site a week earlier. He had disturbing news. The North Koreans had given up hope of getting a light-water reactor from abroad and were building their own.[32]

It was bad enough that the North Koreans were trying to build a type of reactor they had never built before. If not done right, the result could be a mini-Chernobyl. Worse, they would need to produce low-enriched uranium to power the reactor. If they could do that, they could enrich the uranium further to build nuclear weapons.

The next piece of the puzzle fell into place in Pyongyang. Ri Gun, a foreign ministry official they had met many times before, dropped a hint. Their visit reminded him of 2004 when "we showed you the reprocessing and the metal." The name of the game then was "nuclear peek-a-boo" to convince Hecker and skeptics they had mastered the bomb.[33]

It was déjà vu all over again. Unhappy with the collapse of the Clinton nuclear deal in 2004, the North Koreans were now unhappy with strategic patience. It "demands us to give up our system, our ideology and our priorities," Ri pointed out.[34] Obama punctuated the point when he criticized the North in a speech just as the three Americans arrived in Pyongyang.

It was the same old issue: time. "While Obama has waited, we have realized the miniaturization of the nuclear weapons and developed the technology to put the nuclear weapon into the delivery means, completing our nuclear deterrent," Ri stated without overt belligerence. Carlin, however, sensed plenty of menace lurking around the edges.[35]

The Americans knew something was up. Hecker took Ri's bait. This trip could clear up ambiguities, he responded, if they were allowed to "visit the construction site, and the site where fuel is manufactured, as well as the uranium enrichment facility."[36]

"We have contacted the agency at Yongbyon and conveyed your requests. You can have detailed discussions on many issues," Ri told them. Over dinner, he hinted that the trio would see North Korea's uranium enrichment plant. "You will have big news," the diplomat said.[37]

The three Americans and their four escorts drove north sixty miles to Yongbyon the next day. Surrounded by hills dotted with hidden antiaircraft guns, the facility's four hundred buildings housed thousands of scientists and their families. A beehive of activity during the 1980s, Yongbyon had been shut down repeatedly because of nuclear deals, then restarted once the deals failed.

The Stanford trio arrived at a three-story guesthouse outside the installation's fenced perimeter. Greeted by scientists and representatives from Pyongyang's nuclear establishment—Hecker had met many of them before—they settled in for a short briefing.[38]

Yongbyon's chief technical official announced they had decided to build their own light-water reactor to generate electricity. The North Koreans had also decided to make their own enriched uranium fuel. (The same facility could be used to produce nuclear material for bombs.) They had announced their decision after the 2009 satellite launch, but "no one believed us including you, Dr. Hecker," the Yongbyon scientist pointed out.[39]

"Construction is completed." The uranium enrichment plant "is operational," he told the trio. They would be "the first to see this facility." It was nuclear peek-a-boo all over again. No one outside of North Korea knew the plant was working, let alone where it was.[40]

The three Americans went on an escorted tour that included a ninety-minute lunch break, but Hecker protested when the end came, and managed to stretch out the tour to three and a half hours.

The first stop was the construction site of the new reactor. Work had just started at the twenty-three-foot-deep hole where the old cooling tower had been. Fifty workers on the concrete floor were dressed in dark coveralls and hard hats. The engineer in charge frequently glanced at his boss to confirm it was all right to answer questions and avoid getting into trouble.

The North Koreans planned to finish the reactor, the first of its type, in 2012, the one hundredth anniversary of Kim Il Sung's birth. Once it mastered the design, North Korea would build bigger versions to feed electricity to its energy-starved economy and advance the country's plan for modernization.[41]

The Americans were alarmed. Even though a banner proclaimed "Safety First—Not One Accident Can Occur," the reactor was a disaster waiting to happen. The 1979 Three Mile Island and 1986 Chernobyl accidents demonstrated that operating these plants was tricky business. No one believed North Korea's regulatory authority would dare to criticize poor concrete, an inexperienced design team, or a wildly optimistic deadline.[42]

I had accompanied Hecker in 2008 to the next stop, a building that produced fuel for the old plutonium reactor but had been shut down as part of Chris Hill's deal. Then we wore white hazmat suits for protection since the building was filled with radioactive debris in plastic bags. This time, it was so clean that the North Koreans asked the Americans to stomp their feet to remove dirt from their shoes before ascending the polished granite steps.[43]

Hecker, Lewis, and Carlin were stunned as they stepped into a second-floor control room located midway in a building as long as a football field. Hecker had thought North Korea's uranium enrichment plant might consist of a couple of dozen old centrifuges. Instead, there were hundreds of modern machines in the hall.[44]

"Oh my God, they actually did what they said they were going to do," he marveled. The control room was new, filled with computers, as well as LED displays of what appeared to be data from operations below. The three couldn't tell for sure, however, whether the centrifuges were spinning.[45]

The North Korean engineer, unhappy he had been ordered by his masters in Pyongyang to host the Americans, reluctantly provided information. The visitors carefully checked what he said with their own eyes, backed up by Hecker's technical knowledge.

According to the engineer, the plant was constructed in eighteen months after the April 2009 satellite launch and had begun producing low-enriched uranium for reactor fuel. "Anyone could tell by the monitors in the control room that the facility was configured for that purpose," he asserted. Others "can think whatever they want," acknowledging that the world would accuse his country of churning out more bomb-making material.[46]

The North Korean briefer also revealed the centrifuges were like European models stolen from the Netherlands in the late 1970s by Dr. A. Q. Khan, the father of Pakistan's nuclear bomb program. Hecker confirmed that visually. He believed the plant could power the new reactor or produce enriched uranium for one or two nuclear bombs every year. It was small but dangerous.[47]

The troubling implications of what the three Americans saw hit home during the return to Pyongyang. No one, not American or Chinese intelligence, had thought the North Koreans had finished a modern uranium enrichment plant.

The speed of construction was also disturbing. It seemed impossible unless they already had experience with a similar plant that no one knew about. If this was true, the decades-old global attempt to stop Pyongyang's acquisition of nuclear technology had been a dismal failure.

Firm believers in diplomacy, the three Americans concluded it was more important than ever to reach a deal limiting Pyongyang's nuclear progress. Revealing the plant probably meant it could be sacrificed, but many Americans would see it as another reason not to talk to the North Koreans.

Ri Yong Ho, the newly appointed vice foreign minister, was calm, precise, insightful, and only as tough as necessary at dinner that evening. Carlin was angry when he viewed the new enrichment plant, but had had time to compose himself. As someone who knew Ri, who had been a regular participant in official and unofficial meetings with Americans, Carlin was determined to give him an honest reaction.[48]

People in Washington had begun to realize Obama's policy was not working, but that reassessment "will be crushed under the weight of these new developments," Carlin told Ri. There would be an outcry that his country had lied about its enrichment program all along, and a strong push against diplomacy.[49]

A calm Ri responded, "I voiced my concerns when the decision was made to construct the new reactor and the uranium enrichment plant," but "we reached the conclusion that America's Korea policy will not change. We had to find a way out."[50]

He also asserted, "Strategic patience is not bad for us. It gives us time to finish the light water reactor and produce the fuel for it." The vice foreign minister added, "We can wait. Time is what we need."[51]

But he couldn't resist striking an ominous note. Ri didn't "know if the military [would] ask the Yongbyon people to take the technology for their own use." He was doing his "best" to see that it didn't happen.[52]

The door would still open. Despite Washington's hostility, Ri asserted, "We are ready for dialogue, not just for the sake of dialogue but for dialogue with results."[53] It was time for Obama to "live up to his campaign promise to sit down with any country's leaders to solve important problems."[54]

Hecker proposed a solution that he called the "three no's:" no nuclear testing, no more production of bomb-making material, and no exports of nuclear technology. Ri hinted Pyongyang might look favorably on his proposal.[55]

The dinner ended on a positive note. "The DPRK was driven to develop nuclear weapons. Since it wasn't our choice, we can do something," Ri told the Americans.[56]

Aside from the explosive nuclear revelations, there were other disturbing signs that strategic patience wasn't working. Traffic in Pyongyang, the proliferation of cell phones, fully lit streets and government buildings, and new tractors plowing the fields—some even displaying Japanese brand names—showed that the North Koreans were getting the goods they needed.[57]

The Americans didn't say anything to the waiting press about the new centrifuge plant when they arrived back in Beijing. Instead, the trio rushed to their hotel and fired off emails to Steve Bosworth.

"The visit to the DPRK was a shocker," Hecker wrote as he described what they had seen. Carlin emailed that it almost felt like Ri was saying, "'Help us out here because we can't keep a lid on this situation much longer.'"[58] Hecker thought it was imperative they meet with Hillary Clinton.[59]

The secretary was having her own doubts about strategic patience. Clinton had failed to drum up global support for sanctions after the March sinking of the *Cheonan*. When the furor died down, the State Department sent a secret message to the North Koreans urging them to turn the page and restart dialogue.

Then, on July 21, the day the United States imposed its own sanctions, Clinton announced that Washington was ready to talk if Pyongyang sent a "positive signal." Behind the scenes, Steve Bosworth was pushing for a new initiative.[60]

In August, Clinton's Policy Planning staff, the in-house think tank, added North Korea to its list of study sessions with private experts for her.[61]

State's Asia bureau, interested in tight ties with South Korea and Japan, wanted to exclude supporters of engagement. In the end, pundits with a wide range of views convened in State's operations center.[62]

Predictably, experts on China argued it had leverage over Pyongyang. Experts on sanctions wanted more restrictions. Experts on North Korea added it couldn't be bribed with incentives. The one point everyone agreed on was that strategic patience was failing. More diplomacy had to be part of the mix. Clinton listened, took notes, and agreed.[63]

"Very disturbing," she responded to an aide's report on the Stanford trio's Yongbyon visit. As the details trickled in, the secretary decided, "We need to see Hecker." November 22 was the day.[64]

Hecker wanted to keep news of the enrichment plant secret to head off a public uproar. But the White House caught wind of a leak to David Sanger, the *New York Times* reporter, and tried to head him off. Nevertheless, Sanger's article sensationalized the discovery. The former lab director raced to get his own report out. However, it was too late; the tainted news had spread like wildfire.[65]

Hecker and Carlin met Secretary Clinton in her office on the seventh floor of the State Department. The two men had participated in the secretary's "deep dive," so they knew they were preaching to the choir.

Obviously, strategic patience was a failure. They argued their trip had demonstrated what every expert knew: how easy it was to hide a uranium enrichment plant. The United States would never know how much bomb-making material the North could produce. It could move forward unchecked.[66]

The new plant would make the situation on the peninsula much more volatile. Hecker believed that North Korea was trying to emulate Pakistan, which had developed smaller nuclear weapons to be used early in any clash against superior Indian conventional forces.[67]

Time did not favor Washington. The United States needed to halt North Korea's nuclear program, and then push for denuclearization. Clinton seemed open to Hecker's proposal, the "three no's."[68] Two years later, American spies uncovered solid information that North Korea had a larger enrichment plant than the Yongbyon facility.[69]

As Carlin feared, the trio's trip reinforced the view that diplomacy was a waste of time. Steve Bosworth wanted to move ahead with talks, but the Obama White House grew more skeptical. "There was gridlock," Hecker recalled.[70]

None of that mattered, however. Hours after Hecker and Carlin met Clinton, the Obama administration faced a new, even more dangerous challenge than Pyongyang's expanding nuclear program. Word arrived in Washington that North Korea had attacked South Korea.

"We are at your side, but don't do anything stupid."

November 23, 2010, began like any other day on the island of Yeonpyeongdo in the Yellow Sea, twice the size of New York's Central Park, and some seventy-five miles off the coast of South Korea but just eight miles from North Korea. Most of its people lived in 930 houses clustered around a port on the southeastern shore.[71]

A portion of the sea surrounding the island, belonging to South Korea, was also claimed by North Korea. The inhabitants—many from families who had fled the North—lived their lives in the shadow of war. "We are always afraid every day," a South Korean resident confessed, "but you get used to living in fear."[72]

Concern over the *Cheonan* eight months earlier had died down. South Koreans were mesmerized by the tearful reunion of hundreds of elderly North and South Koreans eager to see loved ones before they died, a small sliver of the millions separated by the war. People yearned for more conciliatory steps.[73]

Those hopes were crushed on November 23 by one of the most dramatic confrontations since the Korean War. South Korea had conducted at least sixty-five live-artillery-fire exercises since 2006, including three in 2010. The North Koreans had never responded, but on that day, a live-fire drill became a live-fire exchange.[74]

As the sun rose at 7:30 A.M., the South Korean Marines prepared to fire artillery shells into the disputed territorial waters. An hour later, the North Korean military warned of a "resolute physical counterstrike" if they didn't cancel the exercise.

The South Koreans dismissed the threat even though North Korean artillery moved into firing positions, aircraft took to the skies, and patrol boats left their bases. The exercise began at 10:15 A.M. and lasted three hours.[75]

The North Korean barrage commenced not long after the exercise ended. From 2:34 P.M. to 2:46 P.M., 150 shells rained down on the Marines, the villages, and the seas surrounding the island. Screaming and shouting civilians hurried to bomb shelters and docks on the southeast coast. An elderly fisherwoman recounted, "I was 12 during the Korean War and we saw planes fly overhead, but nothing like this happened."[76]

Yeonpyeongdo on fire caused by North Korea's shelling, November 23, 2010.
Featured in the 2010 ROK Defense Photo Magazine, property of the Republic
of Korea Army. CC Attribution-Sharealike 2.0 Generic.

"I did what Marines do," the commander recalled. His unit had the
same fighting tradition as its American counterparts. With shells landing
all around them, his men moved their six self-propelled howitzers into firing position. Two guns didn't work and the radar that pinpointed the origin of incoming shells also failed.

By 2:47 P.M., one minute after the barrage ended, they began firing
fifty rounds at targets they already knew. Eight minutes elapsed. The Marines fired thirty more rounds after their equipment was fixed.[77]

At 3:10 P.M., the North Koreans fired again, perhaps because the South
Korean response had struck a barracks, killing a number of soldiers. The
village's loudspeakers had already urged everyone to evacuate after the first
salvo. One resident made it to the harbor. He "jumped down behind the
sea wall," relieved that "they didn't hit the cars parked there or there would
have been a big explosion."[78]

At 3:41 P.M., the second North Korean barrage ended. The exchange
had lasted just an hour. They had fired 170 shells and the South Koreans, 80.

Miraculously, no residents died, although fifty-two were wounded.
Villagers had been out in their boats fishing. Others hid in underground
shelters. Inaccurate North Korean shells, most of which couldn't penetrate
concrete walls, landed in the sea.

"We were surprised they were so powerless," a South Korean official recalled.[79]

Two mainland construction workers perished. They were still outside after explosions sent their crew rushing into the basement of a half-finished building. They were burned beyond recognition.[80]

Only two South Korean Marines were killed and six wounded. Still, the emergency room of the local hospital was a "sea of blood," a medic recalled.[81]

Hundreds scrambled to escape to Incheon. Dozens cowered in cold, dark shelters for days without blankets and with only bread to eat. Most people stayed away for months, living with relatives in motels and in a hangar-sized bathhouse converted into a refugee center.[82]

One hundred and ten miles away in Seoul, President Lee convened an emergency meeting in a Blue House bunker. After all the good news that month—family reunions, an economic summit, and President Obama's first visit to South Korea—the attack was a shock.

Could this be the start of an all-out clash? They wouldn't dare, Lee thought. It would mean the end of North Korea. The Chinese wouldn't allow it. How to respond? Deep in thought, the president entered the bunker filled with his advisors, mesmerized like millions of Koreans by a live national broadcast of the bombardment, courtesy of civilians with cell phones on the ground.[83]

An aide ran in and whispered to Lee's chief of staff. The president had been reported as urging "restraint to prevent escalation into war." The normally calm Lee raised his voice: "Where did they hear that? Who said that? Our territory is being attacked."

He issued a statement promising "strenuous retaliation" if there were more provocations. But the damage was done; the Bulldozer appeared to be backing down.[84]

Lee wasn't just angry with the North Koreans. He was angry with Kim Tae-yong, a former general and his defense minister. Linked by a video camera to the military command center, Lee could see the staff scurrying about. But Kim wasn't there. He had learned of the attack while testifying at the National Assembly, found a phone, ordered retaliation, and rushed to his office, and then to the Blue House. Lee scolded him for not coming sooner.[85]

While the president wanted to order overwhelming retaliation, the South Korean military wanted to avoid a wider conflict. Its rules of engagement were meant to prevent that from happening. The military was under strict orders to only fire back twice the number of the same weapons at the forces that launched an attack.

"North Korea shot 200 rounds; why did we shoot only 80 rounds? Even double that wouldn't be enough," Lee demanded to know. Since the military's assessment was that 40 to 50 rounds had landed on the island, "80 rounds were fired in response according to the rules of engagement . . . with the same type and quantity of weapons," Minister Kim responded.[86]

"It was mind-boggling," Lee recalled. Provocations required a decisive response: launching a counterstrike with aircraft, not counting the number of shots the North Koreans had fired.

But the defense minister resisted. Rear units armed with bombs had to be called up. The sun was setting. The pilots—with limited training for a night attack—could only promise to do their best, which was hardly reassuring. An airstrike could also escalate out of control since the planes would have to destroy air defense installations to get to the targets.[87]

The Bulldozer paid a surprise visit to the Defense Ministry that evening, to squash rumors that he was avoiding a counterattack. He expected to hear options for a decisive response, but all the military talked about was how the attack had violated the armistice ending the Korean War.

"You are soldiers, not lawyers!" an angry Lee admonished them. "Mobilize all of our land, sea and air forces" to deliver a "punishment that goes beyond the rules of engagement" if the North attacks again, he demanded. His outburst, leaked to the press, was intended to deflect blame onto the military.[88]

The next day, a thorough assessment of North Korean shells fired, and South Korea's counterstrike, proved that the response had fallen short of the rules of engagement. "In a time of crisis, we needed a guy with more guts," a Lee advisor recalled. The president accepted the defense minister's resignation.[89]

The North Korean assault came as a complete surprise to the Americans. Steve Bosworth was passing over South Korea's offshore islands on his way to Beijing after briefing Seoul and Tokyo on the Yongbyon uranium revelation. All was quiet.

His Blackberry erupted with news of the barrage when he landed some ninety minutes later. Concerned that a second Korean War was about to begin, Bosworth rushed to his hotel to call his wife.[90]

Kathleen Stephens, the American ambassador in Seoul, was about to leave the downtown embassy for Thanksgiving in Arizona. Her driver exclaimed, "There has been an attack on Yeonpyeongdo."

After she arrived at Incheon Airport, where Koreans huddled around cell phones and video screens watching the attack unfold a few miles away, the State Department gave her the go-ahead to travel. Stephens, however, was ordered back to Seoul the day after she arrived home.[91]

Walter "Skip" Sharp, the top American general in Korea, was briefing a NATO delegation at his headquarters in central Seoul. An aide interrupted: "Sir, we need to talk to you right now." Sharp hesitated. "Right now," the aide repeated. The general stepped outside, was informed of the attack, and rushed to call the secretary of defense.[92]

In Washington, Tom Donilon, Obama's national security advisor, woke the president just before 4:00 A.M. to inform him that South Korea had been attacked. Obama tried to phone President Lee, but the Bulldozer had gone to bed after scolding his military. When they finally connected, Obama offered solace, condolences, and encouragement.[93]

The artillery attack was worrisome. The sinking of the *Cheonan* could be explained as payback for past clashes. An attack on South Korean soil led one White House aide to wonder, "Was this a tail-wagging-the-dog situation? Was it related to Kim Jong Il's poor health?"[94]

American intelligence had reported months earlier that Kim Jong Un, out to prove himself, had pushed for an attack. His father had said "No." Given his stroke and diminished capacity, however, the elder Kim may have given in to his son.

A strike also could have shored up military support for the succession. There were unconfirmed reports that the two had inspected the units that launched the strike just hours earlier. If true, such a visit would reinforce that conclusion.

If this was the new normal, how could the United States and South Korea defend themselves against a much more aggressive North Korea without triggering a larger conflict? And as the administration was about to discover, how could it restrain Seoul from a massive retaliation that could escalate into a full-scale war?[95]

The first order of business was to head off more attacks. Obama and Lee agreed to "hold combined exercises and enhanced training." Slated to visit the East Sea off North Korea's coast, the aircraft carrier USS *George Washington* was rerouted to the West Sea, the site of the artillery attack.

However, the calculated move to send a message to North Korea and China threatened to drag the United States into a confrontation. After the South Koreans had been already shamed by the *Cheonan*'s sinking, the Yeon-pyeongdo attack "poured gasoline on the South Korean military's bonfire," according to one American officer. It hatched a plan for another live-fire drill and expected North Korean artillery units to respond. This time the South Koreans had enlisted backup, an American carrier task force.[96]

"What they wanted to do was a postmortem retaliation, not self-defense," the American officer recalled. An Obama advisor remembered that "the carrier could have dragged us into something we didn't want to be dragged into at that stage."

The American military rejected Seoul's plan. The naval exercise in the West Sea went ahead. The live-fire drill set for November 30 as the exercise wound down was "delayed."[97]

President Lee, however, was still "mad as hell and politically vulnerable," according to an Obama aide. Proportional response was discarded and replaced by the threat of massive counterstrikes—one hundred times greater—against targets beyond military units that initiated attacks.[98]

Chun Yung-woo, Lee's conservative but pragmatic security advisor, and Kim Kwan-jin, the new defense minister who reminded observers of Donald Rumsfeld, discounted the danger of escalation. "All we have to do is hit the North Koreans hard and they will back down," they argued.[99] Were the North to respond, "We will teach them a lesson." That's "better for building a sustainable peace."[100]

The South Koreans concocted another plan to conduct an artillery drill like the one that triggered the North Korean strike, backed up this time by their own threat of massive retaliation. Ambassador Stephens and General Sharp repeatedly asked Chun, "Do you really need to do this?"[101]

The South Koreans "bulked up," according to an American officer. Fifty aircraft, essentially the first package of planes that would be rushed into a real war, would back up the artillery. They would fly north, take up stations close to Yeonpyeongdo, and respond to any North Korean military moves.[102] Local commanders could retaliate if the North Koreans interfered with the exercise, including against targets that were at the heart of Pyongyang's military.[103]

The South Koreans didn't consider Murphy's Law: Anything that could go wrong, would go wrong. They assumed the North Koreans wouldn't view hundreds of shells landing in waters they claimed, backed up by an air armada just a few miles from their border, as provocative.

Anyone looking at a map would also see that North Korea's surface-to-air missiles could blanket nearby Incheon International Airport, South Korea's global hub. Almost six thousand passengers arrived every hour.

Intentions didn't matter; a civilian airliner could be shot down, igniting a war.[104]

President Obama understood Lee's predicament and agreed that inaction wasn't an option. Provoking conflict over an artillery drill, however, wasn't an option either. Some American officials compared the brewing confrontation to the Cuban Missile Crisis of 1962.[105]

Inside the administration, a debate broke out. One side argued against any exercise since it could drag the United States into a war. The other countered that Washington had to back an ally that had just been attacked.[106] The White House split the difference. "We weren't going to jerk the choke chain, but we weren't letting the South off either," one aide recalled.[107]

There were "so many meetings, so many mixed messages, back and forth" with Seoul, a senior commander remembered.[108] Civilian micromanagement of the military made it more complicated. American decision-makers pored over maps and satellite photos scrutinizing targets "as if everyone was an analyst," a Pentagon official observed.[109]

Admiral Mike Mullen, chairman of the Joint Chiefs of Staff, traveled to Seoul the first week in December. He promptly reassured the public and President Lee, "We are at your side," while privately admonishing the South Koreans, "but don't do anything stupid." Allowing local commanders to retaliate left open the possibility that "a bunch of generals might feel pressure to show they were tough," according to a Pentagon official.[110]

The allies found a solution by mid-December. The pragmatic Chun proposed that South Korea fire shells into undisputed waters rather than disputed waters. Washington decision-makers huddled over a map and drew boundaries for the new target area.[111]

The American and South Korean militaries would stand ready, but aircraft would avoid taking threatening flight paths north of the island. The targets, however, still "went well beyond just 'some' artillery," one officer recalled.[112]

The two allies also launched a diplomatic offensive to convince China to restrain the North Koreans. Beijing had refused to agree to sanctions after the *Cheonan* incident, but this time, Obama and Lee had better luck.[113]

The Bulldozer turned up the heat during a session with Dai Bingguo, China's top diplomatic troubleshooter. Lee warned that if North Korea were to act again, "We will severely retaliate and punish them."[114] Lee knew that Dai, slated to go to Pyongyang soon, would pass on his threat.[115]

President Obama then called Hu Jintao on December 6, just before Dai left. He urged Hu to restrain the North Koreans. This time, the Chinese leader didn't complain about naval exercises in the Yellow Sea or blame Washington for not talking to the North Koreans. It was a positive sign.[116]

Although Dai previously had confessed to the Americans that he didn't dare be candid with Kim, the envoy "conveyed a very stern warning" to the North Korean dictator. China would not come to North Korea's aid if there was an armed conflict.[117]

Tensions mounted as the December window for the live-fire drill approached. Rumors spread in Korea that the United States might evacuate hundreds of thousands of expats, a sure sign war was imminent. People watched General Sharp's daughter's Facebook page to see if her family was still going to visit Seoul for Christmas.[118]

With the drill approaching, diplomats tried to head off a war. On December 18, Russia convened an emergency session of the UN Security Council, hoping to send an envoy to the region to ease tensions. When Ambassador Stephens and General Sharp asked a senior ROK (Republic of Korea) official if Seoul was still determined to go ahead, he replied, "What is the US veto for?"[119] The Russian envoy warned that war could break out in a few hours.[120]

In Pyongyang, Bill Richardson, the former UN ambassador, appealed to the North Koreans in a last-ditch effort to avoid a conflict. They apparently agreed to shut down their Yongbyon uranium enrichment plant. But the South's defense minister still informed General Sharp, "We are firing tomorrow. There is no changing it."[121]

Sung Kim, Bosworth's deputy, met the North Koreans in New York to warn them what was coming. While American intelligence monitoring Pyongyang's military units had seen no signs of the threatened strong response, there was always a danger of miscalculation.[122]

At 9:05 A.M. on December 20, hours after the UN debate ended, loudspeakers on Yeonpyeongdo informed the 280 civilians, officials, and reporters still there that "a maritime firing drill [is] scheduled to take place today. All residents must move to nearby air raid shelters."[123] After a fog delay, the South Koreans fired hundreds, maybe thousands, of rounds into the water in just ninety minutes.

Deputy National Security Advisor Denis McDonough and his staff monitored the action in the White House Situation Room. The shells plunged into South Korean waters, but at least one appeared to have splashed down in waters claimed by North Korea. "There was a lot of eye-rolling," an aide recalled. "You mean after all this, you aren't aiming?" They all held their collective breath.[124]

At the Pentagon, Admiral Mullen and Michael Schiffer, the top Asia expert, weren't as concerned. "We were going to kill a bunch of waves," one recalled. But no one could be sure what the North Koreans would do, especially after a shell went astray.[125] America's spy satellites and planes spotted nothing unusual.

The North Korean military issued a communiqué later that day stating, "We felt it was not worth reacting one-by-one to military provocations."[126]

Life returned to Yeonpyeongdo, with a South Korean destroyer nearby and jets flying overhead for protection. Evacuees returned to homes still surrounded by charred buildings and piles of rubbish. The ferry connecting the island to the mainland began operating again. "I feel good. I am scared though," one resident admitted to a reporter.[127]

Was the Korean Peninsula about to be engulfed in a second Korean War? Secretary Gates recalled that "South Korea's plans for retaliation were . . . disproportionately aggressive." He worried that "the exchanges could escalate dangerously."[128]

Other officials believed the South Koreans may have had a "hold me back" mentality; "they really didn't want to fight."[129] At the very least, Washington's intervention reduced the chances of a devastating conflict.

Jeff Bader argued that the results "generally vindicated" strategic patience. Washington "sent the strongest possible message that we would not resume the old cycle and that North Korea needed to adjust." The United States also proved it could work with China. The White House aide believed the crisis set the stage for a "freeze and degrade strategy" in talks.[130]

While Washington failed to appreciate the pressing need to reverse the slow-motion deterioration on the peninsula, it may have been obvious to President Lee. In fact, his secret diplomacy with North Korea had already made more progress than anyone had expected.

Indescribable Anxiety

Ambassador Kim Sook crossed the DMZ three months after the *Cheonan* incident and three months before the November shelling. He left a farewell letter for his wife in his study, unsure if he would return from his secret mission.[131]

The "Cold War's last divide" was anything but demilitarized. Littered with hundreds of thousands of mines and barbed-wire fences, it was night-marishly hard to navigate. South Koreans crossed through the zone at the Joint Security Area, a cluster of blue buildings straddling the border. All comings and goings were recorded by troops guarding the area.[132]

A high-ranking official in South Korea's spy agency, Kim was not a spy. He was a respected diplomat with a three-decade-long career, in-cluding a stint at the Beijing multilateral talks as South Korea's nuclear negotiator.

Smart, meticulous, and experienced, Kim had to accept President Lee's appointment as deputy director of Seoul's spy agency. Leon Panetta, the American CIA director, paid him a backhanded compliment after an hour-long chat. He warned an aide, "Don't trust this guy. He will steal your wallet."[133]

South Korea's National Intelligence Service had a long, sordid history. Originally called the KCIA after its American counterpart, Seoul's mili-tary rulers used the agency to investigate, detain, and torture whoever they pleased as well as to kidnap dissidents abroad. It also raised funds through extortion, stock manipulation, and bribery of individuals and foreign governments.

The KCIA was reformed and renamed as South Korea transitioned from dictatorship to democracy, eventually becoming the National Intel-ligence Service, or NIS. When Ambassador Kim moved into its up-to-date facilities in southern Seoul, sixty thousand employees were spread across thirty-nine headquarters and regional offices.[134] Once he was put in charge of foreign intelligence, Kim's most important job was to open his own "goon channel" to North Korea.

South Korea's spies had been meeting North Korean spies since 1972. Feeling "a kind of anxiety" that was "quite indescribable," the then KCIA director had slipped into Pyongyang to see Kim Il Sung, not sure if he would return. However, his meeting led to the first communiqué issued by the two Koreas, a sign that peace was possible. Spies later played impor-tant roles in arranging inter-Korean summits.[135]

President Lee turned to the NIS at the end of 2009 after talks between North and South collapsed. The agency had failed in his first year in of-fice to establish a channel with the North Koreans. Kim Sook started small. He recruited a private citizen who knew their way around Pyongyang to help establish the means to communicate with the North Koreans in case of a crisis. No one knew about it except his boss and President Lee.

When the *Cheonan* was sunk, Kim had the perfect opportunity to test his strategy. He warned the North Koreans his country would thwart any more attacks, but also proposed face-to-face talks. Several months later, they invited the surprised diplomat-turned-spy to Pyongyang.[136]

Ambassador Kim and an aide crossed the DMZ in the dark, then climbed into a waiting car for the three-hour trip escorted by the North Korean secret police. As the convoy sped north, occasional pedestrians holding flashlights walked on the side of the road, lighting up the deserted four-lane highway. Hills and tunnels gave way to flatlands surrounding Pyongyang and to the city itself.[137]

Kim's July visit was the first of three in as many months. The negotiators were squirreled away in a Pyongyang guesthouse and others outside the capitol, where meetings stretched out for three days at a time. No one knew Kim was there except President Lee, his boss, and the North Koreans. Worried that he might be spotted, his minders refused his request to visit a famous restaurant that served cold buckwheat noodles, a favorite summertime meal.[138]

General Ryu Kyung, fresh from his triumph arranging Bill Clinton's session with Kim Jong Il, was waiting for Kim Sook. By now, everyone knew he was the leader's right-hand man. If they didn't, "the Young General" made sure they did. Ryu boasted he was more important than the American national security advisor. He alone was responsible for relations with the United States, South Korea, and Japan.[139]

The Young General had more in mind than calming tensions. His job was to arrange a summit with President Lee. All South Korea had to do was provide hundreds of thousands of tons of rice to help feed North Korea, and fertilizer for its crops.[140]

General Ryu's proposal may have seemed surprising coming after the *Cheonan*. But it was the same old story, the same demand the North Koreans had made before two past summits and again in late 2009. President Lee couldn't accept it, and neither could his envoy, especially after forty-six sailors had been killed, and the Bulldozer had labeled North Korea as his country's "archenemy."[141]

The South Koreans demanded that North Korea first admit its guilt, apologize, and punish those responsible for the attack. But Pyongyang couldn't apologize for something it claimed it didn't do. Moreover, the North Koreans had never had an easy time saying they were sorry.[142]

Ryu was willing to express regret for the loss of life on behalf of his fellow North Koreans, but not as the culprit. The North had already issued a statement on the "regretful accident," muddied by an assertion that the crew had been forced to live "a tiresome life in the puppet army."[143]

While Pyongyang's statement was unacceptable, the experienced South Korean diplomat glimpsed a sign that Ryu's boss really wanted a summit. Kim went home and wrote an apology for the North Koreans himself rather than wait for them to come up with one guaranteed to be unacceptable. His move was a standard diplomatic tactic, getting the first draft on the table to serve as the basis for a deal.[144]

Kim crossed the DMZ again a month later. The Young General was waiting. His straightforward draft expressed deep regrets about the sinking, and condolences to "the victims and bereaved families." It concluded, "The DPRK will do its utmost to make this tragic incident not happen again and will endeavor with concerned parties for the purpose of lasting peace and stability on the Korean peninsula."[145]

"This means we did it!" the Young General protested, probably after showing the language to Kim Jong Il. The North's intention was to express regret, not as criminals but as brethren.[146]

The South Koreans presented a new draft on their next trip, using Korean grammar to omit "the DPRK" as the subject of the statement. Ryu rejected it again. This time, his indignation was fueled by President Lee's proclamation a few days earlier that "reunification will definitely come." The Bulldozer even proposed creating a special tax to finance the cost.[147]

The new tax implied "absorption by the South," Ryu thundered.[148] He was right. President Lee's advisors believed Kim Jong Il wouldn't live much longer and that North Korea would collapse once he was gone. The secret talks ended then and there.

President Lee still pressed forward. He told the *New York Times* in early November that he was flexible when it came to an apology.[149] In private, the Bulldozer decided to cut through the haggling and propose an unconditional summit. The North Koreans only needed to agree when and where the two leaders would meet. Everything and anything—an apology, food assistance, even denuclearization—could be on the agenda.[150]

The November 23 artillery attack shattered the relative calm just as Ambassador Kim was about to leave for Pyongyang with the new proposal. He still traveled to the North even though the two countries traded threats and the danger of war loomed. Kim's secret trip just days after the attack was unnerving.[151]

The atmosphere was tense as Kim and Ryu exchanged harsh threats. The soft-spoken South Korean diplomat warned that one of their two countries would disappear if there was a war. His meaning was clear: the North was no match for South Korea's firepower.

The Young General countered that firepower was not the only factor that determined victory. North Korea had brilliant leadership, an expression of his devotion to Kim Jong Il.[152]

But the mood quickly changed. With threats and counterthreats on the table, the two men switched to planning for a summit. Let the leaders meet and talk about everything freely rather than haggling over preconditions, the South Koreans told Ryu. His boss could raise the issue of assistance and Lee could talk about denuclearization. The Young General agreed. The two men set a target date for February 2011.[153]

Where would the leaders meet? The South Koreans wanted Seoul since the first two summits had been in Pyongyang. Ryu said "No," even though the North Korean leader had earlier agreed to come south "at an appropriate time." The South Koreans proposed other cities in their country, as well as Vladivostok in the Russian Far East, a neutral site the North's dictator had visited in 2002.[154] Ryu told him it was Pyongyang or nothing.

Kim Jong Il may have been afraid a trip outside his country would jeopardize his health or his regime. Yet he later visited Russia just before his death.[155] More likely, the summit venue dispute reflected the decades-old struggle between the two Koreas. Appearances mattered. The talks ended without an agreement.

Two weeks later, General Ryu traveled to Seoul. No one knew he was in town except Ambassador Kim, the director of the NIS, and President Lee. Like the North Korean envoys who had visited after Kim Dae-jung died, the Young General wanted to see the Bulldozer. And like those envoys, he was probably carrying a message from Kim Jong Il.[156]

The stakes were high. After months of meeting with Ryu, the South Korean diplomat-turned-spy believed Kim Jong Il was serious about a summit. He was inclined to recommend that the president see the envoy since that could clinch the deal.[157]

The risk was real that Lee would appear to be caving in to blackmail if he agreed to a summit after the North Korean shelling. Moreover, a political firestorm could erupt if word of his meeting with Ryu leaked. On the other hand, Lee would miss a promising opportunity if he didn't see the envoy.[158]

General Ryu waited. Lee deliberated, and finally decided to fob him off on Kim's boss, a former Seoul subway manager and vice mayor who knew nothing about North Korea. Predictably, their meeting was a bust.

A disappointed Ryu returned home, presumably still carrying a message from the dictator in his back pocket.[159]

The CIA passed on startling news a few weeks later, just before the South Koreans requested another meeting. Ryu Kyung had been shot as a spy, reportedly with a machine gun at, or after, a party hosted by Kim Jong Il.[160]

No one in Washington or Seoul knew why, but they had lost a valuable negotiating partner. Ryu, promoted to the rank of three-star general and appointed an alternative member of the Workers' Party central committee, appeared to be parlaying his relationship with Kim Jong Il into a steady climb up the leadership ladder.[161]

His return from Seoul empty handed, however, was disastrous. According to intelligence reports, Kim Jong Il was furious he hadn't clinched a deal. Ryu may have added insult to injury by meeting a low-level functionary rather than returning to Pyongyang immediately. The Young General's performance also may have given jealous rivals an opening.[162]

To Kim Sook, Ryu Kyung was a dedicated, tenacious, and pragmatic adversary—a clever opponent who fell victim to a man he considered more than a father.[163] Both men had brought the two Koreas to the brink of a historic third summit only to fail. Ryu's execution was a sobering reminder of the brutality of North Korea's system.

CHAPTER SEVEN

"We've got them right where
we want them."

THE TWO HUNDRED SEATS in the RAND Corporation's Santa Monica, California, auditorium were nearly filled. James Steinberg, the deputy secretary of state, was the headliner. A RAND researcher twenty years earlier, he had been passed over for the job of Obama's national security advisor and named Secretary Clinton's Number Two instead. She liked him, her aides suspected he was a White House mole, and bureaucrats thought he was brilliant, grouchy, and arrogant.[1]

Steinberg's recipe for success in dealing with North Korea—and Iran—was simple: diplomacy backed by stronger measures. "We've got them right where we want them," the confident deputy secretary told two surprised audience members afterwards. If anything, the mounting North Korean nuclear threat and a near war had demonstrated just the opposite.[2]

Steinberg, however, may have had reason to think his pronouncement made perfect sense. In 2010, China had cooperated on North Korea and other common interests, in exchange for U.S. acceptance of China's rise as a global power. Steinberg and Jeff Bader thought the task now in 2011 was to press ahead with China, building on what had been accomplished.[3]

Secretary Gates had warned the Chinese a few weeks earlier in Beijing that North Korea now posed a "direct threat" to the United States because its missiles could reach beyond the region. If Pyongyang didn't restart negotiations and stop building better rockets, Washington might have to stage a military buildup near China's borders.[4]

Nonetheless, his meeting with Xi Jinping, the Chinese heir apparent, was cause for optimism. Born to a life of privilege, Xi dug ditches after his father, a senior party leader, had been imprisoned during the Cultural Revolution and his sister committed suicide. He joined the communist party once the upheaval ended and had become a member of the Politburo by 2007. One Asian leader compared him to Nelson Mandela, "a person with enormous emotional stability who does not allow his personal misfortunes or sufferings to affect his judgment."[5]

Confident, self-assured, and blunt, Xi spoke frankly and fluently, without notes, a breath of fresh air compared to the scripted Hu Jintao. Rather than repeat the standard line about the importance of diplomacy, Xi was skeptical Pyongyang would give up its nuclear weapons. His anti–North Korean comments telegraphed positions Xi would adopt as China's leader, an encouraging glimpse into the future for the Americans.[6]

After President Obama threatened Hu Jintao during a trip to Washington, the Chinese leader deigned to express "concern" about the North's uranium enrichment program. "That was attention-getting," an American official recalled. Steinberg told the press in Seoul that the joint communiqué would "help drive the message home" to the North.[7]

Confident that patience was working, the White House tightened its grip on policymaking. The newly established Deputies Small Group, or DSG, only included a few top officials rather than the usual interagency gaggle. It was intended to foster collaboration, encourage out-of-the-box thinking, and "prevent leaks to the press by twentysomethings sitting in on meetings." Instead, the group "insulated the decision-making process and helped avoid bureaucratic pressures to do something," according to one official.[8]

"What did the DSG decide?" bureaucrats who weren't part of the group often asked each other after it met. "I don't know" was the usual response. Sanctions experts received nonsensical directives. The Pentagon was stymied when instructed to examine defenses against North Korean missiles. None of its experts were part of the conversation.[9]

Perhaps no agency felt the tug of the White House leash more than the State Department, still haunted by Clinton's campaign clash with Obama. One exasperated Clinton advisor wrangled an invitation to the DSG, only to be turned away at the White House gate and forced to walk back to the department in the pouring rain.[10]

Still, Steve Bosworth was hopeful talks might resume. Secretary Clinton wanted to stop careening from crisis to crisis on the peninsula. Even a White House architect of strategic patience about to retire told his successor, "We have got to come to the table. There has to be a serious negotiation."[11]

There was another reason for cautious optimism: the North Koreans. Pyongyang desperately needed food after torrential rains, floods, and landslides the previous summer, followed by an outbreak of livestock disease and a brutal winter. Reaching out to the global community for aid could lower tensions and help smooth the way for Kim Jong Il's son to take over once he died.[12]

"We don't want to visit with them. We want to visit with you."

Joe DeTrani believed in diplomacy. The time seemed right again after the March 2010 *Cheonan* sinking and the November artillery attack.

As the head of the intelligence community's National Counterproliferation Center, DeTrani's job was to "protect the American people from weapons of mass destruction," according to its website. Terrorist groups were the main target, but North Korea was also in the intelligence community's crosshairs. Quiet persuasion was one tool at its disposal.[13]

While North Korea had racked up billions of dollars in missile sales, earning the moniker "Missiles R-Us," an even bigger nightmare came true in 2007.[14] Pyongyang was caught helping Syria build a nuclear reactor that could have produced bomb-making plutonium. Washington breathed a collective sigh of relief when Israeli warplanes destroyed the unfinished facility.[15]

DeTrani was worried about a new nuclear cash crop: North Korea's growing stockpile of enriched uranium. Easy to export since it was harder to detect than plutonium, it also made it easier to build a bomb. The nuclear device dropped on Hiroshima, which killed one hundred thousand people in 1945, was so elementary that the United States never bothered to test it.[16]

His solution was more talks with North Korea. Coincidentally, the White House wanted to reactivate the goon channel to de-escalate tensions and prepare for the possibility of instability when Kim Jong Il died. The channel was perfect. Its hardliners played a central role in proliferating weapons and could play a critical role in the North Korean succession.[17]

The CIA dialed Pyongyang after the White House approved its plan. The same spies who had arranged the Singapore meetings agreed to organize sessions with their leaders. DeTrani and a colleague boarded a flight from Washington to Beijing in late January, and then the Air Koryo shuttle to Pyongyang, ending up in a state-owned guesthouse for two days.[18]

The Americans got the first hint their visit was important at dinner that evening. Their gracious host, Woo Dong Cheuk, was head of the Security Ministry—and much more. A philosophy major, general, and spy hunter, he was one of a handful of people chosen to groom Kim Jong Un for leadership. Woo had accompanied his father to dinner with Bill Clinton. He also probably would report to the leader on DeTrani's time in Pyongyang.[19]

The next day, the two Americans met Kim Yong Chol, North Korea's equivalent of the CIA director and soon to be its top intermediary with the United States. Rumored to have masterminded the *Cheonan* incident and the attempted assassination of North Korean defectors, he had also negotiated major deals with Seoul.[20]

Arrogant, pugnacious, and combative, Kim was more than ready to denounce the United States and South Korea for hours at a time. And he knew the details of American policy more precisely than the Americans knew North Korean policy. "You would not want him as an enemy since he knew you better than you knew yourself," one visitor to Pyongyang recalled.[21]

The two CIA officials were ushered into Kim's empty office in a walled, heavily guarded military compound. They sat at a conference table across from his desk. The spymaster and a North Korean he introduced as the scientist responsible for "our nuclear program" joined them.[22]

The American spies wanted Kim to promise that North Korea wouldn't sell nuclear technology to bad actors and would stop missile exports. They reminded him that the United States knew about Pyongyang's uranium enrichment program.[23]

The bellicose general pushed back: North Korea would never sell anything nuclear, had nothing to do with the Syrian reactor, and wasn't producing uranium for bombs. As for missile sales, he scolded the Americans, exclaiming, "Stop the accusations!" The United States sold more missiles than anyone else.[24]

When they told Kim that Washington wanted to try to work out these problems, the general abruptly switched gears. He repeated more than once that North Korea was prepared to talk.[25]

In the next session, the Americans met Jang Song Thaek, Kim Jong Il's brother-in-law. A session with him was the next best thing to seeing the leader himself. The ambitious Jang had been purged more than once but had been appointed head of the council established to spearhead his nephew's succession. He was the odds-on favorite to become the power behind the throne once the elder Kim passed from the scene. There was even speculation that Jang might push the son aside.

The Americans repeated their talking points about North Korea's objectionable WMD activities but added that the United States wanted to move toward better relations with Pyongyang.[26]

Jang smoothly countered the accusations. He also reaffirmed, however, that his country desired good relations with the United States.[27]

Sightseeing for the visiting spies included a visit to the Juche Tower, a monument to the North Koreans' philosophy of self-reliance. Located on the east side of the river that split the city, the tower faced Kim Il-Sung Square, home of the Ministry of Foreign Affairs.[28]

"Would you like to go visit them?" the spies asked the Americans, sardonically hinting at their rivalry with the diplomats over who would lead the charge in handling the United States. "We don't want to visit with them. We want to visit with you," the Americans responded.[29]

A week later, DeTrani sat across from Barack Obama, Joe Biden, and their top aides in the Oval Office. Everyone wanted to know, Are the North Koreans serious? Do they want to move forward?[30]

Much of the forty-five-minute conversation focused on Jang. DeTrani, a China hand, likened him to Deng Xiaoping, who had followed Mao. Both had been purged, and then staged comebacks. Biden joked to Obama, "You better not do that to me." Like Deng, Jang had been interested in economic reform, and supported a less confrontational path with the United States.[31]

The trip was worthwhile. The administration sent a message to the North Koreans about weapons proliferation and resuming talks. Meeting Jang spoke volumes. The two countries seemed on the threshold of another thaw.

"We like you, Ambassador King. We don't like your title."

North Korea had suffered from chronic food shortages since its founding over six decades earlier. Mountainous terrain limited the amount of arable land. Droughts, typhoons, heat waves, and widespread frosts were constant threats. North Korean planners had embraced costly, inefficient farming methods that depended on cheap fuel and fertilizer from Russia and China. Some experts thought Pyongyang's crops were planted in more chemicals than soil.[32]

Shortages skyrocketed in the mid-1990s when North Korea encountered the perfect storm of Kim Il Sung's death and a collapse of foreign subsidies and imports. The Soviet Union had splintered, and China demanded fair prices the North couldn't pay. Heavy rains fell, triggering flooding of biblical proportions, followed by drought. Grain production dropped drastically, the public distribution system disintegrated, and as many as one million people may have died.[33]

President Ronald Reagan once proclaimed that "a hungry child knows no politics." But as one congressional staffer recalled, "funding the spread of leprosy would have been more popular than aid for North Korea." The Clinton administration did help pull Pyongyang out of its 1990s nosedive, although the shortages weren't obvious until after the 1994 nuclear deal was done. President George W. Bush helped only after progress in nuclear talks.[34]

When another flood triggered fears of more famine, Jon Brause, a civil servant at Bush's Agency for International Development, hatched a plan to go "big for big." The United States would provide five hundred thousand tons of aid if the North Koreans allowed outsiders to ensure it reached the right people. He sold his idea to the White House, and then to the North Koreans over coffee and cookies in Pyongyang. They signed a twenty-two-page single-spaced, detail-filled document.[35]

A consortium of private American organizations and the United Nations–run World Food Programme was given unprecedented access to cities and villages that hadn't been seen by outsiders since the Korean War. During three thousand visits, they watched aid move from ports to remote villages, often by wheelbarrow. They visited seven warehouses, 973 nurseries, 266 kindergartens, an orphanage, and a hospital in one of the two provinces targeted by the program, all to make sure the aid reached its recipients: pregnant women, children, and the elderly.[36]

The outsiders learned about North Koreans' daily lives. In return, the North Koreans received a different perspective on the United States after their steady diet of anti-American diatribes. Since the "Stars and Stripes" was plastered on every bag of corn, a condition for aid that the North Koreans themselves had originally suggested in the 1990s, the villagers knew where it came from and appreciated the help.[37]

The foreign monitors came away with a better understanding about why North Korea was so resilient. Bureaucrats worked as many as fifteen hours per day without complaint to make sure that food reached people. They often improvised. Since they didn't have barbed wire to keep the rats in warehouses at bay, they wove plant stems with sharp thorns around the food bags. Perhaps the North Koreans' ingenuity explained how a country short on resources could develop nuclear weapons.[38]

All of that came to an end with Kim Jong Il's stroke in August 2008. Scrutiny tightened. The foreigners found it difficult to do their jobs. They were finally expelled in March 2009 just before the distribution of the remaining aid and the April satellite launch.[39]

Six months later, Robert "Bob" King, a soft-spoken Wyoming native, was named the State Department's human rights envoy. King had spent two decades working for Tom Lantos, the chair of the House Foreign Affairs Committee, before his boss passed away. His responsibilities also included dispensing aid to North Korea, even though there wasn't any to dispense.[40]

The new envoy spent his first year on the job spotlighting North Korea's abuses, but he came up with a small aid package when heavy rains and flooding hit again in fall 2010. The package changed everything for King, who was going nowhere because the North Koreans didn't want to deal with human rights and hadn't realized he oversaw humanitarian assistance.[41]

King was invited to the North Korean mission in New York by Ambassador Han Song Ryol. His job had nothing to do with the United Nations, however. Smart, perceptive, and attuned to the ins and outs of his country's authoritarian system, Han was the "New York channel," the line of communication between Washington and Pyongyang. His invitation to King wasn't a surprise; North Korea needed help to prevent a famine.[42]

Brause had already begun to formulate a new aid package, smaller than his first plan, but still hundreds of thousands of tons of food and supplies. Like before, the plan required on-site verification of aid reaching those in need, not the elite or the military. Nutritional assistance and grains would be distributed to children, pregnant women, mothers of young children, and the elderly.

This time, the North Koreans had to allow the measurement of the mid–upper arm circumference of children suffering from malnutrition to record whether the aid was working. Also, they had to allow visits to private markets that had sprouted up after the government's food distribution system failed. Finally, better monitoring was required to ensure the food wasn't being diverted from its intended recipients.[43]

"We like you, Ambassador King. We don't like your title," a wary Han told him after he was informed of the new demands. Some North Korean officials opposed inviting King because of his title, but he "had a wonderful personality for engagement," a colleague recalled.[44] The trip was approved; it was the first time an American human rights envoy had been invited to North Korea.

King's mission got off to a bumpy start. His flight from Beijing to Pyongyang on an ancient Air Koryo airplane suddenly plunged into a nosedive. Flight attendants screamed. Passengers' faces turned ashen. The pilot managed to climb out of the dive only to take an even steeper one. But he managed to pull out again. "We are about to arrive in Pyongyang," a cheery flight attendant announced moments later. The plane landed without using its brakes and coasted the full length of the two-mile-long runway.[45]

After the American delegation settled into its hotel, the aid experts fanned out to see what was happening in the countryside.[46] They met local officials, and visited farms, pediatric wards, nurseries, daycare centers, clinics, and households. They took arm measurements of some 170 children, and asked questions about their case histories.[47]

"If I can't see it, I can't report it," the team leader, unhappy about frequent restrictions, cautioned the North Korea escorts. Still, they were able to gather enough information to estimate how much aid to send.[48]

While the team roamed the countryside, the American negotiators in Pyongyang informed the North Koreans that "a new level of transparency and cooperation" had to go beyond the failed 2008 agreement. The Americans also wanted compensation for aid the North Koreans distributed after they left the country in 2009.[49]

Ri Gun, a veteran of past talks with the Americans, accepted the Bush agreement as the jumping-off point for the negotiations. The next four days and four nights were spent haggling over Washington's new demands.

Neither side made promises, but a reassuring King told the North Koreans, "We believe we can work out a program." Ri Yong Ho, the vice foreign minister and Ri's boss, urged King and Brause to "seize the opportunity to move forward." The North Koreans, however, proved to be immovable.[50]

The farewell banquet on the last evening, attended by Kim Kye Gwan, the veteran negotiator who still had a "crackerjack mind," was held at the

Americans' hotel.[51] King reminded him they had met in 2005, when Congressman Lantos, fresh from a session with Libyan leader Muammar Gaddafi, who had agreed to give up his nascent WMD program, urged the North Koreans to follow his lead.

"See what happened to Libya," Kim pointed out. The Arab Spring had just rocked the regime and would end in Gaddafi's execution. He shook his finger at King and declared, "We will not follow the example of Libya."[52]

The Americans expected an evening of heavy drinking. Since King was a Mormon committed to sobriety, Brause became his designated drinker. Ri Yong Ho, the vice foreign minister, pitched in, repeatedly filling King's glass with water before anyone else could serve him.[53]

Early in the dinner, Kim surprised the Americans by starting a conversation about his country's least favorite subject, human rights. "There were no perfect countries," Kim admitted. Both countries had prisoners, but "you have so many prisoners, it's obscene!"[54]

When the conversation turned to Pyongyang's treatment of women, Kim claimed North Korea did a better job than the United States. King gently suggested, "Why don't we try to have a meeting on the rights of women in both countries just as an opener?"

Kim was interested. With one understated exchange, King had started the ball rolling for the first-ever human rights dialogue between the United States and North Korea. He made sure to mention that accomplishment during testimony before a skeptical Congress.[55]

The agreement was the second gesture made to the human rights envoy that day. Eddie Jun, a detained Korean American businessman involved in missionary work, was released, and allowed to join the Americans at the hotel.[56]

The dinner was encouraging. Kim appeared confident that the leader was backing the Foreign Ministry. King and Brause departed the next day with Jun sitting across the airplane aisle. They left behind a draft aid deal filled with nitty-gritty for the North Koreans, who seemed eager to keep talking.[57]

The rest of the American team returned home a week later, reporting no evidence of an urgent nationwide crisis, but rather food shortages and acute malnutrition that needed to be factored into an assistance package.[58]

Despite the optimism, a stalemate ensued. More torrential rains, successive floods, and two typhoons inundated southwestern and central North Korea. Again, aid groups found no danger of an urgent nationwide crisis, but there were significant food shortages.[59]

Six months went by. King, Brause, and Ri Gun finally sat down in December at the North Korean embassy in Beijing. "We are fortunate to have this meeting before the end of the year," the caustic North Korean negotiator remarked, kicking off two days of talks.[60]

The North Korean negotiator had a surprise up his sleeve. Suspending operation of the uranium enrichment plant at Yongbyon had been a central topic in nuclear talks between Steve Bosworth and Kim Kye Gwan begun that summer. Now, it moved to the top of the Beijing agenda even though the session was about food.[61]

Ri offered to stop the plant's operation if the Americans met North Korea's assistance demand. When King wouldn't agree, the North Korean negotiator called a recess, presumably to seek new instructions from Pyongyang. State's envoy waited patiently, hoping for the best.[62]

Ri returned, and announced that "nothing is settled until everything is settled." There would be no nuclear deal unless North Korea received the food it demanded.[63]

A Gentlemen's Agreement

Steve Bosworth hadn't signed up to lead a strategically patient policy that assumed Washington could engineer behavior change in North Korea. With its history of defying communist patrons and capitalist enemies, he knew North Korea wouldn't give in. His experience coaxing a dictator in the Philippines to abdicate and running KEDO, however, taught him that engagement could steer the North toward a peaceful path forward.

Bosworth knew times had changed since his stint in the Clinton administration. He had little diplomatic running room, given the negative narrative that had emerged in the United States after the demise of the 1994 deal, the failure of President Bush to reach agreements, and Pyongyang's initial rebuff of Obama. North Korea was now more inclined than ever to guarantee its own security, rather than rely on diplomacy, an everpresent impulse heightened by Kim Jong Il's stroke.

Bosworth was determined to make engagement work from his first day on the job. Addressing it would require the diplomatic equivalent of brain surgery: going beyond the technicalities of getting rid of nuclear weapons to address the root causes of the conflict.[64]

His hands were also bound, however, by the dictums "Don't buy the same horse twice" and "No talks for talks' sake." No one wanted to reward Pyongyang for implementing its 2005 pledge to denuclearize, its agreement to dismantle Yongbyon, and its return to the Six Party Talks. But getting something for nothing was unrealistic. Washington had to find the smallest, most defensible concession. Food aid seemed the best option.[65]

Finally, the administration decided to do something no other administration had done with North Korea: reach a "gentlemen's agreement." Instead of haggling over every comma and period in a written document, each country would issue its own statement explaining what had been agreed. The idea was an oxymoron. No one believed Pyongyang could be trusted. It also ran counter to other negotiations, such as nuclear talks with Iran.[66]

The odds were fifty-fifty between success and failure. Bosworth adhered to the baseball catcher and philosopher Yogi Berra's advice: "When you come to a fork in the road, take it." Bosworth would get started, stick with it, and see what developed.[67]

The Obama administration had come to its own fork in the road in 2011. Strategic patience was still its guiding principle, but the danger remained of another clash in Korea. Washington had tiptoed back to talks. So had the North Koreans, who not only gave DeTrani the green light, but also signaled in March they were even willing to talk to the South Koreans first.[68]

When the two Koreas met on the sidelines of a multilateral summit in Bali, Wi Sung-lac, Seoul's negotiator, told his delegation that their session was part of a tag team wrestling match. The Americans would enter the ring after them and "pin the North Koreans." After the session, Wi believed an agreement could be within reach.[69]

Ambassador Bosworth entered "the ring" days later in New York City. Secretary Clinton sounded a cautious note to reporters, warning against getting embroiled in "protracted negotiations." Arriving at John F. Kennedy Airport, Kim Kye Gwan was more positive, stating, "I am optimistic that the Six Party Talks will come together well."[70]

A media mob jostled outside the stark, white concrete U.S. mission to the United Nations when the Americans and North Koreans arrived on July 28. An architecture critic imagined "unspeakable things going on in [its] soundproof rooms." But the Bosworth-Kim meeting, the first in over eighteen months, held out hope that peace could be at hand.[71]

The talks were free of histrionics. Ambassador Bosworth spelled out a positive future for Korea, if multilateral negotiations resumed and denuclearization was achieved.[72] Kim declared that Pyongyang wanted to resume the Six Party Talks.[73]

The two men quickly got down to business. The North Koreans already knew the American demands. They thought them "too one-sided."[74]

Kim had his own laundry list. He wanted the United States to reaffirm its commitment to eventually provide North Korea with light-water reactors, which was buried in the 2005 statement. After all, Washington couldn't ask the North Koreans to reaffirm their denuclearization pledge without also reaffirming its promises.[75]

He even sweetened the pot, acknowledging that the 2005 declaration covered uranium enrichment. His boss, Kang Sok Ju, had told Bosworth in 2009 that it did not.[76] Kim was also willing to shut down the Yongbyon enrichment plant, one of Bosworth's demands, if the Americans renewed their reactor commitment.[77]

Bosworth wasn't ready to bite, however. He feared a commitment to provide the reactors would lead down a slippery slope to restarting the project.[78]

The North Korean negotiator also zeroed in on sanctions. He wanted relief from them, pushed for a moratorium on new measures, and demanded a public statement by Washington that sanctions were not aimed at the Korean people.[79]

Bosworth countered that the best way for Pyongyang to get what it wanted was to make progress on denuclearization. But he did note that sanctions were not aimed at the Korean people. They were aimed only at North Korea's WMD programs.[80]

The two negotiators also grappled with the perennial problem of satellite launches and whether a missile test moratorium should include them. Kim was candid; North Korea still had launch plans.[81]

Bosworth was "100 percent clear and 100 percent explicit," according to one American. They had to be banned.[82] He proposed that the moratorium could be accompanied by talks that could lead to lifting sanctions.[83]

Kim, however, countered that Washington should send a high-level official to meet Kim Jong Il, the only person who could agree to their demand. After all, Secretary of State Madeleine Albright had traveled to Pyongyang in 2000.

The North Korean negotiator repeated the proposal during his lunch with Bosworth on the last day of talks as well as the proposal his leader had made to Bill Clinton. The secretary of state would fit the bill.[84]

Washington hadn't even considered the idea. All Bosworth could do was nudge Kim's suggestion to the side. He noted that Albright's trip happened only after extensive discussions, including a Washington visit by North Korea's second-ranking official, Marshal Jo.[85]

The New York meeting wasn't all work. The North Koreans serenaded Syd Seiler, the intelligence analyst who was the newly appointed White House Korea expert, with a chorus of "Happy Birthday" on his fiftieth birthday. They probably didn't know Seiler thought the 1994 nuclear deal was a mistake. He believed it was a lifesaver for Pyongyang, which was teetering on the brink of collapse.

The talks adjourned after two days with both delegations encouraged. One American recalled, "We felt like we were moving towards something real."[86] Kim told reporters that "talks were constructive and business-like." The meetings would continue.[87]

However, despite the progress, the White House decided to replace Steve Bosworth, citing the need for a full-time envoy for what was becoming a full-time job.

Some officials believed that proponents of strategic patience seized the opportunity to get rid of Bosworth. His differences with Danny Russel only fed the speculation. Moreover, officials at State viewed his replacement, skilled diplomat Glyn Davies, as Russel's choice.

Bosworth graciously accepted the decision when Hillary Clinton informed him. But he was surprised, disappointed, and angry.[88]

"I thought the whole thing was weird," a senior State Department official recalled. Davies had no experience with the North Koreans. Sung Kim had already left to become the first Korean American ambassador in Seoul. He was replaced by Clifford "Ford" Harte, a Foreign Service China hand, who also lacked experience dealing with Pyongyang.[89]

Ambassador Bosworth had one more shot that fall. Han in New York had told Harte that North Korea was ready to accept Bosworth's demands. In October, Kim Jong Il reaffirmed that he was committed to denuclearization during a rare interview with a foreign journalist.[90]

The New York message seemed too good to be true—and it was. Before the talks convened at the Americans' Geneva mission, Kim remarked that both sides had left New York with a lot of homework. "We may not get an A+, but maybe a B," he told Bosworth.[91]

Kim still wasn't ready to meet the American demand that North Korea suspend operations at the Yongbyon uranium enrichment plant. Washington had to promise to provide North Korea with a timetable for new lightwater reactors, along with the fuel for them, and declare a moratorium on sanctions.[92]

Bosworth argued there could be no deal without suspending operations at the Yongbyon plant. But he was willing to go as far as recommitting to the vague 2005 Beijing pledge to eventually provide reactors.[93]

Regarding sanctions, Bosworth emphasized once more that he couldn't do anything about UN restrictions unless North Korea met the conditions to lift them. That meant progress on WMD issues. All he could do was affirm publicly that American restrictions were not aimed at the North Korean people.[94]

Nailing down the details of a rocket test moratorium remained a serious challenge. Again, Kim balked when it came to including satellite launches. He argued that other countries were allowed to put satellites in space, and that only his country was subject to sanctions.[95]

The North Koreans delayed the second morning of talks, scheduled at their diplomatic compound across Lake Geneva. When the two delegations finally met over a lunch prepared by the North Korean diplomats' wives, the discussion didn't touch on WMD. Shakespeare, World Cup soccer, and the weather were the three favorite topics discussed by a cosmopolitan North Korean diplomat who spoke perfect English.[96]

Finally, the two delegations convened for thirty minutes. It felt like a "rope-a-dope session as the North Koreans ran out the clock," one American recalled. Kim implied he had been waiting for new instructions, but they never arrived. All that was left to do was review the results and go home.[97]

Despite the remaining differences, the Americans felt they "were in the ballpark of the two basic requirements: stopping uranium enrichment, and a test moratorium," one official recalled.[98]

The gap had also narrowed on sanctions. In addition to saying in public that restrictions weren't aimed at the Korean people, Bosworth assured Kim that the United States didn't view the restrictions as permanent. He was prepared to review them if there was progress on the nuclear front.[99]

Kim reminded the Americans that the number three was auspicious in Korean culture, suggesting a third round of talks could lead to success.[100] The normally restrained Bosworth was also optimistic, although he told the press more work was necessary to reach an agreement.[101]

Steve Bosworth, however, wouldn't be there to see it. In his matter-of-fact style, before the talks adjourned, he had introduced Glyn Davies to the North Koreans. They weren't surprised since State had already announced his departure. Pyongyang's diplomats exchanged pleasantries with Davies and sized him up during breaks.[102]

Bosworth was disappointed, though he may have also been relieved. Lingering suspicions at the White House about the Clinton-appointed envoy and periodic clashes with advocates of strategic patience had taken their toll. Fewer and fewer meetings with the secretary drove home the point that diplomacy with Pyongyang wasn't a priority.

Even Bosworth's farewell party reflected his isolation. He wasn't accorded a sendoff by Clinton, his boss. Nor was he thrown a farewell party by the head of the Asia bureau. Instead, Bosworth's party was held in the Office of Korean Affairs, another step down in the bureaucratic pecking order.[103]

"How could a part-time envoy deal with the nuclear challenge posed by Pyongyang?" critics had asked after he was appointed in February 2009. Bosworth's part-time status and his calm, deliberate style may have been a handicap despite his frequent travel to Washington and Northeast Asia. After all, Chris Hill, the Bush envoy, had spent every waking moment negotiating with North Korea.

Full-time Clinton-appointed envoys fared little better, however. Richard Holbrooke, seen as aggressive and badgering, quickly wore out his welcome at the White House. One pundit described both men's predicament well: "How could you have a special representative who was not special and not representative of the president?"[104]

Bosworth also had to take on the South Koreans. He found the close relationship between Obama and Lee Myung-bak disturbing. Lee had demolished the legacy of Kim Dae-jung, a man Bosworth respected and admired. The droll envoy observed after attending a White House fête for the Bulldozer that the "man-crush" was now closer than ever.[105]

Steve Bosworth concluded by the time he left the administration that Washington had grossly underestimated how much it would take to change Pyongyang's nuclear trajectory. He believed the United States would eventually reach another fork in the road: it would have to accept North Korea as a nuclear power or fight a war to prevent it.[106]

"Everything is on the table."

In late November 2011, I led a delegation bound for Track 2 talks in Pyongyang. Our visit took place after the September nuclear negotiations. The timing was lucky. Momentum was growing and the first nuclear deal with the North Koreans since 2008 seemed in sight.

"Everything is on the table," Choe Son Hui had told us the previous March at the Berlin Hilton, setting the stage for the first round of the Bosworth-Kim nuclear negotiations in July. She also signaled a tough road ahead. The North Koreans were fixated on building new light-water reactors and didn't want to stop launching satellites.[107]

Like on my previous trips to Pyongyang, the Koryo Hotel was our November home base. A twin-towered forty-three-story building, its refurbished lobby, with bright lights as well as mirrored walls and ceilings, was like a scene from *Disco Fever.*[108]

Aside from daily unescorted jogs before sunrise to nearby Kim Il Sung Square, and evenings sipping Johnny Walker Blue in the hotel bar, we attended the circus featuring skating monkeys and bears in gaudy costumes. We visited the Korean war museum with its shocking display of the blood-stained uniforms of American soldiers, and toured the Pyongyang Film Studio, where our excited young escort spotted a North Korean movie star.

Hopeful, realistic, and often sardonic, Ms. Choe remarked at our first meeting that the White House wanted "dialogue for dialogue's sake" because of the upcoming presidential election, mimicking Secretary Gates's phrase describing Pyongyang's tactic.[109]

Despite their suspicions, Choe and Ri Yong Ho, her boss, struck an optimistic tone during six hours of talks stretched over three days. Ri believed the next round of negotiations could produce a breakthrough, leading to the resumption of multilateral denuclearization negotiations in Beijing.[110]

But the North Korean's preview of coming attractions was still cause for concern. "If the US provides guarantees of a light-water reactor, then everything comes to an end immediately as early as tomorrow," Choe stated. She had made the same comment in Berlin; Kim Kye Gwan made it in New York as well as in Geneva; and the official media repeated it the day our delegation arrived in Pyongyang.[111]

Choe claimed she could put together a denuclearization road map overnight if the United States agreed to provide reactors. But she knew that bar was high.

When we told Ri that North Korea would also have to give up its nuclear weapons if it wanted new reactors, his response was vague: "They could be dismantled in the context of better U.S.-North Korean relations." The North Koreans weren't going to reveal all their thoughts.[112]

"What if the United States helped North Korea build its experimental light-water reactor?" one American asked. The Foreign Ministry officials hinted they would prefer their country end that project. "How about re-starting the KEDO reactor project since the foundations had already been poured?" Choe asked. Our engineers thought that was impractical.[113]

New reactors weren't the only tough issue for future denuclearization talks; inspections had to be part of the disarmament process.

Ri and Choe had thought long and hard about allowing outsiders to peer into places spy satellites couldn't see. That requirement was now even more important since a uranium enrichment program was easy to hide. They were concerned inspections would be a cover for spying. The United States and Soviet Union shared that concern during disarmament talks but worked out a solution. Still, inspections would be hard for the North to swallow.[114]

We also held a long session with North Korean nuclear scientists in a hotel conference room next to the bar. The Clinton administration had regular contacts with the scientists until the 1994 deal collapsed. They made a comeback after Chris Hill's agreements, but then ended except for the Stanford trio's periodic visits.[115]

Another Ri Yong Ho, a scientist from Yongbyon, kicked off the meeting. He explained that since the United States had reneged on its promise in 1994 to build new reactors, North Korea was doing it on its own. When the discussion quickly shifted to North Korea's uranium enrichment program intended to produce fuel, Ri smiled and replied, "I thought it could be the first topic between us."[116]

He disclosed that the North Koreans were having problems operating the facility. It had been built "so fast, so quickly." That wasn't surprising. Every country faced difficulties during the start-up phase. But Ri's comment could have meant North Korea didn't have as much experience operating a plant as everyone thought. Moreover, the amount of enriched uranium produced may have been less than what everyone had thought.[117]

The North Koreans also lifted the veil from how they guarded their nuclear material. It was natural not to worry about security in an authoritarian country, but anything could happen—and did. Unanticipated instability in the Soviet Union had created enormous risks that its bombs, technology, and material could fall into the wrong hands.[118]

Ri wouldn't talk about bomb-making materials, a sensitive subject in any country. He did provide a rare, reassuring glimpse into how North Korea had protected almost one hundred tons of reactor fuel rods containing a much smaller amount of plutonium for bombs. They were locked up and guarded by armed personnel with small quick-response forces less than ten minutes away, measures on par with those of other countries.[119]

The North Koreans mouthed all the right words when the discussion turned to reactor safety. Like the Stanford trio, however, we all looked at each other in disbelief when they said construction of the new Yongbyon reactor had been given the go-ahead four months after applying for permission. Normally, the certification process lasted years in the West.[120]

The session also brought us face to face with a younger generation of North Korean scientists. They seemed eager to cooperate with outsiders.[121] We proposed relationship-building exchanges, but Ri wasn't enthusiastic. Choe admitted, "We may need more time."[122]

Although he was cordial and relaxed, the North Korean scientist didn't miss the chance to warn us that his country would produce more bombs if the energy shortage continued. "We should replace the cooling tower and recruit operational personnel. It would only take three months." Two years later, North Korea did exactly that, surprising the international community.[123]

Our meetings also provided a brief glimpse into the debate in Pyongyang over whether to shut down the uranium enrichment plant at Yongbyon. The Foreign Ministry had argued a shutdown could be reversed if negotiations failed. The technicians countered that it would be hard to restart the plant. Our experts agreed with the diplomats. Still, the Foreign Ministry's Ri had a fight on his hands.[124]

We briefed administration officials on our talks when we returned to Washington, even though the Obama White House was dismissive of Track 2 meetings. A National Security Council expert told one audience that Choe and her bosses would spin everything from "the weather in Tibet and the price of grapes in France" to suit their purpose.[125] Danny Russel, Obama's top Asia advisor, later warned Bob Gallucci that he was wasting his time going to a Track 2 meeting in Europe.

It was absurd to think, however, that the North Koreans were following a script intended to "spin" the Americans, given the level of detail and the give-and-take in talks. Moreover, former U.S. officials weren't so naïve as to swallow everything hook, line, and sinker. A discerning listener could learn a great deal about the good, the bad, and the ugly in Pyongyang.

Just as Steve Bosworth never had a chance to make his case to President Obama, neither did Americans who undertook unofficial diplomacy with North Korea. The president met outsiders once for a ninety-minute session in April 2013. Stage-managed by Seiler, the gathering only included supporters of strategic patience and hawks who thought diplomacy was a trap.[126]

CHAPTER EIGHT

"Maybe I will get a crystal ball for Christmas"

G LYN DAVIES'S MOVE FROM the grind of multilateral diplomacy at the International Atomic Energy Agency (IAEA) in Vienna to fast-paced talks with North Korea was a Cinderella experience.
Like with Cinderella, however, not everyone was happy with his success. His State Department colleagues resented that his appointment had been engineered by the White House. Newspapers accused him of being soft on North Korea. Private experts harped on his inexperience. Replacing Steve Bosworth, one of the best diplomats of his generation, was akin to trying on the glass slipper meant for someone else.[1]

While the intelligence community had concluded that Pyongyang's accommodating approach was only a ploy, two long-dormant initiatives gained new traction.[2] Three days of hard bargaining at a Bangkok luxury hotel produced an agreement to restart joint missions to retrieve the remains of thousands of Americans missing or killed in the Korean War.[3]

Kim Jong Il's pet project, a visit to the United States by the Pyongyang State Orchestra, was also resuscitated in 2011. Rob Spring, a Korean-speaking Arizona rancher and humanitarian, had completed arrangements by New Year's Day for the visit.[4]

Glyn Davies cautiously balanced his optimism and pessimism. "Maybe I will get a crystal ball for Christmas, but I don't have one yet so I can't predict the future," he told reporters.[5] Bob King's December talks only stoked anticipation, however.[6]

"Is this true?" Secretary Clinton emailed an aide after reading a press clipping headline, "N. Korea Agrees to Suspend Uranium Enrichment." It wasn't. The North Koreans had only suggested they would suspend the program if Washington forked over enough food aid. However, a deal seemed close.[7]

Seven thousand miles away, events would drastically change the course of American relations with North Korea.

"Dear viewers, dear viewers!"

North Korean television started later than normal, a few minutes after 9:00 A.M., on December 19, 2011. After a 10:00 A.M. rerun of a documentary on Kim Jong Il's "on-the-spot guidance" visits in October, an anchor announced, "Dear viewers, dear viewers! There will be a special message broadcast at noon." Five more reminders followed. Something important was about to happen.

A female announcer in a traditional black mourning dress appeared at noon, the same one who had broken the news seventeen years earlier that Kim Il Sung had died. After a solemn five-second pause, she intoned the list of the North Korean leader's titles, and then informed her audience that "respected comrade Kim Jong Il passed away at eight hours thirty minutes on December 17." Like his father, he had died of a heart attack caused by "physical and mental exhaustion" as his train traveled to another inspection. A military orchestra played sorrowful music.[8]

Speculation about Kim's health had dogged him since his 2009 dinner with Bill Clinton. He had all the predictable problems of a nearly seventy-year-old man who had suffered a serious stroke. He was able to stop drinking but kept smoking.

Touring Siberia in his armored train three months before he died, Kim seemed jollier than usual—sightseeing, exploring business opportunities, and reaffirming his commitment to nuclear negotiations. He told President Dmitri Medvedev, "We are having a fun trip." But pictures showed him leaning on a bodyguard as he ducked into a hospital for thirty-six hours.[9]

Kim Jong Il also had been busy at home during his last months. He had inspected defense plants, observed military exercises, watched figure skating, visited a youth fair, and attended art performances by the Korean People's Army.[10]

The dictator began his final day of appearances at 6:00 A.M. on December 15. He spent two hours at a joint venture with a Western firm, followed by a visit to a shopping center scheduled to open that month. Kim signed his last document the next day: an order to supply the people of Pyongyang with pollack and herring for the coming New Year.[11]

Just as there had been speculation about his health in life, there was speculation about his death. Officially, Kim had passed away pursuing his duties. South Korean intelligence agencies, however, spied his train parked in its special Pyongyang depot the day he died.[12] One expert believed Kim had attended a weekly family dinner at his daughter's house and experienced a "major health incident" after taking a nap.[13]

Then there was the mystery of a two-day delay before his demise was announced. The same thing had happened after his father's sudden death in 1994, apparently to allow breathing room to arrange the funeral and a smooth transition. But, unlike 1994 when Kim Jong Il had been running the country for a decade, his son didn't occupy any senior positions, except as one of two vice chairmen of a military body where he was outranked.[14]

Even so, the signs that Kim Jong Un was poised to take over were there for all to see. A CIA study of official photos completed just before his father died concluded the regime was moving "gingerly and incrementally in portraying him as an increasingly active player second only to his father." The two men even wore the same clothes at times. By September, the stage was set for the son to handle daily matters while the father retained veto power. Kim Jong Il had had the same arrangement with his father.[15]

Within hours of Kim's death, the country shut down, the border with China was closed, and guards were doubled. There was probably at least one meeting of top leaders during which Kim Jong Un inherited absolute power. His father's passing was announced at noon the next day, and a funeral committee was named, led by the "Great Successor."[16]

Crowds paid their respects, some mourners kneeling, some wailing, others beating the ground with their fists despite the freezing cold. The emotions weren't all spontaneous. Workplaces and government offices organized meetings to create a proper atmosphere of mourning. It also may not have been as heartfelt as for his father. People had suffered through the 1990s famine under Kim Jong Il's rule.[17]

Like everyone else, the American and the South Korean governments found out what had happened on December 19. Up until then, their best guess was he had five years to live after his stroke, although one American official had speculated that he might linger on like Fidel Castro.[18]

President Obama was briefed shortly afterwards.[19] He called President Lee Myung-bak to reassure him that Washington stood ready to help in case of a provocation, or worse.[20] The Clinton administration had worried that Kim Il Sung's death would bring chaos, although his son, reputed to be a heavy drinker and womanizer, had been running the show for years.[21] The Obama administration was worried because Kim Jong Un was young and unproven.

December 19 was President Lee's seventieth birthday. He was mistaken if he had been looking forward to celebrating. His national security advisor ran to the president's office when the news broke. Lee had already placed the military on high alert, even though the North Koreans were unlikely to attack while they were in mourning. Still, Lee's experience in 2010 taught him anything was possible.[22]

Seoul mirrored Washington's approach: to "stay calm, watch closely, avoid provocation, coordinate closely," according to the American ambassador. Secretary Clinton talked to her aides on the phone, who reported no signs of instability or unusual military movements.[23]

A State Department task force kept close tabs on North Korea. Weeks passed, and the U.S. embassy in South Korea still had to send daily updates, prompting one official to mutter to himself, "Kim is still dead."[24]

There were bigger issues at stake, however. A guessing game played out in the intelligence community, the White House Situation Room, the Oval Office, and the Blue House. Would Kim Jong Un stand or fall by the wayside in a power struggle? Would North Korea disintegrate? What did Kim Jong Il's death mean for American policy?

Washington had sought answers to similar questions after Kim Il Sung's death years earlier. Then, America's intelligence operatives "had no idea what they were talking about when they predicted collapse after Kim Il Sung died," a Clinton aide observed. The same was true in 2011.[25]

Most American intelligence analysts thought Kim Jong Un unlikely to last. Odds favored the elders led by Jang Song Thaek, his powerful uncle, leaving a marginalized, manipulated Kim as a figurehead. Some thought he wouldn't last more than six months.

A power struggle between Kim and the elders could lead to a nightmare scenario: the collapse of North Korea. Victor Cha, a former Bush official, argued that "whether it comes apart in the next few weeks or over the several months, the regime will not be able to hold together."[26]

A disintegrating North Korea leaking refugees and WMD would plunge Northeast Asia into unprecedented chaos. A dying regime could lash out and start a war. Or hundreds of thousands of American, South Korean, and Chinese troops could rush in to protect their interests and clash. One Pentagon official observed that "there are only two ways to be prepared for North Korea's collapse: to be ill prepared, or really ill prepared."[27]

The CIA's Open-Source Works, or OSW, dissented. Relying on public documents rather than top-secret information, its veteran analysts concluded Kim Jong Un would consolidate power, get rid of the elders, and rule for decades. "We got such pushback it was unbelievable," one analyst recalled.[28]

OSW's prediction was also a nightmare for Washington. Instead of an experienced septuagenarian despot, the United States would have to cope with a young, energetic, inexperienced dictator who could reinvigorate a flailing regime. "We would come out in the worst place," one of the president's intelligence advisors recalled.[29]

The unpopular prediction meant it was even more important to understand Kim Jong Un. The Western media speculated that, because of his formative years in Switzerland, he might become a North Korean Gorbachev. Kim might institute dramatic reforms, establish a more open society, and become a member in good standing of the international community.

A secret CIA analysis, based on interviews with "his classmates, the chefs and the drivers" during his time in Switzerland, came to a different conclusion, according to one official. Kim was "the spoiled brat son of a dictator who kicked his dog, broke pool cues over his friends' heads and cheated on his taxes."[30]

President Obama took intelligence community predictions with a grain of salt.[31] His skepticism was reinforced by "good intelligence hedging," a series of questions rather than answers, a top aide recalled.[32]

Nevertheless, when North Korean WMD tests mounted a few years later, David Sanger criticized Obama in the *New York Times* for not understanding Kim Jong Un's "bellicose nature." Obama made his way to the back of Air Force One and, not finding Sanger, unburdened himself to a colleague.

He told the reporter that he had never harbored any illusions about the younger Kim, didn't know what he would be like, and didn't think anyone else did, either. He had decided to wait and see.[33]

Obama and his advisors did not have to wait long.

"Game, set, match."

Kim Jong Il's death changed everything and nothing. Ambassador Davies, bags packed, had been on the verge of buying an airplane ticket. One more session with the North Koreans could wrap up a nuclear deal. Now, an agreement might be delayed or, even worse, the North Koreans could back out of talks.

Then, Ford Harte received a surprising phone call from Ambassador Han Song Ryol in New York, one day after Kim's death had been announced. North Korea wanted to move forward with talks to "find common ground for agreement on issues, including a moratorium and food aid," he told Harte.[34]

Both in life and death, Kim Jong Il had set North Korea on an unalterable course. In 1994, he had moved forward with negotiations even after his father died and reached a denuclearization deal three months later. Kim Jong Il had a game plan for 2011 that started the diplomatic ball rolling in January. Like Glyn Davies, his objective was to reach an agreement by the end of the year.

Even if the "Great Successor" wanted to—and there is no evidence that he did—ditching his father's plan would have been a risky move before he was in control. Kim Jong Un led his father's funeral, mourning ended the next day, and he was appointed supreme commander of the Korean People's Army a day later. By then, Han had made his phone call.

"One moment it seemed something was impossible and then a switch was flicked, and they were ready to go," an American negotiator recalled. President Obama remained open minded. Other officials wondered if Han's call meant Kim Jong Un had a positive vision for relations with the United States.[35]

Ambassador Davies left for Beijing a few days before the negotiations were set to resume on February 24, 2012. Han's phone call was encouraging. So was an article published in Pyongyang's media recalling the good old days of Kim Jong Il's engagement with Bill Clinton.[36]

In a gesture Davies found touching and Syd Seiler found amusing, the North Koreans bought Starbucks coffee for everyone just before the talks convened.[37] Kim Kye Gwan's opening statement was also reassuring.

"As long as the United States abandoned its hostile policy and respected the DPRK's sovereignty, the North did not need to bother the United States, and the nuclear issue could be resolved," Pyongyang's negotiator stated as he outlined the new supreme commander's foreign policy.[38]

Davies reciprocated. He reiterated an offer made by Hillary Clinton after Kim Jong Il's death to "help the North Korean people," as well as her commitment "to usher in a new era of peace, prosperity and lasting security on the Korean peninsula."[39]

Kim highlighted past progress and then caved in on his demand for light-water reactors. Operation of the uranium enrichment plant at Yongbyon could be suspended without Washington giving in. An agreement finally seemed to be within reach.[40]

The North Korean negotiator also accepted the American offer of 240,000 tons of food aid with the important caveat that more help could be provided in the future. Ri Gun's December threat that Washington had to meet North Korea's demand for 300,000 tons of food aid became an afterthought.[41]

One significant issue stood in the way of a final deal: satellite launches. The Americans tried different formulations, including a secret understanding. None worked. Davies fell back on a diplomatic sleight-of-hand, a unilateral assertion that the United States would consider launches as covered by the test moratorium. Washington expected Pyongyang not to violate its assertion.[42]

Seiler, a Korean speaker, pressed Kim in his own language to make sure he understood. The North Korean nodded, smiled, and replied, "Yes, we understand," according to a delegation member. Davies made it clear again, prompting Kim to respond, "Yes, yes, I know, let's move on," another American recalled.[43]

When Davies conferred with Washington, the White House rolled the dice. "Even if it's written down, so what, North Korea wouldn't hesitate to violate deals recorded on paper," an administration skeptic observed. The White House gambled that the new North Korean leader was more interested in an agreement with the United States than in launching satellites.[44]

A gentlemen's agreement began to take shape. Kim presented a written draft, the standard way of doing business, but Davies argued it would be too difficult to negotiate. Kim accepted his suggestion, instead, that each country should issue "parallel press statements" that addressed "the other's concerns."[45]

More haggling followed. The "extra innings" lasted into the next morning. The final deal had something in it for both sides, although the United States gave away little besides a few hundred thousand tons of food aid. It wasn't hard to meet other North Korean demands, such as public statements that the United States had no hostile intentions and that sanctions weren't aimed at its people.

In return, the Americans thought they had secured a moratorium on nuclear testing, long-range missile tests, and satellite launches. The agreement also specified that international inspectors would verify a halt in operations of the Yongbyon plutonium-producing reactor and the uranium enrichment plant.[46]

Washington insisted Davies return home for a final blessing. Presumably, Kim had to do the same. With an eye on public relations, Davies proposed to delay an announcement for five days until February 29. The "Leap Day" deal had a nice ring to it. A pause would also give the two negotiators time to get approval at home. Kim agreed.[47] But that meant Davies had to fend off reporters' questions about whether he had a deal.[48]

Back in Washington, the American negotiator explained the agreement in Situation Room sessions chaired by Denis McDonough. The deputy national security advisor clearly knew the danger of approving an agreement that wasn't in writing. He had been warned by one experienced White House aide that the administration was inviting disagreement on how to interpret it.[49]

There was "no wandering around the soccer field when McDonough ran a meeting," one official noted. He made sure Davies had a plan for implementing the deal, working with allies, messaging the public, and selling the agreement. Satisfied with Davies's explanations, everyone seemed on board.[50]

The stage was set to announce the Leap Day deal. Ambassador Han notified the State Department that North Korea had given its final approval and was ready. Slated to unveil the arrangement to the public, Secretary Clinton told Davies, "If you feel you've got it, let's go," when he returned from Beijing.[51]

Last-minute glitches threatened to upend his game plan, however. It turned out Clinton couldn't make February 29 because she was slated to testify on Capitol Hill. Worried the deal would collapse if Washington "dialed 1-800-Pyongyang and said, 'the day is going to shift,'" Davies came up with a solution.[52] The secretary could lead off her testimony with an announcement. She agreed.[53]

Then Davies heard the deal might leak to the press before Clinton testified. He quickly suggested that State announce the agreement at 9:00 A.M., late evening Pyongyang time, just before Clinton appeared on the Hill. After she was assured, "You can be part of the story," the secretary agreed, replying, "Early is better."[54]

"Before I begin, I want to say a few words about North Korea," the secretary of state told a packed hearing room. A cautious Clinton characterized the agreement as a modest first step. Pyongyang announced the deal at almost the exact same moment. Both came in under the wire, less than an hour before Leap Day ended in Korea.[55]

The press swallowed Davies's catchy label hook, line, and sinker. Charges that the administration had bought "the same horse for a third time" were overshadowed by echoes of Washington's cautious spin. *The Economist*, quoting one expert, speculated that Kim Jong Un's first decision was "a conciliatory, indeed concessionary, not belligerent gesture."[56]

The twin announcements also set off alarm bells, however. There were discrepancies between the two, including a new North Korean line that building light-water reactors would be the priority when talks resumed. Bob Carlin wrote in an email to a colleague that he had never seen "so much of a gap in public presentations about agreements at talks." The gentlemen's agreement began to fray.[57]

Davies dismissed the differences. The moving pieces in the agreement seemed ready to go. International inspectors prepared to leave for Yongbyon. Bob King met the North Koreans in Beijing to set the food shipments in motion. Pentagon personnel slated to recover American soldiers' remains arrived in China to pick up their visas. Ships carrying their supplies began to enter North Korean ports.

The North Koreans also seemed ready. Ri Yong Ho told a Track 2 meeting in New York headlined by Henry Kissinger that his "new leadership does not want to fight the United States; it wants peace." The North Koreans even hinted that an alliance with the United States was possible.[58]

However, by mid-March, Davies grew concerned. The moving pieces seemed stuck. When a chain-smoking Japanese academic who frequently met North Korean officials visited his office, Davies asked him why Pyongyang was stalling.[59]

Like Carlin, he had spotted problems. The biggest had to do with satellite launches. North Korean officials had told him the deal didn't include them. Davies had heard the same message from a Chinese academic, but his response was the same. The North Koreans had promised not to launch satellites.[60]

Five hours later, Pyongyang's NASA announced it would launch a weather observation satellite in a few weeks to mark the centenary of Kim Il Sung's April 15 birth. An American official recalled thinking, "Game, set, match."[61]

The announcement came as a shock even though the gentlemen's agreement was "so inconsistent with how the administration started out, which was 'we don't want to get taken for schmucks again,'" one official recalled. All Washington could do was show indignation.[62]

"It's my way or the highway."

Three men boarded a plane at Anderson Air Force Base on Guam, a thirty-mile-long island in the western Pacific, early in the morning of April 7, 2012. The United States had used the base to mount punishing air strikes against Japan during World War II and turned to it again during the Korean War and the grinding conflict in Vietnam. Anderson also was used for episodic shows of force when North Korea conducted military provocations. This time, however, the three men had been dispatched by the White House to meet its leaders.[63]

The unusual team had spent their professional lives doing highly classified work in the intelligence community. Joe DeTrani had held clandestine talks with North Korean spies before. Now about to retire, he agreed to one more mission. Syd Seiler had recently moved to the White House and was a key player in the Leap Day debacle.

The third man, Michael Morrell, was in charge. He had spent three decades at the CIA fighting terrorism and the spread of WMD, as well as dealing with the Arab Spring, the rise of China, and cyberthreats. Morrell had briefed George W. Bush during the 9/11 terrorist attacks and then risen to the top as acting head under President Obama.

Their secret mission was a last chance to head off the satellite launch and the collapse of the Leap Day deal. Even if it could not be averted, Washington hoped to avoid an action-reaction cycle that could lead to yet another crisis and confrontation.

It took just a phone call to Pyongyang. When the CIA officials got the North Koreans on the line, the spies scolded them because they hadn't heard from them in a long time. But they agreed to the CIA's request.[64]

A two-thousand-mile trip through South Korean and Japanese airspace required filing a flight plan and requesting clearance. However, the Morrell mission was so secret that few American officials, and fewer still South Koreans and Japanese, knew about it. So few, in fact, that an embarrassed State Department official had to fend off a Japanese threat to shoot down the mysterious aircraft. Then, a South Korean general held up the plane as it flew over his country's waters. His president's security advisor, one of the few who knew about the mission, ordered him to let the plane pass.[65]

Washington had tried to recover its footing in the weeks before the three men landed in Pyongyang. The mid-March announcement came like a bolt from the blue, even though Ambassador Han had warned the State Department hours ahead of time. One White House official thought the North Koreans might cheat, but not before the ink on the deal was even dry.[66] It was clear that Pyongyang was moving forward when spy satellites finally spotted launch preparations.[67]

The North Koreans tried to disguise their move as peaceful space exploration by announcing a launch window and notifying international authorities. Perhaps reflecting the style of the new leader, they invited foreign experts and journalists to verify that the launch was peaceful. But a rocket able to propel a satellite into space could also carry nuclear warheads.[68]

Davies moved quickly. He recruited his government counterparts in Japan, China, Russia, and South Korea to join the rising chorus of condemnation. Washington also contacted the North Koreans to make it "clear six ways to Sunday, please don't do this; it's not worth it," one official recalled. They wouldn't listen.[69]

Instead, Kim Kye Gwan had a suggestion. North Korea could go forward with part of the deal: suspending uranium enrichment at Yongbyon in return for food assistance.[70] But Davies admonished him that a launch would be "an act of bad faith," and that "there would be consequences." The choice was North Korea's to make.[71]

During a visit to Seoul for a multilateral summit, President Obama bluntly warned Pyongyang that it would "achieve nothing by threats or provocations." When President Hu Jintao, also in Seoul, tried to convince Obama not to throw the deal away, one aide recalled, "I have never seen the president so angry." Hu dropped the suggestion.[72]

Every accomplishment since January 2011 had evaporated by March 28. It did not take long for Morrell's mission in Pyongyang likewise to go off the rails.

Hoping to meet Kim Jong Un, the three Americans had nothing new to offer—just a warning the North Koreans had heard and rejected before: continuing to build bombs and missiles would result in a significant American military threat and total isolation, while negotiating away its weapons would produce a normal relationship with the United States. His message was "It's my way or the highway," one official recalled.[73]

The American spies' warning met with a defiant response during a session with Kim Yong Chol, the bullying general–turned–spy chief. A meeting with Kim Jong Un was out of the question. They would not even get to see his powerful uncle whom DeTrani had met a year earlier.[74]

Five days later, a North Korean rocket lifted off at 7:40 A.M. local time, flew south, broke up at four hundred thousand feet, and tumbled into the West Sea. The public relations campaign was also a bust. The foreign visitors were hustled to the unveiling of a new statue of Kim Jong Il just before the launch. After the regime admitted failure—for the first time ever, shocking ordinary North Koreans—officials in the press center were nowhere to be found.[75]

"People wanted to run from it"

A predictable chain of events followed the failed North Korean satellite launch. The United States and North Korea backed out of the Leap Day deal. The Security Council condemned the launch and warned Pyongyang not to carry out more tests. Spy satellites spotted suspicious activities at North Korea's nuclear test site. What happened then, however, wasn't predictable. There was no test.[76]

Exactly why may have been an important clue that explained events since Kim Jong Il had died. Ambassador Han relayed a message to the State Department soon after the UN acted. His government had decided to refrain from any further "concrete action," taking into consideration the concerns "raised by the American side." Despite everything, the North Koreans wanted to keep hope alive.[77]

While some administration officials thought the North Koreans never intended to reach a Leap Day deal, the real answer probably had less to do with that hypothesis or Morrell's secret mission than with the dead dictator.

Looking ahead to 2011, Kim Jong Il had devised a strategy to accomplish two contradictory objectives. On the one hand, he knew a satellite launch in mid-April 2012 to commemorate the one-hundredth anniversary of his father's birth would anger the Americans. On the other, Kim wanted to tamp down tensions with Washington to help ensure a smooth leadership transition, and the modernization of his economy. Hence his shift to diplomacy.[78]

Kim Jong Il's strategy was all about leverage. By mid-March 2012, when he planned to announce a launch, Kim could well have anticipated that inspectors would have returned to Yongbyon, a nuclear freeze and missile test moratorium would be in place, food aid would have started flowing, and relations with Washington would have begun to thaw. The United States would have to accept the launch or give up everything that had been accomplished. It could be a win-win proposition for Kim.

The odds favored that the North Korean leader would launch, but he could have held off. Kim could use his new leverage to demand more than the minimal gains in the Leap Day deal, possibly the meeting with Hillary Clinton he had sought in his session with her husband. Kim Kye Gwan had also mentioned her visit in his July 2010 lunch with Bosworth, hinting that might secure a moratorium on satellite launches.

Of course, Kim Jong Il couldn't have anticipated his death. He would have had four months from the day a deal was signed to put his strategy in motion, but his son only had two weeks. The final round of nuclear negotiations happened two months after Kim died in December. Implementation was just getting started on March 16, the day the launch was announced. Since the Americans had nothing to show for their trouble except an exchange of press statements, it was easier for them to back out.

Kim Jong Un had another problem. The talks with the Americans had become wrapped up with his transition to power. His father may have had the option of postponing the satellite launch, but he did not. The new leader had to move forward with his father's master plan as he was consolidating his base.[79]

Some U.S. administration officials speculated that the new leader was in the dark about the talks. But just before reaching the Beijing deal, Kim Kye Gwan was called up to the reviewing stand after a military parade on February 16, Kim Jong Il's seventieth birthday. He huddled with the new leader in freezing, overcast weather. At the very least, the thirty-minute session meant Kim Jong Un knew what was happening. He may have told his negotiator to hold firm on satellite launches but keep diplomacy alive.[80]

If North Korea put off a nuclear test after Morrell's disappointing mission and UN condemnation, that would fit in nicely with what may have been Kim Jong Il's strategy. Dangling a nuclear freeze in front of Davies after announcing the satellite launch, and then delaying a nuclear test, would stop mounting tensions from getting out of control, an objective the North Koreans shared with the Americans.

Kim Jong Il's strategy was also reflected in his son's maiden speech, delivered at a military parade on April 15. Most pundits saw it as hardline, but the speech was quite measured. "There was no chest beating, no threats, no anti-US rhetoric or no anti-ROK rhetoric," one expert observed. A measured tone made sense if North Korea was trying to dampen tensions.[81]

However, the Americans made a near-fatal mistake in waiting four months before sending Morrell back to Pyongyang. The North concluded that Washington was more interested in dialing up its hostile intent than finding a new deal. That perception was clear when I met Ms. Choe at the Singapore Hilton at the end of July, before Morrell left for his second trip to Pyongyang.[82]

Our meeting started on what seemed a positive note. Choe declared, "There are no eternal friends or eternal enemies." But it was all downhill from there.[83]

Her new leadership had concluded there was no hope of recovering the Leap Day deal or any part of it. Moreover, Pyongyang was reexamining its commitment to denuclearization enshrined in the 2005 Beijing agreement. She implied her country would build more missiles and bombs.[84]

Choe asserted that talks could restart only after the United States made the first move, and when the North Koreans were satisfied. She knew that was an impossible demand. No one in Washington was going to step onto that ledge after the Leap Day debacle.[85]

It was obvious the North Koreans were confident they had weathered strategic patience. It also didn't make sense for them to reach out to either Washington or Seoul with election season about to start in both countries. They had shut the door to diplomacy.

Our delegation left Singapore believing Kim Jong Un wasn't going to be pushed around. With Pyongyang's WMD programs gaining momentum, North Korea could well have the tools to highlight nuclear weapons as the cornerstone of its security policy. The session didn't bode well for the United States.

When Mike Morrell and Syd Seiler returned to Pyongyang two weeks later, they got a frosty reception. No surprise there since we had warned Washington that there was trouble ahead. Just to make sure everyone got the message, Ms. Choe sent an email with an alarming account of our Singapore session to the South Korean press.

Moreover, the two Americans appeared to have had little new to say, other than recalling Obama's 2009 pledge to hold out his hand to any country that unclenched its fist. The North Koreans, however, preferred to wait until after the fall election. One American official recalled that their briefing afterwards was "more like a travelogue." They didn't hear anything that mattered.[86]

Obama doubled down on the "two paths" message after his reelection during a speech in Myanmar, another pariah state, but one whose military rulers had embarked on reform. His message, however, was drowned out by a move he had made weeks earlier. In 1979, Washington agreed to provide

Seoul with missile technology if it limited the range of its weapons. Despite State Department objections, the president had decided to allow South Korea to increase the range of its missiles able to attack the North.[87]

Two days after his decision, Pyongyang denounced the deal, blamed Obama, and went public with the secret exchanges. "The situation gives a lie to all the U.S. messages," the North Koreans concluded. Whether they were serious about the secret talks or not, Obama's move was the straw that broke the camel's back.[88]

The North Koreans announced on December 1 that they would launch another satellite. Eleven days later the rocket lifted off after slight delays caused by freezing temperatures, light snow, and breezy winds. Pyongyang's first winter launch succeeded. Hundreds of thousands of North Koreans celebrated, believing Kim Jong Un had made the miracle happen.[89]

A year that had started with promise ended with an administration already skeptical of diplomacy empty handed. Gambling on a sleight-of-hand, "a gentlemen's agreement" with North Korea, had been rash.

With Iran and previously with Pyongyang, the White House had insisted on written, detailed agreements. Its new approach was especially surprising since it would leave the president open to criticism in an election year, even if foreign policy wasn't a big issue with American voters.

The White House had a ready-made rebuttal. The National Security Council's Korea expert told a think-tank audience that the administration had engaged Pyongyang "in a way that there was a little bit of political exposure, but not a penny, not one ounce of goods got into North Korea for actions it didn't take."[90]

Obama was a "hard ass on North Korea," an aide recalled. Diplomatic failure allowed Washington to pivot and impose more sanctions. The administration had followed the same strategy—embarking on a campaign to secure China's support for crushing restrictions—after its first nuclear deal with Iran collapsed in 2009.[91]

The White House's secret diplomacy with Pyongyang was minimal. After 2012, spies who didn't think diplomacy had a chance were armed with boilerplate messages, making yearly pilgrimages to Pyongyang to secure the release of detainees, but with nothing new to say about the nuclear confrontation.

In contrast, the president's secret outreach to Iran was striking. After the 2009 deal collapsed, talks continued. Seasoned American diplomats were constantly harangued by the Iranians. But Washington persisted, and eventually paved the way for the landmark 2015 nuclear agreement.

Could the Obama administration have salvaged the Leap Day deal working with a new North Korean leader who was still consolidating power? Patient, continuous contacts, and a willingness to compromise on both sides, would have been necessary; however, "at this point, the White House was inherently skeptical of everything about North Korea," a State Department official noted.[92]

Instead, the Leap Day deal quietly sank beneath the waves. Some officials blamed Davies and Harte. As a general proposition, "people wanted to run from it," a top Clinton aide recalled. The president and the secretary of state didn't mobilize the government to say "'All hands on-deck.'" If it had been Iran, which was a priority for the White House given the danger its nuclear program posed in the Middle East, "we would have had a process six ways to Sunday."[93]

Glyn Davies's first five months on the job had been action packed. Once the Leap Day deal collapsed, he knew "winter was coming."[94] Davies would spend the next three years shuffling paper, parsing words, writing press releases, giving speeches, testifying before Congress, and consulting South Koreans, Japanese, Russians, and the Chinese. He would never again see another North Korean.

CHAPTER NINE

"We weren't going to deal with those assholes anymore"

ITH EIGHT HUNDRED THOUSAND Americans crammed onto the National Mall and millions more watching on livestreams around the world, President Barack Obama's second inaugural address on January 21, 2013, included a few sentences hinting that diplomacy was on his mind.[1]

After a decade of war and three years of cleaning up the mess left by President Bush, Obama told his advisors in private that it was time to restore "the hope side of the equation." They focused on diplomacy with Iran, Cuba, and Myanmar. North Korea, however, didn't make the cut. Even as a foreign policy dumpster fire, it couldn't compete with Hafez al-Assad gassing his own people.[2]

No one was pushing diplomacy with Pyongyang, although John Kerry, the new secretary of state, wasn't a fan of strategic patience. His immediate impulse was to go to North Korea to "talk to those guys," an aide recalled. The peripatetic Kerry, however, quickly turned his attention to the Middle East and Europe.[3]

Dennis Rodman, the former Chicago Bulls basketball player and renowned eccentric, was a far less credible advocate. After he met Kim Jong Un in Pyongyang—Kim's family were big Bulls fans—Rodman told ABC News that the young leader wanted Obama to call him. The president confided in an aide that he was willing to reach out to the leaders of Iran, Cuba, and Myanmar, but drew the line at the North Korean dictator.[4]

Kim didn't even mention Washington in his New Year's speech, three weeks before the president's inaugural address. Observers speculated that he was either hoping to prevent a downturn in relations after the successful December satellite launch or waiting to see how the UN sanctions debate turned out.[5]

The answer came in rapid-fire succession the day after Obama's address, the same day China agreed to new sanctions. The North Koreans proclaimed denuclearization dead, codifying Choe's Singapore warning. Pyongyang also threatened to "target" the United States and detonate a third "higher-level nuclear test." The stark message was underscored in a YouTube video depicting New York skyscrapers under fire by a hail of missiles.[6]

Kim then staged three meetings with his top aides, a hint that something was brewing. On February 12, the North Koreans announced they had tested "a miniaturized and lighter nuclear device with greater explosive force than previously."[7]

Washington responded. Obama tweaked his State of the Union address to add that the North could "only achieve security and prosperity by meeting its obligations," that provocations would "further isolate them," and that the United States would "lead the world in taking firm action in response to these threats."[8]

Revising a speech was just the beginning. The one-two punch of a successful satellite launch and North Korea's claim it had miniaturized a nuclear warhead might mean that Pyongyang could attack American cities. In fact, when the Pentagon's intelligence agency conjectured North Korea could build a warhead, Obama was forced to issue a denial.[9]

Kim raised the crisis to a fever pitch in late March.[10] In a dramatic, publicized session with his top generals in his secret war room, Kim ordered them to "mercilessly strike the US mainland," as well as bases in the Pacific and South Korea in the event of any "reckless US provocations." In fact, Pyongyang didn't have the weapons to do it. But his threat grabbed headlines around the world and made clear that Kim Jong Un would not be intimidated.[11]

A day later, the young leader, who had demonstrated a flair for drama, pivoted to cool tensions and announced a new policy called *byungjin*. It placed an even-greater emphasis on developing nuclear weapons. But the purpose was to build a better shield to protect Pyongyang while he modernized its economy. In short, Kim Jong Un was telling Barack Obama that he wasn't going to choose between developing his weapons or improving his economy. He would do both.[12]

Interviewed in April, President Obama could not explain Kim's motives. "I am not a psychiatrist," he responded. The president added, however, that "you don't get to bang your spoon on the table and somehow get your way," echoing a comment made by George W. Bush about Kim's father. Obama's description in private of North Korea as a crime family bent on extortion was often used by neoconservatives opposed to diplomacy.[13]

The president hinted that the United States would let Kim blow off steam, and then try to reengage the North Koreans to "work out diplomatically some of these issues so that they can get back on a path where they are actually feeding their people."[14] The *New York Times* pointed out, however, that he didn't say "under what conditions it would take place," nor did he repeat the promise made during his first campaign to "engage the North unconditionally."[15]

In fact, the Obama administration had decided to deal with North Korea by not dealing with North Korea. It was a policy of paralysis cloaked in a virtuous posture of patience. The White House considered regime change, but as one official observed, "How serious could that be? We don't have the means to bring it about." Slamming Pyongyang for human rights abuses was another option. It might have "felt good in the short run, but in the long run, it wasn't going to help," a State Department opponent recalled.[16]

The biggest shift came on the nuclear front. Glyn Davies had told Congress the administration would pursue "authentic and credible negotiations." Given the Leap Day debacle, however, North Korea would have to go well beyond its restrictions and stop its entire nuclear weapons program before talks could even begin.

Supporters like Syd Seiler argued that the North Koreans could just flip a switch at all their facilities. Another White House aide, however, saw this as a ruse to prevent talks. North Korea would never give in.[17]

As Washington doubled down on patience, the threat to millions of Americans grew and the president focused elsewhere. William Burns, Obama's deputy secretary of state, later said, "Strategic patience had a deceptively reassuring ring to it but only seemed to narrow our strategic choices and fueled long-term impatience on all sides—especially after Kim Jong Un succeeded his father."[18]

A less diplomatic top U.S. official recalled, "Strategic patience during the second term meant we weren't going to deal with those assholes anymore."[19]

"Honor the threat"

"We are the 300 protecting the 300 million," proudly proclaimed the motto of the Forty-Ninth Missile Defense Battalion. An Army base since World War II, Fort Greely, Alaska, was home to ground-based missile interceptors called GBIs, designed to collide with and destroy incoming nuclear warheads. They weren't foolproof, but they were America's last line of defense against North Korea.[20]

As the spring 2013 crisis with North Korea mounted, Chuck Hagel—the newly confirmed secretary of defense—announced a $1 billion initiative to protect the United States from Pyongyang's "irresponsible and reckless provocations." The money would buy fourteen more interceptors to be deployed at Greely by 2017, resuscitating a plan by President George W. Bush that Obama had rejected.[21]

His announcement capped a three-year uphill struggle by a few determined officials. James "Jim" Miller, a top Pentagon aide since 2009, led the fight. An innovative, problem-solving perfectionist, he had guided reviews of America's nuclear arsenal and missile defenses, as well as its strategy for arms control talks with the Russians.

A long-time congressional defense expert, Miller worked for a president who had ditched Bush's initiative soon after taking office. Most Democrats were skeptical about missile defenses since success required perfection. Relying on technically deficient interceptors was highly risky, especially since a shield would have to be perfect to stop incoming nuclear-armed weapons from killing millions of civilians.[22]

A second reason for the administration's skepticism was the long history of bad intelligence estimates about North Korea. According to the new director of the Pentagon's Missile Defense Agency in April 2009, projections from 2002 of "what the threat would be today" were "off by a factor of 10 to 20." Secretary Gates had "good confidence" that the already-fielded ground-based interceptors were enough to deal with North Korea's missiles.[23]

A February 2010 study run by Miller reinforced that conclusion. Protecting American troops and allies overseas against a missile attack, including from North Korea, was the top priority. Intelligence estimates believed the threat to the United States was still a decade off, prompting one official to call the North Korean ICBM "a myth."[24]

"Sometimes, well, almost always, intelligence is wrong," a top Pentagon official asserted, however. With that in mind, Gates, General James

Defense Secretary Robert Gates peers out of a Silo Interface Vault to view an operational ground-based interceptor during a visit to the Missile Defense Complex at Fort Greely, Alaska, on June 1, 2009. Photo by Sgt. Jack W. Carlson III.

"Hoss" Cartwright—the second-ranking officer in the military—and Miller decided to hedge their bets and mothball the fourteen silos constructed to house the Bush interceptors. This way, they could be reactivated if necessary.[25]

Sure enough, a new estimate concluded that a long-range rocket called the Taepodong-2, which had blown up after its first test in 2006, might be ready sooner than expected. In January 2011, then-secretary Gates made headlines announcing that North Korea could attack American cities in as few as five years, not ten.[26]

With the ground shifting under his feet, Miller sought help from Tom Ehrhard, a retired veteran of the Strategic Air Command, which had been in charge of America's nuclear-armed bombers. While colleagues thought Ehrhard was paranoid, he had three virtues. He wasn't afraid to speak his mind, didn't engage in wishful thinking, and would stop at nothing to uncover the truth.[27]

Ehrhard drilled through layers of bureaucracy. He talked directly to missile analysts and arranged for them to meet Miller, often in secret since their supervisors tried to obstruct his snooping. They gave Miller and Ehrhard a clearer glimpse into the future—one the two men didn't like.[27]

For years, the Pentagon had been fixated with fighting terrorists to prevent attacks like 9/11 and counterinsurgency wars like in Afghanistan. Russia and China were off the radar screen, and few believed that a backward hermit country like North Korea could build missiles able to fly thousands of miles and wipe out American cities.[28] In particular, it would require an extensive testing program.

Ehrhard questioned this last assumption. The United States and Russia tested their missiles extensively before fielding them, but maybe China was a better template. Beijing—poor and with limited resources—had conducted fewer tests than the two superpowers but still fielded a small missile force. The Chinese claimed the force dissuaded its enemies from launching an attack or engaging in nuclear blackmail.[29]

Miller and Ehrhard felt vindicated when American intelligence agencies began to pick up signs that North Korea was working on a new long-range missile, the KN-08. Unlike the stationary Taepodong-2, the new weapon could roam the countryside mounted on a large vehicle.

Washington had expected North Korea to capitalize one day on rocket technology sold to it by cash-poor scientists after the Soviet Union disintegrated, but the timing was a surprise, even an embarrassment.[30]

Pyongyang's program had been hidden in plain sight. Starting in October 2010, a Chinese company's website announced an agreement to export "large off-road vehicles" for "transporting timbers" to the North Korean Forestry Ministry. Since the Chinese firm also built missiles, it must have known what was up. Deliveries were underway by May 2011 and more followed that fall.[31]

Even more surprising, Pyongyang bought the vehicles before the missile was tested, reversing the traditional order of building a mobile weapon system. Before he left his job in June 2011, Secretary Gates told *Newsweek*, "I never would have dreamed they would go to a road-mobile before testing a static ICBM."[32]

The KN-08 missile, mounted on six modified Chinese vehicles, made its debut in April 2012 in a massive parade celebrating the one hundredth anniversary of Kim Il Sung's birth. "That was a seminal event for us," an American officer recalled. Some pundits argued the missiles were only mockups and therefore a hoax. The Pentagon knew better, however. The models were a part of the process to build a new weapon.[33]

It also didn't make sense for the North Koreans to spend millions of dollars on Chinese trucks to haul logs. When Glyn Davies urged Wu Dawei, the Chinese nuclear negotiator, to punish the corporation, he parried, "It was just a logging truck." A skeptical Davies replied, "So a space launch corporation is now making logging trucks?" Even the Chinese laughed.[34]

The mobile KN-08 presented a problem for the Pentagon, tasked with thwarting a North Korean attack. As General Cartwright told Congress in 2009, a stationary missile could be destroyed "before launch if you desire." However, mobile missiles were more likely to survive any attempt to strike them on the ground, raising the real possibility that they could overwhelm America's missile defenses.[35]

While doubters wondered whether to believe the new estimate, Miller and Ehrhard pressed ahead. They needed a game plan and an organization within the Pentagon to get the interceptors built. No one, however, wanted to take the mission on, not even the Missile Defense Agency, the logical candidate, which was already under financial siege. The uniformed services opposed any new funding for the organization since it took away from their own budgets.[36]

Miller and Ehrhard found an important military ally, Admiral James "Sandy" Winnefeld Jr. The newly appointed vice chairman of the Joint Chiefs of Staff in 2011, Winnefeld had been responsible for protecting

American territory against missile threats in his last job. His wife joked that Pyongyang always launched rockets on holidays, dragging him back into the office. The four-star admiral vowed to take care of the problem.[37]

Winnefeld prodded the Pentagon to set priorities based on common sense, "a hierarchy of national interests." North Korea qualified as an important threat. The admiral feared that its nuclear-armed missiles could land on West Coast cities like Seattle.[38]

To illustrate the danger, Winnefeld devised a convincing graph that showed how a growing North Korean arsenal could overwhelm America's interceptors. Countering the threat meant fielding more interceptors that were more capable. Restoring the Bush plan to deploy more GBIs would help narrow the gap.[39]

By mid-2012, a consensus had emerged to "honor the threat," according to one official. Miller convinced Leon Panetta, who had replaced Gates as secretary of defense, that America's missile defenses had to be bolstered.[40]

The April 2012 parade had also set off alarm bells in the White House. President Obama had been concerned about the North Korean ICBM threat.[41] The President's Daily Brief highlighted the KN-08's appearance, although the intelligence community didn't believe the missile would work until it was successfully tested. However, Obama sent an unequivocal message to Pentagon officials: "I have to defend this country. I want you to take this seriously," one recalled.[42]

Miller had to clear another hurdle before a final decision was made to deploy more ground-based interceptors. Russia might hesitate to sign a new arms reduction treaty since additional interceptors could also destroy more of its missiles. Miller argued that the small number of new GBIs wouldn't be a concern, convincing Denis McDonough, the deputy national security advisor, to finalize the plan to upgrade America's missile defenses.[43]

A few weeks later, Pyongyang's successful December satellite launch was "a big wake-up call," one Pentagon official remembered.[44] A senior Obama aide accosted an intelligence official and asked, "Why didn't you guys warn us?" Astounded, he replied. "We've been warning you for years. You haven't been listening."[45]

Spy satellites spotted the KN-08 roaming the countryside early in the new year, despite the fact it had never been tested. The North set off another nuclear blast in February, claiming its goal was to miniaturize warheads for the ICBMs to be used against the United States.[46]

Miller, Winnefeld, and Ehrhard finally won their battle when Secretary Hagel mounted the Pentagon podium in March 2013. But the menace from North Korea's ICBMs had just begun.

"Everything depended on Xi."

Weeks after President Obama started his second term, China elected Xi Jinping as its new leader in a choreographed, once-in-a-decade transition of power.[47]

At the close of the twelve-day session in the Great Hall of the People, Xi conveyed Napoleonic self-confidence in the importance of his mission and its inevitable success, and a willingness to "go to the mattresses for the system," a former CIA analyst recalled. He called on the 1.37 billion people of his country to achieve a great rejuvenation, "the dream of the whole nation as well as of every individual."[48]

How Xi's vision would transform domestic and foreign policy was still an open question. He favored stamping out corruption, protecting China's sovereignty in territorial disputes, and revitalizing the economy. Xi's three predecessors had called for a similar ideal. But he would eventually embrace policies that parted ways with them at home and abroad.[49]

The new leader didn't have much experience abroad, but he had visited the United States five times by 2013.[50] His visits weren't a coincidence. Xi's main challenge was to "create more space for a frustrated China while at the same time avoiding confrontation with the United States," according to one expert.[51] Revered as the "architect of modern China," Deng Xiaoping had prescribed, "Hide your light and bide your time." That is, stay close to the United States.[52]

By 2013, China had the world's second largest economy and a growing military, two defining features of national power. The gap between China and the United States was shrinking. The smiling, friendly Xi reminded one American, who accompanied him during his 2012 visit, of a boxer looking for signs of an opponent's weakness.[53]

Xi's challenge was to avoid the "Thucydides trap." The Greek historian had observed that the rise of Athens, and the fear it instilled in Sparta, made war inevitable. China and America were the "Athens and Sparta of today," according to a Harvard scholar.[54]

The Chinese leader's solution was a "new model of major power relations," drawing on more than a decade of Chinese thinking. Confrontation could be avoided through dialogue, but both countries also had to refrain from challenging each other's "core interests." In effect, he was inviting the United States to step back from Asia and let China assume the mantle of dominant regional power.

Once Xi took office, a decision was made to sacrifice North Korea to further cooperation based on the assumption that Pyongyang could be controlled, and Washington prodded to resume talks. The mounting crisis in 2013, however, tested that assumption, threatening to rip open what one Chinese official called "a long-term seam of US-China relations," and to torpedo Xi's hopes.[55]

The crisis triggered a debate in Beijing. Some scholars advocated working with Washington. Others distrusted the West but were still open to more cooperation. Still others wanted to stick with China's traditional support for Pyongyang.[56] One eye-popping article in an influential party journal argued that the North might even use its nuclear weapons against China.[57]

More importantly, Xi had made no secret of his disdain for Kim Jong Un. Kim didn't defer to the Chinese, like his father had. He argued that if China could have nuclear weapons, so could North Korea. He asserted that Xi should travel to his country before he visited China—a rude demand given that China was North Korea's "big brother" and Xi was Kim's elder by over two decades.[58]

On top of all that, the two men were "princelings," members of their country's ruling elite. Kim didn't think he owed the Chinese anything. "Unlike Hu Jintao, who was the manager of the shop, Xi thought he was the owner," one Chinese scholar observed.[59]

Pyongyang's satellite launch and nuclear blast angered Beijing since it didn't consider China's interests. The nuclear test had upset the Lunar New Year holiday when a tremor felt in China forced the government to calm public fears of radioactive contamination. Hostile posts by Chinese netizens, such as one that read, "North Korea, the dog, has been raised to be an ingrate wolf," were allowed to stand.[60]

As the crisis mounted, President Xi warned, "No one should be allowed to throw the region and even the whole world into chaos for selfish gain." Beijing insisted the warning was aimed at both the United States and South Korea, not North Korea. But enhanced Chinese cooperation at the UN, stepped-up border inspections of North Korea–bound cargo, and Beijing's severing ties between Pyongyang and the Bank of China after new sanctions fueled speculation.[61]

While Xi was the leader-in-waiting, the Obama administration had decided to assign Vice President Biden a new job. His mission was to "get an understanding of where Xi might take China," and to give him a "sense of where we wanted the relationship to evolve," according to one aide.[62]

The two men would spend more time together than any American and Chinese leaders since Nixon and Kissinger met Mao Zedong and Zhou Enlai in the 1970s. They met in Beijing, Washington, and California. One encounter over dinner lasted ten hours.

Biden seemed to admire Xi. The former provincial official talked about repairing sewers, fixing ports, and improving China's education system. He quizzed Biden about the American system of government and civilian control of the military. But Xi "held his cards close to his chest," perhaps because he wasn't in charge yet and didn't want to get "ahead of his skis," one Biden aide remembered.[63]

Xi didn't hide his negative feelings about Kim, opening the door to an interesting possibility. Could he be convinced that North Korea, not the United States, was the real threat to Chinese interests? "If that's your real concern, let's work together to deal with this source of instability," Biden reasoned, according to an aide.

Convincing the Chinese, however, would require a painstaking dialogue that could lead to nothing less than rearranging the geopolitical landscape in Northeast Asia. The Americans had to demonstrate that Beijing's interests would be preserved even if the North collapsed under pressure and the peninsula was reunified under South Korea, an American ally.

Solving that equation might mean the United States reducing its decades-old military presence in South Korea. The Americans had thought about it before. Kissinger had told Zhou that if relations improved, "most, if not all, American troops will be withdrawn from Korea" before the end of Nixon's second term.[64]

The downside was that a successful dialogue with Xi could open a bigger Pandora's policy box. What if China pinched North Korea's feeding tube and accidently pushed Pyongyang over the brink? Collapse would pit Washington, Seoul, and Beijing against one another in a scramble for control. Dealing with that danger and building cooperation could prove tricky, especially given the years of distrust between the two powers.

The vice president floated the idea with Xi of a dialogue on the North Korean endgame to reassure him that the United States would take China's interests into account. The moment seemed right. The crisis in 2013 bolstered the narrative that North Korea, not the United States, was the real danger. Moreover, Xi appeared to favor the Americans when he lectured a North Korean envoy in May that denuclearization, not stability on the peninsula, was his top priority.[65]

"The timing of this is important," Tom Donilon observed. A detail-oriented advisor to Democratic presidential candidates since 1976, Obama's top national security aide believed that "Beijing might be at a policy tipping point." Xi's remarks, the debate in China, negative comments about Pyongyang by Beijing's diplomats, and reports that China had tightened the spigot on oil to North Korea, all pointed in that direction.[66]

Washington launched the first of two initiatives intended to capitalize on China's discontent in April 2013. The State Department invited Wu Dawei, China's chain-smoking nuclear envoy, to Washington. He rarely traveled to the United States because of the thirteen-hour smoke-free flight from Beijing. The Americans joked with Wu that he should consider wearing a nicotine patch.[67]

The Chinese envoy's mission, to discuss "denuclearization of the region," suited Glyn Davies. He knew relations with North Korea would enter a deep freeze after the Leap Day debacle, but was determined to keep trying, if only to prevent rising tensions on the peninsula. Since the North wouldn't agree to Washington's preconditions, enlisting China to help was the next best thing.[68]

It may have been "premature to demand that Xi deliver so much on North Korea right after his inauguration," one Chinese insider recalled. Beijing offered to cooperate, however, for the sake of great-power relations.[69]

China had mediated only once before between Washington and Pyongyang, helping devise the 2005 Joint Statement issued at the Beijing multilateral nuclear talks.[70] Wu Dawei soon found himself flying between capitals, reminiscent of American diplomats enlisted to calm tensions in the Middle East.

The second American initiative was to build on Vice President Biden's bridge to Xi. Obama and the Chinese leader were slated to meet in September 2013, but Donilon pressed for an earlier informal get-together tailored to Xi's informal style. The two men would spend hours alone together in small meetings, meals, and private walks. The Chinese, anxious to repair their most important relationship, agreed.

An informal summit called for an informal setting. The former winter home of the late billionaire Walter Annenberg, Sunnylands, nestled in the

President Barack Obama takes a walk with President Xi Jinping
of China on the grounds of the Annenberg Retreat at Sunnylands
in Rancho Mirage, California, June 8, 2013.
Official White House photo.

Southern California desert and surrounded by the San Jacinto Mountains, was now a site for high-level meetings.

The two-hundred-acre estate was "a magical place and a wonderful place to talk," according to George Shultz. the former secretary of state, who often joined Republican presidents there. It featured a twenty-five-thousand-square-foot structure with twenty-two bedrooms, a golf course, eleven artificial lakes, three guest cottages, a tennis court, and landscaped grounds.[71]

The White House announced Obama would meet Xi in early June to figure out how to enhance cooperation and to manage differences covering a wide range of subjects, including North Korea. The president would try to turn the Chinese leader against Pyongyang. One White House aide recalled, "Everything depended on Xi."[72]

Animated, personable, and confident, Xi bantered with Obama without the binders filled with instructions that Hu Jintao always carried with him. He didn't get emotional, swear, raise his voice, or pound the table, but Xi trashed Kim Jong Un. "This guy is pissed off like us," a White House aide thought.

Obama came away encouraged. Donilon was "super excited," according to one official. He saw North Korea as a promising area for "enhanced cooperation," as did Secretary Kerry.[73]

Other American officials weren't convinced. Xi may have shared his frustration with Kim, but whether it was an "issue of style [or] substance was another thing," a State Department official noted. There was a lot more work ahead.[74]

The skeptics proved right. Steering the course charted at Sunnylands became harder as months went by. Tensions mounted in the East and the South China Seas. Moreover, the Chinese realized the Americans hadn't really accepted Xi's "new model" prescription. They weren't willing to go along with its premise that Beijing would eventually replace the United States as the great power.[75]

Despite his disdain for Kim, Xi found it hard to dismiss a legacy of ideological affinity, North Korea's position as a buffer state that had led to Mao's intervention in the Korean War, and historical, cultural, and emotional memories. He invoked a Chinese proverb during a meeting with Obama in Russia that fall: "A barefoot person does not fear those who wear shoes." Xi's point was that pressure on an already poor North Korea wouldn't work.[76]

All bets were off when Kim Jong Un executed Jang Song Thaek—the one North Korean leader who had enjoyed a warm relationship with China—that fall. Beijing had hoped his demise was just domestic politics, but there was no escaping rumors that Jang was executed after asking President Hu what he would do if Kim were swept from power. "When you have a gas leak, you want to be careful not to set off any sparks," a Chinese insider remarked.[77]

Wu's diplomacy wasn't going well. Since his April visit to Washington, the Chinese envoy had traveled to the United States again, met Glyn Davies five times in Beijing, and talked to the North Koreans five times, including three times in Pyongyang. The Americans assured him they had "all types of PowerPoint slides," showing good things for them if the North Koreans met their preconditions. But they weren't interested.[78]

"Still energetic and enthusiastic, but not hopeful," according to a South Korean diplomat, Wu invited the two parties to a tenth-anniversary celebration of the Six Party Talks just before Jang's demise.[79] The North Koreans showed up, but the Americans didn't. They were unwilling to meet unless Pyongyang capitulated.[80]

Wu's mediation finally hit a diplomatic brick wall during a visit to Pyongyang in early 2014. He toured a suburban equestrian riding center and shooting facility but didn't meet anyone who had anything to do with the nuclear issue. Foreign Minister Wang Yi confided to Davies that Wu had been treated as a persona non grata.

"How much money do you want us to waste on airplane tickets to Pyongyang to get told they are not denuclearizing?" one Chinese official complained to American diplomats.[81]

The same dismal fate awaited White House hopes for a dialogue with China on Korea's future. One senior American official argued that someone close to Obama who could reason with China's leaders had to handle the dialogue. Bureaucrats would only mouth "whatever their script was" and move on. Henry Kissinger and Hillary Clinton supported the idea, as did Biden, who found a "big play" intriguing, according to an aide.[82]

Susan Rice, however, Donilon's successor as Obama's national security advisor and the obvious candidate, seemed risk adverse. She seemed unwilling to lose Chinese cooperation on priorities like climate change and an Iran nuclear deal by pushing Beijing on North Korea. If Pyongyang wouldn't give up its nuclear weapons and China couldn't force it to, why push?[83]

Left to bureaucrats, the dialogue languished. Chinese relations with Pyongyang may have reached a low, but Beijing was guided by an old proverb: "Don't trouble trouble till trouble troubles you."[84] Meeting the American demand to abandon the North was out of the question.

Later, two Obama aides observed that Washington had a history of an "outsized sense of its ability to change China's course." The Sunnylands summit was a perfect example. One State Department official recalled "the myth of Tantalus, the figure whom Zeus condemned to go forever thirsty and hungry in Hades, despite standing in a pool of water and almost within reach of a fruit tree."[85]

"Trying is more beautiful than the result."

Bob Carlin and Hyon Hak Bong, North Korea's ambassador to Great Britain, sat together at Jim Hoare's seventieth birthday celebration. The former British ambassador in Pyongyang had been a strong supporter of the 1994 nuclear deal. But he had had the misfortune of transmitting the message from Jim Kelly to Washington in 2002 that helped trigger its demise.[86]

Conversation turned to an important statement issued by North Korea's National Defense Commission the previous day, June 16. Military men known for hardline rhetoric had reversed a Foreign Ministry declaration that Pyongyang would never give up its weapons.[87] They said that denuclearization was at the "behest" of Kim Il Sung, his son, and Kim Jong Un.

A surprised Hyon emphasized the importance of the statement. "The situation is going to get worse" unless the Americans talked to his leader, he warned Carlin. The North Koreans certainly weren't going to denuclearize right away, but the former intelligence analyst interpreted the statement as an "invitation to the dance."[88]

The White House issued a near-instantaneous rejection, however. The administration was convinced strategic patience was working. New sanctions, and what appeared to be a negative shift in China's attitude, had put Kim Jong Un on the defensive again, concerned that the two powers were going to gang up on him.

In fact, the spring 2013 crisis had an entirely different meaning for the North Koreans. "We actually won because we completely deterred U.S. aggression," North Korean officials told a Japanese academic.

They could then pivot to the more forward-looking proposal, which was also a nod to President Obama's aspirational goal of achieving a nuclear-free world. "If Obama is serious, then surely the Americans should talk to us without preconditions," the Japanese expert's contacts reasoned.[89]

Even if Washington wanted to reach out, relations were so bad that the North Koreans at the UN refused to answer the phone. The State Department resorted to sending faxes it knew would be forwarded to their Pyongyang bosses.[90]

Three former U.S. special envoys took the lead in testing the diplomatic waters: Robert Gallucci, the architect of the 1994 nuclear deal; Joe DeTrani, the Bush negotiator and spy channel impresario; and Steve Bosworth, Obama's former envoy. I also participated in unofficial dialogues, along with others.

The Hotel N'vY in Geneva, advertised as "artsy, cozy and trendy," located a stone's throw from the lake, was an unlikely venue for our first secret meeting.[91] We would lay the groundwork for a main event in September. Marquee-name North Koreans like nuclear negotiator Ri Yong Ho and Ms. Choe didn't attend. Neither did Gallucci, Bosworth, or DeTrani.

An Myong Hun, the head of the North Korean delegation, was a veteran of multilateral diplomacy, including two tours in Geneva. He had played a minor role in the Clinton denuclearization talks. An bought Mc-Donald's hamburgers that his wife distributed to the American negotiating team, prompting laughs all around and breaking the ice.[92]

The Geneva meeting, our first encounter with North Koreans since the rocky Singapore session in the summer of 2012, came on the heels of Pyongyang's June pronouncement. While we were concerned that An wouldn't be as open as Choe Son Hui, he proved to be straightforward, well-informed, and less combative.[93]

An was also frustrated. "A zero-sum game will never work," he asserted, after we told him "things had never been so bad in Washington." The North Korean diplomat asked, "What can be done?" then answered his own question: "The only way is to hold talks." We agreed.[94]

An explained that the June 16 statement was a green light to resume negotiations.[95] The North Koreans had hoped the Obama administration would "think seriously about our proposal, but it failed to do so," he commented.[96]

Discussion of the June pronouncement also dominated the second day of talks. We explained that an observer attuned to deciphering Pyongyang's cryptic statements knew it was important. But the North Koreans' message had been drowned out in a welter of contradictory statements and actions during the spring crisis.[97]

An offered advice on how to conduct a successful dialogue. First, the United States had to avoid the American narrative that the North Koreans reached agreements, reaped benefits, and then violated them. Pyongyang also had to avoid its own narrative of focusing on a cycle of "negotiation, agreement, implementation, a new administration and then a new crisis."[98]

"Everything is on the table," An proclaimed, although what he offered was nothing new. Denuclearization, starting with delaying the resumption of the production of bomb-making plutonium announced that spring, could be discussed. He also proposed stopping nuclear and missile tests.[99]

The next discussion, held at the Mercure, a budget hotel in Berlin's former eastern sector, came close to a breakthrough. Reporters stalked nuclear negotiators Ri Yong Ho and Choe Son Hui, as well as Bob Gallucci and Steve Bosworth.[100] Some even booked hotel rooms and roamed the hallways looking to corner any North Koreans also staying there.[101]

Ri, Bosworth, and Gallucci, with decades of negotiating experience, took stock of the situation during our first session. The always understated but straightforward Bosworth said, "Because of its major disappointments with the North, the administration has decided by necessity and prefer-ence to deal with other problems," namely the Syrian civil war, Iran's nuclear program, Putin's Russia, and Xi's China.[102]

An equally low-key Ri waxed philosophical about missed opportunities, especially the Leap Day deal. "Both parties were surprised and disappointed with the sudden breakdown," he remarked. Reading between the lines, our delegation concluded that the deal's failure was a setback for Kim Jong Un or the Foreign Ministry or both.[103]

How did this happen? "What we have here is a failure to communicate," Gallucci said, quoting from a Paul Newman movie. The former dean of the Georgetown School of Foreign Service had even played that line back to the actor during dinner at his New York apartment.[104]

The problem, in Ri's words, was historical and cultural differences, as well as "deep-rooted mindsets" and a "lack of trust," a favorite North Korean theme that had the ring of truth.[105]

The North Koreans were puzzled. Why had the Obama administration adopted a policy of strategic patience? "What are you waiting for?" Ri wondered aloud. It didn't make sense; time was on his side. Washington had said North Korea was a grave threat, but "it doesn't seem to pay a lot of attention to us."[106]

Ri searched for a hidden meaning and speculated that the United States welcomed North Korea's growing arsenal as an excuse to justify a military buildup in the region. Chinese experts and government officials also shared his theory.[107]

"It would be nice if there was consistency between resources expended and declarations about threats, but we aren't that good," Gallucci countered.

Bosworth chimed in: "There is no interest in preserving a state of conflict. We want stability." He and Gallucci added that most Americans knew regime change was a fantasy and warned Ri not to be so logical.[108]

The Americans, in turn, wondered about the hyperbolic turn of events in Pyongyang beginning in spring 2013. The North Koreans related that much of the hoopla was because Kim Jong Un had taken over before he had established a personal network of supporters. In a rush to demonstrate loyalty, many North Koreans had issued exaggerated threats.[109]

Kim also had to show Washington he was tough. "People thought the existing arsenal may not be enough to deter the American threat" with the "nuclear blackmail" of bombers flying over the peninsula. "Byungjin was the response," Ri explained. "Once we are convinced that we're not in danger anymore, we can think of new things."[110]

After a cordial lunch, Gallucci got right to the heart of the matter. "I am often asked; will North Korea give up its nuclear weapons? Americans are skeptical." Ri had been asked a similar question in Pyongyang: "Do you really think the Americans will change their policy towards North Korea?"[111]

"There might be pessimism, but that doesn't mean the problem should remain forever," Gallucci argued. Ri agreed. Kang Sok Ju, the negotiator of the 1994 nuclear deal, often quoted from *Gone with the Wind* to make a point. Ri turned to Sidney Sheldon, the American author of romantic suspense novels, and responded, "Trying is more beautiful than the result."[112]

"Nuclear weapons will be on the table" if talks were to resume, Ri remarked, although he added a familiar caveat: The United States would have to withdraw its nuclear umbrella over South Korea by withdrawing its troops. We also knew Kim Jong Il had been willing to drop that condition if relations with Washington improved, but there was no guarantee his son would, too.[113]

"We are just thinking out loud here," Ri continued, a sign he was about to table more far-reaching ideas than what we had heard in Geneva. What followed was a startling North Korean road map that would end Washington's "hostile policy," and result in Pyongyang giving up its nuclear arsenal.[114]

First, Washington would declare a list of steps it would take to demonstrate that it was dropping its hostile policy by lifting sanctions, holding peace talks, and helping Pyongyang develop nuclear energy for economic needs. In return, North Korea would freeze its nuclear buildup.[115]

As the United States implemented its declaration, North Korea would disable its nuclear weapons program and make sure none of its facilities would ever be used again. Finally, after all the actions were implemented, his country would dismantle its facilities and weapons.[116]

Our delegation quickly spotted the flaws in Ri's proposal. For example, the United States would never finish all its moves before Pyongyang dismantled its nuclear program. However, Ri was flexible, suggesting that "I don't think the order of things is important. It's up to U.S. convenience."[117]

Some of his demands would also be hard, if not impossible, to meet, like building new reactors. "We could build peaceful nuclear energy by ourselves," or "we can discuss energy cooperation," Ri allowed. However, that could mean providing North Korea with another multibillion-dollar reactor project.[118]

Despite the challenges, Ri's road map was familiar as a starting point for serious talks. Gallucci had been through this before when he negotiated the 1994 nuclear deal. "If you can say this, that's a big deal," he told the North Koreans.[119]

There was another important speed bump that couldn't be avoided. Ri was still unwilling to halt satellite launches, the issue that had upended the Leap Day deal.[120]

Gallucci had an idea: "Could you just maintain your sovereign right to peaceful space exploration but say it will not be exercised?"

Bosworth chimed in. Washington had done that before when it was deemed to be in our national interest. Their suggestion seemed to address Kim Kye Gwan's concern during the Leap Day talks that all states had a sovereign right to peacefully explore space.[121]

Ri thought for a moment and answered, "Where there is a will, there is a way." His response was cryptic, but at least it left room for further discussion.[122]

London was the next stop for a two-day session in early October at the five-star Athenaeum Hotel. Gallucci and I dropped out while Bosworth stayed on. DeTrani also joined the talks. The North Korean delegation remained the same.[123]

My friend Leon Sigal, a twenty-year veteran of unofficial talks who hadn't been in Berlin, led the American delegation. A former academic who had taught at Wesleyan, Princeton, and Columbia universities, Lee had served in the Carter State Department and as a member of the *New York Times* editorial board.

Much of the back-and-forth in London covered the same ground about denuclearization, reinforcing the point that the Foreign Ministry was testing Ri's idea out on American experts.[124]

The talks also picked up on Gallucci's suggestion about satellite launches. This time Ri was more positive: "I'm optimistic that it's possible." One American described his answer as a kind of "hook-baiting."[125]

The Geneva, Berlin, and London sessions reminded the former American negotiators of past talks. These meetings, however, were free of polemics and the tedious repetition of official positions. They were brainstorming sessions, not the last—and maybe not the most important—word in Pyongyang, but a ray of hope in a bleak diplomatic landscape.

The contrast between face-to-face dialogue and Washington's attempt to use China to advance unilateral demands was striking. Ri and his staff unveiled a proposal to take positive steps early in talks, maybe even on the thorny problem of satellite launches. They also tabled new denuclearization ideas.

Bob Gallucci and Steve Bosworth coauthored a *New York Times* op-ed, "Reasons to Talk to North Korea," after returning home. The two argued that Pyongyang was ready to put its nuclear weapons "on the negotiating table." They concluded, "It is imperative that the United States turn its attention to quickly resolving this dangerous situation."[126]

The White House and the State Department dismissed what the North Koreans had said. According to administration officials, they were experts at deceiving naïve Americans.

CHAPTER TEN

"No news is okay news."

E IGHT MINUTES INTO A twenty-minute YouTube interview—part of a strategy to reach out to millions of subscribers after President Obama's 2015 State of the Union speech—one interviewer asked Obama, "How should the United States deal with Pyongyang's human rights atrocities?"[1]

North Korea had been in the news over a cyberattack on Sony Pictures. Obama repeated the standard mantra, "North Korea is the most isolated, the most sanctioned, the most cut off nation on Earth."[2] But then he predicted that it would eventually collapse because of the Internet. Obama appeared to be joining a long list of wishful thinkers, who were patiently waiting for North Korea's inevitable demise.[3]

The president's pronouncement reflected his experience watching the Internet trigger the Arab Spring, but also discussions with private experts in his one and only session on North Korea. The supporters of strategic patience suggested the United States foment unrest in the North by making sure the average citizen knew how much better life was in the outside world.[4]

In the two years since Kim Jong Un had threatened American cities with destruction, the Obama administration had focused on other foreign policy challenges. No one wanted to risk a post–Leap Day deal fiasco. Years had passed since the last WMD test, so the prevailing attitude was "No news is okay news," one official recalled.[5]

Doubts about strategic patience continued to grow, however, as information poured in on Pyongyang's WMD programs. Some policymakers thought the Asia experts who pushed patience didn't know what they were doing. Some viewed the intelligence community's insisting that North Korea would never give up its nuclear weapons as preemptive capitulation. Some had a gnawing hunch that the Deputies Small Group was decision-making gone bad.[6]

Even Obama and his top aides were tiring of patience. The White House embarked on the first of three policy reviews in 2014. The minor adjustments recommended by the reviews prompted Denis McDonough to complain to his staff that they were not serving the president well.[7]

Without a new vision, Washington dabbled in old, ineffective initiatives. One program, costing hundreds of millions of dollars, was designed to use the "seeping in" of information—including the outlandish idea of concealing it in hollowed-out soap bars—to undermine the regime. The North Koreans fielded tools to check that effort.

Another plan was to "use human rights to go after bad guys." An American-backed UN commission concluded that Kim should be tried for crimes against his people. Predictably, China and Russia blocked implementation.[8]

Washington's successes—freeing a record eight detained American citizens—had nothing to do with WMD. But one incident may have been a missed opportunity to restart nuclear talks. The administration had inundated Pyongyang with requests to free Kenneth Bae, a Korean American missionary arrested in 2012. As a result, the North Koreans sarcastically referred to the New York channel as the "the Kenneth Bae channel."[9]

Pyongyang was in the hunt for big game. "Gruff, direct, outspoken and seasoned," James Clapper, Obama's director of national intelligence, or DNI, had a long history with North Korea dating back to the 1970s. He was almost shot down later when his helicopter mistakenly crossed the DMZ. Still, a visit to Pyongyang was on his bucket list. He checked off that box in November 2014.[10]

Avril Haines, the CIA's first female deputy director, visited Pyongyang weeks before Clapper, presumably to pave his way. She returned with gifts of beauty products, not the detainees. When the CIA analyzed them, concerned the North Koreans might try to poison her just as it had tried to poison Fidel Castro, they didn't find anything. Soon afterwards, an American tourist detained for leaving a Bible in his hotel bathroom was released.[11]

As for Bae, the North Korean spies were willing to let him go if a member of Obama's cabinet came to fetch him. But there was one condition: an invitation for the minister of state security to visit Washington. The Americans didn't promise anything, only to relay the request to the White House. That was good enough for the North Koreans.[12]

Clapper seemed ideal. He had Korea experience, held a cabinet-level job, and had a good relationship with Obama, "who liked to needle him for always dropping paper clips on the rug in the Oval Office." As an intelligence official and not a policymaker, he wasn't itching to negotiate.[13]

But in this instance, the DNI warned the White House that strategic patience was "flawed." Talking could lead to "a McDonald's moment."[14] Clapper recalled, "The United States was treating North Korea as a noisy aggravation, and neither side had anything resembling diplomacy with the other." His trip could change all that.[15]

The DNI wanted to establish diplomatic outposts in each capital—the two nations hadn't formally acknowledged the other's existence for six decades—to break the ice. Clapper's proposal, however, was more than the White House could bear. Like Bill Clinton, he was cautioned, "Don't bow, don't smile, don't accept flowers," one official recalled.[16]

Clapper left for Pyongyang in early November on a mission that was "comical in a slapstick kind of way," a delegation member observed. His Air Force Boeing 737 broke down twice. Angered by the delay, the North Koreans accused the Americans of "stringing them along," and threatened to revoke their landing permit.[17]

The DNI was met at the Pyongyang Airport by the minister for state security and driven to a guesthouse in a 1990s-vintage Mercedes. Right from the start, the North Koreans were clear they were expecting a breakthrough in relations. They raised the possibility of a summit between President Obama and Kim Jong Un.[18]

The next stop was a thirteen-course dinner in a bowling alley dining room with Kim Yong Chol, the diplomatic wolf warrior who had met Morrell and DeTrani. The DNI endured a diatribe laced with accusations that the Americans were "criminals and warmongers." When Clapper responded in kind, Kim bristled. The DNI's assistant quickly suggested "a head call" before the clash got out of hand.[19]

When Clapper returned, he blurted out, "The United States has no permanent enemies." Whether deliberately or not, he struck the same positive note as had Kim Jong Un.

The North Korean spy chief reversed course and responded that Clapper "could foster that transformation by negotiating the normalization of relations," exactly what he had hoped to propose. All the DNI could do was insist that North Korea had to denuclearize first.[20]

While the Americans were confined to their guesthouse, informed that angry people were waiting outside to shoot them, Bae and a twenty-five-year-old Californian detainee, Matthew Miller, were handed over. The Americans boarded their plane, after promising to relay the request for a return visit by the minister for state security. They had no intention of following through.[21]

Clapper's trip was a missed opportunity. The North's security operatives thought that he was the right person to arrange negotiations, and that they were the right people to handle them. After all, Pyongyang's spies had arranged Bill Clinton's session with Kim Jong Il in 2009. However, when he was asked by a reporter whether the release gave him a better understanding of Kim's strategy, the president had a single-word answer: "No."[22]

The North Koreans tried again on January 10, 2015, after Kim Jong Un called for a positive change in relations with South Korea in his New Year's speech. Their UN mission called the State Department to propose that Pyongyang would halt nuclear tests if the United States canceled an upcoming military exercise with South Korea. Those temporary steps would create a better atmosphere for talks.[23]

The proposal shouldn't have come as a surprise. The administration had been informed in spring 2014 that the plan was brewing in Pyongyang. Ri Yong Ho raised the idea during a Track 2 meeting with me and other experts, which we had reported upon our return.[24]

But the State Department still rejected it right away, even though the United States had canceled exercises in the past. Washington argued that the exercise was a legitimate activity, while Pyongyang's nuclear tests violated sanctions. One American official confidently concluded, "We knew they weren't going to test." He was wrong.[25]

Pyongyang tried again and again. A North Korean diplomat in New York stated a few days later, "If the United States needs dialogue as regards this issue, the former [i.e., North Korea] is ready to sit with the US anytime." They suggested in mid-February that the exercise could just be postponed for a few days so it wouldn't overlap with a reunion of families separated by the Korean War.[26]

The whole episode reminded Sung Kim, who had just replaced Glyn Davies, that he had a tough road ahead. His job was "to get something going with North Korea," a colleague commented.[27] As the top aide to Chris Hill and Steve Bosworth, Kim had witnessed their trials and tribulations.

He didn't have to contend only with the North Koreans. "There was tension between him and advocates of strategic patience," one official recalled. Danny Russel had moved to State from the White House as the top Asia hand. Syd Seiler, who nominally worked for Kim, also moved over. They quickly rejected Pyongyang's proposal before the new envoy, taking his daughter off to college, could weigh in.[28]

The North Koreans persisted. During a meeting in Singapore with Steve Bosworth a week later, Ri Yong Ho pointed out that his country hadn't conducted a WMD test in fifteen months and had recently released a number of detainees. Reducing the size, scale, or frequency of the exercises was also acceptable.[29]

"Sung Kim has similar aspirations," Bosworth responded. It was understood that the new envoy was sending a message through his old boss. Talks could start without preconditions. Kim seconded Bosworth's message through the New York channel.[30]

Not long afterwards, the North Koreans invited Sung Kim to visit Pyongyang. He could meet with anyone he wanted and talk about anything. The White House was ready to accept but changed its mind when the conservative Park administration in South Korea stepped in and opposed the visit. Instead, Kim offered to meet anywhere in Asia except Pyongyang.[31]

By then, after the president's YouTube interview, the North Koreans had had enough. "If President Obama doesn't talk to us, we will just wait for the next president," Ri Yong Ho warned a visitor. Kim Jong Un was going to be around for a long time. A State Department official recalled, "Those were years we needed. I wished we could get them back and we can't."[32]

"It will be like tying a time bomb that may explode at any time on the backs of the hostile forces."

Starting in 2014, a sprawling facility shaped like an atom began to rise on an islet in the river running through Pyongyang. Within the year, a shiny science and technology complex was completed. Some observers thought the building was a reminder that North Korea would never denuclearize.[33]

Just a few weeks earlier, Kim Jong Un had visited another prize project, which pundits also thought had a not-so-hidden meaning. The six-lane street, lined with tall buildings decorated with atoms, planets, and scientific iconography, featured shops, recreation facilities, and even a pizzeria, and housed thousands of families from a university renowned for its nuclear expertise.[34]

Regardless of whether his construction projects signaled Kim Jong Un's devotion to building a nuclear arsenal, there was no debate about his reinvigorating Pyongyang's equivalent to the Manhattan Project. Change was already in the works as younger scientists had stepped into the limelight while his father was still alive.[35]

Kim Jong Un was replacing geriatric masterminds, many in their eighties, with a younger generation that had grown up in a thriving country and then experienced the 1990s' desperate food shortages. He promoted them, met them, and relied on them, a hands-on approach that may have contributed to the faster development of better bombs and missiles.[36]

Kim Jong Un still kept some of his older scientists around. Men like seventy-year-old Ri Hong Sop, the former director of Yongbyon, and Hong Sung Mu, also a Yongbyon veteran, were given pride of place.[37] They often accompanied the leader on inspection tours, an honor reserved for Kim's closest advisors. Ri was put in charge of the Nuclear Weapons Institute, believed to design new bombs. Hong probably supervised the 2013 nuclear test.[38]

However, younger technicians dominated the missile elite. Kim Jong Sik, a forty-something civil aeronautics expert, figured out why the April 2009 rocket launch failed, and managed the successful December 2012 test. Jang Chang Ha, a mystery man in his fifties, oversaw the development of advanced weapons. Ri Pyong Chol, the Air Force commander and a relative of the young leader's wife, helped run the missile program.[39]

Despite the slow-motion progress made by his WMD programs, the elder Kim had planted technological seeds that blossomed when his son took over. Not satisfied with his father's sluggish pace, the younger Kim conducted two satellite launches in 2012 (his father had launched two in ten years), unveiled a mobile long-range missile—also developed under Kim Jong Il—and conducted a nuclear test in February 2013.

Even so, American decision-makers didn't immediately understand the growing danger since there were no more tests for almost two years. In public pronouncements, scientific journals, construction at WMD installations, and efforts to acquire foreign technology, however, Kim made clear that he wanted more bombs, better bombs, more powerful rockets, a strategy for using them, and a military to take charge of them.

Building more bombs meant producing more nuclear material. The uranium enrichment plant at Yongbyon, visited by the Stanford trio in 2010, had doubled in size by August 2013. It appeared poised to double the production of bomb-making material.[40]

One hundred and fifty miles to the south, not far from the DMZ, a nondescript plant near a uranium mine was also being refurbished. The facility turned raw ore into enriched uranium, a process that continued at Yongbyon where the almost-finished product was made.[41]

Building more powerful hydrogen bombs, just like almost all the other nuclear powers had done, was a natural next step. Despite skeptics who thought North Korea was too backward to do it, Pyongyang began in 2010 to publicly muse about "boosting" the yield of an atom bomb. That was the first step in building a hydrogen weapon.[42]

North Korea's interest in producing lithium 6, a key ingredient in a hydrogen bomb, was first revealed in its scientific literature. Then, Pyongyang signed a contract in China in 2012 for equipment and materials to build a production plant. Four years later, the North attempted to sell lithium metal to an overseas customer.[43]

A closer look at Yongbyon in 2014 revealed construction of a new facility in its southwest corner. Analysts suspected the plant might separate small amounts of tritium, a radioactive isotope also used in building H-bombs, from fuel rods coming out of the installation's nuclear reactor.[44]

More powerful bombs were useless, however, unless they could be reduced in size and placed on top of missiles. First-generation explosives typically weighed tons. North Korean scientists were probably working hard using data gathered from nuclear tests—failures and successes—to refine their designs. If they had to detonate a new design, the nuclear test site stood at the ready.

Even if the North Koreans succeeded in building more powerful, smaller bombs, missiles had to carry them thousands of miles to targets in the United States. These missiles needed big engines; safe, efficient, and powerful fuels; and the ability to escape attempts to destroy them before they could be launched. North Korean engineers were trying to overcome those hurdles on their own, but it didn't hurt to shop overseas for technology.[45]

The KN-08 missile featured in the April 2012 Pyongyang parade was mobile, powered by more advanced Russian rocket engines, and launched off Chinese-built trucks. It still couldn't reach the entire United States. Work underway at Pyongyang's space launch center to raise the height of the gantry, however, seemed to indicate that North Korea could test technologies for a bigger rocket with greater range.[46]

But bigger missiles could be cumbersome, less mobile, and more vulnerable to attack. North Korean rocket scientists had to master another challenge. They had to build mobile missiles the same size as, or smaller than, the KN-08 that could also fly greater distances.

One way to do that was to use better fuel. The Soviet Union, China, and other countries produced unsymmetrical dimethylhydrazine, or UDMH, a powerful liquid propellent. It wasn't secret, but it wasn't easy to produce. A North Korean journal published three articles related to UDMH in 2013, including one by a scientist who worked at a chemical complex that would have been a perfect place to churn out the fuel.[47]

Another way to increase range was to build more powerful engines. The collapse of the Soviet Union decades earlier had reopened doors for the North Koreans. Along with Chinese, Iranians, and Iraqis, they descended on the Ukrainians—once a key cog in Russia's missile program—desperate for deals. "It was like the Star Wars bar scene," one American official recalled.[48]

North Koreans claiming to be tourists viewed one showroom filled with satellites and rocket engines in the early 2000s. "It's just a guess," a retired Ukrainian scientist, Viktor Moisa, later told a reporter, "but they were probably dreaming of becoming a missile power."[49]

Two North Korean officials were caught trying to photograph advanced rocket designs, including engines, at another facility in 2011. The Ukrainians insisted it was the first time the North Koreans had tried to steal information, but, as one local told an American, "We would rather be making missiles and satellite launchers than buses." Six years later, Pyongyang tested a new ICBM with a powerful liquid-fueled engine that only Ukraine and Russia could build.[50]

While more powerful liquid fuel engines would do the trick, most countries developing a mobile ICBM transitioned to solid fuel. The rockets were easier to operate, didn't require a train of fuel trucks, and could be launched in minutes, not hours. There were disadvantages, however. Even the slightest cracks in the propellant, for example, could lead to an explosion.

By the time Kim Jong Un took over, the North Koreans had years of experience with solid fuel, mainly for very short-range artillery rockets. They purchased a Russian-made solid fuel missile from Syria in the late 1990s, then produced a model able to fly one hundred miles, and tested a longer-range version. Since this was still a far cry from reaching targets thousands of miles away, acquiring more experience was essential in building "bigger and bigger and bigger," according to one rocket scientist.[51]

The North Koreans had also gone shopping overseas for solid fuel technology. An American scientist discovered his hotel registry was filled with names of North Koreans during a visit to a Russian plant in 1999 to help destroy excess engines. Whether they had succeeded in acquiring technology or hiring financially strapped scientists was unclear.[52]

Just as Kim Jong Un took over, satellite photos of the No. 17 Explosives Plant near Hamhung, the country's second largest city, revealed suspicious activity. Two years later, a new factory able to produce solid fuel engines for large rockets was finished. A nearby facility on eighteen acres along the East Sea to test those engines was also completed.[53]

Perhaps Kim Jong Un's biggest WMD surprise was the development of one of the most complicated technologies imaginable: submarine-launched ballistic missiles. Established nuclear powers had fielded fleets. Nascent powers were trying to build them.

Cash-strapped, experienced Russian scientists apparently made their way to North Korea and Iran during the 1990s.[54] Satellite pictures of a military shipyard northeast of Pyongyang in late 2014 revealed a submarine with a conning tower that could house one- or two-missile launch tubes. The Russia connection later became obvious when the North tested a submarine-launched missile based on its technology.[55]

Building a new nuclear arsenal was one thing; figuring out how to use it another. A "mutual assured destruction" doctrine, or MAD, emerged after the 1994 nuclear deal collapsed. As their arsenal grew, the North Koreans hinted they might have to use weapons early in a conflict to stop more powerful invaders. European countries, backed by the United States and confronting a more powerful Soviet Union, had adopted the same approach. So did Pakistan, faced with India's larger army.[56]

Finally, any respectable nuclear power needed a military organization to run its arsenal. The United States had its Strategic Air Command, which had been renamed the U.S. Strategic Command, and the Soviet Union had the Strategic Rocket Forces. Kim Jong Il had his Strategic Rocket Forces Command, which he reportedly boasted was a unit that "I care for like a son." Two years after Kim Jong Un visited the unit in 2012, he put his own stamp on the organization, renaming it the "Strategic Command."[57]

What did the American intelligence community know about North Korea's WMD iceberg and when did it know it? Even though the testing lull may have created a false sense of security, the community knew something was up.[58]

"All of a sudden, we were seeing their program on a more accelerated track," one senior official recalled. "They were a lot closer to having the capability to marry a weapon to an ICBM that could hit us." In short, "we had underestimated the pace of the threat."[59]

Kim Jong Un was the wild card. No one realized that, unlike his father, who thought failures made North Korea look bad, the younger Kim was willing to learn from mistakes. And no one ever heard of him executing scientists.

Failures, partial successes, and successes were the new norm as Pyongyang resumed tests in mid-2015. Kim was closely involved. He was reported to have praised a new submarine-launched missile, saying, "It will be like tying a time bomb that may explode at any time on the backs of the hostile forces."[60] The danger to millions of Americans was growing.

"We were just ankle-biting."

Weeks after North Korea's February 2013 nuclear test, the United States barred the Foreign Trade Bank, Pyongyang's primary overseas bank, from doing business with its financial institutions. American officials believed they were about to relive the glory days of 2005 when crippling sanctions imposed on Banco Delta Asia instantly transformed North Korea into a global pariah.

The new sanctions were a big win for Danny Glaser, a Columbia University–trained lawyer. He had been part of the Treasury team that unleashed a new era of financial warfare after 9/11 intended to stop funding for terrorists and to punish perpetrators of financial crimes. Glaser hoped the Foreign Trade Bank restriction was the next Banco Delta Asia.[61]

The sanctions seemed to have an immediate impact. Beijing's four largest state-owned commercial institutions closed their doors to North Korea. The *New York Times* heralded "the strongest public Chinese response yet" to North Korea's defiance of Beijing and its continuing WMD program.[62]

But the longer-term effect was murky. Much of Pyongyang's trade with China was settled in barter or cash with money brought in by couriers carrying suitcases stuffed with dollars. One Chinese bank manager explained to a British reporter, "We just sent across 15,000 pounds to Pyongyang; it's that easy."[63]

Even more shocking, the Foreign Trade Bank eventually operated in China on a much grander scale. Five years later, the U.S. Justice Department revealed that North Korean and Chinese citizens had set up more than 250 shell companies run by the bank's branches to launder over $2.5 billion with the money flowing back to Pyongyang.[64]

Glaser finally realized the days of precision strikes to disable North Korea's financial network were over. The only sanctions that would work had to threaten North Korea's very existence. That path led straight to China, its primary economic partner, but no one wanted to confront Beijing after the Sunnylands summit. "We don't have a Korea policy; we have a China policy," a State Department official told a Treasury colleague.[65]

The next three years felt like a scene from the movie *Groundhog Day*. The United States planned how to respond to the next WMD test that never came. Instead, "We would get an intelligence briefing about North Korean smuggling and everyone would be upset." Nothing more than a "shrugging of shoulders" resulted, one official recalled.[66]

As for short-range missile tests and sanctions violations, all Washington could do was report them to the UN. Protests went nowhere because of Russian and Chinese intransigence. A White House aide recalled, "Our biggest response was a harshly written letter."[67]

However, there was some method to the Americans' madness. The UN Panel of Experts, with eight members from different countries, investigated charges of sanctions violations. If the charges stuck, the case could be kicked upstairs to another committee, which might recommend new restrictions.

Washington sent lists "with ten, twenty, thirty sets of people and organizations to sanction," but the Chinese would whittle them down, one American recalled. They didn't want to provoke the North Koreans. One request, however, led to the case of the *Mu Du Bong*, a rust bucket whose fate would embroil Pyongyang, Washington, and Mexico City in a tug-of-war that lasted almost two years.[68]

It all started in July 2013 when another North Korean ship, the *Chong Chon Gang*, left Cuba for home, and was stopped for a drug inspection as it passed through the Panama Canal. Hidden in its hold were everything from artillery shells to two jet fighters. According to Treasury, it was "the most substantial consignment of DPRK-related arms and related materiel interdicted" since sanctions had been enacted in 2006.[69]

The Panel of Experts' investigation led to an innocuously named Vladivostok-based firm, Ocean Maritime Management, or OMM, which provided the captain and crew. Its 14 ships were part of an illicit network that one study estimated included 147 vessels, 167 individuals, and 248 companies.[70]

After a stupefyingly slow investigation, during which Washington was ready to throw in the towel, the Chinese allowed the UN to name OMM as contributing to activities it prohibited. Treasury followed with its own sanctions. Still, OMM continued to operate after renaming ships, reregistering them under foreign "flags of convenience," and re-naming itself.

The *Mu Du Bong*, however, didn't escape the UN's clutches. The vessel, which normally plied the coast of China, had crossed the Pacific, and transited the Panama Canal in mid-June on its way to Cuba. After the ship ran aground in July on a protected Mexican coral reef (OMM hadn't paid thirty dollars for updated charts), it was towed to a nearby port.[71]

It was "the worst timing ever," according to a White House official. There were no weapons on board, but the vessel was subjected to an asset freeze. Since no one had ever done that before, it was left to the unlikely trio of Mexico, North Korea, and the United States to sort out the details.[72]

"We spent a ton of time trying to convince the Mexicans to seize the ship," a White House official recalled. The Mexicans offered to send the North Koreans home, but the crew refused to go. Pyongyang's diplomats in New York threatened to "take the necessary measures to make the ship leave immediately."[73]

The Mexicans were ready to give up, so Washington threatened them.[74] A tense standoff finally ended a year later when the crew left for home. Mexico declared the rusting ship "abandoned," and sold it for scrap.[75]

The episode proved to be a Pyrrhic victory. OMM lost a ship and more sanctions were slapped on three companies linked to the firm. The Americans circulated a list of vessels countries shouldn't let into their ports. However, OMM was replaced by two new firms that managed its fleet.[76]

The Obama administration's whack-a-mole campaign was also waged on land. Just like other countries that had set out to build nuclear weapons, North Korea had also relied on individuals to smuggle technologies to build bombs and missiles.

None could match A. Q. Khan, the Dr. No–like Pakistani scientist who stole nuclear technology from Europe, returned home to build the bomb, and ran his own one-stop shopping operation to help other countries. Many of these individuals didn't need the money. They wanted to impress colleagues, friends, and family.[77]

Alex Tsai had been on the American intelligence community's radar since the late 1990s. Born in an impoverished region of Taiwan, he had made his way to Taipei, worked in a customs job, and then become a successful businessman. He was later described as a model citizen by his lawyers, who didn't mention that Tsai, and his wife, daughter, and son, also sold technology to North Korea.[78]

The Americans tried repeatedly to convince the Taiwanese to arrest Tsai. His company, Trans Merits, had done business with the Korean Mining Development Trade Corporation, Pyongyang's arms dealer, since 1999.[79] But he had managed to stay free.[80]

When Tsai was finally arrested, convicted, fined a pittance, and given a suspended sentence in July 2008, he shrugged it off. Even when Treasury imposed new sanctions on him and his company, Tsai set up a new firm with a new name and a new wrinkle.[81]

His thirty-seven-year-old son Gary, a permanent resident of the United States and accomplice in past illegal exports from California, Ohio, and Michigan, established a branch in Illinois. Nice people, according to their neighbors, the younger Tsai and his wife were "pursuing the American dream," his lawyers later pleaded.[82]

In August 2009, father and son arranged the illegal export of precision tools from Illinois to North Korea to help produce nuclear bombs. While Gary slipped up and provided the firm with a business card saying he worked for his father's company, it never bothered to check out the father-son business relationship.[83]

The FBI's Counter Proliferation Center, tasked with stopping the spread of WMD, was on the case. It was housed in a "Sensitive Compartmented Information Facility" in downtown Washington, DC, where nearly one hundred analysts scoured information for clues on proliferation. Each had three computers: one for unclassified browsing of the Internet and sending emails, one for the secret FBI-net, and one for Top Secret information.[84]

The Center identified criminal activity, forwarded leads to field agents, and helped build court cases. FBI investigators operating out of the Counter Proliferation Center and the Bureau's office in Chicago obtained eight search warrants in the case of the Tsais. They covered five of their six email accounts and others held by third parties.[85]

The FBI's main job was to "arrest someone," according to a former bureau analyst. Some violators were "turned," however, and helped the bureau track illegal shipments or sabotage weapons. Others were targeted by undercover sting operations in the United States and overseas.[86]

"Nine out of ten operations overseas involved already planned foreign travel," according to a law enforcement official. In other cases, Bureau assets lured criminals with fake prize vacations or invitations to conferences in countries that had an extradition treaty with the United States. Sometimes, the smuggler would take the bait.[87]

That may have happened to Alex Tsai, who was arrested in spring 2013 while vacationing with his wife in Tallinn, Estonia. His son was taken into custody in Illinois the same day. The father was sent to the United States in October to stand trial.[88]

The Tsais insisted they were innocent, but eventually pleaded guilty. Alex got off easy after nineteen meetings with federal authorities, telling them everything he knew about smuggling. He was sentenced to time served plus two months, far short of the maximum sentence of five years. His fine of $100 was laughable compared to the maximum of $250,000. Alex returned to Taiwan after he was freed.[89]

Gary Tsai was sentenced a month later. Fired from his job, divorced by his wife, and confined for two years in his home, he pleaded, "I love the United States of America and I would never do anything to hurt America." The judge believed him. Gary was sentenced to three years of probation and a $250 fine.[90]

There was some justice, however. A federal court decided in 2019 that Alex should forfeit almost $150,000. The funds had been traveling through the American banking system in his daughter's name from Hong Kong to Taiwan when they had been blocked seven years earlier.[91]

Assistant Attorney General John P. Carlin insisted that "sanctions are meant to raise the cost for WMD proliferators to do business and deter others from proliferating." But, according to one official, the only smugglers caught were "dumb criminals who made some stupid mistake."[92]

It all amounted to "just throwing sand in North Korea's gears," a White House aide recalled, a conclusion seconded by a State Department official: "We were just ankle-biting."[93]

"If they launch a nuclear weapon at San Francisco, we will nuke them."

When John Plumb moved from the Pentagon to the White House in 2013—he hadn't been part of Jim Miller's campaign to counter North Korea's ICBM—he discovered how little the United States was prepared for the danger. Pyongyang's advances hadn't set off alarm bells yet, but they were very close.

The Pentagon's attitude that "We've got it," after Secretary Hagel's March 2013 announcement, ignored inconvenient truths. Despite the planned upgrade in defenses, the United States would have to fire more and more interceptors at increasingly greater cost to stop a devastating nuclear attack. "I don't think any serious person would say it looks good to me," one official concluded.[94]

There were also important unanswered questions. Secretary Hagel had assumed forty-four interceptors could stop a salvo of six mobile KN-08s. But the system would be overwhelmed if the threat grew faster than expected. The warheads could also evade the interceptors. A Google search generated thousands of possibilities, including something as simple as inflated balloons that looked like warheads to radars tracking the missiles.

Complacency set in again. Warnings of a growing danger "became a little bit of a broken record," one official observed. The KN-08 missile still hadn't been flight tested. Even in a worst-case scenario, Pentagon officials reasoned, "If they launch a nuclear weapon at San Francisco, we will nuke them."[95]

Plumb was horrified. The solution to the growing threat shouldn't be sacrificing tens of thousands of Americans or vaporizing millions of North Koreans. Like Miller, Ehrhard, and Winnefeld, he spent the next two years trying to shift an unwieldy Pentagon bureaucracy into action.

He wasn't alone. President Obama had been following North Korea's missile program, certainly since the KN-08's coming-out party in the April 2012 parade. Concerned that the ground-based interceptors were inadequate to deal with a larger ICBM menace, Obama ordered the National Security Council to review the defenses against an attack.[96]

Plumb, an aerospace engineer who had coauthored the Pentagon's 2010 missile defense review, was perfect for the job. Skeptics resisted, but the review concluded North Korea could deploy more than six KN-08s, maybe as many as twenty to thirty missiles over the next five years. They could easily overwhelm the missile defenses Hagel had announced.[97]

Something had to be done. In late 2014, Susan Rice forwarded a memo from President Obama ordering the Pentagon to consider the missile operational—even if it hadn't been tested—and to develop a plan to defend the United States. Obama didn't want the military to "bring him another rock," a senior officer recalled. He was interested in "taking these missiles out" before they could be launched.[98]

The fight to find a solution had an important new ally. Robert "Bob" Work, a Marine Corps veteran of twenty-seven years, had served as a top Navy civilian before starting his job as the deputy secretary of defense. Work was also "very wonky," according to an observer, always looking for cutting-edge technologies.

He quickly focused on the danger, with the help of Tom Ehrhard, who had remained behind after Jim Miller left the Pentagon. Work didn't want to repeat his experience with the Navy. He had watched the service resist efforts to counter the imminent threat of a Chinese missile that could destroy U.S. aircraft carriers. When the missile was tested, there was a mad rush to catch up.[99]

While Jim Miller had only been able to cajole others to do the right thing, the deputy secretary held sway over everything bureaucrats cared about, from building weapons to funding. A "bigger hammer meant they became more resistant," one official observed, however. Work led the charge to counter Pyongyang's arsenal, supported by Admiral Winnefeld, while Plumb and Ehrhard waged a quiet insurgency.[100]

Since America's interceptors couldn't stop all North Korea's ICBMs from destroying American cities, and killing millions of North Koreans was unpalatable, how could the United States defend itself? The alternative was to prevent as many of the missiles as possible from leaving the ground, what the Pentagon called "left of launch." Hopefully, the remaining ones would be destroyed "right of launch," in flight by interceptors.

Destroying mobile missiles was hard. The Allies only stopped one German V-2 rocket before liftoff during World War II. None were destroyed during the 1991 "Great SCUD Hunt" for Saddam's mobile missiles. If the United States was to succeed, it had to learn from the past. For example, almost nothing had been done to dissect missile operations—key to tracking them—before the Gulf War.[101]

Technology advances had also ushered in a new age of transparency. Satellites, piloted aircraft supplemented by stealthy drones, and improved sensors able to track movements more precisely, were aided by a huge increase in the speed of data transmission to zero in on the target. New weapons—some fast, precise, and flying at almost fifteen times the speed of sound—could destroy mobile missiles before they were moved or launched.[102]

More exotic "left of launch" technologies had also been refined. The possibilities seemed endless, ranging from contaminating guidance systems with a virus to be activated by satellite or ships offshore, to cyberstrikes that could disable computers that controlled the weapons.[103]

Work and Winnefeld had their own experts examining this new tool kit. The deputy secretary's Special Missile Defeat Group looked at "all things to counter the KN-08," a Pentagon official recalled. Winnefeld's shop dissected missile programs from design to operations, what they called the "chain of chains," to "mess with it."[104]

Their recommendations were funneled upwards in the bureaucracy. A committee run by Work, Winnefeld, and Stephanie Sullivan, a top intelligence official, was the first stop. The community played a critical role in finding mobile missiles. The next and last stop was the Deputy's Management Action Group, run by Work and Winnefeld. Its recommendations ended up on the desk of the secretary of defense.[105]

Much of the Pentagon was fixed on the exotic to the exclusion of the pragmatic. An eye-opening, but misleading, *New York Times* article claimed in 2017 that "left of launch" cyberattacks had stopped North Korean missile tests dead in their tracks. Exotic technologies, however, were only "1 percent of the answer," according to a senior official.[106]

There was no substitute for old-fashioned detective work, tracking and blowing up Pyongyang's rockets. Ehrhard had experienced that drudgery as a young Air Force captain assigned the job of figuring out how to destroy Soviet mobile missiles.[107]

The American intelligence community had been monitoring the North's missiles. But the spies still had to figure out "everything we need to do every day to understand better what they do, and to make it hard for them to sneak around," one official recalled.[108]

The Joint Chiefs of Staff had promised Congress in 2013 the military would prevent adversaries "from effectively employing any of [their] offensive air and missile weapons."[109] Still, the Pentagon missed two deadlines for reports to the White House on plans to counter the North Korean threat. Even when the reports were finally forwarded, they were bounced back.

"It's not good enough. I want another version," Rice commented after seeing the first report. "Is that enough, what else can you do?" White House officials asked during briefings on the ICBM-busting plan. The pressure helped Work push the envelope. His staff threatened Defense bureaucrats that their boss would "cloud up and rain all over them" unless they fell in line.[110]

Just as a worn-out Plumb was about to leave government in May 2015, the Joint Chiefs of Staff organized a half-day-long secret war game. The objective was to see if they could stop Kim Jong Un from rolling the dice and launching a suicidal attack to destroy American cities.

The exercise tried to answer serious questions. How much progress had the Pentagon made in thwarting an attack? Would the president have time to make a considered decision to launch a pre-emptive strike in an escalating crisis? What about the likelihood that U.S. allies would face almost certain destruction?[111]

Presidents had confronted that dilemma ever since Richard Nixon considered retaliation after North Korea shot down a Navy spy plane in 1969. Kim Jong Un had far more destructive weapons that he could use against South Korea and Japan, even if his ICBMs were destroyed on the ground.

The answers fell far short of what Obama wanted. All the Pentagon was willing to say was, "We will do the best we can, we are just not sure we can catch everything," according to one aide. The result would either be "a full-scale war on the Korean Peninsula or nothing."[112]

Obama reminded his advisors that the United States didn't know Osama Bin Laden's whereabouts when he became president. "We organized ourselves, cracked that nut and got him. Why aren't we putting the same effort into this bigger challenge?" an aide heard him argue. "You've got to be working harder."[113]

The pressure never stopped. "What do you need? How many people? How much money? More resources?" Obama asked Pentagon officials. During a National Security Council meeting after Pyongyang's hydrogen bomb test in September 2016, the president asked again if it was possible to launch a preemptive strike supported by cyberoperations.[114]

However, Obama never planned to start a war, contrary to what President Trump later claimed. The president hoped America's military alliances would deter North Korea, but that last remaining bulwark appeared shaky by 2016. If the North seemed ready to roll the nuclear dice, the president wanted whoever was in charge to be equipped with the next-best option: a first strike.[115]

The success of Obama's efforts remains secret. One official estimated a five on a scale of one to ten. Launching a first strike remained a giant roll of the dice. "Even if you get 80 to 90 percent, the potential for a devastating attack on the U.S. homeland, Hawaii, or allies was up there," a White House aide recalled.[116]

As for the North Korean ICBM that triggered the bureaucratic struggle in the first place, the KN-08 was eventually canceled. Soon afterwards, American intelligence picked up signs of bigger and better ICBMs. The year after President Obama left office, Pyongyang's long-range missile tests threatened to plunge the United States and North Korea into the very crisis he had feared.

CHAPTER ELEVEN

"The five stages of grief"

I CHUN HEE, A seventy-three-year-old "passionate, intimidating and exuberant" grandmother, had retired after announcing Kim Jong Il's death. She reappeared on January 6, 2016, to inform TV viewers that North Korea had tested a hydrogen bomb and could now field nuclear-tipped missiles.[1]

Initially, Washington responded that its analysis "was not consistent" with North Korean claims of a successful hydrogen bomb test, even though Pyongyang's media had published Kim Jong Un's handwritten order to open the New Year with "the exhilarating explosive sound of the first hydrogen bomb." Moreover, American intelligence knew the North was producing nuclear material for more powerful weapons.

But after a few weeks, the community's analysts changed their minds. They concluded that "it was as likely as not" that the North Koreans had detonated a hydrogen device, a White House aide recalled.[2]

Coming after a three-year lull, North Korea's blast proved to be the last straw for South Korean president Park Geun-hye, elected in 2013. The conservative daughter of authoritarian modernizer Park Chung-hee had attempted but failed to chart a middle course toward the North, between soft progressives and tough right-wingers.[3]

By January 2016, Park had closed shop. Aside from touting the end of the Pyongyang regime as the only way out of the growing mess, she was under siege. Her administration had mishandled a tragic ferry sinking with over three hundred fatalities. By the end of the year, she would be impeached because of a top aide's influence peddling.

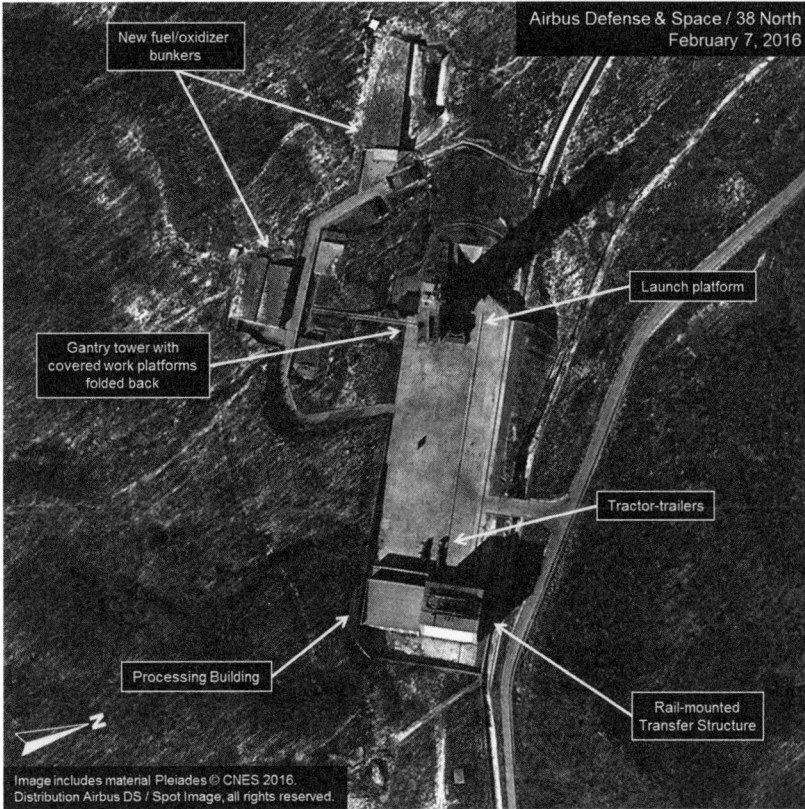

Rocket pad in Sohae just hours after the February 2016 satellite launch
by the DPRK. Image includes material Pleiades © CNES 2016. Distribution
Airbus DS / Spot Image, all rights reserved. Annotation by *38 North*.

If Obama had high hopes for Park when she took office, he was disappointed. After meeting Moon Jae-in, her successor and a supporter of engagement, years later, the former president and an aide wondered what it
would have been like if he had been their partner.[4]

Obama called Park after the January blast. Convinced that it would be
best if North Korea disappeared altogether, she told him to forget about
nuclear talks.

Five weeks later, when a satellite launch followed, Park bluntly
warned her advisors it was an "unacceptable challenge." She predicted
on TV that Pyongyang's pursuit of nuclear weapons would only "hasten
its collapse."[5]

The two presidents agreed on the usual steps: pursuing sanctions, condemning the North, reaffirming Washington's commitment to protect Seoul, and sending a B-52 bomber to fly over the peninsula. However, where Park saw North Korea's collapse as the only way forward, Obama saw the blast as one more sign that strategic patience had failed.[6]

By the end of Barack Obama's second term in 2016, his administration had gone through, according to a senior advisor, "the five stages of grief: denial, anger, bargaining, depression, and acceptance." The White House finally realized its best option was to negotiate a "settlement and deal with it." Obama told Park that he had initiated another policy review.[7]

When the North Korean grandmother reappeared to announce the "completely successful" launch of a satellite, it was clear Kim Jong Un was determined to move forward.[8] He didn't care about international condemnation or failure of the tests. He was interested in results. More launches followed in rapid succession into the summer, including six of a missile able to reach American territory in Guam, and another fired from a submarine.[9]

But Kim also hinted at the first congress of the Korean Workers' Party in four decades that a policy shift was coming. After a "confetti of self-congratulations about his WMD program," North Korea could now focus on "realistic" steps for the future. Kim's father had used a similar formulation to initiate economic reforms under the cloak of renewed talks with the United States.[10]

Still, Madame Ri reappeared on September 9, to announce Pyongyang's second nuclear blast in a single year, the first time that had happened. The test was also its largest detonation ever. Park told her aides that Kim Jong Un's "state of mind had gone out of control," but she was wrong. The North Korean leader knew exactly what he was doing.[11]

Even if the White House had reached the fifth stage of grief and the door to talks was opening again, finding a new path wouldn't be easy. Securing President Park's support was going to be hard. And Beijing would have to be convinced that North Korea, not the United States, was the real threat to its security.

Perhaps the biggest challenge facing President Obama was his own administration. Despite the growing danger, bureaucrats found it hard to chart a new course after seven years of strategic patience. The White House would conduct policy review after review, none of which changed much.

Finally, there was that old problem: time. Susan Rice admonished bureaucrats to "run through the tape" at the race's finish line, the end of the administration. But with the 2016 election just over the horizon, perhaps all she and Obama could hope for was to lay the groundwork for a future president, Hillary Clinton.[12]

"We want to put an end to war."

Susan Rice and her deputy, Avril Haines, arrived in the White House Situation Room soon after the rest of us. I was there with two colleagues to meet the president's national security advisor one month after North Korea's nuclear blast and days after a session with Choe Son Hui.[13]

The setting wasn't a high-tech command center straight out of a Cold War movie. Located underneath the main floor of the West Wing, the windowless room was small with a rectangular table and no video screens, just digital clocks displaying worldwide time zones and the location of the president of the United States.[14]

Our delegation had dined with Choe five days earlier in the Berlin Hilton across from a historic square in the city center. Former government officials and academics were the only Americans meeting the North Koreans regularly since the Leap Day negotiations had collapsed four years earlier.[15]

Kim Jong Un's New Year's speech was the first topic of discussion the next morning. Kim felt he had "strong weapons," according to Choe, so it was time to concentrate on modernizing North Korea's economy. He wanted to calm tensions, and that meant renewing talks.[16]

We believed the blast and a satellite launch in the works were only more likely to shut the door to diplomacy. Choe explained, however, that Kim saw WMD tests as a "shortcut" around holding "talks for talks' sake." He wanted Washington's attention focused on "what we are pursuing."

Pyongyang was frustrated. Its proposal in October 2015 to conclude a peace treaty to end the Korean War had been rejected. For North Korea, the best path to denuclearization was to end the state of belligerency first. For Washington, nuclear talks had to be well underway before peace could be discussed.

This time around, the Obama administration didn't reject the North's idea out of hand. Choe's view, however, was that "the U.S. was clear that talking about denuclearization should come first." The North Koreans took that as a "no," and decided that a nuclear test was the best shortcut.[17]

Their plan made some sense. The need for nuclear weapons diminished when enemies became friends. I pointed out, however, that we could be locked in a room for years trying to resolve issues related to peace, while Pyongyang's nuclear program went ahead unchecked.[18]

"I myself wonder how long it will take to conclude this treaty," Choe admitted. All she wanted was "a kind of positive response, not that denuclearization should come first."[19]

Choe was much less cryptic the next morning, perhaps because I informed her our next stop was the White House to report on our meeting. "We want to put an end to war," she said.[20]

Her proposal turned out to be less complicated than negotiating a peace treaty right away. First, both countries would declare that the period of the 1954 temporary armistice was over. Then, they could negotiate a treaty that would include denuclearization.

Choe also repeated Pyongyang's proposal to halt nuclear tests in return for suspending military exercises. Her objective was to build confidence on both sides. A more modest alternative—scaling back the exercises—could be discussed.

She, however, was concerned about the upcoming election in November 2016. Choe had been through the disastrous Clinton-Bush transition, so she naturally wondered if one president's diplomacy would continue with the next. We didn't know the answer.[21]

Our meeting with Ambassador Rice after the Berlin session seemed like the perfect opportunity to relay Choe's ideas, and to offer advice to Obama's top advisor. It was also unexpected. One colleague muttered to me before the session started, "Now they ask us with only a few months left in office?"[22]

I started my presentation by stating the obvious. The administration's time in office was running out, but it could still set the stage for either Hillary Clinton or Donald Trump.

Choe outlined how to do that during our Berlin meeting. A moratorium on nuclear testing in return for suspending U.S.-South Korean military exercises would build confidence. Then, the two countries would declare that the Korean War was over. They would pursue a peace treaty and denuclearization, rather than haggle over whether "the chicken or the egg" should come first.[23]

Bob Carlin, who was in Berlin, and who had three decades of experience analyzing Pyongyang's moves, stressed that Kim's arsenal was intended to protect his country. But it also would enable him to pivot to his real priority, economic modernization. To do that, he needed a peaceful external environment and talks with the United States.[24]

After Rice listened politely, she turned to two China experts who were present. One, a Princeton professor, urged her to get tough with China. The United States should threaten to blow up Pyongyang's rocket the next time it was about to launch a satellite. No need to worry about starting a war![25]

Our small group tried to keep straight faces following the preposterous suggestion. We waited for Rice to ask about the situation in Pyongyang, our Berlin meeting, and our ideas for next steps. She never did.

Ambassador Rice did reject Choe's proposal to suspend nuclear tests, opining that North Korea only conducted one nuclear test per year, anyway. She proved wrong about 2016, however. North Korea would conduct another blast in September.[26]

As the meeting ended, Obama's national security advisor asked, tongue in cheek, what it would take for Kim Jong Un to give up his nuclear weapons. The Princeton professor immediately swerved out of his lane of expertise, saying, "Guarantee his safety if the regime falls." I wanted to respond, "Just like Gaddafi!" But none of us got a chance to add our views.[27]

Since the session lasted longer than expected, I thought that was a positive sign. A friend pointed out, however, that Rice "had no idea what she wanted."[28] A White House aide later confirmed she was more interested in convincing China to take Washington's side as the solution to North Korea than in working directly with Pyongyang. That was why two China experts had been invited.[29]

Like our delegation, Sung Kim also thought a window had opened. State's envoy scheduled a session with Choe for mid-February in New York City, but the North Koreans pulled out. Washington's sanctions drive probably worsened the bad mood in Pyongyang.

Ambassador Kim tried again. In May, he met with Suzanne DiMaggio, who was on her way to Stockholm to talk to Choe Son Hui. A former vice president of the Asia Society, she had already been to Pyongyang twice. Ever the advocate of strategic patience, Danny Russel tried to dissuade DiMaggio the first time, but she got the go-ahead from the deputy secretary of state, his boss.

Kim surprised DiMaggio. Anxious to get talks started, he asked her to tell the North Koreans that he was willing to meet them without any preconditions.

When she relayed the message, Choe and Ambassador Han, home from New York, seemed interested but wondered whether it was worthwhile to start talks with Obama, who was about to leave office.[30] The

Americans argued they could help lay the foundation for the next administration, especially if Hillary Clinton, the odds-on election favorite, became president.[31]

Unfortunately, the administration failed to anticipate the effect of legislation passed by Congress that spring sanctioning anyone responsible for human rights violations in North Korea. Kim Jong Un was at the top of the list. The White House considered "naming and shaming" him in secret but came up short. In July, the State Department added Kim to a public list of living and dead sanctioned dictators.[32]

Outraged, the North Koreans canceled a meeting with DiMaggio and claimed they would never talk to her or the administration again. After she pushed back, they relented. More Track 2 meetings were fine, but the North Koreans were through with Obama.[33]

"A stalemate of stagnant options"

Avril Haines was given the unenviable job of trying to come up with a new North Korea policy during the Obama administration's last year in office. She wasn't an expert on North Korea, but she was the next best thing for a deputy national security advisor.

Her rise inside the government had been meteoric. A stint at the State Department as an assistant legal advisor preceded a move to the National Security Council, where she wrote a playbook on criteria for drone strikes targeting terrorists. Haines was then appointed the first female deputy director of the Central Intelligence Agency.

She became a member of the policymaking Deputies Small Group. The new CIA deputy director also embarked on at least one secret mission to Pyongyang to free American detainees. Haines agreed with colleagues who argued, "If you take this threat seriously, then you shouldn't be satisfied with the lack of progress."[34]

Once Haines returned to the White House as Susan Rice's deputy, she was assigned the unenviable task of coming up with a new North Korea policy. Past reviews had only led the administration into "a stalemate of stagnant options," one official recalled.[35] "We were on autopilot with the pilot looking out the window to make sure we weren't flying into a storm."[36]

The new deputy national security advisor had to satisfy a dissatisfied president. "This still isn't what I want it to be," Obama commented after one review.[37] A White House aide recalled that "he didn't have an answer for it, didn't want to be bothered, and was half mad all the time."[38] Denis

McDonough, his chief of staff, constantly pressed for everyone to "think the unthinkable," according to one official.[39]

Haines also had to contend with intransigent bureaucrats, especially in Washington's intelligence agencies. Still mired in the intellectual mud of the Cold War, they had asserted for decades that North Korea would never give up its nuclear weapons. In a closed system they were the loudest voices.[40]

The community had a monopoly on information about North Korea. It paid little attention to unclassified sources. In contrast, information on Iran poured in from Europeans, journalists, and experts talking to Iranians, companies interacting with them, and Iranian officials traveling around the world.[41]

That difference made it even more important to take advantage of information from outsiders. The Obama administration, however, had done little or no outreach to the small private community that spent time in North Korea providing humanitarian assistance. The same was true for former government officials, like me.

The intelligence community flourished. American spies were not only the sole source of information but were omnipresent. Its analysts were everywhere in the policy world. They filled positions at the National Security Council, State, and the Department of Defense. The community even held regular White House sessions to educate less experienced officials.[42]

Interagency meetings always went downhill quickly after the opening intelligence briefing. Invariably, the conclusion was that North Korea wouldn't give up its nuclear weapons. Syd Seiler, a career intelligence analyst who worked at the White House, seconded the motion. Everyone concluded, why bother with diplomacy?

Haines had seen this happen during her stint at the CIA. America's spies told everyone that Iran wouldn't negotiate away its nuclear program. The natural response was, "Are we really going to do this?" one official remembered. Yet, negotiations led to a landmark nuclear deal.[43]

She had to make sure no policy stone was left unturned. All hands had to be on deck to sort options. Haines replaced the exclusive Deputies Small Group with its disjointed decision-making. Staff experts participated in a regular series of sessions culminating in National Security Council meetings chaired by Obama. Alternatives to strategic patience would be considered and passed up the chain of command.[44]

The objective was to find the elusive "tipping point." As one official recalled, "Maybe there will be a magic moment when Kim sees that the cost is so high that he would actually be willing to engage in good-faith diplomacy." When that would happen, however, was anyone's guess.[45]

The review was based on two assumptions. First, Kim Jong Un may not have been interested in giving up his nuclear weapons. But he was a rational leader who was genuinely interested in leaving his country and people better off than how he found them. Opening the door to diplomacy with the United States could serve that objective.[46]

Second, the White House believed Kim was vulnerable to pressure. The theory was his hold over North Korea was more tenuous than that of his father and grandfather because he had come to power faster and hadn't had time to build ironclad support among North Korea's elites. The flow of external information about a better life in the outside world to ordinary citizens was another Achilles' heel. It added to the regime's fragility.[47]

Haines and the National Security Council staff embarked on a torturous process to find the tipping point. Interagency meetings produced hundreds of pages examining different options. They were finally boiled down to just a hundred, highlighting decisions for Obama and his top advisors to make.

Officials spent hours in the Situation Room pondering "the wildest things we could do," according to one aide.[48] The "Big-Mac-Attack" option posited the question, "What if there were McDonald's and Apple stores in Pyongyang?" If barriers to trade and commerce were dropped, diplomatic relations established, and peace negotiated, the North wouldn't need nuclear weapons. Kim, however, might just pocket the concessions. Plus, the allies and Congress would go crazy.[49]

The other extreme was to pile on pressure, more sanctions backed by blockades, embargos, and quarantines that would cut Pyongyang's economic lifelines. They could create rifts between Kim and his leadership cadre, causing the North to cry uncle or collapse like the Soviet Bloc. But pressure could also trigger a backlash from China, and cause a stubborn Pyongyang to go down fighting rather than give in.[50]

Haines attempted to chart a middle course instead, something akin to what the administration had done with Iran. The combination of crushing sanctions and easing nuclear demands culminated in the 2015 nuclear deal, one of the highpoints of Obama's foreign policy.

The White House supported a shift into diplomatic high gear. Denuclearization remained the objective, but the demand that the North Koreans had to say that magic word before talks started was dropped. A deal could also be pursued in phases, starting with freezing Pyongyang's WMD capabilities.[51]

The big policy shift, however, was that the White House was now open to thinking about the unthinkable, a "freeze-for-freeze" proposal. North Korea's idea, suspending military exercises for stopping nuclear tests, was still unacceptable, but it might serve as a jumping-off point for negotiations.[52]

There was hardly unanimity on that point. Ash Carter, supported by General Joseph Dunford, the chairman of the Joint Chiefs, predictably argued that "you can't suspend exercises since readiness will go out the window, and it will send a terrible message to the North Koreans and the Chinese." But just in case, the Defense Department drew up plans to make sure readiness didn't suffer if the White House decided that "we're going to do this thing," a Pentagon official admitted.[53]

While Defense argued against the policy change, the State Department, normally the strongest proponent of negotiations, was in disarray. Secretary Kerry supported constraining military exercises if that opened the door to talks, but his attention was episodic. Tony Blinken, his deputy, was more interested in ramping up pressure. "Adamant, inflexible and hardline," Danny Russel, State's Asia expert, thought a freeze was a form of "accommodation" that would lead down a slippery slope to de facto acceptance of a nuclear North Korea.[54]

Still, Haines believed an "interim freeze" in exchange for modifications to the military exercises that "do not reduce our readiness capabilities" should be in the mix. More importantly, the president had no trouble with modifying exercises in exchange for, among other steps, a stop to testing.[55]

The bureaucracy was more willing to line up behind more pressure, but North Korea wasn't Iran. The crushing Iran sanctions, led by the United States and the European Union, were possible with the support of other major powers, including China. However, the "sixty-four-million-dollar question" remained how to convince China, Pyongyang's neighbor and erstwhile ally, to go along with crushing sanctions on the North.

The president believed "we can push China more; they need us more than we need them," an aide noted. Vice President Biden agreed, although he was skeptical that China would move without generating pressure on Beijing to go along with Washington. Just how much punishment to inflict that would "help us" or "push the Chinese away from us" was the key question.[56]

A contentious debate revolved around what are called "secondary sanctions." Primary sanctions are imposed on countries to stop their bad behavior. North Korea's Chinese enablers seemed a logical target for secondary sanctions. Those restrictions put pressure on third parties to stop their activities with the sanctioned country by threatening to cut off access to the sanctioning country. By virtue of its global economic power, the United States had successfully compelled foreign banks to either cut off business with Iran or lose access to American financial institutions.

The Treasury Department, always the loudest voice when it came to sanctions, was of two minds. The sanctionistas, led by Adam Tzubin, a Harvard-trained lawyer who had Stuart Levey's old job, zealously supported a relentless stream of secondary sanctions on China. The restrictions would demonstrate that Washington was willing to accept economic harm to its own companies, even to the global economy, to make its point.[57]

Others at Treasury, led by the undersecretary who oversaw international relations, highlighted the negative impact of harsh secondary sanctions on the U.S.-China trade relationship. Beijing would retaliate.[58]

The White House hit on a compromise, a new tool that could push the Chinese out of their comfort zone, but not so far out that it would tank the bilateral relationship. Even if Chinese individuals or institutions that had violated sanctions weren't located in the United States, the Department of Justice could seize any assets that were.

"Let's give them some berth here." They were "enforcing the law, doing what they're supposed to do," one White House aide remembers Obama saying.[59]

The result was the only practical outcome of Haines's policy review. Washington sanctioned a Chinese firm in fall 2016 for ties to North Korea's WMD program and moved to seize twenty-five of its bank accounts. But, according to one official, "we did a lot of careful stuff and didn't go as far as we could have gone." Department of Justice prosecutors visited Beijing twice before the indictment to inform Chinese officials about the firm's alleged criminal activities.[60]

Avril Haines never finished her last review, despite Susan Rice's admonition to "run through the tape" at the end of the race.[61] Chuck Hagel, Obama's former secretary of defense, observed that the administration in general had "way too many meetings" that were unproductive. The Haines review "took too long for us to all be on the same page internally, and to decide what actually made sense," one participant remembered.[62]

The results would be passed on to the next president, expected to be Obama's former secretary of state. In fact, it might have been better not to have locked Clinton into a policy with which she may or may not have agreed.

Even so, there remained one final opportunity for the Obama administration: an opportunity to strengthen the hand of whichever Republican
or Democrat came next, an opportunity handed to the administration by
North Korea and its renewed WMD tests.

The China Play

Susan Rice believed strategic patience amounted to doing the same thing
over and over again and expecting different results—Einstein's definition
of insanity. She blamed an ossified bureaucracy.[63]

Rice, however, was mired in her own orthodoxy. Her cure for North
Korea was China. Obama's top aide thought she understood the Chinese.
The national security advisor joked that, as UN ambassador, she had spent
more time with them than with her husband.[64]

Rice was convinced that the road to Pyongyang's denuclearization ran
through Beijing. But she also believed that just pushing the Chinese to push
Pyongyang wouldn't work. Beijing was concerned that turning up the pressure might trigger the Pyongyang regime to collapse and reunify under
America's South Korean ally.

Moreover, Rice was responsible for Obama's entire agenda with Beijing, everything from security to climate change. Why risk upsetting that
apple cart, especially since the intelligence community insisted Kim Jong
Un would never give up his weapons?

Finally, a steady hand with Beijing was essential since North Korea's
collapse could trigger a global conflict. Like World War II when the American and Soviet armies rushed toward each other, the same could happen
with China in North Korea, only without coordination. The White House
had even held a simulation to prove the point.[65]

With strategic patience failing, Obama signed a Presidential Decision
Memorandum in April 2016 approving Rice's game plan as a final attempt
to stymie Pyongyang's WMD progress. By then, intelligence estimates were
highlighting "the rapidity with which North Korea was developing the
capacity to deliver a weapon to the United States," according to one senior
official.[66]

Beijing would have to help stop the growing North Korean threat or
face a growing threat from the United States. But Washington would also
help make the Chinese comfortable with getting "more skin in the game,"
one official observed.[67]

The president would meet Xi Jinping twelve times during his second term. Press releases rarely referred to North Korea in an attempt to shield Xi's political ability to move in Obama's direction. Pyongyang remained part of the conversation, however. The two leaders shared what was on their minds in small, private meetings and during meals.[68]

Obama's sessions with Xi were "as close as you would get to a peer-to-peer relationship," according to one White House aide. The Americans had learned from the Sunnylands summit to "disaggregate Xi's encouraging words" about North Korea from "the actual steps he was willing to take." Still, there was genuine give-and-take.[69]

Just as China talked about its core interests in Tibet and Taiwan, Obama talked about Washington's core interest in stopping North Korea's WMD programs. He wanted to work with China. But if Xi was unwilling or unable to get Pyongyang to behave, the United States would take steps Beijing wouldn't like: more missile defenses, military exercises, troops in the region, and sanctions against China.[70]

As time went by, Obama believed he would be able to see if "there was space to engage the Chinese to push for harder action," one aide observed. The two leaders may have shared the goal of denuclearization, but the more they talked, the more Xi revealed his limited willingness to do what the president wanted.[71]

Like Henry Kissinger when he was Richard Nixon's national security advisor, Rice also pursued her own "quiet centralized approach." She met Xi three times in Beijing to pave the way for Obama, six times accompanying the president, and had her own encounters with Xi's top advisors.

Rice started to "peel back the layers of the onion" during her first visit to Beijing in 2014, identifying Chinese concerns, explaining what the United States was trying to do, and figuring out whether the gap could be bridged. She learned that they were worried about the American military presence in Northeast Asia and the implications of a reunified Korea under Washington's ally. "It was more of a diagnosis than a prescription of a solution," an aide recalled.[72]

While the Chinese believed the Americans were exaggerating the North Korean threat, they could see that Washington was serious. Moreover, there was some wiggle room for progress. China's relations with North Korea still hadn't recovered from the jolt of the 2014 execution of Kim's sinophile uncle.

Washington launched several initiatives. A new "sustained and comprehensive pressure" campaign was aimed at undermining Beijing's economic ties with North Korea. The administration would step up its efforts to work with the Chinese, especially at the UN, to come up with new sanctions. But the United States would also "strangle lifelines Kim Jong Un had" with other countries. That would heighten his pain if China was already "turning the spigot down or off," according to one official.[73]

Tony Blinken, Vice President Biden's longtime aide and the newly appointed deputy secretary of state, was a key player. "Let's just stipulate we are freaked out about what's happening in North Korea and talk about what we are doing," he told a group of officials at an interagency meeting.[74]

Blinken was serious. Cho Tae-yong, a top Park advisor, hoped to sit down with him twice a year to work out a game plan. The deputy secretary suggested every three months. The two men planned to squeeze North Korea's top cash earners, including coal and mineral exports, as well as remittances from workers overseas.[75]

Dan Fried had also been waiting for the right moment to step up sanctions. A longtime Foreign Service expert on Russia and Eastern Europe, he had become head of State's sanctions operation in 2013. Frustrated by the calcified logic of strategic patience, Fried had been boxed out of policymaking by State's Asia experts.

He got his chance when Blinken took over. Fried's "Like-Minded Group," established with South Korea, Japan, and Australia to formulate new sanctions, had been restricted to going over the minutiae of implementation. Membership expanded with Blinken's support to include France, Germany, and Britain. The group compiled a database of North Korea's global ties and coordinated steps to cut them.

The campaign began in earnest after Pyongyang's WMD tests in early 2016. Informed by her New York experience, Rice turned to the Chinese, not to allies like Britain and France, to help draft a new UN sanctions resolution. "We needed to find a way to work with the Chinese, not against them," one official recalled. She finalized the draft when Beijing's foreign minister visited Washington.[76]

Resolution 2270, passed in early March, went beyond past WMD restrictions to prohibit imports of North Korea's coal, iron, and iron ore, important pieces of Pyongyang's economic relationship with China. One expert called it "the most comprehensive, legally binding sanctions program imposed on a country since Iraq in the 1990s."[77]

The United States followed up with a series of sessions with Beijing intended to strengthen sanctions enforcement. A Chinese team provided "a lot of granular information on their system, how it worked, and how it didn't work," one American official observed. "We would see them tightening the screws in places."[78]

Washington also scoured the globe looking for more opportunities. It turned its attention to Africa. North Korean front companies, diplomats, and smugglers had been operating there for years, doing multimillion-dollar deals with the help of governments, often violating sanctions. Everything from weapons sales to rhino poaching was up for grabs.

The National Security Council devised an Africa "matrix" that became the guide for a sanctions offensive on the continent. The intricate game plan mapped out each country's ties with Pyongyang and how to cut them.[79]

There were successes and failures, but some countries played both sides of the net. Egypt, for example, seized a ship transiting the Suez Canal carrying North Korean weapons estimated to be worth $26 million. The Egyptians destroyed the cargo, but it turned out they were the buyer, a fact conveniently hidden by canvas covering the crates' labels. Cairo's long-standing relationship with North Korea continued despite American protests.[80]

Washington had better luck stopping the flow of money sent home by Pyongyang's overseas laborers. Tens of thousands in Russia and China, thousands in the Persian Gulf, hundreds in Poland and Southeast Asia, and tens in Peru, Chile, and Uruguay forwarded as much as $2 billion a year. "We cut off four or five hundred million dollars," one official recalled. Every success magnified the growing squeeze on China's ties with the North.[81]

The sanctions campaign shifted back to the UN in September 2016 after North Korea's globally condemned nuclear blast. Washington worked with the Chinese again. The result was Resolution 2321, with far-reaching restrictions that included limits on coal exports—90 percent of which went to China—and reduced earnings by $650 million. A ban on copper, nickel, silver, and zinc exports was expected to cost Pyongyang an additional $100 million.

That fall, Washington also gently, but directly, turned up the heat on Beijing. As a result of Avril Haines's policy review, Washington sanctioned, for the first time, a Chinese firm for ties to North Korea's nuclear weapons program.[82]

Aside from moves to tighten economic restrictions, the administration took steps on the military front that Beijing was guaranteed to dislike. The Terminal High Altitude Area Defense, or THAAD, was perfect for shooting down North Korean missiles. Pentagon officials wanted to send the weapon to South Korea.

Initially, Ash Carter, the secretary of defense, and a skeptic when it came to missile defenses, hesitated. So did General Mark Milley, the Army chief of staff, who wanted to deploy THAAD in the Middle East first. "I thought sending it to Korea was pretty obvious, but he thought I was crazy," a Pentagon official remembered. Carter and Milley eventually agreed.[83]

Susan Rice also initially opposed deploying THAAD in Korea. She was concerned it "would drive the Chinese batshit crazy." They would view the weapon as a threat to their own missiles that would strengthen the American presence near their borders.[84]

However, once the Pentagon made a strong case, Rice pivoted and beat Beijing over the head with it. After the July 2016 announcement that the missile defense system would be deployed by the next year, Rice and Blinken warned the Chinese, "If you don't like THAAD, wait until you see what's next." If they hadn't taken American warnings seriously before, they did now.[85]

As the White House stepped up the pressure, it also stepped up efforts to reassure China. Washington shared "various proposed coordinated strategic approaches" covering "a wide range of contingencies" on the peninsula, according to one official. The logic was that "until they had full confidence and a full picture, they didn't want to take any steps."[86]

Reducing American military forces stationed on its periphery, long a major concern of China, was one possibility. Rice followed in the footsteps of Henry Kissinger, who discussed troop reductions on the peninsula with the Chinese, and Secretary Kerry, who raised the possibility after the Sunnylands summit.

Rice's talks with Yang Jiechi, China's national security advisor, before the November 2016 election, included military postures in Asia and possible arms control agreements. Exactly what was discussed in those talks is unclear. State and Defense were cut out, as were the South Koreans, who, according to one American official, "were suspicious."[87]

Despite a history of reticence, Beijing also agreed to compare notes on how to avoid a clash if the North Korean regime collapsed. Led by Dan Kritenbrink, a China hand who worked for Rice, the talks took place away from prying eyes: at the Naval Academy in Annapolis, in Beijing, and in Dalian, a port on the Yellow Sea.[88]

The soft-spoken Kritenbrink aimed to reassure the Chinese. Washington was not going to send troops to the Yalu River border if North Korea disintegrated, a move that had provoked Beijing during the Korean War.

At first, the Chinese posture was "listen, don't engage and move on," according to one official. They just took a lot of notes.[89]

Gradually, the ice melted. The Chinese volunteered that they wanted the Security Council to take charge of reunification since Beijing was a permanent member with veto power. On the other hand, South Korea planned to take control. The two could clash if there wasn't a solution in place ahead of time.[90]

The Americans had hoped to arrive at understandings that would avoid armed clashes, but time ran out. One participant thought the sessions made the Chinese think more about the subject, but another concluded that "they probably still harbored a degree of skepticism."[91]

At the end of the administration, the jury was still out on whether Susan Rice's China play had worked. Some officials believed the initiative may have laid the foundation for much greater progress in the future. Others thought she was kidding herself. Beijing would tack between Washington and Pyongyang, never going too far in either direction.

If anything, the China play reaffirmed that time was on Pyongyang's side. "We could never convince them to accelerate the pressure to the point that exceeded the progress that North Korea made in its WMD programs," an official conceded.[92]

"Trying to defend oneself with a pebble"

Nuclear weapons had been part of the security equation on the peninsula since Dwight Eisenhower threatened North Korea and its allies with them unless they ended the Korean War. Aside from bombers, missiles, and submarines poised to destroy the communist bloc, almost a thousand "tactical nuclear weapons," on missiles, jeeps, and landmines, were deployed in South Korea by 1969.[93]

The Americans began to realize, however, that they might end up "blowing up what we are trying to save," according to one officer. As part of a worldwide initiative meant to respond to a coup against Mikhail Gorbachev, President Bush removed the last one hundred weapons in 1991.[94]

Up until 2006 and North Korea's first nuclear test, the South Koreans were content to let their ally handle anything nuclear. But, as an American admiral told visitors, "One nuclear weapon changes everything."[95]

South Korean and Japanese leaders became even more nervous after President Obama's April 2009 pledge in Prague to achieve a nuclear-free world. Did his vision mean the end of the American nuclear umbrella protecting their countries? Tokyo took his decision to retire nuclear-armed submarines that could be sent to Asia in stride. Seoul did not.[96]

Problems with allies over nuclear umbrellas were nothing new. NATO established a Nuclear Planning Group in the 1960s after tensions erupted over Washington's stinginess in providing information about weapons on the continent. The Americans remained in control, but the Europeans were reassured that the United States had their best interests at heart.

Instead of replicating the NATO arrangement, which would have gone a long way to addressing Seoul's concerns about being second-class citizens, the Obama administration opted for yearly tutorials for Seoul's bureaucrats.[97] American officials briefed them on how nuclear threats would deter North Korea. Nuclear war games, the first for an ally outside of NATO, helped the South Koreans "work through the options about what to do if a conflict happened," according to one participant.[98]

The South Koreans also went on field trips to see firsthand Washington's nuclear weapons, which one American official characterized as Seoul's "nuclear force." The most dramatic was a visit to Vandenberg Air Force Base, where the South Koreans watched a missile blast off.[99]

Four small concrete-capped silos, the only missile interceptors based outside of Alaska, made an even greater impression. "It was one thing to see a missile test, another to see something on alert that could have been fired at any moment," a Pentagon official recalled. Afterwards, a Korean told the Americans, "I am reassured."[100]

But was he? One official thought the dialogue "significantly raised the South Koreans' deterrence IQ."[101] Another American believed it was "like pouring water into a sieve that filled up, then emptied, and the process had to start all over again."[102] No amount of education could reassure officials from a small country depending on a larger one for its survival, especially Koreans who had been betrayed by big powers before.

Moreover, Washington's tutorials did nothing to calm domestic politics in Seoul, which was driven by Pyongyang's WMD testing. The lure of bringing American tactical nuclear weapons back to South Korea, or South Korea building its own, gradually infected the political bloodstream. One politician compared the North to a "gangster in the neighborhood buying a brand-new machine gun," while the South was "trying to defend oneself with a pebble."[103]

A bigger myth was at play: WMD were the be-all and end-all to solving Seoul's problems. Some believed that South Korean hands on the nuclear steering wheel or even weapons based on the peninsula would force

Pyongyang to stop building its own arsenal. Then, China would have to put more pressure on the North Koreans, and the United States would get serious about stopping them.

Initially, President Park tried to keep the contagion in check and agreed with her aides, who advised her during the 2012 presidential campaign that it didn't matter if nuclear weapons weren't stationed on the peninsula if they could hit their targets. "She had a very firm position on that," one aide remembered.[104]

Still, the South Koreans weren't comfortable that only the president of the United States could decide whether to use nuclear weapons. One South Korean official later admitted, "We wanted to operate the nuclear umbrella to make sure it unfolded correctly."[105] They didn't quite understand that the NATO model wouldn't allow them to open the umbrella.

Pressure mounted when candidate Trump hinted during the U.S. presidential campaign that the allies, South Korea and Japan, would be left to defend themselves. A South Korean politician lamented that his country was "like a candle facing a storm." Bringing nuclear weapons back to the South became part of the ruling conservative party's platform after Pyongyang's September blast.[106]

The Blue House launched "a serious exploration" to return nuclear bombs to South Korea, according to one American official.[107] Others thought it was just a ploy to get something in return. In either case, Washington had to be careful. The exploration could turn into a formal request that would have to be turned down. The result would be a serious rift in the alliance.[108]

There were obvious reasons to say "no." The Park administration was fixated on public opinion and the fact that North Korea had nuclear weapons, not on any military justification. Moreover, one American official observed, "Even if we put a nuclear-armed ICBM in the middle of Seoul for everybody to look at like the Eiffel Tower, it wouldn't fix the problem."[109] A positive response could open the floodgates to endless requests.

American officials also suspected the Korean request was a stalking horse for something far worse: "Would you please deploy weapons here since you don't want us to do it ourselves?" The Americans were concerned. The more President Park emphasized reunification, the more South Koreans involved in top secret planning for the North's collapse pushed for a role in seizing Pyongyang's WMD.[110]

The consequences of a nuclear-armed South Korea would have been catastrophic. It would have to withdraw from the global regimes intended to stop their spread, triggering a backlash that would severely damage South Korea's economy. The United States would be forced to try to stop it and, if it failed, the alliance would be busted. Japan, undoubtedly, would be the next nuclear domino. Tensions would rise with China in a region already beset by periodic confrontations.

Washington's biggest concern was that a nuclear-armed Seoul could stumble into a war. Prone to "speak loudly and carry a big stick," the South Koreans had proclaimed they would wipe out Kim Jong Un and his aides if just "signs" of an attack were detected. They threatened to use nuclear weapons from the get-go in war games, only to recoil when confronted with the destructive consequences.[111]

In April 2016, Deputy Foreign Minister Kim Hyoung-zhin traveled to Washington. The soft-spoken diplomat, who as a junior ministry official had worked on KEDO, told the Americans he was there to gauge their reaction if South Korea requested the return of tactical nuclear weapons. His mission wasn't a surprise; the U.S. embassy in Seoul had already sent a heads-up.[112]

"Ninety-five percent of the people in the Obama administration had an immediate reaction, not just 'no,' but 'Hell no!'" one official recalled. The diplomatic response, however, was, "Very difficult; and let me tell you why."[113]

The White House had just launched an effort to reinvigorate President Obama's 2009 pledge in Prague to achieve a nuclear-free world. Bringing nuclear weapons back to the peninsula would tank that initiative.[114]

More importantly, returning nuclear weapons to the South could make nuclear war more, not less, likely. Pyongyang might feel pressure to strike first. The United States could already destroy North Korea using long-range weapons and bombers. Finally, there were no facilities in South Korea, such as special storage bunkers, to support a nuclear presence.

Pentagon officials warned the South Koreans they shouldn't ask the question, but one American told them, "If there is something you want to know, ask. If you decide you want to do it, let me tell you what that means, and point out the downsides."[115]

Other options to reinforce the nuclear umbrella were available. B-52 bombers could land on the peninsula, not just fly overhead. Missile-armed submarines could visit ports. New F-35 stealth fighter-bombers, slated to be sent to Seoul in the future, could eventually be armed with nuclear weapons controlled by the Americans.

Although the Americans also sent public signals reinforcing the nuclear taboo, the South Koreans persisted. Cho Tae-yong was dispatched to Washington in early October 2016 to meet with Tony Blinken and press Seoul's proposal. The deputy secretary of state didn't slam the door shut, but he sought to dissuade Cho. Since Hillary Clinton was expected to win the presidential election in a month, Washington didn't want to foreclose her options.[116]

Three weeks later, after the annual meeting of top U.S. and South Korean national security officials, the two countries agreed to start a new nuclear dialogue with more senior officials. It still wasn't a NATO-like planning group. But the move was a face-saving step that the South Koreans may have believed brought them one step closer to that model.[117]

The allies also agreed to step up permanent deployments of "US strategic assets" on a "rotational basis," Seoul's defense minister told the press.[118] A nuclear-armed submarine subsequently visited Guam for the first time in twenty-eight years. American forces based there would play a key role in defending Korea. South Korea's top military commander boarded the submarine. It wasn't the Korean Peninsula, but it was close.[119]

The first and last session of the new nuclear dialogue was held in Washington six weeks later. The South Koreans pushed for the group to do "what NATO does." The Americans refused.[120]

CHAPTER TWELVE

"Everyone was trying to piss on the table."

SIX DAYS AFTER DONALD TRUMP'S January 20, 2017, inauguration, Kathleen Troia "K. T." McFarland convened representatives from all the national security agencies in the windowless, wood-paneled White House Situation Room. The session kicked off the administration's first policy review.[1]

An assistant to Henry Kissinger in the Nixon and Ford White Houses, McFarland believed America was ready to reject the traditional Washington establishment. So was she. Trump had picked McFarland as deputy national security advisor after seeing her on Fox News. The president-elect asked her on Thanksgiving to take the job and gave her a first-floor West Wing office reserved for top aides.[2]

McFarland was worried that North Korea would confront the administration with its first crisis. She knew all about Obama's Oval Office warning and had heard Susan Rice deliver the same message to Michael Flynn, Trump's national security advisor.[3]

Her big challenge was turning the president's tweet response to Kim's New Year's threat, "It won't happen," into a policy. Continuing strategic patience was out of the question. McFarland and Matthew Pottinger, a former journalist, Marine, and now Trump's top Asia advisor, thought Obama had just kicked the North Korea can down the road.[4]

Allison Hooker's job was to figure out the details. As a career civil servant, her experience with the North Koreans dated back to President

George W. Bush's Six Party Talks. After moving from the State Department to the National Security Council, Hooker had orchestrated Obama's policy reviews. She was accused by the alt-right of representing "180 degrees of what Trump was trying to do."[5]

McFarland's first meeting with bureaucrats wasn't encouraging. She felt "they had dusted off the old briefing papers and stamped a new date on top." Most were career civil servants or Obama holdovers who hadn't received new instructions. They didn't have a lot of time "to unshackle their creative minds," one official recalled.[6]

McFarland tried to shake them up, get them to abandon past policy mush, think outside the box: everything from "regime change to accepting North Korea as a nuclear weapons state." She didn't realize those options and more had been raked over the coals by the Obama White House. "The menu was the menu," one official observed.[7]

Hooker managed to coax ten options out of papers, memos, and meetings. Most were more of the same, except two new possibilities. One option, to blow up the North Koreans' nuclear installations, was shelved. The other was to hold summits with Kim Jong Un.

A summit with the president of the United States had been Pyongyang's diplomatic pot of gold at the end of its rainbow at least since Bill Taylor's session with Kim Il Sung. They often asked Obama administration officials when their leaders could meet. But one White House aide recalled thinking, "What would Susan Rice say if we did?" There would have been hell to pay.[8]

The Trump review considered the option that Obama wouldn't, listed under the innocuous heading "engagement to change the relationship." That didn't mean "some mid-level State Department guy would spend years chasing the North Koreans," according to a White House official. Knowing the president, it was only a matter of time before he was going to put the idea of a direct meeting on the table.[9]

The secretary of state typically would have been a key player in any policy review. However, Rex Tillerson, nominated by three former Republican secretaries of state, was a big problem. Seemingly perfect for the job, he was absent from the start. The former head of Exxon Mobil "had the charisma, looked like a CEO, was a smooth operator, was well spoken, and already had this experience jetting around the world meeting top leaders," a Trump aide recalled.[10]

But he was alien to government. The secretary surrounded himself with a small praetorian guard of advisors, got rid of longtime employees, failed to fill leadership positions, and ignored career bureaucrats. No one noticed that he had done the same thing at Exxon, cloistering himself in what employees called the "God Pod."[11]

"There is only one secretary of state," Tillerson often proclaimed.[12] Instead of participating in the White House policy review, he took it upon himself to launch a private study run by two members of his guard who didn't know anything about North Korea and believed in "one size fits all" sanctions.[13] No one else at State or any other government agency knew what they were up to.

Tillerson wasn't Hooker's only problem. "Everyone was trying to piss on the table," one White House aide recalled. As a rogue state hostile to the United States, Pyongyang was a perfect target for bureaucrats who wanted to play tough guy. They were only willing to consider pressure, not diplomacy.[14]

Meanwhile, the late-winter action-reaction cycle kicked in on the peninsula. Tens of thousands of American and South Korean troops practiced wiping out North Korea's leaders, nuclear installations, and missiles before an attack could be launched. The US Navy's SEAL Team Six, which had killed Osama bin Laden, participated for the first time, prompting speculation that Kim Jong Un and his WMD were next.[15]

Pyongyang literally launched its own countermoves: twelve tests of rockets during the first six months of 2017. All the tests—successful or not—contributed to weapons development. Kim Jong Un was less visible than during the 2013 crisis, although he presided over an April military drill, and called the units "reminiscent of fierce tigers."[16]

Tensions threatened to take a turn for the worse in mid-April. Spy satellites spotted activity at Pyongyang's nuclear test site. But a week later, personnel were seen playing volleyball there, not a harbinger that a nuclear bomb was about to go off.[17]

Instead, North Korea celebrated the April 15 anniversary of Kim Il Sung's birth with a massive military parade that made the "ground shake." A new improved KN-08 look-alike—the missile that had triggered Obama's preparations for a preemptive strike—was displayed. No one seemed to notice that the parade also included floats highlighting Kim's hope to modernize his economy.[18]

Luckily, the Trump administration's two policy reviews reached the same conclusion. Tillerson's proposal, unveiled in a PowerPoint briefing for fellow cabinet members, called for "maximum pressure in big letters, and engagement in tiny letters," according to one official. He thought his idea was an important pronouncement, but it was more like a "a simplistic East Asia 101 seminar."

Allison Hooker's review reached the same conclusion. While the policy's bumper sticker title, "maximum pressure," was impressive, past administrations had pursued similar approaches. General H. R. McMaster, who replaced Flynn as national security advisor, called the new policy "the three don'ts": don't rush into weak initial agreements, successful diplomacy depends on the will to use force, and don't lift sanctions prematurely to reward the DPRK for just talking.

After Trump approved maximum pressure, the administration acted.[19] Treasury sanctioned North Korean smugglers. An aircraft carrier was dispatched to the peninsula to demonstrate determination to protect American allies. The UN condemned a missile launch. McMaster warned that "all options were on the table," hinting that military force might be used.[20]

All of those moves reminded observers of what a new Clinton administration might have done. Indeed, a *Washington Post* columnist pointed out that Trump's advisors "could fit in a Cabinet put together by, say, Hillary Clinton." He was right. Tillerson, Secretary of Defense James "Mad Dog" Mattis, and McMaster were all members of the establishment.[21]

Donald Trump, however, didn't fit that mold. Inexperienced, unorthodox, and an out-of-the-mainstream thinker, he took, in some cases, a refreshing re-look at old problems like North Korea. In others, such as questioning alliances, his yardstick, "Are we making money, or is it costing us?" was problematic, according to one official.[22]

Trump was enamored of the "madman theory of international politics," used by Richard Nixon and Henry Kissinger to pressure adversaries. In his first meeting with McMaster at the end of February, he told his new national security advisor to make sure North Korea understood that "if they threaten us, they will face a response that is overwhelming."[23]

But Trump also wanted to be unpredictable, unlike Obama, who he thought was entirely predictable. One moment, Trump would warn about a coming war between the United States and North Korea; the next, he would be "honored to meet Kim."[24]

How much of the president's actions reflected being crazy like a fox or just plain crazy remained a topic of debate throughout his four years in office. Former aides thought Trump was more aware than most people knew of how he was perceived at home and abroad. But his outrageous public statements, willingness to go to extremes, fringe ideas, and narcissism only reinforced the view that he was just plain crazy.[25]

So did his stream-of-consciousness musings with whomever was around, as he tried to understand his options. Trump questioned world leaders who had little interest in the subject. He questioned Allison Hooker, since she had visited the North, "Is it a place you would want to live?" He even quizzed Kid Rock, the singer, rapper, and songwriter, who knew nothing about North Korea.[26]

May 2017 brought President Trump a step closer to the moment he had been dreading. The North Koreans test-fired a new version of the KN-08, paraded a month earlier, although they were careful not to test him, or fate. They had tiptoed over the milestone by firing the weapon high into space, not to its full range.[27]

Two leaders—a young dictator determined to sprint across the WMD finish line, and an inexperienced president bent on stopping him—were about to embark on a roller-coaster ride, a game of verbal chicken threatening to bring the United States and North Korea to the brink of nuclear war.

The Honey Badger

The fourth diplomat in eight years to hold the job of special representative for North Korea, Joseph Yun was born in South Korea, educated in England, and joined the Foreign Service in 1985. After tours in Hong Kong, Indonesia, Paris, Seoul, and Thailand, punctuated by work in Washington, he was appointed ambassador to Malaysia in 2013.

While Yun knew his predecessors, Steve Bosworth, Glyn Davies, and Sung Kim, had failed to stop Pyongyang's WMD program, he still decided to take the job. Aside from his personal interest in Korea, the chance to work with old colleagues associated with Hillary Clinton, who seemed set to become president, was too good to pass up. They were skeptical about diplomacy, but Yun believed he could win them over.[28]

A good bet seemed more like a bad one by the time he assumed his post in October 2016. The North Koreans had stopped talking to Washington after Kim Jong Un was sanctioned for human rights violations. Then, Trump's victory meant Yun would be working with strangers, not with his old colleagues.

Still, he decided to take the new job, his last post before retiring. Willing to take risks in the risk-averse State Department, Yun was nicknamed the "honey badger" by his staff after the feisty, tenacious, fearless animal.[29]

Ambassador Yun and I met in late November after Choe Son Hui had offered to resume talks with the incoming administration. "Diplomacy is all about creating an opening," he said. Joe knew he still had to weather the presidential changing of the guard, and heed Choe's warning about the early 2017 U.S.–South Korean military exercise.[30]

Although the Obama administration had been allergic to diplomacy, the White House belatedly recognized that some contact was better than none. Yun reached out to the North Koreans through Sweden, Norway, Switzerland, and Mongolia, countries with ties to Pyongyang. But the North Koreans didn't respond.[31]

The American envoy even phoned Pyongyang's UN mission in New York without permission from his bosses. The diplomat who answered reminded him they couldn't meet until Obama was gone.[32]

Yun just wanted to know how the two countries could start on a positive note when Trump took office. He answered the question himself, asking what if Washington contributed to a UNICEF appeal issued after an August typhoon that had left hundreds dead and missing, as well as thousands homeless? The North Korean admitted Pyongyang wouldn't turn down help.[33]

Yun was able to secure $1 million, which was announced by Secretary Kerry the day before Trump's inauguration. The first assistance provided to North Korea since 2011 came as a surprise, since Washington and Seoul had been stepping up pressure on Pyongyang after its September nuclear test.[34]

The second step in his plan was to secure the release of three detained Americans, a move that proponents of maximum pressure couldn't oppose. Success would then set the stage for talks on denuclearization.[35]

By early 2017, one of those detainees, Otto Warmbier, had become a cause célèbre. Seized after sightseeing and celebrating New Year's in Pyongyang, the Ohio college student was charged with removing a propaganda poster from a wall in a restricted hotel area. He tearfully admitted trying to bring down "the foundation of North Korea's single-minded unity" in a televised confession.[36]

Even though the State Department had warned Fred and Cindy Warmbier, Otto's frustrated parents, to expect a "marathon, not a sprint" in securing his release, Yun pitched in. Like Sung Kim, he turned to Suzanne DiMaggio, the former vice president of the Asia Society, who was slated to go to Pyongyang in February.[37]

Armed with a message from Yun, DiMaggio told Choe Son Hui, "President Trump is an opportunity to think about a new relationship with the United States." State's envoy was ready to meet her without preconditions.[38]

Choe raised the ante with a surprising proposal: "How about a summit between Trump and Kim Jong Un?"[39]

First things first, DiMaggio asked about releasing the American detainees; that would go a long way toward building better relations. At the very least, the North Koreans should permit visits by the Swedish ambassador in Pyongyang to ensure they were all right. Choe promised to consider the request.[40]

The North Korean diplomat bristled, however, when DiMaggio raised another Yun proposal: North Korea could pave the way to nuclear talks if it stopped its WMD tests. Choe replied that the idea could be discussed if the United States suspended its joint military exercises with South Korea. But her country wasn't going to restrain itself just because the Americans asked it to.[41]

Yun was more than pleasantly surprised by DiMaggio's progress. Track 2 talks were planned for late February when Choe was slated to visit New York, as well as a later session in Sweden or Norway. He would see her both times.[42] Choe had also raised the prospect that Trump and Kim might "be in touch," and even meet.[43]

The honey badger, however, was about to learn a lesson his predecessors had learned the hard way: expect the unexpected when it comes to North Korea. The sinking of the *Cheonan* and the attack on Seoul's offshore island in 2010 had ended Steve Bosworth's diplomacy. The April 2012 satellite launch, and the Leap Day deal's collapse, ended Glyn Davies's talks. Sung Kim was upended by Obama's 2015 YouTube interview that predicted North Korea would eventually collapse and disappear.

For Joe Yun, the assassination of reform-minded Kim Jong Nam, the exiled eldest half-brother of the North Korean leader, thousands of miles away while transiting the Malaysian capital of Kuala Lumpur, threatened to end his talks. It was worse still that two women had smeared the elder Kim's face with the nerve agent VX, in what was clearly an act of state-sponsored terrorism.[44]

While Tillerson had ordered Yun and Susan Thornton, State's top Asia expert, to keep the envoy's diplomacy secret from the White House, news of Kim's death made that impossible. State wanted to go ahead with Choe's New York visit, but the White House called it off. Yun realized that the only way to continue his mission was to secure Trump's support.[45]

Early in the administration, Rex Tillerson had set about building "a relationship with the president to advance his own agenda," an aide recalled. The two men had dinners together before their families moved to Washington. Jared Kushner, Trump's son-in-law, also scheduled a weekly lunch for them to help overcome the secretary's "lack of alignment with the president's policy goals."[46]

The secretary went to Trump to get his approval for Yun's diplomacy. Since his transition team had met Warmbier's parents, the president was aware of his predicament. Trump gave Tillerson the go-ahead without consulting his own staff.[47]

DiMaggio and Choe met again in early May, this time in an isolated, government-owned conference center on Oslo's outskirts, away from the prying eyes of the press. The two sketched out the broad outlines of a negotiation that would cover a WMD test freeze, an end to military exercises, and a new North Korean demand to lift sanctions.[48]

The real business, however, took place the next day when Yun and Choe met. She agreed that the release of the detainees would pave the way for nuclear negotiations. But Choe was persistent. She "really wanted a contact" between Trump and Kim Jong Un, a State Department official recalled. The two diplomats scheduled another session in a few weeks.[49]

While the Oslo meeting seemed to "pass the baton from DiMaggio to Yun," something went wrong.[50] The Swedish ambassador was allowed to see only one detainee. Kim Jong Nam's assassination hadn't amounted to more than a pothole in the diplomatic road. The next blow, however, was unexpectedly tragic and opened a chasm.[51]

Yun was summoned to meet Pyongyang's UN diplomats in New York. They informed him that Otto Warmbier was unconscious. "I was completely shocked," he recalled.

The American envoy demanded the student be freed at once and insisted on traveling to Pyongyang to retrieve him. The North Koreans agreed on the condition that "we would have to discuss some of the conditions of getting him out once we got there."[52]

The president "sounded more like a dad" when he backed Yun's ultimatum, a State Department official remembered. Tillerson helped plan the nitty-gritty of the mission, even insisting that State hire a commercial air ambulance rather than use a military aircraft. No one knew what kind of reception the American military would get.[53]

Yun hired the Phoenix Air ambulance service and left for Japan in its Gulfstream G-11 jet upgraded into a flying emergency room. Once the plane arrived, everyone except Yun and Michael Flueckiger, a sixty-seven-year-old doctor with thirty years of trauma center experience, deplaned. The Gulfstream flew on to Pyongyang, dropped them off, and returned to Japan.[54]

The honey badger immediately began negotiations to secure Warmbier's release. When the North Koreans resisted, he demanded to visit the student. Nothing prepared Yun and Flueckiger for what they saw: a pale, inert young man with a feeding tube threaded through his nostrils. Warmbier was breathing on his own, but he had suffered extensive brain damage, and no longer showed signs of awareness.[55]

When Yun threatened to leave with or without Warmbier, the North Koreans gave in. While they probably had been planning to release the college student all along, they understood that there would be serious consequences if the American envoy left without him.

For his part, Yun was willing to do whatever it took, including agreeing to two conditions: The United States had to pay his $2 million hospital bill, and promise not to criticize their country for what had happened to him. Washington did neither once the American student left North Korea.[56]

A motorcade drove the envoy, Flueckiger, and Warmbier from the hospital to the airport. The Gulfstream had flown back from Japan and was waiting on the tarmac. The doctor cradled him, changed his diaper, and whispered that he was free.[57]

Six days after he returned to Ohio, Otto Warmbier died with his parents at his bedside. Exactly what happened to him remains a mystery. There was no intelligence or medical evidence that he had been tortured. There were rumors he had tried to hang himself.

Three thousand people crowded into his high school auditorium and overflow rooms for the funeral. Hundreds of mourners, some waving American flags, lined the streets in the small town of eight thousand to witness his hearse passing by. Students tied ribbons on trees and light posts along the three-mile route to the cemetery in a show of support.[58]

"Our thoughts and prayers are with Otto's family and friends and all who loved him," Trump said in a statement. The words may have sounded hollow coming from someone who often demonstrated lack of empathy for others.

But the president was shaken by Warmbier's death. "Why would they do that?" he asked his staff. Still, Trump couldn't resist making political hay out of the student's death. Trump implied Obama was to blame when he told reporters that Warmbier "should have been brought home a long time ago."[59]

Otto Warmbier would never be far from Trump's thoughts. During a visit to Seoul in November, he accused the North Koreans of torturing Warmbier in a speech to the Korean National Assembly. In the 2018 State of the Union address, he pledged to "honor Otto's memory with total

American resolve." After the June 2018 summit with Kim Jong Un, Trump remarked, "Otto did not die in vain."[60]

Tragic as it was, the Ohio college student's release marked the high point for Joe Yun's diplomacy. Other American officials grew skeptical as North Korean WMD tests ramped up, asking, "You want to talk to them while they were doing this bullshit?"[61]

It didn't help Yun that relations between Tillerson and Trump took a downturn by summer 2017. Their personalities clashed. The risk-averse Tillerson was inclined to manage problems while the president liked to face risk head on. Trump also "grew to dislike Tillerson's swaggering style." The secretary even dared a White House official to "talk back to me freely" since "I am all man," Kushner recalled. On top of everything else, Tillerson often informed Trump of what he was doing, as opposed to asking him what he should do.[62]

North Korea became a bone of contention between them. Every time Tillerson saw the president, Trump asked him, "Did you get a meeting with Kim Jong Un yet?" one official recalled. The secretary kept trying, since "talking to Pyongyang might prevent him from being fired."[63]

Meanwhile, it slowly dawned on the North Koreans that talking to the honey badger—and Tillerson—was a waste of time. Yun and Choe agreed to meet at the UN General Assembly in late September, clearing the way for the secretary to see the North Korean foreign minister. But Trump's notorious rant at the session, calling Kim Jong Un "Little Rocket Man," killed any chance of a meeting.[64]

By late September, Tillerson was clearly on the outs with the president and the North Koreans. After the secretary told the press, "We do talk to them [the North Koreans]," an angry Trump tweeted he was "wasting his time trying to negotiate with Little Rocket Man." The president thought he, not the secretary of state, should meet the North Koreans.[65]

Yun suffered from guilt by association. His attempt to set up a meeting between Tillerson and the North Korean foreign minister in Sweden or Pyongyang before Christmas failed. When Tillerson floated the idea of unconditional talks and the White House shot him down, the North Koreans never responded to his proposal.[66]

If Otto Warmbier hadn't been fatally injured, would his release have propelled Joe Yun's diplomacy forward? Could Yun have arranged a WMD test cessation and even succeeded in arranging a "contact" or an early summit? Perhaps, but jump-starting diplomacy might have been too hard, even for the honey badger.

Joe Yun retired in early 2018 after Rex Tillerson turned down an invitation to attend the Winter Olympics in South Korea. There was a real prospect that the secretary might encounter a senior North Korean official at the games and save his job. But when his advisors urged him to accept, Tillerson decided not to go. He had been to the Olympics before.

"If China is not going to solve North Korea, we will"

For even a casual observer of international politics, April 6, 2017, must have seemed a strange day. At 2:00 P.M., President Xi Jinping and First Lady Peng Liyuan stepped out of an Air China Boeing 747 aircraft at Palm Beach International Airport.[67] The president of the United States and his first lady arrived on Air Force One an hour later, accompanied by Ivanka Trump and her three children.[68]

Their destination was Trump's "Winter White House," Mar-a-Lago. Described by an American official as "a 15th century Florentine Medici palace with Trump as the Renaissance prince," the villa was built for Marjorie Merriweather Post, one of the wealthiest, most glamorous women of her time. She willed the seventeen-acre estate to the government. Mar-a-Lago was then sold to Trump in 1985 for a bargain-basement price. Eight years later, he turned his home into a club that boasted a $200,000 membership fee.[69]

Xi's visit was a surprise. China had been Trump's personal punching bag. He had elevated grievances over its trade surplus, currency manipulation, and stealing millions of American jobs to a campaign centerpiece. Still, President Xi traveled to Florida six weeks after Trump took office. George H. W. Bush was the only president who had met a Chinese leader faster, but he had already had a good relationship with them.

Trump's policy would ultimately be shaped by clashes among hawks, moderates, and a president who wasn't in either camp. Hawks, like Steve Bannon, a White House advisor, were dead set on opposing Beijing, which was "bent on world domination." Moderates, led by Jared Kushner, included Tillerson, Trump advisor and former Wall Street executive Gary Cohn, and Henry Kissinger. They were interested in trying to build more cooperation with Beijing.[70]

Donald Trump may have crowed about China's unfair trade practices, but he saw the two countries as "two giant corporations with Xi as the opposing CEO," according to one observer. He was all about bonding with the Chinese leader and using America's economic might to pressure him to make deals.[71]

For Xi, Trump was a threat and an opportunity. He expected to consolidate power at the Communist Party congress in the fall and take the bold step of being named a "core leader," like Mao Zedong. Xi's plan, however, could be derailed by a trade war with the world's largest economy, a possible clash over the administration's initial skepticism regarding America's "One China" policy that recognized Beijing, not Taiwan, as the legitimate ruler of China, or a confrontation over North Korea.[72]

Seen through the prism of *The Art of the Deal,* Trump's behavior, while volatile and unpredictable, was about softening up Beijing to get a better bargain. An early summit with a volatile leader who had a transactional mentality made sense, one Chinese insider observed.[73]

The China hawks initially had the upper hand. But the moderates stepped in after the White House failed to send the traditional Chinese New Year's greeting. Trump phoned Xi, recognized the "One China" policy, and invited him to come to Mar-a-Lago. Beijing's top diplomat then dropped by the Oval Office in late February to "say 'hi' to the president."[74]

There was one subject all the Americans could agree upon. China wasn't doing enough to pressure Pyongyang to denuclearize. Trump directed his aides to make Xi "pay a price for backing Kim Jong Un." Tillerson informed Xi during a March trip to Beijing, "You guys have to play a much greater role in the denuclearization of the Korean peninsula."[75]

President Trump upped the ante on the eve of the April summit, threatening that "if China is not going to solve North Korea, we will." The United States sending a carrier battle group to the peninsula, and North Korea having tested another missile while Xi was on his way to Florida, punctuated his threat.[76]

The National Security Council (NSC) and State engaged in a "bureaucratic food fight" preparing for the summit. One aide recalled that "Tillerson had all sorts of ideas about how he would exercise authority as secretary of state," including ensuring he was always in the room when Trump met Xi. The final game plan was a tough hill to climb: to set China straight on trade, oppose its moves to achieve regional dominance, and get it to step up pressure on North Korea.[77]

For Donald Trump, however, Mar-a-Lago was a chance to spend time alone with an opposing CEO. The White House staff knew Trump might pull his own schemes out of a hat. They were right. "Nothing went according to plan," one official remembered.[78]

The summit went smoothly at first. Tea and drinks in a formal living room off Mar-a-Lago's central hall featured Trump's two young grandchildren. They performed a popular Chinese folksong and recited verses from a thirteenth-century Chinese text used to educate children, as well as from Tang dynasty poems. Xi was overjoyed. It was all part of Trump's plan to establish a warm family relationship.[79]

The two delegations were slated to discuss U.S.-Chinese relations next, but Trump opted to hold a private confab with Xi. Several hours passed. An anxious Tillerson waited in the library bar across the vestibule, a wood-paneled study with a portrait of Trump in tennis whites titled "The Visionary." He watched the meeting room door, hoping for, but never finding, an opportunity to squeeze in.[80]

While the two leaders talked, Xi's bodyguards were visibly nervous. Club members and guests started to arrive for dinner, including Bob Kraft, the New England Patriots' owner, with a young Asian woman on his arm.[81] The leaders' dinner, however, would be held in a private room, whereas Trump's meal with Japanese prime minister Shinzo Abe a few weeks earlier had been in the members' dining room for all to see and hear.[82]

The leaders' private session finally ended, and dinner started. Candidate Trump had criticized Obama for hosting a state dinner for Xi; this meal was much more lavish, held in a gilded room with chandeliers, golden pillars and molding, and walls painted with scenes of mountains. Guests sampled Trump's favorite dishes—dry-aged steak and whipped potatoes, pan-seared Dover sole with champagne sauce and Thumbelina carrots.[83]

"We had a long discussion already, and so far, I have gotten nothing, absolutely nothing," Trump joked with reporters. Still, he remarked, "long-term, we are going to have a very, very great relationship." Although the specter of Pyongyang loomed, both men ignored questions shouted by the press on North Korea.[84]

The president leaned over as Xi enjoyed what Trump later called "his big, beautiful piece of delicious chocolate cake" near the end of the meal. After his wife passed him a note from General McMaster, he told the stunned Chinese leader that the United States had just fired fifty-nine missiles at Syria's Assad regime, which had used chemical weapons to kill women and children. The strike wasn't just about Syria. Trump had pointed out to his aides it would send a message to China and North Korea, becoming another arrow in his maximum-pressure quiver.[85]

No one knew what had happened during Trump's private meeting with Xi. Only the interpreter was present. But over the morning and during lunch the next day, he haphazardly revealed that his new friend had lectured him on history: not only the history of how the West had mistreated China but also how "Beijing had ruled the [Korean] peninsula" and "knew them [the Koreans] very well," one official recalled.

A few aides tried to inject facts into Trump's version, but "our chins were on the table, we were dumbfounded," a State Department official remembered. Xi nodded and smiled as the president spoke.[86]

"I don't like what you're doing to us, but you're going to help me on North Korea so I will be nicer to you," the president told Xi. The United States wasn't going to accept a tremendous trade deficit. However, solving the problem with North Korea was "worth having deficits," and "worth not having as good a trade deal as I would normally make."[87]

Although the China hawks had warned him not to reach grand bargains, his deal shouldn't have come as a surprise. In January 2016, Trump tweeted that if Beijing "didn't solve the problem [North Korea], we should make trade very difficult for China." He linked the two issues again after his election.[88]

Even the normal practice of issuing a summit communiqué didn't go as planned. Kushner, as well as John Thornton, a moderate ex–business executive, had told the Chinese during a trip to Beijing that the president wanted to move the two countries toward a "strategic partnership." State and the NSC, however, thought that proclaiming any kind of partnership was a bridge too far.[89]

While Trump and Xi sat down for a farewell lunch, Tillerson and the Chinese foreign minister engaged in an argument near the pool over whether to use the word "partnership" in the final communiqué. The Chinese thought it was a slam dunk, but Tillerson was so opposed that he seemed ready to push the minister into the water.

Kushner had to be called out of the lunch to resolve the dispute. When he backtracked on what he had said earlier, the Chinese gave in. Their news agency only published that the two countries "are capable of becoming great cooperative partners."[90]

Did President Trump's gambit pay off? Shocked and dismayed by the February assassination of Kim Jong Nam in Malaysia, Beijing had already suspended all of Pyongyang's $1 billion worth of yearly coal exports to China. The day Trump and Xi met, Beijing ordered companies to send North Korean coal cargoes back. North Korean ships appeared to return to their home port, although four were still in China weeks later.[91]

The Mar-a-Lago deal, called "the Trump incentive" by one Chinese expert, gave Beijing another reason to cooperate. Paving the way for better relations and signing up to the maximum-pressure campaign would hopefully pay off later when Trump returned the favor. According to a Chinese insider, Beijing was willing to "put North Korea on a hotter roof," although not "sacrifice it completely."[92]

One week after the summit, Trump reminded Xi during a phone call that "the way you're going to make a good trade deal is to help us with North Korea." They discussed reports that China had turned away North Korean coal shipments. The president also asked Xi to remind Kim Jong Un that the United States didn't just have aircraft carriers, an allusion to the USS *Carl Vinson*, which had just arrived off the peninsula. It also had submarines that carried nuclear-armed missiles.[93]

A mid-April editorial in a Chinese Communist Party newspaper reflected the new spirit of cooperation. Beijing warned Pyongyang that if it conducted another nuclear test, China would "dramatically decrease" its petroleum exports to North Korea. The threat had teeth since the North relied on Beijing for almost all its oil. By late June, Beijing had completely suspended sales, even though there had been no North Korean nuclear test.[94]

Perhaps even more significant, the editorial warned that China would not help North Korea if the United States launched a preemptive attack. Trump's Syria strike, his periodic threats, and other American officials' warnings that all options "were on the table" may have unsettled the Chinese.[95]

Secret talks continued with China on cooperating if North Korea collapsed, although Tillerson almost scuttled the sessions when he mistakenly mentioned them in public. At one point, Matt Pottinger, a White House hawk who "liked to break crockery sometimes," pushed a map of North Korea across the table to illustrate his points. Nevertheless, the two countries formulated guidelines on how "not to heighten the chances of conflict" if Pyongyang collapsed, according to one participant.[96]

Washington and Beijing also held more meetings in late May on implementing sanctions. Susan Thornton, State's top Asia expert, arrived in China just as Pyongyang accused Beijing of "dancing to the tune of the US." The Chinese tightened restrictions along the North Korean border, and imposed regulations on companies and financial institutions. Afterwards, she told the press that the United States had seen a "shift in emphasis" in China's approach.[97]

If Donald Trump was to make good on his January tweet and stop North Korea's ICBM program, maximum pressure seemed the only option. But there was a limit to how far Beijing would go to support Washington.

Just as the Americans had discovered after the Sunnylands summit in 2013, they had to disaggregate what Xi said from what he did. The Chinese leader had told Obama, "A barefoot person does not fear those who wear shoes," his explanation of why stepped-up pressure wouldn't change Pyongyang's behavior. At a multilateral meeting in July 2017, Xi told Trump the same thing.

CHAPTER THIRTEEN

"Fire and fury"

S PEAKING AT A CONFERENCE in Omaha, Nebraska, General Vincent
Brooks, the commander of United States Forces Korea, or USFK,
asked a question he pondered every day. How could Washington
convince Kim Jong Un he was better off having a conversation
with Rex Tillerson than a confrontation with James Mattis?[1]

The first African American named Cadet First Captain at West Point,
Brooks was the son of a major general, his brother would become a briga-
dier general, and he would rise even higher to the rank of full general. After
three decades of service in South Korea, Kosovo, Iraq, Afghanistan, the Pa
cific, and the Pentagon, he had been appointed to his last command in
2016.[2]

The crew of the general's aircraft was alerted as he flew home six thousand miles, over the Russian Far East, and down the coast to the East Sea
and South Korea. A North Korean ICBM was about to pass overhead.
While a missile tested earlier that July could reach Alaska, this one could
hit Los Angeles or even Chicago. The general's near encounter was ironic,
coming after his Omaha speech.[3]

July 2017 was a pivotal moment for Donald Trump and Kim Jong Un.
The North Korean leader had made good on his New Year's threat to
launch a missile that could destroy American cities. But Trump hadn't made
good on his response, "It won't happen." His threats, the military strike in
Syria, and dispatching a carrier to the peninsula hadn't dissuaded Kim.
Moreover, one American intelligence agency estimated that the North

could start producing long-range missiles "well within the year," sooner than expected.[4]

General Brooks understood that rounding up the usual military suspects wouldn't make Kim Jong Un think twice about testing. American bombers would fly over Korea, tensions would rise, and then the aircraft would go away. "The North Koreans knew we weren't going to attack," one official remarked.[5]

While the Obama White House had held a tight rein on military responses, everything changed once Jim Mattis took over as Trump's secretary of defense. Brooks, as the army commander in the Middle East, with Mattis as his Marine boss, had worked on tougher responses to Iranian provocations. They were ready by the time North Korea tested its ICBM in July.[6]

American and South Korean short-range missiles moved to the peninsula's east coast where they had a clear field of fire into the East Sea. They were launched just twenty hours after the July 3 test. The distance the allies fired their missiles was the same required to attack the ICBM's launch point.

Brooks then announced, "Self-restraint, which is a choice, is all that separates the armistice and war." Silent in public, the North Koreans probably got the message, but that still didn't dissuade them from testing again in late July.[7]

Tensions escalated again. The Americans and South Koreans fired their missiles once more, this time less than six hours after the launch. Brooks issued another warning, but it had no effect.

The UN issued a new set of sanctions in early August after the late July test, and Trump declared, "North Korea best not make any more threats to the United States," or "they will be met with the fire and fury like the world has never seen."[8]

Pyongyang raised the ante, threatening Guam, where seven thousand American troops were based along with a bomber force. The North Koreans dismissed Trump's "fire and fury threat" as a "load of nonsense."[9]

Trump returned the volley: "If anything, maybe that statement wasn't tough enough." Asked what was tougher, he replied, "You'll see."[10]

More WMD tests followed. On August 29, the Japanese government texted its citizens that Pyongyang had launched a missile over their northernmost island. On September 3, Pyongyang detonated a blast ten times larger than that of Hiroshima after photos in the media spotlighted Kim Jong Un inspecting what looked like a hydrogen bomb. North Korea fired another missile over Japan a few weeks later.[11]

President Donald Trump addresses the 72nd Session of the United Nations
General Assembly in New York City on September 19, 2017.
U.S. Department of State video.

The UN issued new sanctions, followed by a new Trump threat. In
his first major address to the UN General Assembly at the end of September, the president warned, "We will have no choice but to totally destroy North Korea" if it continues to threaten the United States. "Rocket
Man is on a suicide mission."[12] No world leader had ever spoken from
that podium about "wiping out a country of 25 million people," the BBC
commented.[13]

Kim quickly responded, "I will surely and definitely tame the mentally
deranged dotard with fire."[14]

Ri Yong Ho, his foreign minister, suggested that North Korea might
test a nuclear weapon over the Pacific Ocean, as well as attack the U.S.
homeland. He had his own nicknames for Trump: "Commander-in-Grief,"
"Lyin' King," and "President Evil."[15]

The president tweeted in response, "If he echoes thoughts of Little
Rocket Man, they won't be around much longer!"[16]

Ri called Trump's salvo tantamount to a declaration of war.[17]

The president seemed out of control, but there was also a method to
his name-calling madness. Before U.S. ambassador to the UN Nikki Haley began negotiations with the Chinese on the September sanctions resolution, he told her, "Tell them every option is on the table. Make them
think I'm crazy."[18]

He also relished the attention. "What do you think of me calling Kim Jong Un 'Little Rocket Man'?" Trump asked Haley before his UN address. She warned him, "This is a very serious crowd," prompting the president to protest, "It's killing it on Twitter."[19]

"You've got to make the earth move to make heavy objects move," one official observed. After Trump's threats, "all sorts of things, good and bad, went into motion." Still, the president had no idea whether his taunts would cow Kim into submission or provoke him.[20]

Trump also hadn't given much thought to how his own advisors might react. General McMaster was on board. The author of a book that concluded America's failed policy in Vietnam was based on fundamentally flawed assumptions, he believed the same was true about Obama's policy toward North Korea.[21]

McMaster thought Kim Jong Un was an irrational dictator who couldn't be deterred and would be prone to start a war once he had an arsenal. The general wasn't squeamish about considering a military strike. "Do you want to bet a mushroom cloud over Los Angeles?" he warned Trump.[22]

Secretary Mattis, however, was "much more deliberate, calculating and strategic," according to a colleague. Early in Trump's administration, he had called North Korea "the crocodile closest to the canoe."[23] But the retired Marine general knew a second Korean War would be bloody and chaotic. He was all about "diplomacy, diplomacy, diplomacy."[24]

Tillerson agreed with Mattis. The two men also found Trump's abandonment of America's commitment to the world order disturbing. They tried to reeducate him just before the second July ICBM test. Trump, however, was fixated on holding a military parade like the Bastille Day procession he had just attended during a visit to France. Mattis shut down with a distant defeated look on his face. Tillerson was reported to have called Trump "a moron" afterwards.[25]

The president's three top advisors also clashed for bureaucratic and personal reasons. While McMaster assured Tillerson in one of their first meetings that he planned to be an "honest broker," the traditional role for a national security advisor, the two secretaries suspected he was bent on directing policy.[26] Tillerson often just ignored him.

As for the secretary of defense, Mattis called McMaster "an unstable asshole" during a three-way phone conversation with the secretary of state, unaware that one of his aides was listening in even though he had been called away.[27] "There were few people who could get under Mattis's skin as the national security advisor," according to one aide.[28]

The clash spilled over into the public. The two secretaries refused to take on the job of defending Trump's "madman" rhetoric. McMaster regularly argued that the North Korea threat could trigger a U.S. military response. A sympathetic colleague recalled that the general found himself a "bit of a barking dog." He was taking a lot of heat.[29]

In August, Mattis and Tillerson took the unusual step of penning a joint *Wall Street Journal* op-ed that called for a "peaceful pressure campaign." They proposed deepening cooperation with allies, stepping up sanctions, and convincing China to support the United States. All those moves could easily have come out of a Democratic administration's playbook.

McMaster believed that their actions were at odds with what Trump wanted. As one senior White House official, recalled, "Nobody in any meetings I was in with the president ever said, 'peaceful pressure.'"[30]

"The machine was quietly moving towards war"

The chaos in Washington had transformed Korea from its traditional description, the "land of the morning calm," into "the land of morning surprises." North Korea had always been a big unknown. South Korea had sometimes surprised its ally. In contrast to past American presidents, Trump was volatile.[31]

Chaos in Washington made General Brooks's job—defending South Korea—harder. Who was driving policy: Trump, Mattis, Tillerson, or Fox News pundits? It was hard to say, so he stayed close to Mattis and General Dunford, the chairman of the Joint Chiefs of Staff.

Brooks updated them regularly. He also participated in the secretary's video conferences with combatant commanders from around the world. But no one could anticipate the daily wild cards dealt by the president.[32]

Trump's negative view of South Korea also made it hard for Brooks. The president was like the brainwashed ex-soldier in *The Manchurian Candidate* who did his communist master's bidding whenever he saw the Queen of Hearts. Trump's automatic response, "We are getting ripped off," was triggered just by mentioning South Korea. He was outraged by the $18 billion trade deficit with Seoul, and what he believed was the outrageous cost of the alliance.

On top of all that, while Trump treated President Moon Jae-in well when they met, he thought the South Korean leader was "a wimp," according to one White House advisor. When Moon suspended the THAAD deployment in spring 2017, Trump exclaimed, "You mean, we paid for it, and they don't even want it?" adding, "Pull it back and put it in Portland."[33]

U.S. Secretary of State Mike Pompeo is greeted by USFK commander
General Vincent Brooks upon arrival to Osan Air Base in Osan, Seoul,
on June 13, 2018. Official State Department photo.

The soft-spoken Moon had prepared himself to deal with Trump. He
had even read *The Art of the Deal.* The South Korean leader was, in fact, a
realist. He had increased defense spending by almost 10 percent, but Moon
also saw American unilateralism as a serious threat, especially after Trump's
"fire and fury" comments. The South Korean leader reminded Washington that there would be no war unless he agreed to it.[34]

Everyone expected the worst when President Trump visited South
Korea in November, but the visit turned out uneventful. Matt Pottinger
had toned down his speech to the National Assembly. President Moon had
also requested a number of changes. During their dinner together, the two
leaders talked mostly to their own wives, not to each other. Trump did comment that the Blue House banquet hall was nicer than most hotels, high
praise coming from a real estate tycoon.[35]

The president snapped back into character during a helicopter flight
over Camp Humphreys, a major military base. General Brooks explained

that a little more than 90 percent of it had been paid for by the Koreans. Trump protested, why didn't they pay for all of it?

Still, Brooks and the South Koreans soldiered on together. When North Korea detonated its hydrogen bomb in September, they were ready with another unprecedented military demonstration intended to dissuade Kim from testing.[36]

Instead of the usual bomber overflight, the Americans put together a "strike package" of some forty warplanes advancing from the south along the North Korean coast to the far northeast. The plan was risky, so they took precautions. The aircraft stayed in international airspace and were staged late at night, not prime time for the North Koreans. Still, they had shot down an American spy plane over the same waters in 1969.[37]

Pyongyang got the message. The region's air defense commander may have been executed. Air defense units were moved to the nuclear test site, also located in the northeast. Foreign Minister Ri threatened on Twitter to shoot down American bombers even in international airspace. The North did not conduct another WMD test for two months. But no one knew whether that was because of the demonstration, or a testing schedule carved in stone.[38]

Soldiering on together meant, above all, preparing to fight a second Korean War. The Time-Phased-Force Deployment Data, known as the TPFDD, required the United States to send hundreds of thousands of troops and weapons by sea and air before hostilities. The time to deploy the troops was not measured in days, or weeks. It was more like months.[39]

The thirty thousand American soldiers and hundreds of thousands of South Koreans already there were supposed to be ready "to fight tonight," USFK's motto. But they weren't. As a lieutenant colonel commanding an infantry battalion near the DMZ in the 1990s, Brooks found that his troops couldn't even repair combat vehicles. Korea was considered the end of the world when it came to spare parts, fuel, or ammunition.[40]

A new TPFDD, emphasizing logistics first, not new troop deployments, made the most sense. First, a long-lasting flow of forces was obsolete. North Korea's nuclear weapons could wipe out ports and airfields where American soldiers and supplies would embark. Second, Pyongyang would be surprised since it expected a prolonged troop buildup before hostilities. Finally, preparations wouldn't be noticed by the Korean public and trigger panic.[41]

Once Secretary Mattis approved the plan, General Dunford diverted resources to Korea from around the world. If everything went according to schedule, the United States and South Korea would be "ready to fight tonight" by spring 2018. Even when Washington, Seoul, and Pyongyang shifted to diplomacy, "the machine was quietly moving towards war," one official recalled.[42]

The second major task for Brooks and the U.S. embassy was to prepare to evacuate American civilians. As the nuclear crisis escalated in 1994, the NEO, or noncombatant evacuation operation, called for flying thousands of Americans out on military aircraft that brought troops in. The logistical hurdles were enormous. Moreover, an NEO was guaranteed to tip off the North Koreans that war was imminent, and panic South Korean civilians.[43]

Since then, the challenge had grown by leaps and bounds. Some two hundred thousand Americans, along with thirty thousand Japanese and civilians from four close allies, would have to be evacuated. Foreign diplomats asked USFK and the embassy how to get their citizens out of the country. And what about the five hundred thousand Chinese citizens in South Korea? Would their air force evacuate them if Beijing was about to intervene on the North's side?[44]

With tensions mounting, USFK staged a drill for the first time ever to fly civilians all the way to the United States. "It wasn't just a rehearsal. It was more about learning what we needed to do better," one officer recalled. While the Department of Health and Human Services was slated to handle repatriation, the deputy secretary's and undersecretary's mouths were agape during a video call when they realized what had to be done.[45]

The U.S. military and the embassy also formulated a plan with the South Koreans. Americans would be transported south on buses and trains out of reach of the North Koreans. They would then be loaded onto boats and planes. All of this would be done while holding off their own citizens trying to flee.

One embassy official concluded that an NEO would require "a healthy sprinkling of fairy dust." Another thought the plan was "doomed from day one." Tens of thousands of Americans would have to shelter in place in the middle of the second Korean War, awaiting rescue.[46]

"We are going to be in a war in six months."

As 2017 ended, "the tension was palpable," according to a White House aide. Army chief of staff General Mark Milley traveled to Asia and warned top-ranking American and allied officers, "We are going to be in a war in six months." Mattis ordered Brooks to "stay on the ramparts"; in other words, don't come home.[47] The secretary also did his best to delay or deflect any military moves.[48]

Part of the problem was that, aside from his threatening public pronouncements, Trump's private ruminations encouraged concerns that he was "just plain crazy." The president mulled over using a nuclear weapon against North Korea and blaming another country. An alarmed John Kelly, a former Marine general and his chief of staff, brought in high-ranking officers to brief him on how easily war could break out, and the enormous consequences.[49]

But Trump wasn't the first president to consider attacking North Korea with nuclear weapons. The American nuclear war plan, the Single Integrated Operational Plan, or SIOP, had included options to launch nuclear strikes against targets in the North for decades. The Nixon White House had mulled over a nuclear strike in 1969 when the North Koreans shot down the American spy plane.[50]

Nor was the Trump administration the first to think about a first strike, although not with nuclear weapons. President Clinton had considered destroying the Yongbyon reactor before plutonium in its fuel rods could be used to build a nuclear bomb. Obama's Pentagon had developed options for a first strike to wipe out the growing North Korean ICBM threat.

Tensions reached a boiling point in late November 2017 when North Korea tested a long-range missile that could reach any city in the United States. After Trump mocked, "Little Rocket Man, he is a sick puppy," Ambassador Haley warned that the launch "brings us closer to war."[51]

The danger was closer than she realized. A "national emergency conference" of Trump's top advisors, held via a secure video link, convened while the rocket still sat on the launch pad. The sessions had a new sense of urgency given Pyongyang's tests of ICBMs. "You never knew where they were going until they were launched; whether it was Japan, American territory in the Pacific, or the United States," one official recalled.[52]

As information flashed on the video screen, the secretary of defense, the chairman of the Joint Chiefs, and military commanders sorted out their options before the launch, since time would be short once the rocket lifted off. They would have only thirty minutes to decide what to do if it was headed toward the United States, and several minutes if headed for American territory in the Pacific or Japan.[53]

What if the missile veered off course, one possibility given North Korea's spotty test record? What if the launch was a deliberate attack? That was unlikely, but the exchange of threats made it seem possible. What if the rocket was carrying a nuclear warhead? No one knew for sure, although Pyongyang boasted it had one. Whatever the case, "if word had come that a missile was inbound for Seattle, we were already launching interceptors," Mattis recalled.[54]

The danger of a second Korean War would become real if the interceptors failed to stop the missile and the United States had to retaliate. "If someone had said, 'Go get Kim Jong Un,' we were postured to do that," according to one official. The North Korean leader had been attending launches, including the November test. If the order was given to destroy the launch site, it would have been "too bad for Kim."[55]

Some White House aides believed his death would paralyze his country, but that required a leap of faith. Everyone, including the North Koreans, knew killing him was part of the war plan. If Pyongyang had a plan to respond, lashing out against Seoul, just across the border, would have been easy. The North could devastate its nine million civilians.[56]

Luckily, the November launch was just a test and didn't veer off course. The flight went higher than both July launches and ended with the rocket landing six hundred miles downrange in the East Sea. The only civilians threatened were pilots on two commercial airliners, who saw flashes, probably the burnout of the first stage and the ignition of the second stage.[57]

Strangely enough, while the November 2017 test could have triggered a second Korean War, the launch inspired hope that the crisis was winding down. Ri Chun Hee appeared on TV once again, this time to announce that Pyongyang had finally "realized the great historic cause of completing the state nuclear force, the cause of building a rocket power."[58]

The U.S. intelligence community believed Pyongyang had reached a turning point. CIA analysts had thought Kim hinted in his New Year's speech that the WMD tests would eventually end. The November launch appeared to signal he was finished. USFK agreed. "We shouldn't be looking for a war. We should be looking to prevent one," one officer observed.[59]

Washington may have missed other signposts throughout 2017. A North Korean pronouncement in May carefully made the point that there were circumstances in which dialogue and "normal relations" could happen. When Pyongyang launched an ICBM on July 4, Kim Jong Un signaled that he was open to talks on his nuclear and missile programs. In September, Pyongyang's announcement that a hydrogen bomb had been detonated also hinted that the North was almost finished with testing.[60]

Still, tension mounted after the November test. Trump and Xi worked together. Before the test, China had already closed the bridge across the Yalu River connecting the two countries and suspended flights to Pyongyang, citing lack of demand.[61] After the test, a Chinese delegation visited Washington to negotiate the details of a tough UN resolution with Steve Mnuchin, the secretary of the treasury.[62]

By January 2018, Washington was in a frenzy. A *Wall Street Journal* article claimed the administration was considering a "bloody nose option." It assumed the United States could launch a strike without fear of retaliation, since a military response could trigger the end of the North Korean regime.[63]

The story gained momentum when the White House withdrew its nomination of Victor Cha to be ambassador to South Korea, reportedly because he opposed the option. Cha's *Washington Post* op-ed, titled "Giving North Korea a 'Bloody Nose' Carries a Huge Risk to Americans," seemed to confirm the speculation.[64]

General Brooks, however, told US representatives and senators visiting South Korea, "It's a construct of the Beltway," the chattering classes in Washington. One senior officer compared North Korea to "a kid on the playground who would get hit in the nose and freak out while others would cower and walk away." You had to be prepared for both reactions.[65]

The administration wasn't blameless for the uproar. For months, Trump and McMaster had stoked tensions, laying the groundwork for speculation. After the November ICBM launch, McMaster warned that new sanctions "might be our last, best chance to avoid military conflict."[66]

He believed a first strike might be necessary to protect civilians, although he argued that wasn't American policy. McMaster grabbed two books from a shelf in his West Wing office that proved his point to show Kang Kyung-wha, Seoul's first female foreign minister.[67] "Let's hope it doesn't come to that," she responded with a nervous laugh.[68]

But McMaster had spent his entire military career rejecting false notions about the use of military force. Anyone who thought North Korea wouldn't retaliate or that bombing could be an element of coercive diplomacy was just plain wrong.[69]

Nevertheless, the fevered speculation reinforced calls for an NEO. Recognizing that an NEO could trigger a conflict, Senator Lindsey Graham withdrew an earlier suggestion that Trump should start moving American dependents out of South Korea. Jack Keane, a retired general whom

Trump watched on Fox News, argued, however, that "the Pentagon should stop sending families there to allow the US to prepare for war."[70]

Trump's advisors had been debating an NEO for months. McMaster wanted USFK to just send its dependents home to show the North Koreans that Washington would not be bullied. Mattis and Tillerson argued that Pyongyang would interpret any NEO, even one focused on a small subset of Americans, as a sign that war was about to begin.

Bob Woodward later claimed that Trump was on the verge of tweeting that "we are going to pull our dependents from South Korea—family members of the 28,000 people there."[71] The president, in fact, had already ordered the Pentagon to stop sending military families to Korea, and to withdraw those already there. That move would have affected hundreds, maybe thousands, not hundreds of thousands of Americans.

Mattis, concerned that the president might do something rash, had been undermining McMaster's efforts to prepare military plans to deal with Pyongyang. He had frustrated McMaster's idea to hold a military "table-top exercise" to prepare for war and his push to enforce sanctions by stopping suspicious ships at sea.[72]

The Pentagon also "slow-rolled" the directive on evacuating military families, an act of insubordination, according to a White House official.[73] Instead, it had come up with a plan to draw down military and embassy civilians over months, to "get them out of there." Like USFK's quiet preparations "to fight tonight," the gradual drawdown would probably not have been noticed by anyone.[74]

While Trump had fired off a tweet before without thinking about the consequences, at least one senior White House aide was confident he wasn't going to do so now. "The president thinks out loud. It was part of the conversation. It wasn't necessarily something he was going to do." The possibility remained, nonetheless.[75]

Mattis and Brooks were probably on the same page. They believed there was only one reason why Washington should initiate an evacuation: as an "information nuke" if military action was the next step. As far as Brooks was concerned, his advice for Washington was to shut the hell up.[76]

While the Trump administration was lost in navel-gazing, Kim Jong Un's New Year's speech for 2018 was rebroadcast nine times. The Western media went for the easy headlines—his claim that he had a "nuclear button" on his desk and Trump's response that he had a "much bigger and more powerful one [that] works."[77]

The CIA was right, however. Kim was done with WMD tests. "I am willing to send a delegation" to the Winter Olympics to be hosted by South Korea next month, the chairman announced. Pyongyang had begun to shift from confrontation to engagement.[78]

"Exquisitely normal activity"

Andrew "Andy" Kim's job was to defuse the crisis. The State Department oversaw diplomacy. The Pentagon was in charge of fighting a war. The Central Intelligence Agency straddled both worlds. It ran the goon channel and helped the Pentagon plan military options. But the CIA also occupied a gray area: trying to convince the North Koreans to back down.

Born in South Korea, Kim had come to the United States as a high school freshman. He had spent almost thirty years as a CIA case officer operating undercover overseas and at the agency's McLean, Virginia, headquarters. Kim had achieved every case officer's dream and became an overseas station chief, then retired as the crisis with North Korea mounted.[79]

No sooner had he left the CIA than he was called back by Mike Pompeo, the new director. First in his West Point class, the conservative Kansas representative had warned that Donald Trump would be "an authoritarian president who ignored our Constitution." By the 2016 Republican Convention, however, Pompeo was "excited for a commander-in-chief who fearlessly puts Americans out front."

The new CIA director's confirmation by the Senate in late January completed his transition from critic to Trump's most loyal foot soldier.[80] Pompeo proudly proclaimed on a trip abroad, "It's an insurgent presidency." One puzzled American ambassador wondered, "What the hell?"[81]

The new intelligence chief fell into lockstep right away with Trump's top priority: eliminating the North Korean threat. He asked Kim, how could the CIA focus its resources on that task? The retired spy pointed out that the agency had talented people, from desk-bound analysts to field operatives, but that they were scattered in different departments. They should be pooled together like the CIA's ten other mission centers.[82]

Pompeo pressed Kim to come back from retirement to run the new operation. When he finally agreed, all Kim asked was, "Will you tell my wife?" Pompeo announced the Korean Mission Center would "more purposely integrate and direct CIA efforts against serious threats to the United States and its allies emanating from North Korea."[83]

Kim's first task was to build a covert action plan. While speculation had been rampant that the CIA was plotting regime change, even the assassination of Kim Jong Un, America's spies were skeptical. Pompeo echoed that sentiment to a think-tank audience. No one knew what was "behind door number three," so trying to get rid of the chairman or his regime was too risky.[84]

Even more important, the CIA's job was to convince the North Koreans to back down if they were contemplating war. The only way to figure out what was on their minds was face-to-face contact. With the exception of the CIA deputy director, Joe DeTrani, and a few top aides, however, none of the desk-bound analysts had met a North Korean during Obama's eight years in office.[85]

The goon channel was the perfect solution. Kim helped DeTrani set it up in 2009 and traveled to North Korea with Avril Haines in 2014. But it had gone cold after the agency's previous counterpart, Pyongyang's minister of state security, had been purged.

The CIA pinpointed Kim Yong Chol, General Clapper's opposite number in 2014, as the new contact. A rising star close to Kim Jong Un who was confident enough to engage American spies, he seemed the right choice. The agency ferreted out his phone number and called him. When the North Koreans responded, the channel was reopened.[86]

American spies held two sessions with the North Koreans in Singapore: one in spring 2017 as the crisis escalated, and another in the fall after more WMD tests and the rhetorical volleys between Trump and Kim Jong Un.

Neither group wasted time mimicking their leaders' exchange of insults. They had other questions in mind. Were the North Koreans serious about attacking the United States? Was President Trump as crazy as people thought he was?[87]

The North Korean spies had a surprising offer. If Trump was serious about having a hamburger with their leader, could the American spies set it up? They made it clear Kim Jong Un was the only person in North Korea who could discuss denuclearization.[88]

The Americans didn't know if Trump's hamburger summit proposal, made in the heat of the campaign, was serious or not. He had a habit of veering from making threats to offering an outstretched hand. They did know that the confrontation couldn't be solved without a decision by both leaders. But the North Koreans had to stop launching missiles first.[89]

The North Koreans also weren't sure if the American spies were the right men to deliver their message, even though Andy Kim worked for Mike Pompeo, a Trump confidant. Their intelligence service had a long history of rivalry with the Foreign Ministry when it came to talking to Americans. They weren't sure whether that same rivalry existed in Washington.

It did. No one knew what was happening in the secret channel except Pompeo and the president. The CIA was "hiding fifty-one of the fifty-two cards in the deck," according to a State Department official. A White House aide complained of "Andy-PTSD."[90]

That didn't stop Pompeo and Kim, however, from visiting Secretary of State Tillerson with an extraordinary proposal. They offered to turn their channel over to him.[91]

One official recalled thinking Tillerson's efforts to set up a meeting with the North Koreans were "way amateurish." The secretary had reached out to North Korean sympathizers in Japan, hoping they could help. But their influence had long since evaporated once the funds they sent to Pyongyang dried up.[92]

Pompeo and Kim met Tillerson and Margaret Peterlin, his chief of staff, in the secretary's seventh-floor suite. Pompeo made his offer when Tillerson mentioned he was trying to set up a session with the North Koreans. The secretary turned him down. He may have suspected it was a trap: the CIA director had been bad-mouthing Tillerson at the White House.[93]

The secretary knew Trump would be angry if he learned that he was trying to set up his own meeting with the North Koreans. Rumor had it that Pompeo had even shared intelligence with the president that Tillerson had asked the Chinese to help him.

The Singapore talks made it clear that the North Koreans were interested in a summit, not in a war. As tensions mounted, Andy Kim reassured South Korean friends, who were worried by Trump's unpredictability, that he had no plans to bring his daughter home from her university in Seoul.[94]

In an interview with Bob Woodward two years later, Trump claimed that Kim Jong Un anticipated a war and was totally prepared. That fit in nicely with the president's narrative that he had prevented a major conflict. The North Korean leader later told Pompeo he had anticipated a war, but the secretary was more discerning: "We never knew whether it was real, or whether it was a bluff."[95]

American intelligence, in fact, hadn't detected any signs that North Korea was preparing for war. Expecting an attack, Kim Jong Il had joined troops in the field in 1993. The intelligence community almost issued a "warning of war" in 1994. In 2015, Pyongyang seemed ready to fight when a crisis erupted at the DMZ. But in 2017, "there was no sign that Kim Jong Un was interested in going to war," a CIA official recalled.[96]

The North Koreans seemed more interested in peace. CBS president David Rhodes flew into Pyongyang in March to negotiate a regular presence, the same arrangement as the Associated Press and Japan's Kyodo News had.

A CBS film crew returned in April as the confrontation heated up. Pyongyang bustled with cars, the skyline bristled with construction, commerce was blossoming, and the zoo was filled with children. One repeat visitor called it "exquisitely normal activity."[97]

In August, Evan Osnos, a writer for the *New Yorker*, traveled to Pyongyang, days after the North Korean threat to attack Guam and Trump's tweet that the U.S. military was "locked and loaded."[98] He ominously noted that whether a nuclear war was imminent depended on the "senescent real-estate mogul and reality television star, and a young third-generation dictator" with less than five years of leadership experience between them.[99]

Everyday life in Pyongyang seemed undisturbed, however, except for the outpouring of anti-Trump, anti-American sentiment. Just like other visitors, Osnos was questioned by his escort about whether Donald Trump was irrational or "too smart." The North Korean sounded like many Americans who hadn't been able to figure Trump out.[100]

On the theory that the best defense was a good offense, Osnos was lectured by one official that "the United States is not the only country that can wage a preventive war." A few months later, a foreign visitor was told by a government official that North Korea wasn't going to wait for an American attack.[101]

Like the CBS team, the *New Yorker* writer found an air of normality, with even "flashes of modernity," including women wearing stilettos and short skirts, "people hunched over cell phones, couples whispering on park benches and a grandmother following a toddler on fresh asphalt." Osnos spotted busloads of foreign tourists and visited the subway surrounded by commuters.[102]

After Trump's September 2017 "Rocket Man" speech, articles didn't exhort the public to prepare for war. Instead, the North Korean leadership urged people to boost economic production.[103]

No one knew it, but Kim Jong Un had a plan percolating to shift from bolstering his defenses to modernizing his economy. If that happened and testing subsided, Pyongyang's door to talks would open again. His shift could only take place if the threat from Washington diminished.[104]

Also, no one knew that Donald Trump had his own pivot in the works.

"I'm here representing the Secretary General for the whole world."

An American diplomat arrived in Pyongyang six days after the November 2017 ICBM launch. However, after almost thirty years in the State Department, Jeffrey Feltman wasn't an American diplomat anymore. He was a top advisor to the UN secretary general.

Feltman felt a sense of "diplomatic nakedness."[105] One minute, he was backed by the most powerful country in the world. The next, he had to rely on his own powers of persuasion. The new envoy soon realized, however, that representing the international community came with a different legitimacy that "cannot be replicated by any one nation, no matter how powerful."[106]

He would have been right to suspect that the UN's good offices meant little to the North Koreans. The Korean War had been fought under its imprimatur. Condemnation after condemnation and sanction after sanction had been issued by the Security Council. The fact that the UN had also sent millions of dollars in humanitarian help to the country's most vulnerable people wasn't enough to erase its long negative record with the North Koreans.

While a visit by a high-ranking official from New York might have appeared part of some grand design, coming so soon after Pyongyang's ICBM test, the trip had been in the works for months. Feltman's staff had proposed a dialogue with the North Koreans earlier in the year to discuss threats to peace on the peninsula.[107]

Nothing happened until September. Ri Yong Ho, the North Korean foreign minister, was slated to meet Secretary General António Guterres and Feltman after Trump's "Rocket Man" speech. When the North's ambassador grabbed Ri and introduced the American diplomat, Ri extended an invitation to visit Pyongyang.[108]

What was the UN for if not to prevent war from breaking out? "Given the grave risks associated with any military confrontation, in exercise of its primary responsibility, the Security Council needs to do all it can to prevent an escalation," Feltman told an emergency session after North Korea launched a missile.[109]

Since political sensitivities were high, the secretary general felt obliged to consult the countries that had attended the multilateral Beijing nuclear talks. Russia, China, and South Korea gave a thumbs-up. Only Japan, led by a conservative government fixated on maximum pressure, opposed the UN envoy's mission.[110]

None of that mattered without approval from a president who had tweeted that the UN was "just a club for people to get together, talk and have a good time."[111] Washington seemed opposed at first. American bureaucrats were only interested in maximum pressure, not in throwing the North Koreans a diplomatic lifeline in the form of a UN envoy. The secretary general decided to delay responding to the invitation.[112]

The subject came up again in October when Guterres met Trump in the Oval Office. The secretary general mentioned that the UN still hadn't responded to a North Korean invitation. Despite his past negative comments, Trump had also praised the secretary general and said that the UN had the "power to bring people together like nothing else." Now, he put that power into action.[113]

Trump leaned over and told Guterres that Jeff Feltman should go to Pyongyang and tell the North Koreans he was willing to sit down with Kim Jong Un. The Portuguese former politician and diplomat must have been shocked. Not only was Trump willing to meet Kim Jong Un. He was also sending the message via the United Nations.[114]

White House aides weren't surprised, given Trump's penchant for personal diplomacy. After an Oval Office briefing, no one else knew it, but he asked Mike Pompeo, "Do we have a way to communicate with the North Koreans?" Trump wanted to get a message to Kim. Pompeo mentioned the goon channel. "Good, call them," he said. "Tell them you want to come see them."[115]

While Feltman agreed to visit Pyongyang the first week in December, after the November 29 ICBM test, "it was really touch and go," one official recalled.[116] Still, his trip was approved, and the envoy was greeted with open arms by the North Koreans. Little gestures, like flying the UN flag at his guesthouse and on his car, showed they were trying.[117]

On his first night in Pyongyang, the deputy foreign minister told him, "I can see you're serious, you're on an important mission. I was expecting this evening to be just a social evening but let's get into the substance."[118]

The next four and a half days were filled with fifteen hours of intense discussions, so intense and so long that some participants were dying for a bathroom break. The sessions weren't a stale exchange of canned talking points. They were engaged in spirited debate, a dialogue Feltman hadn't expected.[119]

The North Koreans were more interested in grilling him about events in Washington than in proposing how to stand down from confrontation. Even more terrifying, they argued that Trump intended to attack them, but "we would go first because that's our only chance."[120] Moreover, the North Koreans claimed that Kim Jong Un would know when Washington was about to go to war. It may have been an empty bluff, but it was a dangerous one.[121]

Feltman warned the Foreign Ministry that the United States wasn't the only country concerned about violations of Security Council resolutions and the global regime intended to stop the spread of nuclear weapons. "I'm here representing the Secretary General for the whole world," he said, playing his strongest card. "You risk sleepwalking into war with the United States."[122]

To punctuate his point, the UN envoy presented the foreign minister with a book, *Sleepwalkers: How Europe Went to War in 1914*. "This is what you are doing. You are going into an accidental war," he emphasized. Feltman delivered a letter from the secretary general to Kim Jong Un reinforcing that point.[123]

He had four suggestions, all designed to help North Korea back away from the brink: The North Koreans should implement Security Council resolutions and stand down from the confrontation. Pyongyang should re-open communication with the United States and South Korea to avoid accidental war. The North Koreans should attend the upcoming Winter Olympics in South Korea as a step to renew dialogue. Finally, they should participate in an upcoming Security Council meeting of senior officials.[124]

Feltman saved his most important message for a private meeting with Ri Yong Ho, the foreign minister. President Trump "would be willing, under the right conditions, to sit down with Kim Jong Un," he informed Ri.[125]

Silent at first, the normally unflappable Ri responded, "I don't believe you. Why should I believe you?"[126]

"Look, I am not asking you to believe me," Feltman replied. "What I am telling you is the UN was entrusted with a message from President Trump. I am the carrier of that message." Nothing more was said.[127]

When Feltman left New York, he had been "deeply, deeply concerned that war was imminent." When he left Pyongyang, he was still "really worried about an accidental move towards conflict." President Trump might feel obliged to react to North Korea's WMD tests.[128]

The Security Council met three times during Feltman's first week back in New York, approving hard-hitting sanctions. General McMaster told CBS News that the restrictions "might be our last best chance to avoid military conflict."[129]

For the first time in years, however, the North Korean ambassador, who had been with the UN diplomat in Pyongyang, showed up. So did Secretary General Guterres and Secretary Tillerson. While the ambassador advanced his government's position—which was not what the other diplomats wanted to hear—his presence was surprising.[130]

Then, the North Korean envoy came to see Feltman, ostensibly to drop off a letter from Ri Yong Ho thanking him for his visit. But he also dropped a hint to pay close attention to the Supreme Leader's New Year's address. Days later, Kim Jong Un announced that "I am willing to send a delegation" to the Winter Olympics to be hosted by South Korea next month.[131]

The North Korean diplomat visited Feltman again, ostensibly to make sure he understood what Kim had said. The ambassador also relayed a personal message from the vice foreign minister who had been Feltman's host in Pyongyang: "I hope you listened carefully [to the speech] and thought of our discussions."[132]

The American diplomat realized that his trip to North Korea may have been the most important mission of his career. Looking back, Feltman had no idea that the three weeks between the visit and Kim's New Year's speech would change everything. "I think we played a useful function. I don't think we played a decisive role," he concluded.[133]

In fact, Kim Jong Un may have already decided to shift gears. The chairman rode his white horse up snow-covered Mt. Paektu the day after Feltman left Pyongyang, mimicking what his grandfather had done when he was fighting the Japanese. It meant Kim was about to make an important decision. The odds-on favorite was that he would move forward with engagement.[134]

Exactly why Pyongyang shifted gears remains a matter for conjecture. If Andy Kim and the CIA were right, the North Koreans had been planning all along to open the door to diplomacy once they had completed their WMD tests. That moment arrived in November.

General McMaster believed maximum pressure forced the North Koreans to switch from confrontation to cooperation.[135] But even if maximum pressure played a role, the switch didn't happen until after the North Koreans had built a missile that could destroy American cities with a nuclear warhead.

The North Korean vice foreign minister, who escorted Feltman to the Pyongyang Airport, may have provided an important clue. "You get to fly back to New York, but I have to prepare a report for our bosses on your visit," he told the envoy. At the very least, Feltman's visit reinforced the case for renewed dialogue.[136]

President Trump's message, however, had to have been the diplomatic equivalent of "shock and awe." No one had expected it. Kim Jong Un now had the prospect of achieving an objective his grandfather and father had pursued for decades: a face-to-face meeting with a sitting American president.

CHAPTER FOURTEEN

"Now, he won't lose his early morning sleep anymore."

PYEONGCHANG COUNTY IN SOUTH KOREA is a popular hiking and skiing destination not far from Seoul and the DMZ. Its long, snowy winters and mountains covering most of its territory made it a natural choice for hosting the 23rd Winter Olympic Games.

The Olympics had been a springboard for diplomacy with North Korea before. The 1988 Seoul summer games helped the South Korean military dictatorship reach out to Pyongyang as it transitioned to a democracy. President Ronald Reagan followed its lead with his own initiative.[1]

History repeated itself with the 2018 Winter Games. South Korea had been sending the North Koreans messages for months through its own secret spy channel, code-named "Moon Road." They only responded "message received."[2] After Kim Jong Un's surprise New Year's pronouncement, the two Koreas were "all of a sudden talking to each other," an American official recalled.[3]

A few days after Kim's speech, Trump and Moon decided to encourage the North Koreans to come to Pyeongchang. They delayed two long-standing joint military exercises. General Dunford also postponed missile tests set for before and after the games.[4]

When the North Koreans confirmed they would show up, the American embassy in Seoul swung into action. The staff fielded urgent requests from South Korea for waivers and exemptions, covering everything from sanctions that prevented North Koreans from traveling South to the UN's ban on North Korea importing luxury items such as hockey equipment that Canada wanted to donate to Pyongyang's team. Everything needed to be in place by February when the games began.[5]

Overseas delegations converged on Pyeongchang. Naturally, everyone expected that talks would ease tensions. Hearing that Kim Yo Jong, the leader's sister, would attend, becoming the first member of the ruling family to visit South Korea, the American embassy figured anything was possible.[6]

The youngest of Kim Jong Il's seven children, she was called "my sweet princess" by her father. Kim Yo Jong sat next to him at family dinners in the chair reserved for his wives. After her mother died, she kept the seat on a permanent basis.[7]

After her father died, she became her brother's tour manager and the driving force behind developing his cult of personality. In 2017, Kim Yo Jong was named only the second woman appointed as an alternate member of the Politburo.[8]

U.S. representation at the games was equally important. But Rex Tillerson turned down an invitation.[9] Instead, the president sent Mike Pence, who shared McMaster's assessment that Kim was mounting a charm offensive to relieve pressure on his regime. The vice president had ignored the Secret Service's advice in 2017 and walked up to the border, folded his arms across his chest, and peered silently into the North. He "thought it was important that people on the other side of the DMZ see our resolve in my face."[10]

Pence's Pyeongchang performance was no different. He skipped a dinner hosted by Moon rather than share a seat at the table with Kim Yo Jong. Then, at the opening ceremony, he sat less than ten feet apart from her, staring straight ahead. Photos of the stony-faced Pence prompted international criticism.[11]

The vice president was deliberately attempting to scuttle South Korea's diplomatic matchmaking. A secret session that President Moon and his staff had brokered for him with Kim after the opening ceremony raised suspicions among his staff.[12] Asked why the North Koreans wanted to meet, the South Koreans told a Pence aide, "It really doesn't matter who wants to meet first."[13]

Already skeptical about any meeting with the chairman's sister, the vice president's staff coached Pence to be disrespectful at the opening ceremony. Then, the North Koreans might pull out. Sure enough, Kim Yo Jong

Vice President Mike Pence and Mrs. Karen Pence attend the 2018 Winter
Olympics Opening Ceremony at the Pyeongchang Olympic Stadium
on February 9, 2018, in Pyeongchang, South Korea. Seated behind them are
Kim Yo Jong and the North Korean delegation while South Korean President
Moon Jae-in and Mrs. Kim Jung-sook are seated next to them, applauding.
Official White House photo by D. Myles Cullen.

informed Moon the next morning she was canceling the session, possibly because her brother may have witnessed the snub.[14]

The South Koreans were more successful in their talks with Pence. President Moon had been trying to persuade Trump, who was seemingly fixated with maximum pressure, to meet Kim Jong Un. This time, Pence agreed to pressure and engagement at the same time. Seoul could also talk to the North Koreans first, raising the prospect that Moon would pull off the first Korean summit in a decade.[15]

He was in luck. The "Ivanka Trump" of North Korea wasn't in Seoul just to flash her "Mona Lisa smile." Kim Yo Jong was there to deliver a summit invitation to Moon. He cautioned her not to forget the Americans. Even though his top advisors were resisting, Trump had informed the South Korean leader a few weeks earlier that he would be willing to meet her brother.[16]

The real Ivanka would attend the closing ceremony. By then the chairman's sister had left, replaced by Kim Yong Chol. No meeting, secret or otherwise, was likely with the "scary dude," according to one American official, even though he sat a few feet away from her.[17] But the president's daughter kept a smile on her face in case of a chance encounter. One canceled session with a North Korean official was enough for her father, who was on a glide path to a summit.[18]

There was no U.S.–North Korea meeting at the Olympics, but the president and the North Koreans still edged toward talks. Kim Yong Chol told the press Pyongyang was open to negotiations. Pence signaled on his way home that preliminary talks were fine. Trump delivered the same message: "We want to talk also," but "only under the right conditions."[19]

Events moved quickly. A few days later, Moon's intelligence chief, Suh Hoon, and his national security advisor, Ambassador Chung Eui-yong, boarded a jet at an airfield near Seoul. Landing in Pyongyang an hour later, the two envoys unpacked at their guesthouse and proceeded to the Workers' Party Headquarters. They would soon be the first South Korean officials to meet Kim Jong Un.[20]

A smiling chairman and his sister greeted them. Over a four-hour dinner, Kim Jong Un presented himself as a man of action, a well-informed problem solver with a keen grasp of world events. He didn't want to cling to old ideas. Kim wanted to be flexible. He wanted to seize the moment.[21]

For the two envoys, seizing the moment meant completing discussions that Kim Yong Chol had started at the Olympics about a summit. They suggested a meeting in Pyongyang, Seoul, or Panmunjom. Kim agreed to the last option. Since time was short, the South Koreans proposed a hotline to connect the two leaders just in case of any problems. Kim agreed.[22]

Chung and Suh also observed that their diplomacy would be short-circuited unless Kim agreed to talk to the Americans and discuss giving up his nuclear weapons. "I know" and "I understand you," the chairman replied. He would do both, even hold a summit with President Trump, whom he knew was interested in meeting.[23]

Kim had two other surprises up his sleeve. He was willing to stop WMD tests to help create a better atmosphere for diplomacy. "I was sorry to hear that President Moon Jae-in had to convene meetings early in the morning because of our missile launches," Kim joked. "Now, he won't lose his early morning sleep anymore."[24]

The chairman also didn't have a problem with the upcoming joint U.S.–South Korean military exercises. That was a relief. Chung and Suh had been worried diplomacy would be derailed if Pyongyang demanded they had to be canceled.

His senior envoy, a general, made it clear in a separate conversation that he and the armed forces did have a problem with the joint military exercises. But his boss's word was final.[25]

The trip was a resounding success. A Korean summit was in the offing, the stage was set for a Trump-Kim meeting, and the North Koreans seemed poised to denuclearize. Kim had also offered to stop WMD testing and wouldn't object if the military exercises moved forward.

The two envoys returned home, briefed President Moon, and held a press conference. Three days later, they were in the Oval Office with President Trump.

"I get it! I get it!"

Ambassador Chung phoned General McMaster before leaving for Washington to fill him in on his meeting with Kim Jong Un. The South Korean envoy had been careful not to tip his hand to the press, but he told McMaster that Kim Jong Un was ready to meet Donald Trump.[26]

The general was all for a summit—it might succeed where past negotiations had failed. But he was also concerned about reducing maximum pressure too soon. Like Pence, he believed Kim was desperate for sanctions relief. Moreover, the ink wasn't dry on the new sanctions passed by the Security Council in December. Pyongyang might think it could revert to the old game of "provocations followed by concessions."[27]

McMaster knew Trump would jump at a summit. The president had been telling his aides, "Wouldn't it be great!" He didn't know the president had already tasked Pompeo to prepare to visit Pyongyang. Slated to be replaced soon, McMaster still wanted to make sure Trump understood the pros and cons of meeting Kim.[28]

The national security advisor choreographed a logical series of meetings over two days. He would meet Chung alone, while Gina Haspel, the deputy director of the CIA, would meet Suh Hoon separately, followed by a session with the president's top advisors. Then, Trump would give Chung and Suh his decision. Tillerson and Pompeo, both out of town, would be back by then and could also weigh in with the president.[29]

As was so often the case, Trump proved to be the wild card. When he heard the envoys were in the White House, the president tweeted, "The World is watching and waiting! May be false hope, but the US is ready to go hard in either direction!" He ordered an aide to bring them up if they were still in the building, cutting short the South Koreans' briefing for a room filled with American officials.[30]

Meanwhile, McMaster and Haspel rushed over to the Oval Office to fill Trump in before they arrived. The general agreed that a summit was the way to go but pointed out the disadvantages of dialing pressure back prematurely. He was cut short when the White House chief of staff, John Kelly, ushered American and South Korean officials into the Oval Office.[31]

Chung and Trump sat in separate chairs in front of the fireplace under a gold-framed portrait of George Washington. Arrayed on two sofas, the rest of the Americans listened as Moon's envoy briefed the president.[32]

"Thank you very much for sending Ivanka to Korea. She was an enormous success," Chung told Trump. "There is even a fan club for her in South Korea."[33]

A happy president looked at his aides and said, "I told you she was the one for the job."[34]

Chung relayed what Kim had promised. He would denuclearize, refrain from WMD tests, not object to the United States and South Korea holding their next joint exercise, and he wanted to meet the president. Chung painted Kim as a well-meaning leader trapped by his authoritarian system and desperately needing a meeting. "A lot of it was horseshit," a White House aide recalled.[35]

The president accepted the invitation on the spot, brushing off objections by exclaiming, "I get it! I get it!" One American official recalled that Trump looked around the room and snapped, "Do you know why Clinton, Bush and Obama failed? Because they were listening to people like you."[36]

"How about April?" Trump asked. They agreed to aim for May after Chung suggested that it would be better to hold the session after the Korean summit slated for that month. The South Koreans hadn't expected Trump to agree to a summit right away or to hold one so soon.[37]

Then, the president surprised everyone again. Would the South Koreans announce he was willing to meet Kim Jong Un? The two envoys agreed. They were instantly hustled off to draft a statement with McMaster, without a chance to report to their boss, President Moon. Standing in the door of the press briefing room, an excited Trump told reporters there would be a major announcement on North Korea. He had never done that before.[38]

At 7:00 P.M., Ambassador Chung exited the West Wing with two other South Korean officials. He told an array of microphones and a crowd of reporters that Donald Trump had agreed to meet Kim Jong Un in May. The White House press secretary tweeted confirmation shortly afterwards.[39]

Trump's sudden, erratic, and shocking move had been in the mix ever since the early 2017 policy review. He had a summit in mind even as his rhetorical battle with Kim Jong Un escalated. And it was more than obvious when Jeffrey Feltman carried Trump's secret message on his trip to Pyongyang.

As for the North Koreans, a summit with the American president had been on their minds at least since Bill Taylor's session with Kim Il Sung in 1992. It wasn't clear if Pyongyang was serious about denuclearization. The big difference was the North Korean threat that now placed American cities in danger.

Critics harped that Trump had made a big mistake in giving Pyongyang a high-profile photo op with an American president. Regardless of his quest to embellish his own reputation, that would be a small price to pay if the WMD threat could be stopped.

Trump's request that the South Korean envoys announce his major policy move was also perplexing. As one White House aide recalled, Ambassador Chung often "characterized things in a way that didn't exactly happen." Perhaps Trump wanted them to own it if anything went wrong.[40]

Just to be sure, Trump asked the CIA to check out the South Korean envoy's story. American spies confirmed with their North Korean counterparts that Kim was willing to stop WMD tests, accept the upcoming military exercises, and meet Trump. But they couldn't reaffirm his intention to denuclearize. Only Kim Jong Un could use that word. Mike Pompeo would have to visit their country to verify what he had said.[41]

"Mr. Chairman, I am still trying to kill you."

Pompeo and Andy Kim flew to Pyongyang in secret over Easter weekend. North Korean fighter jets shadowed their aircraft. Their pilot joked that a rescue team was ready to recover their remains.[42] The mission, as the *Washington Post* described it, was an "extraordinary meeting between one of Trump's most trusted emissaries and the authoritarian head of a rogue state."[43]

The North Koreans rolled out the red carpet. Their top officials, including Kim Yong Chol, Pompeo's new counterpart, lined up at the airport to shake hands. The CIA director and Andy Kim were whisked off in a motorcade traveling through blocked-off roads in the heart of the city. They weren't sure where they were going.[44]

The Americans were welcomed by Kim Yong Chol in their guesthouse conference room. He reaffirmed the chairman's promises to the South Koreans, but also wanted to know what the CIA director was going to say before he met his boss. Pompeo needed face-to-face confirmation. He was also there to deliver a letter from Trump and discuss moving forward. "Get some rest, I will be back," the general responded. He returned a short time later. "I think the chairman is ready to see you."[45]

After a fifteen-minute drive, Pompeo arrived at a heavily armed office building. Tall soldiers armed with machine guns were lined up a meter apart along the final quarter mile. Pompeo and his aide joked that Kim Jong Un was sending a message: "Don't think about a 'bloody nose' strike."[46]

Standing at the end of a long red carpet, Kim Yo Jong, and then her brother, greeted the two Americans. The smiling dictator opened the conversation: "Mr. Director, I didn't think you would show up. I know you have been trying to kill me."[47]

Indeed, Pompeo had publicly mused about "separating the regime" from the North Korean people. Still, he didn't expect a joke about assassination. Determined not to smile so his visit couldn't be used for propaganda, the CIA director still leaned in with his own humor. "Mr. Chairman, I am still trying to kill you."[48]

The young dictator led the Americans into a conference room. He and Kim Yong Chol sat on one side of the table, and the CIA director and his aide sat on the other. Awkward, even nervous at first, Kim Jong Un read from a script, then relaxed and ignored it. The session lasted for hours, interrupted every forty-five minutes or so for him to take a phone call. Pompeo thought that was just an excuse for a cigarette break.[49]

Trump's envoy was straightforward. North Korea should eliminate its weapons of mass destruction and establish a broader peace between North and South. Then, the United States would lift its economic restrictions and encourage other countries to invest in North Korea.

The proposal must have resonated with Kim. He had started the conversation by relating how he intended to redirect North Korea's focus on the military to developing its civilian economy.[50]

Pompeo delivered his "sales pitch," hoping to convince Kim of three things: First, Kim would survive a transition from a nuclear state to a non-nuclear state, unlike Libya's Gaddafi. Second, "a non-nuclear North Korea would survive and prosper." Pompeo described investments that "could go to his dream projects, like a beautiful international tourist resort at Wonsan."[51]

Last, but not least, the CIA director reassured Kim that Washington would protect him against China. When Pompeo told him the Chinese had said he wanted U.S. troops off the peninsula, Kim "laughed, pounded the table with sheer joy and exclaimed they were liars." Pyongyang had made that demand in the past. Like his father at the height of engagement, however, Kim wanted the troops to stay to protect him from China.[52]

Pompeo asked the chairman to confirm the commitments he had made to the South Korean envoys, especially denuclearization. "I have two daughters, and I don't expect them to carry those nuclear weapons in their backpack for the rest of their lives," Kim replied. "So yes, I do want to get rid of it when the time is right."[53]

After Kim praised Trump's "America First" policy as brilliant, he reiterated that he wanted to meet the first president he could trust. That would be a great step to end seventy years of hostility. Pompeo turned over Trump's letter, which said he would be glad to meet Kim. The two agreed to set up talks to discuss the details.[54]

After a farewell dinner, the leader's sister handed over a letter for Trump. "I'm prepared to cooperate with you in sincerity and dedication," the North Korean leader wrote, "to accomplish a great feat that no one in the past had been able to achieve and that is unexpected by the whole world."[55]

Mike Pompeo had successfully navigated his first encounter with North Koreans, with the help of Andy Kim, who warned him not to get bogged down in responding to harsh lectures and endless debates.

Moreover, the trip allowed Pompeo and Andy Kim to take the measure of the international man of mystery. They believed Kim "was no accidental leader." The CIA director thought he was insecure, but his aide bought into the notion that Kim Jong Un was a pragmatic risktaker.[56]

Andy Kim, however, couldn't rescue Pompeo from clashing with Kim Yong Chol, who the CIA director thought was "one of the nastiest guys" he had ever encountered." Pompeo was no slouch, however. Supporters of his opponent in the 2014 congressional campaign proudly wore stickers proclaiming, "Mike Bullied Me."[57]

The two men took an instant dislike to each other. When Pompeo shook Kim Yong Chol's hand after his plane landed, the general didn't even say "hello." He remarked, "We have eaten grass for 50 years. We can eat grass for another 50 years."

Considering that no one in North Korea's elite had to suffer from starvation, Pompeo responded, "General Kim, nice to see you too. I can't wait for lunch. And I prefer my grass steamed."[58]

The North Korean envoy insisted later in the visit that the Americans stay in Pyongyang longer, but the director refused. And when he noticed that an assistant had to help the general make a call on his cell phone, Pompeo whispered to his aide that he would tell Mattis not to worry about the North Korean military.[59]

Pompeo's trip marked the beginning of a new feud with a North Korean, and the end of an old one with Rex Tillerson. As Pompeo moved closer to Trump's inner circle, the secretary of state had drifted further away. Rumors that Tillerson was on his way out took on a name of their own, "Rexit."[60]

The secretary had little credibility left with Trump, the North Koreans, or with his own advisors. After his hard-to-fathom refusal to go to the Winter Olympics, Joe Yun, his special envoy, retired.[61] Tillerson even tried to stop Trump from jumping at a summit, arguing he should hold talks first.[62]

Trump fired the secretary hours after he landed at Andrews Air Force Base on March 13. "We were not really thinking the same," the president told reporters. That had been obvious for months.

"He has my trust. He has my support," Trump remarked, naming Mike Pompeo secretary of state. His appointment as America's top diplomat and encounter with Kim Jong Un had solidified Pompeo's role as the one person the president thought could help him end the North Korean threat.[63]

"A new history begins now."

A week before Mike Pompeo visited Pyongyang, a vintage train, painted a distinctive drab green with bulletproof, dark-tinted windows, pulled into Beijing.[64] Kim Jong Un was in China for his first meeting with Xi Jinping, in fact, his first encounter with any foreign leader.

The two men had good reason to meet with two summits in the offing. China had its own vital interests on the Korean Peninsula despite Xi's Mar-a-Lago encounter with Trump. And Kim wanted Xi's support, especially if diplomacy failed and Trump threatened him again.[65]

At first, the visit was kept secret, given the bad relationship between the two princelings. But Xi and Kim acted like long-lost comrades. Photos of smiling and laughing Chinese officials seated on pink leather couches with the North Korean leader on his train accentuated the positive press coverage.[66]

Evidence mounted that Kim Jong Un was serious about diplomacy even before his visit to Beijing. After the Trump-Kim summit was announced, the state-run media declared "a sign of change" in relations and cut back references to the American threat. Pyongyang also publicized what Kim said in private to Pompeo after his visit, as well as his pledge to suspend WMD tests and shut down the nuclear test site.[67]

Days after Pompeo left Pyongyang, the chairman adopted an "all for the economy" policy, 180 degrees from his father's "all for the military" strategy. His pledge to create an "international environment favorable for the socialist economic construction" was a green light for diplomacy. "Unlike Godot, the North Korean pivot has finally arrived," Bob Carlin observed.[68]

Skeptics argued that North Korea wanted to escape sanctions or make it harder for Trump to threaten him. The WMD test moratorium was reversible. The nuclear test site had been crippled by multiple blasts, anyway. Kim didn't mention denuclearization, wasn't interested in giving up his weapons, and was still producing bombs.[69]

Sig Hecker, the former lab director, believed, however, that the moratorium was "a serious step towards denuclearization."[70] And that the unilateral halt without demanding anything in return was a new twist.

The chairman's April pronouncements only strengthened President Moon's determination to move ahead. His conviction to engage North Korea had been kindled first when he led preparations for Roh Moo-hyun's summit with Kim Jong Il in 2007 and, second, by Kim Dae-jung's dying wishes. Now, he was about to follow in the footsteps of the two South Korean leaders he most admired.

Moon's Blue House established an "inter-Korean preparation committee." His staff proposed that the summit's objective should be to figure out who Kim was as a person. Part of the reason was that, like the U.S. intelligence community, his experts reported that the chairman was someone with whom common sense didn't work.

But Moon replied, "That is not enough." He wanted to include details that built on previous vague inter-Korean agreements that the two sides could implement.[71]

The committee went to work, fine-tuning a summit declaration, choreographing the meeting, and sharpening a public relations campaign to build support. President Moon, the only one in the Blue House with summit experience, frequently attended committee meetings giving tips and orders.[72]

Aside from advancing inter-Korean relations, Moon had to find "middle ground between a cunning enemy to the North and an impulsive ally in the United States," the *New York Times* reported. The South Korean president was determined to make sure that Kim Jong Un understood the importance of his summit with Trump.[73]

Denuclearization was a case in point, where Moon had to tread lightly. Pyongyang had previously insisted on only talking to the United States about it. But the South Koreans also thought the American plan for total nuclear disarmament was "an impossible concept," according to one official.

Seoul hit on middle ground with the idea of playing back Kim Jong Un's words, "complete denuclearization," to its two envoys. The North Koreans couldn't object to that. The phrase would hopefully lay the foundation for talks between Trump and Kim.[74]

The rest of the South's draft covered "bread-and-butter" issues. Measures to assure one another that war wasn't likely or inevitable were important given tensions in 2017. Establishing "liaison offices" to facilitate communication was another priority. The two Koreas had no way of communicating except in sporadic meetings.[75]

Economic cooperation was part of Moon's game plan. The president believed more cooperation would be good for the North. It would also bolster Seoul's gross domestic product. He intended to hand Kim a thumb drive with an explanation of his plan. After the chairman's April announcement, the proposal was tweaked to help him achieve his economic priorities.[76]

The two Koreas also had a common objective fueled by national pride: guaranteeing that the summit would be an all-Korean affair. The United Nations Command, with contributions from twenty-two countries, was responsible for monitoring activities in the DMZ. The South Koreans, seconded by the North, asked, "Can we have everyone out of there except the security detail on both sides?" a UN official recalled. The command stayed out of sight.[77]

Preparations moved forward. Pyongyang's past record of cooperation at the DMZ had been spotty, but both sides were polite, cordial, and committed to success. Even the two security details worked together. No matter how close the cooperation or meticulous the planning, however, Moon's bodyguards were ready if something went wrong. The UN and South Korean troops were prepared to get him out of harm's way, if necessary.[78]

Ironically, the biggest impediment to a successful summit turned out to be a fifty-yard-long footbridge that offered what could be the perfect photo op. The bridge crossed a wetland not far from where a runaway North Korean soldier had been shot in November. Kim and Moon could be photographed as they crossed it conversing.[79]

Upon inspection, however, the bridge was unstable, and only wide enough for two skinny UN monitors to walk side by side to reach their patrol areas. One officer recalled, "I don't think you had to be a genius to figure out that the two leaders, one fairly rotund, wouldn't be able to do that." Workers quickly strengthened, widened, and painted the structure blue, a nod to the UN's colors and the Korean unification flag.[80]

Nature, however, then threatened the photo op with bees swarming dangerously near the bridge hours before the summit. President Moon's bodyguards spotted the bees and wanted to move the stroll. Miraculously, they had vanished by the time the two men arrived, replaced by singing birds. One official observed, "It seemed to be a divine scene."[81]

Final preparations were intense. A declaration was finalized despite shouting, walkouts, and uncomfortable silences. North and South rehearsed. Seoul's publicity slogan, "Peace, a New Start," was set. The world was able to follow the meeting on an online platform and Twitter created a high-five emoji. Over three thousand journalists signed up at the media center. North Korea was ready to broadcast key moments live.[82]

Moon left the Blue House at 8:06 A.M. on April 27 in a long motorcade. Supporters waved South Korean flags and banners proclaiming, "Denuclearization! Best wishes for a successful summit!" His car stopped once, allowing him to assure onlookers he would "do well" today.[83]

Less than an hour later, Moon's motorcade pulled up to the Peace House on the southern side of the border village where the summit would be held.[84]

Kim Jong Un had already left Pyongyang for his one-hundred-mile journey to Panmunjom on the "Reunification Highway." The multilane road, interrupted by checkpoints and with tank traps visible, stretched south from the flatlands around Pyongyang to the DMZ. Signs along the way showed the distance to Seoul.

At 9:25 A.M., President Moon and his aides headed for the red carpet facing the demarcation line that had separated the two Koreas for almost seven decades. Surrounded by his advisors and bodyguards, Kim Jong Un, dressed in his black Mao suit, emerged from a building. They all peeled off as he headed for the border to greet the waiting Moon.[85]

Standing on their respective sides of the line, the two leaders shook hands. An exchange of pleasantries led to the summit's first dramatic choreographed moment. Kim accepted Moon's invitation to step over the demarcation line and became the first North Korean leader to cross into South Korea.[86]

Then came the summit's first unscripted moment. Led by Kim Jong Un, Moon crossed over the line into the North.[87] Even the security team responsible for the president's safety laughed and applauded. Riveted to video screens in Seoul, South Koreans clapped and cheered. The scene was instantly broadcast around the world.[88]

Moon and Kim headed back into the South. They posed for photos with two children who presented Kim with flowers, and then the leaders entered the Peace House, escorted by South Koreans dressed in the traditional costumes of a royal guard. "A new history begins now. At the starting point of a generation and history of peace," the chairman wrote in the visitors' book.[89]

It was time to get down to business. Moon and Kim moved to a reception room where a painting of Mount Kumgang, a South Korean tourist destination in the North that was shut down in 2008, covered one wall. Six chairs, with seatbacks decorated with the outline of the Korean Peninsula, were arrayed around an oval-shaped wooden table. The two men's seats were separated by 2,018 millimeters—a nod to the year of the summit.[90]

The leaders talked in private for the next two hours. Kim was very polite and respectful. He treated the older South Korean like an uncle.

Moon, in turn, advised Kim that he couldn't both keep his nuclear arsenal and develop his economy. If he did, North Korea would remain sanctioned and isolated. The chairman told him he "knew that well."[91]

"How can we trust the Trump administration?" Kim asked. The North Korean leader was really wondering whether he could trust Donald Trump.

"There is no choice but to trust him," Moon replied, according to an aide. "We will be in a facilitating role," but "you are not the only one": a frank admission for an American ally.[92]

Moon and Kim planted a pine tree dating back to 1953—the year the Armistice was signed—after lunch, then walked to the famous footbridge. Video of their conversation aired on worldwide television. Since the microphones were muted, only birds chirping could be heard in the background as Moon and Kim sat on benches after crossing the bridge.[93]

The conversation lasted longer than planned. The South Korean leader recalled that Kim "had a strong will to denuclearize"; however, it would have to be done "step by step" since the weapons protected his regime. In return, the international community should gradually lift sanctions. He asked the South Korean president to relay his message to Washington.

The North Korean leader also kept quizzing Moon about the United States. How could he alleviate skepticism that he was committed to denuclearize? How should a summit with the United States be conducted? According to Moon, Kim worried about North Korea's lack of experience in conducting such a meeting with the United States.[94]

All that was left was to sign the declaration. Moon and Kim reentered the Peace House lobby, sat at a desk, signed, posed for photos holding hands lifted high, bear-hugged, and shook hands with aides. Moon announced that the North Korean leader had confirmed "a completely nuclear-free Korean peninsula is their common goal." The two men also "agreed to end the unstable armistice structure and construct a permanent and strong peace structure through a peace agreement."[95]

Despite laughter and toasts, a ten-course dinner caused an international incident. Dishes from both countries were served. But the two leaders also cracked open "Dokdo" mousses, resulting in a Japanese protest. That was the Korean name of an island group claimed by both countries.[96]

The summit ended a little before 9:30 P.M. after a musical performance outside the Peace House. Then, Kim Jong Un and his wife, who had joined him after the celebrated bridge crossing, boarded their limousine. They rolled down a window and waved as the motorcade passed between two lines of the traditional honor guard and disappeared from view. A Korean American officer texted his family, "I think we have taken the first big step toward a possible peace."[97]

"There was a frenzy the next day that South Korea was in a new era of peace," an American official recalled. President Moon's approval rating shot up to over 70 percent. South Korean tourists flocked to the DMZ. Long lines formed outside restaurants serving Pyongyang-style cold noodles, which had played a starring role at the banquet.[98]

Equally frenetic, President Trump tweeted, "KOREAN WAR TO END." However, his prediction that "something very dramatic could happen" seemed premature. Wendy Sherman, President Clinton's North Korea envoy, dryly remarked, "Dialogue at this moment is certainly better than a march to war."[99]

The summit's rampant symbolism obscured its accomplishments. The Panmunjom declaration achieved exactly what the South Koreans had hoped: lofty pronouncements coupled with specific steps to improve relations and reduce the risk of war. Future talks would build on those steps. The denuclearization pledge might have been vague, but the South Koreans achieved their limited goal: to open the door for more talks between Trump and Kim.[100]

Any doubts that North Korea would implement its provisions were dispelled immediately. Within four days of the summit, North Korea's military tore down its DMZ loudspeakers, used for decades for propaganda purposes. South Korea's military, which had told the Blue House it would take months to dismantle its own loudspeakers, immediately followed suit.[101]

The Panmunjom summit turned out to be a rare occasion when John Bolton, the new national security advisor, agreed with the *New York Times*. Both thought it was "almost substance free." Bolton gave Trump an op-ed penned by a fellow neoconservative who argued the meeting was "P. T. Barnum–style, a sucker-is-born-every-minute diplomacy." Trump's new advisor would do everything he could in the months ahead to derail the president's initiative.[102]

"The father of our nuclear arsenal"

John Bolton's eighteen-month courtship of Donald Trump finally paid off. The president told him, "I've got a job for you that is probably the most powerful job in the White House." The next day, Trump tweeted that John Bolton would be the new national security advisor.[103]

Nationalist, neoconservative, and an uber-hawk, the single-minded Bolton was his party's poster boy for advocating regime change and the use of military force. His big break came when he walked into a Tallahassee library during the Bush-Gore 2000 election clash and declared, "I am here to stop the count." Afterwards, Vice President-elect Cheney reportedly had said that Bolton should get any job he wanted. He did, working for Colin Powell at State.[104]

Bolton was a "kiss-up, kick-down sort of guy" who put intimidation to good use. Bullying the chief monitor of the global treaty banning chemical weapons not to oppose the Bush march to war in Iraq, he shared that the United States knew where his family was.[105]

In an ironic moment, Bolton told Trump on December 7, months before his appointment, that the United States should launch a preemptive attack on the North. The significance of the date seems to have been lost on them. Bolton didn't care about the horrendous consequences of a conflict. Even Trump confided in McMaster, "He is going to get us into a war."[106]

Bolton's history of disloyalty to his bosses should have been another showstopper, particularly for a president obsessed with loyalty and obeisance. Bolton had sabotaged Colin Powell at every turn and cheered when the 1994 deal collapsed. The North Koreans later ironically praised him as "the father of our nuclear arsenal."[107]

Bolton's appointment set the stage for an inevitable clash with Mike Pompeo. "Sick at heart" when he heard that Trump had signed on to a summit with Kim Jong Un, Bolton was determined to stop it.[108] Pompeo, on the other hand, followed Trump's lead. He was president and the secretary's meal ticket should he later decide to run for the top job.[109]

The national security advisor's long-standing hatred of the State Department also fueled his fire. He was a big believer in Senator Barry Goldwater's view: "I'd fire every S.O.B. on the first seven floors (the secretary was on the eighth floor), then start hiring again." During his time at State, Bolton derisively called the Bureau for East Asia and Pacific Affairs, which supported diplomacy with Pyongyang, "E-A-P-sers."[110]

If Bolton and Pompeo could agree on anything, it was how to denuclearize North Korea. For Bolton, Libya was the gold standard. After the 2003 war in Iraq, a scared Muammar Gaddafi abandoned his nascent WMD program. Reintegrating his country into the international community would only come after the program had been entirely dismantled.[111]

Pompeo agreed, after concluding that Washington had been fooled into granting concessions in return for promises that were never kept. He later falsely claimed that President Clinton had naïvely signed the Agreed Framework even though he "knew it wouldn't work." Like Bolton, Pompeo believed "only a massive first step" by Kim to give up his arsenal should result in the lifting of sanctions.[112]

The "Libya model," unfortunately, also featured the eventual overthrow and murder of Gaddafi—something that didn't trouble Bolton, even if it applied to Kim Jong Un and North Korea. Instead, Pompeo latched onto "complete, verifiable, and irreversible denuclearization," or CVID, a term first coined by Bush neocons that meant the same thing.

The bureaucracy went to work. One White House aide recalled, "Bolton wanted everything in it, and the kitchen sink." Pyongyang would have to give up its nuclear, chemical, and biological weapons as well as its ballistic missiles, dismantle its facilities, and submit to inspections. It would all be done in one year, before North Korea would receive any benefits.[113]

Bolton had his job cut out for him if he wanted to head off Trump's summit, however. The president thought Kim's test moratorium was "big progress." Bolton labeled it as "just another propaganda ploy." Trump tweeted, "Thank you, a very smart and gracious gesture," after Kim pledged to dismantle his nuclear test site. Bolton thought it "pure fluff." He saw the Panmunjom declaration as "remarkably anodyne." Trump wanted to hold his own summit earlier.[114]

Pompeo's second trip to Pyongyang in early May moved the president closer to his goal and Bolton further away from his. The secretary accomplished his main mission, retrieving three American detainees, after he made it clear there would be no summit unless they were released before he left at sundown.[115]

Pompeo also unveiled CVID. The secretary told Kim he wanted to "back up a truck and take away his whole stash" before sanctions were lifted. Naturally, the chairman was unhappy. But the secretary felt empowered. The president had just quit Obama's 2015 Iran agreement that stopped its nuclear program. The message was clear: the United States wasn't going to sign up to "crappy deals."[116]

The two sides agreed Singapore seemed to be the best place to hold the summit, although not before considering other options: Pyongyang, Ulaanbaatar, Geneva, Hawaii, and Coronado near San Diego. They all were rejected by one side or the other.[117]

Pompeo's visit also confirmed he wasn't going to have a bromance with Kim Yong Chol. The secretary tried something new: relationship building. He mentioned over lunch that he and friends would relax, have a beer, and watch a ball game on weekends. Kim replied that he liked to study political thought and think about how to best support his leader.[118]

The trip had been a triumph. Even though Pompeo and the three detainees arrived home in the middle of the night, hundreds of people and dozens of TV cameras were waiting. The president was on "cloud nine," Bolton recalled.

Trump tweeted the next day, "The highly anticipated meeting between myself and Kim Jong Un will take place in Singapore on June 12th. We will both make it a very special moment for World Peace."[119]

Bolton tried a different tack. Aware that his remark would trigger a harsh North Korean response, he told the press that the administration was "looking at the Libya model."

The national security advisor later claimed that the president thought he had been "very good," although he didn't like references to Libya because Gaddafi had been overthrown. Pompeo recalled, however, that Trump "blew a gasket" and ordered the secretary to "shut Bolton out of the North Korea process." Trump also agreed with President Moon, who was visiting Washington, that the Libya model was a nonstarter.[120]

The president, however, only made matters worse in a subsequent interview. He denied the Libya model was what he had in mind for North Korea but didn't leave it at that. "We decimated that country. That would happen if we don't make a deal with North Korea." Pence gave Bolton a high five, thinking the president had his back.[121]

Three days later, the vice president chimed in on Fox News that "this will only end like the Libya model ended if Kim Jong Un doesn't make a deal." When the interviewer pointed out that it sounded like a threat, Pence replied, "Well, I think it's more of a fact."[122]

Uncharacteristically restrained up until then, the North Koreans had to respond. Choe Son Hui condemned Pence for his "ignorant and stupid remarks," called the vice president a "political dummy," and said the choice between a summit or a "nuclear showdown" was up to Washington. Still, she didn't aim any insults at Trump.[123]

Nevertheless, her harsh response gave Bolton the opening he needed. He suggested to Trump that he demand an apology, or "at least imply Singapore would be cancelled without one." Bolton gathered more negative press coverage for an 8:00 A.M. phone call with the president the next morning.[124]

"Jesus, that's strong," Trump reacted to the coverage. He agreed to cancel the summit. It was "inappropriate, at this time, to have this long-planned meeting," he wrote in a letter to Kim.[125] Trump hedged his bet, however, continuing, "if you change your mind . . . please do not hesitate to call me or write."[126]

But then Bolton's "roof fell in." The North Koreans issued a statement that came close to an apology.[127] Kim Jong Un even reassured President Moon at a snap DMZ summit that he was committed to denuclearization.[128] A few days later, the chairman told the Russian foreign minister that "Trump can trust me. Our course to denuclearization is straightforward."[129]

The president reversed course, despite a last-ditch attempt by Bolton to convince him to postpone the summit for a month. In fact, the national security advisor's attempt to scuttle the summit only made matters worse. Trump had a new revelation: that diplomacy was a process. Singapore would just be a "getting-to-know-you" meeting. "We will see where it will lead," Trump tweeted.[130]

With Bolton sidelined, Pompeo pressed ahead. He may have thought he could clinch a deal by himself, but soon realized that managing America's global relations was a full-time job. State didn't have an Andy Kim, but it did have Sung Kim, the American ambassador in Manila with a long history of dealing with North Koreans. He was dispatched to meet Choe Son Hui at the DMZ.

Pompeo also invited Kim Yong Chol to New York to work on preparations for the Singapore session. It would have been easier than talking to the general using a phone card since there were no reliable diplomatic channels. The secretary didn't want a repeat of the time the conversation dropped after the operator warned there was only ten minutes left.[131]

General Kim arrived at JFK Airport on a May 30 flight from Beijing. The two haggled over a summit declaration into the early morning hours in an apartment with sweeping views of Manhattan, the East River, and the UN. But the secretary wouldn't budge off CVID.[132]

Their feud continued. Pompeo, a former tank commander, wore socks with green army men holding pistols, rifles, and bazookas. "Was he sending a message?" one reporter speculated.

Pompeo joked the next day, after Kim had asked to see the socks, that his new pair had pictures of a free, nonnuclear Korean Peninsula—and the general in jail. Kim appeared puzzled.[133]

Luckily, the North Korean envoy had another, more important mission than sparring with Pompeo: to personally deliver a message from Kim Jong Un to Donald Trump. The last time that had happened was eighteen years earlier when Marshal Jo met Bill Clinton in the Oval office. Despite his old age, a suddenly rejuvenated Kim Yong Chol recited the message for the secretary. "My grandfather couldn't have done that," one official observed.[134]

Although Trump's advisors, including Pompeo, had misgivings, the president thought the idea was "very elegant" and "genius." Early the next morning, a convoy of black SUVs carrying Kim left his New York hotel and drove south for a 1:00 P.M. meeting at the White House.[135]

Security was tight. A plainclothes Secret Service agent stood outside the Oval Office. Others lined the hallway at staggered distances, and uniformed officers toting weapons patrolled the driveway. Maybe the spy chief, reputedly responsible for the 2010 *Cheonan* sinking, was a dangerous man? Guards had also been everywhere when Pompeo first met Kim Jong Un.[136]

Just as the North Korean envoy and his escort neared the Oval Office, the general realized he had left the chairman's letter in his car. His interpreter retrieved the message and returned. sweating profusely, resulting in another delay while the Secret Service inspected the envelope's contents.

The planned twenty-minute session stretched to more than an hour. Trump didn't stop talking. Finally, a desperate Kim Yong Chol stood, raised his voice, and begged the president to allow him to say something. It seemed rude, but if the general didn't deliver Kim Jong Un's message, he would be in trouble when he arrived back home.[137]

The "America First" policy was brilliant, the general said. Trump was unique. That was why Kim Jong Un thought he would be a great partner. Then came the punchline. The chairman understood that American military exercises with South Korea were defensive, but his people were scared. As the two leaders' relationship grew, would Trump help convince the North Korean public that a new era was coming?

The president took the bait; he riffed on how the exercises were provocative and expensive. He was ready to reduce them. It was then clear they were up for grabs in any negotiation.[138]

Trump, Pompeo, and Kim emerged from the Oval Office, posed for photos, and proceeded to the North Korean's black SUV. The president announced that the summit was back on for Singapore on June 12. "I think it's going to be a process," he told the press, the same line he had used with Bolton.[139]

Trump called Bolton from Camp David the next day. He was now looking forward, not just to Singapore, but to more than one summit. Frustrated by Trump's wild policy swings, the national security advisor was still reluctant to resign after just weeks in office.[140]

Despite being reassured by White House officials and Pompeo, Bolton was suspicious. He had been excluded from the president's meeting with Kim Yong Chol. The press was already speculating that Bolton wouldn't go to Singapore. "Whether even at this early stage there was more to it than that, I can't say," Bolton recalled. He would soon find out.[141]

CHAPTER FIFTEEN

"This wasn't just another negotiation."

THE DAY AFTER THE snap DMZ summit between President Moon and Kim Jong Un, and a few days before Pompeo met Kim Yong Chol in New York, a group of American officials crossed into North Korea. For the first time in its sixty-year history, the fortified no-man's-land had become a hotbed of denuclearization talks.[1]

Time was short and the pressure was on. Sung Kim and Choe Son Hui, the two negotiators, were old adversaries who hadn't seen each other in almost a decade. President Trump had tweeted, "Our United States team has arrived in North Korea to make arrangements for the Summit between Kim Jong Un and Myself."[2]

Three thousand miles away, Joe Hagin, the White House deputy chief of staff, arrived in Singapore to work out summit logistics with Kim Jong Un's top aide, nicknamed "the Butler." They were to remain there until the summit began.[3]

Sung Kim had drafted a summit declaration before leaving for Panmunjom. "This wasn't just another negotiation," one official recalled. The four-page draft reflected "our maximum approach," CVID. Some officials thought it made negotiating sense. Others believed Choe would dig her heels in.[4]

The skeptics were right. The talks dragged on. The Americans had clothes shipped to them or shopped for new outfits in Seoul. Still, they lived "like Saudi princes out of favor" in the Four Seasons Hotel, one recalled.[5]

The delegation left the hotel every morning for the nearby American embassy, where they checked emails, read instructions from Washington, and made secure phone calls back home. They left at 9:00 A.M. for the hour-long, thirty-mile trip to the DMZ, caucused in a conference room on the southern side of the demarcation line, and then crossed into North Korea to meet Choe. When the talks were over, the Americans crossed back, and drove to the embassy in Seoul.[6]

At the end of the first week, Sarah Sanders, the White House press secretary, announced that the "discussions have been very positive and significant progress has been made." In fact, there had been no progress. Neither side budged.[7]

Mike Pompeo received daily reports, not Bolton. The secretary would then brief the president. Ambassador Kim also had a direct line to Pompeo to discuss how to respond to the North's demands.[8]

The national security advisor was worried that State would drop CVID, even though Pompeo had said that Trump wouldn't agree to anything else. But the president was also "eager for success," and the North Koreans had no intention of accepting that formulation.

"We can't have a bunch of doves take over the delegation!" Trump exclaimed after Bolton spun him. "Tell Pompeo I'll have to take this deal over. We have got to discuss denuclearization [in the Singapore communiqué]. Got to have it!" One official recalled, "It was so easy to ramp Trump up with the idea those f—king State Department weenies are screwing you."[9]

"Get the leader of the delegation on the phone," the president ordered. Trump told a surprised Sung Kim, "I'm the one to sell the deal . . . you shouldn't negotiate denuclearization and you should tell them that," he demanded. "You have to say denuclearization with no wiggle room."[10]

It wasn't every day that an American diplomat got a phone call from the president. But a delegation member recalled that one of Ambassador Kim's superpowers was to defuse the ire of leadership. Denuclearization was 100 percent part of the conversation, just not Bolton's formulation.[11]

The American negotiator must have phoned the secretary right away. An upset Pompeo called Bolton a few minutes later. He seemed to agree when the national security advisor explained he was concerned about "weak draft language in the communiqué." Bolton later wondered whether

Pompeo knew what was going on, but the secretary knew exactly what was going on.[12]

Once Trump announced the June 12 summit date, the Americans raced against the clock. Choe still wouldn't budge. Days before the summit, Ambassador Kim told his delegation, "We need to take this to Singapore and use the urgency to get some movement."[13]

On the eve of the summit, more than three out of four American citizens approved Trump's move, even though half of this majority disapproved of everything else he had done. Critics who had railed about his recklessness in 2017 now said he was too anxious to strike a deal. Progressives determined to impeach Trump now supported him on North Korea.[14]

The president only encouraged critics who thought him reckless and impulsive. "It's about the attitude," he boasted, "The first minute I'll know—just my touch, my feel, that's what I do."

In fact, Trump had been prepared. His aides briefed him on North Korea's WMD programs and conventional military forces. Whether the briefings worked or not, their objective was to "scare the bejesus out of him," according to one aide.[15]

Just before he flew to Singapore, Trump berated America's friends at a multilateral meeting in Quebec. But he still had time to warn Kim Jong Un that their summit was a "one-time shot." Trump also instructed his aides to use his Quebec antics to show Kim that "We don't take any shit." Larry Kudlow, a top economic advisor, told CNN that the president wasn't "going to permit any show of weakness on the trip to negotiate with North Korea."[16]

Nothing, however, could mask the fact that the CVID proposal the Americans unveiled at the DMZ was dead on arrival. The success or failure of Trump's summit was up in the air.

"I don't think we're half done, but it was well begun."

"We did not put our hands up for this," Singapore's foreign minister told reporters, as his country raced to turn the city into a giant stage for Trump and Kim.[17]

Strict security measures were imposed. Immigration officers turned away one traveler because his phone revealed internet searches about suicide bombings. They even interrogated Howard X, an Australian Kim Jong Un impersonator, but allowed him into the country.[18]

The Singaporeans also hastily assembled a twenty-three-thousand-square-foot media center for more than 2,500 journalists at a cost of $5 million, one-fourth of the summit expense. Trump later bragged, "I have never seen anything like it. Thousands. Thousands."[19]

Kim Jong Un arrived first on Sunday, June 10, in a Boeing 747 aircraft borrowed from the Chinese government. He was whisked in a thirty-five-car motorcade to the St. Regis Hotel in the popular Orchard shopping district. A cordon of North Korean bodyguards, Singaporean police officers, and hotel staff created a human shield around the entrance.[20]

Air Force One touched down five hours later, thirty-six hours before the summit started. Trump tweeted en route, "I look forward to meeting [Kim] and have a feeling that this one-time opportunity will not be wasted!" The president told reporters he felt "very good," before heading to the Shangri-La Hotel, a half mile from where Kim was staying.[21]

The contrast between the two men was striking. Smiling and relaxed after meeting the Singaporean prime minister, Kim, accompanied by his sister, reappeared the next evening to sightsee. He waved jovially at cheering crowds and took a cell phone selfie with the Singaporean foreign minister.[22]

Scheduled to meet Singapore's prime minister on Monday, and then Kim on Tuesday, Trump chafed at the delay. Sarah Sanders pointed out that moving the summit up meant it would air on Sunday night in the United States. "Sir, you're doing a historic meeting, and you don't want it on prime time?" The president backed down.[23]

Although Trump tweeted, "Great to be in Singapore, excitement in the air," his mood didn't improve on Monday.[24] "I just think it's going to work out nicely," he said for the press to hear during lunch with the prime minister. When the foreign minister argued in private that the summit was a concession to North Korea and China, all Trump could say was he had taken a long flight for a short meeting.[25]

Back at the hotel, the president got more bad news. Negotiations had stalled. John Kelly, the White House chief of staff, thought Trump might walk. Bolton hoped the administration could avoid major concessions. But Trump was still ready to "sign a substance-free communiqué, have his press conference to declare victory and then get out of town."[26]

The president's mood brightened that evening. Dennis Rodman, the former Chicago Bulls star, informed a TV audience that if anyone could reach a deal, it was Donald Trump! Even Sarah Sanders thought it was bizarre. But she did as the president asked, and thanked Rodman the next

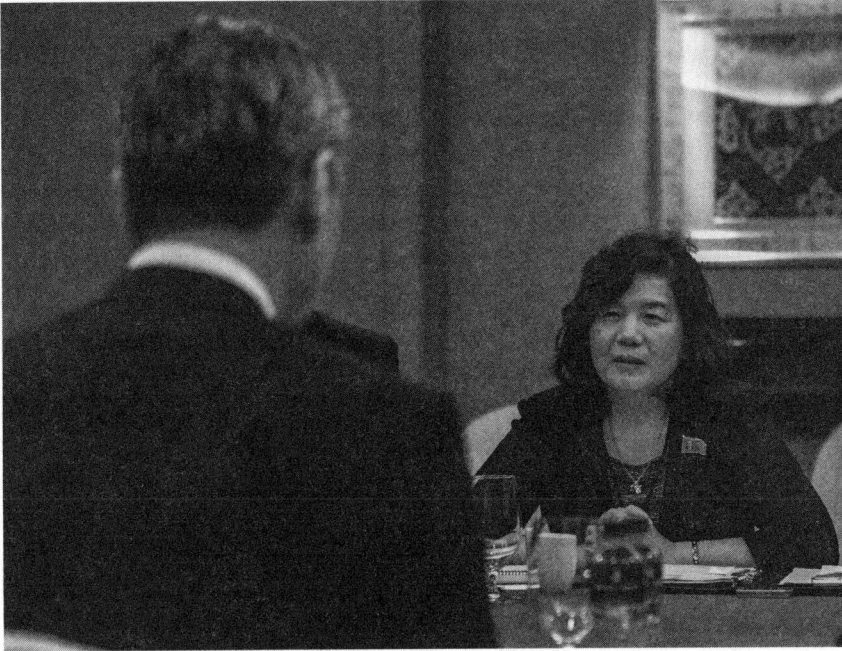

U.S. ambassador to the Philippines Sung Kim participates in meetings with DPRK vice foreign minister Choe Son Hui and DPRK Ministry of Foreign Affairs officials in Singapore on June 10, 2018. Official U.S. Department of State photo.

morning. The former basketball player appeared later on CNN wearing a red MAGA (Make America Great Again) hat and told viewers, "Today is a great day for everybody."[27]

By the time the two leaders arrived in Singapore, Sung Kim had been there for a few days. His round-the-clock talks with Choe at the Ritz-Carlton Hotel went nowhere. Instead of CVID, the best the Americans could hope for was a few new words added to the formulation, "complete denuclearization," agreed to by Kim Jong Un and Moon.

While the State Department was ready to sign off on the language, Bolton wasn't. He berated Randy Schriver, a member of the negotiating team and an old colleague from Colin Powell's State Department. Bolton flatly refused to recommend that the president approve the draft if CVID wasn't in it.[28]

With Trump and the chairman slated to meet at 9:00 A.M. the next day, Pompeo and Kim Yong Chol sat down for a last-ditch negotiating session. They emerged with a short declaration, more like what the North

Koreans had planned all along than the detailed American statement brought to the DMZ.[29]

None of the elements was groundbreaking. Pyongyang agreed to a "firm and unwavering commitment to complete denuclearization," but no CVID. Establishing new relations, the second element, meant normalizing ties. The third element, building "a lasting and stable peace regime," meant declaring the Korean War over and negotiating a peace treaty. The fourth, retrieving the remains of American soldiers from the war, was on Washington's original wish list. Finally, the two leaders agreed their negotiators would start talks right away.[30]

Everyone had doubts. Bolton later complained Pompeo had made too many concessions and "got nothing in return." Sung Kim wasn't sure. Pompeo knew it fell short, but at least the declaration would lead to more talks.[31] Trump emerged from his hotel at 8:00 A.M. after consulting with the secretary. He was satisfied.[32]

The Capella Hotel, the site of the summit, had been the military fortress where the British surrendered to Japan at the beginning of World War II and the Japanese surrendered to them at the end. At the hotel's heart were two colonial bungalows dating back to the 1880s along with two modern wings. Set on manicured grounds surrounded by rain forests, the Capella overlooked the South China Sea.

June 12, the day of the Trump-Kim encounter, was bright and steamy. Stern and unsmiling, dressed in a black Mao suit with his glasses in one hand and a portfolio in the other, Kim arrived first in a black Mercedes-Benz limousine. He was met by his top aides, including Ms. Choe. Then Trump's armored limo, "the Beast," pulled into an opposite driveway. He entered the hotel alone, followed by his team.[33]

The Americans were on edge as they waited in their holding room. Trump asked his assistant if he had any phone calls to return. Only one piqued his interest—Jack Nicklaus, the legendary golfer. After a brief conversation, Trump hung up, stood, and looked at his aides as if to say, "Can you believe this?" Sarah Sanders couldn't. The two countries had seemed on the brink of a nuclear war just months earlier.[34] Now he was talking to Jack Nicklaus before holding a summit with the North Korean dictator.

A few minutes later, Donald Trump and Kim Jong Un walked toward each other on a red carpet from opposite sides of a colonnaded breezeway connecting the two hotel wings. They met in front of alternating American and North Korean flags.

President Donald J. Trump and North Korean leader Kim Jong Un shake hands
as they meet for the first time, June 12, 2018, at the Capella Hotel in Singapore.
Official White House photo by Shealah Craighead.

Smiling, Trump and Kim shook hands for thirteen seconds. "Nice to
meet you Mr. President," Kim said in English. Trump's warm welcome of
a long-time enemy stood in stark contrast to his roughing up of allies only
days earlier in Quebec.[35]

As millions of people around the world watched, the two men made
the most of their historic moment. They posed for photos with somber
expressions. Walking along the hallway of pillars, they stopped again to
chat, shook hands again, and smiled. Trump placed his hand on Kim's back
when they arrived at the meeting room and ushered him into the small
space.[36]

The president gushed to reporters, saying that he felt "really great,"
that the summit was going to be a "tremendous success," and that the two
men were going to have a "terrific relationship." Years later, Trump compared meeting Kim to meeting a woman for the first time: "In one second,
you know whether or not it's all going to happen."[37]

Kim chuckled and nodded at the words "terrific relationship." The two
leaders had overcome a past that "covered our eyes and ears," that prevented
the two countries from "going forward." They shook hands one more time

as camera shutters clicked. The president gave Kim a thumbs-up sign and the press was ushered out.[38]

Alone with their interpreters for the next forty minutes, Trump and Kim talked about North Korea's "tremendous potential." The president reassured the chairman he didn't want to remove him, alluding to Libya's Gaddafi. North Korea could be "one of the great economic powers of the world," Trump told Kim.[39]

To reinforce his point, Trump and Kim watched a slick video on an iPad prepared by the Americans. With an ominous voice-over and a swelling soundtrack, the flick showcased Kim's choice, "to shake the hand of peace and enjoy prosperity like he has never seen" or slide back into "more isolation." The answer was obvious for Trump. The North Koreans could have the "the best hotels in the world right there," he later told the media.[40]

After Trump and Kim emerged and stopped at a balcony, the president rhapsodized some more to reporters. Then, their advisors joined them for the next session.

Kim praised Trump for leadership none of his predecessors had shown, a cue for Trump to criticize them. Obama would have attacked the North Koreans without first talking to them, a reference to his Oval Office warning. Past presidents had been "stupid," but Trump reserved special scorn for Rex Tillerson, who was "like a block of granite."[41]

In a revealing moment, the chairman asked how Trump assessed him. The president "saw Kim as really smart, quite secretive, a very good person, totally sincere with a great personality." Then, Kim let his guard down for a moment, admitting, "In politics people are like actors."[42]

The conversation got around to the reason why they were in Singapore in the first place: North Korea's WMD. Kim had a hard time with the word "denuclearization," but strenuously affirmed his intention to give up his weapons. The chairman blamed "the hostile policies of past US administrations," the standard North Korean explanation for the troubled relationship. Trump agreed, just as he had with President Xi's version of history.[43]

Like the president, the chairman also believed a series of summits could dispel mistrust and accelerate the process. In the meantime, he promised to stop nuclear tests, dismantle his WMD programs in an "irreversible manner"—a nod to the "I" in CVID—and to put Yongbyon on the chopping block.[44]

Kim asked Trump if the United States could reduce or eliminate military exercises held with South Korea, since his people thought they were threatening. He was pushing on an open door. The president promised to override his generals who argued they were essential to maintain troop readiness.

The fact that he didn't consult Bolton dismayed the national security advisor as well as the Pentagon. However, he did consult Pompeo, who thought many of the exercises were not essential to maintain the readiness of troops in Korea.[45]

The morning meetings appeared to reaffirm what Trump had thought all along, that his breezy manner guaranteed success. The president and Kim even had a light-hearted exchange about "Little Rocket Man." Kim had no idea who Elton John was, until Trump explained he had written the iconic song and that the term was a compliment. The chairman replied, "'Rocket Man' okay; 'little' not okay."[46]

After a short break, Trump checked out the media coverage, and then the two leaders reconvened for a lunch. The president and Kim discovered they were both sports fans. They talked about golf, women's soccer, and Kim's favorite basketball players—Kobe Bryant and Dennis Rodman.[47]

There were also awkward moments. When Trump offered Kim some Tic Tac mints just before lunch started, Sarah Sanders thought the chairman hesitated. She fantasized that Kim was worried the president might be trying to poison him. After Trump popped a few in his mouth, the chairman did the same.[48]

Even more awkwardly, Trump tried to encourage a Bolton-Kim bromance. "Once a hawk," Bolton was now "a dove," the president told Kim.

Everyone laughed, but Bolton tried to keep a straight face. "I look forward to visiting Pyongyang. It will certainly be interesting," he said.

Kim replied, "You will be warmly welcomed."

Bolton avoided answering the chairman's question, "Do you think you can trust me?" but Trump didn't stop pushing.[49] He pointed out that Bolton once called "for war with Russia, China and North Korea," but that "it was a lot different on the inside."[50]

The North Koreans laughed again. "We must have a picture so I can show hard-liners that you are not such a bad guy," Kim replied.[51]

After the summit was over, Trump told Bolton, "I rehabilitated you with them," as if that's what he wanted.[52]

In perhaps the most awkward moment at lunch, Sarah Sanders looked up from notetaking and made eye contact with Kim, who nodded and seemed to wink. For the rest of the meeting, a stunned Sanders only looked in the direction of the Americans. "All I could think was, 'What just happened?' Surely, Kim Jong Un didn't just mark me?"[53]

Afterward, Trump and Kim killed some time, strolling around the courtyard garden and inspecting the "Beast."[54] Once the English and Korean versions of the declaration were finished, the doors of the room opened wide, and the two leaders entered, walking in front of eight alternating flags. Trump gestured for Kim to take a seat. The chairman's sister presented him with his pen and the document. Pompeo did the same for Trump.[55]

"We're signing a very important document. Pretty comprehensive document," Trump informed everyone. "We've had a really great time together, a great relationship."[56]

Adjusting his glasses, Kim remarked, "We decided to leave the past behind and are going to sign a historic document that will signal a new beginning." Trump nodded as the two shook hands again. The president exclaimed, "Okay!" and they signed the declaration.[57]

Trump's press conference started in dramatic fashion a few hours later. A Hollywood production crew filmed his remarks. The moment was ruined, however, when a reporter shouted that they had not yet seen the summit document. The oversight was quickly corrected by the president's staff.[58]

Trump was convincing at times. He had avoided a war that "could have lost 20 million, 30 million people." There had been no missile tests or nuclear explosions in seven months, the nuclear test site had been closed, and Pyongyang was about to destroy a rocket-engine test facility. Those accomplishments stood in stark contrast to the diplomatic dry spell under President Obama.[59]

Trump's bragging, however, created the impression he had been snookered. His claim that the North Korean leader's commitment to denuclearization was a "big thing" remained to be seen. Pyongyang had pledged to give up its nuclear arsenal before but didn't.

The president's praise of Kim as "very talented" was disturbing. After all, he had killed his uncle and was held responsible for Otto Warmbier's death. Trump admitted in private that he discerned "a vicious streak" in Kim, but his public praise would reach new heights in the months ahead.[60]

The president's gut feeling that Kim wanted to make a deal, while probably correct, did not inspire confidence. Nor did Trump's claim that he had inherited a nuclear gene from an uncle who was an MIT physicist and a "great, brilliant genius." He later told Kim, "I know every one of your sites better than my people."[61]

Finally, Trump crowed that only he could fix the mess left him. He trashed Bill Clinton, who had been snookered by the North Koreans into giving them "billions of dollars," and "the following day the nuclear program continued." Trump concluded, "I'm not just blaming President Obama," adding, "I was given a very tough hand." There was a grain of truth in that claim.[62]

When the press conference was over, the president walked off the stage, was congratulated by his staff, grabbed a Diet Coke, slapped Sarah Sanders on the shoulder, and invited her to ride to the airport with him. On their way to Air Force One, Sanders admitted to Trump and Kelly that Kim had winked at her during lunch, prompting uproarious laughter.[63]

Trump was elated. He tweeted from his airplane, "Everybody can now feel much safer than the day I took office. There is no longer a Nuclear Threat from North Korea." After he landed, Trump wrote to Kim that the "media for North Korea and you have been fantastic," adding that "they have great respect for you and your country." None of that was true.[64]

International reaction was mostly positive. The North Korean media naturally praised Kim's "proactive peace-loving measures." Ardent advocates of diplomacy, Russia and China couldn't resist "I told you so's." Even Japanese prime minister Abe, a supporter of maximum pressure, wanted to have his own summit with Kim.[65]

The Western media was mostly negative. Nicholas Kristof wrote in the *New York Times* that Trump had been "hoodwinked." An op-ed in the *Washington Post* proclaimed, "Let the Bribery Begin."[66] A more balanced *Financial Times* pointed out the situation on the peninsula was "considerably less alarming than a year ago." Bob Carlin told CBS News, "I don't think we're half done, but it was well begun."[67]

While Republicans believed Trump had made reasonable compromises and Democrats disagreed, independents tilted the public opinion poll balance in favor of his diplomacy. But it was too early to judge whether the summit was a success or to have confidence that talks would lead to a denuclearization of North Korea.[68]

"Even a broken clock is right twice a day," Tony Soprano once told his capos. President Trump was right in focusing on relationship building with Kim, and in thinking there would have to be more summits. It would take more than a few hours to repair relations between two countries that had fought a bloody war and been at loggerheads for decades.

Still, President Moon was disappointed that the summit declaration didn't "reach our hopes that it would be a detailed agreement."[69] One Trump official and skeptic observed, "The document was not insignificant. We had Kim Jong Un's signature on denuclearization." But an erratic president and an inexperienced secretary of state would now have to find the way forward.[70]

"Succeed fast or fail fast"

The State Department announced three weeks after the summit that Mike Pompeo would return to Pyongyang on July 5 for his third trip to North Korea in four months. The secretary later joked when he arrived, "If I come one more time, I will have to pay taxes here."[71]

President Trump thought denuclearization was a done deal. Flying out of Singapore, he called President Moon to seek his advice on how to implement the agreement. He told Prime Minister Abe that it was time to close the deal. Just before Pompeo's trip, Trump tweeted, "We signed a wonderful paper saying they're going to denuclearize the whole thing. It's going to happen."[72]

It was one thing to agree on denuclearization and another to make it happen. North Korea did begin dismantling rocket test facilities, although those steps could easily be reversed. But the Yongbyon nuclear facility was still churning out bomb-making material, and missile production factories were still operating. Moreover, a Pentagon study, leaked to the press before Pompeo's visit, repeated the decades-old line that North Korea would never give up its WMD.[73]

CVID remained Washington's game plan, although Pompeo changed the name to "final, fully verified denuclearization of the DPRK as agreed to by Chairman Kim in Singapore." His attempt to mollify the North Koreans was criticized as backing away from Washington's demands.[74]

Pompeo also became more realistic about achieving denuclearization. Bolton insisted that North Korea had to dismantle its WMD programs in one year. The secretary shifted to two and a half years, and then downplayed the importance of a timeline altogether when he arrived in Pyongyang.[75]

Pompeo's mission was still to "succeed fast or fail fast," according to one official. He planned to demand that Kim give up his weapons in two big installments, starting with twenty-five nuclear bombs, more than half its stockpile. If the North Koreans refused, five would do. If that didn't work, one would be acceptable. Pompeo, Mattis, and Bolton also agreed that Pyongyang had until September 1 to show it was serious.[76]

On the flight to Pyongyang, however, Pompeo and Ambassador Sung Kim, who had been at his post in Indonesia and hadn't been part of the Washington deliberations, changed their minds. Pompeo decided to first seek a full accounting of Pyongyang's WMD programs. Negotiators would nail down the size of his stockpile and Kim could then turn it over.[77]

His proposal was logical, but it was also impractical. Pyongyang had turned over eighteen thousand pages of records—some incomplete—to the George W. Bush administration detailing operations at Yongbyon alone. A declaration covering all of Pyongyang's programs could run into tens of thousands of pages and prove unverifiable.

In return, the Americans would sign off on a declaration that the Korean War was over. Since the armistice had been temporary, making the cessation permanent made sense. Pompeo, Mattis, and Bolton didn't like the idea since it could trigger a rush toward peace and an end to the U.S.-South Korean alliance. But Trump liked it precisely for that reason. Moon was also on board, anxious to move peace forward.[78]

The president's July 3 letter to Kim Jong Un previewed the secretary's priority, an agreement on "taking the first major steps towards final, fully verified denuclearization of the Korean Peninsula." However, it may have set off alarm bells in Pyongyang. There was no mention of what Washington was willing to do in return.[79]

Once their plane touched down, the Americans cooled their heels for two hours at the same guesthouse where Madeleine Albright, two South Korean presidents, and a Japanese prime minister had stayed. Sung Kim made small talk. Pompeo, radiating anger, watched CNN and avoided eye contact with anyone.

When Kim Yong Chol finally showed up with Choe Son Hui, he had a "swelled head" after the successful summit, one American recalled. That spelled trouble.[80]

A session with reporters who had accompanied the secretary started well enough. Posing for cameras, the seventy-three-year-old general remarked, "The more you come, the more trust we can build between one another." Pompeo responded, "Yes, I agree, I look forward to it, and I count on it being very productive," adding his witty remark about paying taxes in North Korea.[81]

Pompeo quickly lost patience, however. Kim Yong Chol just kept talking. The secretary asked his spokesperson to end the session, but the

North Koreans were in charge. One reporter remembered, "Pompeo got owned in that encounter."[82]

With talks off on the wrong foot, the two men fought to a draw over the next five hours, followed by another unproductive session the next morning. The American's declaration-for-declaration proposal went over like a lead balloon.[83]

Angry that Pompeo would bring up the idea of declaring his country's WMD sites, Kim Yong Chol accused the secretary of asking for a target list to attack North Korea's armed forces.[84]

When Kim blurted out, "We can tell you where all of our nuclear weapons, our chemical weapons, our missile sites, our submarines are," a nervous Choe grabbed his arm before he could finish.

"You shouldn't be saying this," she whispered, as Pompeo kept pushing.[85]

The secretary was offering only a little in return. The North Koreans already had the impression from Trump in Singapore that Washington would sign up to the end-of-war declaration. They were hoping for new items on their wish list: lifting sanctions, negotiating a peace treaty, and establishing diplomatic relations. That didn't happen.[86]

Neither of the two tough guys looked for middle ground. Kim Yong Chol stonewalled, claiming "That's for our leader to decide," even over minor matters. He called Pompeo's authority into question. "You might want to check with your president," the general advised. "This is inconsistent with what we've heard from him, and what I heard in the Oval Office."[87]

Pompeo was reduced to asking the general to just implement Kim Jong Un's promise to allow inspections, starting with dismantlement at the rocket launch site.

But the North Korean envoy refused. "There is no need for you to inspect. You can see from the sky," he replied, alluding to spy satellites.[88]

The general even "denied the need for further progress" on denuclearization, arguing that the pledge to destroy the test sites was enough. When he pressed the secretary to do something about American nuclear weapons, which had never been part of the talks, Pompeo was furious.[89]

Contrary to the State Department's description of their dinner that evening as "relationship building" with the two men "cracking jokes and exchanging pleasantries," their clash continued. Kim accused the secretary of having a Chinese agent on his delegation——his Chinese American aide, Alex Wong. Pompeo smiled and replied, "We have all types of people in the United States."[90]

Early the next morning, Pompeo left the guesthouse to phone Trump, Bolton, and Kelly using the British embassy's secure communications line. Five hours of meetings plus dinner had been "incredibly frustrating," producing "almost no progress," he reported.[91]

The Pompeo-Kim cage match resumed after breakfast. The general asked how Pompeo had slept. "We did have very serious discussions on important matters yesterday. So, thinking about those discussions, you may not have slept well."[92]

"Director Kim, I slept just fine," Pompeo replied, reminding him it was important to implement the Singapore declaration and to set off on the "path toward complete denuclearization."[93]

"Of course, it's important," Kim fired back. "There are things I have to clarify," prompting the secretary to respond, "There are things I have to clarify as well." One official discerned Pompeo's undisguised rebuke as a message to "cut the shit."[94]

While the two men met, the American reporters waited to see if Pompeo would see Kim Jong Un. Word was that Trump had autographed a copy of Elton John's "Rocket Man" recording for the secretary to give to him.[95]

Suddenly, there was a knock on one reporter's door. "Hurry up, we're leaving, quick, grab your stuff," a colleague yelled. They were heading to the airport.[96]

There was no meeting with Kim Jong Un, a sign that the talks had not gone well. If there was any doubt, Kim Yong Chol was nowhere to be found when the secretary was seen off at the airport. That job was left to Foreign Minister Ri, who hadn't participated in any of the meetings.[97]

Pompeo put his game face on before boarding the plane. He had had "many hours of productive conversations," the secretary told reporters. Progress was made on "almost all of the central issues."[98]

He was right on one count. Pompeo and Kim Yong Chol had agreed to restart cooperation to retrieve the remains of Americans missing or killed in the Korean War. By the end of the month, the North Koreans had turned over fifty-five boxes of what they said were the remains of an undetermined number of soldiers.[99]

When Pompeo arrived in Tokyo, he phoned Trump with the bad news. North Korea wanted security guarantees before denuclearization, and there would only be "verification" afterwards. Moreover, there was no way they were going to turn over a declaration first. Bolton, also on the call, said that was a nonstarter.

Trump agreed. "This trust-building is horse shit," he concluded. "This is a waste of time. They're basically saying they don't want to denuke."[100]

The North Koreans issued a statement the moment Pompeo left, probably approved by Kim Jong Un, blasting his unilateral demands. They reminded Washington it could take a "shortcut" to denuclearization if it responded positively to Pyongyang's unilateral moves by taking its own steps.[101] They claimed that Trump had been led astray by Bolton and Pompeo.[102]

If the secretary of state's disastrous trip wasn't enough, the Americans also pulled back from Trump's promise in Singapore to cancel "war games." The president ordered Bolton to tell the Pentagon to stand down after he learned it was still planning to continue drills.[103]

Instead, the national security advisor orchestrated an effort, joined by the Pentagon, to suspend but not cancel just the two largest exercises, including one planned for that summer. Smaller drills would make up for the loss. Trump was kept in the dark.[104]

When Mattis mistakenly revealed the plan to reporters, the president lashed out but did nothing to stop the scheme. That failure was one of the North Korean Foreign Ministry's litany of complaints after the secretary's disastrous visit.[105]

By the end of July, Trump's diplomacy had reached a moment of truth. Pompeo and Bolton agreed there was "zero probability of success." They decided to increase the pressure and tighten sanctions.[106]

Neither Trump nor Kim Jong Un, however, was ready to change course. The president wanted to invite Kim to the White House after the chairman wrote at the end of July suggesting they meet again. Instead, Trump's advisors convinced him to send Pompeo to Pyongyang again, even though the president thought it was a bad idea.[107]

He was right. While the chairman responded that he was willing to hold serious talks with Pompeo, Kim Yong Chol sent a nasty message telling him not to come unless he was bringing new proposals. At Bolton's urging, Trump tweeted the trip was off.[108]

The president still wasn't ready to give up on diplomacy, and said in a follow-up tweet, "In the meantime, I would like to send my warmest regards and respect to Chairman Kim. I look forward to seeing him soon."[109]

CHAPTER SIXTEEN

"A rat-shit little country"

ONALD TRUMP WAS PUZZLED when he spoke to President Moon on September 4. Why wasn't North Korea denuclearizing? Singapore had been phenomenal. Moon thought Kim was committed to giving up his weapons, but "Kim Yong Chol and others around him had rude manners." The South Korean leader suggested another summit.[1]

John Bolton had his own explanation. "Singapore hadn't been phenomenal unless you were a North Korean; KJU [Kim Jong Un] didn't make friends with enemies, and there wasn't a real deal." Dripping with sarcasm, Bolton declared that another summit was "just what we needed."[2]

Trump disregarded his own role, his administration's ill-conceived negotiating plan, and a six decades–old hostile relationship. Instead, he blamed Xi Jinping. The Chinese leader had been helpful until 2018, trading support on North Korea for American restraint on trade. Within days of the Singapore summit, however, Washington imposed more tariffs on China, proving to Xi that Trump couldn't be trusted. Moreover, Trump had reached out to Kim Jong Un without informing China.[3]

The president regarded the March 2018 Xi-Kim summit with suspicion. An aide recalled that his reaction was, "Kim Jong Un and Xi, I see you!" He hinted to reporters that the breakdown in preparations for Singapore coincided with another Xi-Kim meeting in May. After Singapore, the president blamed Xi for Pompeo's disastrous July trip. He tweeted that China was behind the canceled August visit.[4]

Trump was right to be suspicious. Xi had urged Kim to go slow on denuclearizing at their second summit. The Chinese also cautioned the North Koreans, "If you agree to anything without us, we cannot be your sounding board," one insider observed. "We cannot be responsible for the future consequences."[5]

He was wrong, however, to think Xi was behind the problems with getting the Singapore declaration off the ground, especially with denuclearization. Kim was following the step-by-step recipe for giving up his arsenal handed down to him by his father and grandfather.

In fact, ten days after Pompeo's August trip was canceled, the chairman sent Trump another letter, perhaps the most important one in their entire correspondence.[6] Trump gushed to his aides that "this is a really nice letter." It also included an apology for his senior envoy's nasty message.[7]

Amid the flattering passages was a plea from Kim to meet again "instead of having another war of words" with Pompeo. Kelly later told Bolton, "It was as if the letter had been written by Pavlovians who knew exactly how to touch the nerves enhancing Trump's self-esteem."[8] The president ordered his aides to set up a summit for after the November midterm elections.[9]

Bolton also reacted predictably. "It was written by the dictator of a rat-shit little country" who didn't deserve another meeting with Trump until he met Pompeo, he argued.[10]

More importantly, Kim Jong Un's letter included significant clues about the future. He asserted that the two leaders should have an "in-depth exchange of views on important issues including denuclearization," hinting that the topic was reserved for them alone. Kim pointed out that "significant progress" could be made if the United States took "more substantive steps and actions."[11]

The chairman elaborated, "We are willing to take further meaningful steps one at a time in a phased manner, such as the complete shutdown of the Nuclear Weapons Institute or the Satellite Launch District and the irreversible closure of the nuclear materials production facility."[12]

His offer to close the Nuclear Weapons Institute was new. In fact, U.S. intelligence agencies only had spotty information on what it did. Just like the American Los Alamos and Livermore labs, it appeared to play a significant role in developing bombs. If the lab was shut down, North Korea might not be able to field nuclear weapons.

The organization made its public debut in March 2016 when Kim Jong Un gave its staff "on-the-spot guidance." Kim examined what was probably a model of a nuclear bomb, accompanied by Ri Hong Sop, the organization's new chief and a former director of Yongbyon.[13]

That September, the institute announced North Korea's fifth blast, suspected to be a prototype hydrogen bomb. A year later, it hailed the next detonation as a "perfect success in the test of a hydrogen bomb for an ICBM."[14] Afterwards, Ri and another advisor showed Kim what appeared to be a peanut-shaped nuclear warhead.[15]

Kim Jong Un's offer was "remarkable," according to Sig Hecker, the former Los Alamos director, especially if it was the "brain center of the North's nuclear program." The institute's role, and exactly when it would be dismantled, were not elaborated in the letter.[16]

Only a few people saw the Trump-Kim correspondence. None were experts who could recognize a potential game changer. Although one State Department staffer found the offer intriguing, neither Trump nor his top advisors appear to have given it any thought. The whole episode remains a mystery.

"A big baby step"

A South Korean aircraft slowed to a halt on the tarmac. Large blue banners welcomed President Moon to Pyongyang. The motto "Let us open up a generation of peace and prosperity through the united strength of our people" appeared in neat white Korean lettering.[17]

The crowd cheered as Kim Jong Un and his wife walked toward the plane. A smiling Moon Jae-in and the First Lady descended from the aircraft. The two men embraced. Moon made history again, as the only South Korean leader to hold three summits with the North Koreans in one year.[18]

As tens of thousands of citizens shouted "Reunification of the fatherland!" the two men waved to the crowds as they stood side by side in the same car.[19] September 18 was the start of a three-day visit.

"I am feeling we've truly become close," Kim Jong Un confessed once he and Moon sat down for lunch.

"I am creating a new generation for inter-Korean and US-DPRK relations with Chairman Kim," Moon gushed.[20]

The leaders talked for two hours. In the meantime, the South Korean delegation—including the First Lady, singers, rappers, composers, a former Olympic table tennis star, and industrialists—fanned out in Pyongyang.[21]

The day ended with a banquet. Some guests drank too much. Some sang duets. One South Korean proposed a toast to Kim. The chairman responded, "We came all the way here, overcoming all kinds of barriers and difficulties. We shouldn't think about going back."[22]

"The Americans really hate you," a delegate from Seoul informed Kim Yong Chol. The wolf warrior's response was predictable.

"We're not a defeated nation. They cannot dictate to us. That's why they don't like me. I don't care."[23]

The summit could have mirrored the Panmunjom meeting, which was heavy on symbolism and light on substance, but hard work in the preceding four months made a difference. After a private chat the next day, the two leaders signed the "Pyongyang Joint Declaration of September 2018," which covered everything from working together on sports to public health. Seoul, however, was limited in what it could do by sanctions. Another Trump-Kim summit would have to lift those restrictions.[24]

The declaration included a detailed pledge on denuclearization, but only after President Moon pushed Kim hard on the one topic that could make or break his next summit with Trump. In fact, the chairman later complained to the president about Moon's "excessive interest."

Kim was frustrated. He had repeatedly promised to give up his nuclear weapons, but his pledge seemed to make no difference.[25] He complained that his unilateral steps to denuclearize got no response from the United States.

Pompeo simply demanded in July that Kim provide a detailed account of Pyongyang's WMD programs, which would have left his country vulnerable to attack. This was why the chairman had insisted in Singapore on easing tensions first.[26]

Kim's biggest problem, however, was that the Americans refused to lift sanctions without complete denuclearization. The North Koreans thought it was unfair that "only when they were completely naked would the US relax sanctions," according to a Moon advisor.[27]

Despite everything, the chairman was willing to sign a detailed WMD pledge, something North Korea hadn't done with Seoul since the early 1990s. The Pyongyang declaration recorded his promise to dismantle Yongbyon and destroy the Sohae rocket test site if the United States reduced tensions.[28]

The declaration was important, but what followed was even more significant. The two defense ministers signed the "Agreement on the Implementation of the Historic Panmunjom Declaration in the Military Domain," capping months of intense negotiations.

The new "Comprehensive Military Agreement," or CMA—shorthand for the awkward longer title—aimed to reduce the rising risk that a crisis, miscalculation, or miscommunication could trigger conflict. The CMA, in the words of a Blue House official, was "a big baby step." It didn't cover nuclear weapons but could help reduce the probability that even small-scale clashes could spiral out of control or disrupt later nuclear talks.[29]

Unlike the first confidence-building deal reached decades earlier between the two Koreas, the CMA was loaded with details. It was formulated by a Blue House official who had traveled secretly along the 151-mile-long DMZ beginning in fall 2017 to gather ideas. Everyone knew tension reduction had to begin there.[30]

The 2018 Panmunjom declaration was a test run. In addition to lofty pronouncements, the South proposed a specific step, that North and South Korea would dismantle speakers along the DMZ that broadcast propaganda into each other's territory. Braving criticism by conservatives, Moon moved forward. The North Koreans agreed, the loudspeakers were dismantled, and the stage was set for more talks.[31]

The Blue House faced three challenges in preparing to negotiate the CMA. First, the South Korean army, responsible for defending the DMZ where many of the measures would have to be implemented, was "not so welcoming," one official recalled.[32]

Second, there were multiple military commands in the loop. The UN Command supervised the DMZ. The Combined Forces Command oversaw the American and South Korean forces in case of war, while USFK was in charge of them in peacetime. However, consulting the three organizations proved easy since General Vincent Brooks led all three.[33]

Third, facing the Korean People's Army, or KPA, across the negotiating table was no mean feat. Working out the details loaded into the draft wouldn't be easy.

At first, the talks went nowhere. The two experienced negotiators, both generals, followed the standard script. They read set speeches while playing to audiences in the Blue House and Pyongyang, who were watching the proceedings via secure video link. "Seven or eight hours of bad language screaming at each other" followed the breaks, according to one official.[34]

To break the ice, the Blue House overrode its own military's opposition and faxed Seoul's seven-page draft of an agreement to the North Koreans.[35] The proposal grew to some thirty pages as faxes flew back and forth, with North Korean additions, deletions, and amendments. They were not easy exchanges.[36]

Moon and Kim Jong Un monitored the negotiations' progress. The South Korean leader understood military issues. He had served as a young soldier stationed at the DMZ and on the National Assembly committee responsible for defense. Briefed regularly on the talks, Moon emphasized that "we cannot compromise our security," according to an aide.[37]

Kim Jong Un also kept tabs on the talks. A stickler for detail, he was obsessed with implementation. The chairman followed the negotiations and was happy with the outcome. At least that's what he told South Korean envoys before the summit, and Moon when they met.[38]

Nonetheless, the CMA talks were on the verge of collapse by early September. The military negotiators couldn't handle a political hot potato, the location of the Northern Limit Line in the West Sea. The North Koreans balked; nothing could be agreed until the problem was resolved. Moon's two envoys, Ambassador Chung and Suh Hoon, traveled to Pyongyang to break the logjam.[39]

When talks resumed nine days later, the two generals reached a deal after twelve hours stretching into the early morning. The North Koreans agreed to establish an amorphous "maritime peace zone," in effect, kicking the NLL dispute down the road.[40]

The last stumbling block was the title. "Agreement on the Implementation of the Historic Panmunjom Declaration in the Military Domain" didn't sound good in Korean, let alone in English. The South Koreans pushed to delete "historic," but the North Koreans refused. The dispute was finally resolved at 3:00 A.M. on September 14 when the South Koreans caved in.[41]

The details of the new deal were striking. Fashioned after agreements between the Soviet Union and Europe at the end of the Cold War, the CMA imposed constraints on military operations, not just greater transparency. Its measures were designed to prevent the kinds of clashes that had threatened to escalate in the past.

The CMA created a ten-kilometer-wide buffer zone on land on both sides of the demarcation line in the DMZ. Potentially dangerous activities, such as major maneuvers, were prohibited. The Joint Security Area at Panmunjom was effectively demilitarized. Some twenty guard posts along the DMZ "almost within a stone's throw of each other," according to one official, were to be dismantled.[42]

The same was true in the air and at sea. A military no-fly zone was established along the DMZ up to forty kilometers from the demarcation line. As part of establishing the maritime zone of peace in the West Sea, the agreement provided for joint patrols to stop illegal fishing.[43]

The CMA was celebrated in Seoul and Pyongyang, but not in Washington, which was determined to keep the pressure on Pyongyang. When a Blue House aide called Matt Pottinger to give him the good news, he had no idea what was going on. Trump's advisor immediately placed a "What the hell happened?" phone call to General Brooks.[44]

Mike Pompeo was also angry. "Why didn't you call me?" he protested to Kang Kyung-wha, implying that Seoul's foreign minister was hiding something. She responded that her government had been keeping General Brooks informed. The secretary later apologized.[45]

Kang was right. Brooks had met the South Korean negotiator before every session with the North Koreans. Moreover, a South Korean general working at the Blue House spoke to Brooks's staff some fifty-eight times about the talks. They did everything possible to keep USFK informed, even working out negotiating positions beforehand.[46]

Brooks, in turn, sent reports up his chain of command to General Dunford, the chairman of the Joint Chiefs of Staff, as well as to Mattis's military assistant. But they apparently didn't make it to the White House.[47]

A Trump aide recalled, "Mattis and Dunford did a really shitty job of keeping us informed." The CMA may have been caught up in the secretary's ongoing effort to slow-roll the White House on Korea. Bolton was also trying to squeeze Mattis out the door by spreading rumors of his imminent departure.[48]

Even more important, the Security Battalion–Joint Security Area, stationed at Panmunjom and in charge of securing the border, was kept in the dark. The Joint Security Area, or JSA, was one of the most dangerous places in the DMZ, a circular patch of land eight hundred meters in diameter, where troops glared at each other. The JSA's demilitarization was a priority.[49]

The soldiers guessed something was up from the newspapers. But none of them expected that the agreement "would involve our unit," an officer recalled. "All of a sudden, the entirety of the CMA fell on us."[50]

Tasked to implement the deal, a group of majors, captains, and sergeants, most of whom had never spoken to a North Korean, sat down with members of the Korean People's Army. Luckily, they were led by an experienced American colonel.[51]

At first, the interaction was "cold and scripted," one officer remembered, but then felt "almost normal." After summits at Panmunjom in April, Singapore in June, and Pyongyang in September, the North Korean soldiers apparently had greater leeway to get down to business.[52]

Removing landmines was a top priority. The North Koreans were responsible for clearing hundreds of dangerous, 1950s-era wooden box mines. They contained a minimum amount of metal, were hard to detect, and had deteriorated due to age.[53]

"We know you are experts, but mines still blow up," one American officer pointed out to the North Koreans and offered a class on tourniquets. But they turned him down.

"You know, you guys are much different from what we were taught," a North Korean officer later admitted. "When my granddaughter learns to count, she learns like this, 'one American bastard, two American bastards.'"

The KPA eventually accepted help after accidentally detonating a mine for the second time.[54]

Trust grew. During a tour of the Joint Security Area, UN Command and KPA officers observed a hollow wooden ramp used to move items in and out of a guard post. It could be a hiding place for weapons. Just as a South Korean soldier was about to demolish the ramp with an axe, the North Koreans told him, "You don't have to do that. We trust you." It was a far cry from the first encounters, an American officer recalled.[55]

Growing cooperation over the three remaining months in 2018 became, in some instances, a competition. When the South Korean military slowed the dismantlement of guard posts, the KPA sped ahead. The South then moved faster. By mid-December, most of the work was done.[56]

Many experts were disappointed with the summit. South Korean conservatives argued that the CMA tied the hands of the military. They failed to mention that the Lee administration had planned to pursue a similar deal.[57] Others pointed out there was no forward movement on denuclearization. But the Blue House believed it had done all it could on a topic reserved for Trump and Kim.

With three summits under South Korea's belt in one year, President Moon had big plans. Regular summits, expanding economic cooperation, and a more far-reaching security deal building on the CMA seemed possible. He needed the United States to agree.[58]

"A new sheriff comes to town"

Mike Pompeo phoned a long-time Republican foreign policy expert on his way home from Singapore to offer him a job. He had to find a full-time negotiator, especially since Sung Kim was slated to return to his day job as ambassador to the Philippines.

The expert, Stephen Biegun, had good ties with Congress, executive branch experience, and fifteen years of doing deals for the Ford Motor Company. Even more important, he hadn't joined the "Never Trump" movement.[59]

While Biegun's bread and butter had been U.S.-Russian relations, as a congressional aide he helped secure funding for the 1994 nuclear deal with North Korea and encouraged cooperation with former secretary of defense Bill Perry's policy review. When President Bush visited the DMZ in 2002, Biegun, then a White House aide, unsuccessfully lobbied to include a line in his speech, "Chairman Kim, tear down this wall," parroting Reagan's Berlin dictum to Mikhail Gorbachev.[60]

As the Ford executive in charge of international affairs, he studied the consequences of a second Korean War for the auto giant's supply chain. A colleague argued that Ford needed a communications network to keep its business going in case of a nuclear attack. "We won't need satellite phones; we're going to need ramen soup and bottled water in the basement," Biegun pointed out.[61]

Trump's shift to diplomacy with Pyongyang intrigued him. A dealmaker like Gallucci, Bosworth, and Yun, he was "attracted to the president's willingness to step outside of convention and test a different way to solve the problem."[62]

One official described his appointment, just before Pompeo's canceled August trip to Pyongyang, with the phrase "a new sheriff comes to town." Denis McDonough, a Democratic colleague of Biegun's on Capitol Hill and one of Obama's top aides, observed, "He listens." The *New York Times* later described the mild-mannered Biegun as the "anti-Pompeo."[63]

McDonough was right. Unencumbered by myths about Pyongyang that had dogged Washington for years, Steve reached out to former government officials and private citizens, including myself. We had several meetings to discuss North Korea during his time in the Trump administration.

Biegun had a tough road ahead, but he had Pompeo's "100 percent ironclad trust," according to one aide. The secretary was skeptical about denuclearization, but he still wanted to give it his best shot. Like Chris Hill, the new envoy had a direct line to the secretary, and through him, to the president. Moreover, Pompeo told Biegun not to worry about politics. He had his back.[64]

The new envoy's job wasn't only to negotiate with North Korea. Biegun was a "bureaucratic ninja who did it with a smile and a very civilized

Stephen E. Biegun, later confirmed as Deputy Secretary of State, meets with Special
Representative for Korean Peninsula Peace and Security Affairs Lee Do-hoon,
in Seoul, Korea, on December 9, 2020. Official U.S. Department of State photo.

manner," one aide observed. Effective in winning allies and in besting foes,
he seized control of policymaking, leaving Bolton in the dark.[65]

CVID was at the top of his hit list. Rather than insist Pyongyang give
up all its weapons and then get benefits, Biegun put together a step-by-
step approach with both sides moving forward together. His plan was keyed
to Singapore's four principles, like "a Christmas tree with us hanging or-
naments on the branches."[66]

Biegun's approach was guaranteed to alienate Bolton. So was his ditching of Bolton's up-front WMD declaration, which "was the cork in the
negotiating bottle" that "we didn't need," a State Department official recalled. The new option was a step-by step declaration as well.[67]

Denuclearization remained the objective, accompanied by transforming relations. Pyongyang would freeze, reduce, and eliminate its WMD
programs. Along the way, the United States would take steps—scaling back
military exercises, establishing diplomatic relations, negotiating a peace
treaty, and lifting sanctions—that North Korea wanted.

When another letter from Kim Jong Un arrived the day after the
September summit, Trump, Pompeo, and Biegun were back in business.

Evidently, the cancellation of the secretary's August trip had caused hand-wringing in Pyongyang. The chairman asked the president to send Pompeo to North Korea "at an early date" to "discuss and plan steps forward, including the time and venue of our meeting."[68]

The secretary's airplane landed in Pyongyang two weeks later, marking his fourth visit in six months, this time with Steve Biegun. Despite the chairman's positive letter, however, the Pompeo–Kim Yong Chol feud erupted on the tarmac even before the aircraft had shut down its engines.[69]

The secretary responded with a forced smile when the general said he couldn't bring his interpreter to the meeting with Kim Jong Un. His armed bodyguard would also have to leave his weapon behind.

"Okay, I hope she [his interpreter] can be there. We will figure out how to make it work," Pompeo replied. As for the "big guy," the secretary laughed and "puffed up his shoulders to imitate the broad physicality of his Secret Service detail," one reporter observed.[70]

The motorcade headed into Pyongyang on a quiet Sunday morning. Only five cars passed the procession during its twenty-minute drive from the airport to the "one hundred flowers" guesthouse where Pompeo had stayed before.[71]

Later that morning, the American delegation gathered for the meeting with Kim Jong Un. Biegun hopped into a limousine with Pompeo. Andy Kim and the secretary's interpreter piled into the car behind them with other aides in trailing vehicles.[72]

Five long minutes passed. Pompeo's bodyguards nervously exchanged glances. North Koreans loitering in the driveway whispered to each other. Finally, the secretary's limousine door opened, and Pompeo spoke briefly with the North Koreans. Moments later, his interpreter stepped out of the car and the motorcade left.[73]

Kim Jong Un warmly greeted the secretary of state for the cameras. The two spoke semiprivately for two hours, a sure sign the chairman wanted to get talks back on track. Biegun and Andy Kim as well as the chairman's sister were on hand, but the North Korean senior envoy wasn't there, a sure sign that he was in the doghouse.[74]

An unexpected lunch together back at Pompeo's guesthouse followed their morning session. The "good Mike," meandering around the halls waiting for Kim to arrive, gave a North Korean a "lighthearted slap" on the back. "It's a very nice day that promises a good future for both countries," the chairman remarked as they sat down for lunch.[75]

Kim Jong Un did most of the talking during the morning and the ninety-minute lunch. He seemed "very confident," one American delegation member observed. While Kim had a "stack of talking points on the table," he didn't glance at them. The chairman seemed pragmatic, but "insistent that his point of view had to be registered."[76]

CVID had been discarded. Instead, the discussion focused on three topics: how to end seventy years of hostility between the United States and North Korea, how to move the Singapore process forward, and arranging for a second summit.[77]

Kim was more than ready to tackle denuclearization. He repeated his past pledge to allow inspectors into test sites and to dismantle Yongbyon in return for "corresponding measures." The Americans assumed that meant lifting sanctions.[78]

The chairman also mentioned something new, hinting that North Korea would consider "much, much more" than just dismantling Yongbyon. Kim may have meant the Nuclear Weapons Institute mentioned in his September 6 letter to Trump. The Americans, however, didn't push on the open door.[79]

Determined to rebuild Singapore's lost momentum, Biegun test-drove a proposal keyed to a past statement by the chairman that his economy could be as advanced as that of Vietnam. What better way to help than for the World Bank, which funded development programs, to provide aid? A puzzled Kim, however, asked, "What is the World Bank?"[80]

The American envoy was "surprised as hell." Kim's response seemed a polite way of saying he wasn't interested. However, one delegation member surmised that the North Koreans knew a lot about the UN organizations that had some connection to them, but nothing about others like the World Bank that didn't.[81]

As for another summit, Pompeo's delegation wasn't ready to nail down a date and venue. There had to be progress on achieving Singapore's four objectives before moving forward. Each side had its own preferences for a location, although Vietnam was high on the list for both.[82]

Over lunch—conch shell soup, mounds of caviar, and the North Korean equivalent of Kobe beef—a relaxed, inquisitive Kim asked the Americans, What do you think of North Korea? What do you think of our food? How hard is it to travel the way you do? A quiet Kim Yong Chol joined the meal after being shut out of the morning session.[83]

The chairman was surprisingly open about infighting in his regime. Kim Yong Chol was temporarily in the doghouse. His diplomats didn't understand what he was trying to do. That was why there were no officials from the Foreign Ministry present and why Foreign Minister Ri had treated nuclear talks like a policy hot potato.[84]

Kim's disdain, however, didn't extend to Choe Son Hui. The chairman had good news for Biegun. She had been assigned to work with him, not as a representative of her ministry, but in a personal capacity. While one American thought that was better than dealing with Kim Yong Chol, the general still had ownership of the portfolio.[85]

Pompeo's delegation was also able to get greater insight into the role of "North Korea's Ivanka Trump," Kim Yo Jong. Her brother relied on her "very, very attentive eye to details," one American observed. Humble but confident, quiet but with a ready smile, she hovered in the background while making sure everything went according to plan. Even Kim Yong Chol was deferential to her.[86]

In the morning, Kim Yo Jong sat to her brother's left taking notes. During lunch, she spoke only when spoken to. While Kim Jong Un shook hands with everyone before departing, his sister raced off to supervise the transfer of photos documenting the visit to a computer disc. She hustled back and delivered a white envelope with the thumb drive to Pompeo before he left for the airport.[87]

After almost six hours on the ground, the secretary flew to Seoul and tweeted, "Had a good trip to Pyongyang to meet with Chairman Kim. We continue to make progress on agreements made at Singapore Summit." Trump added, "I look forward to seeing Chairman Kim again in the near future."[88]

This time around, positive news dominated the headlines. Pyongyang's media was glowing.[89] International outlets featured progress in arranging another summit. But a realistic Pompeo told President Moon in private that his visit was only one step in the right direction. The stage was set for Biegun to get to work.[90]

John Bolton was predictably negative. He ignored Kim's pledge to go beyond dismantling Yongbyon and was unhappy about more talks. That was where the "US concession train would really start steaming along."[91]

The new sheriff in town spelled trouble for Bolton. Biegun was pragmatic. Bolton was an ideologue. Biegun built coalitions. Bolton was polarizing. Biegun was committed to Trump's initiative. Bolton was committed to torpedoing it. In the months ahead, the national security advisor did everything he could to stop the new envoy.

CHAPTER SEVENTEEN

"Looking forward to my next summit with Chairman Kim."

S TEVE BIEGUN'S PHONE RANG one Saturday morning in early January 2019. After months of trying to jump-start talks, the North Koreans had informed the CIA that Kim Yong Chol would travel to Washington in five days to see President Trump. This was short notice to be sure, but welcome news.

Biegun's phone rang again an hour later. Kent Harstedt, Sweden's North Korea envoy, was on the line. Choe Son Hui had accepted an invitation to come to Stockholm for talks with the Americans on the same day Kim Yong Chol would arrive in Washington. She also wanted to see Biegun.[1]

"It was a real head-scratcher," a State Department official recalled. Kim Yong Chol and Choe were jockeying for position and clearly not consulting each other.[2] Biegun couldn't be in two places at the same time, so he offered to meet Choe in Stockholm a day later. He would wrap up in Washington with Kim Yong Chol, grab a military flight from Andrews Air Force Base, and see Choe the next morning.[3]

The months since Pompeo's successful October visit to Pyongyang had been inexplicably quiet. There had been no response when Biegun reached out to Choe. The CIA managed to set up a Pompeo–Kim Yong Chol rematch in New York City, but the meeting was canceled. There was no reply when the Americans tried to reschedule.[4]

Of course, the North Koreans may have been reacting to Pompeo's statements about sanctions, and to the actual sanctioning of three North Korean officials in November.[5]

But other positive elements emerged. In early November, the North Koreans told Biegun's staff that an American who had illegally crossed the border with China would be released. In mid-December, Biegun hinted that the United States would loosen restrictions on humanitarian assistance and travel to North Korea.[6]

Just before Christmas, Kim Jong Un weighed in. After Pompeo told the press he was "counting on" a summit despite the stalemate, the secretary asked a surprised Biegun and Allison Hooker, just back from Seoul, to rush to the White House. Another letter from the chairman had arrived.[7]

President Trump had spent most of the day barking out his frustrations with a partial government shutdown in a stream of tweets. Kim's message was likely a welcome distraction. Filled with the usual unctuous language, it wasn't just another mash note.

The chairman proposed that the two leaders move forward quickly with preparations for a second summit. He also wanted to hold "a senior-level contact between the DPRK and the U.S." to discuss where the two leaders would meet. The twin phone calls to Biegun in early January were a direct result of the proposal.[8]

Trump tweeted a photo of himself at his desk with Biegun and Allison Hooker as well as a message: "Looking forward to my next summit with Chairman Kim."[9] The president was signaling that he wanted to meet Kim and Biegun was the man to arrange it.[10]

Three days later, Trump replied to Kim's letter affirmatively. He agreed that the venue for a summit should not be a problem and mentioned Hanoi as one option. The president added that he was open to a location closer "to you than to me."[11] His offer, however, could have been viewed as a subtle putdown. Kim had borrowed a Chinese plane to fly to Singapore, a reminder of his junior status.[12]

The North Korean leader's secret commitment to an early summit was there for all to hear in his New Year's speech a week later. Dressed in a Western-style suit and tie, the chairman was filmed walking to his office followed by his photogenic sister. He settled into a plush armchair with bookshelves in the background, rather than standing at the usual podium, to deliver a thirty-one-minute prerecorded address.[13]

Kim appeared uncomfortable, however. The clock behind him showed fifty-five minutes had elapsed since he started talking, betraying the fact he may have taken a break or needed several attempts to repeat passages. Even more jarring, taped applause was piped in to give the impression Kim was speaking to a large audience. Instead, observers were reminded of a canned sitcom laugh track.[14]

Nevertheless, he projected an "almost exuberant confidence" that dialogue and cooperation with the United States and South Korea were irreversible.[15] Kim let the world, and perhaps even more importantly, his people, know that he had great expectations for the next summit.[16]

The chairman's speech was leavened with familiar refrains about how to make progress. Kim's "firm will" was to advance toward "complete denuclearization." The best way to proceed was "step-by-step simultaneous action." A "faster pace" was possible if the United States responded to "North Korea's proactive efforts" with "practical actions."[17]

Kim also implied that U.S. troops wouldn't have to leave South Korea after all, which had been a standard North Korean demand in the past. His father had made the same comment when engagement was in full swing. The remark wasn't definitive, but it was intriguing.[18]

Most analysts missed an important clue about why Kim was enthusiastic about the future. The chairman hinted that North Korea's defense industry, which had dominated its economy, would be downsized, and contribute more to modernizing the civilian sector.[19]

Instead, the Western media focused on an imagined threat in his closing. Kim reminded listeners that if sanctions continued, "We may be compelled to find a new way for defending the sovereignty of the country." The press jumped to the eye-popping conclusion that he meant more WMD tests.[20]

In fact, experienced analysts detected a return to a tried-and-true practice of playing great powers off each other. Kim may have sensed that opportunity, given his summits with President Xi in 2018, and renewed trade tensions between the United States and China. The point of his message was, "You are not our only option for security and economic development," one expert observed.[21]

That analysis was proven correct a few days later when a heavily armored train passed over the Chinese border on its way to Beijing. North Korean media confirmed that Kim Jong Un was traveling to China for his thirty-fifth birthday.[22]

The fact that Xi and his wife hosted a birthday dinner for Kim was important. In China, parents did that for their children. The chairman appeared to be implicitly acknowledging Xi as his senior, a far cry from when he first took power. The visit confirmed a Chinese saying, "Your uncle is still your uncle. He is wiser and more experienced."[23]

Beijing was concerned about the upcoming summit. Kim probably tried to reassure Xi and told him what Trump wanted. But he also may have kept his negotiating cards close to his chest. Xi urged him to be careful, although he didn't say what he was probably thinking: that moving too fast with the Americans could diminish China's influence.[24]

Donald Trump was also hurtling toward the summit. Encouraged by Kim's New Year's speech, the president showed off the chairman's recent letter during his first cabinet meeting of 2019.

"We've really established a very good relationship," Trump gushed. "A lot of good things are happening." He then returned to a favorite theme: how he had prevented World War III. An expressionless, stiff John Bolton could be seen in the background.[25]

For Steve Biegun, the time had come to put his new negotiating game plan to the test.

"I don't want him in my f—king building!"

Kim Yong Chol's aircraft landed at Dulles Airport in the early evening on January 18. He was the first top North Korean official to stay overnight in Washington since Marshal Jo had met President Clinton almost two decades earlier.

Kim's visit was a logistical nightmare. He arrived at the Beijing airport with a delegation but no visa or airplane tickets. He did have tens of thousands of dollars to pay for them, but United Airlines wasn't convinced. Only after the State Department promised they would be admitted to the country did the airline relent and allow them to board the flight to Washington.[26]

Once they arrived at Dulles, the North Koreans were whisked to a VIP area. Homeland Security officials, customs agents, and consular officers scrambled to process them, collect their luggage, and organize a motorcade. The North Koreans were annoyed because they had to wait for over a half hour.[27]

Beaming like a proud father, Kim Yong Chol introduced Steve Biegun to a younger colleague, the "Special Representative for the United States." The three men had moved to a sofa when Biegun suddenly realized he would be working with the man sitting next to Kim, not Choe Son Hui.[28]

A career diplomat from an elite family, Kim Hyok Chol was no relation to his boss. After participating in multilateral nuclear talks, Kim was named ambassador to Spain and then expelled as tensions mounted in 2017. He returned home to work for the North Korean leader, which may have explained why his new boss didn't seem to intimidate him.[29]

The sudden switch was puzzling. One minute, Kim Jong Un named Choe; the next, his senior envoy named someone else. If that was the case, why was Choe coming to Stockholm? Perhaps the latest chapter in the conflict between Pyongyang's diplomats and spies, it was also personal. Choe and Kim Yong Chol didn't like each other.

The North Korean delegation arrived at the Dupont Circle Hotel, entering through an alley to avoid the press. After a short reception, the schedule for the next day was finalized: a photo op and morning meeting at the hotel with the secretary of state, a mid-day session with President Trump in the Oval Office, and then lunch with Pompeo and Biegun back at the hotel.[30]

None of the general's meetings were at the State Department, which seemed odd. Kim Jong Il's envoy had had dinner at Foggy Bottom with Secretary Albright, and lunch with the foreign policy establishment. Pompeo, however, told his staff, "I don't want him in my f—king building!"[31]

The tension between the two men was obvious when they met the next morning. Kim Yong Chol began to sketch the outlines of North Korea's price for denuclearization. He bragged that Pyongyang's economy was strong, but his country was open for foreign aid, business, and investment.[32]

Kim specified for the first time what sanctions should be lifted: all the measures that "affected the welfare of the Korean people," including every restriction imposed since the end of the Obama administration. The Americans calculated those sanctions cost the North Koreans almost $5 billion every year.[33]

Pompeo's response was measured but firm. Talking economics was fine, but denuclearization was the priority. Giving up WMD wasn't just about money. Pompeo emphasized that their countries faced a bigger threat: China. Just like Vietnam, which had been transformed into a friend after a costly war, the United States and North Korea should work together against Beijing.[34]

The conversation hit a brick wall. "Don't you want a strong friend?" the general replied, implying, "Don't you want a friend with nuclear

President Donald J. Trump is presented with a letter from Chairman Kim Jong Un
by Kim Yong Chol, vice chairman of the Workers' Party of Korea, January 18, 2019,
in the Oval Office of the White House. Official White House photo
by Shealah Craighead.

weapons?" Even the senior envoy wasn't permitted to talk about denuclearization.[35]

Kim's next stop was the Oval Office, where he handed Trump another
letter from his leader. The two men smiled and posed for a photogra-
pher. Then, the president took his seat behind the *Resolute* desk with
Kim, Pompeo, and Biegun seated opposite him. As was often the case
with Trump, the disjointed conversation lasted longer than anyone had
expected.[36]

The summit was set for Vietnam, but the location remained undecided.
Prompted by the secretary, Trump pushed for Danang, a coastal city that
the Secret Service thought would be easier to secure. The North Koreans
preferred Hanoi. It would be a shorter train ride for Kim, who was already
slated to travel three thousand miles and sixty hours. Pyongyang's embassy
there could also provide him with any support he needed.[37]

Naturally, denuclearization came up. The ex–real estate mogul told
Kim, "I don't want old properties, I want new properties." Presumably he
meant not just the decades-old facilities at Yongbyon, but other facilities

such as Pyongyang's uranium enrichment plant. Kim may have been confused at first but didn't respond.[38]

The general had some positive surprises up his sleeve. He suggested the two countries should establish offices for diplomats in Washington and Pyongyang. Aside from ending six decades of North Korea and the United States refusing to recognize each other, the "liaison offices" would serve as a reliable communications link to help build better relations. They had been a part of the 1994 Agreed Framework, but were never implemented.[39]

Even more surprising, Kim told Trump that North Korea didn't want American troops to leave Korea. The chairman had hinted at this new twist in his New Year's speech. The North Koreans had shifted their position before when relations improved with Washington. They viewed the United States as a counterweight to their Chinese neighbor.[40]

Still, the proposal was ironic. Pundits feared Trump would agree to a North Korean demand that the United States pull out or scale back American troop presence at the upcoming summit. That way, he would save on money spent to protect South Korea. But Kim Jong Un wanted them to stay.

The Pompeo-Kim feud then erupted in front of the president. Pointing at the secretary, Kim accused him of making it hard for Trump to reach his dream deal with Pyongyang. Pompeo visibly stiffened. "I thought he was going to lose it right there," one official recalled.[41]

Payback came during lunch at the Dupont Circle Hotel. Anticipating a clash between their boss and the North Korean envoy, State Department officials had designed a short meal. Sure enough, the secretary "radiated anger like Darth Vader," according to one official.[42]

Kim suggested American inspectors didn't need to come to the nuclear test site despite what the chairman had said. He added that Yongbyon was barely functioning, and that North Korea wasn't producing enriched uranium. The secretary turned to a CIA official at his table and commented, "Don't we have the coordinates for that place?"

Pompeo looked right at Kim and said, "I have a plane. Why don't we go there right now?" The general squirmed. One American recalled that the general seemed to shrink in his chair. Kim told Pompeo there was no need to do that.[43]

Then, the secretary proposed a toast, "To Truth." The two men needed to be honest with each other if they were going to help the president and chairman realize their dream. He was calling Kim a liar and warning him,

Satellite image of the Yongbyon Nuclear Scientific Research Center Area, captured on February 11, 2018. Pleaides © CNES 2018. Distribution Airbus DS. Annotation by *38 North*.

"Wait until I can put you down in front of your leader; see how you like that," a State Department aide observed.[44]

Sitting at the same table as their bosses, Biegun and his new negotiating partner hatched a plan to come up with commitments, not just vague promises. Kim Hyok Chol didn't seem like "the kind of person to deliver the wire brush treatment, the litany of perfidy, sins, and misery that the United States had inflicted on North Korea," one American official remembered.[45]

Biegun's new counterpart suggested they meet the next day, a ploy obviously designed to keep him from a session with Choe thousands of miles away in Stockholm. Evidently, Kim Yong Chol had ordered his delegation to stop Biegun from seeing her. But the American envoy persuaded his partner to sit down together right after lunch instead.

That afternoon, Kim Hyok Chol put his cards on the table, asking, Did the Americans have a plan to bring inspectors to the North Korean missile site? How about the nuclear test site? A plan for dismantling Yong-byon? He wanted to see them.[46]

The North Korean negotiator had his own demands: "We need sanctions relief, sanctions relief, sanctions relief." He asked Biegun to draw up a proposal for what the Americans were prepared to give in return for steps on the WMD front. The two agreed to reconvene in Pyongyang.[47]

Once their late Friday afternoon session was over, Biegun, Allison Hooker, and a few aides rushed to Andrews Air Force Base, boarded a military aircraft, and flew directly to Stockholm. They drove fifty kilometers to a conference center facing a snow-covered lake. Police had cordoned off the area to prevent outsiders from entering.[48]

Choe Son Hui was already there. So were South Korean officials. Technically, the Swedes were hosting the meeting, but they receded into the background to allow the antagonists to talk. Private European experts expounded on topics that might come up in the official negotiations. Some Americans thought the lectures were helpful; others didn't.[49]

The first encounter between Biegun and Choe revealed her to be thoughtful, careful, confident, and well informed with a mischievous, sardonic sense of humor. Choe was equally comfortable over dinner talking about American spirituals or ABBA, the Swedish pop group.[50]

It was unclear why she had stepped back from negotiating a landmark deal with the United States, arguably the role of a lifetime. But the fact that Choe was in Stockholm meant she still had clout.

Were the North Koreans happy their rival was leading the charge? the Americans asked. "Half happy, half sad," they replied, relieved and disappointed. There was a hint of disdain for Kim Yong Chol. The Stockholm delegation may have thought they would pick up the pieces after he failed.[51]

Nevertheless, since rumor had it Choe was close to Kim Yo Jong, the Stockholm session was an opportunity to send a message to the leader. "The president is serious. This is the best chance you are going to have to reach a lasting deal with the United States; let's get it done," one American told Choe.[52]

Talks were finally moving forward. The Washington and Stockholm sessions started to fill in the blanks for a summit deal. Denuclearization, inspections, improved political and economic ties, and sanctions lifting were on the table. The North Koreans might even agree that American troops could remain on the peninsula. The appearance of a new negotiator who wanted to get the job done was also encouraging. President Trump tweeted afterwards, "Great meeting this week with top Reps. Looking forward to meeting Chairman Kim at the end of February."[53]

The North Koreans were expecting great things from Trump. Just before leaving for Beijing, Kim Yong Chol asked an American official, "Who was the most famous, beloved president?" His escort hesitated. Maybe Lincoln, Washington, FDR? A surprised Kim responded, "Why not Donald Trump?"[54]

Once home, the North Korean media published a photo of Kim Yong Chol and his new negotiator briefing the chairman in his book-lined office at the Central Committee headquarters. The message was clear. A summit was going to happen.[55]

"President Trump is ready to end this war. It is over. It is done."

Steve Biegun hatched a plan over a late-night drink in Stockholm. A major speech on North Korea would put to rest the speculation swirling around Trump's initiative, not to mention the confusion caused by his erratic tweets and remarks. It would also send a clear message to Pyongyang, which often struggled to understand the Washington babble.[56]

Biegun dictated a draft into his cell phone early one morning after he returned home. His staff cleaned it up and the speech was forwarded to Secretary Pompeo. A reporter recalled, "They were telling us, 'You've really got to watch this. It's going to be a big deal.'"[57]

Hours after the State Department announced Biegun would travel to North Korea, the American envoy stood at a podium at Stanford University on January 31. Palo Alto, California, seemed the right place for the speech, far enough from Washington to escape the political hothouse and close enough to Asia to make the morning headlines. Moreover, Biegun had turned to Sig Hecker and Bob Carlin—John Lewis had passed away—to be part of his kitchen cabinet.[58]

"The President of the United States is convinced that it's time to move past 70 years of war and hostility on the Korean peninsula," Biegun told the audience. Washington and Pyongyang were at an "inflection point." He announced, "President Trump is ready to end this war. It is over. It is done."[59]

Biegun didn't say it out loud, but so was CVID. His new plan, a step-by-step approach to denuclearization, was keyed to the provisions in the Singapore summit statement. The United States would also take steps along the way to end "hostility." Lifting sanctions before Pyongyang had denuclearized was now possible.

The speech was grounded in reality. Biegun didn't mimic Trump's over-the-top salesmanship. Diplomacy might not succeed, but it was worth a try. Given that time was short before the next summit, elaborating on the Singapore statement would be challenging.

Still, the American envoy was only partially successful. Pyongyang was encouraged because Biegun's approach was more like its own. But the media only got some of it right, in part because the press wasn't steeped in the nuances of diplomacy. Reuters even suggested that Pyongyang would be angered by his demands. Just the opposite was true.[60]

John Bolton would later accuse the envoy of pursuing a personal agenda and speculate that Pompeo was "ignorant of it." In fact, Bolton was the bureaucratic outlier. No one showed him an advance copy, not even his own staff. "We didn't really care what Bolton thought," one official said. "It was up to Pompeo and the president."[61]

The national security advisor had been his own worst enemy. Bolton made no effort to orchestrate policy; he isolated himself in his office to read memos. Moreover, he thought everyone else was about to sell out the country. Another sarcastic official remarked, "We really didn't get into the business of selling out the country until December."[62]

Six days after the Stanford speech, just as President Trump announced in his State of the Union address that he would meet Kim in three weeks, a plane carrying Steve Biegun and his fifteen-member delegation landed in Pyongyang. They knew only that their aircraft was set to depart in three days.[63]

As the Americans' motorcade turned onto the street leading to the Koryo Hotel, they were informed that talks would start right away. The delegation was confined to the thirty-seventh and thirty-eighth floors of the hotel, which were self-contained with guest, conference, and dining rooms. There would be no sightseeing.[64]

Any optimism, however, evaporated when Biegun and Hooker met an angry Kim Yong Chol. The general accused Trump of planning to hold a summit with his boss and then one with Xi, reducing the chairman to a prop in a photo op. He threatened to end talks before they even started.[65]

"It felt like he was taking the newspaper to the puppy's nose," one American recalled. Rather than argue, Biegun and Hooker assured him that the president had the best of intentions. They would relay his concern to Trump.[66]

Once the talks began, Kim Hyok Chol, the previously can-do partner, transformed into a haranguing apparatchik. Maybe it was because the meetings were bugged or because Kim Yong Chol had read him the riot act.

In any case, the general was running the show even if he wasn't in the room. North Koreans shuttled in and out of the talks, feeding messages to the negotiator. Sometimes he would shift his tone, double down on a point, or call for a break, often looking frazzled when he returned. One message dropped to the floor, but a North Korean stomped his shoe on it before an American could pick it up.[67]

There was another problem. The American delegation included a nuclear scientist, a missile expert, and lawyers. Biegun had asked the North Koreans to bring experts, but the same old diplomats and bureaucrats showed up. "We probably knew more about their WMD programs than the people sitting across the table from us," an American official noted.[68]

Since the conference room was too small to hold everyone, Biegun's experts took turns at the table. His nuclear experts talked about denuclearization. His missile experts talked about giving them up. Legal experts talked about lifting sanctions and establishing diplomatic relations.[69]

The discussion was civil and often constructive, especially when it came to North Korea's priority of transforming relations. Declaring the Korean War over and eventually signing a peace treaty were at the top of the North Korean agenda. So was working together on the American proposal to help Pyongyang achieve a "brighter future."[70]

Setting up embassies—proposed by Kim Yong Chol in the Oval Office—was also important since it would signal that the two countries were ready to live with each other. The North Koreans took Biegun on a guided tour of the former East German embassy that would house American diplomats. I had visited the same building, with a bomb shelter basement and an escape hatch into an adjacent garden, decades earlier.[71]

Transforming relations also meant building stronger humanitarian ties. Biegun suggested new programs besides the Singapore commitment to resume joint recovery of the remains of American soldiers killed or missing in the Korean War. One idea—combating virulent strains of tuberculosis that had plagued North Korea—had been a favorite of John Lewis.[72]

Hopes for quick progress on denuclearization, however, were dashed. Chairman Kim had agreed to allow inspections of his nuclear test site, but North Koreans had warned Biegun in Stockholm that it would be hard even to get inspectors into their country.

This time, the North Koreans rejected Biegun's proposal, which included a request for soil samples. One American recalled, "It was like we were asking for the crown jewels."[73] Soil samples would have been one piece in the jigsaw puzzle that would establish the size of Pyongyang's stockpile. But the North Koreans may have also been reminded of 1992 when they were called out as lying after inspectors analyzed samples.[74]

As Biegun feared, Kim's diplomats and bureaucrats couldn't discuss dismantling the Yongbyon nuclear facility. The Americans brought their plan, just as Kim Hyok Chol had requested in Washington. The real work could only begin after the two sides agreed on which of the facility's hundreds of buildings would be torn down. But the North Koreans didn't know anything about the site except its name. "What are you going to give us?" they kept asking.[75]

Kim's delegation wouldn't discuss Biegun's WMD road map, or even acknowledge the end point of "final, fully verified denuclearization." Biegun argued that passengers on a train had to know all the stops as well as its last stop. The North Koreans argued that passengers would be satisfied with taking the train to the next station.[76]

The U.S. envoy even reiterated a key point in his Stanford speech, that sanctions lifting could start once Pyongyang moved forward with denuclearization. Kim Hyok Chol was happy to accept the lifting of restrictions on his country's coal exports but unwilling to give up anything in return.[77]

The summit's location was the only issue settled in a separate conversation between Dan Walsh, the White House deputy chief of staff, who had accompanied the American delegation, and Kim Jong Un's closest aides. Walsh tried one last time to convince the North Koreans to hold the meeting in Danang but settled for Hanoi.[78]

With the Pyongyang talks about to end and no summit declaration in sight, another session had to be scheduled quickly. Kim Yong Chol waxed poetic about his boyhood and freezing winters at the foot of Mount Paektu, the sacred mountain of the revolution, for much of the farewell dinner.

The general still found time to propose reconvening in Pyongyang, which would have made it easy for him to retain control. Biegun, however, insisted on moving to Hanoi since time was short. Kim finally agreed.[79]

As the American delegation's plane landed in South Korea, President Trump tweeted that the Pyongyang talks had been a "very productive meeting," even though they weren't. With the summit set for Hanoi at the end of February, Biegun admitted to the press, "We have some hard work to do with the DPRK."[80]

"If nuclear weapons didn't exist, the draft declaration would have been very good."

A few weeks later, in late February, Kim Hyok Chol and Steve Biegun reconvened at the Hotel Du Parc in Hanoi's historic district. The conference area had been roped off for the negotiations, but one American official suspected that "a dozen countries had planted microphones" to eavesdrop.[81]

Some three thousand journalists descended on the city. Reporters chased Kim Hyok Chol's sedan down city streets during the ten-minute drive from a government guesthouse to the hotel. Biegun's car was mobbed by motorcycles and film crews wherever he went.[82]

With just a few days left before Trump and Kim Jong Un would arrive, the prognosis was worse than uncertain. The Americans brought their entire team again. The North Korean diplomats and bureaucrats showed up one more time. Right away, it was clear that, according to one American, "they had zero authority to discuss nuclear issues."

Moreover, Kim Hyok Chol was still "remote-controlled" by his boss even though he was thousands of miles away in Pyongyang. North Koreans shuttled in and out of the conference room with messages.[83]

The general made his presence known right off the bat. Kim Hyok Chol threatened to cancel the summit unless Washington immediately agreed to lift sanctions. His threat had to be taken seriously whether it was real or not. The chairman hadn't boarded his train yet.[84]

Biegun responded that the United States wasn't prepared to meet their demand, and the North Koreans filled the first day of talks with heavy hints about Kim Jong Un. Finally, Biegun told his counterpart, "I will inform Washington this evening and tell you our reply tomorrow," one aide recalled.[85]

The answer arrived the next morning. Trump called the North Koreans' bluff. The United States was not going to lift sanctions before the summit started. Kim Hyok Chol requested a break to report to Pyongyang. Or at least he said he did.[86]

"Where are we on the agenda?" the North Korean negotiator asked when he returned, acting as if nothing had happened. "He looked like the weight of the world had been lifted off his shoulders," a member of the U.S. delegation observed.[87]

Then came a pleasant surprise. After the Americans tabled a draft declaration, the North Koreans tabled their own. Even more surprising, their draft mirrored many of the American presentations made in Pyongyang.

Still, the North Korean proposal was nowhere near where it needed to be. Denuclearization was the biggest problem. There was a blank space where it should have appeared in the document.[88]

Steve Biegun and Kim Hyok Chol worked for the next three days— some meetings lasted twelve hours—to merge the two drafts. They weren't horse-trading. The sessions were constructive, even cooperative. Biegun emerged from the hotel during one break. He refused to speak to reporters but gave a thumbs-up gesture they took to mean the talks were going well.[89]

The two men made remarkable progress, drafting road maps that solved almost every challenge that had surfaced during decades of talks. Most of the provisions focused on ending American "hostility" toward North Korea, an enduring objective for Pyongyang.[90]

Washington's "hostile policy" was not an idle or abstract complaint for the North Koreans. The absence of diplomatic relations was a sign of political hostility. Sanctions were a sign of economic hostility. Preservation of the temporary 1954 armistice in lieu of a declaration that the war was over and a peace treaty reflected security hostility.[91]

All this had been discussed in Pyongyang, but the Hanoi session sealed the deal. Biegun and Kim agreed to issue a declaration that the Korean War was over, and to begin negotiations on a treaty that would codify peace. Despite Bolton's, Pompeo's, and Mattis's earlier opposition, the Pentagon had finally approved the provision Biegun negotiated.[92]

The two negotiators agreed to establish liaison offices, a signal that political hostility was coming to an end. Hanoi seemed appropriate to the occasion since Washington had taken the same approach when it ended its enmity with Vietnam. The State Department had already started looking for diplomats to staff its new Pyongyang office.[93]

Strengthening people-to-people contacts would help spur normalization. The Americans proposed, and the North Koreans agreed to, an umbrella program that would lead cultural and other exchanges. The White House envisioned Ivanka Trump would play a role in those exchanges.

Kim Jong Il's dream of sending the Pyongyang State Orchestra to the United States was about to happen. Biegun's staff had already contacted the Kennedy Center in Washington to arrange a performance on June 12, the anniversary of the Singapore summit.[94]

Korean American lobbying for family reunions—a fixture of relations between North and South since 1985—paid off. Millions of Koreans had fled during the war and tens of thousands had moved to the United States while thousands of family members remained in North Korea. The negotiators agreed to meetings between Korean Americans and their North Korean relatives. Video conferences seemed the way to go.[95]

The draft even included an American promise to send a professional basketball team to North Korea. Kim Song Hye, the deputy negotiator, was especially keen. She knew that the leader's family were big fans of the Chicago Bulls and that the chairman had met Dennis Rodman twice during the Obama years.[96]

As for helping Pyongyang achieve a "brighter future," two international conferences would be held, first with the North Koreans as observers, then as participants, to discuss how the global community could help.[97] Visits to North Korea from International Monetary Fund and World Bank experts were also in the mix.[98]

All these steps served North Korean interests, but building better relations was the key to unlocking the denuclearization door. As the confrontation with Washington receded into history, Kim Jong Un would be able to shift resources from his enormous defense budget to modernizing his economy.

By the time Air Force One was on its way to Hanoi, two glaring omissions remained in the multi-page draft: denuclearization and North Korea's demand that sanctions be lifted.[99] One official observed, "If nuclear weapons didn't exist, the draft declaration would have been very good."[100]

With the summit about to begin, the North Koreans insisted that Kim Jong Un would arrive with a "big" present for President Trump that "just the chairman knows." The Americans, however, "couldn't agree to something we couldn't see."[101]

Biegun pressed the North Koreans to nail down Yongbyon's boundaries. He even brought a CIA map of the facility to coax the North Koreans forward. But Kim Hyok Chol was a diplomat. That wasn't his business.[102]

The American envoy tried another ploy to suss out what the chairman meant by "more than Yongbyon." He spread a newspaper article out in front of Kim detailing a site suspected of producing enriched uranium. The North Koreans dismissed the report as idle speculation.[103]

Biegun urged them to present a more detailed denuclearization road map. Kim Song Hye, the deputy negotiator, who was cut from the same abrasive cloth as Choe Son Hui, insisted that if it were up to her, she wouldn't give up their weapons. But her leader wanted to do it.[104]

She argued the North Koreans were trying to sell Biegun a car and he wasn't buying it. A former Ford vice president, State's envoy responded, "If you're going to buy a car, you lift the hood, check the engine, go for a test drive, and know what you are getting for the price." The North Koreans still wouldn't budge.[105]

Finally, Biegun and Hooker threatened, "You can't play this game with Trump." If the North Korean delegation wouldn't address denuclearization, the summit would fail. Their prophetic warning fell on deaf ears.[106]

The North Koreans didn't know it, but Biegun was primed to start lifting sanctions once Kim Hyok Chol budged on WMD. His delegation reconvened late one night in a windowless room in the basement of the ramshackle U.S. embassy. They sent a message to Pompeo asking for the go-ahead to start lifting $1 billion worth of restrictions. While Biegun got the green light, he needed Kim Hyok Chol to move first.[107]

He never budged. The North Koreans were under enormous pressure to deliver on sanctions, but they were powerless on denuclearization. Kim Hyok Chol kept threatening, "If you don't do this, Kim Jong Un may not come," even when the chairman was on his train heading south.[108]

Finally, Biegun called it quits. He inserted the American version of denuclearization into the draft's blank space. If the North Koreans wanted to meet again, all they had to do was call. The unfinished declaration "didn't end up on the cutting room floor, but it didn't go any further," he recalled.[109]

Nevertheless, the talks had made astonishing progress. Everything now depended on Donald Trump and Kim Jong Un.

CHAPTER EIGHTEEN

"A little bit of desperation
on the president's part"

H OURS BEFORE HE LEFT on his eight-thousand-mile trip to Hanoi, President Trump painted a rosy picture of the future for North Korea if it gave up its nuclear weapons. He had sent a handwritten letter and four photos of the Singapore summit to the chairman a week earlier, gushing, "I look forward to seeing you next week. It will be great."[1]

Just talking to Kim should have been considered a victory according to the White House, but Trump's relentless impulsiveness, exaggeration, optimism, and self-promotion stoked fears he would go off half-cocked.[2] Everyone knew the president was in the hunt for a Nobel Peace Prize to match Obama's. He had recently been nominated for one by Japanese prime minister Abe for meeting Kim.[3]

Looming congressional investigations were another wild card. Trump's former lawyer and fixer Michael Cohen was scheduled to testify before the House Oversight Committee just as the summit began. Special Counsel Robert Mueller was expected to release his report on possible ties between his campaign and Russian election interference a few days after that.

On top of everything else, Trump's diplomacy had been under constant attack from the media, pundits, and Congress since his January Oval Office session with Kim Yong Chol. Long-time Korea expert Victor Cha suggested the summit reflected "a little bit of desperation on the president's part."[4]

On the other hand, General Vincent Brooks, the recently retired commander of United States Forces Korea, argued, "Without conversation we go right back to where we were in 2015 and 2017 with the great potential for miscalculation." Brooks knew what he was talking about since he had been on the front lines of the confrontation. But his message was drowned out by the armchair generals.[5]

Still, most of the American public approved of Trump's policy for the first time since the crisis in 2017. The president's reminder in the State of the Union address that the United States would be in a "major war with North Korea" if he hadn't been elected may have also resonated with the public.[6]

The imminent summit only motivated John Bolton. Worried that State was "spinning out of control," he orchestrated briefings for the president with the theme that "no deal is better than a bad deal."[7] Trump could do worse than emulate Republican icon Ronald Reagan, who walked away from a 1986 summit with Mikhail Gorbachev. Bolton believed their last session was a "successful conclusion to our briefing efforts."[8]

He was in for a big surprise. As Bolton's aircraft made its way to Hanoi, the draft document Biegun had negotiated arrived in his inbox. Approved by Pompeo but kept from Bolton, "It read as if drafted by the North Koreans," he recalled.[9] Its vague statement on denuclearization was more evidence of a "massive process foul."[10]

Bolton's new right-hand man, Charles Kupperman, showed the draft to White House Chief of Staff Mick Mulvaney and Stephen Miller, Trump's domestic advisor. Neither knew anything about North Korea, but they agreed the draft violated the "established interagency process." Vice President Pence was also alerted and agreed with them.[11]

Flying across the Pacific on Air Force One, Trump was warned by Bolton's staff that State was freelancing. The statement was a huge deviation from his policy. In fact, the draft was a huge deviation from Bolton's "Libya model," discarded months earlier by Pompeo and Biegun. The national security advisor's aides took the opportunity to urge Trump once again to adopt his model.[12]

Rumor had it that after landing in Hanoi, Bolton even buttonholed reporters to get out his message. Fox News reporter John Roberts tweeted that everyone in the government thought Biegun was "getting too far over his skis."[13]

Bolton, however, had already been outmaneuvered. Pompeo had kept Trump informed about State's negotiating approach but kept him in the dark. The president hadn't seen Biegun's negotiated draft only because it had been a work in progress.[14]

Trump queried Dan Walsh, who had traveled with Biegun to Pyongyang. The White House deputy chief of staff told the president that State's envoy was "killing it" for him, one official recalled. Bolton would later claim the president was unhappy. But State heard that Trump thought the draft looked pretty good although the nuclear issue still had to be worked out.[15]

Bolton's argument that the State Department had violated the established decision-making process was rich. Maureen Dowd wrote in the *New York Times* that he had been the "fifth column in the Bush State Department—there to lurk around and report back on flower child Colin Powell." Another round in the bureaucratic fight had gone to Pompeo and Biegun. There were more to come.[16]

As Air Force One neared Hanoi, Kim Jong Un's yellow-and-green armored train approached the end of a 2,500-mile trip from Pyongyang to China's border with Vietnam. Despite his campaign to stop smoking in his country, Kim had been spotted taking a predawn cigarette break at China's Nanning train station. A woman who appeared to be his sister was holding a crystal ashtray. The leader of a famous North Korean girl band, Hyon Song Wol, rumored to be Kim's former mistress, and Choe Son Hui were also spotted on the platform.[17]

When the chairman's train reached the border town of Dong Dang, he switched to his black armored Mercedes for the one-hundred-mile drive to Hanoi. Thousands of soldiers and police had been mobilized to guard Highway One, which was closed to traffic. The motorcade traveled through provinces where hundreds of North Korean soldiers had fought during the Vietnam War. Some were probably buried there.[18]

But Kim almost didn't make it. Somebody on his train, perhaps the chairman himself, had been watching media coverage from Hanoi. Reporters were standing in front of cameras on the rooftop of Kim's hotel. The North Koreans threatened that their leader would go home if the press wasn't expelled.[19]

In fact, they were the ones who had messed up. Kim's staff had tried to reserve rooms at a five-star hotel, but the cost was too high. Their only option was the less expensive Melia where reporters had set up the American press center. Biegun got frantic calls from the Vietnamese and the North Koreans to help resolve the problem, but there was nothing he could do.[20]

The Vietnamese tweeted with a three-megaphone emoji that the "American press center" would be moved. Troops boxed up the equipment, and the seventh floor was cleared out. The center was relocated to an ornate Soviet-style venue, normally hired out for weddings and concerts.[21]

Kim Jong Un arrived in Hanoi that afternoon, Tuesday, February 26. Security swarmed around his hotel. The surrounding block was completely closed. Four armored personnel carriers guarded by soldiers were parked nearby. The lobby, which now featured a metal detector, had been cleared and window shades were pulled down. Reporters staying at the Melia were warned not to bother the North Koreans.[22]

Air Force One landed at Noi Bai International Airport that evening. President Trump's motorcade arrived a half hour later at the J. W. Marriott Hotel, just five miles from where Kim would be staying.[23]

"It was as CNN as it gets in North Korea."

Donald Trump and Kim Jong Un strode toward each other the next evening, shook hands for the first time since June 2018, exchanged a few words, and answered questions from the press.

"I think it will be very successful. We have a great relationship. I think it will be very successful," Trump proclaimed. Skeptics wondered whether anything would come out of it.[24]

The Vietnamese breathed a collective sigh of relief. The summit had been announced during their most important festival, leaving only three weeks to prepare. Streets were cleaned, construction sites tidied up, and Vietnamese, American, and North Korean flags were hung from the city's light poles. Police, anti-riot units, and the military were mobilized.[25]

By the time Trump and Kim shook hands, the city had a "summer camp vibe." There were celebratory concerts. Children wearing traditional Korean dress practiced songs to welcome Kim. Street vendors sold T-shirts emblazoned with his face and the "Rocket Man" nickname.[26]

The summit venue, the Metropole Legend, was a French colonial–style hotel built in 1901. With its white stucco, green shutters, hardwood floors, ceiling fans, and iron filigree, the Metropole was a favorite haunt of celebrities and politicians. Charlie Chaplin honeymooned there in 1936. Jane Fonda spent two weeks there during her 1970s anti–Vietnam War campaign. Trump himself stayed at the hotel in 2017.[27]

President Donald J. Trump is greeted by Kim Jong Un, chairman of the Workers'
Party of Korea, February 27, 2019, at the Sofitel Legend Metropole hotel in Hanoi,
for their second summit meeting. Official White House photo by Shealah Craighead.

A confident White House announced the two leaders would sign an
agreement. Yet when Pompeo tried to meet Kim Yong Chol to finalize the
declaration, just as he had in Singapore, he failed.[28]

The North Koreans probably thought they could get a better deal with
Trump. Besides, only Kim Jong Un could negotiate the details of denuclearization. Pompeo waited several hours for his counterpart to change
his mind, then finally turned in.[29]

Cocky in public, Trump was uncertain in private. He saw three possible outcomes: a small deal with a first step toward denuclearization, which
he thought would weaken sanctions; a big deal, which wasn't going to happen because Kim wasn't ready; or "I walk."[30]

The Trump-Kim handshake was a prelude to a private dinner in the
Spice Garden, the hotel's first-floor restaurant. The two leaders sat side by
side with their advisors at a large round table. Clusters of American and
North Korean flags were arranged behind them. John Bolton was conspic-
uously absent; the North Koreans had excluded him.[31]

The chatter was relaxed. After the Americans explained why each star
on the flag stood for a state, Kim Yong Chol asked if there were plans to

add more.[32] Some Americans joked that Greenland was up for sale, but others made it clear that the United States wasn't going to add new states. Little did the North Koreans know, Trump had already asked about buying the Danish territory.[33]

The president hadn't planned to discuss nuclear weapons at dinner. Still, Biegun launched into his offer to dismantle Yongbyon, only part of Pyongyang's nuclear program, in return for lifting all the sanctions. He appeared surprised when Trump rejected his proposal.[34]

Foggy and overcast, Thursday, February 28, was the big day. The leaders wound through streets guarded by the Vietnamese en route to the Metropole. Bystanders waved North Korean and American flags. The Secret Service parked "the Beast" in a tent and surrounded it; Kim's bodyguards protected his armored limousine close by.[35]

Trump was irritable after watching Michael Cohen's explosive congressional testimony all night. He canceled a presummit session with his advisors. In the car with Bolton, Pompeo, and Mick Mulvaney, Trump had wondered out loud whether "walking away or agreeing to a small deal would be a bigger story," and how to explain "taking a walk." Pompeo suggested a positive spin: they had made progress and would meet again.[36]

The two leaders returned to the same room where they had met the night before, seated at a round table, once again with flags arrayed behind them, poised to answer reporters' questions. An optimistic Trump took up most of the six-minute session, although he added once again that he was in no rush to get a deal. Getting the "right deal" was more important.[37]

Kim said little, although he answered a question shouted at him, the first time ever as far as anyone knew. Was he confident about the negotiations? Kim paused, then replied, "I will not make rash decisions but from my instincts, I believe good results will come out."[38]

Trump and Kim met alone for the next forty minutes. The chairman pushed his Yongbyon proposal again, and was frustrated and angry when Trump still wouldn't agree to it. The president appeared tired and annoyed.[39]

After a short stroll in the hotel's inner courtyard, the two leaders were joined poolside by Pompeo and Kim Yong Chol. They headed into a greenhouse for a scheduled ten-minute break. It lasted almost an hour. The chairman repeated his proposal. Trump rejected it. Pompeo recalled that Kim stared at his envoy "with an expression that required no translation: WTF?"

Back in the holding room, the president snarled at Pompeo, "Do we have to stay for lunch?" It was just two hours into the day-long summit. They agreed the afternoon could be cut short.[40]

Returning to the talks, Trump, Kim, and their advisors held a brief photo op for the media.[41] Playing master of ceremonies for the press, Trump quipped, "Is everyone having a good time?" A reporter asked Kim, "Are you ready to denuclearize?" He replied, "From what I feel right now I do have a feeling that good results will come out."[42]

A surprised Trump observed, "That's probably the best answer you've ever heard."[43] After the reporters left, he asked Kim, "Does the press give you a hard time?" The chairman laughed as he replied, "I don't have that burden."[44]

One floor above the two leaders, the State Department had set up a war room ready to provide quick-reaction analysis.[45] Trump would consult with Pompeo and Biegun during breaks. They, in turn, would query the war room for information and suggestions.[46]

Trump pushed Kim and Kim pushed back for the next ninety minutes, trying to reach a deal. The exchange was never acrimonious, angry, or confrontational, although the chairman added emphasis to his voice on one or two occasions.[47]

The president was ready to accept a small deal, just not Kim's small deal. The problem was a simple trade: How much of the nuclear program would North Korea give up and how many sanctions would the United States lift? "Trump would have been happy to accept a deal if Kim requested less or offered more," an aide recalled.[48]

The two leaders reached a moment of truth after a break. Trump pressed Kim on his Yongbyon proposal: "What you have asked for isn't going to work, but let's talk about it. Can you do more? Or how about a percentage reduction in sanctions rather than removing them?"[49]

That was beyond a doubt the worst moment for Bolton. "If Kim had said, 'Yes, I'll take a 50 percent reduction,' Trump would have thumped the table and said, 'Deal!'" Another official believed the horse trading would have started. If Kim said he could give Trump all of Yongbyon, more than the president thought he would get, yet another official believed, "We might have got a pause in the conversation, a break, and then a more substantive conversation at lunch."[50]

But the chairman just kept saying he couldn't do it—his people wouldn't let him—and repeated his offer. One American described him as a "robotic, thirty-five-year-old inexperienced leader." Another believed he may have miscalculated and thought the president needed a deal.[51]

Trump switched tacks. He asked Kim whether he would give up his missiles that were able to attack the United States. The president's proposal was a clear sign he wasn't listening to Bolton. The national security advisor had warned Trump that South Korea and Japan also wanted to eliminate shorter-range weapons that were able to strike their countries.[52]

In fact, Trump hadn't been listening to Bolton since the summit began. He carried a copy of the "Libya model" in his pocket to dinner the first night but didn't bring it up. The next day, after Bolton hounded the president, Trump flipped the plan across the table to Kim with the almost derisory comment that he might want to look at it. Trump didn't say, "We want this," one official remembered.[53]

When the president asked a surprised Bolton in front of the North Koreans what he thought about giving up long-range missiles, his advisor pivoted to an idea near and dear to his heart: an up-front, comprehensive WMD declaration. Trump shot Bolton down; that was too complicated.

In any case, the chairman wasn't buying any of it.[54] The president later told Bob Woodward that he "instinctively knew Kim wasn't ready to get where he needed to go" to give up enough nuclear sites without asking for too much sanctions relief.[55]

But just to make sure, Trump checked with Pompeo all along. He also huddled with the secretary, Biegun, Bolton, Mick Mulvaney, Allison Hooker, and Matt Pottinger. They all agreed and told him so. He couldn't accept Kim's deal.[56]

Disaster loomed. Separate statements or no summit statement at all would mean they couldn't agree on anything. One official imagined that a visibly frustrated Kim was thinking, "We have to sign something." With his full propaganda contingent present and expecting a deal, "It was as CNN as it gets in North Korea."[57]

Trump could see Kim was disappointed. He hesitated but then tried to put the North Korean leader at ease by agreeing to support a joint statement. When Bolton pointed out that would risk showing "we hadn't achieved anything," Trump shot him down again in front of everyone. The president wanted to demonstrate the two leaders could cooperate.[58]

Surprisingly, Kim agreed with Bolton. One American remembered the chairman's reaction: "I don't think there is going to be any purpose served by a joint statement of any kind."[59]

Trump wanted to try something, anything. He proposed that Pompeo and Kim Yong Chol come up with a statement. But "Kim Yong Chol turned purple. He must have been thinking, 'Great, what I am going to do about this?'" an American official remembered. Instead, the president volunteered Pompeo and his team to produce a first draft.[60]

Once the North Koreans left, a tired Trump dictated the gist to Biegun and Hooker—literally two sentences—along the lines of what Pompeo recommended: the two leaders had met, discussed the following issues, and agreed their teams would continue to talk.

Trump asked Biegun and Hooker if they got it. "Yes sir," they replied.[61]

The two negotiators retired to the holding room to find a laptop. After a few minutes, Trump and Pompeo came in. The president looked over the draft and gave the go-ahead. He thought the North Koreans would agree and the meeting would be over.[62]

As the summit clock was running out, Choe Son Hui suddenly showed up and asked to see Biegun. No one had seen her since January in Stockholm, but she had traveled to Hanoi. Choe had been spotted on the platform when Kim's train stopped in Nanning and was featured in a newspaper photo of Kim Jong Un being briefed on the eve of the summit.[63]

She had been lying low until the right moment but now was obviously stepping forward to try to save the deal. Biegun and Hooker handed Choe their draft and informed her Trump had approved the language.[64]

Choe had her own draft, which the Americans assumed came from the chairman. She translated the two-page proposal into English while Biegun and Hooker took notes. It repeated the trade of shutting down Yongbyon for lifting sanctions and added a continuation of the WMD test moratorium—nothing new there.[65]

But Choe explained the North Koreans were not demanding that every restriction imposed since 2016 be lifted, only individual provisions that hurt the "livelihood" of their people. It may have been a very small crack in opening the sanctions-lifting door.[66]

In a new twist, North Korea was also willing to accept "snapback" sanctions. They had been part of the nuclear deal with Iran and were also embedded in Biegun's negotiating road maps. Such sanctions could be reimposed if Pyongyang didn't fulfill its end of the bargain. But Biegun hadn't tabled them yet.

Choe understood the United States couldn't tell the other members of the UN Security Council what to do. She just wanted Washington to lend its support in case of a deal.[67]

"What now?" the Americans wondered. Choe had put a new proposal on the table at the last moment. First things first, though.

"What do you mean by Yongbyon?" Biegun asked. The installation covered acres of land and hundreds of buildings. Did the North Koreans mean parts or all of it? He had asked their bureaucrats and negotiators the same question day after day without getting an answer.[68]

Choe look at him quizzically and admitted she didn't know either. She rushed back to the North Korean holding room where the chairman was waiting, presumably to ask him, and returned. It meant everything, she responded. Biegun replied that this is what we need to talk about, what we are including and how we move forward.[69]

Choe retorted, "Chairman Kim doesn't understand your method of calculation." For one thing, why wouldn't the Americans lift the sanctions he had requested? It was a logical question if the North Koreans were considering a step-by-step road map that included denuclearization and corresponding American measures.[70]

Before Biegun could answer, Trump swept by, heading for the exit. He stopped for a final handshake, a few words of encouragement, and a pat on the arm for the smiling Kim, who appeared shell-shocked. We will do this again, Trump assured him.

He even offered the chairman a lift home on Air Force One, a surprising but friendly gesture since Kim had a long train ride ahead of him. Only two other world leaders had ever flown on Air Force One before. Kim politely declined.[71]

When the chairman realized that Trump wasn't going to hang around for lunch, he begged him to stay so they could talk more. The president instead offered to get the two teams together again in thirty days. Kim wasn't ready to agree, however.[72]

Time was up. "It wasn't about Kim. It was more about who Trump is," an American official observed. "We're done? We're done. Why are we here? Let's go. He couldn't sit still anywhere for anything."[73]

Trump's departure triggered a mad American rush for the door. Biegun alerted the staff in State's war room, who grabbed all the computers, including one owned by the hotel that now contained secret documents. The Metropole charged the administration $1,000 extra.[74]

Despite the progress they had made, Biegun informed Choe he had to leave. When he offered to get back together again, she wasn't encouraging.[75] Biegun and Hooker rushed to make the last van back to Trump's hotel. They were almost hanging out the door as the motorcade left.[76]

A storm cloud descended over a lake near the Metropole, whipping up the wind but shedding no rain as Trump's motorcade sped past crowds lining the streets and journalists stationed on a café rooftop. Motorbikes escorting Kim switched their engines on, then off, then on again as he left the Metropole. Kim stormed back to his hotel room, slammed the door, and spoke to no one.[77]

The White House announced at 1:40 P.M. that "no agreement had been reached," despite "very good and constructive meetings." Chat groups blew up online. Trump's press conference had been moved up to 2:00 P.M. Then, he would leave on Air Force One.[78]

Biegun and Hooker stood on the sidelines of Trump's press conference, waiting for it to start. They wondered whether they should have kept talking to Choe. But a senior White House official told them their last-minute back-and-forth with her wasn't enough to extend the summit. Trump's last words to Kim had shut the door.[79]

The president and Pompeo arrived fifteen minutes late. They walked to a podium on a blue-curtained stage with banners in front and back proclaiming the Hanoi summit. Trump tried to be positive.

"He has a certain vision and it's not our vision, but it's a lot closer than it was a year ago."[80]

"You always have to be prepared to walk," Trump observed, repeating a line that would have made Bolton proud. "I could have 100 percent signed something today . . . but it just wasn't appropriate. I want to do it right. I would much rather do it right than do it fast."[81]

Trump explained, "They were willing to denuke a large portion of the area that we wanted," referring to Yongbyon, "but we couldn't give up all the sanctions for that." He added, "If they wanted all the sanctions removed, they would have to do more than that."[82]

Nonetheless, Trump called President Moon the minute Air Force One lifted off, and asked him to "talk to Kim Jong Un, see how he feels, then come to Washington," a South Korean official recalled. He repeated his request six times.[83]

The president's aides shared his concern. "I wouldn't say I was naïve as to the likelihood of turbulence after the summit," one recalled, "but we still harbored the hope that we could get back with the North Koreans."[84]

Kim Jong Un seemed fine the next day. According to the North Korean media, he thanked Trump for "making positive efforts and promised a next meeting." Kim appeared confident and poised as his limousine rolled beneath fluttering North Korean and Vietnamese flags. Large crowds jammed Hanoi's streets.[85]

But the chairman cut short his stay the following morning. His motorcade sped to the Chinese border, where he boarded his train. Kim may have put on a smiling public face, but there were signs of trouble ten hours after Trump's Thursday afternoon press conference.[86]

Still in Hanoi, Foreign Minister Ri and Choe Son Hui held their own session with the media. The polite, soft-spoken foreign minister pointed out that the chairman hadn't asked for the lifting of all sanctions, only five out of the eleven UN resolutions. Biegun agreed. Trump, as usual, had exaggerated.[87]

Choe was blunt. Her remarks may have reflected the chairman's anger. The Americans had missed a "once in a thousand-year opportunity." What would come next was unclear. "We have not decided on a next summit or discussion," she concluded and left the room.[88]

"The two-minute man"

No one—not American officials, foreign diplomats, pundits, nor the media—predicted the summit would end the way it did. Local bars filled up after Trump left. Journalists buzzed. It had been a great news day.[89]

The American public supported the talks even as Democrats and Republicans in Washington were united in praising the president's decision to cut the meeting short.[90] They recited the standard wisdom: no deal was better than a bad deal.[91]

Why did the summit fail? Many believed Bolton had engineered the collapse. Others blamed President Trump's misplaced confidence. Still others surmised the Cohen hearings had adversely affected the president. Plenty of blame was reserved for Kim Jong Un.

John Bolton was happy to take the credit in his book *The Room Where It Happened.* He claimed his three forty-five-minute sessions with Trump had done the trick, especially their spotlight on how Ronald Reagan had walked out of the 1986 summit. Bolton argued that the issue was whether Kim Jong Un was ready to agree to a "big deal," and he wasn't.[92]

The national security advisor's description of what happened in Hanoi left one reporter who covered the summit dumbfounded. Bolton portrayed it as a victory over Pompeo, "the moment when he [Bolton] was successfully able to steer Trump." But the idea that they were deep-state bureaucrats acting without the president's say-so was "total baloney."[93]

In fact, Bolton had been in the dark all along. He didn't know that Pompeo had kept Trump informed about State's negotiating strategy, didn't know about Biegun's Stanford speech, and wasn't in the loop on his Pyongyang talks. He didn't know about the draft Hanoi statement or that Trump approved it.[94]

To his credit, the national security advisor admits in his book that the president dismissed his advice at every turn in Hanoi. Trump passed his Libya model proposal to Kim but didn't press it. He rejected all of Bolton's ideas, including limiting North Korea's short-range missiles, requiring a declaration of WMD programs, and avoiding a joint statement at the end of the summit.[95]

Trump also didn't need Bolton's advice to understand that Kim's Yong-byon proposal was unacceptable. He may not have known all the details. But he knew enough. Just to make sure, the president asked all his advisors and they agreed.

As for walking out of meetings, Donald Trump had done that long before he met John Bolton. He had walked out of two divorce proceedings as well as a recent session with Democratic congressional leaders Nancy Pelosi and Chuck Schumer.[96] Trump didn't turn to Bolton in Hanoi and ask him, "Is now the right time to walk out?" an aide recalled.[97]

In fact, the president had "walked out" on the North Koreans before, just not in person. He called off the Singapore summit in spring 2018 after Choe verbally attacked Mike Pence. He abruptly cancelled Pompeo's trip to Pyongyang in August 2018. The North Koreans reversed themselves both times.

The *Washington Post* observed that Trump "supposed that his personal and improvisational diplomacy, featuring unwarranted and unseemly flattery of a murderous tyrant would make possible the substantive steps towards disarmament that the regime has resisted for decades." His flattery of other authoritarians like Putin reinforced the point.[98]

Donald Trump wasn't the first president who believed it possible to charm dictators. He also wasn't the first to discover it didn't work. Franklin Roosevelt thought he could win over Joseph Stalin at the end of World War II but failed. John F. Kennedy believed he could charm Nikita Khrushchev, but the Soviet leader "savaged" him, in the president's own words.[99]

Trump's most serious character flaw was that "he had no attention span," according to his former ghostwriter. Dr. Anthony Fauci reportedly said that Trump was like "a kindergartener who can't sit still in a classroom," and that "his attention span is like a minus number." One confidant called him "the two-minute man."[100]

Ironically, Donald Trump resembled another Republican president in this regard. Ronald Reagan once remarked, "Mike Deaver in his book said that I have a short attention span," adding, "Well, I was going to reply to that, but what the hell, let's move on to something else." Yet, Reagan sat through eight hours of talks over four days during the failed Reykjavik summit.[101]

Who knows how the Hanoi summit would have turned out if Trump had mustered the same patience? He didn't plan to talk about substance during dinner the first night, but Kim did. The two started the next day at 9:00 A.M. and met on and off privately and with their aides for a few hours. Then, Trump said good-bye to Kim, held a news conference, and left Hanoi. Talks lasted less than half a day.

Was Trump irked by the Cohen hearings? One congressional staffer speculated that "he was pissed so he acted out." Trump blamed his failure to cut a deal on Michael Cohen's testimony, which absorbed his attention, day and night, throughout his short time in Hanoi. Instead of news coverage portraying him as a statesman, it was "one of the most epic trolls in Trump's life," a *Washington Post* article noted.[102]

But an aide asserted that "part of the secret of doing the job is compartmentalizing." Trump was doing just that. In short, it's hard to say whether the president would have behaved differently if the hearing hadn't happened.[103]

Joe Yun, the retired special envoy, feared that Trump would try to deliver something spectacular, or nothing at all. Bolton was afraid he would reach a small deal to "drown out Cohen's hearing in the media."[104] Neither was right. Trump pursued a pragmatic path to a deal, a path that might have led to an agreement if he had stuck around.

Experts argued there was too little preparation for the summit in too little time. Ambassador Thomas Pickering, a respected diplomat, observed that summits were successful when leaders "have only two or three of the hardest issues left to decide when they are face to face." Despite the popular misconception, the almost-ten-page draft statement negotiated by Steve Biegun solved everything except the two most important issues: denuclearization and sanctions lifting.[105]

Many blamed Kim Jong Un for the failed summit. Pundits argued he was just seeking attention, stalling, trying to relieve pressure, or biding time until his next round of WMD tests. This view discounted Kim's new emphasis on economic modernization, unilateral actions on the nuclear and missile fronts, and commitments to denuclearize. The evidence overwhelmingly suggests that Kim wanted a deal, thought one was within reach, and was just as surprised as everyone else when the summit collapsed.

Perhaps even more important, Pyongyang's media hype before Hanoi signaled to his people that he had great expectations. The rapid progress before Kim arrived was approved and telegraphed by a publicized pre-summit meeting with his negotiating team. Finally, the chairman was visibly disappointed and angry when the summit collapsed.

Was Kim Jong Un overconfident, inexperienced, the victim of bad advice, or some combination of the three? The *Guardian* wrote in 2018 that Kim came "away from Singapore interpreting Trump's gushing behavior as a sign of a desperation to strike a deal."[106] Steve Biegun believed the North Koreans' "shoot the moon" strategy at the leader level explained why they wouldn't talk to him about WMD.[107]

Going straight to Trump, who had demonstrated he was a diplomatic wild card, was obviously the best approach. But only Kim Jong Un could touch the third rail of his country's security and negotiate away Pyongyang's WMD arsenal. It had to be done by the two leaders.

Why did Kim think his Yongbyon proposal was an offer Trump couldn't refuse? American officials blamed the South Koreans. President Moon, his aides, and his intelligence service had been pitching a Yongbyon deal since the September 2018 summit, despite Washington's warning that the facility was only part of a solution. The South Koreans, however, seemed to be "simply looking for a deal for the sake of a deal," one American official recalled.[108]

The North's anger aimed at Seoul after the Hanoi summit seemed to confirm it felt duped by the South Koreans. In addition to public condemnation, the North Koreans withdrew their staff from the jointly manned liaison office in Kaesong, the first full-time, person-to-person contact between the two in five decades.[109]

In all fairness, Seoul was on to something. Yongbyon had expanded and included a new uranium enrichment plant, as well as other plants that probably produced ingredients for hydrogen bombs. Kim was willing to dismantle all of that, perhaps to be followed by his "and more" promise, including the Nuclear Weapons Institute, which may have been the heart and soul of the North Korean nuclear program.

The Yongbyon fixation also fit in nicely with Pyongyang's expectations for Hanoi. Two weeks after the summit, North Korean officials told a Japanese academic, Professor Hajime Izumi, that they had expected a "modest agreement" since time was short, "not something too eye-catching which would have been impossible to get." They anticipated "a series of summits and believed President Trump thought the same way."[110]

While all these factors may have explained Kim's Yongbyon fixation, what accounted for his "robotic" behavior? In terms of experience, he had only stepped onto the world stage in 2018, meeting Xi, Putin, Trump, and Moon. None of those summits, even the first with Trump, would have prepared him for the president's rapid-fire questions, proposals, and ideas.

He may have also faced internal pressures. While observers dismissed the notion that North Korea had domestic politics, the elite was allowed to express their views within limits. Kim had hinted at dissention in letters to Trump, in his meetings with Americans in Pyongyang, and in Hanoi. "Please help me with my opponents" was a standard Negotiating 101 tactic, but his hints may have contained a grain of truth.

Kim also may have been determined to hang tough. Stopping WMD tests and starting unilateral dismantlement might have been dismissed by skeptics, but the chairman thought they were important gestures. In any case, hanging tough was standard North Korean negotiating behavior. He could also move quickly if he wanted to.

Sending Choe to find Biegun with his own proposal for how to move forward was a last-minute gambit that showed a willingness to compromise. In a few moments, they accomplished more on denuclearization and sanctions lifting than in the many hours Biegun had spent with powerless negotiators.

So why did Hanoi fail? The summit was a bust when it came to denuclearization and sanctions lifting. But three sessions—January in Washington, February in Pyongyang, and Hanoi before the summit—resolved a raft of issues in less than two months that had separated the United States and North Korea for decades.

Trump's unorthodox summitry had hit the diplomatic nail on the head. But the president couldn't sit still long enough to close the deal.

"You are my friend and always will be."

A spy satellite passing over Pyongyang's equivalent to Cape Kennedy before the Hanoi summit revealed an undisturbed dusting of snow. Afterwards, however, the North Koreans started to rebuild the facility they had dismantled after the Singapore summit in 2018, finishing the work two days later.[111]

Kim Jong Un was sending a subtle signal. He was running out of patience. President Trump told reporters three times he would be "very disappointed" if North Korea launched a satellite, but nothing more happened.[112]

Still smiling when he left Hanoi, the chairman nonetheless wasn't happy. Kim didn't bother to stop in China. There was nothing to talk about. Arriving in Pyongyang over sixty hours later at 3:00 A.M., the North Korean leader was greeted by a cheering crowd and officials waiting to shake his hand.[113]

The public was kept in the dark at first. A television feature hit the highlights of his eleven-day journey, putting a positive spin on the trip. It didn't mention the lack of an agreement. That was left to the party newspaper five days later.[114]

Choe Son Hui, seated on a stage with photos of Kim Il Sung and Kim Jong Il in the background, underscored to Pyongyang-based reporters and diplomats how serious the situation was. She repeated her Hanoi formulation, "We believe the United States had missed a one-in-a-thousand years opportunity this time."[115]

"We have neither the intention to compromise with the US in any form nor much less the desire or plan to conduct this kind of negotiation," Choe pronounced. The United States had to change its "method of calculation," the phrase she had used in her hallway encounter with Biegun.[116]

The WMD test moratorium hung in the balance, according to Choe. North Korea had launched its own policy review and, ominously, was investigating the people involved. The chairman would decide soon whether to drop more WMD shoes.[117]

There was one bright spot in Choe's bleak picture. "The chemistry is mysteriously wonderful" between Kim and Trump, she observed, punctuating her comment by repeating "chemistry" in English. Pompeo and Bolton, on the other hand, had created a "stumbling block" to achieving results.[118]

Contact with Washington ceased. Biegun's attempts to reach out to Choe as well as the North's UN Mission got no response. An unsuspecting North Korean diplomat picked up the phone when the State Department called but cut the conversation short.[119]

Trump's letter to the chairman on March 22 went unanswered. "You are my friend and always will be," and together, they had made "tremendous progress," he wrote. One expert later concluded, "If Kim [Jong Un] didn't laugh out loud at that line, then surely he was slack-jawed."[120]

The president tried to send a message in public. Trump told reporters after meeting President Moon on April 11 that he was open to "various smaller deals," negotiations could be "step by step," and a third summit was possible.[121]

Trump, however, insisted that sanctions would only be lifted when Pyongyang agreed to eliminate its weapons. Nothing was said about gradually rolling them back, although that had been part of Biegun's game plan all along.[122]

Kim Jong Un mounted the podium at the Fourteenth session of North Korea's Supreme People's Assembly the next day. He delivered a very different message to the four thousand delegates than his positive New Year's speech.

The United States "came to the talks only racking its brain to find ways that are absolutely impracticable," Kim asserted. It did "not ready itself to sit with us face-to-face and settle the problem." He warned Washington, "Sitting down with us a hundred times or a thousand times will not make us budge."[123]

Kim still had hopes for diplomacy, however, especially since the two leaders had "excellent relations." Trump had until the end of 2019 to make a "bold decision." Then, North Korea would have to explore a new path to defend itself, a repetition of his ominous line in the New Year's speech.[124]

Personnel shifts in Pyongyang fueled speculation that diplomacy was not well, but still alive. Choe was named to North Korea's top policy-oriented leadership body. Reportedly executed, Kim Hyok Chol was just in custody. Kim Yong Chol disappeared. A smiling Pompeo gloated, "It does appear the next time we have serious conversations that my counterpart will be someone else." The general would reappear, just not as senior envoy.[125]

Kim calibrated a harder line after his April 12 speech. Days later, he attended Pyongyang's first test in over eighteen months, the firing of a very short-range antitank missile. Kim also watched pilots fly jets previously grounded because of fuel shortages. He supervised the first of three tests of short-range missiles in early May. Still, the moves were not as threatening as firing long-range missiles or nuclear tests.[126]

The North Koreans also escalated their attacks on their favorite American punching bags. Choe slammed Bolton as "dim-sighted," an obvious reference to his eyeglasses, after he said North Korea had to decide to give up its nuclear weapons before a third summit. She also fired back at Pompeo after he made a similar remark.[127]

By mid-May, a debate was underway in Pyongyang's official media. Supporters of diplomacy painted a positive picture of the Hanoi summit and raised the possibility of restarting talks. A June 4 Foreign Ministry statement noted Kim Jong Un's personal commitment to engagement.[128]

Skeptics argued that "no amount of fawning upon powers" would save North Korea from "falling into a bloody civil war and national calamity." An article published on the June 12 anniversary of the Singapore summit suggested Kim needed a rest since his "mental and physical overwork" had accumulated. The notion had been advanced before, but given the ongoing back-and-forth, it was eye-opening.[129]

No one knew exactly what was going on. The to-and-fro may have meant Kim hadn't made up his mind. His appearances at military drills and defense industry factories, after he had downplayed their roles in 2018, may have signaled a shift. Or maybe Kim wanted it understood that after Hanoi, diplomacy would not be drawn out, and might not succeed.[130]

The chairman tried to line up support from abroad. He met Vladimir Putin in April. Kim asked for help to get around sanctions on Pyongyang's loggers in Russia who sent home millions of dollars. He also requested more food aid and stepped-up trade. Putin was happy to provide public support, but nothing more.[131]

President Xi arrived in Pyongyang on June 20 for his first state visit since Kim took over. The two leaders agreed Trump was a problem. They also reaffirmed their commitment to "avoid tensions," and to "create conditions for solving problems on the peninsula." The Chinese promised Kim more food aid but nothing more. He had checked another diplomatic box, although the practical results were sparse.[132]

Whether Xi knew it or not, the chairman had already decided to pivot back to the United States. Kim used the twin occasions of the June 12 Singapore summit anniversary and the president's birthday two days later as excuses to finally send him a letter. Once again, Trump described the message as "beautiful," prompting the media to describe it once again as meaningless.[133]

But the letter came close to extending an invitation to meet again. Kim wrote, "I believe one day will come sooner or later when we sit down together to make great things happen with the will to give another chance to our mutual trust."[134]

Trump's quick positive response was just what Kim was looking for. The president highlighted the Singapore declaration—the North Korean leader "committed to completely denuclearize" while Trump "committed to provide security guarantees." He concluded on a high note: "We both committed to establish new relations for our two countries and build a lasting and stable peace regime on the Korean peninsula."[135]

Two days after President Xi departed, a front-page photo of Kim Jong Un, reading Trump's letter in his book-lined office, appeared in the North's media. He commented, "It contains excellent content," and promised to "seriously contemplate" the message.[136]

The next day, June 23, Trump confirmed in public that he had responded with a "very friendly letter" to the chairman's note wishing him a happy birthday. "It would be a great thing for us to meet again," the president wrote. Kim and Trump were ready to walk through the diplomatic door one more time.[137]

CHAPTER NINETEEN
"I want to pour
the concrete myself"

BOB CARLIN AND SIG HECKER had been to the secretary of state's suite once before to meet Hillary Clinton in 2010 after their visit to North Korea's new uranium enrichment plant. They returned in May 2019, after the collapse of the Hanoi summit and Kim Jong Un's first missile test in almost eighteen months.[1]

Pompeo was combustible. But he had been Trump's cheerleader, depicting Hanoi as a positive development even though he was angry about the outcome. He had predicted the two leaders would meet again and downplayed Kim's recent missile tests. The secretary had also been a constant source of support for Biegun.

The seventh-floor session got off to a good start and lasted longer than expected. The two Stanford-based experts believed Kim Jong Un's offer to dismantle Yongbyon was a golden opportunity. Pompeo listened patiently and nodded as Hecker and Carlin pitched their views on what to do after Hanoi.[2]

Then "bad Mike" exploded. Pompeo didn't believe the North Koreans would give up their weapons. He said if they did, "I want to pour the concrete myself," to make sure their facilities never operated again. Pompeo turned out to be not much different from John Bolton. Beneath the smiling veneer, he thought the president's policy was bullshit.[3]

To Steve Biegun and his team, however, Hanoi seemed like just another pothole in Trump's diplomatic road. "Back to the drawing board. Let's

President Donald J. Trump and President Moon Jae-in of the Republic of Korea
pose for a photo with Secretary of State Mike Pompeo and National Security
Advisor John Bolton on April 11, 2019, in the Oval Office of the White House.
Official White House photo by Shealah Craighead.

see if we can be in contact. Let's see if they will talk to us. Let's see what
the president wants," a White House official recalled thinking. The obvious next move was to reconnect with the North Koreans. But they weren't
responding.[4]

The news wasn't encouraging when President Moon visited Washington on April 11. He had also failed to connect to the chairman. Determined
to rekindle diplomacy, Moon urged Trump to take a "dramatic approach
to generate momentum" for "the summit of the century." He suggested an
unprecedented trilateral meeting. Moon probably thought if he were
there, he could help avoid another debacle.[5]

Trump hesitated. He had received "a lot of credit for how Hanoi
turned out," but "no one wanted to walk away twice." Moon pushed back.
Diplomats couldn't deal with denuclearization. There had to be another
summit.[6]

While Trump, Pompeo, and Biegun were determined to "do no harm"
after Hanoi, Bolton was intent on doing just the opposite.[7] His best bet
was sanctions. The Trump administration had originally believed maximum

pressure would help reach a good deal. When diplomacy took off in 2018, however, the Americans focused on better enforcement, not imposing new restrictions.[8]

Mark Lambert, a veteran Foreign Service officer, traveled the world to convince other countries to do better. North Korean Internet thefts in Bangladesh and Angola, Pyongyang's exports of traditional Asian medicines to Nepal and Mozambique, and ship-to-ship transfers of petroleum bound for North Korea were all fair game. "We see what Lambert is doing around the world, and we hate it," the North Koreans later told American officials.[9]

Washington could also resort to other measures to bolster enforcement. "Routine designations" warned the international community not to deal with individuals and organizations in North Korea or other countries that traded with Pyongyang. The Americans also issued "advisories" outlining the North's deceptive practices.[10]

An interagency team run by Alex Wong, Biegun's deputy, had cranked out seven major actions since the Singapore summit. After Hanoi, the group "designated" two Chinese shipping companies and issued an advisory on how North Korea tried to evade sanctions. No one would have noticed except that John Bolton tweeted about them, did an interview with a right-wing network, and instructed his staff to brief the media. Eye-catching headlines followed.[11]

The national security advisor acted without consulting anyone, including the president. A White House official concluded Bolton "wanted to stick it to the North Koreans" and "spike any future progress with them."[12] The State Department warned Bolton's staff that Trump "was going to smash them." He did just that and reversed the announcement in a tweet.

"Why Trump wanted to roll back these latest enforcement actions was anybody's guess, other than he was feeling Kim Jong Un's pain," Bolton later sneered.[13]

The joke was on him, however. Advertising the new restrictions made it harder to get Treasury and other agencies to develop new designations. They were afraid the president would come down hard on them. The episode fueled a public narrative that Trump's policy was based on tweets. That was a problem, but so were Bolton's attempts to sabotage a president he didn't agree with.[14]

North Korea handed the national security advisor another chance to upend diplomacy when it resumed missile tests in May. Trump and Pompeo downplayed their significance. Bolton, however, pissed all over the president's policy in a meeting with a sympathetic Prime Minister Abe. The president's aide said in public that the launches violated sanctions. Standing beside Trump at a press conference in Tokyo, the Japanese leader repeated the same line.[15]

By summer 2019, Trump was fed up with Bolton and Bolton with Trump. "If it was up to John, we would be in four wars now," the president complained. According to the French ambassador in Washington, Bolton was "dreaming of going to war with Iran," but Trump reversed a decision to launch strikes against Teheran for downing an unmanned drone. Bolton had already typed a two-sentence resignation letter when Trump tried, but failed, to set up a meeting with the Iranian foreign minister.[16]

All his attempts to kill diplomacy after the Hanoi encounter failed to stop the president. With Trump set to visit Japan and South Korea at the end of June, expectations mounted. Pompeo told the press that "we're literally prepared to go at a moment's notice." But no one anticipated another summit.[17]

"You go to the third tree and make a right."

After a fourteen-hour flight and a grueling day of meetings, Steve Biegun turned off his cell phone and settled into his room at the Grand Hyatt Hotel, minutes from downtown Seoul. Trump and Pompeo would arrive the next day. They wanted him to participate in the session with President Moon.

Biegun's assistant roused him at 6:00 A.M. on June 29. The secretary of state was calling from Osaka. During the ride back to his hotel from dinner the night before, the president had wondered whether to personally reach out to Chairman Kim.[18]

Trump had told Prime Minister Abe that Kim had been "writing him beautiful letters and birthday cards." The North Koreans "hated Bolton, Pence and Pompeo" but "loved him." Trump suggested to Germany's chancellor, Angela Merkel, that he might meet Kim at the DMZ. The chairman "wanted to do something but didn't know how to get it started."[19]

The president was right. Kim "wasn't just sprinkling pixie dust," one aide recalled. While Bolton claimed that was the first time anyone had heard that Trump wanted to meet Kim on this trip, the president was actually testing out Moon's April suggestion.[20]

"Trump was Trump," a White House official recalled. "There were off-hand comments that it wouldn't be surprising if he wants to see Kim Jong

Un." No one expected him to do it. But the Secret Service preadvanced a visit to the DMZ, if only because Trump's last attempt to go there had been aborted due to bad weather.[21]

Biegun was skeptical. Would a snap summit help or hurt? It was hard to say, but it would be risky, he told Pompeo. Would the North Koreans agree? Biegun didn't think they would. Could a summit be organized in just one day? There was no easy way to communicate with the North. Pompeo said he would talk it all through with the president.[22]

Trump also consulted Ivanka, who was at a summit in Osaka with the leaders of the world's largest economies to talk about women's empowerment issues. "My team tells me it will be hard to communicate with him," he explained. "But I have heard that Kim follows my Twitter account, so maybe I will just tweet. . . . Who knows?"[23]

"Dad, that would certainly be your way of doing things," she replied.[24]

When Biegun flipped on the television before brewing his first cup of coffee, CNN was flashing "breaking news." President Trump had tweeted, "If Chairman Kim of North Korea sees this, I would meet him at the Border/DMZ just to shake his hand and say Hello(?)!"[25]

Bolton and Mick Mulvaney, the White House chief of staff, were flabbergasted. Once he realized the president meant it, Bolton did everything he could to derail the plan. He failed. Insult followed injury when he learned only Pompeo would be allowed in a Trump-Kim meeting. Bolton traveled to Seoul before the summit with the chairman but then flew off to Mongolia for other meetings.[26]

Time was short. Biegun rushed to organize the snap summit. Tweets weren't enough. He had to make sure the North Koreans saw Trump's message. But the spy channel was dead, no one was answering the phone at Pyongyang's UN mission, and State had failed to launch its own secret channel after Hanoi.[27]

Luckily, the North Koreans followed Trump's tweets. Five hours later, Choe Son Hui replied via the official media that "although we view this as an extremely interesting proposal, we have not received a formal invitation." Pyongyang's fixation with formality wasn't a surprise. As the nuclear negotiations drew to a close in 1994, the North Koreans insisted that a letter from Bill Clinton be typed on White House letterhead with his title. "For a second time that day, I thought this was going to happen," Biegun recalled.[28]

The Americans rushed to meet Choe's request. Already in Seoul, Allison Hooker, Trump's Korea expert, drafted an invitation and sent it to

Osaka to be printed on White House letterhead. The president signed the invitation, and it was scanned and sent back to her. "It was extraordinary," one official remembered.[29]

But how to get the invitation to Kim Jong Un? Twitter wouldn't work. A military hotline connecting the DMZ to Pyongyang seemed the best option, although the North Koreans almost never answered the phone. State's envoy imagined there were "a couple of North Korean corporals sitting in this room with the phone ringing, looking at each other and thinking, 'I'm not answering it.'"[30]

There was the old-fashioned way, a megaphone. In the past, American officers literally walked up to the demarcation line with an interpreter and yelled messages while a North Korean videotaped them. General Brooks, however, had instructed his soldiers not to yell if a North Korean was standing a few feet away.

The megaphone worked. The hotline was activated, and the letter transmitted. The North Koreans later explained they hadn't answered before because "the ringer was off."[31]

While Trump had dinner with President Moon, Biegun and Hooker hopped on a helicopter for the thirty-five-mile flight to the DMZ to talk to Choe's colleagues. They were met by an American colonel and driven to South Korea's Freedom House. There was no road. "You go to the third tree and make a right," Biegun recalled. It seemed dangerous, but "everyone there knows what they are doing."[32]

The two Americans passed Trump's formal invitation to the North Koreans. Still, they needed more information, asking, "What did President Trump want to discuss?" Biegun wasn't sure so he improvised something about moving diplomacy forward. Did the Americans have an agenda? They didn't. The North Koreans suggested they couldn't move forward unless they received an agenda by midnight.[33]

The Americans jumped back on their helicopter, landed in Seoul, scripted an agenda, and sent it to Pyongyang via the hotline. Everyone went to bed unsure if the summit was going to happen.[34]

The phone rang at 7:30 A.M. the next morning, June 30. General Robert Abrams, the commander of US Forces Korea, had assigned some of his best officers to stay up all night to watch the DMZ.[35] He reported that uniformed North Koreans had poured out of thirteen buses and scurried to clean the area. Biegun thought, for the third time in twenty-four hours, "This is going to happen."[36]

With only a few hours left, Dan Walsh and "the Butler," the two men who had organized the Hanoi summit, met. They hammered out how many flags would be placed in the meeting room, how many bodyguards would be allowed, where to position the press, the choreography of the leaders' encounter, and much more.[37]

There was one hitch, however. The Americans proposed a big meeting with the leaders and their top aides, followed by a small session with Trump and Kim attended by the two foreign ministers. That way, Pompeo could steer the president in the right direction. The North Koreans, however, wanted one small meeting with just the two leaders—not surprising since they considered Pompeo a bad influence.[38]

There was no turning back after Trump told the press before leaving for the DMZ that he would be meeting with Kim. The Americans agreed to a fifteen-minute session between the two leaders, and then Pompeo and Ri Yong Ho would join them.[39]

Walsh and the Butler toured the site one last time. They found themselves in a small closet when the North Korean's cell phone rang. Kim Yo Jong, the chairman's sister, was on the line—confirmation that she was in charge.[40]

With two hours to go, even a North Korean vice foreign minister got his hands dirty. Freedom House "was a mess with cobwebs everywhere," one official recalled. A minor crisis erupted when the American flags to be placed behind the leaders weren't all the same size. Some didn't even have tassels.[41]

Minutes before showtime, Hyon Song Wol, the singer and band leader rumored to have been Kim's teenage sweetheart, appeared. Contrary to reports that she had been shot, Hyon was on the Central Committee and helped set up North Korea's participation in the Winter Olympics.

The meeting room had been meticulously prepared, but Hyon still ordered North Koreans to "vacuum this, fix the flag, make sure of this, make sure of that," an American remembered. Officials accustomed to giving orders jumped. She was important.[42]

Trump and Moon left Seoul in the early afternoon for the DMZ. Moon's helicopter, Trump on Marine One, five U.S. military choppers, and a decoy crossed the Imjin River, which flowed north to south. They flew over the "Bridge of No Return," used to repatriate prisoners of the Korean war that was located on the demarcation line between the two Koreas, and landed.[43]

Before moving on to the summit, Trump visited a panorama overlooking North Korea. He was briefed by the same U.S. Army officer who had escorted Biegun to his DMZ session. "What do you think about all this?" Trump asked him. The officer replied, "Your legacy in all this can be peace."

As he was leaving, Trump pointed at him and said, "Peace can be my legacy."

The scene turned chaotic as the two leaders arrived at the nearby Freedom House. President Trump, in a navy-blue suit and a red tie, stepped out of the black van and Moon led him up the steps into the building.[44]

Moments before the president was to meet Kim, Trump huddled with his advisors. Walsh explained the summit's choreography while he asked basic questions.[45]

"How high are the stones on the border?" Trump wanted to know. "Is it going to be hard to get across?

The president seemed to have doubts. "Do I go across?" he asked again.

Walsh replied, "You can take a step or two into North Korea but the Secret Service has no control once you do." Ivanka advised, "Why don't you play it by ear and see how it feels." Trump just nodded.[46]

It was showtime. The president headed down the Freedom House steps alone. Chairman Kim emerged from a pavilion across the way, slowly coming into view and leading his top aides.[47]

The two men headed straight for the border and each other, their first face-to-face encounter since the Hanoi summit. Marked by a low concrete curb separating South and North, the area was no more than fifteen feet wide, surrounded by temporary blue buildings running parallel to each other.[48]

Moving at a brisk pace, Trump reached the demarcation line first. He seemed to be enjoying the moment. Kim also moved quickly. Tucker Carlson, who was nearby, later reported that the overweight Kim sounded like an "emphysema patient whose health was rapidly deteriorating."[49]

Trump stood in the South and Kim in the North as they shook hands across the line separating the two Koreas. "Good to see you again. I never expected to meet you here," Kim said as if they had met by chance. Photographers jostled to record the encounter.[50]

Both men recognized the significance of the moment. Holding Kim's hand, Trump pointed to the North Korean side of the border while the chairman gestured to where he was standing and said, "If you step forward, you will be the first president to cross this line." Kim knew how it felt. He had been the first North Korean leader to cross into the South in April 2018 during the Panmunjom meeting with Moon.[51]

Donald Trump, dressed in his business suit—a stark contrast to past American politicians who often wore bomber jackets and carried binoculars when they visited the DMZ—stepped into North Korea at 3:45 P.M.

President Donald J. Trump steps into the territory of North Korea through
the Joint Security Area with Chairman of the Workers' Party of Korea
Kim Jong Un on June 30, 2019. Official White House photo.

He stood next to Kim, patted the younger man's arm, and made history.
Jimmy Carter and Bill Clinton had traveled to North Korea, but only after
they left office.[52]

"Pretty cool, you know. Pretty cool, right?" an excited Trump recalled
in an interview.[53]

The chairman led the president a few yards beyond the area bordered
by the blue buildings onto the road running in front of the North Korean
pavilion, then burst into applause with a large smile. Trump joined in as
Kim offered his hand again. North Korean camera operators, dressed in
black suits and white shirts, sprinted to record the moment.[54]

Trump gestured to the demarcation line as they shook hands. Western photographers zoomed in from the other side of the line, shouting at
the North Korean cameramen to get out of the way.[55]

The chairman asked Trump if they should take another photo after
they had walked back to the border at a leisurely pace. He nodded as they
stood side by side, unsmiling, facing the reporters on both sides.[56] Trump
crowed that he felt really good, and that this was a "big moment, big moment. Big progress, tremendous progress."[57]

They crossed into South Korea, surrounded by security personnel trying to contain the surging press, and stopped again. "I was in Japan and then I was supposed to come here," Trump told Kim, who chuckled as the president touched him on the arm, "and you said 'yes,' and I said 'good.'"[58]

Smiling, they turned and walked towards Freedom House as the press gaggle shouted, "How does it feel, President Trump?"[59]

"I feel great. It's a great honor to be here. Great honor," he repeated. With reporters and security agents jostling and shouting, Kim told Trump, "As you can see, this shows that nobody has expected this."[60]

"How do you feel, Chairman Kim?" a reporter yelled. The two men stopped again. With hand gestures and swinging arms, Kim replied, "President Trump just walked across the demarcation line that made him the first US president to visit our country."[61]

Trump patted him on the back, saying, "I believe just looking at this, this is an expression of his willingness to eliminate all the unfortunate past and open a new future." It was "a very courageous and determined act."[62]

Trump chattered on about how he wanted to "call Chairman Kim" and how "a lot of progress has been made; a lot of friendships have been made." When Trump repeated that the invitation was made on short notice, Kim chuckled.[63]

A reporter shouted one last question for Trump. Would he invite Kim to the United States? "I would invite him right now to the White House, absolutely," the president answered.[64]

In what was ostensibly a three-way summit among Trump, Kim, and Moon, the South Korean president was like a third wheel. "This was really about Trump and Kim," one American pointed out. Moon, however, insisted on being present since the summit was taking place in his country.[65]

The South Korean leader walked from the Freedom House steps and joined a smiling Trump and Kim. Tense bodyguards surrounded them, pushing back reporters who were struggling to capture the meeting with cameras held above their heads.[66]

The three leaders enjoyed the moment. The two Koreans laughed. "When the time is right and President Trump has a chance to visit Pyongyang, it will leave a great mark on the political history of the world," Kim said.[67]

They chatted, smiled for the cameras, and then headed to the Freedom House steps when the photo shoot was over.

As the party climbed the steps, Kim Yo Jong trailed behind her brother carrying a briefcase.[68]

President Donald J. Trump and Republic of Korea president Moon Jae-in bid
farewell to Kim Jong Un, June 30, 2019, at the demarcation line separating
North and South Korea at the Korean Demilitarized Zone. Official White House
photo by Shealah Craighead.

The lobby was filled with journalists, staff, and officials, including unsmiling North Koreans dressed in black suits, white shirts, and their bright
red lapel pins.[69]

Moon said his good-byes as Trump and Kim headed to another press
session. Since the cozy room wasn't large enough for the crowd, the reporters stampeded toward the door. The North Korean bodyguards, trying to protect Kim, were blamed by the media when the new White House
spokesperson, Stephanie Grisham, was bruised in the melee. In fact, they
were just doing their job.[70]

After lengthy remarks by the two smiling leaders, Kim Jong Un shook
hands with Ivanka Trump, Jared Kushner, Secretary of the Treasury Steven Mnuchin, and Harry Harris, the U.S. ambassador to South Korea.[71]

The DMZ encounter was "classic Trumpian stage management," the
BBC reported, guaranteeing headlines and a large audience. Luring North
Korea away from its nuclear ambition, however, would take more than stag-
ing a historic reality show.[72]

"It's good for North Korea, it's good for America, it's good for the world."

President Trump and Kim Jong Un settled into their soft chairs. They were slated to spend fifteen minutes together, but Pompeo pushed into the room through the crowd of reporters, aided by Dan Walsh, who threw a body block. He yelled for someone to get Ri Yong Ho. A State Department aide grabbed the North Korean foreign minister, who was determined to follow the original plan. But Ri relented and joined the three other men.[73]

With the collapse of the Hanoi summit still on everyone's mind, the Americans hoped the DMZ meeting would be a chance to reassure Kim that the United States was still committed to diplomacy. They wanted the same from him.[74]

The smiles, laughter, and poses for cameras ended once the press left. The chairman was unhappy. Not given to histrionics, Kim was respectful, but "he doesn't do theater very well. What you see is what you get," one official observed.[75]

The North Korean started with a list of grievances. Hanoi had been a disappointment. He wanted the United States to stop military exercises. That would help meet North Korea's need for security guarantees and show him Washington was serious about addressing his concerns.[76]

His biggest complaint, however, was that, despite months of hints in his letters, in his public pronouncements, and in his advisors' statements, Kim felt that "we were simply taking and not giving," one American official recalled. He had halted long-range missile launches, shut down his nuclear test site, and started dismantling his satellite launch center. The United States hadn't done anything.[77]

Trump painted his usual picture of a bright economic future for North Korea and professed he was willing to compromise. But he and Pompeo didn't know where the chairman was heading.

Would Kim drop everything, travel to the DMZ for a summit, and then walk out? It didn't make sense, although Trump had done that in Hanoi. Thirty minutes into the session, there appeared to be a new negative twist to the positive reality show.[78]

Then, Kim shifted gears. Good news always came after a laundry list of complaints. He still wanted diplomacy to work. The conversation refocused on opportunities and ended when the two leaders agreed to appoint negotiators, empowered to reach a deal, who would meet in a few weeks.[79]

While the drama played out inside the small Freedom House room, Jared Kushner, Ivanka Trump, Steve Mnuchin, Mick Mulvaney, top-ranking South Korean and North Korean officials, security guards, and reporters mingled outside. "It was the most surreal thing I had ever seen," one American official recalled.[80]

Ivanka Trump and Jared Kushner started a short conversation with Choe Son Hui, who was standing off to the side trying to be invisible. As she was the top female diplomat in North Korea, with close ties to the chairman's influential sister, talking to her made sense. A student of American popular culture, Choe seemed to be enjoying standing next to the glamorous couple.[81]

More importantly, Choe and Steve Biegun encountered each other again. In an open space with eavesdropping bystanders milling about, they talked more about the weather than denuclearization.[82]

Nonetheless, Choe hinted diplomacy might pick up again with her in charge. The two chatted about the age-old problem that had plagued the run-up to the DMZ meeting: how to communicate. She asked Biegun why he didn't use the New York channel. The answer was obvious. Ten times out of ten the North Koreans had been unresponsive.[83]

Choe disclosed, however, that the channel had been "turned on" last week. She had ordered her aides to stay up all night and to answer any messages from Washington. That was good news.[84]

She also probed for information about the presidential election just eighteen months away. The North Koreans had to calculate whether there was still time to strike a deal with Trump and whether it would last if he lost.[85]

Trump and Kim emerged after fifty-three minutes. Joined by President Moon, the two men escorted the chairman back to the border. As they said good-bye to him and returned to Freedom House to meet the press again, Biegun inched toward the exit. No one wanted to be left behind once the president's motorcade left.[86]

Someone shouted his name, however. Trump was looking for Biegun. The president wanted the envoy to stand behind him to make the point that Biegun was his negotiator. One can only wonder what John Bolton in far-off Ulaanbaatar was thinking. Trump told Biegun to move fast, get a deal, and he would sign it.[87]

With Moon standing by his side, Trump bragged relations with North Korea were no longer a "fiery mess" and "nothing but trouble" like they were when he took office. His relationship with Kim had saved the day.[88]

Trump announced that the two leaders had agreed to start negotiations "over the next two or three weeks." Biegun would lead the Americans. The president then flew by helicopter to address soldiers at Osan Air Force Base, south of Seoul, and boarded Air Force One for home.

"It's good for North Korea, it's good for America, it's good for the world," Mike Pompeo informed reporters, in a statement that sounded like Bill Clinton when he announced the 1994 nuclear deal. Pyongyang's media said new breakthroughs were possible and hailed the snap summit as an "amazing event."[89]

Donald Trump's "Hail Mary" pass appeared to have paid off. The snap summit was a mesmerizing reality show, for which there had been no preparation. Its only purpose was to get negotiations rolling again. But without Trump punching through the stalemate, the post-Hanoi diplomatic deep freeze could have lasted months longer.

The State Department followed up through the New York channel to schedule new talks. As Choe promised, the North Koreans responded right away. Then, there was radio silence. Something had gone wrong again.[90]

"A long lament of raw emotion and unrelenting woe"

Was Kim Jong Un's DMZ promise to restart talks real or just a ruse? Or did the United States do something to derail negotiations? The answer wasn't obvious at first.

Washington's military exercises with South Korea turned out to be the problem once again. Trump had promised in Singapore to cancel the "war games." However, Bolton, Pompeo, and Mattis simply scaled them down to make them appear less threatening. One hundred small drills were conducted afterwards.

The military drill scheduled for the August after the DMZ summit had always been a major exercise. Two years earlier, jets ripped through the skies, tanks rumbled down roads, and Marines stormed beaches. The upcoming drill, however, would feature mainly officers sitting at computers. The "greatest risk was someone would spill a cup of coffee on their keyboards," one official observed.[91]

Two weeks after the snap summit, the North Koreans issued an official statement. They claimed President Trump had promised at the DMZ summit to suspend military exercises, a personal commitment he had also made at the 2018 Singapore meeting. The North Koreans threatened to resume WMD tests if the August maneuvers went ahead.[92]

Pyongyang punctuated its threat with action. In mid-July, the North Koreans conducted four rounds of missile launches, mostly short-range weapons, accompanied by solemn warnings for the United States and South Korea not to go ahead with the August drill. Twin launches on July 25 were "personally organized" by Kim. The North Koreans also unveiled a new submarine that could launch nuclear-armed missiles, the first of its kind.[93]

Predictably, Trump minimized North Korea's moves, arguing the chairman "will do the right thing because . . . he does not want to disappoint his friend, President Trump!"[94]

North Korea's actions, however, still begged the question, Why did it have such a strong reaction to a scaled-down exercise the North Koreans knew wasn't a threat? The answer was clear. Trump had not only promised to suspend military exercises. Kim Jong Un believed the president had promised at the DMZ summit not to hold the August drill and then went ahead anyway.

Pyongyang's public pronouncement was mild compared to an extraordinary secret letter from Kim to Donald Trump on August 5, the day the exercise began. His letter was not beautiful, but rather "a long lament of raw emotion and unrelenting woe," according to one expert.[95]

Kim recalled the president's promise at the summit to resume talks, but he pointed out that "the current environment is different from that day." The United States had gone ahead with "provocative combined military exercises" despite Kim's understanding they "would either be canceled or postponed" ahead of the negotiations.[96]

"Who are they [the exercises] intended to defeat and attack?" the chairman asked and then answered his own question. The target was "our own military." He condemned "these paranoid and hypersensitive actions," which threatened his country's security and were to blame for "the headache of 'missile threats.'" Kim warned that "until these elements are eliminated, no changed outcome can be anticipated."[97]

"I am clearly offended, and I do not want to hide this feeling from you," the chairman complained. "I am really very offended." Every time they met, Trump had praised his unilateral moratorium on nuclear and missile tests.[98]

Kim further lamented, "I have done more than I can at this present stage, very responsively and practically, in order to keep the trust we have." He had nothing to show his people. "Have actions been relaxed or any of my country's external environments been improved?" Kim asked. "Have military exercises been stopped?"[99]

In as direct a statement from a leader as anyone could imagine, Kim wrote, "If you do not think of our relationship as a steppingstone that only benefits you, then you would not make me look like an idiot that will only give without getting anything in return."[100]

"If this were like Hanoi, just a few months ago, when I held on to the dream of hastening the start of a better life, it would be different." Now, "we are not in a hurry."[101]

Still, Kim couldn't bring himself to completely slam the door on Trump. He would reach out to discuss talks when the exercise was over. While the chairman had a positive feeling about their relationship, it would take an "even greater effort to protect my faith in you," a warning that talks would not be easy.[102]

Was Kim's anger justified? The president's willingness to cancel war games was obvious to everyone, including the North Koreans who had seen him cross his aides in Singapore. Perhaps that was why they had pushed to get him alone in the DMZ, and why Pompeo made sure he was there with the president.

An unhappy Kim complained at the summit about the military exercise. He also probably knew how Trump would respond: with a steady stream of invectives and what seemed to be a promise to stop them. While a senior Blue House official recalled Trump did indeed promise to cancel the exercise, one White House official believed Pompeo thought he "put up a guardrail."

A few days after the summit, the secretary of state confided to Bolton that Trump had reverted to wanting to leave the peninsula entirely, but "we didn't let anything out of the bag with Kim." The chairman thought otherwise.[103]

Even as the drama played out with the North Koreans, the DMZ summit gave Bolton more opportunities to spike the president's diplomacy.

The national security advisor was incensed by a *New York Times* article published soon afterwards that claimed the administration was about to stage a "major retreat from the goal of rapid denuclearization" and accept a nuclear freeze as a "first step." He blamed Biegun.[104]

However, as one official pointed out, "Bolton was not simply an outsider with the president. He was an outsider to his own team." A freeze had been the starting point, and denuclearization the end point, since Biegun's Stanford speech in January.

Pompeo finally put his foot down. The administration's envoy was "a lot closer to the president than you are," he told Bolton. The secretary ordered Biegun not to attend any meetings chaired by the national security advisor.[105]

Bolton then tried a different tack. Trump had instructed Bolton to stop the August exercise since it "agitated the ever-sensitive Kim Jong Un." Drills, however, were also a pawn in another Trump gambit. He was determined to force South Korea and Japan to pay billions of dollars more to support American troops on their soil by threatening to withdraw them altogether.[106]

Bolton traveled to Asia and persuaded the allies to pay more. Then, he convinced Trump to let the August exercise go forward. The president even saw an upside to North Korea's renewed missile tests. "John got it to one billion dollars this year. You'll get it to five billion dollars because of the missiles," he told other aides in private.[107]

Publicly, however, Trump agreed with the North Koreans. The exercises were "a total waste of money," but he told his aides, "I don't want to interfere. . . . You can do them, if you think it's necessary." Kim must have been puzzled about why the president of the United States couldn't order his aides to carry out his wishes.[108]

Trump may have thought he was being clever, even though Kim's August 5 letter was a sure sign he wasn't. He made a promise he didn't keep. Bolton didn't know it at the time, and neither did the president, but he had finally succeeded in spiking Trump's diplomacy.

John Bolton was fired in a tweet that fall, the same unceremonious end as Rex Tillerson. Pompeo and Mnuchin had "shit-eating grins on their faces" at a press conference afterwards, according to a reporter. Trump ordered Pompeo to make sure he told the press that "Bolton is a scumbag loser."[109]

The twenty-seven letters Trump and Kim exchanged in 2018 and 2019 were more than a flirtation. One expert observed they contained "tactical feints, unctuous flattery and psychological ploys" that resembled other correspondence between leaders throughout history. Still, they were indispensable in advancing diplomacy.[110]

The chairman remained open to talks, perhaps for old times' sake. But August 5 was the last time Donald Trump would hear from Kim Jong Un.

"It felt like a break-up date."

In September 2019, I met Steve Biegun in his office on the State Department's prestigious seventh floor. Nothing had happened for more than two months after Trump and Kim had agreed to resume talks in "two or three weeks."[111] Now, a new round of negotiations was just over the horizon, but barely.

We discussed the upcoming talks. What if the North Koreans stuck to their Hanoi small deal: extensive sanctions relief in return for just dismantling Yongbyon? Or worse, what if they insisted the United States and South Korea cancel all military exercises? On top of that, Biegun thought Kim Jong Un was inexperienced. That didn't bode well for the future if it was true.[112]

These known unknowns led to an inescapable conclusion. Reading intelligence reports and scouring the North Korean official media to divine policy tea leaves weren't enough. Periodic encounters were no substitute for regular talks. But these talks were proving elusive.[113]

I mentioned two ideas that might help jump-start regular negotiations. Biegun could offer a Trump visit to Pyongyang if the North Koreans would conclude a nuclear agreement. Or Washington could come up with the unilateral steps Kim had sought since 2018.[114]

Despite the upcoming talks, the atmosphere was fragile. Before the August U.S.-South Korean military exercise, Pyongyang had punctuated its verbal attacks with more missile tests. After the drill, Pompeo labeled North Korea a "rogue state." Foreign Minister Ri Yong Ho called him "the diehard toxin of US diplomacy."[115]

Biegun and Choe guided the conversation in a more positive direction. "We are very curious about the background of the American top diplomat's thoughtless remarks, and we will watch what calculations he has," she responded in the North Korean media to Pompeo.[116]

The American envoy delivered a speech at the University of Michigan, his alma mater, that highlighted the goals of ending hostile relations and achieving denuclearization. Biegun even speculated military exercises could stop and U.S. troops would protect both Koreas—two issues that had been on the North Koreans' minds—if tensions declined. None of that could happen, however, unless the two sides talked and talked often.[117]

Still, diplomacy was hanging by a thread. Choe responded that North Korea was willing to meet "at a time and place to be agreed late in September." She warned, however, that if Washington "fingers again the worn-out scenario," the "DPRK-US dealings may come to an end."[118]

President Trump commented to reporters that a "new method," the step-by step approach, showed Washington's heart was in the right place. The president even hinted that a fourth summit could happen soon despite little evidence for it.[119]

Kim Myong Gil, who had years of experience dealing with Americans and was the North's new negotiator, praised Trump's "wise political determination," although he pointed out that the "new method" wasn't new. Kim was right. Like Choe, he also warned that Washington had to "come up with a proper calculation in the U.S.-North Korea negotiations."[120]

Choe sounded a negative note shortly before the negotiations finally were to start in early October in Stockholm, stating that the talks would last only one day, not enough time for a serious discussion. Soon afterwards, Pyongyang tested a longer-range sea-launched missile to make sure the message was received.[121]

The Americans remained hopeful, although Pompeo admitted in public that "a lot of work needs to be done."[122] Biegun thought he had diplomatic running room, although yellow lights were flashing in Pyongyang.[123]

Before leaving for Stockholm, the American delegation pondered which approach would be most effective. They could build on the detailed draft statement negotiated in Hanoi, but the North Koreans might say "Take it or leave it." The talks could end quickly if they weren't prepared to compromise on sanctions lifting and denuclearization.[124]

They could respond to Kim Jong Un's long-standing complaint and offer unilateral steps on exercises. But the Americans believed they had already "gone far enough" by replacing large military drills with smaller ones. They weren't going to "throw unilateral gestures against the wall to see what sticks," one official recalled.[125]

Biegun chose a third approach: to smoke the North Koreans out by once again going over the road maps discussed during the February 2019 talks in Pyongyang. They would be new to Kim Myong Gil. It would be hard, however, to portray them as a different "method of calculation."[126]

Four delegation members from each side worked out a schedule the day before the negotiations began on October 5. The Americans hoped to inch the North Koreans away from their default position of "If we don't get what we want, we go home." They even brought Swedish sweet buns to the session.[127]

The North Koreans, however, tabled a disturbing new caveat. They would only meet in the morning, and then decide at lunchtime whether to continue.[128]

The police closed off the approaches to the venue the next day. Two motorcades, escorted by police vans, entered the secluded Villa Elfvik Strand, located on one of fourteen islands straddled by Stockholm. Kim Myong Gil and Steve Biegun arrived in separate cars.[129]

"Where is Alex Wong?" the North Koreans asked as the talks convened in one of the many conference rooms overlooking the adjacent woods or the Baltic Sea. He had been at every meeting since 2018.[130] When they were told he was home expecting the birth of his second child, the North Koreans replied that the baby portended peace.[131]

For the next five hours, the United States and North Korea explored how to move forward. The conversation was lopsided. Aside from an opening statement by Ambassador Kim, filled with quotes and statements from the chairman, Biegun did almost all the talking.[132]

He repeated everything he had said in the Pyongyang talks, presenting a framework for transforming relations and achieving denuclearization, from first reciprocal steps to final destinations. Both would be accomplished in a steady stream of meetings stretching into 2020.[133]

Biegun also tried to convince the North Koreans that the exercises weren't a threat, especially since they had been scaled back after the Singapore summit. The recent August drill had only been conducted on computers. The North Koreans didn't seem to believe him, and if they did, they pretended not to.[134]

Ambassador Kim and his delegation listened, nodded, asked questions, voiced restrained demands, and took notes. A tape recorder on the table in front of them ensured they had a verbatim transcript. Their demeanor was "Tell us what you got," one American recalled.[135]

One official thought they were in good spirits. Another didn't know "where it was going to end up."[136] The fact that the North Koreans were mostly listening wasn't necessarily bad. They had taken the same approach in Pyongyang and that led to progress in Hanoi.

But this time was different. For instance, the North Koreans were under strict instructions: no chitchat during breaks, and no meals with the Americans, normally occasions to explore ways forward.[137]

When the two delegations broke for lunch at half past noon, the North Koreans declined a Swedish invitation to join them and the Americans for a meal. Instead, they promised to return at two thirty and went back to their embassy.[138]

Any uncertainty about where the talks were heading faded fast when Biegun's team got a tip from the media. The North Koreans had scheduled a news conference for later that afternoon. The flashing yellow light had turned red. The Americans knew nothing good would come from it.[139]

After lunch, Biegun continued to lay out Washington's vision for the future. The North Koreans continued to ask questions, make comments, and take notes. A tape recorder still sat on the table in front of them.[140]

Near the end of the afternoon, Ambassador Kim asked to take a break so he could phone Pyongyang. His request wasn't necessarily a positive sign or the kiss of death. But since the North Koreans had scheduled a press conference, chances were it wasn't a good sign.[141]

Kim returned thirty minutes later. Once Biegun finished speaking, the ambassador pulled a long statement from his binder. The text couldn't have been prepared during the lunch break. He had brought it from Pyongyang.[142]

A litany of complaints about Washington's empty promises followed, how it had violated the spirit of the Singapore declaration and demonstrated bad faith. The tape recorder took on added significance, insurance to prove to Kim's superiors he had followed their instructions to the letter.[143]

The North Koreans stared at their shoes, their papers, even a spot on the wall, as Kim denounced Biegun. He also lambasted Mark Lambert, the sanctions enforcer, who was a member of the American delegation.[144]

When his turn came to respond, Biegun took the high road. He looked the North's envoy in the eye as he replied, "Ambassador Kim, you and your team and I and my team know that this in no way reflects what was discussed here today, or the potential for what was discussed today."[145]

The American envoy added, "We're prepared to continue to work at this." Kim didn't say they wouldn't meet again, but one American recalled, "It felt like a break-up date."[146]

The North Koreans rushed to their embassy. Kim informed the waiting reporters, "The negotiations have not fulfilled our expectation and finally broke off." Despite President Trump's statement about a "new method," the Americans "brought nothing to the negotiating table."[147]

Nuclear talks would only resume "when the United States responds sincerely to the measures we first took for denuclearization and trust-building." Kim also criticized the United States for holding the military drills Trump had promised to stop.[148]

The State Department spokesperson took the high road and claimed the two countries had good talks. Overcoming "a legacy of 70 years of war and hostility on the Korean peninsula" required more than a "single Saturday."[149] While the statement wasn't true, it was intended to show the Chinese, whose support for sanctions was essential, that Washington was trying to make diplomacy work.

The North Koreans were infuriated. With two-thirds of his airplane's seats filled with reporters, Kim Myong Gil had a ready audience when it stopped in Beijing. Stockholm was "very bad and sickening," he asserted.

Kim repeated that the end of the year was the deadline for Washington to change course.[150]

American officials puzzled over what had happened. It was a safe bet Kim had come from Pyongyang carrying his statement. Did he have orders to read it no matter what? Was this the final act in the talks? Or was Stockholm payback for Hanoi and the DMZ debacle? In that case, more talks could follow.

Could Biegun have avoided the talks' collapse? Replaying negotiating road maps was a weak reed to lean on. The North Koreans had switched gears before, however, so recycling them wasn't doomed to fail. A "new method" of calculation, either countering Choe's Hanoi proposal or coming up with unilateral steps, might have had a better chance of succeeding. But maybe not.

In the final analysis, Donald Trump's loose lips sank his ship. Kim Jong Un thought Trump had lied to him at the DMZ summit. Two weeks later, Biegun accepted a Swedish invitation to reconvene. The North Koreans didn't. The Stockholm talks were the last time negotiators would meet after twenty-five years of diplomacy.[151]

Days after the debacle, Kim Jong Un once again was photographed riding a white horse up snow-covered Mount Paektu, ready to make an important decision. The odds-on favorite was he would move forward with his WMD programs.[152]

Speculation ended after the chairman took yet another ride accompanied by a flurry of public warnings.[153] He announced North Korea was no longer bound by its WMD test moratorium and promised to field a new strategic weapon soon. Diplomacy was over, at least for the moment.[154]

When the world turned inward in January 2020, caught in the grips of a global pandemic, North Korea was no exception. Neither was the United States. The mounting crisis was put on hold.

CHAPTER TWENTY

"Not only a return to strategic patience, but a lot darker"

S TEVE BIEGUN HAD BLOWN through almost one million frequent flyer miles in the failed pursuit of a nuclear deal. Despite the imminent danger of a December surprise, he still thought the window to talks remained open. The question was how to make them work. Regular discussions were essential. Biegun also toyed with the idea of emphasizing a fundamental change in U.S.-North Korean relations rather than the technical ins and outs of denuclearization.

For Donald Trump, the solution was simple. "Push harder," he instructed Biegun during a December 2019 meeting in the Oval Office. It seemed, however, that Kim Jong Un had become disillusioned with a president who said one thing and did another.[1]

But Trump's "pushing harder" fell flat. He offered Kim help dealing with the coronavirus and a plan to "propel relations" forward. Kim didn't reply.[2] Trump claimed in July 2020 that the North Koreans "want to meet again, and we would certainly do that." The chairman's sister replied that another summit would be "useless," although denuclearization was still possible if the United States took "large-scale irreversible measures."[3]

While Trump's push fell flat, possibly because of the blowups in Hanoi and the DMZ, the upcoming November presidential election, and North Korea's shutdown due to COVID-19 in 2020, the winds of change had started blowing in Pyongyang. Kim Jong Un may have been calculating whether a Trump or Biden win would benefit him more. He avoided provocative tests of long-range rockets or nuclear weapons, confining himself to short-range missile launches. Once Joe Biden was elected, Kim still left the door to diplomacy open a crack.

The President-elect, however, was not the second coming of Donald Trump. Although he had presided over the Senate Foreign Relations Committee for twelve years, Biden focused on Europe and the Middle East. He had only traveled once to Asia, visiting China, Taiwan, and South Korea in 2001.[4]

Like other Democrats, Biden supported negotiations with North Korea, especially during the chaotic George W. Bush years, and admired President Kim Dae-jung, the architect of the Sunshine Policy. During lunch with Kim in 2001, the senator complimented the Nobel Prize winner's tie, even after the South Korean spilled soup on it. Kim gave it to Biden. "You should wear this when you are president," he prophetically told the visiting senator.[5]

Biden's support for diplomacy, however, was a mile wide and an inch deep. As a father and grandfather, he was a strong supporter of food aid to feed starving children in North Korea; on negotiating with the regime, he thought it was probably fruitless.[6] Candidate Biden lambasted Trump during the 2020 campaign for his "photo-op" summit at the DMZ.[7] Once in office, when Biden's aides questioned whether an early meeting with Vladimir Putin was worthwhile, since a summit would enhance the Russian leader's global standing, he responded, "Where have you been? This isn't Kim Jong Un."[8]

The president also was surrounded by skeptics. Kurt Campbell, the White House's new Asia czar, had believed for years that diplomacy with North Korea was a waste of time. The only official who had dealt with Pyongyang before, Wendy Sherman, was slated to become deputy secretary of state. But she had other important responsibilities.

President Moon Jae-in, still in office, tried to steer Washington onto the right course. However, as one former South Korean official recalled, the new administration's policy review was "not only a return to strategic patience, but a lot darker."[9]

Seoul had two requests: First, the South Koreans urged the Biden team to engage North Korea quickly and seriously, perhaps through clear indications by the president or the secretary of state, so as not to lose whatever momentum was left from Trump's diplomacy. Second, the Blue House urged the White House to appoint a new special envoy with stature, to capture Pyongyang's and the public's attention.[10]

The U.S. administration's response fell far short on both counts. Washington streamed messages at Pyongyang via email and telephone through the New York channel. Wendy Sherman even contacted Choe Son Hui, now the North Korean vice foreign minister. But Choe brushed them off lightly in the state-run media, although not rejecting the idea of dialogue altogether. After all, Kim Jong Un had been personally engaged with Donald Trump.[11]

Initially, the new administration didn't see the need to appoint any envoy, let alone someone with stature, since there weren't any talks. Washington finally tapped Sung Kim, who wasn't high profile, but at least had years of experience dealing with Pyongyang. He already had a full-time job as ambassador to Indonesia, however. The point wasn't lost on the South or North Koreans.[12]

President Biden's March 2021 summit with Moon put to rest any uncertainty about the administration's policy. The South Korean leader explained during a private lunch with Biden what had been accomplished during the Trump years, hoping to convince him to be more proactive with Pyongyang. Still, Biden was skeptical about diplomacy.

The South Koreans pushed hard to convince the Americans to include in the summit communiqué a favorable reference to Trump's 2018 Singapore statements, as well as their own summits with the North Koreans. The Americans finally gave in to their ally's wishes.[13]

The release of Washington's policy review in May confirmed that the handwriting on the wall was true. In cautious, hair-splitting phrases, the administration portrayed its approach as the "golden mean" between the Trump and Obama approaches. It wasn't going to seek "everything for everything" like Trump—a characterization that was way off the mark—or "nothing for nothing" like Obama, which was also an unfair bumper sticker.

Instead, Washington would "offer relief for particular steps" with the "ultimate goal of denuclearization." Summits were out. Talks between low-level diplomats were in. The approach sounded reasonable enough, but it was by no means a serious call for action.[14]

While Kim Jong Un's signal that he might return to talks in June had become barely perceptible, events that summer and fall, completely unrelated to the Biden administration's North Korea policy, closed the door. Washington's precipitous withdrawal from Afghanistan in August was seen in Pyongyang as heralding America's global retreat.

North Korea shifted closer to its traditional allies, China and Russia. By the time presidents Putin and Xi met in February 2022, and Russia invaded Ukraine, the new alignment had solidified. The North Korean Politburo was already focused on "countermeasures against the United States."[15]

Washington's pivot away from China and Russia occurred just as North Korea was moving closer. Jake Sullivan, who would become Biden's national security advisor, and Kurt Campbell argued in a 2019 article that "the era of engagement with China has come to an unceremonious end."[16] By fall 2021, Washington's effort to build a stable relationship with Moscow had run aground. Putin warned Biden that relations could completely rupture after Biden told him that the United States and NATO would respond "decisively" to an invasion of Ukraine.[17]

Pyongyang piled on, ending its WMD test moratorium. The pace of North Korea's short-range missile tests picked up in early 2022, followed by two longer-range launches that appeared to be preparation for firing an ICBM. A new long-range missile was launched in March, ending Kim's commitment to Trump to stop testing. Pundits believed a nuclear test was imminent, but that Beijing possibly had restrained the North Koreans.[18]

Diplomacy sputtered until the end of the year. The Moon administration tried to salvage something before it left office. At the Blue House's urging, Washington agreed in the text of a declaration that the Korean War was over. Seoul hoped to jump-start talks and pave the way for the next South Korean president to continue engagement. The draft, approved by Wendy Sherman and Vice Foreign Minister Choi Jong-kun during his November 2022 visit to Washington, was sent to Pyongyang. There was no response. Engagement was dead.[19]

"Deal with the North Korean government as it is, not as we might wish it to be"

The Biden administration's policy toward North Korea was the latest chapter in a decades-long history of failure to stop Pyongyang from building a nuclear arsenal. This book has told the story of how North Korea, which was barely able to muster one nuclear weapon and had only a few missiles that could reach Japan at the beginning of the Obama administration, eventually built an arsenal able to strike cities in the continental United States. That was preventable. Four American administrations had multiple opportunities to stop Pyongyang but failed.

The Clinton administration's 1994 nuclear deal with Pyongyang was the first real chance to stop its nuclear program, as well as turn the corner on the Cold War confrontation with North Korea. Time ran out on President Clinton during his second term as he was poised to hold the first-ever summit with a North Korean leader, a meeting that could have clinched a thawing relationship.

Washington's policy sunk to a disastrous low under George W. Bush, an inexperienced president surrounded by hawkish advisors too confident in American power. The administration torpedoed the 1994 deal instead of using the leverage provided by the agreement to curtail or eliminate Pyongyang's secret uranium enrichment program. Washington failed to replace the agreement with anything more than wishful thinking. Ironically, Bush tried in his second term to re-establish what he had jettisoned in his first term, but failed.

The Obama administration had a chance to stop North Korea. However, for almost eight years, a president who had pledged to reach out to dictators clung to a policy of "strategic patience," only once rolling the diplomatic dice on an unwise "gentleman's agreement" that unraveled quickly. Instead, the administration relied on calculated pressure to change Pyongyang's behavior. Washington missed multiple opportunities to hold talks and potentially head off North Korea's WMD buildup. The White House finally concluded that it had to cut a deal, but time ran out on the administration. The fact that North Korea was the main topic of Obama's only meeting with President-elect Donald Trump spoke to the growing threat and his failure to stop it.

If the Obama administration must accept much of the blame for the emergence of the North Korean threat, Donald Trump must accept the blame for his failure to head it off. He was inexperienced, narcissistic, and, at times, apparently dangerous.

But to use an old, hackneyed phrase, there was a method to Trump's madness. Even during heightened tensions in 2017, when the world believed that the United States and North Korea were on the verge of war, Trump was pondering a far-reaching diplomatic initiative. By the end of the year, he had entrusted a UN envoy about to visit North Korea with a message that he was willing to meet Kim.

Trump's three summits with Kim Jong Un, starting in 2018, were roundly criticized. He was on the right track, however, concluding that they were the only way to stop Pyongyang's WMD programs, not to mention give him an international spotlight.

Trump, however, fell on his own sword; the "two-minute man" walked out just as Kim Jong Un appeared to be giving ground on a nuclear deal at the Hanoi summit. At the DMZ summit a few months later, Trump succeeded in reviving diplomacy. Then, the president put it back on life support when he broke his promise to Kim to cancel an upcoming joint military exercise with South Korea.

Washington is not solely to blame for this sad history. While Pyongyang decided in the early 1990s to switch gears from Cold War confrontation to seek accommodation with the United States, North Korea's road ahead was anything but smooth. Pyongyang was torn all along about whether it was prudent to depend on nuclear weapons for its survival or to reach peace with a long-time enemy.

More often than not, North Korea's behavior encouraged the United States to give the worst possible interpretation to everything it said and did. After fighting a bloody war with the United States and maintaining a hostile relationship for decades, North Korea believed the only way to be taken seriously was to demonstrate that it was a threat. Pyongyang didn't understand that the more it tried to do that through "provocations" such as WMD tests, the more the United States believed that dealing with North Korea was a waste of time. Pyongyang's behavior created a negative feedback loop dominated by the view that it couldn't be trusted.

Understanding the reality of what was going on inside North Korea was also essential. Protecting the regime from external dangers was important. However, three Kim family dictators were motivated to modernize their stagnating economy. Their only road to economic reform led through accommodation with Pyongyang's main enemy, the United States, and the global community. That meant putting the North's WMD programs on the diplomatic chopping block.

Why did Washington fail to grasp all of this? For one thing, there was very little, if any, learning from history. Don Oberdorfer and Robert Carlin published in their landmark survey that "the news from and about Korea has been marked by a remarkable absence of historical context, background or basis for understanding."[20]

That has been a persistent challenge facing American foreign policy. Ernest May, a prominent Harvard scholar, once noted that while "history is an enormously rich resource for people who govern . . . such people usually draw upon this resource haphazardly or thoughtlessly."[21]

But the problem runs deeper than that, rooted in the conduct of America's foreign relations since the end of the Cold War. It is too simplistic to excuse failure because Korea is the land of lousy options. Many, if not most, foreign policy challenges are not easily solved. It is just as simplistic to claim, as many experts have, that Washington has been outfoxed by a wily foe in Pyongyang. Stephen Walt, a prominent scholar, has observed that American foreign policy in the post–Cold War era did not fail "because the United States faced a legion of powerful, crafty, and ruthless adversaries whose brilliant stratagems repeatedly thwarted Washington's noble intentions and well-crafted designs."[22]

Walt argues, instead, that an "increasingly dysfunctional foreign policy community" has "pursued a series of unwise and unrealistic objectives" intended to "change the world," and "refused to learn from its mistakes." This pursuit has been based on an overwhelming belief in American primacy.[23]

While a senior Bush administration official once remarked, "We're an empire now, and when we act, we create our own reality," reality can be stubborn.[24] A State Department veteran, reflecting on his thirty years of failing to end the Israeli-Palestinian conflict, recently observed, "We saw the world the way we wanted it to be, not the way it was."[25]

Successive administrations have failed to follow the advice of William Perry in his 1998 policy review for President Clinton, that the United States had to "deal with the North Korean government as it is, not as we might wish it to be."[26]

Washington consistently overrates its ability to influence other countries. Failing to understand those countries and what shapes their behavior has led to a host of U.S. foreign policy failures, in places such as Vietnam, Iraq, and Afghanistan. North Korea, because of the nuclear threat it poses, could be the most dangerous example of that failure.

One result of this unwavering belief that Washington can create its own reality is that the United States has become increasingly uninterested in compromises, relying instead on pressure and force to get what it wants.

Diplomacy has been a casualty of this mind-set. As one prominent columnist observed, Vice President Richard Cheney's philosophy was often summarized as "we don't negotiate with evil, we defeat it," a standard that included dealing with the Kim family dictatorship.[27] Diplomacy with unsavory leaders has become akin to appeasement.

The deal with North Korea I helped negotiate, Bill Clinton's 1994 nuclear agreement, was roundly condemned in the United States as appeasement. Winston Churchill, however, once stated that "appeasement from strength is magnanimous and noble and might be the surest and

only path to world peace."[28] North Korea at that time was a small, struggling country opposed by the world's only superpower allied with two regional dynamos, South Korea and Japan.

Arrogance explains much of Washington's failed efforts to stop Pyongyang from advancing its nuclear program. The Bush administration's disastrous first-term decision to withdraw from the 1994 nuclear deal assumed
that Pyongyang would essentially surrender. It didn't. President Obama's
policy of strategic patience assumed Pyongyang would have no choice but
to eventually return to talks under conditions imposed by the United States
and strike a deal. Instead, North Korea's WMD programs under Kim Jong
Un literally took off.

Ignorance is also to blame. It wouldn't be the first time that American
decision-makers didn't understand what shaped another country's behavior. Top-level officials had nowhere to turn except to rely on myths about
Pyongyang. Firsthand experience with North Koreans accrued from face-
to-face encounters under President Clinton was frittered away during the
Bush administration. The American intelligence community moved to center stage as the only bureaucracy with "expertise" on Pyongyang. But that
expertise was based on outdated and bookish notions from the Cold War,
not on firsthand experience.

In that context, Donald Trump had it right, at least when it came to
reaching out to Kim Jong Un. After reviewing thousands of tapes of high-
level Iraqi meetings, Steve Coll, a well-known journalist, has argued that
the 2003 invasion of that country might have been avoided if the United
States talked directly to Saddam Hussein.[29]

Trump's meetings and correspondence with Kim—as well as the dictator's encounters with Mike Pompeo and Moon Jae-in—helped avoid miscalculation and painted a valuable picture of a young dictator willing to talk.

The solution to this problem—the lack of understanding of other
countries' interests—is no secret. Former U.S. officials and academics have
called for "strategic empathy," or "understanding the interests and motivations of others in order to shape their behavior in support of one's national interests."

Former secretary of defense Robert McNamara, architect of America's failed strategy in Vietnam, admitted that his first lesson learned was
the need to "empathize with your enemy." Another former secretary of defense, Robert Gates, has observed that U.S. failures in Afghanistan resulted
from policymakers being "profoundly ignorant about our adversaries and
about the situation on the ground."[30]

What If?

Today, a mounting arms race in Northeast Asia is threatening to spiral out of control. Pressures are growing for countries to arm themselves with nuclear weapons. More than ever, they are willing to launch weapons at a moment's notice, raising the danger of war by accident or miscalculation. The unwillingness to negotiate measures to control arsenals or to lessen the risk that war might break out multiplies the dangers.

The "New Cold War" divide that has emerged between the United States, South Korea, and Japan on the one hand, and North Korea, Russia, and China on the other, further intensifies the tensions and the risks. Given that divide, Russia and China now see geopolitical advantages to a growing North Korean array of weapons aimed at the United States and its allies.

Pyongyang is the centerpiece of this combustible situation. With the death of engagement, Kim Jong Un has embarked on a relentless drive to increase his WMD arsenal. In addition to an unprecedented number of missile tests, recent studies project that, with an all-out effort, North Korea's stockpile could reach three hundred weapons by 2028, leapfrogging the arsenals of Great Britain and France, both nuclear powers for over six decades.[31]

Perhaps even more disturbing are Kim's public pronouncements that he would use his weapons "anywhere and anytime" if his country were threatened. In September 2022, the North Korean leader announced five conditions under which he would launch a preemptive strike, including if Pyongyang's leaders believed that preparations were being made to wipe them out with conventional weapons by the combined American and South Korean militaries. War could start because of miscalculation if the leaders' judgment proved wrong.[32]

In fact, North Korea's contribution to tensions has led some experts to believe that Pyongyang is preparing for war. Kim Jong Un's declaration ending North Korea's long-standing goal of reunification, and his redefinition of South Korea not only as a "foreign state" but also as a main enemy, have prompted speculation that the move could help legitimize a future attack against South Korea.[33]

The shock waves caused by the growth of Pyongyang's arsenal have naturally caused military responses. In Seoul, conservative president Yoon Suk-yeol, elected in 2022 but impeached in 2024, emphasized deterring the threat by bolstering South Korea's "3K Defense System," weapons that could attack Pyongyang's missiles before they are launched, as well as wipe out North Korea's leadership. South Korea has developed a wide variety of ballistic and cruise missiles, aircraft, and defensive missile systems to implement this strategy.[34]

In a major break with Tokyo's post-war strategy based on self-defense, Japan has also stepped up its ability to strike targets in North Korea, with one eye on the threat posed by China. Tokyo has signed an agreement to buy four hundred long-range cruise missiles, able to destroy targets up to 1,600 kilometers away, from the United States. In addition, it will also develop its own missiles that can be launched by ships or aircraft to attack targets up to 1,000 kilometers away.[35]

Even more disturbing, pressures are growing for countries to "go nuclear." South Korea is the prime candidate. Those pressures were obvious at the end of the Obama administration when the Park administration explored the possibility with Washington.

Now that the hiatus in Pyongyang's WMD testing has ended, the pressures have resumed. They resulted in an extraordinary statement by President Yoon in January 2023 that if North Korea's nuclear threat grows, South Korea might either build its own nuclear weapons or ask the United States to re-deploy them in the South. While he quickly retracted his remark and Yoon was removed from office in 2024, those pressures remain. It's worth noting that his remarks reflect the view of not only conservatives, but also nationalist progressives. [36]

The dangerous reality in Northeast Asia was recently acknowledged by a former senior American officer who has prophesied that "we are one bad decision away from nuclear war."[37] A single nuclear blast could kill almost eight hundred thousand people in Seoul and seven hundred thousand citizens in Tokyo, not to mention millions of casualties in both cities.[38] The devastation of two of the world's largest economies could trigger a worldwide depression. Moreover, a North Korea about to suffer defeat and destruction wouldn't hesitate to attack American cities. A single blast over Los Angeles would kill almost half a million people with twice that number as casualties.

It's natural to speculate what might have happened if events had taken a different course. While many historians have dismissed "counterfactual history" as intellectually irrelevant, some have argued it is relevant as "a kind of thought experiment that allows scholars and the public alike to better understand causality, sharpen their awareness of the variables that contributed to a historical outcome," and view the past from "altered perspectives."[39]

What if Bill Clinton had met Kim Jong Il in 2000 and clinched a new agreement? What if the Bush administration pursued a new nuclear deal strengthening the 1994 Agreed Framework that also solved the uranium enrichment cheating issue rather than triggering its collapse? What if the Obama administration pursued a WMD agreement with North Korea with the same zeal that it sought one with Iran? And, perhaps the most important missed opportunity, what if Donald Trump had reached an agreement with Kim Jong Un at the Hanoi summit?

Of course, even with such agreements, the path to peace would probably have been bumpy. The North Koreans themselves may have hesitated, fearing that the momentum behind engagement could have undermined the regime's control. If my own personal experience overseeing implementation of the 1994 nuclear deal is any guide, negotiating an agreement with the North is only half the challenge. Inevitably, there will be difficult hurdles at every step of the way. Yet, significant progress is achievable.

China may also have tried to act as a brake on an accelerating positive relationship between Washington and Pyongyang. Beijing would have assumed that its influence in North Korea would be undercut by a better relationship with the United States.

There will always be unanticipated twists and turns. North Korea's shutdown in the face of the 2020 global pandemic was bound to have a negative effect. It's unclear if and how President Biden would have taken advantage of success in Hanoi. Even if he could have, implementation of existing agreements, or reaching new ones, could have easily faced significant political, budgetary, and technical challenges. Aside from the North Koreans, some of the biggest hurdles in implementing the 1994 deal came from trying to forge common positions with the partners, South Korea and Japan, assisting in the effort.

One immediate outcome of a deal negotiated at the Hanoi summit would have been to shut down and dismantle the Yongbyon nuclear installation. Key facilities could be disabled quickly, but dismantlement, which would be time consuming, costly—to the tune of hundreds of millions of dollars—and technically difficult, could have lasted a decade. Periodic disputes with the North Koreans would have been inevitable, slowing the process even further. A decision to convert Yongbyon into a peaceful research facility where North Korean scientists and technicians would be employed would add another complicated layer to implementation, although it would also give the North Koreans added incentive to move forward.

Proceeding further down the road to denuclearization would probably have meant nailing down Kim Jong Un's commitment to dismantle "more" made during Mike Pompeo's visit to Pyongyang in fall 2018. So would following up on Kim's September 2018 letter to President Trump that raised the possibility of dismantling the Nuclear Weapons Institute, possibly the heart of Pyongyang's program. Negotiations would have been difficult. New deals may have required on-site inspections, which Pyongyang had strongly resisted in the past, to help verify restrictions. Whether North Korea, like the Soviet Union in past negotiations, would have found an acceptable path to such measures remains unclear.

While the 2018 WMD testing moratorium would have continued, the United States and North Korea would have almost certainly extended negotiations to the unfinished business of limiting Pyongyang's ballistic missiles. One immediate possibility would have been banning the deployments of long-range and medium-range missiles threatening the United States and targets in Northeast Asia. Washington might have run into problems with South Korea and Japan, who would want any limits to include short-range weapons that could attack their territory. But, in the near term, including those weapons in any agreement would be hard to achieve since they are already deployed with North Korea's armed forces.

The flip side of the Hanoi deal would have been growing momentum behind ending the hostile U.S.-North Korean relationship. Lifting sanctions would have been indispensable. While it is hard to predict how many would be lifted and how fast, it's worth remembering that Biegun's team in Hanoi had in its back pocket a proposal to lift sanctions that were estimated to cost Pyongyang $1 billion every year. More would have followed as denuclearization gathered momentum. Both the Americans and North Koreans envisioned that "snapback" sanctions would be part of the mix. Some restrictions could be lifted quickly, but many would require jumping political and legal hurdles.

The draft document negotiated by Steve Biegun covered a wide range of issues in the bilateral relationship. The United States and North Korea would have opened liaison offices, the first step in establishing normal diplomatic relations. As sanctions were gradually lifted, both countries would move forward, along with the participation of the international community, in modernizing North Korea's economy. People-to-people contacts would have also increased, as well as a wide variety of cultural contacts.

A successful Hanoi summit would have improved the chances that positive momentum could have continued in relations between the two

Koreas. It's possible that President Yoon would have still reversed the Moon administration's course and pursued a distinctly muscular approach to Pyongyang. After all, Lee Myung-bak stepped away from the engagement policies of his predecessors. But Yoon would have had to have done so probably against Washington's wishes. In fact, he might not have even won the 2022 election—Yoon squeaked by an engagement-minded opponent—if President Moon's policy had been a success.

The Hanoi summit would have opened a path to several possible next steps in the process of building a peaceful relationship. Economic interactions could have accelerated. Flagship projects, such as the Kaesong Industrial Zone—a collaborative economic development initiative in North Korea that was shut down in 2016—may have been reinvigorated. The two Koreas would have initiated new negotiations for a follow-on deal to the Comprehensive Military Agreement, possibly including thinning out forces confronting each other at the DMZ. Finally, communication between the two Koreas would have expanded, including various hotlines between government agencies, and regular summits between the two leaders. Once again, the road forward would have been anything but smooth, but a path toward progress, nonetheless.[40]

If the Hanoi summit had been successful, today's expanding partnership between North Korea and Russia might never have happened. Pyongyang may still have sought to maintain good relations with Moscow as a hedge against problems with Washington. But having won his big bet on a better relationship with the United States, Kim Jong Un would have tilted toward his new friend in Washington's growing global conflict with Moscow. Pyongyang would not have sent Russia ten thousand shipping containers of ammunition or ballistic missiles in 2024 to be used in the war against Ukraine. Nor would North Korean military personnel have been sent to participate in Moscow's war against Ukraine.

Whether the North would have sought Russian assistance for its missile programs, modernizing its army, or in building up its defense industrial base is unclear. But Pyongyang also would have had to consider the danger of jeopardizing ties with Washington.[41]

Epilogue

"I think he'll be happy to see I'm coming back."

WITH THE REELECTION OF Donald Trump to a second term in office, American policy toward North Korea is poised to come full circle. The president of the United States is ready to resurrect his summitry with Kim Jong Un.

Trump telegraphed his intentions as soon as he took office. The president gave a shoutout to the North Korean dictator while speaking during a video call to some of the thirty thousand service members stationed in South Korea. "How's Kim Jong Un?" he asked them from the stage at the Commander-in-Chief inaugural ball. The next day, Trump observed, "I think he'll be happy to see I'm coming back." He added during a Fox News interview, "I'll reach out to him again."[1]

Still, Trump may not contact Kim right away. His foreign policy plate appears to be full, whether it's his interest in acquiring Greenland, the Panama Canal, and Canada as the fifty-first state, building a garden spot in Gaza, or imposing tariffs on friends and foes overseas. An even more important priority, ending the war in Ukraine and engineering a reversal in U.S.-Russian relations, is likely to take up much more of his time than he thought.

When Trump does reach out to Kim, he will find a very different Korean Peninsula than during his first term in office. The chairman's pivot away from thirty years of trying to reach a normalized relationship with the United States is in full force. Firmly entrenched in a close relationship with Washington's global rivals—especially Russia but also China—Kim has embarked on a relentless buildup of his nuclear-armed missile arsenal. Tensions have mounted between the two Koreas as engagement has collapsed.

Understanding how the situation has changed will be essential to formulating a new approach to Pyongyang. Trump's secretary of state, Marco Rubio, appears to understand reality. During his January 2025 Senate confirmation hearing, after he recognized a "decade of bipartisan failure," Rubio added that "we can start to work on something else."[2]

While it was too soon for him to say what that something else might be, Rubio did note that the United States needs to focus on preventing a crisis and avoiding inadvertent war, perhaps a recognition that North Korea isn't going to give up its nuclear arsenal anytime soon as well as an acknowledgment of the growing tensions. He also observed that Washington must avoid encouraging other states to pursue their own nuclear weapons programs, once again an implicit hint that there was a risk that any new approach could trigger the acquisition of nuclear weapons by other countries in the region to protect themselves.[3]

It's encouraging that Trump's second administration includes members of Steve Biegun's first-term team. They understand that the situation has changed. For example, Allison Hooker, Trump's first-term Asia expert, has been nominated to be undersecretary of state for policy, the third-ranking position in the department. Still, it's unclear how much influence experienced hands will have, especially since Trump has appointed nine special envoys to deal with key foreign policy challenges, including North Korea.[4]

Whether the president will listen to expert advisors is also in doubt. His administration is no longer populated by aides—like Jim Mattis and others—who felt duty-bound to constrain his worst impulses. His second-term aides seem ready to amplify them without question.

Moreover, the second-term Trump almost certainly is confident that he knows more about Kim Jong Un and North Korea than anyone else. On top of that, the president's personality quirks will make a difficult situation even more difficult. Commenting on his recent experience dealing with Trump on tariffs, John Ford, the premier of the Canadian province of Ontario, observed, "He wakes up and the goal posts change."[5]

Then, of course, there is the nagging issue of whether Kim Jung Un would be happy to see Donald Trump again. They seem to have developed a good personal relationship during the president's first term. But the fact that Kim believes he was burned twice by Trump at the Hanoi and DMZ meetings would appear to make summitry unlikely during the president's second term. The North Koreans avoided personal criticism of Trump, but the chairman's anger after he walked out of one summit and lied to him at another was palpable.

If all politics were personal, Kim would avoid Trump. However, Pyongyang practices power politics at home and abroad. The chairman could well change his mind and do it with a straight face if he thought a summit would serve his geopolitical interests. After all, in one of his less guarded moments at the Hanoi meeting, Kim observed that all politics is about acting.

What if a Trump summit invitation is preceded by a warming in U.S.-Russian relations, a resolution of the war in Ukraine, and a Trump-Putin summit where they agree to encourage the countries in Northeast Asia to tamp down tensions? A shift in relations between Washington and Moscow would catch Kim's attention, give him pause, and hopefully alter his strategic calculus, since Russia has become his major ally. It might help open the door to renewed engagement with the United States.

That geopolitical shift might not be enough to reignite summitry, however, especially if Trump's invitation comes out of the blue without any hints that Washington has changed its policy toward Pyongyang. But what if the president's feeler is preceded or accompanied by important changes in American policy that Kim finds attractive?

Trump has at his disposal steps that he could take to show he is serious about renewed talks. Aside from his public pronouncements, the president could renew the leaders' private exchange of letters. They could include valuable clues about how Trump hopes to proceed in moving negotiations forward.

The president might even consider a phone call to Kim as a first step to reignite their relationship. Phone conversations between friendly leaders have been an invaluable way of conducting diplomacy. They take place with enemies, usually only after relations have begun to thaw. It is easy to see Trump seizing on such a grand gesture.

The president also could directly address Pyongyang's past concerns about American hostility. He could establish diplomatic relations with North Korea or begin to lift sanctions imposed on Pyongyang, which would be a clear sign the United States is moving away from political hostility. And the president has been more than willing to opt for suspending U.S.-ROK military exercises, which he sees as wasteful, and which the North Koreans claim are threatening.

If Kim agrees to meet Trump, a second challenge will be for each side to figure out its negotiating "sweet spot," what it wants out of talks, what the other side wants, and what it is willing to give. Times have changed since the height of Trump's summitry in 2019, not the least of which is the growth of North Korea's nuclear-armed missile stockpile. Moreover, Pyongyang passed a law in 2022 that it is a nuclear weapons state, with Kim insisting that this designation is "irreversible."[6]

While the Trump administration still appears to cling to denuclearization in public, these developments call into question that decades-old basic objective. Some experts believe "it is time for the United States to face reality." They argue that the unrealistic goal of insisting North Korea give up its nuclear arsenal should be dropped altogether to clear the way of a major obstacle to progress in talks.[7] Indeed, leaving his job as the Obama's administration's special envoy in 2011, a pessimistic Steve Bosworth thought the United States would have to accept North Korea as a nuclear power or fight a war to stop it.

A strong argument can be made that Washington should pursue another near-term goal, reducing the risk of nuclear war, just as Secretary Rubio suggested. The need to halt the spiraling regional arms race and the dangers of a war triggered by miscalculation or miscommunication is more pressing.

The two objectives—denuclearization and risk reduction—are not mutually exclusive. For example, slowing or stopping the growth of Pyongyang's WMD arsenal, by halting missile and nuclear tests, could be the first step in moving toward denuclearization while also calming tensions and reducing the risk of war.

A strong argument can also be made that denuclearization should remain as a long-term objective of engagement with North Korea. Dropping it altogether could prove risky. The international community today is already faced with the growing danger that the global diplomatic regime to prevent the spread of nuclear weapons is unraveling. That danger has increased dramatically with President Trump's "America First" foreign policy, which has convinced old allies that Washington is backing away from its commitment to their security.

The tremors are already obvious in a Europe whipsawed by the president's coziness with President Putin, his harsh critique of long-time NATO allies for not spending enough to defend themselves, and his launch of a tariff war against them. Recent alarming hints from Poland that it might consider building its own nuclear arsenal, for example, are the direct result of growing doubts about America's security guarantee.[8]

Once the president turns his attention to U.S. allies in Asia, if his first term is any indication—Trump had a reflexive negative reaction whenever South Korea was mentioned—Seoul is in for a rough ride. He claimed in a recent speech to Congress that the South charges four times higher tariffs than the United States, a claim that Seoul has countered is false. Nevertheless, one recent analysis of the "trade risk" faced by 173 countries with the Trump administration ranked South Korea as the most vulnerable.[9]

The president's negativity is certain to extend to the security alliance. That was obvious throughout his first term, in his constant questioning of whether South Korea was paying sufficient money to support the U.S. military commitment, the need to conduct what he believed were wasteful joint military exercises, and the cost of stationing twenty-eight thousand troops on the peninsula.

Dropping the goal of denuclearization, combined with an American president who takes steps to undermine Washington's alliance with South Korea, could ignite a dangerous cascade of WMD proliferation in Northeast Asia. The combination might convince Seoul to protect itself against a nuclear North Korea by embarking on its own nuclear program. Japan might follow, even though it was the sole victim of an atomic attack during World War II. In short, the region would be populated by countries armed with nuclear weapons and hostile to one another. It would be a prescription for disaster.

Is there a path forward for Washington that would, as Secretary Rubio observed in his confirmation hearing, thread the needle of focusing on the short-term goal of reducing the risk of nuclear war, which falls short of denuclearization but avoids the nightmare scenario of proliferation? Perhaps the best that could be done is to push forward with pragmatic measures to tamp down the risk of war; reduce, but not eliminate, the danger of North Korea's nuclear weapons; and avoid a breakdown in America's alliances with South Korea and Japan.

On the first count, there is a large menu of measures—political, security, and economic—that could be taken to achieve that objective. Many of those measures have been mainstays of U.S.-North Korean talks for decades. Many appeared in Biegun's Hanoi draft, which built on the 2018 Singapore summit declaration, but ended up on the cutting-room floor.

They include opening diplomatic relations between the United States and North Korea, negotiating a peace treaty, lifting U.S. and international sanctions imposed on Pyongyang, providing the North with economic aid—largely through international institutions—to help modernize its economy, and establishing a program of people-to-people exchanges, including reunions of families separated by the Korean War.

There may also be new avenues to reach agreements. For example, given President Trump's fixation with rare earth minerals, crucial for use in modern technologies, developing North Korea's extensive deposits could be one avenue. An Australian mining company concluded in 2013 that North Korea has the world's largest deposits of rare earth minerals, totaling some 216 million tons. While their size will have to be verified, they remain underground, largely because of sanctions targeting North Korea's mineral exports.[10]

The 2025 U.S.-Ukraine agreement to mine rare earth minerals could serve as a template for working with North Korea. A percentage of the revenues would be deposited in a fund to be used to modernize Pyongyang's economy. Other countries may participate.[11] China's support will be essential since it dominates the global market and has an effective monopoly over processing many major rare earth minerals. Finally, significant investment by the private sector will be important to set up the infrastructure to mine the minerals.

Establishing a rare earth mineral fund as the centerpiece of engagement will also require accompanying steps familiar from past talks between Washington and Pyongyang to get the project off the ground. Once again diplomatic relations will have to be established between the two main players, the United States and North Korea. International sanctions banning North Korean mineral exports and joint ventures with Pyongyang will have to be lifted. American financial sanctions will also need to be lifted or at least waived, as will restrictions on participating North Korean organizations, to make an investment and move forward with the work.

Just as in the Ukraine deal, private mining companies are likely to be hesitant to make a long-term investment given the ongoing security risks on the Korean Peninsula. As a result, any agreement will have to be accompanied by steps by all parties to reduce regional tensions and establish stability. They should also be designed to meet Washington's and its allies' concerns about the North Korean challenge.

At the top of the list will be measures to reduce the dangers posed by Pyongyang's unconstrained WMD programs. Denuclearization may be a distant objective, but initial constraints, especially a halt to nuclear and missile tests, will be essential to tamp down tensions and constrain technological improvements in the North's weaponry.

The United States and its allies could also take steps to reduce tensions if necessary. These might include halting tests of South Korean and Japanese missiles able to cover North Korean territory. Washington could limit or pause the visits of nuclear-armed submarines and bombers to the peninsula, intended to reassure Seoul of its commitment to defend the South but found threatening by the North.

Beyond initial moves related to WMD, all the interested parties, especially the two Koreas, will have to work to calm regional tensions. On the first count, establishing talks to reduce the danger of nuclear war would allow the participants, starting with the United States and North Korea, and then broadening out to include Russia, China, South Korea, and Japan, to air their gripes. The objective would be to come up with confidence-building measures to alleviate those concerns.

As for the two Koreas, returning to the heyday of President Moon's three summits with Kim Jong Un might no longer be possible, given the nosedive in relations that began in 2020. But calming tensions might at least be possible if President Yoon, who has been impeached, is removed from office. If a new progressive president is elected, Seoul would undoubtably seek to engage Pyongyang.

Whether the North Koreans would respond positively is unclear. It would probably depend on improved relations with Washington and the views of Pyongyang's friends, Russia and China. If engagement between the two Koreas resumes, one place to start would be to formulate measures to avoid serious clashes in the DMZ and along the NLL in the West Sea, perhaps even resurrecting some measures from the now-defunct Comprehensive Military Agreement, which has been abandoned by both countries.

Perhaps the most challenging piece of a policy Rubik's Cube that could help forestall the dangerous nuclearization of the region will be how President Trump handles the long-standing American alliance with South Korea. Maintaining a strong relationship would be the best path forward to forestalling the further spread of nuclear weapons, withdrawing American troops the worst.

South Korea has been preparing sweeteners to stave off Trump's expected onslaught. They range from offering expertise in helping the U.S. to revive its shipbuilding industry—crucial to countering the Chinese military—to a willingness to "achieve a more balanced and mutually beneficial relationship" on trade and economics.[12]

If Seoul fails, however, the key issue then will become whether the United States will pack up and go home or agree to a new security arrangement other than a treaty-based alliance. As two defense experts have noted, "The US has implied a 'virtual' security commitment with a number of countries . . . with whom it does not have a formal security commitment and where the American peacetime military presence is minimal."[13]

For example, the alliance could focus on "places, not bases," like it does with Australia, Singapore, and Thailand, enabling U.S. forces to use existing facilities owned and operated by allies and partners that could be used in a crisis or conflict. Another option is "more offshore balancing light," which would establish a greater "over the horizon" presence with more combat assets in Japan and Guam.[14]

Stage-managing a policy that maintains a loose security commitment to South Korea, makes progress in constraining North Korea's weapons programs, and tamps down tensions would seem to be the best approach. However, even a deft administration in Washington would find implementation challenging.

If the Trump administration's performance during his first months in office is any indication, it's in serious doubt whether a supremely confident president will be able to navigate through these policy shoals. As one columnist has observed, "So much of what Mr. Trump does abroad, just like what he does at home, is ham-handed, shortsighted and cruel."[15]

Notes

Preface

1. The story of the Kumchang-ri inspection is based on the author's recollection, as well as contemporaneous notes.

2. David Sanger, "North Korea Site an A-Bomb Plant, U.S. Agencies Say," *New York Times*, August 17, 1998, https://www.nytimes.com/1998/08/17/world /north-korea-site-an-a-bomb-plant-us-agencies-say.html.

3. John Gittings, "North Korea Fires Missile over Japan," *Guardian* (London), September 1, 1998, https://www.theguardian.com/world/1998/sep/01/ northkorea.

4. Philip Shenon, "Panel Urges Stepped-Up Attention to Ties with North Korea," *New York Times*, September 15, 1999, https://www.nytimes.com /1999/09/15/world/panel-urges-stepped-up-attention-to-ties-with-north -korea.html.

5. Robert L. Gallucci and Joel S. Wit, "North Korea's Real Lessons for Iran," *New York Times*, April 10, 2015, https://www.nytimes.com/2015/04/11 /opinion/north-koreas-real-lessons-for-iran.html.

6. Susan Braudy, "He's Woody Allen's 1-1-Silent Partner," *New York Times*, August 21, 1977, https://www.nytimes.com/1977/08/21/archives/hes-woody -allens-notsosilent-partner.html.

7. Author's personal notes as head of U.S. delegation, 1999; and Philip Shenon, "Suspected North Korean Atom Site Is Empty, U.S. Finds," *New York Times*, May 28, 1999, https://www.nytimes.com/1999/05/28/world /suspected-north-korean-atom-site-is-empty-us-finds.html.

8. Don Oberdorfer and Robert Carlin, *The Two Koreas: A Contemporary History* (New York: Basic Books, 2014), Kindle; Joel S. Wit, Daniel B. Poneman, and Robert L. Gallucci, *Going Critical: The First North Korean Nuclear Crisis* (Washington, DC: The Brookings Institution, 2014); and Mike Chinoy, *Meltdown: The Inside Story of the North Korean Nuclear Crisis* (New York: St. Martin's Press, 2008).

9. William Faulkner, *Requiem for a Nun* (New York: Vintage International, 2011), ebook edition.

Chapter One. "How silly do you think we are?"

1. Michael Madden, "Pyongyang's Leading Ladies: A Short Study on Choe Son Hui and Kim Yo Jong" (program associate, US Intelligence Community, National Intelligence Council, National Intelligence Officer For North Korea, unpublished paper, December 2019).
2. Author's recollection, US-DPRK Track 2 meeting, Berlin, March 2016.
3. Author's observation.
4. Peter Jones, *Track Two Diplomacy in Theory and Practice* (Stanford, CA: Stanford University Press, 2015), 7–54.
5. Hilde Henriksen Waage, "Norway's Role in the Middle East Peace Talks: Between a Small State and a Weak Belligerent," *Journal of Palestine Studies* 34, no. 4 (Summer 2005): 6–24.
6. Author's notes, "Transcript of US-DPRK Track 2 Meeting," November 17–19, 2016, Geneva, Switzerland; and "U.S.-DPRK Track 2 Meeting Briefing Memo," November 17–19, 2016, Geneva, Switzerland.
7. Rachel Cao, "Trump Once Said He'd 'Negotiate Like Crazy' with North Korea," CNBC, August 9, 2017, https://www.cnbc.com/2017/08/09/trump -once-said-hed-negotiate-like-crazy-with-north-korea.html.
8. Ko Dong-hwan, "Trump Up for 'Hamburger Talk' with Kim Jong-un," *Korea Times*, June 16, 2016, https://www.koreatimes.co.kr/www/nation/2024/06 /501_207133.html; "Trump Warns North Korea of 'Fire and Fury,'" CNN, August 9, 2017, https://transcripts.cnn.com/show/nday/date/2017-08-09 /segment/03; and "Donald Trump: N Korea's Kim Jong-un a 'Smart Cookie,'" BBC, April 30, 2017, https://www.bbc.com/news/world-asia-39764834.
9. Interviews with former White House officials, June 20, 2018; February 2, 2018; and December 13, 2017.
10. Edward Wong, "Michael Flynn, a Top Trump Advisor, Ties China and North Korea to Jihadists," *New York Times*, November 26, 2016, https://www .nytimes.com/2016/11/30/world/asia/michael-flynn-trump-adviser-china -north-korea.html.
11. K. T. McFarland, *Revolution: Trump, Washington and We the People* (New York: Post Hill Press, 2020), 164.
12. Interview with former White House official, January 10, 2018.
13. Interview with former White House official, July 13, 2018.
14. Charles M. Blow, "Obama Lives in Trump's Head," *New York Times*, May 17, 2020, https://www.nytimes.com/2020/05/17/opinion/trump-obama.html.
15. Ben Rhodes, *The World as It Is: A Memoir of the Obama White House* (New York: Random House, 2018), 404–405; and interview with former White House official, January 10, 2018.

16. Interview with former White House official, January 4, 2018.

17. The White House, Office of the Press Secretary, "Remarks by President Obama and President-elect Trump after Meeting," November 10, 2016, https://obamawhitehouse.archives.gov/the-press-office/2016/11/10/remarks-president-obama-and-president-elect-trump-after-meeting.

18. Jonathan Karl, *Front Row at the Trump Show* (New York: Dutton, 2020), 95.

19. Associated Press, "WATCH: Trump Says Obama Administration Left Him a 'Mess' in Dealings with North Korea," *PBS NewsHour*, October 22, 2020, https://www.pbs.org/newshour/politics/watch-trump-says-obama-administration-left-him-mess-in-dealings-with-north-korea.

20. Interview with former Pentagon officials, February 27, 2018, and October 3, 2018; Peter Baker, "The War That Wasn't: Trump Claims Obama Was Ready to Strike North Korea," *New York Times*, February 19, 2019, https://www.nytimes.com/2019/02/16/us/politics/trump-obama-north-korea.html.

21. Interviews with former White House officials, April 23, 2018, and December 29, 2020.

22. Joel S. Wit, Daniel B. Poneman, and Robert L. Gallucci, *Going Critical: The First North Korean Nuclear Crisis* (Washington, DC: Brookings Institution Press, 2004), 192–220.

23. Robert Farley, "No Evidence Kim Jong Un Rebuffed Obama's Begging," Factcheck.org, July 2, 2019, https://www.factcheck.org/2019/07/no-evidence-kim-jong-un-rebuffed-obamas-begging/.

24. Interview with former White House official, January 4, 2018.

25. David Nakamura and Anne Gearan, "Obama Warned Trump on North Korea. But Trump's 'Fire and Fury' Strategy Wasn't What Obama Aides Expected," *Washington Post*, August 9, 2017, https://www.washingtonpost.com/politics/obama-warned-trump-on-north-korea-but-trumps-fire-and-fury-strategy-wasnt-what-obama-aides-expected/2017/08/09/f3f02e0e-7d19-11e7-9d08-b79f191668ed_story.html.

26. National Committee on North Korea, "Kim Jong Un's 2017 New Year's Address," Washington, DC, January 1, 2017, https://www.ncnk.org/resources/publications/kju_2017_new_years_address.pdf/file_view.

27. "Trump Tweetwatch: N Korea Nuclear Plans 'Won't Happen,'" BBC, January 3, 2017, https://www.bbc.com/news/world-us-canada-38496070.

28. Tony Munroe and Jack Kim, "North Korea's Kim Says Close to Test Launch of ICBM," Reuters, January 2, 2017, https://www.reuters.com/article/us-northkorea-kim/north-koreas-kim-says-close-to-test-launch-of-icbm-idUSKBN14L0RN/.

29. Interview with former Department of Defense official, October 3, 2018.

30. Interview with former State Department official, February 1, 2019.

31. Interview with former State Department official, February 1, 2019.

Chapter Two. "The world around us is changing."

1. William J. Taylor, "North Korea: A Visitor's First Impressions," trip report, 1991; "Reports on Bill Taylor's Second Trip to North Korea, 18–24 February 1992," trip report; "Report on Bill Taylor's Third Trip to North Korea, 23–29 June 1992," trip report; and "Reflections on President Kim Il Sung," trip report.

2. Harrison E. Salisbury, "North Korean Leader Bids U.S. Leave the South as Step to Peace," *New York Times*, May 31, 1972, https://www.nytimes.com /1972/05/31/archives/north-korean-leader-bids-us-leave-the-south-as -step-to-peace-north.html.

3. The Association for Diplomatic Studies and Training, Foreign Affairs Oral History Project, "Congressman Stephen Solarz," interview by Charles Stuart Kennedy, November 18, 1995, 78–81; and "Record of Meeting with Cong. Stephen J. Solarz and President Kim Il Sung," trip report, attached to a letter from Congressman Stephen J. Solarz to Zbigniew Brzezinski, President Carter's national security advisor, August 4, 1980. (Notation at top says "copy to Carter Library.")

4. Private communication from Robert Carlin to author, March 12, 2019.

5. Mark P. Barry, "Partial List of Americans Who Met Kim Il Sung," *Mark P. Barry's Blog*, August 3, 2018, accessed February 29, 2024, https://mark-p -barry.com/?s=partial+list+of+americans.

6. "Transcript of Meeting with Kim Il Sung, December 1991," trip report, January 2017.

7. Former U.S. official, interview by Wit, 2003, cited in Joel S. Wit, Daniel B. Poneman, and Robert L. Gallucci, *Going Critical: The First North Korean Nuclear Crisis* (Washington, DC: Brookings Institution Press, 2004), 14.

8. Interview with former U.S. delegation member, May 13, 2019.

9. Wit, Poneman, and Gallucci, *Going Critical*, 14.

10. Taylor, "Report on Bill Taylor's Third Trip to North Korea"; and Taylor, "Reflections on President Kim Il Sung."

11. Taylor, "Reflections on President Kim Il Sung."

12. Taylor, "Reflections on President Kim Il Sung."

13. Taylor, "Reflections on President Kim Il Sung."

14. Taylor, "Reflections on President Kim Il Sung"; and Central Intelligence Agency, "North Korea Pursues Strategic Goal of Changing the 'U.S. Hostile Policy," Open Source Works, unclassified, September 11, 2009, 2.

15. Taylor, "Report on Bill Taylor's Third Trip to North Korea, 23–29 June 1992."

16. Taylor, "Report on Bill Taylor's Third Trip to North Korea, 23–29 June 1992."

17. "SDF Head Opposes Foreign Pressure on DPRK," *Kyodo News*, March 18, 1993, cited in Wit, Poneman, and Gallucci, *Going Critical*, 34.

18. Wit, Poneman, and Gallucci, *Going Critical*, 34–39.
19. Charles Krauthammer, "Opinion: North Korea's Coming Bomb," *Washington Post*, November 4, 1993, https://www.washingtonpost.com/archive/opinions/1993/11/05/north-koreas-coming-bomb/82756d7a-d56f-42bc-9cf3-c6ce76b90bf7/.
20. Wit, Poneman, and Gallucci, *Going Critical*, 51–63.
21. Wit, Poneman, and Gallucci, *Going Critical*, 52.
22. Interview with former State Department official, June 23, 2006.
23. Wit, Poneman, and Gallucci, *Going Critical*, 55–63.
24. Wit, Poneman, and Gallucci, *Going Critical*, 169–170.
25. Wit, Poneman, and Gallucci, *Going Critical*, 175–182.
26. Michael D. Mosettig, "20 Years Later, Commemorating a War Averted," *PBS NewsHour*, October 23, 2014, https://www.pbs.org/newshour/world/20-years-later-commemorating-war-averted.
27. Wit, Poneman, and Gallucci, *Going Critical*, 209.
28. Wit, Poneman, and Gallucci, *Going Critical*, 241.
29. Interview with former U.S. government official, February 15, 2001, cited in Wit, Poneman, and Gallucci, *Going Critical*, 68.
30. Wit, Poneman, and Gallucci, *Going Critical*, 221–238; and Jimmy Carter, "Report of Our Trip to Korea, June 1994," unpublished trip report.
31. Wit, Poneman, and Gallucci, *Going Critical*, 222–223.
32. Wit, Poneman, and Gallucci, *Going Critical*, 223–224.
33. Wit, Poneman, and Gallucci, *Going Critical*, 226.
34. Wit, Poneman, and Gallucci, *Going Critical*, 228.
35. Wit, Poneman, and Gallucci, *Going Critical*, 231–235.
36. Wit, Poneman, and Gallucci, *Going Critical*, 255–260.
37. Wit, Poneman, and Gallucci, *Going Critical*, 265–271.
38. Wit, Poneman, and Gallucci, *Going Critical*, 275.
39. Wit, Poneman, and Gallucci, *Going Critical*, 271.
40. Wit, Poneman, and Gallucci, *Going Critical*, 296–303.
41. Wit, Poneman, and Gallucci, *Going Critical*, 307–310.
42. Wit, Poneman, and Gallucci, *Going Critical*, 334.
43. "Rodong Sinmun 1994," *Rodong Sinmun* (Worker's Daily), December 1, 1994.
44. David E. Sanger, "Clinton Approves Plan to Give Aid to North Koreans," *New York Times*, October 18, 1994, https://www.nytimes.com/1994/10/19/world/clinton-approves-a-plan-to-give-aid-to-north-koreans.html.
45. U.S. Department of State, "North Korean Missile Proliferation," January 6, 1999, secret, declassified, U.S. Department of State Case N. F-2016-08654, Doc No. C06092445, August 30, 2017; and Sheryl Wudunn, "North Korea Fires Missiles Over Japanese Territory," *New York Times*, September 1, 1998, https://www.nytimes.com/1998/09/01/world/north-korea-fires-missile-over-japanese-territory.html?mcubz=1.

46. Interview with former U.S. intelligence official, October 9, 2017; and interview with member of the Rumsfeld Commission on Missile Proliferation, October 3, 2017.

47. David Isenberg, "Atomic Market: What Benazir Knew," UPI, https://www.cato.org/commentary/atomic-market-what-benazir-knew; and David Albright and Paul Brannan, "Taking Stock: North Korea's Uranium Enrichment Program," Institute for Science and International Security, October 6, 2010, https://isis-online.org/uploads/isis-reports/documents/ISIS_DPRK_UEP.pdf.

48. Interviews with former State Department officials, October 2006 and November 8, 2022.

49. Don Oberdorfer and Robert Carlin, *The Two Koreas: A Contemporary History* (New York: Basic Books, 2014), chap. 16, Kindle.

50. "Script of Talking Points for William J. Perry," version 5 as delivered, May 21, 1999, secret, declassified October 19, 2006, Case ID 2000601240.

51. Oberdorfer and Carlin, *The Two Koreas*, chap. 16.

52. Taylor Branch, *The Clinton Tapes* (New York: Simon and Schuster, 2009), 626–627.

53. Interview with former State Department official, November 24, 2021.

54. Mike Chinoy, *Meltdown: The Inside Story of the North Korean Nuclear Crisis* (New York: St. Martin's Press, 2008), 25–26.

55. Office of the Spokesman, U.S. Department of State, "U.S.-DPRK Joint Communique, October 12, 2000," https://1997-2001.state.gov/regions/eap/001012_usdprk_jointcom.html.

56. Interviews with former U.S. officials, 2006, 2010, 2015, 2022.

57. U.S. Department of State, "U.S. Ambassador Stephen Bosworth Updates Secretary of State Madeleine Albright on South Korean Public Opinion on the Eve of North-South Summit Conference," June 9, 2000, U.S. Declassified Documents, https://nsarchive.gwu.edu/document/16108-document-16-cable-amembassy-seoul-3037.

58. Madeleine Albright, *Madame Secretary: A Memoir* (New York: Miramax Books, 2003), 465; and Chinoy, *Meltdown*, 18.

59. Chinoy, *Meltdown*, 29; and Konstantin Pulikovksy, *Orient Express: Across Russia with Kim Jong Il* (Moscow: Gordetz, 2002).

60. Albright, *Madame Secretary*, 465; "Secretary Albright Briefs President Kim on DPRK Trip and Impressions of Kim Jong Il," secret cable, October 25, 2000, declassified, July 5, 2018, Case No. M-2014-13564; and interview with a former State Department Official, April 2, 2019.

61. Chinoy, *Meltdown*, 26–28.

62. Chinoy, *Meltdown*, 30.

63. Oberdorfer and Carlin, *The Two Koreas*, chap. 16.

64. Albright, *Madame Secretary*, 467–469.

65. Chinoy, *Meltdown*, 29.

66. Albright, *Madame Secretary*, 467–469.

67. Interview with former State Department official, November 2020.

68. Albright, *Madame Secretary*, 470; Ambassador Wendy Sherman, *Not for the Faint of Heart: Lessons in Courage, Power and Persistence* (New York: Public Affairs, 2018), 107–108; and interview with former State Department official, September 15, 2010.

69. Interview with former State Department official, July 21, 2021.

70. Interviews with two former State Department officials, April 2, 2019.

71. Interview with former White House official, July 31, 2021.

72. Chinoy, *Meltdown*, 32; and interview with expert attendee at Albright dinner, April 18, 2019.

73. Interview with former State Department official, 2010.

74. Sherman, *Not for the Faint of Heart*, 107.

75. Chinoy, *Meltdown*, 29; Samuel Chamberlain, "Bill Clinton Says, "I Regret Missed Chance to 'End' North Korea Missile Program," Fox News, June 7, 2018, https://www.foxnews.com/politics/bill-clinton-says-i-regret-missed -chance-to-end-north-korea-missile-program; and Bill Clinton, *Citizen: My Life after the White House* (New York: Knopf Doubleday Publishing Group, 2024), chap. 23, Kindle.

76. Leon Sigal, email communication to author, April 18, 2019, based on meetings with Eli Segal (2003) and Sandy Berger (2007).

77. Chamberlain, "Bill Clinton Says"; Bill Clinton, *My Life* (New York: Alfred A. Knopf, 2004), Kindle; and Clinton, *Citizen*, chap. 3.

78. Chinoy, *Meltdown*, 32.

79. Sherman, *Not for the Faint of Heart*, 105.

80. Oberdorfer and Carlin, *The Two Koreas*, chap. 16.

81. Karen DeYoung, *Soldier: The Life of Colin Powell* (New York: Alfred A. Knopf, 2006), chap. 1, Kindle; and Martin Plissner, "The Most Trusted Man in America," CBS News, February 4, 2003, https://www.cbsnews.com/news /the-most-trusted-man-in-america.

82. Glenn Kessler, "From the Shadows," NBC News, October 5, 2004, https:// www.nbcnews.com/id/wbna6181546.

83. Bob Woodward, *Bush At War* (New York: Simon and Schuster, 2002), 340; and Condoleezza Rice, "Campaign 2000: Promoting the National Interest," *Foreign Affairs*, January 1, 2000, https://www.foreignaffairs.com/united -states/campaign-2000-promoting-national-interest.

84. Chinoy, *Meltdown*, 44.

85. Chinoy, *Meltdown*, 48–49.

86. Barton Gellman, *Angler: The Cheney Vice Presidency* (New York: Penguin Press, 2008), 240; and interview with former U.S. government official, October 10, 2006.

87. Chinoy, *Meltdown*, 52–55; and Condoleezza Rice, *No Higher Honor: A Memoir of My Years in Washington* (New York: Crown Publishers, 2011), chap. 3, Kindle.

88. U.S. Embassy Seoul, "EU Readout on Pyongyang Visit," confidential, State 0811269, May 2001, unclassified U.S. Department of State Case N. F-2014-15749, October 12, 2017.

89. Interview with former U.S. government official, June 20, 2006; and Chinoy, *Meltdown*, 63.

90. Rice, *No Higher Honor*, chap. 11.

91. Chinoy, *Meltdown*, 71.

92. "President Bush Visits Demilitarized Zone: Remarks by the President at Dorasan Train Station," press release, February 20, 2002, George W. Bush White House Archives, https://georgewbush-whitehouse.archives.gov/news/releases/2002/02/text/20020220-2.html.

93. Charles L. Pritchard, *Failed Diplomacy: The Tragic Story of How North Korea Got the Bomb* (Washington, DC: Brookings Institution Press, 2007), 21; and interview with former U.S. official, February 20, 2006.

94. Interview with former U.S. official, February 20, 2006; and Chinoy, *Meltdown*, 80.

95. Central Intelligence Agency, untitled classified document to Congress, November 2002, National Security Archive, https://nsarchive2.gwu.edu/NSAEBB/NSAEBB87/nk22.pdf; and Pritchard, *Failed Diplomacy*, 31.

96. Chinoy, *Meltdown*, 83.

97. Chinoy, *Meltdown*, 104.

98. Rice, *No Higher Honor*, chap. 11.

99. Interview with former State Department official, May 23, 2005.

100. Interview with former State Department official, May 23, 2005.

101. Interview with former State Department official, May 23, 2005; and "Summary of Private Briefing on Meetings with DPRK with Vice Foreign Minister Kim Gye Gwan," Beijing, China, August 13–14, 2003.

102. Interview with former State Department official, 2005; and interview with former U.S. official, October 15, 2005.

103. Interview with former State Department official, 2005; and private communication with former State Department official, March 2020.

104. Oberdorfer and Carlin, *The Two Koreas*, chap. 17, Kindle.

105. Pritchard, *Failed Diplomacy*, 42; and Chinoy, *Meltdown*, 140–141.

106. Interview with former State Department official, May 23, 2005.

107. Gellman, *Angler*, 229.

108. DeYoung, *Soldier*, chap. 21; and interview with former U.S. official, May 23, 2005.

109. Senate Committee on Foreign Relations Hearing on "Visit to the Yongbyon Nuclear Scientific Research Center in North Korea," Siegfried S. Hecker, Senior Fellow, Los Alamos National Laboratory, University of California, January 21, 2004, https://nonproliferation.org/wp-content/uploads/2022/09/2004_hecker_senate_hearing_testimony.pdf.

110. Rice, *No Higher Honor*, chap. 23.

111. Richard Holbrooke, *To End War: The Conflict in Yugoslavia—American's Inside Story—Negotiating with Milosevic* (New York: Modern Library, 1999), 80; and author's private communication with a State Department reporter, 2006.

112. Norimitsu Onishi, "North Korean Leader Signals Willingness to Resume Talks," *New York Times*, June 17, 2005, https://www.nytimes.com/2005/06 /17/international/asia/north-korean-leader-signals-willingness-to-resume -talks.html.

113. "Joint Statement of the Fourth Round of the Six Party Talks Beijing," U.S. Department of State Archive, September 19, 2005, https://2001-2009.state .gov/r/pa/prs/ps/2005/53490.htm.

114. Christopher Hill, *Outpost: A Diplomat at Work* (New York: Simon and Schuster, 2014), 242.

115. Author's communication with State Department reporter, October 28, 2006; and Chinoy, *Meltdown*, 289.

116. "Interview with Fuji Television," February 27, 2008, U.S. Department of State Archive, https://2001-2009.state.gov/secretary/rm/2008/02/101379. htm.

117. Associated Press, "Raw Video: North Korea Destroys Reactor Tower," video, June 27, 2008, https://www.youtube.com/watch?app=desktop&v =zfj6DDsEFWQ.

118. Hill, *Outpost*, 277–278.

119. Larry Niksch, "North Korea's Nuclear Weapons Development and Diplomacy," Congressional Research Service, 10, https://sgp.fas.org/crs/nuke /RL33590.pdf.

120. Rice, *No Higher Honor*, chap. 38.

121. "President Bush Holds News Conference," CNN, October 11, 2006, https:// transcripts.cnn.com/show/cnr/date/2006-10-11/segment/02; and George W. Bush, *Decision Points* (New York: Crown Publishers, 2010), 425–426.

122. Pritchard, *Failed Diplomacy*, 161.

Chapter Three. "John Bolton was right?"

1. Interview with Bosworth family member, July 18, 2017.

2. Michele Kelemen, "Clinton's Brand of Diplomacy on Display in Asia," *Day to Day*, NPR, February 20, 2009, https://www.npr.org/2009/02/20/1009 19589/clintons-brand-of-diplomacy-on-display-in-asia.

3. Interview with former senior State Department official, February 27, 2018.

4. David Fernández Puyana and Daphné Richemond-Barak, eds., *The Shimon Peres Legacy of Peace through Fourteen Historical Speeches: On the Occasion of the 100th Anniversary of Shimon Peres' Birth* (San José: UPEACE Press, 2023), 68, https://upeace.org/wp-content/uploads/2024/08/Fernandez-The -Shimon-Peres-legacy-on-peace-2024.pdf.

5. Interview with State Department official, March 5, 2018.

6. Sam Roberts, "Stephen W. Bosworth, U.S. Diplomat Who Helped Oust Ferdinand Marcos, Dies at 76," *New York Times*, January 8, 2016, https://www.nytimes.com/2016/01/09/world/americas/stephen-w-bosworth-us-diplomat-who-helped-oust-ferdinand-marcos-dies-at-76.html; interview with Ambassador Stephen Bosworth, Association for Diplomatic Training and Foreign Affairs Oral History Project, February 24, 2003, http://www.loc.gov/item/mfdipbib001521; and Bosworth family member, email to author, May 20, 2020.

7. Mitchell Reiss, "Steve Bosworth: An Appreciation," *38 North*, January 8, 2016, https://www.38north.org/2016/01/mreiss010816/.

8. Reiss, "Steve Bosworth: An Appreciation."

9. Interview with Bosworth family member, February 24, 2017.

10. Jay Solomon and Siobhan Gorman, "U.S. Believes North Korea May Be Preparing Long-Range Missile Test," *Wall Street Journal*, February 3, 2009, https://www.wsj.com/articles/SB123369457060044717; and Jon Herskovitz, "North Korea Issues New Year Denuclearization Pledge," Reuters, January 1, 2009, https://www.reuters.com/article/idUSTRE5000E6/.

11. U.S. Department of State, Office of the Historian, "Ambassador Stephen W. Bosworth, Special Representative for North Korea Policy," Special Envoys and Representatives Oral History Project, interviewed by Tiffany H. Cabrera, February 23, 2012, 13.

12. Lee Sigal, "Notes on Track II Meetings in Pyongyang," trip report, February 3–5, 2009.

13. Sigal, "Notes on Track II Meetings in Pyongyang."

14. Sigal, "Notes on Track II Meetings in Pyongyang."

15. Lauren Bohn, "Special Envoy Stephen Bosworth," *Time*, March 3, 2009, https://time.com/archive/6945873/special-envoy-stephen-bosworth/.

16. Jeremy Glick, "Obama's Jewish CIA Director: Anthony Lake," *Moment*, November 7, 2008, https://momentmag.com/obamas-jewish-cia-director-anthony-lake/; and interview with Obama campaign advisor, August 2, 2019.

17. Steven Mufson, "A 'Rogue is a Rogue' Is a State of Concern," *Washington Post*, June 20, 2000, A16; Robert S. Litwak, *Rogue States and U.S. Foreign Policy: Containment after the Cold War* (Washington, DC: Woodrow Wilson Center Press, 2000), 241; and Anthony Lake, "Confronting Backlash States," *Foreign Affairs* 73, no. 2 (Spring 1994): 46.

18. David Mendell, "Obama Would Consider Missile Strikes on Iran," *Chicago Tribune*, September 25, 2004, https://www.chicagotribune.com/news/ct-xpm-2004-09-25-0409250111-story.html; and Barack Obama, *The Audacity of Hope: Thoughts on Reclaiming the American Dream* (New York: Crown Publishers, 2006), 294.

19. Interview with Obama campaign advisor, February 2020.

20. David E. Sanger, "Kerry Says Bush Has Ignored North Korean Threat," *New York Times*, September 13, 2004, https://www.nytimes.com/2004/09/13

/politics/campaign/kerry-says-bush-has-ignored-north-korean-threat
.html; "John McCain Criticizes Clintons on North Korea," ABC News, October 11, 2006, https://abcnews.go.com/GMA/Story?id=2552913&page
=1; and Sheryl Gay Stolberg, "Parties Trade Blame in Wake of Korea Claim,"
New York Times, October 11, 2006, https://www.nytimes.com/2006/10/11
/us/politics/11politics.html.

21. Mike Allen, "Don't Do Stupid Sh—[Stuff]," *Politico*, June 1, 2014, https://
www.politico.com/story/2014/06/dont-do-stupid-shit-president-obama
-white-house-107293.

22. "MTP Transcript for Oct. 22," NBC News, October 19, 2006, https://www
.nbcnews.com/id/wbna15304689.

23. Barack Obama, *A Promised Land* (New York: Crown, 2020), 99.

24. Joel Roberts, "CBS Poll: Lack of Experience Hurts Obama," CBS
News, August 18, 2007, https://www.cbsnews.com/news/cbs-poll-lack-of
-experience-hurts-obama/; and "Poll: Clinton Firmly Positioned as Democratic Front-Runner," CNN, August 9, 2007, http://www.cnn.com/2007
/POLITICS/08/09/2008.dems.poll/index.html.

25. "Democratic Presidential Candidates Debate at the Citadel in Charleston,
South Carolina," American Presidency Project, July 23, 2007, http://www
.presidency.ucsb.edu/documents/democratic-presidential-candidates
-debate-the-citadel-charleston-south-carolina.

26. "Democratic Presidential Candidate Debate."

27. Interview with former Obama campaign advisor, February 9, 2017.

28. Anne E. Kornblut and Dan Balz, "The Clinton-Obama Debate Point That
Won't Die," NBC News, July 27, 2007, https://www.nbcnews.com/id
/wbna19989655.

29. Ben Rhodes, *The World as It Is: A Memoir of the Obama White House* (New
York: Random House, 2018), 15.

30. Rhodes, *The World as It Is*, 15.

31. Remarks of Senator Barack Obama, "The War We Need to Win," Woodrow Wilson Center for International Scholars, Washington, DC, August 1,
2007, http://www.wilsoncenter.org/sites/default/files/media/documents
/event/obamaspo807.pdf.

32. Interview with former congressional staffer, September 6, 2018; and Editorial Board, "Removing the Nuclear Threat in North Korea," *New York Times*,
November 16, 2007, https://archive.nytimes.com/theboard.blogs.nytimes
.com/2007/11/16/removing-the-nuclear-threat-in-north-korea/.

33. Interview with former congressional staffer, September 6, 2018.

34. Former Obama campaign advisor, email exchange with author, October
2019.

35. "The First Presidential Debate," *New York Times*, May 23, 2012, 16–17,
https://archive.nytimes.com/www.nytimes.com/elections/2008/president
/debates/transcripts/first-presidential-debate.html.

36. "McCain Sings 'Bombs' to Iran," Reuters, August 9, 2007, https://www .reuters.com/article/us-usa-iran-mccain-idUSN1929196820070419/.

37. Author's email exchanges with member of U.S. delegation, August 19,2019.

38. Author's email exchanges with member of U.S. delegation, August 19, 2019.

39. Dai Bingguo, *Strategic Dialogues: A Memoir of Dai Bingguo* (Beijing: Renmin Press, 2016), 148.

40. Author's email exchanges with members of U.S. delegation, 2019–2020.

41. Interview with Frank Jannuzi, February 9, 2017; author's email exchanges with members of U.S. delegation, July 20, 2019.

42. Author's email exchanges with members of U.S. delegation, July 20, 2019.

43. Author's personal experience in Track 2 meetings with North Korean government officials, 2009–2016.

44. Bob Woodward, *Obama's Wars* (New York: Simon and Schuster, 2010), 9.

45. Woodward, *Obama's Wars*, 9.

46. Interview with former Obama transition team member, February 9, 2017.

47. Interview with former Obama transition team member, August 2, 2019.

48. Interview with former State Department official, September 10, 2018.

49. Interview with former Obama transition official, July 23, 2019.

50. Julian Borger, "Obama Inauguration: Themes of the Inaugural Address," *Guardian* (London), January 20, 2009, https://www.theguardian.com/world /2009/jan/20/barack-obama-inaugural-address-speech.

51. Christopher Hill, *Outpost: A Diplomat at Work* (New York: Simon and Schuster, 2015), 291–292; and interview with former Clinton aide, February 27, 2018.

52. Interview with former State Department official, August 5, 2019; and interview with former Bush administration official, March 19, 2018.

53. Interview with former Clinton aide, June 18, 2019; and interview with former Bush administration official, March 19, 2018.

54. U.S. Department of State, "Fox News Interview: North Korea and the Six-Party Talks: Interview with Hillary Rodham Clinton," interview by James Rosen, Fox News, February 20, 2009, https://2009-2017.state.gov/secretary /20092013clinton/rm/2009a/02/119426.htm; Jeffrey Bader, *Obama and China's Rise: An Insider's Account of America's Asia Strategy* (Washington, DC: Brookings Institution Press, 2013), 29–30; and interview with former U.S. official, July 13, 2018.

55. Former U.S. official, email exchange with author, February 15, 2018.

56. Interview with former Clinton aide, June 18, 2019, and February 27, 2018; Bosworth family member, phone conversation with author, August 29, 2019; and Bosworth family member, email exchange with author, April 8, 2018.

57. Interview with former Clinton aide, June 18, 2019.

58. U.S. Department of State, Office of the Historian, "Ambassador Stephen W. Bosworth," 5–7.

59. U.S. Department of State, Office of the Historian, "Ambassador Stephen W. Bosworth"; and interview with former U.S. official, July 13, 2018.

60. Interview with former U.S. official, July 13, 2018.
61. U.S. Department of State, "U.S.-Asia Relations: Indispensable for Our Future: Hillary Rodham Clinton, Secretary of State," remarks at the Asia Society, New York, February 13, 2009; and former U.S. official, email exchange with author, January 4, 2019.
62. Michael Elleman, "Prelude to an ICBM? Putting North Korea's Unha-3 Launch into Context," *Arms Control Today*, February 2013, https://www .armscontrol.org/act/2013-02/prelude-icbm-putting-north-koreas-unha -3-launch-into-context; and "North Korea Newsletter No. 43," Yonhap News Agency, February 26, 2009, https://en.yna.co.kr/view/AEN2009 0225005300325.
63. Mark Landler, "Clinton Reshapes Diplomacy by Tossing the Script," *New York Times*, February 20, 2009, https://www.nytimes.com/2009/02/21/world /asia/21diplo.html?action=click&contentCollection=AsiaPacific&module =RelatedCoverage&region=EndOfArticle&pgt; Mark Landler, "Clinton, Heading Abroad, Takes Softer Tone on North Korea," *New York Times*, February 15, 2009, https://www.nytimes.com/2009/02/16/washington/16diplo .html; interview with former Clinton aide, June 2019; Richard Spencer, "Hillary Clinton Sends Strong Warning over Future of North Korea," *Telegraph* (London), February 20, 2009, https://www.telegraph.co.uk/news /worldnews/asia/northkorea/4731079/Hillary-Clinton-sends-strong -warning-over-future-of-North-Korea.html; and interview with American reporter, September 11, 2018.
64. "Secretary's Visit to Seoul a Huge Success," U.S. Embassy Seoul, confidential, Seoul 000290, February 26, 2009, http://wikileaks.org/cable/2009/02 /09SEOUL290.html; interview with former Clinton aide, June 2019; interview with former senior U.S. Embassy official, June 22, 2018; and interview with former senior ROK [Republic of Korea] official, November 23, 2017.
65. Former U.S. official, email exchange with author, February 15, 2018; "Chinese President Meets U.S. Secretary of State," *People's Daily Online*, February 22, 2009, https://web.archive.org/web/20180628224105/http://en .people.cn/90001/90776/90883/6598048.html; Richard Spencer, "Hillary Clinton Has Told China That the US Considers Human Rights Concerns Secondary to Economic Survival," *Telegraph* (London), February 20, 2009, https://www.telegraph.co.uk/news/worldnews/asia/china/4735087 /Hillary-Clinton-Chinese-human-rights-secondary-to-economic-survival .html; Mark Landler, "Clinton Paints China Policy with a Green Hue," *New York Times*, February 21, 2009, https://www.nytimes.com/2009/02/22 /world/asia/22diplo.html; and interview with former Clinton aide, August 5, 2019.
66. Interview with former U.S. official, July 13, 2018; and Mark Landler, "Clinton Warns N. Korea on Missiles," *New York Times*, February 17, 2009, https://www.nytimes.com/2009/02/17/washington/17diplo.html.

67. Don Oberdorfer and Robert Carlin, *The Two Koreas: A Contemporary History* (New York: Basic Books, 2014), chap. 19, Kindle; "North Korea Announces Rocket Launch Under Preparation," Radio Free Europe/Radio Liberty, February 24, 2009, https://www.rferl.org/a/North_Korea_Announces _Rocket_launch_Under_preparation/1498476.html; and "Preparations for Launch of Experimental Communications Satellite in Full Gear," Korean Central News Agency, February 24, 2009, https://kcnawatch.org/newstream /1451886778-794620942/preparations-for-launch-of-experimental -communications-satellite-in-full-gear/.

68. Interview with former U.S. official, February 26, 2018, and May 13, 2019.

69. U.S. Department of State, "Stephen Bosworth, Special Representative for North Korea Policy, Arrival at Incheon Airport, Seoul," March 7, 2009, https://2009-2017.state.gov/p/eap/ris/rm/2009/03/12021.htm; and "Report: US Eyes Talks with N. Korea," CNN.com, March 7, 2009, https:// edition.cnn.com/2009/WORLD/asiapcf/03/07/us.nkorea/index.html.

70. "National Aerospace Technology Administration," Wikipedia, last modified February 8, 2025, 01:26 (UTC), https://en.wikipedia.org/wiki/National _Aerospace_Technology_Administration.

71. Bader, *Obama and China's Rise*, 32–33.

72. Bader, *Obama and China's Rise*, 31; interview with former senior State Department official, March 6, 2018; and interview with former White House official, July 13, 2018.

73. Bader, *Obama and China's Rise*, 31.

74. Interview with former White House official, May 25, 2017.

75. Robert M. Gates, *Duty: Memoirs of a Secretary at War* (New York: Alfred A. Knopf, 2014), 339; "US Destroyers Set Sail ahead of DPRK launch," *China Daily*, March 30, 2009, www.chinadaily.com.cn/world/2009-03/30/content _7631686.htm; "DASD Sedney's March 1–3 Security Policy Meetings in Seoul," U.S. Embassy Seoul, SECRET, Seoul 000445, March 20, 2009, http://wikileaks.org/cable/2009/03/09SEOUL445.html; and "21st Security Policy Initiative Meeting," U.S. Embassy Seoul, confidential, Seoul 000446, March 20, 2009, http://wikileaks.org/cable/2009/03/09SEOUL446.html.

76. Oberdorfer and Carlin, *The Two Koreas*, chap. 19.

77. Ronan Farrow, *War on Peace: The End of Diplomacy and the Decline of American Influence* (New York: W. W. Norton, 2018), 288–289; interview with Bosworth family member, June 11, 2017; and interview with former senior State Department official, March 6, 2018.

Chapter Four. "Rules must be binding. Violations must be punished. Words must mean something."

1. David Axelrod, *Believer: My Forty Years in Politics* (New York: Penguin Books, 2015), 412.

2. Ben Rhodes, *The World as It Is: A Memoir of the Obama White House* (New York: Random House, 2018), 42.

3. Rhodes, *The World as It Is*, 42.

4. Rhodes, *The World as It Is*, 42.

5. The White House, Office of the Press Secretary, "Remarks by President Barack Obama in Prague as Delivered," April 5, 2009.

6. Interview with former U.S. official, March 19, 2018.

7. James Pearson and Ju-min Park, "Behind North Korea's Nuclear Weapons Programme: A Geriatric Trio," Reuters, January 8, 2016, https://www.reuters .com/article/us-northkorea-nuclear-trio-idUSKBN0UL0ZC20160107/; "Tracing the Origin of North Korea's Nuclear Weapons Program," *Japan Times*, January 8, 2016, https://www.japantimes.co.jp/news/2016/01/08/asia -pacific/science-health-asia-pacific/aging-physicist-general-late-pakistan -linked-broker-called-prime-pyongyang-nuke-players/; and US-Korea Institute, Johns Hopkins School of Advanced International Studies, private intern research note, July 2018.

8. "Gen. O Kuk Ryol," *North Korea Leadership Watch*, https://www.nkleader shipwatch.org/leadership-biographies/gen-o-kuk-ryol/; and "O Kuk Ryol Notes/Clippings," US-Korea Institute, Johns Hopkins School of Advanced International Studies, intern research note, 2018.

9. "The Godfather of North Korea's Nuclear Development is Kim University Professor Suh Sang Guk" [in Korean], *Daily NK*, October 13, 2006, https://www.dailynk.com/%EB%B6%81%ED%95%9C-%ED%95%B5 %EA%B0%9C%EB%B0%9C%EC%9D%98-%EB%8C%80%EB% B6%80%EB%8A%94-%EA%B9%80%E5%A4%A7-%EC%84%9C% EC%83%81%EA%B5%AD/; and telephone interview with Michael Madden, November 10, 2019.

10. Kim Joo-won, "Nuclear Weapons Development and Jon Pyong Ho," Radio Free Asia [in Korean], January 31, 2017, https://www.rfa.org/korean/weekly _program/ae40c528c77cac00c758-c228aca8c9c4-c9c4c2e4/hiddentruth -01312017095418.html; "Jon Pyong Ho (Cho'n Pyo'ng-ho) (1926–2014)," *North Korea Leadership Watch*, https://nkleadershipwatch.wordpress.com /leadership-biographies/jon-pyong-ho/; "Chief Architect of North Korea's Nuclear Programme Dies," *Guardian* (London), July 11, 2014, https://web .archive.org/web/20140726050259/https://www.theguardian.com/world /2014/jul/09/chief-architect-north-korea-nuclear-programme-dies; and Michael Madden, email exchange with author on KCTV film on prominent deceased senior officials, January 2, 2019.

11. Joseph Bermudez, "Overview of North Korea's NBC Infrastructure," North Korea Instability Project, US-Korea Institute, Johns Hopkins School of Advanced International Studies, June 2017, 23.

12. *North Korea: Status Report on Nuclear Program, Humanitarian Issues, and Economic Reforms: A Staff Trip Report to the Committee on Foreign Relations, United*

States Senate, 108th Cong., 2nd sess., February 2004 (Washington, DC: U.S. Government Printing Office, 2004); and Glenn Kessler, "N. Korean Evidence Called Uncertain," *Washington Post*, January 22, 2004, A1.

13. "Jon Pyong Ho (Cho'n Pyo'ng-ho) (1926–2014)" "N.K. Missile's 'Failure' Thrown into Question," *Hankyoreh*, July 7, 2006, https://english.hani.co.kr /arti/english_edition/e_international/139372; James Pearson, "Jon Pyong Ho: Nuclear Expert Who Was Individually Named by United Nations in Sanctions against North Koreans," *Independent* (London), July 10, 2014, https://www.independent.co.uk/news/obituaries/jon-pyong-ho-nuclear -expert-who-was-individually-named-by-the-united-nations-in-sanctions -against-the-north-koreans-9598925.html; and Associated Press, "Dud or Deception? Experts Examine N. Korea claims," CNN, October 10, 2006, https://web.archive.org/web/20061028102616/http://www.cnn.com/2006 /WORLD/asiapcf/10/10/korea.building.bomb.ap/index.html.

14. S. S. Hecker, R. L. Carlin, and E. A. Serbin, "A Technical and Political history of North Korea's Nuclear Program over the Past 26 Years" (Center for International Security and Cooperation, Stanford University, May 24, 2018), 44.

15. U.S. Embassy Seoul, "MND: DPRK Military Rhetoric and National Defense Commission Changes Are About Succession," confidential, Seoul 000672, April 27, 2009, https://www.theguardian.com/world/us-embassy -cables-documents/204174; Don Oberdorfer and Robert Carlin, *The Two Koreas: A Contemporary History* (New York: Basic Books, 2014), chap. 19, Kindle; and "Chronological List around KJI Health, Transition Planning and Hereditary Succession, 2001–2009," *North Korea Leadership Watch*, private research note by author, March 2019.

16. North Korea expert, email exchange with author, February 2020.

17. Evan Osnos, "Why a Nuclear Test? Ask the Sushi Chef," *New Yorker*, May 26, 2009, http://www.newyorker.com/news/evan-osnos/why-a-nuclear-test-ask -the-sushi-chef.

18. "Chronological List around KJI Health"; "In North Korea, Ailing Kim Begins Shifting Power to Military," Fox News, May 1, 2009, https://www .foxnews.com/politics/in-north-korea-ailing-kim-begins-shifting-power -to-military; and interview with former ROK intelligence official, March 10, 2021.

19. "Chronological List around KJI Health."

20. "Chronological List around KJI Health."

21. "Chronological List around KJI Health," citing a DPRK state media essay about Kim Jong Il's visit to the Pyongyang Grand Theater in early April 2009.

22. "Chronological List around KJI Health."

23. Hecker, Carlin, and Serbin, "A Technical and Political History," 24, 29–30.

24. Rebecca Frankel, "The Five Most Infamous Rahm Emanuel Moments," *Foreign Policy*, November 6, 2008, https://foreignpolicy.com/2008/11/06/the -five-most-infamous-rahm-emanuel-moments/.

25. Interviews with former U.S. official, September 13, 2019, and March 15, 2017.

26. Robin Wright, "Stuart Levey's War," *New York Times Magazine*, October 31, 2008, https://www.nytimes.com/2008/11/02/magazine/02IRAN-t.html.

27. Interview with former U.S. official, September 13, 2019; and Juan Zarate, *Treasury's War: The Unleashing of a New Era of Financial Warfare* (New York: Public Affairs, 2015), 319–323.

28. Interviews with former U.S. official, July 27, 2017, and May 25, 2017.

29. Interview with former U.S. official, September 13, 2019.

30. George P. Shultz, "Moral Principles and Strategic Interests: The Worldwide Movement to Democracy," Landon Lecture Series on Public Issues, Kansas State University, April 14, 1986, https://www.k-state.edu/landon/speakers/george-shultz/transcript.html.

31. "U.N. Condemns North Korean Rocket Launch," CNN, April 13, 2009, http://www.cnn.com/2009/WORLD/asiapcf/04/13/north.korea.un/index.html.

32. Jake Sullivan and Secretary of State Hillary Clinton, email exchange, April 11, 2009, Department of State, unclassified, Case No. F-2014-20439, Doc No. C05760804, June 30, 2015.

33. "Obama: N. Korean Acts Pose 'Great Threat' to World Peace, Security," *Los Angeles Times*, May 25, 2009, https://www.latimes.com/archives/blogs/top-of-the-ticket/story/2009-05-25/opinion-obama-n-korean-acts-pose-great-threat-to-world-peace-security.

34. "Barack Obama on Solving Problems and Building Culture," *INBOUND*, January 31, 2023, https://www.inbound.com/blog/barack-obama-inbound.

35. Interview with former U.S. official, May 13, 2019.

36. "WikiLeaks Row: China Wants Korean Reunification, Officials Confirm," *Guardian* (London), November 29, 2010, https://www.theguardian.com/world/2010/nov/30/china-wants-korean-reunification.

37. "US Embassy Cables: China Reiterates 'Red Lines,'" *Guardian* (London), November 29, 2010, https://www.guardian.com/world/us-embassy-cables-documents/204917.

38. Josh Rogin, "The End of the Concept of 'Strategic Reassurance,'" *Foreign Policy*, November 6, 2009; and Jeffrey Bader, *Obama and China's Rise: An Insider's Account of America's Asia Strategy* (Washington, DC: Brookings Institution Press, 2013), 37–38.

39. Foster Klug, "US Looking at Its Own Sanctions on North Korea," Associated Press, June 5, 2009, https://www.sandiegouniontribune.com/sdut-us-us-nkorea-060509-2009jun05-story.html.

40. Susan Rice, *Tough Love: My Story of the Things Worth Fighting For* (New York: Simon and Schuster, 2019), 259.

41. Neil MacFarquhar, "U.N. Security Council Pushes North Korea by Passing Sanctions," *New York Times*, June 12, 2009; The White House, Office of the Press Secretary, "Briefing by Press Secretary Robert Gibbs and UN

Ambassador Susan Rice, June 12, 2009," 3; and Editorial Board, "Will Sanctions Ever Work on North Korea?," *New York Times*, June 12, 2009.

42. Peter Grier, "Whither the Kang Nam, North Korea's Suspect Cargo Ship," *Christian Science Monitor*, June 22, 2009, https://www.csmonitor.com /USA/Foreign-Policy/2009/0622/p02s04-usfp.html; and Wikipedia, "Kang Nam 1," last modified February 19, 2025, 06:03 (UTC), https://en.wikipedia .org/wiki/Kang_Nam_1.

43. Sanjib Kumar Roy, "India to Inspect North Korean Ship in Bigger Port," Reuters, August 20, 2009, https://www.reuters.com/article/idUSTRE57J1QJ /; and "No Nuke Material on Detained North Korean Ship," *Rediff.com*, August 14, 2009, https://www.rediff.com/news/report/no-nuke-material-on -detained-north-korean-ship/20090814.htm.

44. Interview with former U.S. official, August 4, 2017; and Mark Landler, "Envoy to Coordinate North Korea Sanctions," *New York Times*, June 27, 2009, 7.

45. Interview with former U.S. official, September 13, 2017; and interview with U.S. official, August 4, 2017.

46. Interview with former U.S. official, August 4, 2017, and interview with former U.S. official, July 19, 2017.

47. Interview with former U.S. official, July 19, 2017.

48. Ron Kampeas, "Stuart Levey: The Man Trying to Make Anti-Iran Sanctions Work," Jewish Telegraphic Agency, June 29, 2010, https://www.jta.org/2010 /06/29/united-states/stuart-levey-the-man-trying-to-make-anti-iran -sanctions-work; and Jonathan Schanzer, "Foreign Policy: Let the Treasury Make Sanctions," NPR, May 17, 2010, https://www.npr.org/2010/05/17 /126884228/foreign-policy-let-the-treasury-make-sanctions.

49. Interview with former U.S. official, October 17, 2017.

50. Interview with former U.S. official, July 11, 2017.

51. Interview with former U.S. official, July 11, 2017.

52. Interview with former U.S. official, September 19, 2017.

53. Interview with former U.S. official, July 27, 2017.

54. Interview with former UN official, September 13, 2017.

55. Interview with former U.S. official, July 11, 2017, and interview with former U.S. official, September 19, 2017.

56. Interview with former U.S. official, September 19, 2017.

57. Interview with former U.S. official, October 19, 2017.

58. Bader, *Obama and China's Rise*, 39.

59. Interview with former U.S. official, July 11, 2017.

60. NHK, "North Korea Pursues Mysterious 'Nuclear Procurer'" [in Japanese], *Diamond Online*, October 30, 2009, https://diamond.jp/articles/-/4399.

61. John Park and Jim Walsh, "Stopping North Korea Inc.: Sanctions Effectiveness and Unintended Consequences" MIT Security Program, Cambridge, MA, August 2016.

62. Katsuhisa Furukawa and Naoko Noro, "Nexus between Illicit Networks and WMD Proliferation: The Case Studies of North Korea," Council of Asian

Transnational Threats, October 2010; and *Drugs, Counterfeiting, and Weapons Proliferation: The North Korean Connection: Hearing before the Financial Management, the Budget, and International Security Subcommittee of the Committee on Governmental Affairs, United States Senate*, 108th Cong, 1st sess., Senate hearing 108-157, May 20, 2003 (Washington, DC: U.S. Government Printing Office, 2003), 29, https://www.govinfo.gov/content/pkg/CHRG-108shrg88250/pdf/CHRG-108shrg88250.pdf.

63. "North Korea's Search for Western Technology: How Well Is Pyongyang Doing?," Central Intelligence Agency, secret, February 1988, declassified in part—sanitized copy approved for release, November 14, 2012, iii.

64. "North Korea's Search for Western Technology," iii; and Sebastien Roblin, "This Is How North Korea Smuggled In 87 U.S. Scout Helicopters," *National Interest*, October 8, 2017, https://nationalinterest.org/blog/the-buzz/how-north-korea-smuggled-87-us-scout-helicopters-22638.

65. "The Gray Market in Nuclear Materials: A Growing Proliferation Danger, An Intelligence Assessment," Central Intelligence Agency, secret, July 1984, sanitized copy approved for release, May 18, 2011; and interview with former UN official, May 21, 2020.

66. Interview with former U.S. official, March 2018; and interview with John Park, October 17, 2017.

67. Former U.S. official, email exchange with author, February 8, 2018; interview with Vienna-based reporter, August 29, 2018; interview with Fred McGoldrick, March 5, 2018; "DPRK: Eurochemic and Calder Hall Clones," *Nuclear Monitor* 411 (May 6, 1994), https://www.wiseinternational.org/nuclear-monitor/411/dprk-eurochemic-and-calder-hall-clones; and David Lowry, "What Theresa May Forgot: North Korea used British Technology to Build Its Nuclear Bombs," *Ecologist*, July 26, 2016, https://theecologist.org/2016/jul/26/what-theresa-may-forgot-north-korea-used-british-technology-build-its-nuclear-bombs.

68. Bill Gertz, *Treachery: How America's Friends and Foes Are Secretly Arming Our Enemies* (New York: Crown Forum, 2004).

69. Interview with Fred McGoldrick, March 5, 2018.

70. "The Science of Spying: How the CIA Secretly Recruits Academics," *Guardian* (London), October 10, 2017, https://www.theguardian.com/news/2017/oct/10/the-science-of-spying-how-the-cia-secretly-recruits-academics.

71. Interviews with former UN official, September 6, 2017, and May 21, 2020.

72. Jay Solomon, "North Korean Pair Viewed as Key to Secret Arms Trade," *Wall Street Journal*, August 31, 2010, https://www.wsj.com/articles/SB10001424052748704741904575409940288714852.

73. "North Korea's Search for Western Technology," iv., 9, 11; and U.S. Department of the Treasury, "Swiss Company, Individual Designated by

Treasury for Supporting North Korean WMD Proliferation," press release, March 30, 2006, https://home.treasury.gov/news/press-releases/js4144.

74. David Albright and Paul Brannan, "Taking Stock: North Korea's Uranium Enrichment Program," Institute for Science and International Security, October 8, 2010, 11–15, citing German customs investigation of Hans Werner Truppel, July 18, 2003; and Joby Warrick, "N. Korea Shops Stealthily for Nuclear Arms Gear," *Washington Post*, August 15, 2003.

75. Jay Solomon, "North Korean Pair Viewed as Key to Secret Arms Trade," *Wall Street Journal*, August 31, 2010, https://www.wsj.com/articles/SB1000142405274870474190457409940288714852.

76. Robin Wright and Joby Warrick, "Purchases Linked N. Korea to Syria," *Washington Post*, May 11, 2008, https://www.washingtonpost.com/wp-dyn/content/article/2008/05/10/AR2008051002810.html; and interview with former UN official, May 21, 2020.

77. Interview with former U.S. official, September 13, 2019.

78. Park and Walsh, "Stopping North Korea Inc.," 20–21.

79. Park and Walsh, "Stopping North Korea Inc.," 22–27; interview with academic expert, October 17, 2017.

80. Park and Walsh, "Stopping North Korea Inc.," 22–27; interview with academic expert.

81. Park and Walsh, "Stopping North Korea Inc.," 22–27; interview with academic expert.

82. Interview with former U.S. official, September 19, 2017.

83. David Thompson, "Risky Business: A System-Level Analysis of the North Korean Proliferation Financing System," CA4ADS, June 12, 2017, https://c4ads.org/reports/risky-business/.

84. "In China's Shadow: Exposing North Korea's Overseas Networks," Asan Institute and C4ADS, August 2016, 24–42; Chun Han Wong and Jay Solomon, "U.S., China Moves Against Firm Suspected of Aiding North Korean Nuclear Program," *Wall Street Journal*, September 10, 2016, https://www.wsj.com/articles/i-s-china-move-against-firm-suspected-of-aiding-north-korean-nuclear program-1474300834; and Jane Perlez and Chris Buckley, "China Announces Inquiry into Company Trading with North Korea," *New York Times*, September 20, 2016, https://www.nytimes.com/2016/09/21/world/asia/north-korea-china-inquiry-hongxiang.html.

85. "Stopping North Korea, Inc.: Sanctions Effectiveness and Unintended Consequences," Brookings Institution Center for East Asia Policy Studies, panel discussion, November 7, 2016, https://www.brookings.edu/wp-content/uploads/2017/05/20161107_north_korea_sanctions_corrected_transcript.pdf.

86. Gregory So Kam-leung, "United Nations Sanctions Regulations (e37)," Hong Kong Commerce and Economic Development Bureau, Announcement no. 555, February 12, 2013, https://www.msoa.hk/docs/circulars/20130226/cgn20131705555.pdf.

Chapter Five. "Please, please, please, we're sorry, we're foreigners."

1. Laura Ling and Lisa Ling, *Somewhere Inside: One Sister's Captivity in North Korea and the Other's Fight to Bring her Home* (New York: Harper Collins Publishers, 2010), 12.

2. Wikipedia, "Tumen, Jilin," last modified February 27, 2025, 04:21 (UTC), https://en.wikipedia.org/wiki/Tumen,_Jilin.

3. Ling and Ling, *Somewhere Inside*, 12; and "Ling Sisters Recount Laura's Capture in North Korea," *NPR Fresh Air*, May 19, 2010, https://www.npr.org/transcripts/126613763, p. 3.

4. Hamilton Nolan, "The Work of Laura Ling and Euna Lee," *Gawker*, June 10, 2009, https://www.gawkerarchives.com/5285869/the-work-of-laura-ling-and-euna-lee; Jon Matsumoto, "Taking News Personally," *Los Angeles Times*, November 13, 1997, https://www.latimes.com/archives/la-xpm-1997-nov-13-ca-53130-story.html; John L. Mitchell, "Mitchell Koss: Jailhouse Views," *Los Angeles Times*, June 20, 1993, https://www.latimes.com/archives/la-xpm-1993-06-20-tv-5009-story.html; and Ryan Tate, "It's Time for Current TV to Talk About What Happened to Their Captured Reporters," *Gawker*, August 5, 2009, https://web.archive.org/web/20090827060304/http://gawker.com/5330750/its-time-for-current-tv-to-talk-about-what-happened-to-their-captured-reporters.

5. Ling and Ling, *Somewhere Inside*, 14.

6. Euna Lee and Lisa Dickey, *The World Is Bigger Now: An American Journalist's Release from Captivity in North Korea* (New York: Broadway Books, 2010), 4–5.

7. "Ling Sisters Recount Laura's Capture in North Korea," 4; Lee and Dickey, *The World Is Bigger Now*, 4–7; and Ling and Ling, *Somewhere Inside*, 15–16.

8. Ling and Ling, *Somewhere Inside*, 16; and Dorothy O'Donnell, "Telling Stories Behind the Headlines," *Academy Art U News*, December 2015, https://web.archive.org/web/20161104041955/http://academyartunews.com/newspaper/2015/12/90.html.

9. U.S. Embassy Seoul, "DPRK Plotted Capture of U.S. Journalists" [in Korean], confidential, Seoul 001387, August 2009, Wikileaks Korea, http://www.wikileaks-kr.org/news/articleView.html?idxno=12665, September 1, 2017.

10. "Ling Sisters Recount Laura's Capture," 11–12; and Lee and Dickey, *The World Is Bigger Now*, 205–207.

11. "Swedish Ambassador Meets Detained Journalists in Name of US," France 24, May 16, 2009, https://www.france24.com/en/20090516-swedish-ambassador-meets-detained-journalists-name-us-north-korea.

12. "Bill Clinton—Activities First Half of 2009," US-Korea Institute, Johns Hopkins School of Advanced International Studies, private research note by the author, March 2019.

13. "The Life of an Ex-president after Leaving Office," *PBS NewsHour,* January 24, 2017, https://www.pbs.org/newshour/show/life-ex-president-leaving -office; Jennifer Epstein, "Bill Clinton Made $75 Million for Speeches," *Politico,* July 12, 2011, https://www.politico.com/story/2011/07/bill-clinton -made-75m-for-speeches-058770; and Wikipedia, "Post-presidency of Bill Clinton," last modified February 19, 2025, 18:50 (UTC), http://en.wikipedia .org/wiki/Post-presidency_of_Bill_Clinton.

14. Jeffrey Bader, *Obama and China's Rise: An Insider's Account of America's Asia Strategy* (Washington, DC: Brookings Institution Press, 2013), 37.

15. Bader, *Obama and China's Rise,* 37.

16. Ling and Ling, *Somewhere Inside,* 188–189, 206.

17. Ling and Ling, *Somewhere Inside,* 53.

18. Interview with former Bush administration official, 2006.

19. Interviews with former White House aide, May 13, 2019, and January 9, 2019.

20. Mark Landler and Mark Mazzetti, "In North Korea, Clinton Helped Unveil a Mystery," *New York Times,* August 18, 2009, https://www.nytimes.com /2009/08/19/world/asia/19korea.html; and interview with former official, December 27, 2019.

21. Interview with former State Department official, July 10, 2017.

22. Lee Se-won, "Who Is 'Mr. X,' the Key Man of DPRK-Japan Negotiations?" [in Korean], Yonhap News Agency, June 1, 2014, https://www.yna .co.kr/view/AKR20140601072100073; and Ken E. Gause, *North Korean House of Cards: Leadership Dynamics Under Kim Jong-un* (Washington, DC: Committee for Human Rights in North Korea, 2015), 224, https://www .hrnk.org/wp-content/uploads/2024/07/Gause_NKHOC_FINAL_WEB .pdf.

23. Interviews with former official, November 22, 2017, and February 20, 2018.

24. Interviews with former official, December 20, 2018, and December 27, 2019.

25. Interview with former official, December 27, 2019.

26. Interview with former official, December 27, 2019.

27. Interview with former official, December 27, 2019.

28. Interview with former State Department official, January 18, 2019.

29. Bader, *Obama and China's Rise,* 36–37; and interview with former U.S. official, July 13, 2018.

30. Bader, *Obama and China's Rise,* 36; and interview with former U.S. official, July 13, 2018.

31. Ling and Ling, *Somewhere Inside,* 261.

32. Interview with former U.S. official, July 13, 2018.

33. Bader, *Obama and China's Rise,* 36; interviews with former U.S. official, July 13, 2018, and May 13, 2019; and interview with former State Department official, June 18, 2019.

34. Interview with former official, December 27, 2019.

35. Interview with former official, December 27, 2019.

36. Interview with former U.S. official, July 13, 2018.

37. Bader, *Obama and China's Rise*, 36; interview with former U.S. official, July 13, 2018; interview with former State Department official, January 18, 2019; interview with former U.S. official, May 13, 2019; and interview with Bosworth family member, December 17, 2019.

38. Interview with Bosworth family member, June 1, 2017.

39. CBS, "Bill Clinton Wants Trump to Succeed with North Korea," *The Late Show with Stephen Colbert*, video, June 6, 2018, https://www.youtube.com/watch?v=odxGjyeNQRw.

40. CBS, "Hillary Clinton Tells the Story Behind Bill Clinton's Mission to North Korea," *Late Night with Seth Meyers*, video, December 11, 2015, https://www.youtube.com/watch?v=YPndj6ulN3c; "Clinton Used Plane Owned by Millionaire Hollywood Producer for North Korea Visit," Fox News, August 5, 2009, https://www.fox.news.com/politics/clinton-used-plane-owned-by-millionaire-hollywood-producer-for-north-korea-visit; "N. Korea Says Bill Clinton Visiting Pyongyang," Yonhap News Agency, August 4, 2009; and "Former President Bill Clinton Arrives in Pyongyang for Surprise Visit," AP Archives, video, August 4, 2009, https://www.youtube.com/watch?v=DetGdqMjOEg.

41. Bill Clinton, *Citizen: My Life after the White House* (New York: Knopf Doubleday Publishing Group, 2024), chap. 3, Kindle.

42. Lee and Dickey, *The World Is Bigger Now*, 62–65; and, Clinton, *Citizen*, chap. 3.

43. "Moon To Stay in Paekhwawon Guest House Known for Hosting VIPs," Yonhap News Agency, September 18, 2018, https://en.yna.co.kr/view/AEN20180918004200315; "Draft Report on Meeting with Kim Yong Nam, President," Presidium of the Supreme People's Assembly, August 4, 2009; Wikileaks, the Podesta Emails, "CLOSE HOLD: Draft Report on Kim Yong Nam Meeting," August 6, 2009, https://wikileaks.org/podesta-emails/emailid/56939; "The John Podesta Emails Released by Wikileaks," CBS News, November 3, 2016, https://www.cbsnews.com/news/the-john-podesta-emails-released-by-wikileaks; Elizabeth Shim, "Leaked Memo Shows North Korea's Kim Jong Il Sought Friendlier U.S. Relations," UPI, October 31, 2016, https://www.upi.com/Top_News/World-News/2016/10/31/Leaked-memo-shows-North-Koreas-Kim-Jong-Il-sought-friendlier-US-relations/9371477964869/; Jesse Johnson, "Hacked Memo Reveals Details of Bill Clinton's 2009 Meeting with North Korea's Kim Jong Il," *Japan Times*, October 30, 2016, https://www.japantimes.co.jp/news/2016/10/30/world/politics-diplomacy-world/hacked-memo-reveals-details-bill-clintons-2009-meeting-north-koreas-kim-jong-il/; "Bill Clinton Suggested N. Korea Pursue Direct Talks with US in Tandem with Six Party Talks," *Korea Times*, October 31, 2016, https://www.koreatimes.co.kr/www/news/nation/2016/10/485_217134.html; "Memorandum of Conversation, President Clinton and Kim Jong Il," Conference Room, Paekwawon Guest

House, Pyongyang, August 4, 2009; and interview with Clinton delegation member, January 22, 2020.

44. Clinton, *Citizen*, chap. 3.

45. Christina Pazzanese, "Clinton Reflects on Foreign Policy Triumphs and Challenges," *Harvard Gazette*, April 8, 2021, https://news.harvard.edu /gazette/story/2021/04/clinton-reflects-on-foreign-policy-triumphs-and -challenges/.

46. Clinton, *Citizen*, chap. 3.

47. "Memorandum of Conversation, President Clinton and Kim Jong Il," 3; "Hyundai Chairwoman on DPRK Trip, Kim Jong Il," American Embassy Seoul, confidential, August 2009; and "Hyundai Chairwoman on DPRK Trip, Kim Jong Il," U.S. Embassy Seoul, confidential, Seoul 1386, August 28, 2009, https://wikileaks.org/plusd/cables/09SEOUL1386_a.html.

48. "Memorandum of Conversation, President Clinton and Kim Jong Il."

49. "Memorandum of Conversation, President Clinton and Kim Jong Il," 4.

50. Clinton, *Citizen*, chap. 3.

51. "Memorandum of Conversation, President Clinton and Kim Jong Il," 7.

52. Interview with Clinton delegation member, January 22, 2020.

53. Interview with Clinton delegation member, January 22, 2020.

54. Interview with Clinton delegation member, January 22, 2020.

55. Interview with Clinton delegation member, January 22, 2020.

56. Interview with Clinton delegation member, January 22, 2020; and interview with former U.S. official, July 13, 2018.

57. Interview with Clinton delegation member, January 22, 2020.

58. "Bill Clinton's Doctor 'Took a Close Look at Kim Jong-il,'" *Chosun Daily*, September 17, 2009, http://english.chosun.com/site/data/html_dir/2009/09 /17/2009091700392.html?related_all; Kenneth B. DeKleva, "Kim Jong Il's 'Flowers for Kim Il Sung,'" *38 North*, August 19, 2010, https://www.38north .org/2010/08/kim-jong-il's-"flowers-for-kim-il-sung"/; and interview with Clinton delegation member, January 22, 2020.

59. Mark Landler and Peter Baker, "Bill Clinton and Journalists in Emotional Return to U.S.," *New York Times*, August 5, 2009, https://www.nytimes.com /2009/08/06/world/asia/06korea.html; and Ling and Ling, *Somewhere Inside*, 301.

60. Landler and Baker, "Emotional Return to U.S."; Ling and Ling, *Somewhere Inside*, 300–305; The White House, Office of the Press Secretary, "Press Background Briefing on North Korea by Senior Administration Official," August 4, 2009; "Homeward Bound: Bill Clinton Leaves North Korea with Pardoned U.S. Journalists," ABC News, August 5, 2009, http://abcnews.go .com/Politics/International/story?id=8245688; and "US Journalists Released from North Korea: Bill Clinton Did Not Issue Apology," *Telegraph* (London), August 5, 2009, https://www.telegraph.co.uk/news/worldnews /asia/northkorea/5975450/US-journalists-released-from-North-Korea -Bill-Clinton-did-not-issue-apology.html.

61. Interview with Clinton delegation member, January 22, 2020.

62. Interview with Clinton delegation member, January 22, 2020.

63. Interview with U.S. official, July 13, 2018.

64. Interview with former State Department official, January 18, 2019; and "President Bill Clinton Shares Insights on Foreign Policy and Diplomacy," *Belfer Center Spring 2021 Newsletter,* April 13, 2021, https://www.belfercenter .org/publication/president-bill-clinton-shares-insights-foreign-policy-and -diplomacy.

65. Gordon G. Chang, "Mr. Clinton Goes to Pyongyang," *Wall Street Journal,* August 5, 2009, https://www.wsj.com/articles/SB100014240529702043136 04574329662762687616; John Bolton, "Clinton's Unwise Trip to North Korea," *Washington Post,* August 4, 2009; and Maureen Dowd, "Let the Big Dog Run," *New York Times,* August 4, 2009, https://www.nytimes.com/2009 /08/05/opinion/05dowd.html.

66. John Burgess, "S. Korean Leader Won Nobel Peace Prize," *Washington Post,* August 19, 2009, https://www.washingtonpost.com/archive/local/2009/08 /19/s-korean-leader-won-nobel-peace-prize/5c024b98-bac2-472d-b72e -ff56e2c2f774/; "Former S. Korean Leader Kim Dae-jung Dies," CBS News, August 18, 2009, https://www.cbsnews.com/news/former-s-korean-leader -kim-dae-jung-dies/; "Kim Dae-jung, Former South Korean President, Dies Age 85," *Guardian* (London), August 18, 2009, https://www.theguardian .com/world/2009/aug/18/kim-dae-jung-dies; Wikipedia, "Kim Dae-jung," last modified March 1, 2025, 18:23 (UTC), https://en.wikipedia.org/wiki /Kim_Dae-jung; John Gittings, "Kim Dae-jung," *Guardian* (London), August 18, 2009, https://www.theguardian.com/world/2009/aug/18/obituary -kim-dae-jung; and "Somber Reaction to Kim Dae-Jung's Death," U.S. Embassy Seoul, confidential, August 19, 2009, Wikileaks, https://wikileaks.org /plusd/cables/09SEOUL1327_a.html.

67. Shin Seung-keun, "Bill Clinton: A Lifelong Friend" [in Korean], *Hankyoreh,* August 23, 2009, https://www.hani.co.kr/arti/politics/politics_general /372641.html; Hwang Jun-ho, "The Path of Kim Dae-Jung Was History Itself" [in Korean], *Pressian,* August 18, 2009, http://www.pressian.com /pages/articles/96419; Lee Sook-yi, "Though My Body Is Old and Sickly, I Could Not Simply Watch On for the Sake of the Poor Citizens" [in Korean], *SisaIn,* August 24, 2009, https://www.sisain.co.kr/news/articleView .html?idxno=5121; Choi Kyung-hwan, "The Last 4 Calls of Former President Kim Dae-Jung before His Death" [in Korean], *OhMyNews,* December 14, 2009, https://www.ohmynews.com/NWS_Web/View/at_pg.aspx ?CNTN_CD=A0001281262; and Choe Sang-Hun, "South Korea Elects Moon Jae-in, Who Backs Talks with North, as President," *New York Times,* May 9, 2017, https://www.nytimes.com/2017/05/09/world/asia/south-korea -election-president-moon-jae-in.html.

68. "2007 ROK Possible Presidential Candidates Profiled," U.S. Embassy Seoul, confidential, Seoul 2492, July 25, 2006, https://wikileaks.org/plusd/cables

/06SEOUL2492_a.html; "GNP Candidate Lee Myung-bak Takes Aim toward December," U.S. Embassy Seoul, confidential, August 22, 2007, http://wikileaks.org/cable/2007/08/07SEOUL2539.html; "Anything But Roh Carries the Day for President-elect Lee Myung-bak," U.S. Embassy Seoul, confidential, December 20, 2007, http://wikileaks.org/cable/2007/12 /07SEOUL 3579; "Who Is President-elect Lee Myung-bak?," U.S. Embassy Seoul, confidential, Seoul 3575, December 19, 2007, http://wikileaks .org/cable/2007/12/07SEOUL 3574.html; Shin Hae-in, "GNP Candidate Puts 'Economic Community with N.K. On Agenda," *Korea Herald*, September 11, 2007; Lee Jae-myung, "Lee Myung-bak's North Korea Policy" [in Korean], *Hankyoreh*, August 27, 2007, https://www.hani.co.kr/arti /PRINT/231873.html; and Ser Myo-ja, "Sunshine Policy Gets Rained On by Lee," *Korea Joongang Daily*, September 2, 2008, https://koreajoongangdaily .joins.com/2008/09/02/politics/Sunshine-Policy-gets-rained-on-by-Lee /2894394.html.

69.	Interview with former Lee campaign advisor and ROK official, November 23, 2017; and Lee Myung-bak, *President's Time* [in Korean] (Seoul: RHK, 2015), unpublished English translation.

70.	Robert M. Gates, *Duty: Memoirs of a Secretary at War* (New York: Alfred A. Knopf, 2014), 416.

71.	Interview with former ROK presidential aide, December 21, 2017.

72.	Interview with former ROK presidential aide, December 21, 2017.

73.	Lee, *President's Time*, 118.

74.	Lee, *President's Time*, 119–120; "Lee Myung-bak Okays Obama-Kim Jong-il Summit," *AsiaNews.it*, November 11, 2008; interview with former senior ROK official, November 26, 2017; and interview with former ROK presidential aide, December 21, 2017.

75.	Interview with former ROK presidential aide, December 21, 2017; Lee, *President's Time*, 131; Michael D. Shear and Debbi Wilgoren, "Obama Discusses N. Korean Missile at G-20," *Washington Post*, April 2, 2009, http:// www.washingtonpost.com/wp-dyn/content/article/2009/04/02 /AR2009040200595_pf.html; and "N. Korea Warned Over Rocket Launch," BBC, April 2, 2009, http://news.bbc.co.uk/2/hi/asia-pacific/7978397.stm.

76.	Lee, *President's Time*, 132–136; Mary Kissel, "South Korea's Bulldozer Heads for the White House," *Wall Street Journal*, June 13, 2009, https:// www.wsj.com/articles/SB124484758194711341; and Dave Cook, "Obama and Lee Myung-bak Both Condemn North Korea," *Christian Science Monitor*, June 16, 2009, https://www.csmonitor.com/USA/Politics/2009/0616 /obama-and-lee-myung-bak-both-condemn-north-korea.

77.	Lee, *President's Time*, 140–141; and interview with ROK presidential aide, December 21, 2017.

78.	Helene Cooper and Martin Fackler, "Obama Takes Stern Tone on North Korea and Iran," *New York Times*, November 18, 2009, http://www.nytimes .com/2009/11/19/world/asia/19prexy.html; and "Barack Obama: The President's News Conference with President Lee Myung-bak of South Korea in South Korea," American Presidency Project, November 19, 2009, https://www.presidency.ucsb.edu/documents/the-presidents-news-conference-with-president-lee-myung-bak-south-korea-south-korea.

79. "Hyundai Chairwoman on DPRK Trip, Kim Jong Il," U.S. Embassy Seoul, confidential, August 2009, Wikileaks, https://wikileaks.org/plusd/cables/09SEOUL1379_a.html; "Kim Dae-Jung and North Korea: A Glint of Sunshine," *The Economist*, August 22, 2009, http://www.economist.com/node/14259036#print.

80. "Farewell Sunshine," *The Economist*, August 18, 2009, http://www.economist.com/node/14254430; Donald Kirk, "Pyongyang Plays 'Funeral Diplomacy,'" *Asia Times*, August 25, 2009; Associated Press, "Even in Death, Kim Dae-jung Unites Koreas," NBC News, August 23, 2009, https://www.nbcnews.com/id/wbna32523290; "S. Korean Head Meets North Envoys," Trend News Agency, August 23, 2009, https://en.trend.az/azerbaijan/society/1526982.html; "N. Korean Delegation Arrives to Honor Kim," CNN, August 21, 2009, https://edition.cnn.com/2009/WORLD/asiapcf/08/21/kim.nkorea/index.html; "N. Korea Envoys Mourn Kim Dae-jung," BBC News, August 8, 2009, http://news.bbc.co.uk/go/pr/fr/-/2/hi/asia-pacific/8213672.stm; and interview with former senior ROK official, November 26, 2017.

81. Interview with former senior official, November 26, 2017.

82. Interview with former senior official, November 26, 2017.

83. Interview with former senior official, November 26, 2017.

84. Interview with former senior official, November 26, 2017.

85. Interview with former senior official, November 26, 2017.

86. Interview with former ROK presidential aide, December 21, 2017.

87. Interview with former ROK presidential aide, December 21, 2017; Park Chul-cung, "[DJ"s Passing] The North's Supreme Leader Sends a Verbal Message" [in Korean], *Hankyung.com*, August 23, 2009, https://www.hankyung.com/article/2009082377711g; "Seoul Must Not Waver In the Face of N. Korean Overtures," *Chosun Ilbo*, August 24, 2009, 35; "North Envoys Meet with Lee for First Time," *JoongAng Daily*, August 24, 2009; and "Ambassador Bosworth's August 23 Meeting with ROK National Security Advisor Kim Sung-hwang," U.S. Embassy Seoul, confidential, Seoul 001364, August 26, 2009, http://wikileaks.org/cable/2009/08/09SEOUL1364.html.

88. Interview with former senior ROK official, November 26, 2017.

89. Shin Suk-ho, "MB Administration Persistent in North Korea Policy, Says It Sees 'Paradigm Shift'" [in Korean], *Dong-A Ilbo*, August 24, 2009, https://www.donga.com/news/article/all/20090824/8770560/1; and "Koreas Talk amid Funeral for Unity Leader," CBS News, August 23, 2009, https://www.cbsnews.com/news/koreas-talk-amid-funeral-for-unity-leader/.

90. Interview with former senior official, November 26, 2017.

91. Interview with former senior official, November 26, 2017.

92. Interview with former senior official, November 26, 2017; interview with former senior Ministry of Unification official, November 21, 2017; Don Oberdorfer and Robert Carlin, *The Two Koreas: A Contemporary History* (New York: Basic Books, 2014), chap. 19, Kindle; "Questions Linger Over Secret Talks on Inter-Korean Summit," *Dong-A Ilbo*, October 26, 2009, https://www.donga.com/en/List/article/all/20091222/264044/1; "Lee Confidant Admits to Secret Meeting with N. K. Official in 2009," Yonhap News Agency, June 20, 2012, https://en.yna.co.kr/view/AEN20120620001700315; "Labor Minister Held Talks on Inter-Korean Summit," *Dong-A Ilbo*, December 21, 2009, https://www.donga.com/en/article/all/20091221/264036/1; Ahn Chang-hyun, "Senior Official: North Korea Demanded Millions in Aid to Participate in Summit," *Hankyoreh*, January 9, 2013, https://english.hani.co.kr/arti/english_edition/e_northkorea/568899; and Choi Byung-muk, "Inter-Korean Summit Transcript Review Report" [in Korean], *Chosun Monthly*, February 28, 2013, http://monthly.chosun.com/client/news/viw.asp?nNewsNumb=201302100009.

93. Interview with former senior Ministry of Unification official, November 21, 2017; interview with former senior ROK official, November 26, 2017; and Lee Jung-eun, "[President Lee Myung Bak's Interview] South Korea-China Summit Has Already Begun Discussions on the Unification of the Korean Peninsula. . . . 'You Need to Relieve Your Concerns'" [in Korean], *Dong-A Ilbo*, February 15, 2013, https://www.donga.com/news/Politics/article/all/20130215/53051554/1.

94. Interview with former senior official, November 26, 2017.

95. "Joint New Year Editorial of Leading Newspapers in DPRK Released," National Committee for North Korea, https://www.ncnk.org/sites/default/files/KCNA_January_2010_New_Years_Editorial.pdf; and "North Korea's New Year's Day Joint Editorial on Peace and the Economy," *Hankyoreh*, January 4, 2010, https://english.hani.co.kr/arti/english_edition/e_northkorea/396917.html.

96. Jeffrey Bader, "Obama Goes to Asia: Understanding the President's Trip," Keynote Address, Brookings Institution, Washington, DC, November 6, 2009, 15.

97. "Chinese DCM on Bosworth Visit, DPRK Currency Crisis," U.S. Embassy Seoul, confidential, Seoul 1932, December 9, 2009, http://wikileaks.org/cable/2009/12/09SEOUL1928.html; and "Deputy Secretary Steinberg's September 29, 2009 Meeting with PRC Vice Foreign Minister Wu Dawei," secret, https://wikileaks.org/plusd/cables/09BEIJING2964_a.html.

98. AmEmbassy Seoul, "Ambassador Bosworth's August 23rd Meeting with ROK National Security Advisor Kim Sung-hwan," confidential, Seoul 001364, August 23, 2009; and Oberdorfer and Carlin, *The Two Koreas*, chap. 19.

99. "S. Korea, U.S. Show United Front on North's Nuclear Weapons," *Chosun Ilbo*, September 7, 2013; and private communication with former U.S. official, April 11, 2017.

100. Interview with academic expert on September 2009 Pyongyang meeting, February 10, 2019; and interview with former Defense Department official, June 23, 2019.

101. Josh Rogin, "The Cable: Quiet Progress Made in U.S.-North Korea Talks," *Foreign Policy*, November 3, 2009, https://foreignpolicy.com/2009/11/03 /quiet-progress-made-in-u-s-north-korea-talks; and author's private communication with Track 2 organizers, February 2019.

102. Choe Sang-Hun, "U.S. Envoy Makes Rare Visit to North Korea," *New York Times*, December 8, 2009, https://www.nytimes.com/2009/12/09/world/asia /09korea.html; Blaine Harden, "U.S. Envoy Stephen Bosworth Arrives in North Korea for Talks," *Washington Post*, December 8, 2009; John M. Glionna, "U.S. Envoy Stephen Bosworth Arrives in North Korea for High-Level Talks," *Los Angeles Times*, December 9, 2009, http://articles.latimes .com/2009/dec/09/world/la-fg-north-korea-bosworth9_send-2009dec09; and U.S. Department of State, "Senior Administration Official on Special Representative Stephen Bosworth's Upcoming Trip to North Korea," December 7, 2009, https://2009-2017.state.gov/p/eap/rls/rm/2009/12/133271 .htm.

103. Interview with former U.S. official and Bosworth delegation member, June 17, 2019.

104. Interview with former U.S. official and Bosworth delegation member, June 17, 2019.

105. Former U.S. official and member of Bosworth delegation, email communication with author, January 5, 2020.

106. Interview with former U.S. official and Bosworth delegation member, June 17, 2019.

107. Interview with former U.S. official and Bosworth delegation member, June 17, 2019.

108. Interview with former U.S. government official, January 25, 2020.

109. Interview with former U.S. government official, January 25, 2020.

110. Interview with former U.S. government official, January 25, 2020.

111. Glenn Kessler, "Obama Wrote Personal Letter to North Korea's Kim Jong Il," *Washington Post*, December 16, 2009; interview with former U.S. official and Bosworth delegation member, June 17, 2019; and interview with former U.S. official and Bosworth delegation member, January 15, 2020.

112. Interview with former U.S. official and Bosworth delegation member, June 17, 2019; and Stephen Bosworth, interview by Robert Carlin, March 7, 2012.

113. Interview with former U.S. official and Bosworth delegation member, January 15, 2020.

114. Interview with former U.S. official and Bosworth delegation member, January 15, 2020.

115. Interview with former U.S. official and Bosworth delegation member, January 15, 2020.

116. Interview with former U.S. official and Bosworth delegation member, June 17, 2019.

117. Interview with former U.S. official and Bosworth delegation member, January 15, 2020.

118. Interview with former U.S. official and Bosworth delegation member, January 15, 2020; Choe Sang-Hun, "North Korea Sees Progress in U.S. Envoy's Visit," *New York Times*, December 10, 2009, https://www.nytimes.com /2009/12/11/world/asia/11korea.html; and U.S. Department of State, "Morning Walkthrough in Beijing," https://2009-2017.state.gov/p/eap/rls /rm/2009/12/133475.htm.

119. Interview with former U.S. official and Bosworth delegation member, January 15, 2020; Choe, "North Korea Sees Progress"; U.S. Department of State, "Morning Walkthrough in Beijing"; interview with Bosworth family member, May 24, 2017; and interview with former U.S. official, March 15, 2017.

120. Interview with former U.S. official and Bosworth delegation member, June 17, 2019; and interview with former congressional staffer, July 23, 2019.

Chapter Six. "If Wi worried, we worried."

1. Michitaka Uda and Mark J. Valencia, "Yellow Sea," *Encyclopedia Britannica*, January 23, 2020, https://www.britannica.com/place/Yellow-Sea; Sankalan Baidya, "30 Yellow Sea Facts You Need for Your Project," *Facts Legend*, September 3, 2017, https://web.archive.org/web/20230129161451/https:// factslegend.org/30-yellow-sea-facts-need-project/; World Wildlife Foundation, "A Yellow Sea," https://wwf.panda.org/knowledge_hub/where _we_work/yellow_sea; and Wikipedia, "Geography of South Korea," last modified February 14, 2025, 00:00 (UTC), https://en.wikipedia.org/wiki /Geography_of_South_Korea.

2. Terence Roehrig, "The Origins of the Northern Limit Line Dispute," *NKIDP e-Dossier*, no. 6 (May 9, 2012), https://www.wilsoncenter.org /publication/the-origins-the-northern-limit-line-dispute; Jon Van Dyke, "The Maritime Boundary between North and South Korea in the Yellow (West) Sea," *38 North*, July 29, 2010, https://www.38north.org/2010/07/the -maritime-boundary-between-north-south-korea-in-the-yellow-west-sea; Central Intelligence Agency, "The West Coast Korean Islands," confidential, January 1974, approved for release 2000/04/18: CIA-RDP84–00825 R000300120001–7; Central Intelligence Agency, "Korean Fishing Areas in the Yellow Sea: Spawning Ground for Maritime Conflict," confidential, May 1975, approved for release 1999/09/26: CIA-RDP86T00608R00 0600140005–7; Wikipedia, "First Battle of Yeonpyeong," last modified February 3, 2025 09:02 (UTC), https://en.wikipedia.org/wiki/First_Battle _of_Yeonpyeong; Wikipedia, "Second Battle of Yeonpyeong," last modi-

fied February 3, 2025 09:07 (UTC), https://en.wikipedia.org/wiki/Second
_Battle_of_Yeonpyeong; and International Crisis Group, "North Korea:
The Risks of War in the Yellow Sea," *Asia Report*, no. 198, December 23,
2010.

3. International Crisis Group, "North Korea: The Risks of War," 22–31; ROK
Ministry of Defense, "Joint Investigative Report on the Sinking of the
Cheonan," Civil-Military Joint Investigation Group, ROK Policy Briefing,
September 13, 2010, 132–145, https://nautilus.org/wp-content/uploads
/2012/01/Cheonan.pdf; Park Min-hyuk, "Submarine Sinks in the Yellow
Sea . . . Around 40 of 104 Passengers Missing" [in Korean], *Dong-A Ilbo*,
March 27, 2010, http://news.donga.com/3/all/20100327/27141433/1; Shin
Seok-ho and Yoon Wan-jun, "Shallow Water Level . . . Strong Explosion . . .
'High chance of sea mine if caused by external factors'" [in Korean], *Dong-A
Ilbo*, March 29, 2010, http://news.donga.com/3/all/20100329/27189085/1;
"Naval Patrol Frigate Sinks in Waters of Yellow Sea, Baengnyeongdo Is-
land . . . 'Low possibility of North attack'" [in Korean], *Chosun Ilbo*,
March 26, 2010, https://www.chosun.com/site/data/html_dir/2010/03/26
/2010032602058.html; Jeong Woo-sang, "[Navy Patrol Ship Sinking] Pos-
sibility of Internal Collision or Mine Explosion . . . It Doesn't Seem like a
Fight" [in Korean], *Chosun Ilbo*, March 27, 2010, https://news.chosun.com
/site/data/html_dir/2010/03/27/2010032700149.html; Lee Yong-in and
Kim Ki-seong, "Reconstruction of the Sinking of the Cheonan by Time
Period" [in Korean], *Hankyoreh*, March 28, 2010, http://www.hani.co.kr/arti
/politics/defense/412825.html; Choe Sang-Hun, "North Korea Warns
South Over Buffer Zone," *New York Times*, March 28, 2010, http://www
.nytimes.com/2010/03/29/world/asia/29iht-korea.html; "South Korea Ship
'Split in Half,'" BBC News, March 28, 2010, http://news.bbc.co.uk/2/hi/asia
-pacific/8591366.stm?ad=1, and Wikipedia, "ROKS *Cheonan* Sinking," last
modified January 28, 2025, 02:03 (UTC), https://en.wikipedia.org/wiki
/ROKS_Cheonan_sinking.

4. ROK Ministry of Defense, "Joint Investigation Report."

5. Rob Crilly, "South Korea Investigates whether North Involved in Ship Sinking," *Telegraph* (London), March 26, 2010, http://www.telegraph.co.uk
/news/worldnews/asia/southkorea/7528520/South-Korea-investigates
-whether-North-involved-in-ship-sinking.html; and Lee Tae-hoon, "More
Questions Raised Than Answered over Sunken Ship," *Korea Times*, https://
www.koreatimes.co.kr/www/nation/2024/07/113_63157.html.

6. Associated Press, "S. Korea Hoists Sunken Warship; Finds Dead Bodies,"
The Hindu, April 15, 2010, https://www.thehindu.com/news/international
/S.Korea-hoists-sunken-warship-finds-dead-bodies/article16372165.ece;
and Park Si-soo and Jung Sung-ki, "Korea, US Mount Largest Joint Rescue Operations," *Korea Times*, March 29, 2010, https://www.koreatimes.co
.kr/www/nation/2024/07/113_63227.html.

7. ROK Ministry of Defense, "Joint Investigation Report."

8. "South Korean Navy Ship Sinks, North Link Played Down," Reuters, March 26, 2010, www.reuters.com/article/us-korea-ship/south-korean-navy -ship-sinks-north-link-played-down-idUSTRE62P30E20100326.

9. Donald Kirk, "South Korea's Lee Vows Answers on *Cheonan* Navy Ship Sinking," *Christian Science Monitor,* April 19, 2010, https://www.csmonitor .com/World/Asia-Pacific/2010/0419/South-Korea-s-Lee-vows-answers -on-Cheonan-Navy-ship-sinking?cmpid=mkt:ggl:dsa-np&gclid=CjoKC; and interview with former ROK presidential aide, December 21, 2017.

10. Interview with former U.S. official, June 17, 2019.

11. "Report: South Korean Navy Ship Sinks," CNN, March 27, 2010, https:// edition.cnn.com/2010/WORLD/asiapcf/03/26/south.korea.ship.sinking /index.html.

12. Interview with former senior U.S. military officer, January 22, 2018.

13. Interview with former senior U.S. military officer, January 22, 2018.

14. ROK Ministry of Defense, "Joint Investigation Report," 220, 243; John Mc-Glynn, "Politics in Command: The International Investigation into the Sinking of the *Cheonan* and the Risk of a New Korean War," *Asia-Pacific Journal* 8, no. 1 (June 14, 2010): 24, https://apjjf.org/john-mcglynn/3372/ article; and Wikipedia, "ROKS *Cheonan* Sinking."

15. Ken E. Gause, "North Korea's Provocation and Escalation Calculus: Dealing with the Kim Jong-un Regime," CNA Occasional Paper, August 2015, 14; Jean H. Lee, "*Cheonan* Attack May Be Tied to North Korean Succession," Associated Press, May 27, 2010, https://www.csmonitor.com/From -the-news-wires/2010/0527/Cheonan-attack-may-be-tied-to-North -Korean-succession; and Joseph S. Bermudez, Jr., "A New Emphasis on Operations against South Korea," *38 North,* June 11, 2010, https://www.38north .org/2010/06/a-new-emphasis-on-operations-against-south-korea/.

16. Wikipedia, "ROKS *Cheonan* Sinking"; Barbara Demick and John M. Glionna, "Doubts Surface on North Korea's Role in Ship Sinking," *Los Angeles Times,* July 23, 2010; "Most South Koreans Skeptical About *Cheonan* Findings, Survey Shows," *Chosun Daily,* September 8, 2010, http://english.chosun .com/site/data/html_dir/2010/09/08/2010090800979.html; and Yeo Junsuk, "Eight Years since *Cheonan* Sinking, S. Korea Still Mired in Controversy," *Korea Herald,* May 4, 2018, https://www.koreaherald.com/view.php ?ud=20180405000692.

17. Interview with former U.S. official, June 17, 2019; and Jeffrey Bader, *Obama and China's Rise: An Insider's Account of America's Asia Strategy* (Washington, DC: Brookings Institution Press, 2013), 86–87.

18. Lee Myung-bak, *President's Time* [in Korean] (Seoul: RHK, 2015), unpublished English translation, 181.

19. Bader, *Obama and China's Rise,* 84–85.

20. Bader, *Obama and China's Rise,* 84–85

21. Interview with former senior ROK official, February 22, 2018; and interview with former senior ROK official, June 8, 2020.

22. Former U.S. official, private remarks to author, summer 2019.

23. "John W. Lewis: An Oral History Conducted by Carla Hanawalt," Stanford Historical Society Oral History Program, Stanford University, 2015; Sam Roberts, "John W. Lewis, China Expert and Vietnam War Critic, Dies at 86," *New York Times*, September 18, 2017; and Christine Foster, "Compassionate Asia Scholar," *Stanford Magazine*, December 2017, https://stanfordmag.org/contents/compassionate-asia-scholar.

24. "John Lewis: An Oral History," 34.

25. Private communication with author by Stanford scholar, March 1, 2020.

26. Gloria Duffy, "Comments at Celebration for Professor John Lewis," Stanford University, November 2, 2017, https://www.commonwealthclub.org/node/117023.

27. Peter Davis, "Hecker Promotes Nuclear Cooperation with Moscow, Despite Ukraine Crisis," Center for International Security and Cooperation, Stanford University, May 1, 2014, https://cisac.fsi.stanford.edu/news/hecker_promotes_nuclear_cooperation_in_moscow_despite_ukraine_crisis_20140501; David Martin, "The American Scientist Who's Seen North Korea's Nuclear Secrets," *CBS Evening News*, April 12, 2018; and Engineering and Technology History Wiki, "Siegfried Hecker: An Interview conducted by Thomas J. Nizolek in 2018 in Los Alamos, New Mexico," AIME Oral History Series, https://ethw.org/Oral-History:Siegfried_S._Hecker.

28. Author's observation as a member of Hecker's delegation, 2008; and Siegfried S. Hecker, "Report of Visit to the Democratic People's Republic of North Korea (DPRK), Pyongyang and the Nuclear Center at Yongbyon, February 12–16, 2008," National Committee on North Korea, March 14, 2008, https://www.ncnk.org/resources/publications/HeckerDPRKreport.pdf.

29. Private communication with author by North Korea expert, March 9, 2020.

30. John L. Lewis, "Stanford Historical Society Oral History Program Interviews (SC0932)," Stanford Historical Society, May 2015, https://purl.stanford.edu/zn669ty7580.

31. David Albright and Paul Brannan, "What Is North Korea Building in the Area of the Destroyed Cooling Tower? It Bears Watching," *ISIS Imagery Brief*, September 30, 2010, https://isis-online.org/uploads/isis-reports/documents/New_Activity_DPRK_Cooling_Tower_30Sept2010.pdf.

32. Private communication by North Korea expert, March 11, 2020; and Nicole Finneman and Jack Pritchard, "North Korea Reveals Uranium Enrichment Facility and Light Water Reactor," *Korea Insight: A Monthly Newsletter from the Korea Economic Institute*, December 2010, https://www.scribd.com/document/78883647/North-Korea-Reveals-Uranium-Enrichment-Facility-and-Light-Water-Reactor-by-Jack-Pritchard-and-Nicole-Finneman.

33. "Meetings with Ri Gun, Director General, Bureau of North American Affairs, Ministry of Foreign Affairs," trip report, Pyongyang, 1000–1200 and 1830–2100, November 10, 2010; and communication by author with North Korea scholar, January 2019.

34. "Meetings with Ri Gun"; and communication by author with North Korea expert, January 2019.

35. "Meetings with Ri Gun"; and communication by author with North Korea expert, January 2019.

36. "Meetings with Ri Gun"; and communication by author with North Korea expert, January 2019.

37. "Meetings with Ri Gun"; and communication by author with North Korea expert, January 2019.

38. Siegfried Hecker, "A Return Trip to North Korea's Yongbyon Nuclear Complex," Center for International Security and Cooperation, Stanford University, November 20, 2010, https://graphics8.nytimes.com/packages/pdf/world/2010/North_Korea_Report.pdf; Siegfried Hecker and Robert Carlin, interview by the author, October 4, 2017; Siegfried Hecker, "What I Saw In North Korea and Why It Matters," transcript from Google Tech Talks Conference, March 28, 2011, cited by S. Pangambam, *Singju Post*, December 27, 2015, https://singjupost.com/what-i-saw-in-north-korea-and-why-it-matters-by-siegfried-hecker-transcript/; and Siegfried Hecker and Robert L. Carlin, "North Korea Nuclear Facility," C-Span, video, November 23, 2010, https://www.c-span.org/video/?296731-1/north-korea-nuclear-facility#.

39. Hecker, "What I Saw in North Korea," 13; and Hecker, "A Return Trip to North Korea," 8.

40. Hecker, "A Return Trip to North Korea," 2.

41. Hecker, "A Return Trip to North Korea," 2–3.

42. Hecker, "A Return Trip to North Korea," 2–3; Hecker and Carlin, "North Korea Nuclear Facility"; and Hecker and Carlin, interview by the author, October 4, 2017.

43. Hecker, "A Return Trip to North Korea," 4.

44. Hecker and Carlin, "North Korea Nuclear Facility"; and Peter Crail, "N. Korea Reveals Uranium-Enrichment Plant," Arms Control Association, December 5, 2010.

45. "U.S. Scientist Amazed by N. Korean Nuclear Facility," CNN, April 24, 2010, https://edition.cnn.com/2010/WORLD/asiapcf/11/23/north.korea.nuclear.facility/index.html; and Hecker, "A Return Trip to North Korea," 4–5.

46. Hecker, "A Return Trip to North Korea," 5.

47. Hecker, "A Return Trip to North Korea," 7.

48. "Dinner Meeting with Vice Minister Ri Yong Ho," trip report, Potangang Hotel, November 12, 2010.

49. "Dinner Meeting with Vice Minister Ri Yong Ho."

50. "Dinner Meeting with Vice Minister Ri Yong Ho."

51. "Dinner Meeting with Vice Minister Ri Yong Ho."

52. "Dinner Meeting with Vice Minister Ri Yong Ho."

53. "Dinner Meeting with Vice Minister Ri Yong Ho."

54. "Dinner Meeting with Vice Minister Ri Yong Ho."

55. "Dinner Meeting with Vice Minister Ri Yong Ho."

56. "Dinner Meeting with Vice Minister Ri Yong Ho."

57. Stanford delegation communication with Stephen Bosworth, November 13, 2010.

58. Stanford delegation communication with Stephen Bosworth, November 13, 2010.

59. Sig Hecker, email to Sung Kim and Steve Bosworth, November 13, 2010, unclassified, U.S. Department of State, Case No. F-2014-20439, Doc No. C05774356, November 30, 2015, https://wikileaks.org/clinton-emails /emailid/21097.

60. Andrew Quinn and Phil Stewart, "U.S. Announces New Sanctions against North Korea," July 21, 2010, Reuters, https://www.reuters.com/article /idUSTRE66I0I8/.

61. Author communication with former member of Policy Planning staff, March 14, 2020.

62. Author communication with former member of Policy Planning staff, October 11, 2017; interview with former State Department official, September 12, 2017; and author communication with former member of Policy Planning staff, September 3, 2017.

63. Mark Landler, "U.S. Considers Possibility of Engaging North Korea," *New York Times*, August 27, 2010; and Stephen Bosworth, private notes on DPRK experts meeting, August 2010.

64. Hillary Clinton, email to Huma Abedin, November 17, 2010, unclassified, U.S. Department of State, Case No. F-2016-07895, Doc No. C06131636, November 3, 2015.

65. David E. Sanger, "North Koreans Unveil New Plant for Nuclear Use," *New York Times*, November 20, 2010, https://www.nytimes.com/2010/11/21 /world/asia/21intel.html; David E. Sanger and William J. Broad, "U.S. Concludes North Korea Has More Nuclear Sites," *New York Times*, December 14, 2010, http://www.nytimes.com/2010/12/15/world/asia/15nukes .html; Hecker and Carlin, interview by the author, October 4, 2017; and Philip J. Crowley, email to Hillary Clinton and James Steinberg, November 20, 2010, unclassified, U.S. Department of State, Case No. F-2014-20439, Doc No. C05771458, November 30, 2015, https://wikileaks.org /clinton-emails/emailid/21124.

66. Interview with North Korea experts, October 4, 2017.

67. Interview with North Korea experts, October 4, 2017.

68. Interview with North Korea experts, October 4, 2017.

69. Interview with former U.S. official, March 11, 2020.

70. Interview with North Korea experts, October 4, 2017.

71. Lee Jeong-ho, "South Korean Islanders Living under the Shadow of the North's Guns Dream of Peaceful Future," *South China Morning Post*, September 18, 2018, https://www.everand.com/article/388906918/South -Korean-Islanders-Living-Under-The-Shadow-Of-The-North-s-Guns -Dream-Of-A-Peaceful-Future; Martin Fackler, "In Clash between Koreas,

Fishermen Feel First Bite," *New York Times*, June 23, 2009, https://www
.nytimes.com/2009/06/24/world/asia/24korea.html; Steven Borowiec,
"Ramshackle South Korean Island Faces a Threat More Urgent Than
North Korea," *Los Angeles Times*, June 17, 2016, https://www.latimes.com
/world/asia/la-fg-korea-fishing-island-adv-snap-story.html; Jon Herskovitz, "Guns and Crabs at Koreas' Cold Way Fishing Zone," Reuters,
March 10, 2009, https://www.reuters.com/article/idUSSP478459/; and
Martin Moore and Peter Hutchinson, "Yeonpyeong Island: A History,"
Telegraph (London), November 23, 2010, https://www.telegraph.co.uk
/news/worldnews/asia/southkorea/8155486/Yeonpyeong-Island-A
-history.html.

72. Fackler, "In Clash between Koreas," 2009.

73. Kwang-tae Kim, "War-Split North and South Korean Families Reunite
after Years Apart," Associated Press, November 4, 2010, https://nwasianweekly
.com/2010/11/war-split-north-and-south-korean-families-reunite-after
-years-apart/; and Mark McDonald, "After 6 Decades of Separation in
Korea, a Meeting," *New York Times*, October 29, 2010, https://www.nytimes
.com/2010/10/30/world/asia/30iht-reunion-html.

74. United Nations Security Council, "Special Investigation into the Korean
People's Army Attack on Yeonpyeong-Do and the Republic of Korea Marine
Corps' response on 23 November 2010," Annex to Letter dated 19 Decem-
ber 2010 from the Permanent Representative of the United States of Amer-
ica to the United Nations addressed to the Secretary General, S/2010/648
(December 19, 2010).

75. United Nations Security Council, "Special Investigation," 6.

76. "S. Korea Decries 'Inhumane Atrocities' in Clash," CBS/AP, November
23, 2010, www.cbsnews.com/news/s-korea-decries-inhumane-atrocities-in
-clash/; Evan Ramstad and Jaeyeon Woo, "North Korea Fires Rockets at
South," *Wall Street Journal*, November 25, 2010, https://www.wsj.com
/articles/SB10001424052748703904804575631763523837910; and Martin Frackler, "South Korea Experiences a Stirring for Revenge," *New York
Times*, November 28, 2010, https://www.nytimes.com/2010/11/28/world
/asia/28island.html.

77. Joseph S. Bermudez Jr., "The Yeonpyeong-Do Incident," *38 North*, Special
Report 11–1, January 11, 2011, 6; interview with former USFK [United
States Forces Korea] staff, December 22, 2017.

78. Damian Grammaticas, "Soldiers Move In as Locals Evacuate Yeonpyeong Island," BBC News, https://www.bbc.com/news/world-asia-pacific
-11843778.

79. Interview with former senior ROK official, November 23, 2017.

80. Seo Yoonjung and Keith B. Richburg, "2 Civilians Killed in North Korean
Artillery Attack," *Washington Post*, November 24, 2010; Korva Coleman,
"Two Civilians Killed by North Korean Shelling," NPR, November 24,
2010, https://www.npr.org/sections/thetwo-way/2010/11/24/131561429

/two-civilians-killed-by-north-korean-shelling; and interview with former senior ROK official, November 23, 2017.

81. "Marines Recount NKs Deadly Shelling of Yeonpyeong," *Korea Times*, December 15, 2010.

82. "Marines recount"; Wikipedia, "2010 Yeonpyeong bombardment," last modified February 19, 2025, 20:27, https://en.wikipedia.org/wiki/Bombardment_of_Yeonpyeong, 6; and Yu Kil-yong and Kim Mi-ju, "Island in Ruins after Shelling: With Homes Destroyed and Forests Burned, Hundreds of Residents Flee," *JoongAng Ilbo*, November 25, 2010, https://koreajoongangdaily.joins.com/article/view.asp?aid=2928850.

83. Lee, *President's Time*, 219.

84. Lee, *President's Time*, 219–220.

85. Lee, *President's Time*, 219–220; and interview with senior ROK official, February 21, 2018.

86. Lee, *President's Time*, 220.

87. Lee, *President's Time*, 220.

88. Interview with senior ROK official, November 23, 2017.

89. Interview with senior ROK official, November 23, 2017

90. Interview with Bosworth family member, July 17, 2017.

91. Interview with former U.S. official, June 6, 22, 2018.

92. Interview with senior U.S. military officer, January 22, 2018; and interview with senior USFK official, April 6, 2020.

93. Interview with senior ROK official, November 23, 2017; and Kim Ghattas, "Barack Obama's North Korean Conundrum," BBC News, November 24, 2010, https://www.bbc.com/news/world-us-canada-11825868.

94. Interview with former U.S. official, June 17, 2019.

95. Interview with former U.S. official, June 17, 2019

96. Interview with former USFK official, April 6, 2020.

97. Interview with two former USFK officials, December 22, 2017; and interview with former U.S. official, July 13, 2018.

98. Interview with former U.S. official, July 13, 2018.

99. Interview with former senior ROK official, November 23, 2017.

100. Interview with former USFK official, April 6, 2020; and interview with former senior ROK official, November 23, 2017.

101. Interview with former USFK official, April 6, 2020; and interview with former senior ROK official, November 23, 2017.

102. Interview with former senior USFK official, April 6, 2020; and interview with two former USFK officials, December 22, 2017.

103. Interview with former U.S. official, July 13, 2018.

104. Interview with two former USFK officials, December 22, 2017.

105. Interview with former U.S. official, June 6, 22, 2018.

106. Interview with former senior U.S. military officer, January 22, 2018; interview with former senior U.S. official, July 13, 2018; Bader, *Obama and China's Rise*, 90; and interview with former U.S. official, June 17, 2019.

107. Interview with former U.S. official, June 17, 2019.
108. Interview with senior U.S. officer, January 22, 2018.
109. Interview with former senior Department of Defense official, April 18, 2020.
110. Interview with former senior Department of Defense official, April 18, 2020.
111. Interview with former senior Department of Defense official, April 18, 2020;
      and interview with former senior ROK official, November 23, 2017.
112. Interview with former senior USFK official, April 6, 2020.
113. Interview with former U.S. official, June 17, 2019.
114. Lee, *President's Time*, 223.
115. Lee, *President's Time*, 186–187.
116. Mark Landler, "Obama Urges China to Check North Koreans," *New York
      Times,* December 6, 2010, http://www.nytimes.com/2010/12/07/world/asia
      /07diplo.html?rref=collection%2Fbyline%2Fmark-landler; and Huma Abe-
      din, email to Hillary Clinton, November 26, 2010, unclassified, U.S. Depart-
      ment of State, Case No. F-201607895, Doc No. C06131647, April 29, 2017.
117. Lee, *President's Time*, 186–187.
118. Skip Sharp and Kathy Stephens, "U.S. Military, Diplomatic Engagement
      with South Korea," *The General and the Ambassador,* produced by Deborah
      McCarthy, podcast (published October 6, 2018), https://generalambassador
      podcast.org/013.
119. Interview with senior ROK official, November 23, 2017.
120. Susan E. Rice, email to (USUN), December 18, 2010, 09:32, unclassified,
      U.S. Department of State; Jacob J. Sullivan, email to Hillary Clinton, De-
      cember 18, 2010, 13:54, U.S. Department of State; Jacob J. Sullivan, email
      to Hillary Clinton, December 18, 2010, 14:39, U.S. Department of State;
      Hillary Clinton, email to Jacob J. Sullivan, December 18, 2010, 2:48, U.S.
      Department of State; Jacob J. Sullivan, email to Hillary Clinton, Decem-
      ber 18, 2010, 16:04, U.S. Department of State; U.S. Department of State,
      Case No. F-2014-20439, Doc No. C05777476, December 31, 2015; and
      Edith Lederer, Associated Press, "UN Fails to Take Action on Korea
      Tensions," *San Diego Union-Tribune,* December 19, 2010, https://www.sandie
      gouniontribune.com/sdut-un-fails-to-take-action-on-korea-tensions
      -2010dec19-story.html.
121. "North Korea: Unofficial US Envoy Urges Pyongyang to Keep Calm,"
      Guardian (London), December 19, 2010, https://www.theguardian.com
      /world/2010/dec/19/north-korea-us-envoy-urges-pyongyang.
122. Sung Y. Kim, email to Kurt Campbell, December 18, 2010, unclassified, U.S.
      Department of State, Case No. F-2014-20439, Doc. No. C05778468, Sep-
      tember 30, 2015, https://wikileaks.org/clinton-emails/emailid/30241; and
      Stephen Bosworth, Jacob J. Sullivan, September 30, 2015, unclassified, U.S.
      Department of State, Case No. F-2014-20439, Doc. No. C057788468, Sep-
      tember 30, 2015.
123. "Yellow Sea Border Islanders Ordered into Air Raid Shelters," Yonhap News
      Agency, December 20, 2010.

124. Bader, *Obama and China's Rise*, 91; and interview with former U.S. official, June 17, 2019.

125. Interview with former senior Department of Defense official, April 18, 2020.

126. "S. Korea to Stage Live-Fire Drill on Border Island Shelled by N. Korea," Yonhap News Agency, December 16, 2010; Park Ji-Hwan, "N. Korea: 'Not Worth Reacting to South's Drills,'" NBC News, December 19, 2010, https://www.nbcnews.com/news/amp/wbna40740105.

127. "Reaction after Live-Fire Exercise; Residents Return Home," Associated Press Archive, private transcript, December 21, 2010, https://www.youtube.com/watch?v=IZAeJEskoZM.

128. Robert M. Gates, *Duty: Memoirs of a Secretary at War* (New York: Alfred A. Knopf, 2014), 373.

129. Interview with former U.S. official, June 17, 2019.

130. Bader, *Obama and China's Rise*, 91–93.

131. Private communication with author, February 21, 2019.

132. Former U.S. officer, telephone interview by the author, February 20, 2020; Thomas Maresca, "The Scariest Place on Earth: What It's Like on the Korean DMZ, the World's Most Dangerous Strip of Land," *USA Today*, December 21, 2017, https://www.usatoday.com/story/news/world/2017/12/20heres-what-its-like-worlds-most-dangerous-strip-land/964977001/; and Wikipedia, "Korean Demilitarized Zone," last updated February 5, 2025, 12:02 (UTC), https://en.wikipedia.org/wiki/Korean_Demilitarized_Zone.

133. Kim Chi-gwan, "MB Autobiography Confirms Ryun-Kung-Kim Sook Exchange of Secret Visits," January 31, 2015, *Tong Il News*, https://www.tongilnews.com/news/articleView.html?idxno=110741; Son Jae-min, "Exclusive Report of Secret Meetings between Ryu Kyung-Kim Sook MB Administration . . . Denied at the Time but Confirmed in Autobiography" [in Korean], February 3, 2015, *Kyunghyang News*, https://m.khan.co.kr/politics/politics-general/article/201502032202105#c2b; Yoshihiro Makino, *North Korea Broadly: Inner Workings of Military, Economic and Hereditary Power* [in Japanese] (Tokyo: Bungeishunju, 2013); and private communication with author, February 21, 2019.

134. "National Intelligence Service: South Korean Intelligence and Security Agencies," Federation of American Scientists, https://fas.org/irp/world/rok/nis.htm; "National Intelligence Service," GlobalSecurity.org, https://www.globalsecurity.org/intell/world/rok/nis.htm; *Wikipedia*, "National Intelligence Service (South Korea)," last updated January 2, 2025, 05:51 (UTC), https://en.wikipedia.org/wiki/National_Intelligence_Service_(South_Korea); and "The NIS's Long History of Political Interference," *Hankyoreh*, July 12, 2013, http://www.hani.co.kr/arti/english_edition/e_editorial/595495.html.

135. Don Oberdorfer and Robert Carlin, *The Two Koreas: A Contemporary History* (New York: Basic Books, 2014), chap. 1, Kindle.

136. "The Future of North-South Relations: Short Term Perspectives," *38 North*, Special Report 9, November 1, 2010, https://www.38north.org/2010/10/the-future-of-north-south-relations-short-term-perspectives/; interview with former official, November 22, 2017; and Son, "Exclusive Report of Secret Meetings."

137. Interview with former official, May 3, 2018.

138. Interview with former official, May 3, 2018; and Wikipedia, "Okryu-gwan," last updated June 17, 2024, 00:54 (UTC), https://en.wikipedia.org/wiki/Okryu-gwan.

139. Son, "Exclusive Report of Secret Meetings."

140. Son, "Exclusive Report of Secret Meetings."

141. David E. Sanger and Choe Sang-Hun, "New Injection of Tension Further Frays 2 Koreas' Ties," *New York Times*, May 26, 2010, https://www.nytimes.com/2010/05/26/world/asia/26korea.html.

142. Interview with former official, February 20, 2018.

143. Interview with former official, February 20, 2018; and Finneman and Pritchard, "North Korea Reveals Uranium Enrichment Facility."

144. Interview with former official, February 20, 2018; and Finneman and Pritchard, "North Korea Reveals Uranium Enrichment Facility."

145. Interview with former official, February 20, 2018; and Finneman and Pritchard, "North Korea Reveals Uranium Enrichment Facility."

146. Interview with former official, February 20, 2018; and Finneman and Pritchard, "North Korea Reveals Uranium Enrichment Facility."

147. Choe Sang-Hun, "South Korean Leader Proposes a Tax to Finance Reunification," *New York Times*, August 15, 2010, https://www.nytimes.com/2010/08/16/world/asia/16korea.html.

148. Choe Sang-Hun, "South Korean Leader"; and interview with former official, February 20, 2018.

149. Mark McDonald, "South Korea Drops Its Call for Apology from North," *New York Times*, November 8, 2010, https://www.nytimes.com/2010/11/09/world/asia/09korea.html.

150. Son, "Exclusive Report of Secret Meetings."

151. Son, "Exclusive Report of Secret Meetings."

152. Son, "Exclusive Report of Secret Meetings."

153. Son, "Exclusive Report of Secret Meetings."

154. Associated Press, "North Korean Leader Kim Jong Il to Visit South at "Appropriate Time," July 4, 2004, https://www.newson6.com/story/5e367dca2f69d76f620910e1/n-korean-leader-kim-jong-il-to-visit-south-at-appropriate-time; and James Brooke, "Putin Greets North Korean Leader on Russia's Pacific Coast," *New York Times*, August 24, 2002, https://www.nytimes.com/2002/08/24/world/putin-greets-north-korean-leader-on-russia-s-pacific-coast.html.

155. Associated Press, "Kim Jong Il Visits Russia for Talks with Dmitri Medvedev," *Guardian* (London), August 23, 2011, https://www.theguardian.com/world/2011/aug/23/kim-jong-il-visits-russia.

156. Interviews with former official, November 22, 2017, and February 20, 2018.
157. Son, "Exclusive Report of Secret Meetings."
158. Son, "Exclusive Report of Secret Meetings."
159. Interview with former official, February 20, 2018.
160. Interviews with former official, November 22, 2017, and February 20, 2018; and Michael Madden, email exchange with author, April 6, 2018.
161. Madden, email exchange with author, 2018.
162. Madden, email exchange with author, 2018.
163. Interview with former official, November 22, 2017; and interview with former official, February 20, 2018.

Chapter Seven. "We've got them right where we want them."

1. Email exchange with former State Department official, January 18, 2020.
2. Telephone interview with former State Department official, July 5, 2018; and "Above the Fray: U.S. Diplomat Surveys a World of Progress," Perspectives—A Forum for RAND Guest Voices, *RAND Review*, Spring 2011, https://www.rand.org/pubs/periodicals/rand-review/issues/2011/spring/perspectives1.html.
3. Jeffrey Bader, *Obama and China's Rise: An Insider's Account of America's Asia Strategy* (Washington, DC: Brookings Institution Press, 2013), 91–92.
4. Robert M. Gates, *Duty: Memoirs of a Secretary at War* (New York: Alfred A. Knopf, 2014), 524–527; U.S. Department of Defense, "Media Roundtable with Secretary Gates from Beijing, China," January 11, 2011, https://web.archive.org/web/20150905182047/http://archive.defense.gov/transcripts/transcript.aspx?transcriptid=4751; Jim Garamone, "Gates: North Korea Becoming Direct Threat to U.S.," American Forces Press Service, January 11, 2011; and interview with former senior Department of Defense official, May 9, 2020.
5. Alfred L. Chan, "Childhood and Youth: Privilege and Trauma, 1953–1979," in *Xi Jinping: Political Career, Governance and Leadership, 1953–2018* (New York: Oxford Academic Books, 2022), https://doi.org/10.1093/oso/9780197615225.003.0002; and Graham Allison, "Sharing the World with a Rising China," China.org.cn, October 16, 2013, http://www.china.org.cn/opinion/2013-10/16/content_30308432.htm.
6. Interview with senior Department of Defense official, May 9, 2020.
7. Bader, *Obama and China's Rise*, 115–129; Mark Landler and Martin Fackler, "China to Rein In North Korea," *New York Times*, January 20, 2011, http://www.nytimes.com/2011/01/21/world/asia/21diplo.html?,cubz=1; John Pomfret, "Why China Won't Act against a Nuclear North Korea," *Washington Post*, March 22, 2013; David E. Sanger and Michael Wines, "China Leader's Limits Come Into Focus as U.S. Visit Nears," *New York Times*, January 16, 2011, https://www.nytimes.com/2011/01/17/world/asia/17china.html; "For China and U.S., Summit Gets Passing Grade," *Washington Post*, January 21, 2011; and James B. Steinberg, Deputy Secretary of State,

"Remarks at the Ministry of Foreign Affairs and Trade," Diplomacy in Action, January 26, 2011, https://2009-2017.state.gov/s/d/former/steinberg/remarks/2011/169309.htm.

8. Interview with former senior U.S. military officer; interview with former U.S. official, July 13, 2018; interview with former Department of Defense official, October 10, 2017; interview with former White House aide, January 30, 2018; and interview with former senior Department of Defense official, May 9, 2020.

9. Interview with former senior Department of Defense official, May 9, 2020; interview with former State Department official, July 11, 2017; and interview with former White House aide, January 30, 2018.

10. Interview with former senior State Department official, October 15, 2020.

11. Elise Labott, "Can Clinton Remake U.S. Diplomacy?," CNN, February 16, 2011, http://www.cnn.com/2011/POLITICS/02/16/clinton.sweep/index.html; and interview with former U.S. official, July 13, 2018.

12. Mark Landler, "On North Korea, U.S. Shifts toward Talks," *New York Times*, January 6, 2011, https://www.nytimes.com/2011/01/07/world/asia/07korea.html.

13. Wikipedia, "National Counterproliferation Center," last modified February 29, 2024, 10:17 (UTC), https://en.wikipedia.org/wiki/National_Counterproliferation_Center; and Office of the Director of National Intelligence, "We Protect the American People from Weapons of Mass Destruction," https://www.dni.gov/index.php/ncbc-home.

14. "DPRK Missile and Arms Sales, 1970s–1980," private research note by intern, U.S.-Korea Institute, June 2018; Matthew McGrath and Daniel Wertz, "North Korea's Ballistic Missile Program," *NCNK Issue Brief*, August 2015; Jonathan McLaughlin, "North Korea Missile Milestones, 1969–2017," Wisconsin Project on Nuclear Arms Control, January 23, 2018; U.S. Department of State, "Interview with Michele Kelemen of NPR," Diplomacy in Action, July 22, 2009; and Graham T. Allison Jr., "North Korea's Lesson: Nukes for Sale," *New York Times*, February 12, 2013, https://www.nytimes.com/2013/02/12/opinion/north-koreas-lesson-nukes-for-sale.html.

15. Joshua Pollack, "North Korea's Nuclear Exports: On What Terms?," *38 North*, Special Report 9, October 14, 2010, https://www.38north.org/2010/10/north-koreas-nuclear-exports-on-what-terms/; and "CNN: U.S. Pleased by Israel's Syria Flyover," Jewish Telegraphic Agency, September 11, 2007, https://www.jta.org/2007/09/11/default/cnn-u-s-pleased-by-israels-syria-flyover.

16. Allison, "North Korea's Lesson."

17. Interview with former official, July 27, 2020.

18. Interview with former official, July 27, 2020.

19. Michael Madden, email communication with author, August 3, 2021.

20. "Gen. Kim Yong Chol," *North Korea Leadership Watch*, www.nkleadershipwatch.org/leadership-biographies/lt-gen-kim-yong-chol/.

21. Interview with former official, August 5, 2020.
22. Interview with former official, August 5, 2020.
23. Interview with former official, August 5, 2020.
24. Interview with former official, August 5, 2020.
25. Interview with former official, August 5, 2020.
26. Interview with former official, August 5, 2020.
27. Interview with former official, August 5, 2020.
28. Interview with former official, August 5, 2020.
29. Interview with former official, February 27, 2020.
30. Interview with former official, August 5, 2020.
31. Interview with former official, August 5, 2020.
32. Wikipedia, "Agriculture in North Korea," last modified February 12, 2025, 00:01 (UTC), https://en.wikipedia.org/wiki/Agriculture_in_North _Korea; and Randall Ireson, "Why North Korea Could Feed Itself," *38 North*, May 2, 2010, https://www.38north.org/2010/05/why-north-korea -could-feed-itself/.
33. Steve Coll, "North Korea's Hunger," *New Yorker*, December 21, 2011, https://www.newyorker.com/news/daily-comment/north-koreas-hunger; Wikipedia, "1990s North Korean famine," *Wikipedia*, last modified February 11, 2025, 15:09 (UTC), https://en.wikipedia.org/wiki/1990s_North _Korean_famine; and Marcus Noland, "Famine Deaths Again," *North Korea: Witness to Transformation* (blog), Peterson Institute for International Economics, July 30, 2013, https://www.piie.com/blogs/north-korea-witness -transformation/famine-deaths-again.
34. Mark E. Manyin, "U.S. Assistance to North Korea: Fact Sheet," *CRS Report for Congress*, Congressional Research Service, Library of Congress, January 31, 2006; John Norris, "A History of American Public Opinion on Foreign Aid," *Devex*, August 15, 2017, https://www.devex.com/news/special -feature-a-history-of-american-public-opinion-on-foreign-aid-90732; Mark Manyin and Mary Beth Nikitin, *Foreign Assistance to North Korea*, Congressional Research Service, September 9, 2009, https://www.ncnk.org/sites /default/files/content/resources/publications/Foreign%20Assistance%20 to%20North%20Korea.pdf; and interview with former congressional aide, March 10, 2019.
35. Interview with former USAID official, April 2, 2018.
36. "American Food Monitors in North Korea," paper prepared for *38 North*, spring 2019.
37. Interview with former U.S. food monitor, June 3, 2018.
38. "American Food Monitors in North Korea"; and interview with former U.S. food monitor, May 21, 2020.
39. Interview with former U.S. food monitor, May 21, 2020.
40. Wikipedia, "Robert R. King," last modified February 4, 2025, 09:14 (UTC), https://en.wikipedia.org/wiki/Robert_R._King; and interview with former senior U.S. official, March 3, 2017.

41. Interview with former USAID official, April 2, 2018; Central Intelligence Agency, "North Korea: Assessing the Impact of Flooding on Agricultural Output (U/FOUO)," December 15, 2010; Julian Ryall, "Starving North Korea Sends Out SOS for Food Aid," *Telegraph* (London), February 11, 2011, https://www.telegraph.co.uk/news/worldnews/asia/northkorea/8317726/Starving-North-Korea-sends-out-SOS-for-food-aid.html; and Voice of America, "U.S. to Send Flood Aid to North Korea," September 1, 2010, https://web.archive.org/web/20210615211610/https://www.voanews.com/east-asia/us-send-flood-aid-north-korea.

42. Interview with former senior U.S. official, June 15, 2017; Kim Jung-wook and Moon Gwang-lip, "Pyongyang Asks U.S. to Restore Food Aid," *Korea JoongAng Daily*, February 9, 2011.

43. Interview with former USAID official, April 2, 2018; and former USAID official, private communication with author, May 20, 2018.

44. Interview with former USAID official, April 2, 2018; "Living History with Ambassador Robert King, Part 2," *Beyond Parallel* (blog), *Center for Strategic and International Studies (CSIS)*, https://beyondparallel.csis.org/living-history-with-ambassador-robert-r-king-my-trip-to-north-korea/.

45. Interview with former senior U.S. official, May 28, 2020.

46. Interview with former USAID official, April 2, 2018.

47. Interview with former USAID official, April 2, 2018.

48. Interview with former USAID official, April 2, 2018.

49. Interview with former USAID official, April 2, 2018.

50. Interview with former U.S. official, May 22, 2018.

51. Interview with former U.S. official, May 22, 2018.

52. Interview with former senior U.S. official, March 3, 2017.

53. Interview with former USAID official, May 22, 2018.

54. Interview with former USAID official, May 22, 2018.

55. Interview with former USAID official, May 22, 2018.

56. Former senior U.S. official, email exchange with author, July 26, 2017; interview with former senior U.S. official, May 28, 2020; interview with former senior U.S. official, March 3, 2017; interview with former USAID official, May 22, 2018; "North Korea releases U.S. citizen Eddie Jun Yong-su," BBC News, May 28, 2011, https://www.bbc.com/news/world-asia-pacific-13583136; David Eimer, "North Korea releases American Citizen Eddie Jun after Six Months in Detention," *Telegraph* (London), May 28, 2011, https://www.telegraph.co.uk/news/worldnews/asia/northkorea/8543694/North-Korea-releases-American-citizen-Eddie-Jun-after-six-months-in-detention.html; "U.S. Envoy Leaves North Korea after Getting American Released," CNN, May 27, 2011, http://edition.cnn.com/2011/WORLD/asiapcf/05/27/north.korea.american.released/index.html; and "Family of American Detained in North Korea Cheers His Release," CNN, May 29, 2011, www.cnn.com/2011/WORLD/asiapcf/05/28/north.korea.american.released/.

57. Delegation member notes on King visit to Pyongyang, May 2011.

58. Delegation member notes on DPRK Mission Assessment Report, June 2011; and "North Korea Is Not Suffering from Food Crisis: US Team," *Dong-a Ilbo*, June 20, 2011, https://www.donga.com/en/article/all/20110620/401539/1.

59. Tim Large, "Special Report—Crisis Grips North Korean Rice Bowl," Reuters, October 6, 2011, https://www.reuters.com/article/uk-korea-north -food/special-report-crisis-grips-north-korea-rice-bowl-idUKTRE 7956FW20111006; Matthew Pennington, "U.S. to Provide Emergency Food Aid to North Korea," Associated Press, August 19, 2011; Andrew Quinn, "U.S. Plays Politics with N. Korean Food Aid, NGOs Say," Reuters, October 14, 2011; Choe Sang-Hun, "North Korea's Children in Need of Food Aid, Agencies Warn," *New York Times*, November 25, 2011, https:// www.nytimes.com/2011/11/26/world/asia/north-koreas-children-in-need -of-food-aid-agencies-warn.html; FAO, "FAO/WFP Crop and Food Security Assessment Mission to the Democratic People's Republic of Korea," November 25, 2011, https://www.fao.org/markets-and-trade/publications /detail/ar/c/1447343/; and former U.S. official, private notes by author, June 21, 2011.

60. "N. Korea, U.S. to Hold Talks on Possible Resumption of Food Aid: Source," Yonhap News Agency, December 14, 2011; former U.S. official, notes shared with author, December 2011; William Wan, "U.S., North Korea Resume Talks on Food Aid," *Washington Post*, December 15, 2011, https://www .washingtonpost.com/world/national-security/us-north-korea-resume -talks-on-food-aid/2011/12/15/gIQAjqZowO_story.html; and Choe Sang-Hun, "U.S., North Korea Hold Talks on Humanitarian Aid," *New York Times*, December 15, 2011, https://www.nytimes.com/2011/12/16/world /asia/us-north-korea-hold-talks-on-humanitarian-aid.html.

61. U.S. delegation member notes shared with author, December 2011.

62. U.S. delegation member notes shared with author, December 2011.

63. U.S. delegation notes shared with author, December 2011.

64. Interview with former U.S. official, July 13, 2018.

65. Interview with former U.S. official, July 13, 2018.

66. Interview with former U.S. official, February 22, 2018.

67. Stephen Bosworth, "When You Come to a Fork in the Road, Take It," Freeman Spogli Institute for International Studies, Stanford University, video, February 15, 2013, https://fsi.stanford.edu/multimedia/when-you-come -fork-road-take-it-0.

68. Interview with former South Korean official, June 8, 2020.

69. Interview with former senior ROK official, February 22, 2018; and Choe Sang-Hun, "Chief Nuclear Negotiators from North and South Korea Meet for First Time since 2008," *New York Times*, July 22, 2011, https://www .nytimes.com/2011/07/23/world/asia/23korea.html.

70. U.S. Department of State, "Visit of North Korean Vice Foreign Minister Kim Kae-gwan to New York," press statement by Hillary Rodham Clinton,

Notes to Pages 120–123

July 24, 2011, https://2009-2017.state.gov/secretary/20092013clinton/rm /2011/07/169003.htm; and Kwon Eun Kyoung, "Kim Gye Gwan Optimistic on US Trip," *Daily NK*, July 27, 2011, https://www.dailynk.com/english /kim-kye-gwan-optimistic-on-us-trip/.

71. Justin Davidson, "The Keep," *New York Magazine*, February 6, 2009, https:// nymag.com/news/intelligencer/62373.
72. Former U.S. official, private communication with author, October 2018.
73. Former U.S. official, private communication with author, October 2018.
74. Former U.S. official, private communications with author, October 2018.
75. Former U.S. official, private communications with author, October 2018.
76. Former U.S. official, private communication with author, October 2018.
77. Former U.S. official, private communication with author, October 2018.
78. Former U.S. official, private communication with author, October 2018.
79. Former U.S. official, private communication with author, October 2018.
80. Former U.S. official, private communication with author, October 2018.
81. Former U.S. official, private communication with author, October 2018.
82. Former U.S. official, email exchange with author, July 29, 2020.
83. Former U.S. official, private communication with author, October 2018.
84. Former U.S. official, private communication with author, October 2018.
85. Former U.S. official, private communications with author, October 2018.
86. Interview with former U.S. delegation member, October 10, 2017.
87. "U.S., DPRK Ends Dialogue on six party talks," Xinhua, July 30, 2011; "US and North Korea Conclude 'Constructive Talks,'" *Telegraph* (London), July 29, 2011; and "NK, US End 'Constructive' Talks in New York," *Korea Times*, July 30, 2011, http://www.koreatimes.co.kr/www/news/nation/2011 /07/113_91892.html.
88. Bosworth family member, telephone conversation with author, December 31, 2023.
89. Interview with former senior State Department official, March 6, 2018.
90. Arshad Mohammed, "U.S. and North Korea to Meet, Analysts Skeptical on Progress," Reuters, October 20, 2011, https://www.reuters.com/article /world/us-politics/u-s-and-n-korea-to-meet-analysts-skeptical-on -progress-idUSTRE79I4Q6/.
91. U.S. delegation member, private communication with author, March 2020.
92. U.S. delegation member, private communication with author, March 2020.
93. U.S. delegation member, private communication with author, March 2020.
94. U.S. delegation member, private communication with author, March 2020.
95. U.S. delegation member, private communication with author, March 2020.
96. U.S. delegation member, private communications with author, March 2020 and December 6, 2017.
97. U.S. delegation member, private communication with author, February 22, 2018.
98. U.S. delegation member, private communication with author, February 22, 2018; and former U.S. official, private communication with author, October 2019.

99.   Interview with former U.S. delegation member, July 17, 2018.
100. U.S. delegation member, private communications with author, March 2020.
101. Stephanie Nebehay, "U.S. and North Korea Conclude Geneva Talks," Reuters, October 24, 2011.
102. Interview with former U.S. delegation member, July 17, 2018.
103. Interview with former senior State Department official, March 6, 2018.
104. Mark Landler, *Alter Egos: Hillary Clinton, Barack Obama, and the Twilight Struggle over American Power* (New York: Random House, 2016), 26.
105. Private communication with Steve Bosworth, March 2012.
106. Bosworth family member, telephone communication with author, October 18, 2017.
107. Author's notes, "Track 2 Meeting with the DPRK," Berlin, Germany, March 25–26.
108. Wikipedia, "Koryo Hotel," last modified December 31, 2024, 04:51 (UTC), https://en.wikipedia.org/wiki/Koryo_Hotel; "Koryo Hotel," North Korea Travel Guide, Koryo Tours, https://koryogroup.com/travel-guide/koryo -hotel-north-korea-travel-guide.
109. Author's notes, "Record of Meeting with Ri Yong Ho," November 29, 2011; author's notes, "Record of Meeting with Ms. Choe," November 30, 2011; and "Briefing on NTI Trip to DPRK," November 29–December 3, 2011.
110. Author's notes, "Record of Meeting with Ri Yong Ho"; author's notes, "Record of Meeting with Ms. Choe"; and "Briefing on NTI Trip to DPRK."
111. Author's notes, "Record of Meeting with Ri Yong Ho"; author's notes, "Record of Meeting with Ms. Choe"; and "Briefing on NTI Trip to DPRK."
112. Author's notes, "Record of Meeting with Ri Yong Ho"; author's notes, "Record of Meeting with Ms. Choe"; and "Briefing on NTI Trip to DPRK."
113. Author's notes, "Record of Meeting with Ri Yong Ho"; author's notes, "Record of Meeting with Ms. Choe"; and "Briefing on NTI Trip to DPRK."
114. Author's notes, "Record of Meeting with Ri Yong Ho"; author's notes, "Record of Meeting with Ms. Choe"; and "Briefing on NTI Trip to DPRK."
115. Author's notes, "Record of Meeting with DPRK Technical Experts," December 1, 2011.
116. Author's notes, "Record of Meeting with DPRK Technical Experts."
117. Author's notes, "Record of Meeting with DPRK Technical Experts."
118. Author's notes, "Record of Meeting with DPRK Technical Experts."
119. Author's notes, "Record of Meeting with DPRK Technical Experts."
120. Author's notes, "Record of Meeting with DPRK Technical Experts."
121. Author's notes, "Record of Meeting with DPRK Technical Experts."
122. Author's notes, "Record of Meeting with DPRK Technical Experts."
123. Author's notes, "Record of Meeting with DPRK Technical Experts."
124. Author's notes, "Record of Meeting with DPRK Technical Experts."
125. "Meeting at US Institute for Peace," presentation by U.S. official, Washington, DC, November 8, 2013.
126. "Obama Sought Ideas for N. Korea Strategy from Civilian Experts," *Dong-A Ilbo*, August 23, 2013, https://www.donga.com/en/article/all/20130823

/406850/1; and email exchange with North Korea expert by author, November 28, 2018.

Chapter Eight. "Maybe I will get a crystal ball for Christmas"

1. Josh Rogin, "Obama Administration Ignoring Congress on New North Korea Policy," *Foreign Policy, The Cable,* October 28, 2011, https://foreignpolicy.com/2011/10/28/obama-administration-ignoring-congress-on-new-north-korea-policy/#; and interview with former State Department official, July 9, 2020.

2. Former senior Department of Defense official, email exchange with author, January 4, 2020; interview with former Department of Defense official, October 2, 2017; "Message from the Korean People's Army for the U.S. Department of Defense," unpublished document, September 24, 2009; and Hyung-Jin Kim, "North Korea Threatens to Stop Returning GI Remains If U.S. Keeps Dragging Its Feet," Associated Press, April 5, 2010, http://www.cleveland.com/world/index.ssf/2010/04/north_korea_threatens_to_stop.html.

3. William Wan, "North Korea to Discuss Recovery of POW Remains," *Washington Post,* August 19, 2011; Yonhap News Agency, "N. Korea, U.S. Set Talks on War Dead for October 16–18 in Bangkok," *Korea Times,* October 4, 2011, https://www.koreatimes.co.kr/www/nation/2024/07/113_95996.html; interview with former State Department official, July 8, 2020; and Barbara Slavin, "U.S.-North Korea: Persistence Pays Off with 'Rogue' Regimes," Inter Press Service, October 25, 2011, https://www.ipsnews.net/2011/10/us-north-korea-persistence-pays-off-with-rogue-regimes/.

4. Jeff Baron, "An American NGO . . . in North Korea," *38 North,* December 27, 2012, https://www.38north.org/2012/12/jbaron122712/; Greg Bluestein, "Group Hopes N. Korea Concert Spurs Understanding," Associated Press, March 22, 2012, https://www.washingtontimes.com/news/2012/mar/22/group-hopes-n-korea-concert-spurs-understanding; and interview with American organizer, January 16, 2018.

5. U.S. Department of State, "Remarks by Special Representative Davies in Beijing, China," Diplomacy in Action, December 15, 2011.

6. "More U.S.-N. Korea Talks in the Cards," *Chosun Ilbo,* December 14, 2011.

7. Huma Abedin, email to Hillary Clinton, "Fw: N. Korea 'agrees to suspend uranium enrichment'" (AFP); and Hillary Clinton, email to Kurt Campbell, Jacob Sullivan, "Fw: N. Korea 'agrees to suspend uranium enrichment'" (AFP), December 17, 2011; unclassified, U.S. Department of State, Case No. F-2014-20439, Doc No. C05785725, January 29, 2016, https://wikileaks.org/clinton-emails/emailid/21097.

8. Lee Kyung-tae, "North: Ri Chun Hee Appears in Funeral Dress," Yonhap News Agency, December 19, 2011, https://www.yna.co.kr/view/MYH20111219005600038?section=video/index; "Kim Jong Il Passes

Away," Korean Central News Agency, December 19, 2011; and "Notice to All Party Members, Servicepersons and People," Korean Central News Agency, December 19, 2011.

9. Choe Sang-Hun, "Russia Trip Hints North Korea Ready to Do Business," *New York Times*, August 21, 2011, https://www.nytimes.com/2011/08/22 /world/europe/22moscow.html; Simon Shuster, "Kim Jong Il Goes to Siberia and Likes It!," *Time*, August 25, 2011; and Michael Madden, email exchange with author, March 2021.

10. "Summary of Kim Jong Il's Appearances, 2011," U.S.-Korea Institute, Johns Hopkins School of Advanced International Studies, unpublished document, March 2018.

11. Madden, email exchange with author, July 20, 2017; and Madden, email exchange with author, July 16, 2020.

12. Wikipedia, "Death and State Funeral of Kim Jong Il," last modified February 8, 2025, 11:27 (UTC), https://en.wikipedia.org/wiki/Death_and_state _funeral_of_Kim_Jong_Il.

13. Madden, email exchange with author, March 27, 2018.

14. Fyodor Tertitsky, "Fourteen Days which Shook the Country: The Death of Kim Jong Il," *NK News*, March 29, 2018, 3, https://www.nknews.org/2018 /03/fourteen-days-which-shook-the-country-the-death-of-kim-jong-il/?c =1523366340615; Huma Abedin, email to Hillary Clinton, "Fw: Spot Report The Death of Kim Jong Il," December 19, 2011 (SBU Version); and U.S. Department of State, "Spot Report: The Death of Kim Jong Il," Executive Secretariat, Operations Center, sensitive but unclassified, unclassified, U.S. Department of State, Case No. F-2014-20439, Doc. No. C05786031, October 30, 2015.

15. Telephone interview with U.S. analyst, January 2013.

16. Tertitsky, "Fourteen Days," 3–4; Choi Cheong Ho and Lee Seok Young, "Border Closed Before Announcement, *Daily NK*, December 19, 2011; and Lee Seok Young, "NK Shuts Down on News of Death," *Daily NK*, December 19, 2011.

17. "N. Koreans Pour Out Grief Over Leader Kim Jong Il's Death," Yonhap News Agency, December 19, 2011; "Expert Views, Opinions/Editorials, and Other Reports on North Korea," unclassified news summary, p. 5, December 19, 2011; Lee Seok Young, "People Cried and Wailed," *Daily NK*, December 19, 2011; and Jeong Jae Sung and Choi Song Min, "Halfheartedly Going Along with Atmosphere for Mourning . . . Concerned About the Country's Fate Only," *Daily NK*, December 19, 2011.

18. Interview with former U.S. official, October 4, 2018.

19. Lee Chi-dong, "Obama Vows Efforts for Stability of the Korean Peninsula," Yonhap News Agency, December 19, 2011; and Jennifer Epstein, "After Kim Jong Il's Death, Obama and South Korea Huddle," *Politico*, December 19, 2011, https://www.politico.com/blogs/politico44/2011/12/after-kim-jong -ils-death-obama-and-south-korea-huddle-107981.

20. Lee, "Obama Vows Efforts for Stability"; and Epstein, "After Kim Jong Il's Death."

21. T. R. Reid, "North Korean President Kim Il Sung Dies at 82," *Washington Post*, July 9, 1994; and U.S. Department of State, Bureau of Intelligence and Research, "The Secretary's Morning Intelligence Summary," August 25, 1994, TOP SECRET/ CODEWORD/EXDIS, declassified, Date/Case ID: 07 August 2008, 2004. 037012.

22. Former senior ROK official, email exchange with author, July 21, 2020; Lee Myung-bak, *President's Time* [in Korean] (Seoul: RHK, 2015), unpublished English translation, 224–225.

23. "U.S. Sees No Abnormal Movements in N. Korean Military," Kyodo World Service, December 20, 2011; Jacob J. Sullivan, email to Hillary Clinton, "FW: Seoul Calm," unclassified, U.S. Department of State, Case No. F-2014-20439, Doc No. C05786001, January 7, 2016; and Jacob J. Sullivan, email to Hillary Clinton, "Fw: Update for S," unclassified, U.S. Department of State, Case No. C05786012, February 29, 2016.

24. Interview with former U.S. Embassy official, July 18, 2020.

25. Interview with former U.S. official, February 27, 2018.

26. Victor Cha, "China's Newest Province," *New York Times*, December 19, 2011, https://www.nytimes.com/2011/12/20/opinion/will-north-korea-become-chinas-newest-province.html.

27. Interview with former USFK officer, April 16, 2018.

28. Interview with former U.S. analyst, November 1, 2018.

29. Interview with former U.S. analyst, February 2, 2018.

30. Interview with former U.S. official, February 22, 2018; Adam Entous, Siobhan Gorman, and Jaeyon Woo, "The Death of Kim Jong Il—The Heir: Portrait of New Leader Takes Shape," *Wall Street Journal*, December 20, 2011; and interviews with former U.S. official, February 22, 2018, and October 15, 2020.

31. "US Embassy Cables: China 'Would Accept Korean Reunification,'" SEOUL, Secret, February 22, 2010, https://www.theguardian.com/world/us-embassy-cables-documents/249870.

32. Interviews with senior Obama advisor, January 4, 2019, and November 26, 2018.

33. Mark Landler, *Alter Egos: Hillary Clinton, Barack Obama, and the Twilight Struggle over American Power* (New York: Random House, 2016), xii; and interview with American reporter, September 11, 2018.

34. Interview with former U.S. official, February 22, 2018.

35. Interview with former State Department official, June 14, 2018; and interview with former State Department official, July 9, 2020.

36. Interview with former State Department official, June 14, 2018.

37. Interview with former State Department official, July 17, 2018; and Andrew Quinn, "Insight: Obama's North Korean Leap of Faith Falls Short," Reuters,

March 30, 2012, https://www.reuters.com/article/us-korea-north-usa-leap/insight-obamas-north-korean-leap-of-faith-falls-short-idUSBRE82 T06T20120330.

38. Former U.S. delegation member, communication with author, February–March 2019.

39. Former U.S. delegation member, communication with author, February–March 2019.

40. Former U.S. delegation member, communication with author, February–March 2019.

41. Former USAID delegation member, communication with author, April 2019.

42. Former USAID delegation members, communication with author, April 2019; and former State Department official, communication with author, April 2019.

43. Interview with former State Department official, June 14, 2018.

44. Interview with former U.S. official, June 17, 2019.

45. Interview with former State Department official, June 14, 2018; and former U.S. delegation members, communication with author, April 2019.

46. Interview with former U.S. official, October 17, 2021.

47. Former U.S. delegation member, communication with author, April 2019; and interview with former State Department official, July 9, 2020.

48. U.S. Department of State, "Afternoon Remarks to the Press in Beijing, Glyn Davies, Special Representative for North Korea Policy," Diplomacy in Action, February 24, 2012; and interview with former State Department official, June 14, 2018.

49. Interview with former U.S. official, August 25, 2017.

50. Interview with former State Department official, July 17, 2018.

51. Interview with former State Department official, June 14, 2018.

52. Interview with former State Department official, June 14, 2018; and interview with former State Department official, July 9, 2020.

53. Interview with former State Department official, July 9, 2020.

54. Jacob J. Sullivan, email to Hillary Clinton, "RE: Positive Development," February 28, 2012, unclassified, U.S. Department of State, Case No. F-2014-20439, Doc No. C05791775, December 31, 2015; and Hillary Clinton, email to Jacob J. Sullivan, unclassified, U.S. Department of State, Case No. F-2014-20439, Doc No. C05791775, December 31, 2015.

55. U.S. Department of State, "Budget Hearing for the Department of State and USAID," testimony, Hillary Rodham Clinton, Secretary of State, February 29, 2012; U.S. Department of State, "Background Briefing on the Democratic People's Republic of Korea," special briefing, Senior Administration Office, Office of Spokesperson, February 29, 2012; and "North Korea Agrees to Suspend UEP and Postpone Nuclear-Missile Experiments," Yonhap News Agency, February 29, 2012.

56. "U.S. Cautiously Optimistic after Food Aid Deal with North Korea," CNN, March 1, 2012, https://cnn.com/2012/03/01/opinion/analysis-north-korea -promise/; Allen McDuffee, "North Korea Nuclear-Food Aid Deal: Did the Obama Administration Buy the Same Horse for the Third Time," *Washington Post,* February 29, 2012, https://www.washingtonpost.com/blogs /think-tanked/post/north-korea-nuclear-food-aid-deal-did-the-obama -administration-buy-the-same-horse-for-the-third-time/2012/02/29 /gIQAVqvviR_blog.html; and "Leap of Faith," *The Economist,* March 1, 2012, quoting from Marcus Noland, "North Korea's Surprising Steps: Modest Progress," *Realtime Economics* (blog), Peterson Institute for International Economics, February 29, 2012, https://www.piie.com/blogs/realtime -economic-issues-watch/north-koreas-surprising-steps-modest-progress.

57. Robert Carlin, email to the author, March 1, 2012.

58. Track 2 participant notes shared with the author, March 16, 2012.

59. Interview with Japanese expert, March 26, 2021.

60. Interview with Japanese expert, March 26, 2021.

61. Stephen Haggard and Marcus Noland, "The Missile Launch Announcement," *North Korea: Witness to Transformation* (blog), Peterson Institute for International Economics, March 16, 2012, https://www.piie.com/blogs /north-korea-witness-transformation/missile-launch-announcement; Choe Sang-Hun and Steven Lee Myers, "North Korea Says It Will Launch Satellite into Orbit," *New York Times,* March 16, 2012, http://www.nytimes .com/2012/03/17/world/asia/north-korea-satellite-launch-missile-test -html; and interview with former U.S. official, June 14, 2018.

62. Interview with former senior State Department official, March 6, 2018.

63. Interview with former official, July 27, 2020; interview with former official, July 29, 2020; email exchange between author and former official, February 14, 2019; interviews with senior ROK official, November 15, 2017, and November 21, 2017; Ken Dilanian and Barbara Demick, "Secret U.S.-North Korea Diplomatic Trips Reported," *Los Angeles Times,* February 23, 2013, https://articles.latimes.com/print/2013/feb/23/world/la-fg-us-north -korea-20130224; "US Officials Made Two Secret Visits to Pyongyang in 2012," *AsiaNews.it,* February 25, 2013, https://www.asianews.it/news-en/US -officials-made-two-secret-visits-to-Pyongyang-in-2012-27232.html; Jeffrey Lewis, "Secret US Trip to Pyongyang," *Arms Control Wonk,* May 22, 2012, http://www.armscontrolwonk.com/archive/205249/secret-us-trip -topyongyang/; and "Left in the Dark: Secret U.S. Military Flights Carried Officials, Equipment to N. Korea," *Asahi Shimbun,* February 15, 2013.

64. Interview with former official, July 27, 2020.

65. Interview with former senior State Department official, January 18, 2019; and interview with senior ROK official, February 20, 2018.

66. Interview with former senior White House official, March 15, 2017.

67. Former Obama administration official, email exchange with author, August 7, 2020.

68. "Exclusive: North Korea's Expected Rocket Trajectory," *Northkoreatech*, March 21, 2012, https://www.northkoreatech.org/2012/03/21/exclusive-north-korea- expected-rocket-trajectory; and "North Korea Invites Foreigners to Satellite Launch," CNN, March 17, 2012, https://edition.cnn.com/2012/03/17/world/asia/north-korea-satellite-launch/index.html.

69. Interview with former State Department official, June 14, 2018.

70. Interview with former State Department official, March 22, 2012.

71. Interview with former State Department official, March 23, 2012.

72. Jennifer Epstein, "Obama Warns North Korea," *Politico*, March 25, 2012; and interview with former White House official, March 15, 2017.

73. Interview with former official, July 27, 2020.

74. Interview with former official, July 27, 2020.

75. Choe Sang-Hun and Rock Gladstone, "North Korean Rocket Fails Moments after Liftoff," *New York Times*, April 12, 2012; "A Tumultuous Year, Seen through North Korean Eyes," NPR, December 10, 2012, https://www.npr.org/2012/12/10/166659124/a-tumultuous-year-seen-through-north-korean-eyes; Wikipedia, "Kwangmyŏngsŏng-3," last modified September 14, 2024, 14:29 (UTC), https://en.wikipedia.org/wiki/Kwangmy%C5%8Fngs%C5%8Fng-3; and James Oberg, "Using 'Rocket Science' to Understand North Korea's Space and Missile Efforts," *Space Review*, March 18, 2013, https://www.thespacereview.com/article/2262/1, 5.

76. Paul Brannan, "Satellite Imagery of North Korean Nuclear Test Site Shows Growth in Pile of Material Near Test Shaft; Unclear if Nuclear Test Will Follow," Institute for Science and International Security, April 10, 2012, https://isis-online.org/isis-reports/detail/commercial-satellite-imagery-of-north-korean-nuclear-test-site-shows-growth/10#images; and "North Korean Nuclear Test Preparations: An Update," *38 North*, April 27, 2012, https://www.38north.org/2012/04/punggyeri042712/.

77. Private communication with author, April 2018.

78. Interview with Japanese expert, March 16, 2018.

79. Interview with former U.S. intelligence official, November 1, 2018.

80. Interview with Japanese expert, March 16, 2018.

81. Choe Sang-Hun, "North Korean Leader Stresses Need for Strong Military," *New York Times*, April 15, 2012, https://www.nytimes.com/2012/04/16/world/asia/kim-jong-un-north-korean-leader-talks-of-military-superiority-in-first-public-speech.html; and James Church, "The Paint Dries," *38 North*, April 21, 2012, https://www.38north.org/2012/04/jchurch042112.

82. Author's notes, "Transcript of US-DPRK Track II Meeting," July 31–August 2, 2012, Singapore; and Josh Rogin, "Exclusive: North Korea Threatens to Reconsider 2005 Agreement with U.S.," *Foreign Policy, The Cable*, August 16, 2012, http://foreignpolicy.com/2012/08/16/exclusive-north-korea-threatens-to-reconsider-2005-agreement-with-u-s.

83. Author's notes, "Transcript," July 31–August 2, 2012.

84. Author's notes, "Transcript," July 31–August 2, 2012.

85. Author's notes, "Transcript," July 31–August 2, 2012.

86. Interview with former U.S. official, January 18, 2019.

87. The White House, "Remarks by President Obama at the University of Yangon," Rangoon, Burma, November 19, 2012, https://obamawhitehouse.archives.gov/the-press-office/2012/11/19remarks-president-obama-university-yangon; Howard LaFranchi, "Obama's Myanmar Speech Sends Message to North Korea," *Christian Science Monitor,* November 19, 2012, https://www.csmonitor.com/USA/Foreign-Policy/2012/1119/Obama-s-Myanmar-speech-sends-message-to-North-Korea; Max Fisher, "Obama's Message for North Korea in Visiting Burma: Let's Make Up," *Washington Post,* November 19, 2012; interview with senior White House aide, January 4, 2019; senior ROK official, email communication with author, August 26, 2020; and interview with former senior State Department official, August 25, 2020.

88. "DPRK NDC Reiterates Its Stand to Fight It Out against U.S. and S. Korean Regime," *KCNA Watch,* September 10, 2012, https://kcnawatch.org/newstream/1451892607-439237910/dprk-ndc-reiterates-its-stand-to-fight-it-out-against-u-s-and-s-korean-regime/.

89. Interview with Japanese expert, March 16, 2018.

90. "Meeting at USIP," event memo, November 8, 2011.

91. Interview with senior White House aide, January 4, 2019.

92. Interview with former State Department official, June 18, 2019.

93. Interview with former State Department official, June 18, 2019.

94. Interview with former U.S. official, January 24, 2024.

Chapter Nine. "We weren't going to deal with those assholes anymore"

1. Max Fisher, "The One Substantive Foreign Policy Point in Obama's Inauguration Speech," *Washington Post,* January 21, 2013, https://www.washingtonpost.com/news/worldviews/wp/2013/01/21/the-one-substantive-foreign-policy-point-in-obamas-inauguration-speech/; and James Lindsay, "What Did Obama's Inaugural Address Say About Foreign Policy?," *The Water's Edge* (blog), Council on Foreign Relations, January 22, 2013, https://www.cfr.org/blog/what-did-obamas-inaugural-address-say-about-foreign-policy.

2. Ben Rhodes, "Inside the White House During the Syrian 'Red Line' Crisis," *The Atlantic,* June 3, 2018, https://www.theatlantic.com/international/archive/2018/06/inside-the-white-house-during-the-syrian-red-line-crisis/561887/.

3. Interview with former senior State Department official, October 15, 2020; and interview with former State Department official, November 8, 2018.

4. Hunter Felt, "Dennis Rodman Makes 'Friend for Life' during North Korea Visit," *Guardian* (London), February 28, 2013, https://www.theguardian.com /sport/blog/2013/feb/28/dennis-rodman-meets-kim-jong-un-north-ko rea; "Rodman Says N. Korean Leader Wants President Obama to Call Him," VOA News, March 3, 2013, https://www.voanews.com/a/rodman -says-n-korean-leader-wants-president-obama-to-call-him/1614473.html; and interview with senior White House official, January 4, 2018.

5. Democratic People's Republic of Korea, Permanent Mission to the United Nations, "New Year Address Made by Kim Jong Un," press release, January 1, 2013; Chico Harlan, "In New Year's Speech, N. Korea's Kim Says He Wants Peace with South," *Washington Post*, January 1, 2013, https://www .washingtonpost.com/world/in-new-years-speech-n-koreas-kim-says-he -wants-peace-with-south/2013/01/01/bce3a4dc-53dd-11e2-8b9e -dd8773594efc_story.html; and "North Korea's Kim Jong Un Makes Rare New Year Speech," BBC News, January 1, 2013, https://www.bbc.com /news/world-asia-20880301.

6. "UN Extends North Korea Sanctions over Rocket Launch," BBC News, January 22, 2013, https://www.bbc.com/news/world-asia-21137136; Joshua Rhett Miller, "North Korea Video Shows New York in Ruins after Missile Attack," Fox News, December 9, 2015, https://www.foxnews.com/world /north-korea-video-shows-new-york-in-ruins-after-missile-attack; and David E. Sanger and Choe-Sang-Hun, "North Korea Issues Blunt New Threat to United States," *New York Times*, January 24, 2013, https://www.nytimes .com/2013/01/25/world/asia/north-korea-vows-nuclear-test-as-threats -intensify.html.

7. David E. Sanger and Choe Sang-Hun, "North Korea Confirms It Conducted 3rd Nuclear Test," *New York Times*, February 11, 2013, https://www .nytimes.com/2013/02/12/world/asia/north-korea-nuclear-test.html; and Jack Liu and Nick Hansen, "Post Test Analysis of Punggye-ri: What a Difference a Few Days Make," *38 North*, February 20, 2018, https://www .38north.org/2013/02/punggyerio21713/.

8. The White House, Office of the Press Secretary, "Remarks by the President in the State of the Union Address," February 12, 2013, https://obama whitehouse.archives.gov/the-press-office/2013/02/12/remarks-president -state-union-address.

9. Ernesto Londono, "Pentagon: North Korea Likely Has Nuclear Warhead for Its Ballistic Missiles," *Washington Post*, April 11, 2013, https://www .washingtonpost.com/world/national-security/pentagon-north-korea -could-have-nuclear-missile/2013/04/11/72230dea-a2eb-11e2-82bc -511538ae90a4_story.html; Jethro Mullen, "Obama Says He Doesn't Believe North Korea Has Nuclear Missile," CNN, April 18, 2013, https:// www.cnn.com/2013/04/17/world/asia/koreas-tensions/index.html; and David Albright, "North Korean Miniaturization," *38 North*, February 13, 2013, https://www.38north.org/2013/02/albrighto21313.

10. "In Focus: North Korea's Nuclear Threats," *New York Times*, April 16, 2013, https://archive.nytimes.com/www.nytimes.com/interactive/2013/04/12 /world/asia/north-korea-questions.html; Paik Hak-sun, "North Korea-U.S. Relations in the Second Term of the Obama Administration, 2013–2014," Sejong Institute, unpublished paper; Tania Branigan and Ewen MacAskill, "UN Backs Expansion of North Korea Sanctions after Nuclear Threat," *Guardian* (London), March 7, 2013, https://www.theguardian.com/world /2013/mar/07/north-korea-threat-un-sanctions; and Josh Levs and Jethro Mullen, "U.S. Says U.N. Sanctions 'Will Bite' after North Korea Threatens Nuclear Attack," CNN, March 7, 2013, https://edition.cnn.com/2013 /03/07/world/asia/un-north-korea-sanctions/index.html.

11. Max Fisher, "Photo from Kim Jong Un's War Room Reveals North Korea's 'U.S. Mainland Strike Plan,'" *Washington Post*, March 29, 2013, https://www .washingtonpost.com/news/worldviews/wp/2013/03/29/photo-from-kim -jong-uns-war-room-reveals-north-koreas-u-s-mainland-strike-plan/.

12. Cheon Seong-Whun, "The Kim Jong Un Regime's 'Byungjin (Parallel Development)' Policy of Economy and Nuclear Weapons and the April 1st Nuclearization Law," Online Series, Center for North Korean Studies, Korea Institute for National Reunification (KINU), April 23, 2013, https://repo .kinu.or.kr/bitstream/2015.oak/2227/1/0001458456.pdf; and Scott A. Snyder, "The Motivations behind North Korea's Pursuit of Simultaneous Economic and Nuclear Development," *Asia Unbound* (blog), Council on Foreign Relations, November 20, 2013, https://www.cfr.org/blog/moti vations-behind-north-koreas-pursuit-simultaneous-economic-and-nuclear -development.

13. Mullen, "Obama Says He Doesn't Believe"; and interview with former senior White House official, January 13, 2018.

14. Interview with former White House official, October 17, 2018; Stephen Haggard, "The Obama YouTube Interviews," *North Korea: Witness to Transformation* (blog), Peterson Institute for International Economics, January 30, 2015, https://www.piie.com/blogs/north-korea-witness-transformation /obama-youtube-interviews; and participant in Obama roundtable, email exchange with author, September 16, 2017.

15. Mullen, "Obama Says He Doesn't Believe"; David E. Sanger and Michael R. Gordon, "Obama Doubts That North Korea Can Make a Nuclear Warhead," *New York Times*, April 16, 2013, https://www.nytimes.com/2013/04 /17/us/politics/obama-voices-doubts-on-north-korean-nuclear-warhead. html.

16. Interview with former White House official, March 15, 2017; and interview with former State Department official, September 12, 2017.

17. *U.S. Policy toward North Korea, Hearing before the Senate Committee on Foreign Relations*, March 7, 2013, testimony of Glyn T. Davies, Special Representative for North Korea Policy, U.S. Department of State, 4, https://www.foreign .senate.gov/imo/media/doc/Ambassador_Davies_Testimony.pdf; Syd Seiler,

presentation, Council on Foreign Relations, New York, November 8, 2013; and interview with former White House official, August 25, 2017.

18. William Burns, *A Memoir of American Diplomacy and the Case for Its Renewal* (London: Hurst, 2019), 271.

19. Interview with senior Clinton aide, June 18, 2019.

20. Wikipedia, "Fort Greely," last modified October 6, 2024, 10:24 (UTC), https://en.wikipedia.org/wiki/Fort_Greely; Tim Holoday, "A Look inside the Missile Defense Complex at Fort Greely," *Delta Wind*, May 3, 2018, https://www.deltawindonline.com/news/local/a-look-inside-the-missile -defense-complex-at-fort-greely/article_ae65f33c-4ed3-11e8-b2a1 -0b6737596f22.html; U.S. Army Garrison Fort Greely, https://home.army .mil/greely/; and "Ground-Based Missile Defense (GMD)," Missile Defense Advocacy Alliance, January 31, 2019, https://missiledefenseadvocacy.org /defense-systems/ground-based-midcourse-defense/.

21. Thom Shanker, David E. Sanger, and Martin Fackler, "U.S. Is Bolstering Missile Defense to Deter North Korea," *New York Times*, March 15, 2013, https://www.nytimes.com/2013/03/16/world/asia/us-to-bolster-missile -defense-against-north-korea.html; Anne Gearan, "U.S. Beefs Up West Coast Missile Defense in Face of N. Korea Threat," *Washington Post*, March 15, 2013, https://www.washingtonpost.com/world/national-security /2013/03/15/c5b70170-8d9a-11e2-9f54-f3fdd70acad2_story.html; David Cloud, "Pentagon Plans to Add Missile Interceptors in Alaska," *Los Angeles Times*, March 16, 2013, http://articles.latimes.com/2013/mar/16/nation/la -na-anti-missile-20130316; and U.S. Department of Defense, "DOD News Briefing on Missile Defense from the Pentagon," news transcript, March 15, 2013, https://content.govdelivery.com/accounts/USDOD/bulletins/716156.

22. "Obama Scraps Bush Missile Defense Plan," ABC News, September 17, 2009, https://abcnews.go.com/Politics/obama-scraps-bush-missile-defense -plan/story?id=8604357; Peter Baker, "White House Scraps Bush's Ap- proach to Missile Shield," *New York Times*, September 17, 2009, https:// www.nytimes.com/2009/09/18/world/europe/18shield.html; Andrew Futter, "The Elephant in the Room: US Ballistic Missile Defence under Barack Obama," *Defense and Security Analysis* 28 (April 25, 2012): 3–16, https:// www.tandfonline.com/doi/full/10.1080/14751798.2012.651374; and Mi- chael D. Shear and Ann Scott Tyson, "Obama Shifts Focus of Missile Shield," *Washington Post*, September 18, 2009, http://www.washingtonpost.com/wp -dyn/content/article/2009/09/17/AR2009091700639.html.

23. *Budget Request for National Security Space and Missile Defense Programs, Stra- tegic Forces Subcommittee Hearing, Committee on Armed Services, House of Rep- resentatives*, 111th Cong., 1st Sess. (Washington, DC: U.S. Government Printing Office, 2010), 17.

24. Department of Defense, "Ballistic Missile Defense Review Report," Febru- ary 2010; and interview with former Department of Defense official, March 30, 2018.

25. Interview with former senior Department of Defense official, February 6, 2018.

26. Interview with former senior Department of Defense official, February 6, 2018; David Wright, "Secretary Gates and the North Korean Missile Threat," *38 North*, January 27, 2011, https://www.38north.org/2011/01/secretary-gates-and-the-north-korean-missile-threat/; and Elisabeth Bumiller and David E. Sanger, "Gates Warns of North Korean Missile Threat to the U.S." *New York Times*, January 11, 2011, https://www.nytimes.com/2011/01/12/world/asia/12military.html.

27. Interview with former Department of Defense official, February 28, 2018.

28. Interview with former Department of Defense official, February 28, 2018.

29. Interview with former Department of Defense official, February 28, 2018.

30. Interview with former senior Department of Defense official, February 6, 2018.

31. Jeffrey Lewis, Melissa Hanham, and Amber Lee, "That Ain't My Truck: Where North Korea Assembled Its Chinese Transporter-Erector-Launchers," *38 North*, February 3, 2014, http://www.38north.org/2014/02/jlewis020314/; Katsu Furukawa, communication with author, February 2019; Katsu Furukawa, "Chapter 2: Obstinate China," unpublished book manuscript; "Report of the Panel of experts established pursuant to resolution 1874 (2009)," S/2013/337, https://www.securitycouncilreport.org/atf/cf/%7B65BFCF9B-6D27-4E9C-8CD3-CF6E4FF96FF9%7D/s_2013_337.pdf.

32. John Barry, "Robert Gates Exit Interview: Concerns about U.S. Supremacy, Nuclear Proliferation, More," *Daily Beast*, June 21, 2011, https://www.thedailybeast.com/robert-gates-exit-interview-concerns-about-us-supremacy-nuclear-proliferation-more/.

33. Interview with former senior U.S. officer, February 27, 2018.

34. Interview with former State Department official, July 17, 2018.

35. *President Obama's New Plan for Missile Defenses in Europe and the Implications for International Security, Committee on Armed Services, House of Representatives*, 111th Cong., 1st sess., hearing held October 1, 2009 (Washington, DC: U.S. Government Printing Office, 2010), 1–3.

36. Wikipedia, "Ground-Based Midcourse Defense," last modified January 24, 2025, 01:38 (UTC), https://en.wikipedia.org/wiki/Ground-Based_Midcourse_Defense; David Mosher, "Understanding the Extraordinary Cost of Missile Defense," Arms Control Association, https://www.armscontrol.org/act/2000-12/features/understanding-extraordinary-cost-missile-defense; David Willman, "$40 Billion Missile Defense System Proves Unreliable," *Los Angeles Times*, June 15, 2014, https://www.latimes.com/nation/la-na-missile-defense-20140615-story.html; and Kingston Reif, "Missile Defense Can't Save Us from North Korea," *War on the Rocks*, May 29, 2017, https://warontherocks.com/2017/05/missile-defense-cant-save-us-from-north-korea/.

37. Interview with former senior U.S. officer, February 27, 2018.

38. Michael Morell and James A. Winnefeld Jr., "U.S. Should Adopt Interest-based Approach to National Security," *Belfer Center Analysis and Opinions*, Harvard Kennedy School, August 4, 2016, https://wwwbelfercenter.org /node/89170; and interview with former senior U.S. officer, February 27, 2018.

39. Interview with former senior U.S. officer, February 27, 2018.

40. Interview with former senior Department of Defense official, February 6, 2018.

41. Interview with former senior U.S. officer, February 27, 2018.

42. Interview with former senior U.S. officer, February 27, 2018.

43. Interview with former senior Department of Defense official, February 6, 2018; and interview with former senior State Department official, September 21, 2020.

44. Interviews with former Department of Defense official, February 28, 2018, and March 30, 2018.

45. Interview with former senior U.S. intelligence official, November 26, 2018.

46. Thom Shanker and David E. Sanger, "Movement of Missiles by North Korea Worries U.S.," *New York Times*, January 17, 2013, http://www.nytimes .com/2013/01/18/world/asia/north-koreas-missile-movements-worry-us. html; Bill Gertz, "North Korea Making Missile Able to Hit U.S.," *Washington Times*, December 6, 2011, https://www.washingtontimes.com /news/2011/dec/5/north-korea-making-missile-able-to-hit-us/; "N. Korea Tested Long-Range Missile Engine before Nuke Blast: Sources," Yonhap News Agency, February 17, 2013, https://en.yna.co.kr/view/AEN2013 0217003300315?section=print; and David Wright, "A North Korean Mobile ICBM?," *38 North*, February 12, 2012, https://www.38north.org/2012/02 /dwright021212/.

47. "Xi Jinping Named President of China," BBC News, March 14, 2013, https://www.bbc.com/news/world-asia-china-21766622; Bill Idle, "Xi Jinping Becomes China's President," Voice of America, March 14, 2013, https:// www.voanews.com/a/chinas-xi-jingping-given-forma-title-of-president /1621201.html; "China Convenes the 12th National People's Congress," https://www.csis.org/analysis/china-convenes-12th-national-people's-con gress; and William Wan, "Xi's Election to Presidency Completes China's Leadership Transition," *Washington Post*, March 14, 2013, https://www .washingtonpost.com/world/xis-election-to-presidency-completes-chinas -leadership-transition/2013/03/14/d35c8248-8c58-11e2-9f54-f3fdd 70acad2_story.html.

48. Tao Xie, "Opinion: Is President Xi Jinping's Chinese Dream Fantasy or Reality?," CNN, March 14, 2013, https://edition.cnn.com/2014/03/14 /world/asia/chinese-dream-anniversary-xi-jinping-president/index.html.

49. Jeremy Page, "For Xi, a 'China Dream' of Military Power," *Wall Street Journal*, March 3, 2013, https://www.wsj.com/articles/SB10001424127887324

1285045783487740405463 46; Ian Johnson, "A Promise to Tackle China's Problems, but Few Hints of a Shift in Path," *New York Times*, November 15, 2012, https://www.nytimes.com/2012/11/16/world/asia/new-chinese-leader-offers-few-hints-of-a-shift-in-direction.html; "Transcript: Chris Johnson Talks with Michael Morell on 'Intelligence Matters,'" CBS News, November 6, 2019, https://www.cbsnews.com/news/transcript-chris-johnson-talks-with-michael-morell-on-intelligence-matters/; and, Xie, "President Xi Jinping's Chinese dream."

50. Xi Jinping, "'Old Friends': The Xi Jinping-Iowa Story," https://www.xijinpingiowamemoir.com/; "Backgrounder: Xi Jinping's Previous Visits to the United States," *New China*, April 6, 2017, www.xinhuanet.com//english/2017-04/06/c_136187771.htm; and "Why Iowa Is Xi Jinping's Favorite Corner of America," *Down on the Farm*, special report, May 16, 2019.

51. Kerry Brown, *CEO, China: The Rise of Xi Jinping* (London: Bloomsbury Publishing, 2016), 191.

52. Quora, https://www.quora.com/When-did-Deng-Xiaoping-say-hide-your-strength-bide-your-time.

53. Interview with former senior State Department official, October 15, 2020.

54. Graham Allison, "Thucydides Trap Has Been Sprung in the Pacific," *Financial Times*, August 21, 2012, https://www.ft.com/content/5d695b5a-ead3-11e1-984b-00144feab49a; and Wikipedia, "Thucydides Trap," last modified February 1, 2025, 01:07 (UTC), https://en.wikipedia.org/wiki/Thucydides_Trap.

55. Jinghan Zeng, "Constructing a 'New Type of Great Power Relations': The State of the Debate in China (1998–2014)," *British Journal of International Relations* 18, no. 2 (2016): 422–442; Andrew Nathan, "The New Type of Major Power Relationship: An Analysis of the American Response" (remarks at the 28th Asia-Pacific Roundtable, June 2–4, 2014, Kuala Lumpur, Malaysia); David M. Lampton, "A New Type of Major Power Relationship: Seeking a Durable Foundation for U.S.-China Ties," National Bureau of Asian Research (NBR), https://www.nbr.org/publications/element.aspx?id=650; interview with senior Chinese scholar, October 10, 2018; and interview with Chinese expert, December 12, 2017.

56. "Shades of Red: China's Debate Over North Korea," International Crisis Group, *Asia Report*, no. 179 (November 2, 2009): 5–11; and Yu Tiejun, Ren Yuanzhe, and Wang Junsheng, "Chinese Perspectives towards the Korean Peninsula in the Aftermath of North Korea's Fourth Nuclear Test," *Henry L. Stimson Center Report*, June 2016.

57. Jane Perlez, "Chinese Editor Suspended for Article on North Korea," *New York Times*, April 1, 2013, https://www.nytimes.com/2013/04/02/world/asia/chinese-suspend-editor-who-questioned-north-korea-alliance.html.

58. Interview with Chinese expert, December 12, 2017.

59. Interview with Chinese expert, December 12, 2017.

60. Post cited in "Fire on the City Gate: Why China Keeps North Korea Close," International Crisis Group, *Asia Report*, no. 254 (December 9, 2013): 5.

61. "Fire on the City Gate," 6–10.

62. "Jeffrey Bader: Part Two," *U.S.-China Dialogue Podcast*, produced by the Georgetown University Initiative for U.S.-China Dialogue on Global Issues, June 20, 2019, https://uschinadialogue.georgetown.edu/podcasts/jeffrey-bader-part-two; interview with former Biden aide, June 14, 2018; interview with former Biden aide, December 5, 2017; and interview with former Biden aide, December 13, 2017.

63. Interview with former Biden aide, June 14, 2018; interview with former Biden aide, December 5, 2017; and interview with former Biden aide, December 13, 2017.

64. U.S. Department of State, *Foreign Relations of the United States*, "Memorandum of Conversation, July 9, 1971" (Washington, DC: U.S. Government Printing Office, 2006), 390; and interview with former Biden aide, December 13, 2017.

65. Jane Perlez, "China Bluntly Tells North Korea to Enter Nuclear Talks," *New York Times*, May 24, 2013, www.nytimes.com/2013/05/25/world/asia/china-tells-north-korea-to-return-to-nuclear-talks.html/; and Jane Perlez, "North Korea Glosses Over Tensions after Its Special Envoy Visits China," *New York Times*, May 25, 2013, www.nytimes.com/2013/05/25/world/asia/china-tells-north-korea-to-return-to-nuclear-talks.html/.

66. Mark Landler, "Detecting Shift, U.S. Makes Case to China on North Korea," *New York Times*, April 5, 2013, https://www,nytimes.com/2013/04/06/world/asia/us-sees-china-as-lever-to-press-north-korea.html; Mark Landler, "Obama's Journey to Tougher Tack on a Rising China," *New York Times*, September 20, 2012, http://www.nytimes.com/2012/09/21/us/politics/obamas-evolution-to-a-tougher-line-on-china-html; Josh Rogin, "Former Top U.S. Official Getting Fed Up with North Korea," *Foreign Policy, The Cable*, April 5, 2013, https://web.archive.org/web/20150701080728/http://foreignpolicy.com/2013/04/05/former-top-u-s-official-china-getting-fed-up-with-north-korea/; and interview with former senior U.S. intelligence official, November 26, 2018.

67. "China to Send North Korea Envoy to Washington," Reuters, April 19, 2013, https://www.reuters.com/article/us-korea-north-china/china-to-send-north-korea-envoy-to-washington-idUSBRE93I0EG20130419; "Wu Dawei Set for Rare Trip to U.S. for Talks on N. Korea," Yonhap News Agency, April 19, 2013; and interview with Chinese expert, December 12, 2017.

68. Interview with former U.S. official, July 17, 2018.

69. Interview with Chinese expert, October 25, 2017.

70. Interview with Chinese Foreign Ministry official, November 5, 2005.

71. Wikipedia, "Sunnylands," last modified March 1, 2025, 18:47 (UTC), https://en.wikipedia.org/wiki/Sunnylands; and Jackie Calmes, "Expansive

Setting for Obama's Meeting with Xi," *New York Times*, June 7, 2013, https://www.nytimes.com/2013/06/08/us/politics/an-expansive-setting-for-obamas-talks-with-chinas-leader.html.

72. Interview with former White House official, January 10, 2018.

73. Jackie Calmes and Steven Lee Myers, "U.S. and China Move Closer on North Korea, but not on Cyberespionage," *New York Times*, June 8, 2013, https://www.nytimes.com/2013/06/09/world/asia/obama-and-xi-try-building-a-new-model-for-china-us-ties-html?pagewanted=all; interview with former White House official, October 30, 2017; and interview with former senior State Department official, October 15, 2020.

74. Interview with former senior State Department official, October 15, 2020.

75. Stephanie Kleine-Albrandt, "China's North Korea Policy: Backtracking from Sunnylands," *38 North*, July 2, 2013, https://www.38north.org/2013/07/skahlbrandt070213/.

76. Javier C. Hernandez, "After Nuclear Test, China Resists Pressure to Curb North Korea," *New York Times*, January 15, 2016, https://www.nytimes.com/2016/01/16/world/asia/north-korea-xi-jinping-obama.html.

77. Interview with Chinese expert, December 12, 2017; email exchange between author and Chinese expert, August 13, 2020; "Secret Taping Said to Have Worsened North Korea-China Tie," *NHK World Japan*, February 13, 2018, https://www3.nhk.or.jp/nhkworld/en/news/backstories/115/; Mu Chun-shan, "China's Official Response to Jang Song-Thaek's Execution: An Analysis," *The Diplomat*, December 21, 2013, https://thediplomat.com/2013/12/chinas-official-response-to-jang-song-thaeks-execution-an-analysis; and Christopher Bodeen, "The Execution of Kim Jong Un's Powerful Uncle Leaves China in a Very Delicate Position," Associated Press, December 13, 2013.

78. Travel of the Delegation Led by Special Representative Davies to Seoul, Beijing, and Tokyo, unpublished research note by author, January 23, 2013–July 30, 2015, U.S.-Korea Institute.

79. Interview with former ROK diplomat, February 21, 2019.

80. "Retrospect & Outlook: A Decade of the Six-Party Talks" (Commemorative Seminar for the 10th Anniversary of the Six-Party Talks, China Institute of International Studies, Beijing, September 18, 2013); "Notes on Proceedings of September 18 meeting," private document by author; and "China Proposes Holding Informal Six-Party Meeting on N. Korea," Yonhap News Agency, September 5, 2013, https://en.yna.co.kr/view/AEN20130905009000315.

81. Interview with former U.S. official, February 22, 2018; interview with former State Department official, July 17, 2018; and Adam Cathcart, "Tuning Out Beijing's Six-Party Drumbeat: Wu Dawei in Pyongyang," *SinoNK*, April 1, 2014, http://sinonk.com/2014/04/01/wu-dawei-pyongyang-six-party/.

82. Interview with former senior White House official, June 18, 2019.

83. Interview with former senior White House official, June 18, 2019.

84. Interview with Chinese expert, December 12, 2017.

85. Kurt Campbell and Ely Ratner, "The China Reckoning," *Foreign Affairs*, February 13, 2018; and interview with former State Department official, September 12, 2017.

86. James Hoare, email communication with author, October 28, 2020.

87. Robert Carlin, note to author, August 2013; Choe Sang-Hun, "North Korea Proposes High-Level Talks," *New York Times*, June 15, 2013, https://www .nytimes.com/2013/06/16/world/asia/north-korea-proposes-talks-with-us .html; Scott Snyder, "North Korea's Defiant Proposal for Denuclearization Talks," *Asia Unbound* (blog), Council on Foreign Relations, June 17, 2013, https://www.cfr.org/blog/north-koreas-defiant-proposal-denuclearization -talks; and Stephen Haggard, "North Korea Offers Talks: Risks and Opportunities," *North Korea: Witness to Transformation* (blog), Peterson Institute for International Economics, June 6, 2013, https://web.archive.org/web /20220715023103/https://www.piie.com/blogs/north-korea-witness-trans formation/north-korea-offers-talks-risks-and-opportunities.

88. Robert Carlin, email communication with author, January 2014.

89. Interview with Japanese expert, March 16, 2018.

90. Jean Lee, "North Korea Changes Tack and Tells U.S.: Let's Talk," Associated Press, June 15, 2013, https://www.usatoday.com/story/news/world /2013/06/15/nkorea-proposes-nuclear-talks/2427457/.

91. Hotel N'vY website, https://www.hotel.NVYGeneva.com.

92. Author's notes, "Transcript of US-DPRK Track II Meeting," August 6–7, 2013, Geneva, Switzerland; and "Briefing on US-DPRK Track II Meeting," August 6–7, 2013, Geneva, Switzerland.

93. Author's notes, "Transcript of US-DPRK Track II Meeting," August 6–7, 2013.

94. Author's notes, "Transcript of US-DPRK Track II Meeting," August 6–7, 2013.

95. Author's notes, "Transcript of US-DPRK Track II Meeting," August 6–7, 2013.

96. Author's notes, "Transcript of US-DPRK Track II Meeting," August 6–7, 2013.

97. Author's notes, "Transcript of US-DPRK Track II Meeting," August 6–7, 2013.

98. Author's notes, "Transcript of US-DPRK Track II Meeting," August 6–7, 2013.

99. Author's notes, "Transcript of US-DPRK Track II Meeting," August 6–7, 2013.

100. Berlin delegation member, note to author, October 28, 2020.

101. Berlin delegation member, note to author, October 28, 2020.

102. Author's notes, "Transcript of US-DPRK Track II Meeting," September 25–26, 2013, Berlin, Germany; and "Briefing on US-DPRK Track II Meeting," September 25–26, 2013, Berlin, Germany.

103. Author's notes, "Transcript of US-DPRK Track II Meeting," September 25–26, 2013.

104. Author's notes, "Transcript of US-DPRK Track II Meeting," September 25–26, 2013.

105. Author's notes, "Transcript of US-DPRK Track II Meeting," September 25–26, 2013.

106. Author's notes, "Transcript of US-DPRK Track II Meeting," September 25–26, 2013.

107. Author's notes, "Transcript of US-DPRK Track II Meeting," September 25–26, 2013.

108. Author's notes, "Transcript of US-DPRK Track II Meeting," September 25–26, 2013.

109. Author's notes, "Transcript of US-DPRK Track II Meeting," September 25–26, 2013.

110. Author's notes, "Transcript of US-DPRK Track II Meeting," September 25–26, 2013.

111. Author's notes, "Transcript of US-DPRK Track II Meeting," September 25–26, 2013.

112. Author's notes, "Transcript of US-DPRK Track II Meeting," September 25–26, 2013.

113. Author's notes, "Transcript of US-DPRK Track II Meeting," September 25–26, 2013.

114. Author's notes, "Transcript of US-DPRK Track II Meeting," September 25–26, 2013.

115. Author's notes, "Transcript of US-DPRK Track II Meeting," September 25–26, 2013.

116. Author's notes, "Transcript of US-DPRK Track II Meeting," September 25–26, 2013.

117. Author's notes, "Transcript of US-DPRK Track II Meeting," September 25–26, 2013.

118. Author's notes, "Transcript of US-DPRK Track II Meeting," September 25–26, 2013.

119. Author's notes, "Transcript of US-DPRK Track II Meeting," September 25–26, 2013.

120. Author's notes, "Transcript of US-DPRK Track II Meeting," September 25–26, 2013.

121. Author's notes, "Transcript of US-DPRK Track II Meeting," September 25–26, 2013.

122. Author's notes, "Transcript of US-DPRK Track II Meeting," September 25–26, 2013.

123. Lee Sigal, "Track II Meeting notes," London, October 1–2, 2013.

124. Sigal, "Track 2 Meeting notes," London, March 2021.
125. Sigal, "Track 2 Meeting notes," London, March 2021.
126. Stephen Bosworth and Robert L. Gallucci, "Reasons to Talk to North Korea," *New York Times*, October 27, 2013, https://www.nytimes.com/2013 /10/28/opinion/reasons-to-talk-to-north-korea.html.

Chapter Ten. "No news is okay news."

1. David Erickson, "Missoula YouTube Star Hank Green Interviews Obama," *Missoulian*, January 23, 2015, https://missoulian.com/news/local/missoula -youtube-star-hank-green-interviews-obama/article_a11596a2-79de-52cd -9436-4748518baa17.html; Stephen Haggard, "The Obama YouTube Interviews," *North Korea: Witness to Transformation* (blog), Peterson Institute for International Economics, https://www.piie.com/blogs/north-korea -witness-transformation/obama-youtube-interviews, January 30, 2015; and "Obama, on YouTube, Says North Korea Likely to Collapse and NET May Play a Role," *Japan Times*, January 24, 2015, https://www.japantimes.co.jp /news/2015/01/24/world/obama-youtube-says-north-korea-likely -collapse-net-may-play-role/.
2. "Obama on YouTube."
3. Aidan Foster-Carter, "Obama Comes Out as an NK Collapsist," *38 North*, January 27, 2015, https://www.38north.org/2015/01/afostercarter012715/.
4. Interview with former White House official, October 17, 2018; Haggard, "The Obama YouTube Interviews"; and participant in Obama roundtable, email exchange with author, September 16, 2017.
5. Interview with former State Department official, July 24, 2018.
6. Interview with former senior U.S. official, January 17, 2018.
7. Interview with former White House official, July 18, 2019.
8. Interview with former senior Obama administration official, January 11, 2019; interview with former State Department official, July 9, 2020; Anna Fifield, "North Korean Regime Is Finding New Ways to Stop Information Flows, Report Says" *Washington Post*, March 1, 2017, https://www .washingtonpost.com/world/asia_pacific/north-korean-regime-is-finding -new-ways-to-stop-information-flows-report-says/2017/02/28/7e7cefd0 -d605-427b-b37f-8ec8e266017d_story.html; "Commission of Inquiry-Operations and its Consideration in the UN," US-Korea Institute, Johns Hopkins School of Advanced International Studies, private research note by author; interview with former State Department official, September 12, 2017; Nick Cumming-Bruce and Choe Sang-Hun, "North Korea Faces Pressure from U.N. on Human Rights," *New York Times*, March 10, 2013, https://www.nytimes.com/2013/03/11/world/asia/north-korea-faces -pressure-from-un-on-human-rights.html; and Wikipedia, "Report of the Commission of Inquiry on Human Rights in the Democratic People's Republic of Korea," last modified December 31, 2024, 10:56 (UTC), https://en

.wikipedia.org/wiki/Report_of_the_Commission_of_Inquiry_on_Human
_Rights_in_the_Democratic_People%27s_Republic_of_Korea.

9. Author's notes, "Transcript of US-DPRK Track II Meeting," September
   25–26, 2013, Berlin, Germany.

10. James Clapper, *Facts and Fears: Hard Truths from a Life in Intelligence* (New
    York: Viking, 2018), 33–34, 43–47; and James Clapper, "Ending the Dead
    End in North Korea," *New York Times*, May 20, 2018, https://www.nytimes
    .com/2018/05/19/opinion/sunday/clapper-north-korea.html.

11. Interview with former senior U.S. official, June 14, 2018.

12. Interview with former U.S. official, November 5, 2021.

13. Ben Rhodes, *The World as It Is: A Memoir of the Obama White House* (New
    York: Random House, 2018), 228.

14. Interview with former U.S. intelligence official, October 9, 2017.

15. Clapper, *Facts and Fears*, 270.

16. Interview with former U.S. official, January 7, 2019; Clapper, *Facts and Fears*,
    272; and interview with former U.S. official, May 3, 2020.

17. Interview with former U.S. official, May 3, 2020.

18. Interview with former White House official, May 3, 2020.

19. Clapper, *Facts and Fears*, 276–277.

20. Clapper, *Facts and Fears*, 276–277.

21. Clapper, *Facts and Fears*, 279–281; and interview with former U.S. official,
    November 5, 2021.

22. Barbara Demick, "Why Did North Korea Release Kenneth Bae and Mat-
    thew Todd Miller?," *New Yorker*, https://www.newyorker.com/news/news
    -desk/north-korea-release-kenneth-bae-matthew-todd-miller.

23. Choe Sang-Hun, "North Korea Offers U.S. Deal to Halt Nuclear Test,"
    New York Times, January 10, 2015, https://www.nytimes.com/2015/01/11
    /world/asia/north-korea-offers-us-deal-to-halt-nuclear-test-.html.

24. Author's notes, "Transcripts of US-DPRK Track II Meeting," Ulaanbaatar,
    Mongolia, May 23–25, 2014; and "KCNA Report," Korean Central News
    Agency, January 10, 2015, http://www.kcna.co.jp/item/2015/201501/news10
    /20150110-12ee.html.

25. Interview with former U.S. official, February 22, 2018; Robert Carlin, "The
    Meaning of a Missed Opportunity to Talk," *Global Asia* 1, no. 1 (March 2015),
    https://globalasia.org/v10no1/debate/the-meaning-of-a-missed-oppor
    tunity-to-talk_robert-carlin; Agence France Presse, "US: North Korea's
    Nuclear Offer 'A Threat,'" DW, January 10, 2015, https://www.dw.com/en
    /n-koreas-offer-to-suspend-nuclear-tests-is-a-threat-us/a-18183795; and
    "N. Korea Hints at Halting Nuke Tests for No Seoul-U.S. Drills," *Korea
    Times*, January 11, 2015, https://www.koreatimes.co.kr/www/nation/2024
    /06/103_171467.html.

26. Robert Carlin, "Shall We Dance?," *38 North*, February 13, 2014, https://
    www.38north.org/2014/02/rcarlin021314/.

27. Interview with former senior State Department official, January 29, 2021.

28. Interview with former Obama administration official, March 2015; interview with former State Department official, 2019; and interview with former senior State Department official, January 29, 2021.

29. Author's notes, "Track II Meeting in Singapore," January 18–19, 2015.

30. Author's notes, "Track II Meeting in Singapore," January 18–19, 2015.

31. Jack Kim and Kahyun Kang, "North Korea Says U.S. Rejects Invitation to Pyongyang," Reuters, February 1, 2015, https://www.reuters.com/article /idUSKBN0L515O/; and interview with former State Department official, May 3, 2018.

32. Demick, "Why Did North Korea Release?"; and interview with former State Department official, July 24, 2018.

33. David Sim, "North Korea: Kim Jong-un Opens Atom-Shaped Science and Technology Building," *International Business Times*, December 30, 2015, https://www.ibtimes.co.uk/north-korea-kim-jong-un-opens-atom -shaped-science-technology-building-photos-1526161; and "North Korea Opens Atom-Shaped Science and Technology Centre—In Pictures," *Guardian* (London), October 29, 2015, https://www.theguardian.com /world/gallery/2015/oct/29/north-korea-atom-nuclear-science-centre -pictures.

34. "Ceremony Opens Mirae Scientists Street in Pyongyang," *North Korea Leadership Watch*, https://nkleadershipwatch.wordpress.com/2015/11/04 /ceremony-opens-mirae-scientists-street-in-pyongyang; "Mirae Future Scientist Street—DPRK Guide," North Korea Tours, https://www.young pioneertours.com/mirae-future-scientist-street/; Wikipedia, "Mirae Scientists Street," last modified December 26, 2024, 13:11 (UTC), https://en .wikipedia.org/wiki/Mirae_Scientists_Street; and "Mirae Scientist Street: A Symbol of Self-Reliance and Socialist Prosperity in DPRK," Explore DPRK, https://exploredprk.com/articles/mirae-scientist-street-a-symbol-of-self -reliance-and-socialist-prosperity-in-dprk/.

35. Michael Madden, "Meet Kim Jong Un's New Nuclear Warriors," *Foreign Policy*, September 22, 2014, https://foreignpolicy.com/2014/09/22/meet-kim -jong-uns-new-nuclear-warriors.

36. Michael Madden, "Five Revolutionary Generations" (unpublished paper, January 2020); and Michael Madden, "The Passing of the Nuclear Torch: The Next Generation of WMD Scientists," *38 North*, September 22, 2014, https://www.38north.org/2014/09/mmadden091914/.

37. Ju-min Park and Soyoung Kim, "North Korea's Nuclear Scientists Take Center Stage with H-bomb Test," Reuters, September 4, 2017, https://www .reuters.com/article/idUSKCN1BF1XE/.

38. "North Korea's Kim Jong Un Fetes Nuclear Scientists, Holds Celebration Bash," Reuters, September 9, 2017, https://www.reuters.com/article/id USKCN1BL01H/.

39. "Hong Sung Mu," *North Korea Leadership Watch*, www.nkleadership watch.org/leadership-biographies/hong-sung-mu; and Wikipedia, "Hong

Sung-mu," last modified February 2, 2025, 13:04 (UTC), https://en
.wikipedia.org/wiki/Hong_Sung-mu.

40. David Albright and Robert Avagyan, "Recent Doubling of Floor Space at
North Korean gas Centrifuge Plant: Is North Korea Doubling Its Enrichment Capacity at Yongbyon?," Institute for Science and International Security, August 7, 2013, https://isis-online.org/isis-reports/detail/recent
-doubling-of-floor-space-at-north-korean-gas-centrifuge-plant/10; and
Choe Sang-Hun, "North Korea Learning to Make Crucial Nuclear Parts,
Study Finds," *New York Times*, September 24, 2013, https://www.nytimes
.com/2013/09/24/world/asia/north-korea-learning-to-make-crucial
-nuclear-parts-study-finds.html.

41. Jeffrey Lewis, "Recent Imagery Suggests Increased Uranium Production in
North Korea, Probably for Expanding Nuclear Weapons Stockpile and Reactor Fuel," *38 North*, August 12, 2015, https://www.38north.org/2015/08
/jlewis0812/215/.

42. Jeffrey Lewis, "Can North Korea Build the H-Bomb?," *38 North*, June
11, 2010, https://www.38north.org/2010/06/can-north-korea-build-the
-h-bomb; Jeffrey Lewis, "Did Somebody Say H-bomb?," *38 North*,
December 14, 2015, https://www.38north.org/2015/12/jlewis/21415/; and
"North Korea's H-Bomb Claim Dismissed by US," BBC News, December 10, 2015, https://www.bbc.com/news/world-asia-35066203.

43. David Albright, Sarah Burkhard, Mark Gorwitz, and Allison Lach, "North
Korea's Lithium 6 Production for Nuclear Weapons," Institute for Science
and International Security, March 17, 2017, https://isis-online.org/isis
-reports/detail/north-koreas-lithium-6-production-for-nuclear-weapons
/10.

44. David Albright and Serena Kelleher-Vergantini, "Update on North Korea's
Yongbyon Nuclear Site," Institute for Science and International Security,
September 15, 2015, https://isis-online.org/uploads/isis-reports/documents
/Update_on_North_Koreas_Yongbyon_Nuclear_Site_September15_2015
_Final.pdf.

45. "DPRK 26 August Report: Kim Jong Un Guides Meeting of WPK Cen-
tral Military Commission; No Date Given" [in Korean], Korean Central
Broadcasting Station, August 25, 2013; and Lee Yoon Gul, "North Korean
Nuclear-Missile Development under the Era of KJU and the State of the
Command System" [English translation], Sejong Institute Unification Strat-
egy Laboratory, March 10, 2017, 12.

46. "North Korea's Sohae Satellite Launching Station: Major Upgrade Program
Completed; Facility Operational Again," *38 North*, October 1, 2014, https://
www.38north.org/2014/10/sohae100114.

47. Jeffrey Lewis, "Domestic UDMH Production in the DPRK," *Arms Control
Wonk*, September 27, 2017, https://www.armscontrolwonk.com/archive
/1204170/domestic-udmh-production-in-the-dprk/.

48. Former U.S. government official, conversation with author, October 2018.

49. Simon Shuster, "How North Korea Built a Nuclear Arsenal on the Ashes of the Soviet Union," *Time*, February 1, 2018, 1, https://time.com/5128398/the-missile-factory/.

50. Interview with American scientist, January 16, 2018; William J. Broad and David E. Sanger, "North Korea's Missile Success is Linked to Ukrainian Plant, Investigators Say," *New York Times*, August 14, 2017, https://www.nytimes.com/2017/08/14/world/asia/north-korea-missiles-ukraine-factory.html; and UN Security Council, "Note by the President of the Security Council," S2013/317 (June 11, 2013).

51. Interview with American scientist; Broad and Sanger, "North Korea's Missile Success"; UN Security Council, "Note by the President of the Security Council."

52. Interview with American scientist; Broad and Sanger, "North Korea's Missile Success"; UN Security Council, "Note by the President of the Security Council."

53. Joseph S. Bermudez, Jr., "North Korea's Sold Propellant Rocket Engine Production Infrastructure: The No. 17 Factory in Hamhung," *38 North*, January 30, 2018, https://www.38north.org/2018/01/no17factory180130/.

54. Joby Warrick, "Documents Shed Light on North Korea's Startling Gains in Sea-Based Missile Technology," *Washington Post*, December 27, 2017, https://www.washingtonpost.com/world/national-security/documents-shed-light-on-north-koreas-startling-gains-in-sea-based-missile-technology/2017/12/27/dd82878a-e749-11e7-ab50-621fe0588340_story.html.

55. Joseph S. Bermudez Jr., "North Korea's SINPO-class Sub: New Evidence of Possible Vertical Missile Launch Tubes; Sinpo Shipyard Prepares for Significant Naval Construction Program," *38 North*, January 8, 2015, https://www.38north.org/2015/01/jbermudez0108; Joseph S. Bermudez Jr., "North Korea: Development of Submarine Launched Ballistic Missile Continues," *38 North*, October 14, 2015, https://www.38north.org/2015/10/jbermudez101415/; and Joseph S. Bermudez Jr., "The North Korean Navy Acquires a New Submarine, *38 North*, https://www.38north.org/2014/10/jbermudez101914/.

56. Shane Smith, "North Korea's Evolving Nuclear Strategy," *38 North*, North Korea's Nuclear Future Series, US-Korea Institute at SAIS, August 2015, https://www.38north.org/wp-content/uploads/2015/09/NKNF_Evolving-Nuclear-Strategy_Smith.pdf; and Joseph S. Bermudez Jr., "North Korea's Development of a Nuclear Weapons Strategy," *38 North*, North Korea's Nuclear Future Series, August 2015, https://www.38north.org/wp-content/uploads/2015/08/NKNF_Nuclear-Weapons-Strategy_Bermudez.pdf.

57. Lee, "North Korean Nuclear-Missile Development," 5, 9.

58. David E. Sanger, "U.S. Commander Sees Key Nuclear Step by North Korea," *New York Times*, October 24, 2014, https://www.nytimes.com/2014

/10/25/world/asia/us-commander-sees-key-nuclear-step-by-north-korea .html; and Jeffrey Lewis, "North Korea's Nuclear Weapons: The Great Miniaturization Debate," *38 North*, February 5, 2015, https://www.38north .org/2015/02/jlewis020515/.

59. Interview with former senior U.S. official, January 11, 2019.

60. "Kim Jong Un Watches Strategic Submarine Underwater Ballistic Missile Test-Fire" [in Korean], Korean Central News Agency, May 9, 2015, https:// www.kcna.kp/kp/article/q/56253f84daf42bf3d03911a00c6a9d4c.kcmsf.

61. Interview with former White House official, December 6, 2017; and interview with former U.S. official, March 19, 2018.

62. Keith Bradsher and Nick Cummings-Bruce, "China Cuts Ties with Key North Korean Bank," *New York Times*, May 7, 2013, https://www.nytimes .com/2013/05/08/world/asia/china-cuts-ties-with-north-korean-bank .html; and Park Hyun, "New Unilateral Sanctions Target North Korean Banks," *Hankyoreh*, March 14, 2013.

63. Katie Benner, "North Koreans Accused of Laundering $2.5 Billion for Nuclear Program," *New York Times*, May 28, 2020, https://www.nytimes.com /2020/05/28/us/politics/north-korea-money-laundering-nuclear-weapons .html; Spencer S. Hsu and Ellen Nakashima, "U.S. Brings Massive N. Korean Sanctions Case, Targeting State-Owned Bank and Former Government Officials," *Washington Post*, May 28, 2020, https://www.washingtonpost .com/local/legal-issues/us-brings-largest-ever-n-korean-sanctions-case -targeting-state-owned-bank-and-senior-government-officials/2020/05 /28/3b23f616-a02b-11ea-b5c9-570a91917d8d_story.html; and Malcolm Moore, "China Breaking UN Sanctions to Support North Korea," *Sunday Telegraph* (London), April 13, 2013, https://www.telegraph.co.uk/news /worldnews/asia/northkorea/9991907/China-breaking-UN-sanctions-to -support-North-Korea.html.

64. United States of America v. Ko Chol Man et al., No. 1:20-cr-00032-RC, document 1, U.S. District Court for the District of Columbia, February 5, 2020, https://www.ballardspahr.com/-/media/files/articles/china-korea -indictment.pdf; and interview with former State Department official, September 21, 2018.

65. Interview with former U.S. official, March 19, 2018.

66. Interview with former U.S. official, March 19, 2018.

67. Interview with former White House official, January 17, 2018.

68. Interview with former White House official, January 17, 2018.

69. Hugh Griffiths and Roope Siirtola, "Full Disclosure: Contents of North Korean Smuggling Ship Revealed," *38 North*, August 27, 2013, https://www .38north.org/2013/08/hgriffiths082713; Melissa Hanham, "North Korea's Cuban Missile Crisis," *38 North*, August 1, 2013, https://www.38north.org /2013/08/mhanham080113/; "Treasury Sanctions DPRK Shipping Companies Involved in Illicit Arms Transfers," U.S. Department of the Treasury, July 30, 2014, https://home.treasury.gov/news/press-releases/jl2594#:~:text

=The%20illicit%20cargo%20aboard%20the,1718%20was%20ad-opted%20in%202006; and UN Security Council, "Note by the President of the Security Council," S/2015/131 (February 23, 2015), 53–63.

70. "In China's Shadow: Exposing North Korean Overseas Networks," C4ADS and Asian Institute for Policy Studies, August 2016, https://foreignpolicy .com/wp-content/uploads/2017/06/bdd87-inchina27sshadow.pdf.

71. Ramón Rodriguez Rangel, "To Save 30 Dollars, North Korea Must Pay Mexico Almost 15 Million Dollars" [in Spanish], *El Financiero*, July 8, 2015.

72. Interview with former White House official, January 17, 2018; Axel Plasa, "Mu Du Bong: A Ghost Ship in Veracruz" [in Spanish], *Contralinea*, September 29, 2015, https://contralinea.com.mx/interno/featured/mu-du-bong -barco-fantasma-en-veracruz/; and Claudia Rosett, "North Korean Ship Tests the Waters Near America's Shores, *Forbes*, July 13, 2014, https://www .forbes.com/sites/claudiarosett/2014/07/13/north-korean-ship-tests-the -waters-near-americas-shores/?sh=56e598585c55.

73. Interview with former White House official, January 17, 2018; and Associated Press, "North Korea Blames U.S. for Blocking Release of Ship by Mexico," *New York Times*, April 8, 2015.

74. Interview with former White House official, January 17, 2018.

75. "Sailors from the North Korean Ship Detained in Tuxpan 'Mu Du Bong' Shout, 'No Food!'" [in Spanish], *Transporte.mx*, April 13, 2015; and "Detained North Korean Ship to be Scrapped," *Maritime Executive*, April 15, 2016, https://maritime-executive.com/article/detained-north-korean-ship -to-be-scrapped.

76. Interview with former White House official, January 17, 2018; and UN Security Council, "Note by the President of the Security Council," S/2015 /131 (February 23, 2015), 63/313.

77. Interview with former U.S. law enforcement official, October 17, 2017.

78. Andrea Stricker, *Case Study: United States Busts Likely North Korean Transshipment Scheme*, Institute for Science and International Security Report (May 24, 2013), 2.

79. U.S. Department of State, "Following Up with Taiwan on Trans Merits," SECRET, July 30, 2008, https://wikileaks.org/plusd/cables/08STATE82164 _a.html; U.S. Embassy Singapore, "GOS Releases Precision Lathes to Shipper," SECRET NOFORN, January 31, 2007, http://wikileaks.org/plusd /cables/07/SINGAPORE224_ahtml; "MTAG: Taiwan BOFT on Seized Lathes," SECRET, January 4, 2007, https://wikileaks.org/plusd/cables /07TAIPEI117_a.html; "MTAG: Trans Merits Lathes from Taiwan," SECRET, January 11, 2007, https://wikileaks.org/plusd/cables/07TAIPEI72_a .html; Taiwan American Institute Taiwan, Taipei, "Taiwan Investigation of Export Control Cases," unclassified, September 18, 2008, http://wikileaks .org/plusd/cableso8AITTAIPEI/1374_a.html; U.S. Embassy Singapore, "DPRK Proliferation-Related Transaction in Singapore," SECRET, April 14, 2009, https://wikileaks.org/plusd/cables/09STATE36855_a.html;

and U.S. Department of State, "Proposed North Korean Entities and Individuals for EU Designation," for official use only, November 6, 2009, https://wikileaks.org/plusd/cables/09STATE115240_a.html.

80. "MTAG: Trans Merits Lathes from Taiwan."
81. Taiwan American Institute, "Taiwan Investigation of Export Control Cases."
82. Annie Sweeney, "Glenview Man Charged in North Korean Trading Scheme," *Chicago Tribune*, May 7, 2013.
83. United States of America v. Yueh-hsun Tsai (also known as Gary Tsai), U.S. District Court, Northern District of Illinois, Eastern Division, A0 91, criminal complaint, April 19, 2013, 5, https://www.justice.gov/sites/default/files/usao-ndil/legacy/2015/06/11/pro506_01b.pdf.
84. Interview with former U.S. law enforcement official, October 17, 2017; and "FBI Counterproliferation Center," FBI, https://www.fbi.gov/about/leadership-and-structure/national-security-branch/fbi-counterproliferation-center.
85. United States of America v. Yueh-hsun Tsai (also known as Gary Tsai), 5.
86. Aaron Arnold and Daniel Salisbury, "The Long Arm: How U.S. Law Enforcement Expanded Its Extraterritorial Reach to Counter WMD Proliferation Networks" (discussion paper, Managing the Atom Project, Belfer Center, February 2019), 34–40, https://www.belfercenter.org/publication/long-arm; interview with former law enforcement official, October 17, 2017; and Heather Maher, "How the FBI Helps Terrorists Succeed," *The Atlantic*, February 26, 2013, https://www.theatlantic.com/international/archive/2013/02/how-the-fbi-helps-terrorists-succeed/273537/.
87. Arnold and Salisbury, "The Long Arm," 38–39.
88. FBI, Chicago Division, "Taiwanese Father and Son Arrested for Allegedly Violating U.S. Laws to Prevent Proliferation of Weapons of Mass Destruction," U.S. Attorney's Office, Northern District of Illinois, May 6, 2013; Sweeney, "Glenview Man"; and Stricker, "Case Study."
89. United States of America v. Hsien Tai Tsai, No. U.S. District Court, Northern District of Illinois, Eastern Division, plea agreement, October 10, 2014, https://www.justice.gov/sites/default/files/usao-ndil/legacy/2015/06/11/pr1010_01a.pdf; and Jason Meisner, "Banned Businessman Gets 2-year Prison Term for Shipping Machinery Overseas," *Chicago Tribune*, March 16, 2015, https://www.chicagotribune.com/2015/03/16/banned-businessman-gets-2-year-prison-term-for-shipping-machinery-overseas/.
90. United States of America v. Yueh-Hsun Tsai (also known as Gary), No. 1:12-cr-00829, document #89, U.S. District Court, Northern District of Illinois, Eastern Division, "Defendant Gary Tsai's Position Paper on Sentencing," April 18, 2015; and United States of America v. Yueh-Hsun-Tsai (also known as Gary Tsai), No. 1:12-cr-00829, U.S. District Court, Northern District of Illinois, Eastern Division, plea agreement, December 16, 2014.
91. U.S. Attorney's Office, District of Columbia, "United States Wins Civil Forfeiture Suit against Taiwanese National Accused of Laundering Funds

through the United States to Assist Syrian and North Korea Regimes with Procuring Goods," April 3, 2019, https://www.justice.gov/usao-dc/pr/united -states-wins-civil-forfeiture-suit-against-taiwanese-national-accused -laundering.

92. Interview with former law enforcement official, October 17, 2017; and U.S. Attorney's Office, Northern District of Illinois, "Taiwan Businessman Sentenced to 24 Months for Conspiring to Violate U.S. Laws Preventing Proliferation of Weapons of Mass Destruction," March 16, 2015, https://www .justice.gov/usao-ndil/pr/taiwan-businessman-sentenced-24-months -conspiring-violate-us-laws-preventing.

93. Interview with former law enforcement official, October 17, 2017; interview with former White House official, January 30, 2018; and interview with former State Department official, July 10, 2018.

94. Interview with former U.S. official, March 30, 2018.

95. Interview with former U.S. official, March 30, 2018.

96. Interview with former U.S. official, March 30, 2018.

97. Interview with former U.S. official, March 30, 2018; and interview with former White House aide, April 23, 2018.

98. Interview with former senior U.S. officer, February 27, 2018; and interview with former senior U.S. official, October 3, 2018.

99. Interview with former senior U.S. official, October 3, 2018.

100. Interview with former Department of Defense official, February 28, 2018.

101. William Rosenau, "Special Operations Forces and Elusive Enemy Ground Targets," *RAND Monograph Report* (2001): 29–43, https://www.rand.org /pubs/monograph_reports/MR1408.html; Sebastian Robbin, "What the Great SCUD Hunt Tells about a War with North Korea," *The Buzz* (blog), *The National Interest*, October 6, 2017, https://nationalinterest.org/blog/the -buzz/what-the-great-scud-hunt-tells-about-war-north-korea-22637; and Austin Long and Brenden Rittenhouse Green, "Stalking the Secure Second Strike: Intelligence, Counterforce, and Nuclear Strategy," *Journal of Strategic Studies* 38, nos. 1–2 (2015): 38–73, http://dx.doi.org/10.1080 /01402390.2014.958150.

102. John Keller, "DARPA Seeks to Attack Enemy Relocatable Targets with Air Defense-Penetrating Smart Munitions," *Military + Aerospace Electronics*, January 26, 2018, https://www.militaryaerospace.com/uncrewed/article /16726519/darpa-seeks-to-attack-enemy-relocatable-targets-with-air -defense-penetrating-smart-munitions; and R. Jeffrey Smith, "Hypersonic Missiles Are Unstoppable. And They're Starting a New Global Arms Race," *New York Times Magazine*, June 19, 2019, https://www.nytimes.com/2019 /06/19/magazine/hypersonic-missiles.html.

103. *Hearings before the Committee on Armed Services, United States Senate on S. 2943, Part 7. Strategic Forces*, 114th Cong., 2nd sess., statement by Admiral William E. Gortney, commander, U.S. Northern Command and commander, North American Aerospace Defense Council (February 9, 23;

April 13, 2016), 147, 151; Department of Defense and Joint Chiefs of Staff, "Declaratory Policy, Concept of Operations, and Employment Guidelines for Left-of-Launch Capability," unclassified, Report to Congress, May 10, 2017; and "Left of Launch," Missile Defense Advocacy Alliance, March 16, 2015, https://missiledefenseadvocacy.org/alert/3132/.

104. Interview with senior former U.S. officer, February 27, 2018; and interview with former senior U.S. official, October 3, 2018.

105. Interview with former Department of Defense official, February 28, 2018; interview with former senior US official, October 3, 2018; U.S. Department of Defense, Performance Improvement Officer and Director of Administration and Management, "Deputy's Management Action Group (DMAG)," https://dam.defense.gov/Resources/Deputys-Management-Action-Group/; and Wikipedia, "Deputy's Advisory Working Group," last modified March 15, 2020, 20:51 (UTC), https://en.wikipedia.org/wiki/Deputy%27s_Advisory_Working_Group.

106. David E. Sanger and William J. Broad, "Trump Inherits Secret Cyberwar Against North Korean Missiles," *New York Times*, March 4, 2017, https://www.nytimes.com/2017/03/04/world/asia/north-korea-missile-program-sabotage.html; interview with former senior US official, October 3, 2018; and interview with former U.S. official, March 30, 2018.

107. Long and Green, "Stalking the Secure Second Strike."

108. Interview with former Department of Defense official, February 28, 2018.

109. Joint Chiefs of Staff, "Joint Integrated Air and Missile Defense: Vision 2020," December 5, 2013.

110. Interview with former senior U.S. official, October 3, 2018; and interview with former Department of Defense official, February 28, 2018.

111. Interview with former senior U.S. official, October 3, 2018; interview with former senior White House official, April 23, 2018; and interview with former U.S. official, March 30, 2018.

112. Interview with former senior White House official, April 23, 2018.

113. Interview with former White House official, November 14, 2017.

114. Interview with former senior U.S. official, October 3, 2018; and Bob Woodward, *Fear: Trump in the White House* (New York: Simon and Schuster, 2019), 92–93.

115. Interview with former senior White House official, April 23, 2018.

116. Interview with former U.S. official, March 30, 2018; and interview with former senior White House official, April 23, 2018.

Chapter Eleven. "The five stages of grief"

1. Michael Lester, "The Face of North Korean Television," *New York Times*, January 6, 2016, https://www.nytimes.com/video/world/100000004128692/the-face-of-north-korean-television.html.

2. Interview with former U.S. official, March 9, 2021.

3. Seong-ho Sheen, "Dilemma of South Korea's Trust Diplomacy and Unification Policy," *International Journal of Korean Unification Studies*, December 31, 2014, https://repo.kinu.or.kr/bitstream/2015.oak/8906/5/0001477 385.pdf.

4. Interview with former senior U.S. official, January 4, 2019.

5. Kim Kwang-tae, "Park: N. Korea's Nuclear Program to Hasten Its Collapse," Yonhap News Agency, April 3, 2016, https://en.yna.co.kr/view ?AEN20160403001800315.

6. Interview with former U.S. official, November 14, 2017.

7. Interview with former senior U.S. official, February 2, 2018.

8. Anna Fifield, "North Korea Launches 'Satellite,' Sparks Fears about Long-Range Missile Program," *Washington Post*, February 6, 2016, https://www .washingtonpost.com/world/north-korea-launches-satellite-sparks-fears -about-long-range-missile-program/2016/02/06/0b6084e5-afd1-42ec -8170-280883f23240_story.html.

9. Mark E. Manyin, Kurt Smith, and Mary Beth Nikitin, "North Korea: A Chronology of Events from 2016–2020," Congressional Research Service, May 5, 2020, https://www.everycrsreport/files/20200505_R46349_6307d9 4932ea867fid6c287e740681164c6f83bd3.pdf.

10. Robert Carlin, "Some Rabbit, Some Hat!," *38 North*, May 31, 2016, https:// www.38north.org/2016/05/rcarlin053116/.

11. Derek Hawkins, "Count on North Korea's 'Pink Lady' Broadcaster for Joyful News of Bombs and Missiles," *Washington Post*, September 5, 2017, https://www.washingtonpost.com/news/morning-mix/wp/2017/09/05 /north-koreas-pink-lady-broadcaster-once-again-serves-up-earth-shaking -news-with-a-smile/; and Choe Sang-Hun, "South Korea's President Warns of More Provocations from North," *New York Times*, September 12, 2014, https://www.nytimes.com/2016/09/13/world/asia/south-korea-north -nuclear-threat.html.

12. Interview with former U.S. official, January 24, 2018.

13. Author's Notes, "Transcript of US-DPRK Track II Meeting, February 1–3, 2016, Berlin, Germany.

14. Author's notes, "Transcript of US-DPRK Track II Meeting."

15. Author's notes, "Transcript of US-DPRK Track II Meeting."

16. Author's notes, "Transcript of US-DPRK Track II Meeting."

17. Author's notes, "Transcript of US-DPRK Track II Meeting."

18. Author's notes, "Transcript of US-DPRK Track II Meeting."

19. Author's notes, "Transcript of US-DPRK Track II Meeting."

20. Author's notes, "Transcript of US-DPRK Track II Meeting."

21. Author's notes, "Transcript of US-DPRK Track II Meeting."

22. Author's notes, "That Cassandra Feeling Again," NSC meeting, February 2016.

23. Author's notes, "That Cassandra Feeling Again."

24. Author's notes, "That Cassandra Feeling Again."

25. Author's notes, "That Cassandra Feeling Again."
26. Author's notes, "That Cassandra Feeling Again."
27. Author's notes, "That Cassandra Feeling Again."
28. Author's notes, "That Cassandra Feeling Again."
29. Author's notes, "That Cassandra Feeling Again."
30. Interview with U.S. delegation member, April 28, 2021.
31. Interview with U.S. delegation member, April 28, 2021.
32. Interview with former senior U.S. official, February 2, 2018.
33. Interview with U.S. delegation member, April 28, 2021.
34. Interview with former U.S. official, May 31, 2018.
35. Interview with former U.S. official, July 19, 2018.
36. Interview with former U.S. official, November 14, 2017.
37. Interview with former senior U.S. official, February 2, 2018.
38. Interview with former U.S. official, May 3, 2021.
39. Interview with former U.S. official, July 18, 2019.
40. Interview with former U.S. official, July 18, 2019.
41. Interview with former U.S. official, July 18, 2019.
42. Interview with former U.S. official, May 31, 2018.
43. Interview with former U.S. official, July 27, 2018.
44. Interview with former U.S. official, January 24, 2018; and interview with former senior U.S. official, February 2, 2018.
45. Interview with former senior U.S. official, February 2, 2018.
46. Avril Haines, "The Path Forward for Dealing with North Korea: Keynote Presentation," Brookings Institution, October 12, 2017, https://www.youtube.com/watch?v=9K2uqPNAzAo&ab_channel=Brookings institution.
47. Haines, "The Path Forward."
48. Interview with former U.S. official, November 14, 2017.
49. Interview with former U.S. official, November 14, 2017.
50. Interview with former senior U.S. official, February 2, 2018.
51. Interview with former senior U.S. official, July 27, 2018.
52. Haines, "The Path Forward."
53. Interview with former U.S. official, July 18, 2019.
54. Interview with former U.S. official, July 18, 2019.
55. Haines, "The Path Forward."
56. Interview with former senior U.S. official, February 2, 2018.
57. Interviews with former U.S. official, January 24, 2018, and February 7, 2018.
58. Interview with former senior U.S. official, February 2, 2018.
59. Interview with former senior U.S. official, February 2, 2018.
60. Interview with former senior U.S. official; and AFP, "US Sanctions Chinese Company for Alleged Support of North Korea," *Guardian* (London), September 26, 2016, https://www.theguardian.com/us-news/2016/sep/26/us-sanctions-china-north-korea-dandong-hongxiang.
61. Interview with former U.S. official, January 24, 2018.

62. Dan De Luce, "Hagel: The White House Tried to 'Destroy' Me," *Foreign Policy*, December 18, 2015, https://foreignpolicy.com/2015/12/18/hagel-the-white-house-tried-to-destroy-me/; and interview with former senior U.S. official, February 2, 2020.

63. Interview with senior former U.S. official, June 20, 2018.

64. David Ignatius, "In Kissinger's Footsteps, Susan Rice Steers Smooth U.S.-China relations," *Washington Post*, September 1, 2016, https://www.washingtonpost.com/opinions/susan-rice-embraces-kissingers-approach-to-china/2016/09/01/7d440a5c-706b-11e6-9705-23e51a2f424d_story.html.

65. Antony Blinken, "Will Rex Tillerson Pass North Korea's Nuclear Test?," *New York Times*, March 15, 2017, https://www.nytimes.com/2017/03/15/opinion/will-rex-tillerson-pass-north-koreas-nuclear-test.html.

66. Interview with former U.S. official, January 16, 2023; and interview with former senior U.S. official, June 14, 2018.

67. Interview with former U.S. official, November 14, 2017.

68. Interview with former White House official, October 30, 2017.

69. Interview with former White House official, October 30, 2017.

70. Interview with former White House official, October 30, 2017.

71. Interview with former White House official, October 30, 2017.

72. Interview with former White House official, October 30, 2017.

73. Interview with former U.S. official, January 11, 2019.

74. Interview with former U.S. official, January 30, 2018.

75. Interview with former ROK official, February 21, 2019.

76. Interview with former U.S. official, October 27, 2017.

77. Leonardo Borlini, "The North Korea's Gauntlet, International Law and the New Sanctions Imposed by the Security Council," *Italian Yearbook of International Law* 26, no. 1 (2017): 319–345, http://dx.doi.org/10.1163/22116133-90000168a.

78. Interview with former U.S. official, June 14, 2018.

79. Interview with former U.S. official, January 30, 2018.

80. Declan Walsh, "Need a North Korean Missile? Call the Cairo Embassy," *New York Times*, March 3, 2018, https://www.nytimes.com/2018/03/03/world/middleeast/egypt-north-korea-sanctions-arms-dealing.html.

81. Interview with former U.S. official, January 11, 2019.

82. Chang Jae-soon, "US Imposes First Ever Sanctions on Chinese Firm for Assisting N. Korea with WMD Programs," Yonhap News Agency, September 27, 2016, https://en.yna.co.kr/view/AEN20160927000353315.

83. Interview with former U.S. official, July 18, 2019.

84. Interview with former U.S. official, July 18, 2019.

85. Interview with former U.S. official, July 18, 2019.

86. Haines, "The Path Forward."

87. Interview with former U.S. official, January 29, 2021.

88. Interview with former U.S. official, January 16, 2023.

89. Interview with former U.S. official, June 14, 2018.
90. Interview with former U.S. official, June 14, 2018.
91. Interview with former U.S. official, October 30, 2017.
92. Interview with former U.S. official, October 30, 2017.
93. Hans M. Kristensen and Robert S. Norris, "A History of U.S. Nuclear Weapons in South Korea," *Bulletin of the Atomic Scientists* 73, no. 6 (2017): 349, https://www.tandfonline.com/doi/pdf/10.1080/00963402.2017.1388656?.
94. Peter Hayes, *Pacific Powderkeg: American Nuclear Dilemmas in Korea* (Lanham, MD: Lexington Books, 1991), 162–163, https//nautilus.org/wp-content /uploads/2011/04/PacificPowderkegbyPeterHayes.pdf.
95. Author's email exchange with North Korea expert, January 2018.
96. Taewoo Kim, "Combatting North Korea's Nuclear Blackmail: Proactive Deterrence and the Triad System," in *Nuclear Security 2012: Challenges of Proliferation and Implications for the Korean Peninsula*, ed. Jung-Ho Bae and Jae H. Ku (Seoul: Korea Institute for National Reunification, 2010), 95–122, https://repo.kinu.or.kr/bitstream/2015.oak/1598/1/0001423021.pdf.
97. Interview with former Department of Defense official, February 26, 2021.
98. Interview with former Department of Defense official, March 29, 2019.
99. Interview with former Department of Defense official, February 26, 2021.
100. Interview with former Department of Defense official, February 26, 2021.
101. Interview with former Department of Defense official, February 26, 2021.
102. Interview with former Department of Defense official, April 16, 2019.
103. Jung Ho-sun, "Korean Peninsula's Military Balance 'Shaky' . . . Review of Strategy" [in Korean], SBS News, February 13, 2013, https://news.sbs.co .kr/news/endPage.do?news_id=N1001630741.
104. Interview with former ROK official, February 19, 2019.
105. Interview with former ROK official, February 19, 2019.
106. Kang Dong-won, "Hong Joon-pyo: 'Moon's Policy Is "Candle in a Storm," National Security'" [in Korean], TV Chosun, January 22, 2018, https://news .tychosun.com/mobile/svc/article.amp.html?contid=2018012290134; and Kwon Ran, "Nuclear for Nuclear vs. 'Childish Argument' . . . Parties Fire Shots on Redeployment of Tactical Nuclear Weapons" [in Korean], SBS News, September 5, 2017, https://news.sbs.co.kr/news/endPagae.do?news _id=N1004380020.
107. Interview with former U.S. official, March 15, 2021.
108. Interview with former U.S. official, March 19, 2019.
109. Interview with former Department of Defense official, February 26, 2021.
110. Interview with former Department of Defense official, March 18, 2021.
111. Interview with former Department of Defense official, March 29, 2021.
112. Interview with former U.S. official, March 9, 2021.
113. Interview with former Department of Defense official, March 29, 2019.
114. Interview with former U.S. official, November 14, 2017.
115. Interview with former Department of Defense official, April 16, 2019.
116. Interview with former U.S. official, March 3, 2019.

117. U.S. Department of State, "Joint Statement of the 2016 United States-Republic of Korea Foreign and Defense Ministers Meeting," October 19, 2016, https://2009-2017.state.gov/r/pa/prs/ps/2016/10/263340.htm.

118. Chang Jae-soon and Choi Kyong-ae, "S. Korea, U.S., to Consider Deploying U.S. Strategic Assets to Deter N. Korea," Yonhap News Agency, October 21, 2016, https://en.yna.co.kr/view/AFN20161020011851315.

119. U.S. Department of Defense, "Joint Statement for the Inaugural Meeting of the Extended Deterrence Strategy and Consultation Group," December 20, 2016, http://dod.defense.gov/Portals/1/Documents/pubs/Joint-Statement-for-the-Inaugural-Meeting-of-the-Extended-DEterrence-Strategy-and-Consultation-Group-pdf.

120. U.S. Department of Defense, "Joint Statement for the Inaugural Meeting."

Chapter Twelve. "Everyone was trying to piss on the table."

1. K. T. McFarland, *Revolution: Trump, Washington and "We the People"* (New York: Post Hill Press, 2020), 215.

2. McFarland, *Revolution*, 4–5.

3. McFarland, *Revolution*, 164.

4. McFarland, *Revolution*, 214; and Maggie Haberman and David E. Sanger, "'It Won't Happen,' Donald Trump Says of North Korean Missile Test," *New York Times*, January 2, 2017, https://www.nytimes.com/2017/01/02/world/asia/trump-twitter-north-korea-missiles-china.html.

5. Jung Min-kyung, "Allison Hooker: Low-Key Figure Who Could Pave the Way for US-NK Talks," *Korea Herald*, February 24, 2018, https://www.koreaherald.com/view.php?ud=20180224000088; and "Obama Holdovers Still in Dozens of Key National Security Council Jobs," *Daily Caller*, August 14, 2017, https://dailycaller.com/2017/08/14/exclusive-obama-holdovers-still-in-dozens-of-key-national-security-council-jobs/?utm_campaign=atdailycaller&utm_source=Twitter&utm_medium=Social.

6. McFarland, *Revolution*, 215; and interview with former White House official, May 3, 2020.

7. McFarland, *Revolution*, 215–216; and interview with former White House official, May 3, 2020.

8. Former Obama administration official, telephone conversation with the author, January 25, 2024.

9. Interview with former White House official, May 3, 2020; and interview with former senior White House official, June 1, 2022.

10. Interview with former senior White House official, November 9, 2022.

11. Dexter Filkins, "Rex Tillerson at the Breaking Point," *New Yorker*, October 6, 2017, 13, https://www.newyorker.com/magazine/2017/10/16/rex-tillerson-at-the-breaking-point.

12. Interview with former senior White House official, November 9, 2022.

13. Interview with former senior White House official, November 9, 2022; interview with former senior State Department official, September 26, 2018; interview with State Department official, May 24, 2020; and Nahal Toosi, "Leaked Document Shows Tillerson Power Play," *Politico*, October 26, 2017, https://www.politico.com/story/2017/10/26/tillerson-diplomats-policy-state-department-244190/.

14. Interview with former White House official, May 3, 2020.

15. "Seal Team That Took Out Osama bin Laden Joins Drills in Korea," *Korea JoongAng Daily*, March 3, 2017, https://koreajoongangdaily.joins.com/2017/03/13/politics/SEAL-team-that-took-out-Osama-bin-Laden-joins-drills-in-Korea/3030894.html; and Franz-Stefan Gady, "Deterring Pyongyang: US, South Korea Conclude Military Exercise," *The Diplomat*, March 28, 2017, https://thediplomat.com/2017/03/deterring-pyongyang-us-south-korea-conclude-military-exercise/.

16. "Kim Jong Un Observes and Guides SOF Contest," *North Korea Leadership Watch*, April 13, 2017, https://www.nkleadershipwatch.org/2017/04/13/kim-jong-un-observes-and-guides-sof-contest.

17. James Griffiths, "Satellite Photos Show North Korean Nuclear Site 'Primed and Ready,'" CNN, April 13, 2017, https://www.cnn.com/2017/04/13/asia/north-korea-nuclear-site-punggye-ri/; and Joseph S. Bermudez Jr., "The Games People Play: Has the Punggye-ri Nuclear Test Site Transitioned to Stand-by Status?," *38 North*, April 19, 2017, https://www.38north.org/2017/04/punggye041917.

18. Ankit Panda, "North Korea's 2017 Military Parade Was a Big Deal. Here Are the Major Takeaways," *The Diplomat*, April 15, 2017, https://thediplomat.com/2017/04/north-koreas-2017-military-parade-was-a-big-deal-here-are-the-major-takeaways/; and "Rare Live Report from North Korea Military Parade," BBC News, April 15, 2017, https://www.bbc.com/news/av/world-asia-39607343.

19. H. R. McMaster, *At War with Ourselves: My Tour of Duty in the Trump White House* (HarperCollins, 2024), chap. 4, Kindle; interview with former senior White House official, June 1, 2022; interview with former White House official, May 3, 2020; and interview with former senior State Department official, September 26, 2018.

20. Kevin Bohn, "McMaster: All Options Are on the Table in regard to North Korea," CNN, April 16, 2017, www.cnn.com/2017/04/16/politics/hr-mcmaster-north-korea/index.html; and Jeremy Diamond and Kevin Liptak, "Trump, Xi 'Candid,' 'Positive' Talks in Florida," CNN, https://www.cnn.com/2017/04/07/politics/trump-xi-candid-talks/index.html.

21. Charles Krauthammer, "Trump and the 'Madman Theory,'" *Washington Post*, February 23, 2017, https://www.washingtonpost.com/opinions/trump-and-the-madman-theory/2017/02/23/d4f10f30-f9f4-11e6-be05-1a3817ac21a5_story.html.

22. Interview with senior State Department official, January 5, 2022.

23. McMaster, *At War with Ourselves*, chap. 4.

24. Krauthammer, "Trump and the 'Madman Theory'"; James D. Boys, "The Unpredictability Factor: Nixon, Trump and the Application of the Madman Theory in US Grand Strategy," *Cambridge Review of International Affairs* 34, no. 3 (December 4, 2020): 430–451, https://doi.org/10.1080/09557571.2020.1847042; Jeremy Diamond and Zachery Cohen, "Trump: I'd Be 'Honored' to Meet Kim Jong Un under the 'Right Circumstances,'" CNN, May 2, 2017, https://www.cnn.com/2017/05/01/politics/donald-trump-meet-north-korea-kim-jong-un/index.html; James Hohmann, "The Daily 202: Donald Trump Embraces the Risky 'Madman Theory' on Foreign Policy," *Washington Post*, December 20, 2016, https://www.washingtonpost.com/news/powerpost/paloma/daily-202/2016/12/20/daily-202-donald-trump-embraces-the-risky-madman-theory-on-foreign-policy/58583391e9b69b36fcfeaf47/; and James Hohmann, "The Daily 202: Trump Suggests His Embrace of the 'Madman Theory' Brought North Korea to the Table," *Washington Post*, February 26, 2018.

25. Hohmann, "The Daily 202: Donald Trump Embraces."

26. Martin Pengelly, "Kid Rock Says Donald Trump Sought His Advice on North Korea and Islamic State," *Guardian* (London), March 22, 2022, https://www.theguardian.com/music/2022/mar/22/kid-rock-donald-trump-north-korea-islamic-state; and interview with former White House aide, May 3, 2020.

27. Choe Sang-Hun, "North Korea Test Appears to Tiptoe over a U.S. Tripwire," *New York Times*, May 15, 2017, https://www.nytimes.com/2017/05/15/world/asia/north-korea-missiles.html.

28. Interview with former senior State Department official, September 26, 2018.

29. Interview with former Obama administration official, September 2, 2021.

30. Interview with former senior State Department official, September 26, 2018.

31. Interview with former senior State Department official, September 26, 2018; and interview with former Obama administration official, September 2, 2021.

32. Interview with former senior State Department official, September 26, 2018.

33. Interview with former senior State Department official, September 26, 2018.

34. Baik Sung-won, "US Humanitarian Aid Goes to North Korea Despite Nuclear Tensions," Voice of America, January 25, 2017, https://www.voanews.com/a/united-states-humanitarian-aid-goes-to-north-korea/3692811.html.

35. Interview with former senior State Department official, September 26, 2018.

36. Nash Jenkins, "How Otto Warmbier Made It out of North Korea," *Time*, June 14, 2017, https://time.com/4817541/otto-warmbier-north-korea-us/.

37. Interview with former State Department official, November 28, 2018; Jay Solomon, "Top North Korean Nuclear Negotiator Secretly Met with U.S. Diplomats," *Wall Street Journal*, June 18, 2017, https://www.wsj.com/articles/top-north-korean-nuclear-negotiator-secretly-met-with-u-s-diplomats-1497783603; and interview with North Korea expert, April 28, 2021.

38. Interview with North Korea expert, April 28, 2021.
39. Interview with North Korea expert, April 28, 2021.
40. Interview with North Korea expert, April 28, 2021.
41. Interview with North Korea expert, April 28, 2021.
42. Interview with North Korea expert, April 28, 2021.
43. Interview with North Korea expert, April 28, 2021.
44. Richard C. Paddock and Choe Sang-Hun, "Kim Jong-nam Was Killed by VX Nerve Agent, Malaysians Say," *New York Times*, February 23, 2017, https://www.nytimes.com/2017/02/23/world/asia/kim-jong-nam-vx-nerve-agent-.html; and Doug Bock Clark, "The Untold Story of Kim Jong-nam's Assassination," *GQ*, September 25, 2017, https://www.gq.com/story/kim-jong-nam-accidental-assassination.
45. Anna Fifield, "North Korean Officials Are Preparing to Come to U.S. for Talks with Former Officials," *Washington Post*, February 19, 2017, https://www.washingtonpost.com/world/asia_pacific/north-korean-officials-are-preparing-to-come-to-us-for-talks-with-former-officials/2017/02/19/3f853c04-f6a8-11e6-9b3e-ed886f4f4825_story.html; Anna Fifield, "North Korea-U.S. Talks Called Off after Death of Kim Jong Un's Half Brother," *Washington Post*, February 25, 2017, https://www.washingtonpost.com/world/north-korea-us-talks-called-off-after-death-of-kim-jong-uns-half-brother/2017/02/25/68377910-c5b1-43e0-8391-79e81b54eacc_story.html; Jane Perlez, "Trump Administration Cancels Back-Channel Talks with North Korea," *New York Times*, February 25, 2017, https://www.nytimes.com/2017/02/25/world/asia/white-house-north-korea-talks.html; interview with former senior State Department official, September 26, 2018; interview with White House official, May 3, 2020; and interview with former senior White House official, November 9, 2022.
46. Interview with former senior State Department official, February 1, 2019; and Jared Kushner, *Breaking History: A White House Memoir* (New York: Broadside Books, 2022), chap. 10, Kindle.
47. Interview with former senior State Department official, September 26, 2018; and interview with former White House official, May 3, 2020.
48. Interview with participant in talks, April 23, 2021.
49. Interview with former senior State Department official, September 26, 2018; and Doug Bock Clark, "The Untold Story of Otto Warmbier, American Hostage," *GQ*, July 23, 2018, https://www.gq.com/story/otto-warmbier-north-korea-american-hostage-true-story.
50. Reuters, "Senior North Korean Diplomat Says Country Is Open to Dialogue with U.S. under Right 'Conditions,'" *Japan Times*, May 13, 2017, https://www.japantimes.co.jp/news/2017/05/13/asia-pacific/senior-north-korean-diplomat-says-country-open-dialogue-u-s-right-conditions/.
51. Clark, "The Untold Story."
52. Clark, "The Untold Story."

53. Clark, "The Untold Story"; and interview with former Trump administration official, September 2, 2021.

54. Clark, "The Untold Story."

55. Clark, "The Untold Story."

56. Clark, "The Untold Story."

57. Clark, "The Untold Story."

58. Jonathan Kaiman, "Otto Warmbier Dies; American Was Released in a Coma by North Korea," *Los Angeles Times*, June 19, 2017, https://www.latimes.com/world/la-fg-otto-warmbier-dies-north-korea-20170619-story.html; Agence France-Presse, "Otto Warmbier Funeral: Thousands Gather to Mourn Loss," *Guardian* (London), June 22, 2017, https://www.theguardian.com/us-news/2017/jun/22/otto-warmbier-funeral-us-north-korea; and Amy Held, "Mourners Remember Otto Warmbier at Hometown Funeral," NPR, June 22, 2017, https://www.npr.org/sections/thetwo-way/2017/06/22/533987796/mourners-remember-otto-warmbier-at-hometown-funeral.

59. Alan Lockie, "Trump Responds to 'Tragic' Death of Otto Warmbier, Saying North Korea Is a 'Brutal Regime' and 'We'll Be Able to Handle It,'" *Business Insider*, June 19, 2017, https://businessinsider.com/trump-statement-otto-warmbier-2017-6; interview with former White House official, May 3, 2020; and "Trump: Warmbier Should Have Been Brought Home a Long Time Ago," CNN, June 20, 2017, https://www.cnn.com/2017/06/20/politics/trump-otto-warmbier-north-korea/index.html.

60. Clark, "The Untold Story"; "State of the Union 2018: Read the full transcript," CNN, January 31, 2018, https://www.cnn.com/2018/01/30/politics/2018-state-of-the-union-transcript/index.html; "Trump's Speech to South Korea's National Assembly," CNN, November 7, 2017, https://www.cnn.com/2017/11/07/politics/south-korea-trump-speech-full/index.html; and Dartunorro Clark, "Trump Credits Otto Warmbier for North Korea Summit: 'Otto did not die in vain,'" NBC News, https://www.nbcnews.com/politics/white-house/trump-credits-otto-warmbier-north-korea-summit-otto-did-not-n882276.

61. Interview with former senior State Department official, September 26, 2018.

62. Kushner, *Breaking History*, chap. 10.

63. Kushner, *Breaking History*, chap. 10; and interview with senior State Department official, April 27, 2018.

64. Interview with former senior State Department official, September 26, 2018.

65. David E. Sanger, "U.S. in Direct Communication with North Korea, Says Tillerson," *New York Times*, September 30, 2017, https://www.nytimes.com/2017/09/30/world/asia/us-north-korea-tillerson.html; and Emily Tillet, "Trump Says Tillerson 'Is Wasting His Time Trying to Negotiate with Little Rocket Man,'" CBS News, October 1, 2017, https://www.cbsnews.com/news/trump-tweets-rex-tillerson-is-wasting-his-time-on-negotiating-with-n-korea/.

66. Interview with senior State Department official, September 26, 2018.

67. "Chinese President Xi Jinping Arrives in West Palm Beach," CNBC, April 6, 2017, https://www.cnbc.com/video/2017/04/06/chinese-president-xi-jinping-arrives-in-west-palm-beach.html.

68. "Trump Arrives in Florida for Summit with Chinese President," *Palm Beach Post*, April 6, 2017, https://www.youtube.com/watch?v=5iIm1uwUBaM.

69. McFarland, *Revolution*, 175; Sam Dangremond and Leena Kim, "A History of Mar-a-Lago, Donald Trump's American Castle," *Town and Country*, December 22, 2017, https://www.townandcountrymag.com/style/home-decor/a7144/mar-a-lago-history/; Wikipedia, "Mar-a-Lago," last modified February 15, 2025, 17:03 (UTC), https://en.wikipedia.org/wiki/Mar-a-Lago; "Mar-a-Lago," US-Korea Institute, private research note by author; and Steve Holland, "For Trump, Mar-a-Lago Is Place to Break the Ice with Xi," Reuters, April 5, 2017, https://www.reuters.com/article/idUSKBN1772N5/.

70. Josh Rogin, *Chaos Under Heaven: America, China and the Battle for the 21st Century* (New York: Mariner Books, 2021), xxv; and Adam Entous and Evan Osnos, "Jared Kushner Is China's Trump Card," *New Yorker*, January 19, 2019, 2, https://www.newyorker.com/magazine/2018/01/29/jared-kushner-is-chinas-trump-card.

71. Rogin, *Chaos Under Heaven*, 8–11.

72. Wikipedia, "19th National Congress of the Chinese Communist Party," last modified February 5, 2025, 21:47 (UTC), https://en.wikipedia.org/wiki/19th_National_Congress_of_the_Chinese_Communist_Party.

73. Interview with Chinese expert, March 25, 2022.

74. Katie Hunt, "Ivanka: Trump's Secret Weapon with China?," CNN, April 7, 2017, https://www.cnn.com/2017/04/06/politics/china-ivanka-trump/index.html; Betsy Klein, "First Granddaughter Sings Chinese New Year Song in Mandarin," CNN, February 2, 2017, https://www.cnn.com/2017/02/02/politics/ivanka-trump-daughter-mandarin/index.html; Rogin, *Chaos Under Heaven*, 41–44; Kushner, *Breaking History*, chap. 10; and Shannon Tiezzi, "High-Ranking Chinese Envoy Visits Trump's Washington: What's on the Agenda?," *The Diplomat*, February 28, 2017, https://thediplomat.com/2017/02/high-ranking-chinese-envoy-visits-trumps-washington-whats-on-the-agenda/.

75. Dagyum Ji, "U.S. Can 'Compel' China to Comply with Sanctions on N. Korea: Tillerson," *NK News*, January 12, 2017, https://www.nknews.org/2017/01/u-s-can-compel-china-to-comply-with-sanctions-on-n-korea-tillerson/; and Ronan Farrow, *War on Peace: The End of Diplomacy and the Decline of American Influence* (New York: W. W. Norton, 2018), 289.

76. Matthew Weaver, Benjamin Haas, and Justin McCurry, "Trump Says US Will Act Alone on North Korea if China Fails to Help," *Guardian* (London), April 3, 2017, https://www.theguardian.com/us-news/2017/apr/02/donald-trump-north-korea-china; and Mark Landler and Michael D. Shear,

"Trump Administration to Take a Harder Tack on Trade with China," *New York Times*, April 6, 2017, https://www.nytimes.com/2017/04/06/us/politics/trump-xi-jinping-china-summit-mar-a-lago.html.

77. Entous and Osnos, "Jared Kushner Is China's Trump Card"; and interview with former senior State Department official, April 27, 2021.

78. Entous and Osnos, "Jared Kushner Is China's Trump Card"; and interview with former senior State Department official, April 27, 2021.

79. Sidney Leng, "Trump's Granddaughter Diplomacy? Arabella, 5, Sings and Recites Chinese Poetry for Xi Jinping and Wife," *South China Morning Post*, April 8, 2017, https://www.scmp.com/news/china/diplomacy/article/2086029/trumps-granddaughter-diplomacy-arabella-5-sings-and-recites.

80. Interview with former senior State Department official, April 16, 2019; and interview with former senior State Department official, April 27, 2021.

81. Interview with former senior State Department official, April 16, 2019.

82. Rogin, *Chaos Under Heaven*, 46–47.

83. Annie Karni, "Trump Offers Xi Steak, not a Big Mac, at Mar-a-Lago," *Politico*, April 6, 2017, https://www.politico.com/story/2017/04/trump-xi-jinping-mar-lago-host-dinner-236972.

84. Ali Vitali, "Trump Dines with China Leader: 'We Have Developed a Friendship,'" NBC News, April 6, 2017, https://www.nbcnews.com/politics/white-house/trump-dines-china-leader-we-have-developed-friendship-n743626.

85. McMaster, *At War with Ourselves*, chap. 6; Joshua Berlinger, "Trump-Xi Summit Overshadowed by US Strike on Syria," CNN, April 7, 2017, https://www.cnn.com/2017/04/07/politics/xi-trump-summit-syria.

86. Rogin, *Chaos under Heaven*, 50; interview with former senior State Department official, April 16, 2019; and interview with former senior State Department official, April 27, 2021.

87. Gerard Baker, Carol E. Lee, and Michael C. Bender, "Trump Says He Offered China Better Trade Terms in Exchange for Help on North Korea," *Wall Street Journal*, April 12, 2017, https://www.wsj.com/articles/trump-says-he-offered-china-better-trade-terms-in-exchange-for-help-on-north-korea-1492027556.

88. Rogin, *Chaos under Heaven*, 49; and Mark Landler, "Trump Says China Will Get Better Trade Deal if It Solves 'North Korea Problem,'" *New York Times*, April 11, 2017, https://www.nytimes.com/2017/04/11/world/asia/trump-china-trade-north-korea.html.

89. Rogin, *Chaos under Heaven*, 67–68.

90. Interview with former senior State Department official, April 27, 2021; interview with former State Department official, April 16, 2019; and Tian Shaohui, "Xi Says Ready to Boost China-U.S. Ties from New Starting Point with Trump," Xinhua, April 7, 2017, http://www.xinhuanet.com/english/2017-04/07/c_136190556.htm.

91. Susan V. Lawrence and Mark Manyin, "China's February 2017 Suspension of North Korean Coal Imports," *CRS Insight*, April 25, 2017; John Ruwitch

and Meng Meng, "North Korean Ships Head Home after China Orders Coal Returned," Reuters, April 11, 2017, https://www.reuters.com/article/us-china-northkorea-coal-exclusive-idUSKBN17D0D8/; and Leo Byrne, "Four N. Korean Ships, Three with Troubled Pasts, Allowed into Chinese Coal Port," *NK News*, April 20, 2017, https://www.nknews.org/2017/04/four-n-korean-ships-three-with-troubled-pasts-allowed-into-chinese-coal-port/.

92. Interview with Chinese expert, March 25, 2022.
93. Steve Holland, "Trump Says Prepared to Take On North Korea without China If Needed," Reuters, April 13, 2017, https://www.reuters.com/article/idUSKBN17E2PN; and Gerard Baker, Carol E. Lee, and Michael C. Bender, "Trump Says He Offered China Better Trade Terms in Exchange for Help on North Korea," *Wall Street Journal*, April 12, 2017, https://www.wsj.com/articles/trump-says-he-offered-china-better-trade-terms-in-exchange-for-help-on-north-korea-1492027556.
94. Brian Padden, "US and China Intensify Pressure on North Korea," Voice of America, April 24, 2017, https://www.voanews.com/a/us-china-pressure-north-korea/3822871.html.
95. Padden, "US and China Intensify Pressure."
96. Interview with former senior White House official, January 24, 2023.
97. Christopher Bodeen, "China Tightens Border Controls with N. Korea: US Diplomat," *USA Today*, May 26, 2017, https://www.usatoday.com/story/news/world/2017/05/26/china-tightens-border-controls-n-korea-us-diplomat/102182938/; and Sue-Lin Wong and Joseph Campbell, "Evidence of Strained Ties on China-North Korea Border," Reuters, April 3, 2017, https://www.reuters.com/article/idUSKBN1752OY/.

Chapter Thirteen. "Fire and fury"

1. Harrison Menke, "2017 USSTRATCOM Deterrence Symposium," INSS Event Report, July 26–27, 2017; and interview with former U.S. official, August 11, 2021.
2. Wikipedia, "Vincent K. Brooks," last modified December 19, 2024, 14:12 (UTC), https://en.wikipedia.org/wiki/Vincent_K_Brooks.
3. Interview with former U.S. official, August 2, 2021.
4. Bob Woodward, *Fear: Trump in the White House* (New York: Simon and Schuster, 2018), 177.
5. Interview with former U.S. official, August 2, 2021.
6. General (ret.) Vincent K. Brooks and Dr. John Park, "Micro Deterrence Signaling: Policy Innovation During the 2017 Korean Missile Crisis," Harvard Kennedy School, Belfer Center, March 2022, https://www.belfercenter.org/sites/default/files/2022-09/Micro%20Deterrence%20Signaling.pdf; and interview with former U.S. official, August 11, 2021.
7. Brooks and Park, "Micro Deterrence Signaling," 9–11.

8. Brooks and Park, "Micro Deterrence Signaling," 12; Rick Gladstone, "U.N. Security Council Imposes Punishing New Sanctions on North Korea," *New York Times*, August 5, 2017, https://www.nytimes.com/2017/08/05/world /asia/north-korea-sanctions-united-nations.html; and Jeff Zeleny, Dan Merica, and Kevin Liptak, "Trump's 'Fire and Fury' Remark Was Improvised but Familiar," *CNN*, August 9, 2017, https://www.cnn.com/2017/08 /09/politics/trump-fire-fury-improvise-north-korea/index.html.

9. Robin Wright, "The Way Out of Trump's Ad-Lib with North Korea," *New Yorker*, August 10, 2017, https://www.newyorker.com/news/news-desk/the -way-out-of-trumps-ad-lib-war-with-north-korea.

10. Wright, "The Way Out."

11. Melissa Hanham, "Kim Inspects 'Nuclear Warhead': A Picture Decoded," BBC, September 3, 2017, https://www.bbc.com/news/world-asia-41139741; "North Korea Nuclear Test Was 10 Times Bigger than Hiroshima Blast, U.S. Says," CBS News, September 6, 2017, https:///www.cbsnews.com /news/north-korea-nuclear-test-was-10-times-bigger-than-hiroshima -blast-u-s-says/; and "North Korea Fires Second Ballistic Missile over Japan," BBC, September 15, 2017, https://www.bbc.com/news/world-asia -41275614.

12. David Nakamura and Anne Gearan, "In U.N. Speech, Trump Threatens to 'Totally Destroy North Korea' and Calls Kim Jong Un 'Rocket Man,'" *Washington Post*, September 19, 2017, https://www.washingtonpost.com /news/post-politics/wp/2017/09/19/in-u-n-speech-trump-warns-that-the -world-faces-great-peril-from-rogue-regimes-in-north-korea-iran/.

13. Barbara Plett Usher, "Trump UN Speech: Why His Rhetoric Was a Game-Changer," BBC, September 19, 2017, https://www.bbc.com/news/world -us-canada-41329112.

14. "North Korea: Trump and Kim Call Each Other Mad," BBC, September 22, 2017, https://www.bbc.com/news/world-asia-41356836.

15. Stephen Haggard, "Kim Jong Un and Ri Yong Ho Speak," *North Korea: Witness to Transformation* (blog), Peterson Institute for International Economics, September 28, 2017, https://www.piie.com/blogs/north-korea-witness -transformation/kim-jong-un-and-ri-yong-ho-speak; and Justin McCurry, "Ri Yong Ho: The North Korean Diplomat Who Ridicules Donald Trump," *Guardian* (London), September 24, 2017, https://www.theguardian.com /world/2017/sep/24/ri-yong-ho-north-korean-diplomat-defuse-crisis.

16. William Cummings, "Trump Threatens 'Little Rocket Man,' Says Kim May 'Not Be Around Much Longer,'" *USA Today*, September 23, 2017, https:// www.usatoday.com/story/news/politics/onpolitics/2017/09/23/trump -threatens-little-rocket-man-says-kim-may-not-around-much-longer /697452001/.

17. Edith M. Lederer, "North Korean Diplomat Says Tweet by Trump 'Declared War,'" Associated Press, September 26, 2017, https://apnews.com /article/e5846c33e572498ba94983c6f6935235.

18. Nikki R. Haley, *With All Due Respect: Defending America with Grit and Grace* (New York: St. Martin's Press, 2019), 126.

19. Haley, *With All Due Respect*, 129.

20. Interview with former U.S. official, August 11, 2021.

21. H. R. McMaster, *At War with Ourselves: My Tour of Duty in the Trump White House* (New York: HarperCollins, 2024), chap. 3, Kindle.

22. Woodward, *Fear*, 184–185.

23. McMaster, *At War*, chap. 5.

24. Interview with former U.S. official, August 11, 2021.

25. Guy M. Snodgrass, *Holding the Line: Inside Trump's Pentagon with Secretary Mattis* (New York: Sentinel, 2019), 68–82.

26. McMaster, *At War*, chap. 5.

27. McMaster, *At War*, chap. 13.

28. McMaster, *At War*, chap. 13; and David Choi, "Mattis Got So Annoyed on Calls with H. R. McMaster That He Pretended the Line Got Disconnected," *Business Insider*, October 25, 2019, https://www.businessinsider.com/jim-mattis-phone-call-hr-mcmaster-book-holding-the-line-2019-10.

29. Interview with former U.S. official, August 11, 2021.

30. Jim Mattis and Rex Tillerson, "We're Holding Pyongyang to Account," *Wall Street Journal*, August 13, 2017, https://www.wsj.com/articles/were-holding-pyongyang-to-account-1502660253; and interview with former senior White House official, February 15, 2022.

31. Interview with former U.S. official, August 2, 2021.

32. Interview with former U.S. official, August 2, 2021.

33. Interview with former U.S. official, May 14, 2020.

34. Moon Jae-in, *From the Periphery to the Center: Moon Jae-in Memoirs of Foreign Affairs and Security* [in Korean] (Paju, South Korea: Kimyoungsa, 2024), 29–30; and interview with former U.S. official, August 2, 2021.

35. Interview with White House official, May 14, 2020; interview with senior U.S. Embassy official, July 7, 2021; Moon, *From the Periphery*, 67; and Julie Hirschfeld Davis, Mark Landler, and Choe Sang-Hun, "No War Threats from Trump, Who Tells Koreans 'It Will All Work Out,'" *New York Times*, November 7, 2017, https://www.nytimes.com/2017/11/07/world/asia/trump-korea-south-north.html.

36. Brooks and Park, "Micro Deterrence Signaling," 11–12; interview with former U.S. official, August 2, 2021; and interview with former U.S. official, August 11, 2021.

37. Interview with former U.S. official, August 2, 2021; and interview with former U.S. official, August 11, 2021.

38. Interview with former U.S. official, August 2, 2021; interview with former U.S. official, August 11, 2021; and Carol Morello, "North Korea Threatens to Shoot Down U.S. Warplanes," *Washington Post*, September 25, 2017, https://www.washingtonpost.com/world/national-security/north-korea

-asserts-its-right-to-shoot-down-us-bombers/2017/09/25/74da66c4-a204
-11e7-8cfe-d5b912fabc99_story.html.

39. Former Department of Defense official, email exchange with author, May 4, 2022; and interview with former USFK planner, March 4, 2021.

40. Interview with former U.S. official, August 11, 2021.

41. Interview with former U.S. official, August 11, 2021.

42. Interview with former U.S. official, August 11, 2021.

43. Joel S. Wit, Daniel B. Poneman, and Robert L. Gallucci, *Going Critical: The First North Korean Nuclear Crisis* (Washington, DC: Brookings Institution Press, 2004), 215–217.

44. "Foreign Expat Community in Korea," U.S.-Korea Institute, Johns Hopkins School of Advanced International Studies, unpublished research note by author; interview with former U.S. Embassy official, June 23, 2021; and interview with former U.S. official, August 2, 2021.

45. Interview with former U.S. official, August 11, 2021.

46. Interview with former senior U.S. Embassy official, July 7, 2021.

47. Interview with former senior White House official, June 1, 2022.

48. Peter Bergen, *Trump and His Generals: The Cost of Chaos* (New York: Penguin Publishing Group, 2019), 216; and Fred Kaplan, *The Bomb: Presidents, Generals, and the Secret History of Nuclear War* (New York: Simon and Schuster, 2020), 265.

49. Bess Levin, "Report: Donald Trump Wanted to Nuke North Korea and Then Blame It on Another Country," *Vanity Fair*, January 12, 2023, https:// www.vanityfair.com/news/2023/01/donald-trump-wanted-to-nuke-north -korea-and-blame-someone-else.

50. Kaplan, *The Bomb*, 266; and Chris McGreal, "Papers Reveal Nixon Plan for North Korea Nuclear Strike," *Guardian* (London), July 7, 2010, https://www .theguardian.com/world/2010/jul/07/nixon-north-korea-nuclear-strike.

51. Michael Elleman, "The New Hwasong-15 ICBM: A Significant Improvement That May Be Ready as Early as 2018," *38 North*, November 30, 2017, https://www.38north.org/2017/11/melleman113017/; Cristiano Lima, "Trump: North Korea's Kim a 'Sick Puppy,'" *Politico*, November 29, 2017, https://www.politico.com/story/2017/11/29/trump-north-korea-kim-jong -un-sick-puppy-270135; Alex Pappas, "H. R. McMaster: Potential for War with North Korea Increases 'Every Day,'" Fox News, December 2, 2017, https://www.foxnews.com/politics/h-r-mcmaster-potential-for-war-with -north-korea-increases-every-day; and Mark Moore, "Nikki Haley: North Korea Missile Launch 'Brings Us Close to War,'" *New York Post*, November 29, 2017, https://nypost.com/2017/11/29/nikki-haley-north-korea -missile-launch-brings-us-closer-to-war/.

52. Interview with former U.S. official, August 11, 2021.

53. Interview with former U.S. official, August 11, 2021.

54. Bob Woodward, *Rage* (New York: Simon and Schuster, 2020), 72.

55. Interview with former U.S. official, May 13, 2022.

56. Interview with former U.S. official, May 13, 2022.

57. Austin Ramzy, "Jet Pilots Say They Saw North Korean Missile in Flight," *New York Times,* December 5, 2017, https://www.nytimes.com/2017/12/05/world/asia/north-korea-missile.html.

58. Mark Landler and Choe Sang-Hun, "North Korea Says It's Now a Nuclear State. Could That Mean It's Ready to Talk?," *New York Times,* November 29, 2017, https://www.nytimes.com/2017/11/29/world/asia/north-korea-nuclear-missile-.html; and interview with former U.S. official, May 13, 2022.

59. Interview with former U.S. official, May 13, 2022.

60. "Rodong Sinmun Commentator Reveals Truth of 'Maximum Pressure and Engagement,'" Korean Central News Agency, May 25, 2017; "Kim Jong Un Supervises Test-Launch of Inter-continental Ballistic Rocket Hwasong-14," Korean Central News Agency, July 5, 2017; and "DPRK Nuclear Weapons Institute on Successful Test of H-bomb for ICBM," Korean Central News Agency, September 3, 2017.

61. Yonhap News Agency, "Trump: We Have to Denuclearize N. Korea," *Korea Herald,* November 16, 2017, https://www.koreaherald.com/view.php?ud=20171116000120.

62. "Trump Promises 'Major Sanctions' in Response to North Korea ICBM Test," Voice of America, November 29, 2017, https://www.voanews.com/a/donald-trump-promises-major-sanctions-north-korea-icbm-test/4141851.html; Don Tse and Larry Ong, "Why Trump Treats Xi and China Differently," *Real Clear Defense,* December 19, 2017, https://www.realcleardefense.com/articles/2017/12/19/why_trump_treats_xi_and_china_differently_112807.html; and former senior State Department official, email exchange with author, April 29, 2022.

63. Gerald F. Seib, "Amid Signs of Thaw in North Korea, Tensions Bubble Up: Trump Administration Weighs a Risky Strategy as Seoul and Pyongyang Prepare to Meet," *Wall Street Journal,* January 9, 2018, https://www.wsj.com/articles/amid-signs-of-a-thaw-in-north-korea-tensions-bubble-up-1515427541.

64. Victor Cha, "Opinion: Giving North Korea a 'Bloody Nose' Carries a Huge Risk to Americans," *Washington Post,* January 30, 2018, https://www.washingtonpost.com/opinions/victor-cha-giving-north-korea-a-bloody-nose-carries-a-huge-risk-to-americans/2018/01/30/43981c94-05f7-11e8-8777-2a059f168dd2_story.html; and "White House Drops Victor Cha As Candidate for Ambassador to South Korea," *All Things Considered,* January 31, 2018, https://www.npr.org/2018/01/31/582240496/white-house-drops-victor-cha-as-candidate-for-ambassador-to-south-korea.

65. Interview with former U.S. officer, August 2, 2021.

66. Greg Milam, "World Faces Last Best Chance to Avoid War with North Korea, US General Warns," Sky News, December 13, 2017, https://news

.sky.com/story/world-faces-last-best-chance-to-avoid-war-with-north -korea-us-general-warns-11168427.

67. Former senior State Department official, email exchange with author, October 23, 2020; interview with former senior U.S. official, February 15, 2022; interview with former senior State Department official, April 16, 2019; and interview with former senior State Department official, April 27, 2021.

68. Interview with former senior State Department official, April 27, 2021.

69. Interview with former senior U.S. official, August 11, 2021; and interview with former senior U.S. official, February 15, 2022.

70. Billy Perrigo, "'It's Crazy.' Lindsey Graham Says It's Time to Move Americans Out of Korea," *Time*, December 4, 2017, https://time.com/5047454 /lindsey-graham-time-move-military-families-south-korea/; Courtney Kube and Carol E. Lee, "Trump Weighs Barring U.S. Military in South Korea from Bringing Families," NBC News, February 2, 2018, https://www .nbcnews.com/news/world/trump-weighs-barring-u-s-military-south -korea-bringing-families-n844041; and Woodward, *Fear*, 302.

71. Agence France-Presse, "Trump 'almost sent tweet that North Korea would have seen as warning of attack,'" *Guardian* (London), September 10, 2018, https://www.theguardian.com/us-news/2018/sep/10/trump-almost-sent -tweet-north-korea-imminent-attack.

72. McMaster, *At War*, chap. 16.

73. Interview with senior White House official, June 1, 2022.

74. Interview with former U.S. officer, May 13, 2022.

75. Interview with senior White House official, February 15, 2022.

76. Interview with former senior U.S. officer, August 2, 2021.

77. Simon Denyer, "North Korean Leader Says He Has 'Nuclear Button' but Won't Use It unless Threatened," *Washington Post*, January 1, 2018, https:// www.washingtonpost.com/world/north-korea-leader-says-he-hasnuclear -button-but-wont-use-unless-threatened/2017/12/31/af3dc188-ee96 -11e7-90ed-77167c6861f2_story.html.

78. Choe Sang-Hun, "Kim Jong-un Offers North Korea's Hand to South, While Chiding U.S.," *New York Times*, December 31, 2017, https://www .nytimes.com/2017/12/31/world/asia/north-korea-kim-jong-un-olympics .html; and Robert Carlin, "A New Enchilada," *38 North*, January 2, 2018, https://www.38north.org/2018/01/rcarlin010218/.

79. Wikipedia, "Andrew Kim," last modified January 21, 2025, 10:37 (UTC), https://en.wikipedia.org/wiki/Andrew_Kim.

80. Tim Weiner, "Political Books Are Often Bland. Mike Pompeo's Is Savage," *Washington Post*, January 24, 2023, https://www.washingtonpost.com/books /2023/01/24/pompeo-trump-attack-memoir-review/; and Aishwarya Kumar, "Pompeo: Trump 'Fearlessly Puts America out in Front,'" *Wichita Eagle*, July 20, 2016, https://www.kansas.com/news/politics-government/election /article90786197.html.

81. Interview with former U.S. official, June 24, 2021.

82. "CIA Establishes Korea Mission Center," Central Intelligence Agency, May 10, 2017, https://www.cia.gov/stories/story/cia-establishes-korea-mission-center/.

83. "CIA Establishes Korea Mission Center"; and Mike Pompeo, *Never Give an Inch: Fighting for the America I Love* (New York: Broadside Books, 2023), chap. 2, Kindle.

84. Eli Watkins, "CIA Chief Signals Desire for Regime Change in North Korea," CNN, July 21, 2017, https://www.cnn.com/2017/07/20/politics/cia-mike-pompeo-north-korea/index.html.

85. Andrew Kim, "A Historical Review of the U.S. Intelligence Community's Role in Dealing with North Korea," *Belfer Center for Science and International Affairs, Practitioner Observation Series*, no. 1 (July 2021): 4.

86. Michael Gordon and Warren P. Strobel, "U.S. and North Korean Spies Have Held Secret Talks for a Decade," *Wall Street Journal*, January 21, 2019, https://www.wsj.com/articles/u-s-and-north-korean-spies-have-held-secret-talks-for-a-decade-11548091335; Mark Landler, "Spies, Not Diplomats, Take Lead Role in Planning Trump's North Korea Meeting," *New York Times*, March 16, 2018, https://www.nytimes.com/2018/03/16/us/politics/north-korea-cia-trump.html; Anna Fifield, "South Korea Asks: Who Is That Mystery Man with Pompeo and Kim?," *Washington Post*, May 17, 2018, https://www.washingtonpost.com/world/asia_pacific/south-korea-asks-who-is-thatmystery-man-with-pompeo-and-kim/2018/05/17/od4281b4-58f6-11e8-8b92-45fdd7aaef3c_story.html; and interview with former official, October 4, 2021.

87. Interview with former U.S. official, October 4, 2021; and Woodward, *Fear*, 89.

88. Interview with former U.S. official, October 4, 2021; and Woodward, *Fear*, 88.

89. Interview with former U.S. official, October 4, 2021; and Woodward, *Fear*, 89.

90. Interview with former U.S. official, October 4, 2021.

91. Interview with former U.S. official, October 4, 2021.

92. Interview with former U.S. official, October 4, 2021.

93. Interview with former U.S. official, October 4, 2021; and interview with former State Department official, May 3, 2024.

94. Interview with former official, May 20, 2022.

95. Woodward, *Fear*, 82.

96. Alex Ward, "What Trump Got Right—and Wrong—with North Korea, Explained by a Former Intel Official," *Vox*, October 14, 2020, https://www.vox.com/21515145/north-korea-trump-usa-nuclear-war-interview.

97. "U.S. CBS President Here," Korean Central News Agency, March 14, 2017, https://kcnawatch.xyz/newstream/271830/u-s-cbs-president-here; and interview with CBS delegation member, May 24, 2022.

98. Dan Merica, Kevin Liptak, and Agela Dewan, "Trump Warns North Korea: US Military 'Locked and Loaded,'" CNN, August 11, 2017, https://www.cnn.com/2017/08/10/politics/trump-north-korea/index.html.

99. Evan Osnos, "On the Brink: Could Kim Jong Un and Donald Trump Goad Each Other into Nuclear War?," *New Yorker*, September 18, 2017, 36, https://www.newyorker.com/magazine/2017/09/18/the-risk-of-nuclear-war-with-north-korea.

100. Osnos, "On the Brink," 38.

101. Former EU official, email exchange with author, September 10, 2021.

102. Osnos, "On the Brink," 40.

103. "DPRK Backlash against Trump," unpublished research note by author, August-October 2017.

104. Robert L. Carlin and Rachel Minyoung Lee, "Understanding Kim Jong Un's Economic Policymaking: Defense Versus Civilian Spending," *38 North*, September 2021, https://www.38north.org/2021/09/understanding-kim-jong-uns-economic-policymaking-defense-versus-civilian-spending/.

105. David Bosco, "The Nakedness of U.N. Diplomacy," *Foreign Policy*, July 15, 2013, https://foreignpolicy.com/2013/07/15/the-nakedness-of-u-n-diplomacy/.

106. Bosco, "The Nakedness of U.N. Diplomacy."

107. Interview with UN official, July 12, 2021.

108. "Trump Takes on the World," BBC Select, 2021, https://www.bbcselect.com/watch/trump-takes-on-the-world/.

109. Ankit Panda, "Top U.N. Official to Visit North Korea," *The Diplomat*, December 6, 2017, https://thediplomat.com/2017/12/top-un-official-to-visit-north-korea/.

110. Interview with UN official, July 12, 2021.

111. Juliet Eilperin, "Trump Calls U.N. 'Just a Club for People' to 'Have a Good Time,'" *Washington Post*, December 27, 2016, https://www.washingtonpost.com/news/post-politics/wp/2016/12/26/trump-calls-u-n-just-a-club-for-people-to-have-a-good-time/.

112. Interview with senior State Department official, April 27, 2021; interview with White House official, May 3, 2020; interview with UN official, July 12, 2021; and "Trump Takes on the World."

113. Ken Thomas, "Trump: UN Has Tremendous Potential under New Leadership," Associated Press, October 20, 2017, https://apnews.com/united-states-government-67c305c448bd4e45a28d16e36f4299aa.

114. "Trump Takes on the World"; and interview with UN official, July 12, 2021.

115. Pompeo, *Never Give an Inch*, chap. 2.

116. Interview with UN official, July 12, 2021.

117. Interview with UN official, July 12, 2021; and Jennie Oh, "U.N. Political Chief Meets North Korean Vice Foreign Minister," UPI, December 6, 2017, https://www.upi.com/Top_News/World-News/2017/12/06/UN-political-chief-meets-North-Korean-vice-foreign-minister/1751512557681/.

118. Interview with UN official, July 12, 2021; and Oh, "U.N. Political Chief."
119. Interview with former UN official, December 20, 2018.
120. Interview with former UN official, December 20, 2018; and interview with UN official, July 12, 2021.
121. Interview with former UN official, December 20, 2018; and interview with UN official, July 12, 2021.
122. Interview with former UN official, December 20, 2018.
123. Interview with UN official, July 12, 2021.
124. Interview with UN official, July 12, 2021.
125. "Trump Takes on the World."
126. "Trump Takes on the World."
127. "Trump Takes on the World."
128. Mick Krever and Joshua Berlinger, "UN Official Who Visited North Korea Sees 'High Risk" of Miscalculation," CNN, December 15, 2017, https://www.cnn.com/2017/12/14/world/north-korea-jeffrey-feltman-amanpour/index.html.
129. Milam, "World Faces 'Last Best Chance.'"
130. Interview with UN official, July 12, 2021.
131. Interview with former UN official, December 20, 2018.
132. Interview with former UN official, December 20, 2018.
133. Interview with former UN official, December 20, 2018.
134. "Kim Jong Un Climbs Mt. Paektu," Korean Central News Agency, December 9, 2017, https://kcnawatch.xyz/newstream/1512774040-418926616/kim-jong-un-climbs-mt-paektu/.
135. McMaster, *At War*, chap. 8.
136. Interview with former UN official, December 20, 2018.

Chapter Fourteen. "Now, he won't lose his early morning sleep anymore."

1. Robert Carlin and Joel S. Wit, "How the Olympics Could Help Defuse the North Korea Crisis," *The Atlantic*, January 8, 2018, https://www.theatlantic.com/international/archive/2018/01/winter-olympic-games-south-korea-opportunity-for-diplomacy-with-north-korea/549893/.
2. Moon Jae-in, *From the Periphery to the Center: Moon Jae In Memoirs of Foreign Affairs and Security* [in Korean] (Paju, South Korea: Kimyoungsa, 2024), 42, 144.
3. Interview with former senior U.S. Embassy official, July 7, 2021; and interview with former U.S. Embassy official, July 2, 2021.
4. Bob Woodward, *Rage* (New York: Simon and Schuster, 2020), 308; and Dan Lamothe and Simon Denyer, "Trump Agrees to Delay Military Exercise with South Korea until after Winter Olympics," *Washington Post*, January 4, 2018, 1–3, https://www.washingtonpost.com/news/checkpoint/wp/2018/01

/04/trump-agrees-to-delay-military-exercise-with-south-korea-until-after
-winter-olympics/.

5. Interview with former U.S. Embassy official, July 2, 2021; and interviews with former senior U.S. Embassy official, July 7, 2021, and July 15, 2021.

6. Interview with former senior U.S. Embassy official, July 7, 2021.

7. Interview with North Korea expert, January 8, 2021.

8. Wikipedia, "Kim Yo Jong," last modified February 23, 2025, 04:32 (UTC), https://en.wikipedia.org/wiki/Kim_Yo_Jong.

9. Interviews with former senior State Department official, April 7, 2021, and April 23, 2021.

10. Josh Rogin, "Pence: The United States Is Not Seeking Negotiations with North Korea," *Washington Post*, April 19, 2017, https://www.washingtonpost .com/news/josh-rogin/wp/2017/04/19/pence-the-united-states-is-not -seeking-negotiations-with-north-korea/.

11. Tim Kelly and Hyonhee Shin, "Pence Heads to Olympics Leaving Open Chance of Talks with North Korean Officials," Reuters, February 5, 2018, https://www.reuters.com/article/olympics-2018-pence/wrapup-4-pence -heads-to-olympics-leaving-open-chance-of-talks-with-n-korea-officials -idUSL2N1PW07E/; Ashley Parker, "Pence Was Set to Meet with North Korean Officials during the Olympics before Last-Minute Cancellation," *Washington Post*, February 20, 2018, https://www.washingtonpost.com /politics/pence-was-set-to-meet-with-north-korean-officials-during-the -olympics-before-last-minute-cancellation/2018/02/20/89392dfe-1684 -11e8-942d-16a950029788_story.html; and Samantha Raphelson, "Amid Olympic Détente, Pence Snubs North Koreans in Visit to Pyeongchang," NPR, February 10, 2018, https://www.npr.org/sections/thetorch/2018/02 /10/584863661/amid-olympic-d-tente-pence-snubs-north-koreans-in -visit-to-pyeongchang.

12. Interview with former senior U.S. Embassy official, July 7, 2021.

13. Interview with former U.S. official, October 4, 2021.

14. Interview with former U.S. official, October 4, 2021; Gardiner Harris and Choe Sang-Hun, "North Korea Dropped Out of Meeting with Pence at Last Minute, U.S. Says," *New York Times*, February 2, 2018, https://www .nytimes.com/2018/02/20/us/politics/pence-north-korea-meeting.html.

15. Josh Rogin, "Opinion | Pence: The United States Is Ready to Talk with North Korea," *Washington Post*, February 11, 2018, https://www.washing tonpost.com/opinions/global-opinions/pence-the-united-states-is-ready -to-talk-with-north-korea/2018/02/11/b5070ed6-0f33-11e8-9065 -e55346f6de81_story.html.

16. Motoko Rich and Choe Sang-Hun, "Kim Jong-un's Sister Turns On the Charm, Taking Pence's Spotlight," *New York Times*, https://www.nytimes .com/2018/02/11/world/asia/kim-yo-jong-mike-pence-olympics.html; Anna Fifield, "The 'Ivanka Trump of North Korea' Captivates People in

the South at the Olympics," *Washington Post*, February 10, 2018, https://www
.washingtonpost.com/world/the-ivanka-trump-of-north-korea-captivates
-people-in-the-south/2018/02/10/d56119fc-0e65-11e8-baf5-e629fc1cd21e
_story.html; Park Si-soo, "Kim Jong-un's Sister in South for Historic 3-day
Trip," *Korea Times*, February 9, 2018, https://www.koreatimes.co.kr/www
/nation/2024/03/103_243881.html; and H. R. McMaster, *At War with Ourselves: My Tour of Duty in the Trump White House* (New York: HarperCollins,
2024), chap. 17, Kindle.

17. "Winter Olympics 2018: North Korea's General Kim Yong Chol to Attend,"
BBC, February 22, 2018, https://www.bbc.com/news/world-asia-43153976;
Choe Sang-Hun, "Ivanka Trump, in South Korea, Calls for Pressure on the
North," *New York Times*, February 23, 2018, https://www.nytimes.com/2018
/02/23/world/asia/ivanka-trump-south-korea.html; and Mark Landler, "An
Envoy Who Can Rival 'North Korea's Ivanka,'" *New York Times*, Febru-
ary 21, 2018, https://www.nytimes.com/2018/02/21/us/politics/ivanka
-trump-south-korea-pence.html.

18. Interview with senior White House official, February 15, 2022.

19. Hyung-jin Kim and Kim Tong-hyung, "North Korean Envoy, in South,
Opens Door to US Talks," Associated Press, February 25, 2018, https://
apnews.com/article/e594920ca8f947d8994d2e7148e3aaad; Rogin, "The
United States Is Ready to Talk"; and Sarah Kim, "Trump Willing to Talk to
North," *Korea JoongAng Daily*, February 27, 2018, https://koreajoongangdaily
.joins.com/news/article/Article.aspx?aid=3045002.

20. Choe Sang-Hun, "South Korea Names 2 Envoys to Meet with Kim Jong-un,"
New York Times, March 4, 2018, https://www.nytimes.com/2018/03/04
/world/asia/south-north-korea-talks-nuclear-trump.html; Jeong Woo-sang,
"S. Korean Envoys Have Dinner with Kim Jong-un," *Chosun Daily*, March 6,
2018, english.chosun.com/site/data/html_dir/2018/03/06/2018030600825
.html; Ser Myo-ja, "Moon Envoys meet Kim Jong-un," *Korea JoongAng
Daily*, March 5, 2018, https://koreajoongangdaily.joins.com/2018/03/05
/politics/Moon-envoys-meet-Kim-Jongun/3045258.html; and interview
with former Moon administration official, June 22, 2022.

21. Interview with former Moon administration official, June 22, 2022.

22. Interview with former Moon administration official, June 22, 2022.

23. Interview with former Moon administration official, June 22, 2022; and Ser
Myo-ja, "S. Korean Envoys."

24. Interview with former Moon administration official, June 22, 2022; Ser
Myo-ja, "S. Korean Envoys"; and "N.K. Leader: Moon Will No Longer
Have to Wake Up Early to Discuss N.K. Missile Launches," Yonhap
News Agency, March 9, 2018, https://en.yna.co.kr/view/AEN201803090
10100315.

25. Interview with former Moon administration official, June 22, 2022.

26. Interview with former senior White House official, February 15, 2022; and
"South Korean Envoys Head to US to Discuss North Korean Offer," Voice

of America, March 8, 2018, https://www.voanews.com/a/south-korean-envoys-head-to-us-to-discuss-north-korean-offer/4285742.html.

27. Interview with former senior White House official, February 15, 2022.
28. Interview with former senior White House official, February 15, 2022.
29. Interview with former senior White House official, February 15, 2022.
30. Emily Tillett, "Trump Responds to North Korea Talks: 'We cannot let that situation fester,'" CBS News, March 6, 2018, https://www.cbsnews.com/news/trump-responds-to-north-korea-talks-the-world-is-watching-and-waiting/.
31. McMaster, *At War*, chap. 17.
32. Joanne Lee, "White House Visit by Chung-Eui-yong and Suh Hoon in March 2018," unpublished research note, March 28, 2022.
33. Interview with former ROK government advisor, June 3, 2019.
34. Interview with former ROK government advisor, June 3, 2019.
35. Interview with a former senior White House official, June 1, 2022; Peter Baker and Choe Sang-Hun, "With Snap 'Yes' in Oval Office, Trump Gambles on North Korea," *New York Times*, March 10, 2018, https://www.nytimes.com/2018/03/10/world/asia/trump-north-korea.html; and Hwang Ho-jun, "Play-by-Play: S. Korean Envoys Got Trump's Nod for Kim Jong-un Summit," *Arirang News*, online video, March 9, 2018, https://www.dailymotion.com/video/x6fzwmc.
36. Baker and Choe, "With Snap 'Yes' in Oval Office"; interview with former ROK government advisor, June 3, 2019; and Woodward, *Rage*, 91.
37. Interview with former U.S. official, June 22, 2022.
38. Lee Seung-jun, "Not Even Time to Report to the President . . . Swift '5 Hours at the White House,'" *Hankyoreh*, March 9, 2018; Sarah Huckabee Sanders, *Speaking for Myself: Freedom and the Fight of Our Lives Inside the Trump White House* (New York: St. Martin's Press, 2020), 128; and Woodward, *Rage*, 97.
39. Ken Schwartz, "White House: Trump Accepts North Korean Invitation," Voice of America, March 8, 2018, https://www.voanews.com/a/north-korean-dictator-kim-jong-un-invites-trump-for-talks/4287191.html.
40. Interview with former senior White House official, June 1, 2022; and interview with White House official, July 23, 2021.
41. Interview with former U.S. official, November 5, 2021; Mark Landler and Matthew Rosenberg, "Mike Pompeo, CIA Director, Met with Kim Jung-un in North Korea," *New York Times*, April 17, 2018, https://www.nytimes.com/2018/04/17/world/asia/trump-japan-north-korea-summit-talks.html; and Karoun Demirjian and Shane Harris, "Pompeo's North Korea Trip Set the Table for Trump's Planned Meeting with Kim Jong-un," *Washington Post*, April 18, 2018, https://www.washingtonpost.com/powerpost/pompeos-critics-offer-grudging-praise-for-north-korea-meeting/2018/04/18/857f505c-430d-11e8-8569-26fda6b404c7_story.html.

42. Mike Pompeo, *Never Give an Inch: Fighting for the America I Love* (New York: Broadside Books, 2023), chap. 1, Kindle.

43. Pompeo, *Never Give an Inch*, 40; Shane Harris, Carol D. Leonnig, Greg Jaffe, and David Nakamura, "CIA Director Pompeo Met with North Korean Leader Kim Jong Un over Easter Weekend," *Washington Post*, April 18, 2018, https://www.washingtonpost.com/politics/us-china-trade-dispute -looms-over-trump-summit-with-japans-abe/2018/04/17/2c94cb02-424f -11e8-bba2-0976a82b05a2_story.html.

44. Interview with former U.S. official, October 4, 2021; and Pompeo, *Never Give an Inch*, 2.

45. Interview with former U.S. official, October 4, 2021; Pompeo, *Never Give an Inch*, 2; and Woodward, *Rage*, 98–99.

46. Interview with former U.S. official, October 4, 2021; and Pompeo, *Never Give an Inch*, 4.

47. Pompeo, *Never Give an Inch*, chap .1.

48. Pompeo, *Never Give an Inch*, chap. 1.

49. Interview with former U.S. official, November 5, 2021; and Pompeo, *Never Give an Inch*, 40–41.

50. Pompeo, *Never Give an Inch*, chap. 2.

51. Pompeo, *Never Give an Inch*, chap. 2.

52. Pompeo, *Never Give an Inch*, chap. 2.

53. Andrew Kim, "Remarks Delivered at Stanford's Shorenstein Asia-Pacific Research Center," February 22, 2019, https://fsi.stanford.edu/news /transcript-andrew-kim-north-korea-denuclearization-and-us-dprk -diplomacy.

54. Interview with former U.S. official, November 5, 2021; and Pompeo, *Never Give an Inch*, chap. 2.

55. Woodward, *Rage*, 100.

56. Pompeo, *Never Give an Inch*, chap. 8.

57. Pompeo, *Never Give an Inch*, chap. 1; and David Ignatius, "Opinion: Mike Pompeo Has a Belligerent Streak. He Should Be Smart Enough to Fix It," *Washington Post*, January 30, 2020, https://www.washingtonpost.com /opinions/global-opinions/mike-pompeo-has-a-belligerent-streak-he -should-be-smart-enough-to-fix-it/2020/01/30/f5f4a26c-4395-11ea-b5fc -eefa848cde99_story.html.

58. Pompeo, *Never Give an Inch*, chap. 1.

59. Interview with former official, October 4, 2021; and Pompeo, *Never Give an Inch*, chap. 2.

60. Interview with former State Department reporter, June 1, 2021; and Nahal Toosi, "Despite 'Rexit' Rumors, Tillerson Says He's 'Learning' to Enjoy His Job," *Politico*, December 12, 2017, https://www.politico.eu/article/despite -rexit-rumors-tillerson-says-hes-learning-to-enjoy-his-job/.

61. Julian Borger, "Trump's Firings Signal Hawkish Turn on North Korea and Iran," *Guardian* (London), March 18, 2018, https://www.theguardian.com

/us-news/2018/mar/17/donald-trump-tillerson-pompeo-mcmaster-bolton
-iran-north-korea; and Nick Wadhams and Andy Sharo, "Trump's North
Korea Point Man to Step Down," *Bloomberg*, February 26, 2018, https://
www.bloomberg.com/news/articles/2018-02-27/trump-s-north-korea
-point-man-to-quit-as-talks-seem-more-likely?fromNewsdog=1&utm
_source=NewsDog&utm_medium=referral.

62. Interview with former State Department reporter, June 1, 2021.

63. Lauren Fox, Deirdre Walsh, and Laura Korean, "Mike Pompeo Sworn In
as Trump's Second Secretary of State," CNN, April 26, 2018, https://www
.cnn.com/2018/04/26/politics/mike-pompeo-senate-confirmation-vote
-richard-grenell/index.html.

64. Russell Goldman, "Bulletproof, Slow and Full of Wine: Kim Jong-un's Mystery Train," *New York Times*, March 27, 2018, https://www.nytimes.com
/2023/09/11/world/asia/kim-jong-un-armored-train-north-korea.html.

65. Steven Lee Myers and Jane Perlez, "Kim Jong-un Met with X Jinping in
Secret Beijing Visit," *New York Times*, March 27, 2018, https://www.nytimes
.com/2018/03/27/world/asia/kim-jong-un-china-north-korea.html; and interview with former U.S. official, July 9, 2022.

66. Judith Vonberg and Vasco Cotovio, "New Footage Shows Kim Jong Un
Holding Court inside Armored Train," CNN, March 30, 2018, https://www
.cnn.com/2018/03/30/asia/kim-jong-un-china-train-footage-intl/index.
html.

67. Robert Carlin, "Reading North Korean Intent: The Importance of What
Is and Is Not Said," *38 North*, April 3, 2018, https://www.38north.org/2018
/04/rcarlin040318/; Choe Sang-Hun, "North Korea Invites World to Watch
the Closing of Nuclear Test Site," *New York Times*, May 12, 2018, https://
www.nytimes.com/2018/05/12/world/asia/north-korea-nuclear-test-site
.html; "N. Korea Demolishes Nuclear Test Site," Yonhap News Agency,
May 24, 2018, https://en.yna.co.kr/view/AEN20180524001852315; and
Choe Sang-Hun, "'We No Longer Need' Nuclear or Missile Tests, North
Korean Leader Says," *New York Times*, April 20, 2018, https://www.nytimes
.com/2018/04/20/world/asia/kim-jong-un-hotline-korea.html.

68. Robert Carlin, "Kim Jong Un's New Strategic Line," *38 North*, April 23,
2018, https://www.38north.org/2018/04/rcarlin042318/; Rachel Minyoung
Lee, "Kim Jong Un's Tortuous Path to Economic Reform," *War on the Rocks*,
June 8, 2022, https://warontherocks.com/2022/06/kim-jong-uns-tortuous
-path-to-economic-reform/; and Michelle Ye Hee Lee, "Kim Jong Un
Shift from Nuclear Push to Economy Intensified Internal Debates in
Country, Report Says," *Washington Post*, September 22, 2021, https://www
.washingtonpost.com/world/asia_pacific/kim-north-korea-nuclear
-economy/2021/09/21/b12ee8aa-1a93-11ec-bcb8-0cb135811007_story.
html.

69. Harry Kazianis, "North Korea Has No Intention of Giving Up Its Nukes—
And Now We Have Proof," *The Hill*, June 28, 2018, https://thehill.com

/opinion/national-security/394509-north-korea-has-no-intention-of
-giving-up-its-nukes-and-now-we-have/.

70. Siegfried Hecker, "Opinion: Why Did Kim Jong Un Blow Up His Nuclear
Test Site?," *Washington Post*, May 30, 2018, https://www.washingtonpost.com
/news/theworldpost/wp/2018/05/30/north-korea-test-site/.

71. Moon, *From the Periphery*, 181.

72. Interview with former Blue House official, July 13, 2022.

73. David E. Sanger and Choe Sang-Hun, "Korea Talks Begin as Kim Jong-un
Crosses to South's Side of DMZ," *New York Times*, April 26, 2018, https://
www.nytimes.com/2018/04/26/world/asia/korea-kim-moon-summit.html.

74. Interview with former Blue House official, July 13, 2022; and Anna Fifield,
"South Korea Says It Will Lay Groundwork for Trump and Kim to Discuss Nuclear Arms," *Washington Post*, April 18, 2018, https://www.washing
tonpost.com/world/south-korea-says-it-will-lay-the-groundwork-for
-trump-to-talk-to-kim-about-nuclear-weapons/2018/04/18/1a3b7e6a
-42fe-11e8-baaf-8b3c5a3da888_story.html.

75. Interview with former Blue House official, July 13, 2022.

76. Interview with former Blue House official, July 13, 2022; "USB and Foot
Bridge Talk," *Munhwa Ilbo*, July 18, 2022; and Choe Sang-Hun, "South
Korea Hands Kim Jong-un A Path to Prosperity with a USB Drive," *New
York Times*, May 10, 2018, https://www.nytimes.com/2018/05/10/world/asia
/kim-jong-un-north-korea-south-usb-economy.html.

77. Interview with former UN Command officer, June 16, 2021; and interview
with former UN Command officer, June 29, 2021.

78. Interview with former UN Command officer, June 16, 2021; and interview
with former UN Command officer, June 29, 2021.

79. "President Moon Jae In and Chairman Kim Jong Un Will Cross the 'Foot
Bridge' Together," *Huffington Post Korea*, April 26, 2018.

80. Lee Ki-chul, "The Reason Why President Moon Jae In and Kim Jong Un's
'Foot Bridge' of Friendship Is All Blue" [in Korean], *Seoul Shinmun*, April 26,
2018, https://www.seoul.co.kr/news/politics/2018/04/26/20180426500137;
and interview with former UN Command officer, June 29, 2021.

81. Interview with former Blue House official, July 13, 2021.

82. Fifield, "South Korea Says It Will Lay Groundwork"; and Koh Byung-joon
and Song Sang-ho, "Foreign Journalists Hold Out Hope with Subdued Expectations ahead of the Summit," Yonhap News Agency, April 27, 2018,
https://en.yna.co.kr/view/AEN20180427003352315.

83. Joanne Lee, "Description of April 2018 Inter-Korean Summit at Panmun-
jom, July 7, 2022," research note, cites "[Watch Full] Until the Moment
That Leaders of the South and North Meet, Kim Jong Un 'Took 11 Years' . . .
Moon Jae-in 'Let's Catch Up on All We Missed'" [in Korean], Ohmynews
TV, online video, April 27, 2018, https://www.youtube.com/watch?v=GRLQ
HOeKCMo&t=81s.

84. Lee, "Description of April 2018 Inter-Korean Summit."

85. Lee, "Description of April 2018 Inter-Korean Summit."
86. Lee, "Description of April 2018 Inter-Korean Summit."
87. Lee, "Description of April 2018 Inter-Korean Summit."
88. Lee, "Description of April 2018 Inter-Korean Summit."
89. Lee, "Description of April 2018 Inter-Korean Summit"; and Suh Sung-il, "Chairman Kim Jong Un signs the visiting book at Panmunjom, 2018.04.27," digital photo, in Kim Ji-hye, "'New History Begins Now': Kim Jong Un Signs Visiting Book" [in Korean], *Kyunghyang Sinmun*, https://m.khan.co .kr/politics/north-korea/article/201804271147001#c2b.
90. Lee, "Description of April 2018 Inter-Korean Summit"; and Euan McKirdy, "When Kim Met Moon: All the Key Moments from a Historic Day," CNN, April 27, 2018, https://www.cnn.com/2018/04/27/asia/key-moments -korean-summit-intl/index.html.
91. Moon, *From the Periphery*, 192.
92. Interview with former Blue House official, July 13, 2021.
93. "Moon, Kim Plant Pine Tree Together at MDL," *KBS World*, April 27, 2018, https://world.kbs.co.kr/service/news_view.htm?lang=e&Seq_Code =135830.
94. Kim Myung-il, "President Moon Reveals Conversations He Had with Kim Jong-un at the Panmunjom Pedestrian Bridge" [in Korean], *Chosun Ilbo*, April 26, 2022; and Moon, *From the Periphery*, 116.
95. Lee, "Description of April 2018 Inter-Korean Summit"; "Panmunjom Declaration on Peace, Prosperity and Reunification of the Korean Peninsula," ROK Ministry of Foreign Affairs, September 11, 2018, https://www.mofa .go.kr/eng/brd/m_5478/view.do?seq=319130&srchFr=&amp%3BsrchTo =&amp%3BsrchWord=&amp%3BsrchTp=&amp%3Bmulti_itm_seq =0&amp%3Bitm_seq_1=0&amp%3Bitm_seq_2=0&amp%3Bcompany _cd=&amp%3Bcompany_nm=&page=1&titleNm; and Wikipedia, "April 2018 Inter-Korean Summit," last modified February 13, 2025, 19:47 (UTC), https://en.wikipedia.org/wiki/April_2018_inter-Korean summit.
96. Lee, "Description of April 2018 Inter-Korean Summit."
97. Lee, "Description of April 2018 Inter-Korean Summit"; and interview with former UN Command officer, June 16, 2021.
98. Interview with former U.S. official, February 20, 2020; Brian Padden, "South Koreans Hopeful in Wake of Denuclearization Summit," Voice of America, April 30, 2018, https://www.voanews.com/a/south-koreans-react-to -summit/4371903.html; and Park Cho-rong, Yonhap News Agency, April 28, 2018, https://www.yna.co.kr/view/AKR20180428038400004.
99. "Trump Declares in Tweet: 'KOREAN WAR TO END,'" *PBS NewsHour*, April 27, 2018, https://www.pbs.org/newshour/politics/trump-declares-in -tweet-korean-war-to-end; and Robin Wright, "Why Trump's Boasts about the Korean Summit Are Premature," *New Yorker*, April 27, 2018, https://www .newyorker.com/news/news-desk/why-trumps-boasts-about-the-korea -summit-are-premature.

100. "Trump Declares in Tweet"; Wright, "Why Trump's Boasts"; Russell Goldman and Choe Sang-Hun, "North and South Korea Summit is Short on Details, but Long on Theater," *New York Times*, April 27, 2018, https://www.nytimes.com/2018/04/27/world/asia/north-korea-south-border.html; and Paula Hancocks, Jungeun Kim, and Yoonjung Seo, "'Master Manipulators': Why Negotiating with North Korea Is Fraught with Risk," CNN, April 24, 2018, https://www.cnn.com/2018/04/23/asia/north-korea-kim-jong-un-negotation-skills-intl/index.html.

101. Interview with former Blue House official, October 16, 2022; and Joori Roh, "North and South Korea Start to Dismantle Border Speakers, Fulfilling Summit Pledge," Reuters, May 1, 2018, https://www.reuters.com/article/us-northkorea-southkorea-idUSKBN1I22U5/.

102. Goldman and Choe, "North and South Korea Summit"; Nicholas Eberstadt, "North Korea's Phony Peace Ploy," *New York Times*, April 25, 2018, https://www.nytimes.com/2018/04/25/opinion/north-korea-south-korea-peace.html; and John Bolton, *The Room Where It Happened: A White House Memoir* (New York: Simon and Schuster, 2020), 81–82.

103. Bolton, *The Room Where It Happened*, 34–36; and Peter Nicholas, "The Quickest Path to Irrelevance in the Trump White House," *The Atlantic*, September 11, 2019, https://www.theatlantic.com/politics/archive/2019/09/why-boltons-days-were-numbered-from-the-start/597778/.

104. Michael E. O'Hanlon, "What Type of National Security Advisor is John Bolton Likely to Be?," Brookings Institution, March 27, 2017, https://www.brookings.edu/articles/what-type-of-national-security-advisor-is-john-bolton-likely-to-be/.

105. Dexter Filkins, "John Bolton on the Warpath," *New Yorker*, April 29, 2019, https://www.newyorker.com/magazine/2019/05/06/john-bolton-on-the-warpath.

106. Bolton, *The Room Where It Happened*, 27–30.

107. Author's recollection from multiple Track 2 meetings with North Koreans, 2011–2016.

108. Graeme Wood, "Will John Bolton Bring On Armageddon—Or Stave It Off?," *The Atlantic*, April 2019, https://www.theatlantic.com/magazine/archive/2019/04/john-bolton-trump-national-security-adviser/583246/.

109. Bolton, *The Room Where It Happened*, 76.

110. Pat Murphy, "Goldwater, Softer but Still Spicy, Reflects on a Fading Odyssey," *New York Times*, September 22, 1985, https://www.nytimes.com/1985/09/22/us/goldwater-softer-but-still-spicy-reflects-on-a-fading-odyssey.html; and John Bolton, *Surrender is Not an Option: Defending America at the United Nations and Abroad* (New York: Threshold Editions, 2007), 105.

111. Joshua Berlinger, "Bolton Says US Considering Libya Model for North Korean Denuclearization," CNN, April 30, 2018, https://www.cnn.com/2018/04/30/asia/north-korea-bolton-libya-intl/index.html; and Peter Baker, "Libya as a Model for Disarmament? North Korea May See It Very Differ-

ently," *New York Times*, April 29, 2018, https://www.nytimes.com/2018/04
/29/us/politics/bolton-libya-north-korea-trump.html.

112. Pompeo, *Never Give An Inch*, chap. 8.
113. Interview with former U.S. official, June 13, 2021.
114. Bolton, *The Room Where It Happened*, 80–81.
115. Pompeo, *Never Give An Inch*, chap. 8; Nicole Gaouette, "Pompeo's 13 Hours in North Korea," CNN, May 9, 2018, https://www.cnn.com/2018/05/09 /politics/mike-pompeo-north-korea-prisoners-tick-tock/index.html; Carol Morello, "My Journey to North Korea with the Secretary of State," *Washington Post*, May 10, 2018, https://www.washingtonpost.com/world/national -security/my-journey-to-north-korea-with-the-secretary-of-state/2018 /05/10/93f7c90e-5472-11e8-9c91-7dab596e8252_story.html; and Benjamin Haas and Oliver Laughland, "North Korea Releases Three US Citizens in Run-Up to Trump Summit," *Guardian* (London), May 9, 2018, https://www .theguardian.com/world/2018/may/09/north-korea-releases-three-us -citizens-in-run-up-to-trump-summit-mike-pompeo.
116. Pompeo, *Never Give an Inch*, chap. 8.
117. Interview with former U.S. official, February 27, 2023.
118. Member of U.S. delegation, email exchange with author, September 16, 2022.
119. "Trump Summit with Kim Jong Un Set for June 12 in Singapore, Trump Tweets," CBS News, May 10, 2018, https://www.cbsnews.com/news/trump -summit-with-kim-jong-un-set-for-june-12-in-singapore-trump-tweets/; and Bolton, *The Room Where It Happened*, 83–84.
120. "Bolton Says U.S. Looking at 'Libya Model' for North Korea—Full Transcript," *Haaretz*, April 29, 2018, https://www.haaretz.com/us-news/2018-04 -29/ty-article/bolton-says-u-s-looking-at-libya-model-for-north-korea /0000017f-dfod-d856-a37f-ffcdb8a80000; and Pompeo, *Never Give an Inch*, chap. 4.
121. Rick Noack, "Trump Just Contradicted Bolton on North Korea. What's the 'Libya Model' They Disagree on?," *Washington Post*, May 17, 2018, https:// www.washingtonpost.com/news/world/wp/2018/05/16/whats-this-libya -model-north-korea-is-so-angry-about/; and Bolton, *The Room Where It Happened*, 82–83.
122. Sophie Tatum and James Griffiths, "Pence: North Korea Will End like Libya Only if Kim Jong Un Doesn't Make a Deal," CNN, May 22, 2018, https://www.cnn.com/2018/05/21/politics/mike-pence-fox-news-north -korea/index.html.
123. "North Korea Says US Vice-President Pence's Comments 'Stupid,'" BBC, May 24, 2018, https://www.bbc.com/news/world-asia-44234268; and Choe Sang-Hun, "North Korea, Calling Pence Remarks 'Ignorant and Stupid,' Issues New Warning on Summit," *New York Times*, May 23, 2018, https:// www.nytimes.com/2018/05/23/world/asia/north-korea-trump-pence -summit.html.

124. Bolton, *The Room Where It Happened*, 91.

125. Bolton, *The Room Where It Happened*, 91; Mark Landler, "Trump Pulls Out of North Korea Summit Meeting with Kim Jong-un," *New York Times*, May 24, 2018, https://www.nytimes.com/2018/05/24/world/asia/north -korea-trump-summit.html; and John Wagner, "Trump's Cancellation of Summit with Kim Raises Fears of Renewed Tensions, Destabilization," *Washington Post*, May 24, 2018, https://www.washingtonpost.com/politics /trump-cancels-nuclear-summit-with-north-korean-leader-kim-jong-un /2018/05/24/e502d910-5f58-11e8-a4a4-c070ef53f315_story.html.

126. The White House, "Donald Trump's May 24 Letter to Kim Jong Un," May 24, 2018.

127. Camila Domonoske, "Trump Cancels Summit, North Korean Leaders Leave Door Open for Talks," NPR, May 24, 2018, https://www.npr.org /sections/thetwo-way/2018/05/24/614082389/very-perplexed-international -confusion-concern-after-trump-cancels-summit.

128. Choe Sang-Hun, "North Korea Willing to Talk about Complete Denucle-arization," *New York Times*, May 26, 2018, https://www.nytimes.com/2018 /05/26/world/asia/korea-kim-jong-un-summit-meeting.html; Jeong Woo-sang, "Leaders of 2 Koreas in Surprise Summit at Border," *Chosun Daily*, May 28, 2018, english.chosun.com/site/data/html_dir/2018/05/28/2018 052800599.html; and Bolton, *The Room Where It Happened*, 92–93.

129. "Moscow Briefing by Senior Russian Diplomat," private notes by author, summer 2018.

130. Mark Landler and David E. Sanger, "Trump Says North Korea Summit May be Rescheduled," *New York Times*, May 25, 2018, https://www.nytimes.com /2018/05/25/world/asia/trump-summit-north-korea.html; and Bolton, *The Room Where It Happened*, 92.

131. Interview with former State Department official, July 29, 2022.

132. Anna Fifield and John Wagner, "Top North Korean Official on His Way to U.S. for Talks on Trump-Kim Summit," *Washington Post*, May 29, 2018, https://www.washingtonpost.com/world/top-north-korean-official -believed-to-be-on-his-way-to-the-us-for-meetings/2018/05/29/16a7b7e2 -62f6-11e8-b166-fea8410bcded_story.html; Scott Neuman and Bill Chap-pell, "Pompeo Meets with Top North Korean Official in Hopes of Reviv-ing Singapore Summit," NPR, May 31, 2018, https://www.npr.org/sections /thetwo-way/2018/05/31/615691882/pompeo-meets-with-top-north -korean-official-in-hopes-of-reviving-singapore-summi; and Sofia Lotto Persio, "Mike Pompeo Enjoyed Dinner of Steak, Corn and Cheese with North Korea's Kim Yong Chol," *Newsweek*, May 31, 2018, https://www .newsweek.com/mike-pompeo-enjoyed-his-dinner-steak-corn-and-cheese -north-koreas-kim-yong-950600.

133. Pompeo, *Never Give An Inch*, chap. 8.

134. Pompeo, *Never Give An Inch*, chap. 8; and interview with former State De-partment official, September 2, 2021.

135. Bolton, *The Room Where It Happened,* 95–96; and Pompeo, *Never Give An Inch,* chap. 8.

136. Bolton, *The Room Where It Happened,* 96.

137. Bolton, *The Room Where It Happened,* 101; and interview with former U.S. official, October 4, 2021.

138. Interview with former U.S. official, November 5, 2021.

139. The White House, "Remarks by President Trump after Meeting with Vice Chairman Kim Yong Chol of the Democratic People's Republic of Korea," June 1, 2018, https://trumpwhitehouse.archives.gov/briefings-statements /remarks-president-trump-meeting-vice-chairman-kim-yong-chol -democratic-peoples-republic-korea/; and Kevin Liptak, "Trump Says Singapore Summit with Kim Is Back on," CNN, June 1, 2018, https://edition .cnn.com/2018/06/01/politics/trump-north-korea-letter/index.html.

140. Bolton, *The Room Where It Happened,* 98.

141. Bolton, *The Room Where It Happened,* 99.

Chapter Fifteen. "This wasn't just another negotiation."

1. Interview with former U.S. official, June 13, 2021.

2. Elise Labott, Kevin Liptak, and Sophie Tatum, "US Delegation Travels to North Korea for Potential Summit Preparation," CNN, May 28, 2018, https://edition.cnn.com/2018/05/27/politics/us-team-north-korea -summit/index.html.

3. Hyonhee Shin and Lesley Wroughton, "U.S. Team in North Korea for Talks on Summit, Trump Says," Reuters, May 27, 2018, https://www.reuters.com /article/us-northkorea-missiles/u-s-north-korean-officials-meet-for-talks -on-summit-idUSKCN1IS01K/; and Andrew Jeong and Chun Han Wong, "U.S., North Korea Meet to Try to Salvage Summit," *Wall Street Journal,* May 28, 2018, https://www.wsj.com/articles/u-s-north-korea-meet-to-try -to-salvage-summit-1527500643.

4. Interview with former State Department official, August 25, 2021; and interview with former official, November 5, 2021.

5. Interview with former U.S. official, August 25, 2021; interview with former U.S. official, August 31, 2021; and interview with former U.S. official, June 13, 2021.

6. Interview with former US official, June 13, 2021; and "U.S. Officials Held Summit-Planning Talks with North Korean Officials at the DMZ," Reuters, May 27, 2018, https://www.cnbc.com/2018/05/27/us-officials-in-summit -planning-talks-with-north-korea-at-panmunjom.html.

7. The White House, "Press Briefing by Sarah Sanders," June 4, 2018, https:// trumpwhitehouse.archives.gov/briefings-statements/press-briefing-press -secretary-sarah-sanders-060418/.

8. Interview with former State Department official, August 25, 2021; and interview with former U.S. official, June 13, 2021.

9. John Bolton, *The Room Where It Happened: A White House Memoir* (New York: Simon and Schuster, 2020), 94; and interview with former U.S. official, June 13, 2021.

10. Bolton, *The Room Where It Happened*, 94.

11. Interview with former U.S. official, June 13, 2021.

12. Bolton, *The Room Where It Happened*, 94.

13. Interview with former State Department official, August 25, 2021.

14. Ted Barrett, "Democrats Warn Trump on North Korea Deal," CNN, June 4, 2018, https://www.cnn.com/2018/06/04/politics/north-korea -congress-reaction/index.html; Anita Kumar, "Trump's Unlikely Allies on North Korea Talks—Progressive Democrats," *McClatchy*, June 13, 2018, https://www.mcclatchydc.com/news/politics-government/white-house /article212960759.html#cardLink=row1_card1; and "The Surprise Coali- tion of Trump Critics Supporting the Kim Jong Un Meeting," CNN, May 11, 2018, https://www.cnn.com/2018/05/11/politics/poll-trump-critics -north-korea-kim-jong-un-meeting.

15. Bryan Schatz, "Trump Says He'll Use 'My Touch, My Feel' to Assess Kim Jong-un's Nuclear Plans," *Mother Jones*, June 9, 2018, https://www .motherjones.com/politics/2018/06/trump-says-hell-use-my-touch-my -feel-to-assess-kim-jong-uns-nuclear-plans/; and interview with former U.S. official, June 13, 2021.

16. Callum Borchers, "'Within the First Minute I'll Know': Trump's Confident G-7 News Conference, Annotated," *Washington Post*, June 10, 2018, https:// www.washingtonpost.com/news/the-fix/wp/2018/06/10/within-the-first -minute-ill-know-trumps-confident-g-7-news-conference-annotated/; Bolton, *The Room Where It Happened*, 105; and Damian Paletta and Joel Achenbach, "Trump Accuses Canadian Leader of Being 'Dishonest' and Weak,'" *Washington Post*, June 18, 2018, https://www.washingtonpost.com /politics/trump-attacks-canada-to-show-north-korea-hes-strong-aide -says/2018/06/10/afc16c0c-6cba-11e8-bd50-b80389a4e569_story.html.

17. Singapore Ministry of Foreign Affairs, "Edited Transcript of Minister Viv- ian Balakrishnan's Media Doorstop with Singapore Media on 9 June 2018 in Beijing," https://www.mfa.gov.sg/Newsroom/Press-Statements-Transcripts -and-Photos/2018/06/20180609-Edited-Transcript-Beijing.

18. Christine Kim and Joori Roh, "Unprecedented Security Measures Likely to Surround Kim at Summit," Reuters, June 10, 2018, https://www.reuters .com/article/idUSKCN1J604P/; Tan Tam Mei, "Sentosa Island Declared 'Special Event Area' as well," *Straits Times*, June 6, 2018, https://www .straitstimes.com/singapore/trump-kim-summit-will-be-held-at-sentosas -capella-hotel-white-house; Tan Tam Mei and Lee Wen-Yi, "Trump-Kim Summit: Shangri-La Hotel's Vicinity Declared Special Event Area," *Straits Times*, June 5, 2018, https://www.straitstimes.com/singapore/trump-kim -summit-shangri-la-hotels-vicinity-declared-special-event-area; and Siobhan O'Grady, "Kim Jong Un Impersonator Detained at Singapore Airport Days

before U.S.-North Korea Summit," *Washington Post*, June 8, 2018, https://www.washingtonpost.com/news/worldviews/wp/2018/06/08/kim-jong-un-impersonator-detained-at-singapore-airport-days-before-u-s-north-korea-summit/.

19. Royston Sim and Charmaine Ng, "Trump-Kim Summit: Media Centre at F1 Pit Building Opens to Journalists; ST Booth Set Up with Freebies," *Straits Times*, June 10, 2018; and Bob Woodward, *Rage* (New York: Simon and Schuster, 2020), 192.

20. Jamie Taraday, "Kim Jong Un Arrives in Singapore for Historic Summit, Meets Singapore PM," CNN, June 10, 2018, https://www.cnn.com/2018/06/10/asia/kim-jong-un-arrives-in-singapore-intl/index.html.

21. Jacob Pinter, "Trump and Kim Arrive in Singapore For Unprecedented Summit," NPR, June 10, 2018, https://www.npr.org/2018/06/10/618660184/trump-and-kim-arrive-in-singapore-for-unprecedented-summit.

22. Lauren Said-Moorhouse, "Kim Jong Un Goes for Surprise Nighttime Walk ahead of the Summit," CNN, June 11, 2018, https://www.cnn.com/2018/06/11/asia/kim-jong-un-singapore-walk-intl/index.html.

23. Sarah Huckabee Sanders, *Speaking for Myself: Freedom and the Fight of Our Lives inside the Trump White House* (New York: St. Martin's Press, 2020), 133.

24. Brent Griffiths, "Trump: 'Excitement in the Air' in Singapore," *Politico*, June 10, 2018, https://www.politico.com/story/2018/06/10/trump-singapore-korea-nuclear-summit-635360.

25. Bolton, *The Room Where It Happened*, 106.

26. Bolton, *The Room Where It Happened*, 106.

27. Sanders, *Speaking for Myself*, 135.

28. Interview with former U.S. official, June 13, 2021; and Bolton, *The Room Where It Happened*, 107.

29. Interview with former U.S. official, June 13, 2021; and Bolton, *The Room Where It Happened*, 107.

30. Interview with former U.S. official, June 13, 2021; and Bolton, *The Room Where It Happened*, 107.

31. Bolton, *The Room Where It Happened*, 108; and interview with former State Department official, August 25, 2021.

32. Bolton, *The Room Where It Happened*, 108; interview with former State Department official, August 25, 2021; and interview with former U.S. official, June 13, 2021.

33. "Trump-Kim Historic Summit Livestream," Channel News Asia, June 11, 2018, https://www.youtube.com/watch?v=OH50Rv_GSSM.

34. Sanders, *Speaking for Myself*, 136.

35. Joanne Lee, "Description of the Singapore Summit," unpublished research note, Henry L. Stimson Center, July 29, 2022, 2.

36. Lee, "Description of the Singapore Summit," 3.

37. Lee, "Description of the Singapore Summit," 4.

38. Lee, "Description of the Singapore Summit," 4.

39. Woodward, *Rage*, 108.

40. *Billboard*, "Trump Showed Kim Jong Un a Movie Trailer–Like Video at Singapore Summit," Associated Press, June 13, 2018, https://www.billboard.com/music/music-news/trump-movie-trailer-video-kim-jong-un-singapore-summit-8460735/.

41. Bolton, *The Room Where It Happened*, 109.

42. Bolton, *The Room Where It Happened*, 109.

43. Bolton, *The Room Where It Happened*, 109.

44. Bolton, *The Room Where It Happened*, 110.

45. Bolton, *The Room Where It Happened*, 110; and Mike Pompeo, *Never Give An Inch: Fighting for the America I Love* (New York: Broadside Books, 2023), chap. 8, Kindle.

46. Bolton, *The Room Where It Happened*, 111.

47. Bolton, *The Room Where It Happened*, 112; and Sanders, *Speaking for Myself*, 137.

48. Sanders, *Speaking for Myself*, 138.

49. Bolton, *The Room Where It Happened*, 112–113.

50. Bolton, *The Room Where It Happened*, 112–113.

51. Bolton, *The Room Where It Happened*, 112–113.

52. Bolton, *The Room Where It Happened*, 112–113.

53. Sanders, *Speaking for Myself*, 138.

54. Motoko Rich, "Unscripted Moments Steal the Show at Trump-Kim Singapore Summit," *New York Times*, June 12, 2018, https://www.nytimes.com/2018/06/12/world/asia/trump-kim-summit-theatrics.html.

55. Sanders, *Speaking for Myself*, 139.

56. "Trump-Kim Historic Summit Livestream," Channel News Asia, https://www.youtube.com/watch?v=OH50Rv_GSSM&t=22180s.

57. "Trump-Kim Historic Summit Livestream."

58. Jennifer Williams, "Read the Full Transcript of Trump's North Korea Summit Press Conference," *Vox*, June 12, 2018, https://www.vox.com/world/2018/6/12/17452624/trump-kim-summit-transcript-press-conference-full-text.

59. Williams, "Trump's North Korea Summit Press Conference."

60. Bolton, *The Room Where It Happened*, 116.

61. Amy Davidson Sorkin, "Donald Trump's Nuclear Uncle," *New Yorker*, April 8, 2016, https://www.newyorker.com/news/amy-davidson/donald-trumps-nuclear-uncle; and Jamie Gangel and Jeremy Herb, "'A Magical Force': New Trump-Kim Letters Provide Window into Their 'Special Friendship,'" CNN, September 9, 2020, https://www.cnn.com/2020/09/09/politics/kim-jong-un-trump-letters-rage-book/index.html.

62. Williams, "Trump's North Korea Summit Press Conference."

63. Sanders, *Speaking for Myself*, 141–142.

64. Woodward, *Rage*, 109; and letter from Donald Trump to Kim Jong Un, June 15, 2018, in Hanmi Club, "Full English Transcript of Letters: Letter

2018. 4.1.–2019.8.5" [in Korean], *KORUS Journal* 10 (September 2022): 84–132, https://www.rfa.org/korean/in_focus/kjuletters-09302022162829 .html/d2b8b7fcd504-ae40c815c740-ce5cc11c-c601c5b4bcf8-1.pdf.

65. Euan McKirdy, "How Do North Koreans Learn about the Trump-Kim Summit?," CNN, June 13, 2018, https://www.cnn.com/2018/06/13/asia /north-korea-state-media-summit-reporting-intl/index.html; Brian Murphy and Shibani Mahtani, "With Some Reservations, East Asian Countries Welcome the Trump-Kim Summit," *Washington Post*, June 18, 2018, https:// www.washingtonpost.com/news/worldviews/wp/2018/06/12/japan -wanted-kim-jong-un-pledge-to-reopen-issue-of-cold-war-era-abductions -trump-says-they-working-on-that/; Daniel Hurst, "The Trump-Kim Summit: The View from Japan," *The Diplomat*, June 12, 2018, https://thediplo mat.com/2018/06/the-trump-kim-summit-the-view-from-japan/; and Bill Ide and Brian Kopczynski, "China, Moscow See Views Vindicated in Singapore Summit," Voice of America, June 18, 2018, https://www.voanews .com/a/china-moscow-see-views-vindicated-in-singapore-summit /4436925.html.

66. Nicholas Kristof, "Trump Was Outfoxed in Singapore," *New York Times*, June 12, 2018, https://www.nytimes.com/2018/06/12/opinion/trump-kim -summit-north-korea.html; and Isaac Stone Fish, "The Singapore Summit Is Over. Let the Bribery Begin," *Washington Post*, June 13, 2018, https://www .washingtonpost.com/news/global-opinions/wp/2018/06/13/the -singapore-summit-is-over-let-the-bribery-begin/.

67. "Trump-Kim Summit Must Pave the Way to Real Progress," *Financial Times*, https://www.ft.com/content/9b43e962-6e40-11e8-92d3-6c13e5c92914; and "'The Real Challenge Starts Now': Experts Say Trump-Kim Summit a Promising Start," June 15, 2018, in *The Takeout*, produced by CBS News, podcast, https://www.cbsnews.com/video/the-takeout-podcast-north-korea -duyeon-kim-robert-carlin/.

68. Emily Swanson and Catherine Lucey, "Most Americans Approve of How Trump Handled North Korea, New Poll Finds," *PBS NewsHour*, June 21, 2018, https://www.pbs.org/newshour/world/most-americans-approve-of -how-trump-handled-north-korea-according-to-new-poll.

69. Moon Jae-in, *From the Periphery to the Center: Moon Jae In Memoirs of Foreign Affairs and Security* [in Korean] (Paju, South Korea: Kimyoungsa, 2024), 244.

70. Interview with former U.S. official, August 31, 2021.

71. Julian Borger and Justin McCurry, "Mike Pompeo Holds Nuclear Talks with North Korean Officials in Pyongyang," *Guardian* (London), July 6, 2018, https://www.theguardian.com/us-news/2018/jul/05/mike-pompeo -north-kroea-visit-pressure-nuclear-progress.

72. Bolton, *The Room Where It Happened*, 113.

73. Joseph S. Bermudez Jr., "North Korea Begins Dismantling Key Facilities at the Sohae Satellite Launching Station," *38 North*, July 23, 2018, https://www .38north.org/2018/07/sohae072318/; Frank Pabian, Joseph S. Bermudez Jr.,

and Jack Liu, "Infrastructure Improvements at North Korea's Yongbyon Nuclear Research Facility," *38 North*, June 26, 2018, https://www.38north.org/2018/06/yongbyon062618/; and Jonathan Cheong, "North Korea Expands Key Missile Manufacturing Plant," *Wall Street Journal*, July 1, 2018, https://www.wsj.com/articles/north-korea-expands-key-missile-manufacturing-plant-1530486907.

74. Interview with former official, July 6, 2021; and David Brunnstrom, John Walcott, and Hyonhee Shin, "U.S. Softens North Korea Approach as Pompeo Prepares for More Nuclear Talks," Reuters, July 4, 2018, https://www.reuters.com/article/idUSKBN1JU25Y/.

75. Matthew Pennington and Lolita C. Baldor, "Bolton: US Has Plan to Dismantle NK Nuclear Program in Year," Associated Press, July 1, 2018, https://apnews.com/article/85a2e763521c4db1a9446102825030862503086; and Francesco Fontemaggi, "Pompeo: US Hopes for 'Major' North Korea Nuclear Disarmament by 2020," Agence France-Presse, June 13, 2018.

76. Interview with former US official, May 24, 2020; and Bolton, *The Room Where It Happened*, 115.

77. Interview with former U.S. official, May 24, 2020.

78. Interview with former U.S. official, June 13, 2021.

79. Letter from Donald Trump to Kim Jong Un, July 3, 2018, in Hanmi Club, "Full English Transcript of Letters: Letter 2018. 4.1.–2019.8.5"; and Robert Carlin, email exchange with author, May 20, 2021.

80. Interview with former U.S. official, May 24, 2020; and Tara Palmeri, "28 Hours in Pyongyang: Reporter's Notebook," ABC News, July 10, 2018, https://abcnews.go.com/International/28-hours-pyongyang-reporters-notebook/story?id=56471067.

81. Nick Wadhams, "Inside Pompeo's Fraught North Korea Trip," *Bloomberg*, July 8, 2018, https://www.bloomberg.com/news/articles/2018-07-08/one-night-in-pyongyang-inside-pompeo-s-fraught-north-korea-trip.

82. Wadhams, "Inside Pompeo's Fraught North Korea Trip," July 8, 2018; interview with former U.S. official, May 24, 2020; and interview with former U.S. official, July 6, 2021.

83. Interview with former U.S. official, June 9, 2021.

84. Interview with former U.S. official, August 25, 2021.

85. Interview with former U.S. official, August 25, 2021.

86. Interview with former U.S. official, November 5, 2021.

87. Interview with former U.S. official, August 31, 2021.

88. Interview with former U.S. official, May 24, 2020.

89. Interview with former U.S. official, May 24, 2020.

90. Interview with former U.S. official, August 25, 2021; and Borger and McCurry, "Mike Pompeo Holds Nuclear Talks."

91. Bolton, *The Room Where It Happened*, 117–118.

92. Palmeri, "28 Hours"; and interview with former U.S. official, August 25, 2021.

93. Palmeri, "28 Hours"; and interview with former U.S. official, August 25, 2021.

94. Palmeri, "28 Hours"; and interview with former U.S. official, August 25, 2021.

95. Palmeri, "28 Hours"; Davis Richardson, "Mike Pompeo Banned a Journalist from His Plane for Reporting He Ate Processed Cheese," *The Observer*, November 12, 2018, https://observer.com/2018/11/mike-pompeo-banned -journalist-plane-processed-cheese/.

96. Palmeri, "28 Hours."

97. Interview with former U.S. official, August 25, 2021.

98. U.S. Department of State, "Secretary of State Michael R. Pompeo Remarks to Traveling Press," Pyongyang Sunan International Airport, Democratic People's Republic of Korea, July 7, 2018, https://2017-2021 .state.gov/secretary-of-state-michael-r-pompeo-remarks-to-traveling -press/.

99. Bolton, *The Room Where It Happened*, 117–118.

100. Bolton, *The Room Where It Happened*, 118.

101. "North Korean Foreign Ministry Spokesman Criticizes US 'Attitude' at 6–7 July High-Level Talks," Korean Central News Agency, July 7, 2018.

102. "North Korean Foreign Ministry Spokesman."

103. Bolton, *The Room Where It Happened*, 113–114.

104. Bolton, *The Room Where It Happened*, 115–116.

105. Bolton, *The Room Where It Happened*, 123.

106. Bolton, *The Room Where It Happened*, 119–120.

107. Bolton, *The Room Where It Happened*, 120; and letter from Kim Jong Un to Donald Trump, July 30, 2018, in Hanmi Club, "Full English Transcript of Letters: Letter 2018. 4.1.–2019.8.5."

108. Letter from Kim Jong Un to Donald Trump, August 12, 2018, in Hanmi Club, "Full English Transcript of Letters: Letter 2018. 4.1.–2019.8.5"; and Josh Rogin, "Opinion: Why Trump Canceled Pompeo's trip to North Korea," *Washington Post*, August 27, 2018, https://www.washingtonpost.com /news/josh-rogin/wp/2018/08/27/why-trump-cancelled-pompeos-trip-to -north-korea/.

109. Bolton, *The Room Where It Happened*, 120–121; and letter from Donald Trump to Kim Jong Un, September 6, 2018, in Hanmi Club, "Full English Transcript of Letters: Letter 2018. 4.1.–2019.8.5."

Chapter Sixteen. "A rat-shit little country"

1. John Bolton, *The Room Where It Happened: A White House Memoir* (New York: Simon and Shuster, 2020), 124–125.

2. Bolton, *The Room Where It Happened*, 124.

3. Record of White House Briefing for Senate Foreign Relations Committee staffer, spring 2018.

4.   Record of White House Briefing; and Cristiano Lima, "Trump Says North Korea Meeting May Be Delayed, Hints China Is to Blame," *Politico*, May 22, 2018, https://www.politico.com/story/2018/05/22/trump-kim-jong-un-summit-602669.

5.   Interview with Chinese expert, March 25, 2022.

6.   Letter from Kim Jong Un to Donald Trump, September 6, 2018, in Hanmi Club, "Full English Transcript of Letters: Letter 2018. 4.1.–2019.8.5" [in Korean], *KORUS Journal* 10 (September 2022): 84–132, https://www.rfa.org/korean/in_focus/kjuletters-09302022162829.html/d2b8b7fcd504-ae40c815c740-ce5cc11c-c601c5b4bcf8-1.pdf.

7.   Bolton, *The Room Where It Happened*, 125.

8.   Letter from Kim Jong Un to Donald Trump, September 6, 2018; and Bolton, *The Room Where It Happened*, 125.

9.   Bolton, *The Room Where It Happened*, 125.

10. Bolton, *The Room Where It Happened*, 125.

11. Letter from Kim Jong Un to Donald Trump, September 6, 2018; Robert L. Carlin, "The Real Lessons of the Trump-Kim Love Letters," *Foreign Policy*, August 13, 2021, https://foreignpolicy.com/2021/08/13/north-korea-trump-kim-jong-un-love-letters-diplomacy-nuclear-talks/; and Robert Carlin, "Gentlemen Apparently Do Read Other Gentlemen's Mail: Kim Jong Un's Letters to President Trump," *38 North*, September 11, 2020, https://www.38north.org/2020/09/rcarlino91120/.

12. Letter from Kim Jong Un to Donald Trump, September 6, 2018.

13. Max Fisher and Jugal K. Patel, "What One Photo Tells Us About North Korea's Nuclear Program," *New York Times*, February 24, 2017, https://www.nytimes.com/interactive/2017/02/24/world/asia/north-korea-propaganda-photo.html; Lee Se-won, "North Korea's Nuclear Weapons Institute Is a Nuclear Warhead Development Institution. . . . Director Ri Hong Sop Is a Sanctioned Individual" [in Korean], Yonhap News Agency, September 14, 2016, https://www.yna.co.kr/view/AKR20160914031000073; and Kwon Min-seok, "Kim Jong Un Realized Miniaturized Nuclear Warhead . . . Reveals Nuclear Bomb" [in Korean], Yonhap Television News, March 9, 2016, https://www.ytn.co.kr/_pn/0101_201603092204326878.

14. Tariq Rauf, "North Korea's Fifth Nuclear Test," Stockholm International Peace Research Institute, September 9, 2016, https://www.sipri.org/commentary/topical-backgrounder/2016/north-koreas-fifth-nuclear-test.

15. Reuters, "Kim Jong Un's Nuclear Scientists Take Centre Stage after Missile Test," *Guardian* (London), September 5, 2017, https://www.theguardian.com/world/2017/sep/05/kim-jong-un-nuclear-scientists-take-centre-stage-north-korea-missile-test; and Kwon, "Kim Jong Un Realized."

16. Siegfried Hecker, *Hinge Points: An Inside Look at North Korea's Nuclear Program* (Redwood City, CA: Stanford University Press, 2023), 126.

17. Joanne Lee, "Description of Pyongyang Inter-Korean Summit," research note, September 18–20, 2018, citing New China TV, "Live: South Korean

President Arrives in Pyongyang for Inter-Korean Summit," video, September 17, 2018, https://www.youtube.com/watch?v=OoJOVZsxQXE.

18. Lee, "Description of Pyongyang Inter-Korean Summit."
19. Lee, "Description of Pyongyang Inter-Korean Summit."
20. Korea TV, "2018 Inter-Korean Summit Pyeongyang," video, September 21, 2018, https://youtube.com/watch?v=CXJzBIY2MUA.
21. "K-pop Stars Zico, Ailee, Ali in Pyongyang to Attend Inter-Korean Summit," *Straits Times*, September 18, 2018, https://www.straitstimes.com/asia/east-asia/k-pop-stars-zico-ailee-ali-in-pyongyang-to-attend-inter-korean-summit; and interview with former Moon administration official, October 13, 2018.
22. Interview with former Moon administration official, October 13, 2018.
23. Interview with former Moon administration official, October 13, 2018.
24. Interview with former Moon administration official, October 3, 2022.
25. ROK official, private conversation with author, fall 2018; and letter from Kim Jong Un to Donald Trump, September 21, 2018, in Hanmi Club, "Full English Transcript of Letters: Letter 2018. 4.1.–2019.8.5."
26. ROK official, private conversation with author, fall 2018; and letter from Kim Jong Un to Donald Trump, September 21, 2018.
27. Interview with former Moon administration, October 13, 2018.
28. National Committee on North Korea, "Pyongyang Joint Declaration of 2018," September 19, 2018, https://www.ncnk.org/node/1633.
29. Interview with former Moon administration official, August 26, 2022.
30. Interview with former Moon administration official, August 26, 2022.
31. Interview with former Moon administration official, August 26, 2022.
32. Interview with former Moon administration official, August 26, 2022.
33. Interview with former Moon administration official, August 26, 2022.
34. Interview with former Moon administration official, August 26, 2022.
35. Interview with former Moon administration official, August 26, 2022.
36. Interview with former Moon administration official, August 26, 2022.
37. Interview with former Moon administration official, August 26, 2022.
38. Interview with former Moon administration official, August 26, 2022.
39. Interview with former Moon administration official, October 24, 2022.
40. Interview with former Moon administration official, October 24, 2022.
41. National Committee on North Korea, "Agreement on the Implementation of the Historic Panmunjom Declaration in the Military Domain," September 19, 2018, https://www.ncnk.org/sites/default/files/Agreement%20on%20the%20Implementation%20of%20the%20Historic%20Panmunjom%20Declaration%20in%20the%20Military%20Domain.pdf; and interview with former Blue House official, August 26, 2022.
42. Sukjoon Yoon, "North and South Korea's New Military Agreement," *The Diplomat*, October 2, 2018; and Ankit Panda, "At Fifth Inter-Korean Summit," *The Diplomat*, September 19, 2018, https://thediplomat.com/2018/10/north-and-south-koreas-new-military-agreement.

43. Interview with former Blue House official, August 26, 2022; interview with former White House official, November 9, 2022; and interview with former senior U.S. officer, September 23, 2022.

44. Christy Lee, "Inter-Korean Military Pact Leaves Washington Uneasy," *Voice of America*, October 19, 2018, https://www.voanews.com/a/inter-korean-military-pact-leaves-washington-uneasy/4620148.html; and Hyonhee Shin, "South Korea Says Pompeo Complained about Inter-Korean Military Pact," *Reuters*, October 10, 2018, https://www.reuters.com/article/world/south-korea-says-pompeo-complained-about-inter-korean-military-pact-idUSKCN1MK21O/.

45. Interview with former senior U.S. officer, September 23, 2022.

46. Interview with former senior U.S. officer, September 23, 2022.

47. Interview with former White House official, November 9, 2022.

48. Interview with former officer, October 12, 2022.

49. Panmunjom Travel Center, "The Joint Security Area (JSA)," http://panmunjomtour.com/jsa/jsa_4_0.asp.

50. Panmunjom Travel Center, "The Joint Security Area"; and Steve Miller, "The Koreas and United Nations Command Work toward Disarming the DMZ," *Voice of America*, October 22, 2018, https://www.voanews.com/a/disarming-korea-dmz/4623429.html.

51. Interview with former U.S. officer, October 12, 2022.

52. Interview with former U.S. officer, October 12, 2022.

53. Interview with former U.S. officer, October 12, 2022.

54. Interview with former U.S. officer, October 12, 2022.

55. Panmunjom Travel Center. "The Joint Security Area."

56. "S. Korea, DPRK Complete Withdrawal of Weapons from JSA inside DMZ," *Xinhua*, October 25, 2018, https://web.archive.org/web/20181025144921/http://www.xinhuanet.com/english/2018-10/25/c_137557889.htm.

57. "Ex-military Figures' Opposition to Comprehensive Military Agreement Intensifies Controversy," *Hankyoreh*, December 5, 2018, https://english.hani.co.kr/arti/english_edition/english_editorials/873193.html.

58. Interview with former Blue House official, August 26, 2022.

59. Wikipedia, "Stephen Biegun," last modified February 9, 2025, 23:45 (UTC), https://en.wikipedia.org/wiki/Stephen_Biegun; In-Chan Hwang, "Steve Biegun, the Angler of Denuclearization," *Dong A-Ilbo*, December 26, 2018; John Hudson and David Nakamura, "Stephen Biegun Tutored Sarah Palin on Foreign Policy. Now He's Trying to Clinch a North Korea Deal for Trump," *Washington Post*, February 20, 2019, https://www.washingtonpost.com/politics/stephen-biegun-tutored-sarah-palin-on-foreign-policy-now-hes-trying-to-clinch-a-north-korea-deal-for-trump/2019/02/20/2f5fca4e-3529-11e9-af5b-b51b7ff322e9_story.html; Lara Jakes, "Uniting Trumpers, Never Trumpers and Democrats with a New Deputy at the State Department," *New York Times*, February 21, 2020, https://www.nytimes.com/2020

/02/21/us/politics/biegun-trump.html; and "An Interview with Steve Biegun," produced by *NK News*, podcast, July 14, 2021, https://www.nknews.org/category/north-korea-news-podcast/latest/an-interview-with-stephen-biegun-nknews-podcast-ep-191/902590/.

60. Hudson and Nakamura, "Stephen Biegun Tutored Sarah Palin."
61. Interview with former U.S. official, June 9, 2021.
62. Interview with former U.S. official, June 9, 2021.
63. Jakes, "Uniting Trumpers"; and interview with former State Department official, June 13, 2021.
64. Interview with former State Department reporter, June 1, 2021; and interview with former State Department official, May 24, 2020.
65. Interview with former State Department official, June 13, 2021.
66. Interview with former State Department official, June 13, 2021.
67. Interview with former State Department official, June 13, 2021.
68. Letter from Kim Jong Un to Donald Trump, September 21, 2018.
69. Kylie Atwood, "Pompeo's Six Hours in Pyongyang—A Reporter's Notebook," CBS News, October 11, 2018, https://www.cbsnews.com/news/pompeos-six-hours-in-pyongyang-a-reporters-notebook/.
70. Atwood, "Pompeo's Six Hours in Pyongyang."
71. Atwood, "Pompeo's Six Hours in Pyongyang."
72. Atwood, "Pompeo's Six Hours in Pyongyang."
73. Atwood, "Pompeo's Six Hours in Pyongyang."
74. Atwood, "Pompeo's Six Hours in Pyongyang"; and "An Interview with Steve Biegun."
75. Atwood, "Pompeo's Six Hours in Pyongyang."
76. Interview with former U.S. official, June 9, 2021.
77. Interview with former U.S. official, June 9, 2021.
78. Interview with former U.S. official, June 9, 2021.
79. Interview with former U.S. official, June 9, 2021.
80. Interview with former official, November 5, 2021; and interview with former U.S. official, August 25, 2021.
81. Interview with former official, November 5, 2021.
82. Interview with former official, November 5, 2021.
83. Interview with former U.S. official, June 9, 2021.
84. Interview with former U.S. official, June 9, 2021.
85. Interview with former U.S. official, June 9, 2021.
86. "An Interview with Steve Biegun"; and interview with former U.S. official, June 9, 2021.
87. "An Interview with Steve Biegun"; and interview with former U.S. official, June 9, 2021.
88. Benjamin Haas, "North Korea: Kim Jong-un Expects 'Great Progress' after Pompeo Talks," *Guardian* (London), October 7, 2018, https://www.theguardian.com/world/2018/oct/07/mike-pompeo-upbeat-on-successful-morning-in-north-korea.

89. Haas, "Kim Jong-un Expects 'Great Progress'"; and Dagyum Ji, "At Meeting with Pompeo, Kim Jong Un Expressed 'Deep Confidence' in Trump," *NK News*, October 7, 2018, https://www.nknews.org/2018/10/at-meeting -with-pompeo-kim-jong-un-expressed-deep-confidence-in-trump-kcna/.

90. Simon Denyer, "Pompeo, Kim Jong Un Agree to Hold 2nd Summit with Trump as soon as Possible," *Washington Post*, October 7, 2018, https://www .washingtonpost.com/world/pompeo-meets-kim-jong-un-in-north-korea -for-talks-on-denuclearization/2018/10/07/d9832280-c997-11e8-9cof -2ffaf6d422aa_story.html.

91. Bolton, *The Room Where It Happened*, 126.

Chapter Seventeen. "Looking forward to my next summit with Chairman Kim."

1. Interview with former U.S. official, June 9, 2021.

2. Interview with former U.S. official, June 9, 2021.

3. Interview with former U.S. official, June 9, 2021.

4. Michael R. Gordon, Courtney McBride, and Andrew Jeong, "U.S. Surprised as Pyongyang Scraps Talks," *Wall Street Journal*, November 7, 2018, https:// www.wsj.com/articles/u-s-surprised-as-pyongyang-scraps-talksu-s -surprised-as-pyongyang-scraps-talks-1541635954; and Simon Denyer and John Hudson, "Pompeo's Meeting with North Korean Counterpart Called Off at Last Minute," *Washington Post*, November 7, 2018, https://www .washingtonpost.com/world/pompeos-meeting-with-north-korean -counterpart-called-off-at-last-minute/2018/11/07/2c355fca-e252-11e8 -a1c9-6afe99dddd92_story.html.

5. U.S. Department of the Treasury, "Treasury Sanctions North Korean Officials and Entities in Response to the Regime's Serious Human Rights Abuses and Censorship," December 10, 2018, https://home.treasury.gov /news/press-releases/sm568.

6. "An Interview with Steve Biegun," produced by *NK News*, podcast, July 14, 2021, https://www.nknews.org/category/north-korea-news-podcast/latest /an-interview-with-stephen-biegun-nknews-podcast-ep-191/902590/; and interview with former U.S. official, August 25, 2021.

7. Interview with former U.S. official, July 23, 2021; and "Transcript: NPR's Full Interview with Secretary of State Mike Pompeo," NPR, December 20, 2018, https://www.npr.org/2018/12/20/678742858/transcript-nprs-full -interview-with-secretary-of-state-mike-pompeo.

8. Letter from Kim Jong Un to Donald Trump, December 25, 2018, in Hanmi Club, "Full English Transcript of Letters: Letter 2018. 4.1.–2019.8.5" [in Korean], *KORUS Journal* 10 (September 2022): 84–132, https://www.rfa.org /korean/in_focus/kjuletters-09302022162829.html/d2b8b7fcd504 -ae40c815c740-ce5cc11c-c601c5b4bcf8-1.pdf.

9. Sarah Kim, "Trump Counting on Summit with Kim Jong-un," *Korea Joong-Ang Daily*, December 25, 2018, https://koreajoongangdaily.joins.com/2018/12/25/politics/Trump-counting-on-summit-with-Kim-Jongun/3057347.html.

10. Interview with former U.S. official, July 23, 2021.

11. Letter from Donald Trump to Kim Jong Un, December 28, 2018, in Hanmi Club, "Full English Transcript of Letters: Letter 2018. 4.1.–2019.8.5."

12. Robert Carlin, unpublished analysis of Kim-Trump letters provided to the author, August 28, 2021.

13. Ruediger Frank, "Kim Jong Un's 2019 New Year's Address: Dropping a Strategic Bombshell," *38 North*, January 2, 2019, https://www.38north.org/2019/01/rfrank010219.

14. Frank, "Kim Jong Un's 2019 New Year's Address."

15. Frank, "Kim Jong Un's 2019 New Year's Address."

16. Robert Carlin, "Hints for 2019: Kim Jong Un's New Year's Address," *38 North*, January 3, 2018, https://www.38north.org/2019/01/rcarlin010319; and Korea Institute for National Unification, "Analysis of Kim Jong Un's 2019 New Year's Day Speech and Prospects for 2019" [in Korean], North Korean Research Division, Online Series, KINU Repository, CO19–01e.pdf, https://repo.kinu.or.kr/handle/2015.oak/9824.

17. Carlin, "Hints for 2019."

18. Hong Min, Park Hyung-joong, Kim Jin-ha, Oh Kyung-sub, Hong Je-whan, Jung Eun-mi, and Lee Young-ki, "Analysis of Kim Jong Un's 2019 New Year's Address and Political Forecast" [in Korean], Korean Institute for National Unification, *KINU Insight*, no. 1 (2019), https://unibook.unikorea.go.kr/libeka/elec/2019040000000058.pdf.

19. Carlin, "Hints for 2019."

20. Frank, "Kim Jong Un's 2019 New Year's Address"; and Carlin, "Hints for 2019."

21. Frank, "Kim Jong Un's 2019 New Year's Address"; and Carlin, "Hints for 2019."

22. Choe Sang-Hun, "North Korea's Leader, Kim Jong-un, Arrives in China by Train," *New York Times*, January 7, 2019, https://www.nytimes.com/2019/01/07/world/asia/kim-jong-un-china-train-html; James Griffiths and Young Xiong, "China Hosts Surprise Visit by Kim Jong Un amid US Tensions," CNN, January 8, 2019, https://www.cnn.com/2019/01/07/china/kim-jong-un-visit-china-intl/index.html; and Ankit Panda, "Kim Jong Un Makes Fourth Trip to China, At Xi Jinping's Invitation," *The Diplomat*, January 8, 2019, https://thediplomat.com/2019/01/kim-jong-un-makes-fourth-trip-to-china-at-xi-jinpings-invitation/.

23. Interview with Chinese expert, July 9, 2022.

24. Interview with Chinese expert, July 9, 2022.

25. White House, "Remarks by President Trump in Cabinet Meeting," January 2, 2019, video, https://www.youtube.com/watch?v=sohD32-9Oh8.

26. Interview with former State Department official, June 13, 2021; and Reuters, "Top North Korean Officials Reportedly Set for Washington Visit," *Guardian* (London), January 16, 2019, https://www.theguardian.com/world/2019/jan/16/north-korean-officials-washington-kim-yong-chol.

27. Interview with former senior U.S. official, June 9, 2021.

28. "An Interview with Steve Biegun"; and interview with former U.S. official, June 9, 2021.

29. Jihye Lee, "North Korea's Surprise New Nuclear Envoy Key to Trump-Kim Talks," *Bloomberg*, February 23, 2019, https://www.japantimes.co.jp/news/2019/02/23/asia-pacific/politics-diplomacy-asia-pacific/north-koreas-surprise-new-nuclear-envoy-key-trump-kim-talks/.

30. Interview with former State Department official, June 13, 2021.

31. Former U.S. official, email exchange with author, September 23, 2021.

32. Interview with former U.S. official, September 29, 2021; and "North Korea's Kim Yong-chol Meets Mike Pompeo in Washington," BBC, January 18, 2019, https://www.bbc.com/news/world-asia-46901250.

33. Interview with former U.S. official, September 29, 2021; and "North Korea's Kim Yong-chol."

34. Interview with former State Department official, June 13, 2021; and interview with former U.S. official, September 29, 2021.

35. Interview with former U.S. official, June 28, 2021.

36. Interview with former U.S. official, June 28, 2021; Hwang Joon-bum, "Kim Yong-chol's Washington D.C. [Visit], A Positive Signal for 2nd NK-US Summit," *Hankyoreh*, January 21, 2019, https://english.hani.co.kr/arti/english_edition/e_northkorea/879254.html; and Hwang Joon-bum, "Trump Meets with Kim Yong-chol at White House for 90 Minutes," *Hankyoreh*, January 19, 2019, https://english.hani.co.kr/arti/english_edition/e_northkorea/879254.html.

37. Interview with former U.S. official, June 28, 2021.

38. Interview with former U.S. official, September 29, 2021.

39. Interview with former U.S. official, July 31, 2021.

40. Interview with former senior U.S. official, July 13, 2021; and interview with former State Department official, June 13, 2021.

41. Interview with former senior U.S. official, July 13, 2021; and interview with former U.S. official, June 28, 2021.

42. Interview with former State Department official, June 13, 2021.

43. Interview with former senior U.S. official, July 13, 2021; interview with former U.S. official, June 28, 2021; and interview with former U.S. official, September 29, 2021.

44. Interview with former State Department official, June 13, 2021; and interview with former U.S. official, June 28, 2021.

45. "An Interview with Steve Biegun"; and interview with former senior U.S. official, June 9, 2021.

46. "An Interview with Steve Biegun"; interview with former senior U.S. official, June 9, 2021; interview with former State Department official, June 13, 2021; and interview with former U.S. official, September 29, 2021.

47. Interview with former senior U.S. official, July 13, 2021; "An Interview with Steve Biegun"; and interview with former U.S. official, September 29, 2021.

48. Ryan Tebo, "SIPRI Helped Broker Secret Meeting between USA and North Korea," SverigesRadio, July 7, 2016, https://sverigesradio.se/artikel/646 9407; and "Choe and Biegun Meet for First Time in Sweden," *Hankyoreh*, January 21, 2019, https://english.hani.co.kr/arti/English_edition/e_north korea/879255.html.

49. Interview with former senior U.S. official, July 13, 2021; "An Interview with Steve Biegun"; interview with former State Department official, June 13, 2021; and interview with former U.S. official, September 29, 2021.

50. Interview with former senior U.S. official, July 13, 2021; "An Interview with Steve Biegun"; interview with former State Department official, June 13, 2021; and interview with former U.S. official, September 29, 2021.

51. Interview with former U.S. official, April 8, 2021; and interview with former U.S. official, September 29, 2021.

52. Interview with former U.S. official, June 28, 2021.

53. "Trump-Kim Summit in February Expected to Take Place in Vietnam," *Straits Times*, January 21, 2019, https://www.straitstimes.com/asia/east-asia /trump-kim-summit-in-february-expected-to-take-place-in-vietnam.

54. Interview with former U.S. official, July 15, 2021.

55. "An Interview with Steve Biegun."

56. Interview with former State Department official, June 13, 2021; and interview with former U.S. official, July 6, 2021.

57. Interview with former State Department reporter, July 6, 2021

58. "An Interview with Steve Biegun."

59. Stephen Biegun, U.S. Special Representative for North Korea, "Remarks on the DPRK," January 31, 2019, Stanford University, Palo Alto, CA.

60. Leon V. Sigal, "Misreporting the Trump Administration's Boffo Break with the Failed North Korea Policy of the Past," *38 North*, February 5, 2019, https://www.38north.org/2019/lsigal020519/.

61. Interview with former State Department official, June 13, 2021.

62. Interview with former State Department official, June 13, 2021.

63. "North Korea Nuclear Talks: US Envoy Biegun in Pyongyang," BBC, February 6, 2019, https://www.bbc.com/news/world-asia-47126274; Colin Zwirko and Oliver Hotham, "U.S. Special Representative Biegun to Hold Talks in Pyongyang on Wednesday: State," *NK News*, February 4, 2019, https://www.nknews.org/2019/02/u-s-special-representative-biegun-to -hold-talks-in-pyongyang-on-wednesday-state/; and Choe Sang-Hun, "U.S.

Envoy Arrives in North Korea to Prepare for 2nd Trump-Kim Summit," *New York Times*, February 6, 2019, https://www.nytimes.com/2019/02/06/world/asia/trump-kim-north-korea-summit.html.

64. Interview with former senior U.S. official, July 8, 2021.
65. Interview with former U.S. official, July 23, 2021; and interview with former senior U.S. official, July 9, 2021.
66. Interview with former U.S. official, July 23, 2021.
67. Interview with former U.S. official, July 23, 2021; and interview with former senior U.S. official, July 8, 2021.
68. Interview with former U.S. official, July 23, 2021; and interview with former senior U.S. official, July 8, 2021.
69. Interview with former U.S. official, July 23, 2021; and interview with former senior U.S. official, July 8, 2021.
70. Interview with former U.S. official, July 23, 2021; and interview with former senior U.S. official, July 8, 2021.
71. Interview with former U.S. official, July 23, 2021; and interview with former senior U.S. official, July 8, 2021.
72. Interview with former U.S. official, July 23, 2021; and interview with former senior U.S. official, July 8, 2021.
73. Interview with former U.S. official, July 23, 2021; and interview with former senior U.S. official, July 8, 2021.
74. Interview with former U.S. official, July 23, 2021; interview with former senior U.S. official, July 8, 2021; and interview with former State Department official, July 17, 2021.
75. Interview with former U.S. official, July 23, 2021; and interview with former State Department official, July 17, 2021.
76. Interview with former senior U.S. official, July 8, 2021.
77. Interview with former U.S. official, July 23, 2021.
78. Interview with former senior U.S. official, July 8, 2021.
79. Interview with former U.S. official, July 23, 2021; and interview with former senior U.S. official, July 8, 2021.
80. "Biegun Wraps Up Talks in Pyongyang," *Korea Joongang Daily*, February 9, 2019, https://koreajoongangdaily.joins.com/2019/02/08/politics/Biegun-wraps-up-talks-in-Pyongyang/3059180.html.
81. Interview with former senior U.S. official, July 8, 2021; and "Hotel du Parc, Hanoi," https://hotelduparchanoi.com/about-us.
82. Hwang Joon-bum, "Working-Level Talks for Hanoi Summit to Begin Soon," *Hankyoreh*, February 20, 2019, https://english.hani.co.kr/arti/english_edition/e_northkorea/882914.html; Lee Chi-dong, "N. Korea, U.S. continue talks on summit agenda amid some progress," Yonhap News Agency, February 25, 2019, en.yna.co.kr/view/AEN20190225007155315; and interview with former senior U.S. official, July 8, 2021.
83. Interview with former U.S. official, July 23, 2021; and interview with former senior U.S. official, July 8, 2021.
84. Interview with former senior U.S. official, July 8, 2021.

85. Interview with former senior U.S. official, July 8, 2021.
86. Interview with former senior U.S. official, July 8, 2021.
87. Interview with former senior U.S. official, July 8, 2021.
88. Interview with former U.S. official, July 23, 2021; interview with former senior U.S. official, July 8, 2021; and "An Interview with Steve Biegun."
89. Interview with former senior U.S. official, July 8, 2021; and Kim Ji-eun and Gil Yun-hyung, "Preparation for 2nd NK-US Summit in Hanoi in High Gear," *Hankyoreh*, February 25, 2019, https://english.hani.co.kr/arti/english _edition/e_northkorea/883522.
90. Interview with former senior U.S. official, July 8, 2021.
91. During my many meetings over decades with the North Koreans, they explained repeatedly what they meant by America's "hostile policy."
92. Interview with former State Department official, July 17, 2021.
93. Interview with former State Department official, July 17, 2021.
94. Interview with former senior U.S. official, July 8, 2021; and interview with former U.S. official, September 29, 2021.
95. Interview with former senior U.S. official, July 8, 2021; and interview with former U.S. official, September 29, 2021.
96. Interview with former State Department official, July 17, 2021.
97. Interview with former senior U.S. official, July 8, 2021.
98. Interview with former senior U.S. official, July 8, 2021.
99. Interview with former State Department official, July 17, 2021.
100. Interview with former U.S. official, July 23, 2021.
101. "An Interview with Steve Biegun"; and interview with former senior U.S. official, July 8, 2021.
102. Interview with former U.S. official, July 23, 2021; and interview with former State Department official, July 17, 2021.
103. Interview with former senior U.S. official, July 8, 2021; and interview with former State Department official, July 17, 2021.
104. Interview with former U.S. official, December 9, 2021; and interview with former State Department official, July 17, 2021.
105. Interview with former State Department official, July 17, 2021.
106. Interview with former U.S. official, July 23, 2021.
107. Interview with former State Department official, July 17, 2021.
108. Interview with former State Department official, July 17, 2021.
109. Interview with former senior U.S. official, July 8, 2021; and "An Interview with Steve Biegun."

Chapter Eighteen. "A little bit of desperation on the president's part"

1. Bob Woodward, *Rage* (New York: Simon and Schuster, 2020), 174.
2. "Expectations Low as Trump Looks for Win in North Korea Summit," *PBS NewsHour*, February 25, 2019, https://www.pbs.org/newshour/politics /expectations-low-as-trump-looks-for-win-in-north-korea-summit; and

Kevin Fitzpatrick, "Mike Pompeo Carefully Trying to Lower Expectations for a Second Summit," *Vanity Fair,* February 24, 2019, https://www.vanityfair .com/news/2019/02/trump-pompeo-north-korea-summit-hanoi.

3. Roberta Rampton, "Trump Makes His Case for Nobel Peace Prize, Complains He'll Never Get It," Reuters, February 15, 2019, https://www.reuters .com/article/idUSKCN1Q42GN/,

4. Julian Borger, "Trump and Kim Jong-un to Meet Again at Second Nuclear Summit," *Guardian* (London), January 18, 2019, https://www.theguardian .com/world/2019/jan/18/north-korea-kim-yong-chol-pompeo-trump -second-summit; and Paul Blumenthal, "Progressive Democrats Show Support for Trump-Kim Summit with New Call to End Korean War," *Huffington Post,* February 26, 2019, https://www.huffpost.com/entry/trump-kim -summit-korean-war_n_5c75b341e4b062b30eb8cea3.

5. Nick Schifrin, "What a Second Trump-Kim Summit Could Mean for the Push to Denuclearize North Korea," *PBS NewsHour,* January 18, 2019, https://www.pbs.org/newshour/show/what-a-2nd-trump-kim-summit -could-mean-for-the-push-to-denuclearize-north-korea.

6. Dhrumil Mehta, "America Had Warmed to Trump's North Korea Strategy before the Vietnam Summit," *FiveThirtyEight,* March 1, 2019, https:// fivethirtyeight.com/features/america-had-warmed-to-trumps-north-korea -strategy-before-the-vietnam-summit/; and Glenn Kessler, "Trump Exaggerates the Possibility of War with North Korea," *Washington Post,* February 5, 2019, https://www.washingtonpost.com/news/fact-checker/wp/2018/07/02 /president-trumps-exaggerated-claims-about-the-north-korea-deal/.

7. John Bolton, *The Room Where It Happened: A White House Memoir* (New York: Simon and Schuster, 2020), 320.

8. Bolton, *The Room Where It Happened,* 321.

9. Bolton, *The Room Where It Happened,* 323.

10. Bolton, *The Room Where It Happened,* 323.

11. Bolton, *The Room Where It Happened,* 323.

12. Bolton, *The Room Where It Happened,* 323; interview with former U.S. official, July 23, 2021; and interview with former U.S. official, October 15, 2021.

13. Adam Shaw, "Trump Lands in Vietnam for Kim Jong Un Summit," Fox News, February 26, 2019, https://www.foxnews.com/politics/trump-lands -in-vietnam-ahead-of-crucial-summit-with-kim-jong-un.

14. Interview with former senior U.S. official, July 8, 2021; interview with former U.S. official, October 15, 2021; and interview with former U.S. official, October 15, 2021.

15. Interview with former senior U.S. official, July 8, 2021; interview with former State Department official, July 17, 2021; and interview with former U.S. official, October 15, 2021.

16. Maureen Dowd, "Will Trump Be the Sage One?," *New York Times,* May 18, 2019, https://www.nytimes.com/2019/05/18/opinion/sunday/trump-bolton -war.html.

17. "On His Way to Vietnam, Kim Jong Un Took an Early Smoke Break," Associated Press, February 25, 2019, https://www.seattletimes.com/nation-world/nation/tv-footage-shows-kim-jong-un-taking-smoke-break/.

18. Tran Van Minh, "Hanoi Postcard: Vietnam Sees Upside to Media Invasion," Associated Press, February 28, 2019, https://apnews.com/article/9eoddfa-6dac64092a54d8d8a68eb454c; David Nakamura and John Hudson, "In Hanoi, Kim Jong Un and a Culture Clash with the White House Press Corps," *Washington Post*, February 26, 2019, https://www.washingtonpost.com/politics/in-hanoi-kim-jong-un-and-a-culture-clash-with-the-white-house-press-corps/2019/02/26/5a3c02cc-3985-11e9-a2cd-307b06d0257b_story.html; Mike Ives, "Kim Jong-un's Symbolic Vietnam Visit Is about More Than Trump," *New York Times*, February 24, 2019, https://www.nytimes.com/2019/02/25/world/asia/north-korea-kim-vietnam.html; and Doan Loan, "Vietnam to Close 170km Hanoi-China Highway Segment on Saturday," *VN Express*, February 28, 2019, https://e.vnexpress.net/news/news/vietnam-to-close-170km-hanoi-china-highway-segment-on-saturday-3888229.html.

19. Interview with former senior U.S. official, July 8, 2021; Nakamura and Hudson, "In Hanoi"; and Mike Ives, "Breakfast with Kim Jong-un? Some American Reporters Came Close(ish)," *New York Times*, February 26, 2019, https://www.nytimes.com/2019/02/26/world/asia/trump-kim-hanoi-hotel.html.

20. Interview with former senior U.S. official, July 8, 2021.

21. Interview with former senior U.S. official, July 8, 2021.

22. Soyoung Kim and Mai Nguyen, "Bomb Bunker, War Reporters and Charlie Chaplin—Hanoi's Storied Metropole Hosts Trump-Kim Summit," Reuters, February 26, 2019, https://www.reuters.com/article/idUSKCN1QG064/.

23. Justin Sink and Margaret Talev for Reuters, "Trump Lands in Hanoi for Second Kim Summit, Seen Yielding Low Returns," *Bloomberg*, February 25, 2019, https://www.bloomberg.com/news/articles/2019-02-26/trump-s-high-profile-summit-with-kim-seen-yielding-low-returns.

24. "First Day of Hanoi Summit: Evening Session with the Press, February 27, 2019," unpublished research note by author.

25. Hannah Beech, "Vietnam Summit Hosts Offer North Korea a Model: Cozy Up to the U.S.," *New York Times*, February 25, 2019, https://www.nytimes.com/2019/02/26/world/asia/trump-kim-vietnam-summit-north-korea-relations.html; and Michael Tatarski, "Vietnam Won the Trump-Kim Summit," *The Atlantic*, February 28, 2019, https://www.theatlantic.com/international/archive/2019/02/vietnam-won-trump-kim-summit/583834/.

26. James Hookway, "Vietnam Is Big Enough for Only One Kim Jong Un," *Wall Street Journal*, February 25, 2019, https://www.wsj.com/articles/vietnam-is-big-enough-for-only-one-kim-jong-un-11551104557

27. "Sofitel Legend Metropole Hanoi," https://www.lartisien.com/hotel/sofitel-legend-metropole-hanoi; Wikipedia, "Sofitel Legend Metropole Hanoi,"

last modified December 20, 2024, 10:47 (UTC), https://en.wikipedia.org /wiki/Sofitel_Legend_Metropole_Hanoi; Kim and Nguyen, "Bomb Bunker"; and Laignee Barbon, "Trump and Kim Are Meeting One-on-One at This Historic Hanoi Hotel," *Time*, February 27, 2019, https://time.com /5539621/donald-trump-kim-jong-un-metropole-hotel-hanoi/

28. Jim Sciutto, Kylie Atwood, Jeremy Diamond, and Kevin Liptak, "A Snub and a Last Minute Hail Mary. Trump's Tough Lesson in North Korean Diplomacy," CNN, March 6, 2019, https://www.cnn.com/2019/03/06 /politics/trump-kim-hanoi-summit-snub/index.html.

29. Sciutto, Atwood, Diamond, and Liptak, "A Snub and a Last Minute Hail Mary."

30. Bolton, *The Room Where It Happened*, 324.

31. Bolton, *The Room Where It Happened*, 325.

32. Jonathan Karl, *Front Row at the Trump Show* (New York: Dutton, 2020), 296.

33. Karl, *Front Row at the Trump Show*, 296.

34. Karl, *Front Row at the Trump Show*, 296–297; and Bolton, *The Room Where It Happened*, 325.

35. ABC News, "North Korea Summit 2019: Trump, Kim Jong Un Meet in Hanoi, Vietnam for Second Summit," February 27, 2019, video, https://www .youtube.com/watch?v=mHGCZna1IIc.

36. Bolton, *The Room Where It Happened*, 326.

37. Everett Rosenfeld, "On North Korea Giving Up Nukes, Trump Says Again and Again: 'No Rush,'" CNBC, February 27, 2019, https://www.cnbc.com /2019/02/28/trump-heads-into-nuclear -talks-with-north-koreas-kim.html.

38. Caitlin Oprysko, "Trump Leaves North Korea Summit without a Deal," *Politico*, February 28, 2019, https://www.politico.eu/article/trump-kim -summit-unexpectedly-cut-short/.

39. ABC News, "North Korea Summit, 2019," video, February 27, 2019.

40. Mike Pompeo, *Never Give an Inch: Fighting for the America I Love* (New York: Broadside Books, 2023), chap. 8, Kindle; and Bolton, *The Room Where It Happened*, 326–327.

41. ABC News, "North Korea Summit, 2019," February 27, 2019.

42. Oprysko, "Trump Leaves North Korea Summit."

43. ABC News, "North Korea Summit 2019," February 27, 2019; and Bolton, *The Room Where It Happened*, 292.

44. Bolton, *The Room Where It Happened*, 327.

45. Interview with former U.S. official, October 15, 2021.

46. Interview with former U.S. official, October 15, 2021.

47. Interview with former senior U.S. official, July 13, 2021.

48. Interview with former senior U.S. official, July 13, 2021.

49. Bolton, *The Room Where It Happened*, 328.

50. Bolton, *The Room Where It Happened*, 328; interview with former senior U.S. official, July 13, 2021; and interview with former U.S. official, July 23, 2021.

51. Interview with former U.S. official, July 23, 2021; and interview with former senior U.S. official, July 13, 2021.

52. Bolton, *The Room Where It Happened,* 328.

53. Interview with former senior U.S. official, July 13, 2021; and interview with former U.S. official, July 23, 2021.

54. Bolton, *The Room Where It Happened,* 328; and interview with former senior U.S. official, July 13, 2021.

55. Woodward, *Rage,* 175.

56. Interview with former U.S. official, July 23, 2021; interview with former senior U.S. official, July 13, 2021; and "An Interview with Steve Biegun," produced by *NK News,* podcast, July 14, 2021, https://www.nknews.org/category/north-korea-news-podcast/latest/an-interview-with-stephen-biegun-nknews-podcast-ep-191/902590/.

57. Interview with former U.S. official, July 23, 2021.

58. Bolton, *The Room Where It Happened,* 328.

59. Interview with former senior U.S. official, July 13, 2021; and interview with former U.S. official, July 23, 2021.

60. Interview with former U.S. official, December 9, 2021.

61. Interview with former senior U.S. official, July 13, 2021; and interview with former U.S. official, July 23, 2021.

62. Interview with former U.S. official, July 23, 2021; and interview with former senior U.S. official, July 13, 2021.

63. Interview with former U.S. official, July 23, 2021; Korean Central News Agency, February 27, 2019; and *Rodong Sinmun* [in Korean], February 27, 2019.

64. Interview with former U.S. official, July 23, 2021.

65. Interview with former senior U.S. official, July 13, 2021; and interview with former U.S. official, July 7, 2021.

66. Interview with former senior U.S. official, July 13, 2021; and "An Interview with Steve Biegun."

67. Interview with former senior U.S. official, July 13, 2021.

68. Interview with former senior U.S. official, July 13, 2021.

69. Interview with former senior U.S. official, July 13, 2021.

70. Interview with former senior U.S. official, July 13, 2021.

71. Interview with former senior U.S. official, July 13, 2021; Jim Acosta and Paul Leblanc, "Trump Offered Kim Jong Un a Ride Home on Air Force One Following Vietnam Summit, One Source Says," CNN, February 22, 2021, https://www.cnn.com/2021/02/22/politics/trump-kim-jong-un-air-force-one-vietnam-summit/index.html; and interview with former U.S. official, December 9, 2021.

72. Email exchange between former ROK official and the author, December 14, 2022.

73. Interview with former U.S. official, December 9, 2021.

74. Interview with former U.S. official, July 13, 2021.

75.	Interview with former U.S. official, October 15, 2021.
76.	Interview with former U.S. official, December 9, 2021.
77.	BBC analyst, email exchange with the author, March 3, 2019.
78.	Trump White House Archives, "Remarks by President Trump in Press Conference, Hanoi, Vietnam," JW Marriott Hotel Hanoi, February 28, 2019, https://trumpwhitehouse.archives.gov/briefings-statements/remarks-president-trump-press-conference-hanoi-vietnam.
79.	Interview with former U.S. official, January 5, 2022.
80.	Trump White House Archives, "Remarks by President Trump in Press Conference."
81.	Alexander Mallin and Conor Finnegan, "US-North Korea Summit with President Donald Trump and Kim Jong Un Cut Short in Vietnam," ABC News, February 28, 2019, https://abcnews.go.com/Politics/trump-kim-meeting-2nd-summit-us-pushes-concrete/story?id=61368977; and "Trump on Leaving without a Deal with Kim Jong Un: 'Sometimes You Have to Walk,'" CBS News, February 28, 2019, https://www.cbsnews.com/live-news/trump-kim-2019-summit-press-conference-today-2019-02-28-live-updates/.
82.	Trump White House Archives, "Remarks by President Trump in Press Conference," February 28, 2019.
83.	Private meeting with senior ROK official, April 2, 2019; and Uri Friedman, "The Plan to Resurrect the North Korea Nuclear Talks," *The Atlantic*, April 10, 2019, https://www.theatlantic.com/politics/archive/2019/04/south-korea-wants-bring-trump-and-kim-together-again/586894/.
84.	Interview with former U.S. official, December 9, 2021.
85.	Foster Klug, "NKorea Leader Kim Jong Un Tours Hanoi after Summit Breakdown," Associated Press, March 1, 2019, https://apnews.com/article/5d0829c4df3b4c15878e5b03b17d0675; and Foster Klug, "North Korea's Kim Leaves Vietnam after Summit," Associated Press, March 2, 2019, https://apnews.com/article/6e7ef294851f43249bd4beae9de609b4.
86.	"Kim Returns Home to Pyongyang," *Korea JoongAng Daily*, March 5, 2019, https://koreajoongangdaily.joins.com/2019/03/05/politics/Kim-returns-home-to-Pyongyang/3060177.html.
87.	"Kim Jong-un Will Cut His Vietnam Visit Short," *Korea JoongAng Daily*, March 1, 2019, https://koreajoongangdaily.joins.com/2019/03/01/politics/Kim-Jongun-will-cut-his-Vietnam-visit-short/3060037.html.
88.	Rebecca Morin, "North Korea Denies Trump's Account of a Summit Collapse," *Politico*, February 28, 2019, https://www.politico.com/story/2019/02/28/north-korea-press-conference-sanctions-1196561; "An Interview with Steve Biegun"; and Noh Ji-won and Kim Ji-eun, "North Korea Refutes Trump's Claim That It Demanded Removal of All Sanctions," *Hankyoreh*, March 1, 2019, https://english.hani.co.kr/arti/english_edition/e_northkorea/884167.html.
89.	BBC analyst, email exchange with author, March 20, 2019.

90. Brett Samuels, "Fewer Than Half of Americans Said Second Trump-Kim Summit Reduced North Korean Nuclear Threat: Poll," *The Hill*, March 7, 2019, https://thehill.com/blogs/blog-briefing-room/news/433047-less-than -half-of-americans-think-second-trump-kim-reduced.

91. Michael Bowman, "US Lawmakers Back Trump's No Deal Stance at Hanoi Summit," Voice of America, February 28, 2019, https://www.voanews .com/a/us-lawmakers-on-trump-kim-summit-no-deal-better-than-flawed -deal/4807963.html.

92. Bolton, *The Room Where It Happened*, 320–322; and CBS News, *Face the Nation*, March 3, 2019, https://www.cbsnews.com/news/transcript-national -security-adviser-john-bolton-on-face-the-nation-march-3-2019/.

93. Interview with former U.S. official, July 6, 2021.

94. Interview with former U.S. official, July 6, 2021.

95. Bolton, *The Room Where It Happened*, 324–331.

96. Shannon Pettypiece and Margaret Talev, "President Trump Has a Long History of Storming Out of Meetings—and It Has Usually Worked," *Time*, January 10, 2019, https://time.com/5499109/trump-history-storming-out -of-meetings/.

97. Interview with former U.S. official, July 23, 2021.

98. Editorial Board, "The Hanoi Summit Failure Exposes Trump's Weak Diplomacy," *Washington Post*, February 28, 2019, https://www.washingtonpost .com/opinions/global-opinions/the-hanoi-summit-failure-exposes-trumps -weak-diplomacy/2019/02/28/d922faco-3b63-11e9-a2cd-307b06d0257b _story.html.

99. Robin Wright, "As Trump Preps For Singapore, A Look at Past Summits That Succeeded—Or Flopped," *New Yorker*, June 5, 2018, https://www .newyorker.com/news/news-desk/as-trump-preps-for-singapore-which -summits-changed-history-which-flopped; and Daniel Fried, "Framing a Trump-Putin Meeting: A Short Guide to US-Russia Summits Past," *New Atlantacist* (blog), Atlantic Council, June 18, 2018, https://www.atlantic council.org/blogs/new-atlanticist/framing-a-trump-putin-meeting-a -short-guide-to-us-russia-summits-past/.

100. Jane Mayer, "Donald Trump's Ghostwriter Tells All," *New Yorker*, July 18, 2016, https://www.newyorker.com/magazine/2016/07/25/donald-trumps -ghostwriter-tells-all; Woodward, *Rage*, 354; and Steve Benen, "Trump's Attention Span Creates Challenges for Afghanistan Policy," MSNBC, August 7, 2017, https://www.msnbc.com/rachel-maddow-show/trumps -attention-span-creates-challenges-afghanistan-policy-msna1009826.

101. Ronald Reagan, "Remarks at the Annual White House Correspondents Association Dinner," Washington, DC, April 21, 1988, https://www.reagan library.gov/archives/speech/remarks-annual-white-house-correspondents -association-dinner; and U.S. Department of State, "Iceland Chronology," October 14, 1986, secret, declassified, July 31, 1996, https://nsarchive2 .gwu.edu/NSAEBB/NSAEBB203/Document20.pdf.

102. Interview with former Senate staffer, August 20, 2020; Philip Rucker and Josh Dawsey, "Trump's Bid for History in Hanoi Is Overwhelmed by Michael Cohen's Spectacle in Washington," February 27, 2019, *Washington Post*, https://www.washingtonpost.com/politics/thousands-of-miles-away-from-washington-trump-takes-aim-at-cohen/2019/02/27/223ae876-3a6a-11e9-b786-d6abcbcd212a_story.html.
103. Interview with former senior U.S. official, January 5, 2022.
104. Bolton, *The Room Where It Happened*, 295.
105. Wright, "As Trump preps for Singapore"; and Robin Wright, "After All the Swagger, Trump's Talks with North Korea Collapse," *New Yorker*, February 28, 2019, https://www.newyorker.com/news/our-columnists/after-all-the-swagger-trumps-talks-with-north-korea-collapse.
106. Julian Borger, "The Art of No Deal: How Trump and Kim Misread Each Other," *Guardian* (London), February 28, 2019, https://www.theguardian.com/world/2019/feb/28/how-donald-trump-kim-jong-un-misread-each-other-hanoi-summit.
107. "An Interview with Steve Biegun."
108. Interview with senior former U.S. official, July 13, 2021; interview with former State Department official, July 17, 2021; and interview with former U.S. official, July 23, 2021.
109. "President Moon's Policy towards North Korea: Working with the United States for Peace and Security on the Korean Peninsula," unpublished research note by author, February 26, 2019; "North Korea Quits Kaesong Liaison Office with South Korea," BBC, March 22, 2019, https://www.bbc.com/news/world-asia-47665514.
110. Interview with Japanese academic, March 29, 2019.
111. Julian Borger, "North Korea Rebuilds Part of Launch Site It Promised the US It Would Dismantle," *Guardian* (London), March 5, 2019, https://www.theguardian.com/world/2019/mar/06/north-korea-rebuilds-part-of-launch-site-it-promised-the-us-it-would-dismantle; Jack Liu and Jenny Town, "North Korea's Tongchang-ri Rebuilding Commences on Launch Pad and Engine Test Stand," *38 North*, March 5, 2019, https://www.38north.org/2019/03/sohae030519/; and Jack Liu, Peter Makowsky, and Jenny Town, "North Korea's Sohae Satellite Launch Facility: No New Activity Since March 8," *38 North*, March 13, 2019, https://www.38north.org/2019/03/sohae031319.
112. Jeff Mason and David Brunnstrom, "Trump Would Be 'Very Disappointed' in Kim if North Korea Rebuilding Rocket Site," Reuters, March 6, 2019; and Liu, Makowsky, and Town, "North Korea's Sohae Satellite Launch Facility."
113. "Kim Returns Home to Pyongyang," *Korea JoongAng Daily*, March 5, 2019, https://koreajoongangdaily.joins.com/2019/03/05/politics/Kim-returns-home-to-Pyongyang/3060177.html; and "Kim Jong-un Will Cut His Vietnam Visit Short," *Korea JoongAng Daily*, March 1, 2019, https://

koreajoongangdaily.joins.com/2019/03/01/politics/Kim-Jongun-will-cut
-his-Vietnam-visit-short/3060037.html.

114. "N. Korean Media Airs Documentary Film on Trump-Kim Summit,"
Yonhap News Agency, March 7, 2019, https://en.yna.co.kr/view/AEN
20190307002751325?section=nk/nk.

115. Choe Sang-Hun, "North Korea Threatens to Scuttle Talks with the U.S.
and Resume Tests," *New York Times*, March 15, 2019, https://www.nytimes
.com/2019/03/15/world/asia/north-korea-kim-jong-un-nuclear.html; and
Kim Ji-hoon, "[Full text] Statement by North Korean Vice Minister of Foreign Affairs Choe Son Hui at March 15 Press Conference" [in Korean],
Newsis, March 25, 2019, https://mobile.newsis.com/view.html?ar_id=NISX
20190325_0000598643#_PA.

116. Kim, "[Full text] Statement."

117. Kim, "[Full text] Statement."

118. Kim, "[Full text] Statement."

119. State Department official, email communication with the author, May 17,
2019.

120. Robert L. Carlin, "The Real Lessons of the Trump-Kim Love Letters," *Foreign Policy*, August 13, 2021, https://foreignpolicy.com/2021/08/13/north
-korea-trump-kim-jong-un-love-letters-diplomacy-nuclear-talks/.

121. David Nakamura, "In Meeting with South Korea's Moon, Trump Signals
Openness to Smaller Deal with North Korea in Nuclear Talks," *Washington
Post*, April 11, 2019, https://www.washingtonpost.com/politics/in-meeting
-with-south-koreas-moon-trump-signals-openness-to-smaller-deal-with
-north-korea-in-nuclear-talks/2019/04/11/6bebfe32-5c62-11e9-a00e
-050dc7b82693_story.html.

122. Nakamura, "Trump Signals Openness."

123. Ministry of Foreign Affairs, Democratic People's Republic of Korea, "Supreme Leader Kim Jong Un Makes Policy Speech at First Session of SPA,"
April 13, 2019, www.mfa.gov.kp/view/article/91216.

124. Josh Smith and Joyce Lee, "North Korea's Kim Jong Un Gives U.S. to Year-
End," Reuters, April 13, 2019, https://www.reuters.com/article/us-north
korea-usa/north-koreas-kim-jong-un-gives-u-s-to-year-end-to-become
-more-flexible-idUSKCN1RO2PI/.

125. Choe Sang-Hun and Edward Wong, "North Korean Negotiator's Down-
fall Was Sealed When Trump-Kim Summit Collapsed," *New York Times*,
May 31, 2019, https://www.nytimes.com/2019/05/31/world/asia/Kim-Yong
-chol-execution-north-korea.html; Choe Sang-Hun, "North Korea Executed and Purged Top Nuclear Negotiators, South Korean Report Says,"
New York Times, May 30, 2019, https://www.nytimes.com/2019/05/30/world
/asia/north-korea-envoy- execution.html; "Kim Yong-chol: 'Purged' N. Korean Diplomat Appears with Kim," BBC, June 3, 2019, https://www.bbc
.com/news/world-asia-48493702; Will Ripley, "'Executed' North Korean
diplomat is alive, sources say," CNN, June 4, 2019, https://www.cnn.com

/2019/06/03/asia/north-korea-diplomats-intl/index.html; and Dagyum Ji, "North Korea's Legislature Replaces Key Officials in First Meeting since Election," *NK News*, April 11, 2019, https://www.nknews.org/2019/04/north-koreas-legislature-replaces-key-officials-in-first-meeting-since-election/.

126. Jihye Lee, "North Korea Test Was of Ground-Combat Weapon, South Korea Says," *Bloomberg*, April 19, 2019, https://www.bloomberg.com/news/articles/2019-04-19/north-korea-test-was-of-ground-combat-weapon-south-korea-says; Choe Sang-Hun, "North Korea Launches Short-Range Projectiles," *New York Times*, May 3, 2019, https://www.nytimes.com/2019/05/03/world/asia/north-korea-missile.html; Robert Carlin, "DPRK Firing Drill: Message to the Blue House," *38North*, May 5, 2019, https://www.38north.org/2019/05/rcarlin050519/; and "Supreme Leader Kim Jong Un Guides Flight Drill of Unit 1017 of KPA Air and Anti-Aircraft Force," KCNA Watch, April 17, 2019, kcnawatch.org/newstream/1555477238-457893581/supreme-leader-kim-jong-un-guides-flight-drill-of-unit-1017-of-kpa-air-and-anti-aircraft-force.

127. Ankit Panda, "With Diplomacy on Life Support, North Korea Names and Shames Pompeo and Bolton," *The Diplomat*, April 24, 2019, https://thediplomat.com/2019/04/with-diplomacy-on-life-support-north-korea-names-and-shames-pompeo-bolton/; and Choe Sang-Hun, "North Korea Hits a Man with Glasses," *New York Times*, April 19, 2019, https://www.nytimes.com/2019/04/20/world/asia/north-korea-john-bolton.html.

128. Robert Carlin, "Mixed Signals on Engagement," *38 North*, June 10, 2019, https://www.38north.org/2019/06/rcarlin061019; and Robert Carlin, "North Korea: The Pot Still Boiling," *38 North*, June 20, 2019, https://www.38north.org/2019/06/rcarlin062019.

129. Carlin, "The Pot Still Boiling."

130. Carlin, "The Pot Still Boiling."

131. Anna Kireeva and Liudmila Zakharova, "Takeaways from the Long-Awaited Russia-North Korea Summit," *The Diplomat*, April 26, 2019, https://thediplomat.com/2019/04/takeaways-from-the-long-awaited-russia-north-korea-summit/; Natalia Vasilyeva, "Putin, Kim to Meet in Russia's Far East on Thursday," Associated Press, April 22, 2019; Sarah Kim, "Kim Arrives in Vladivostok for Summit with Putin," *Korea JoongAng Daily*, April 29, 2019, https://koreajoongangdaily.joins.com/2019/04/24/politics/Kim-arrives-in-Vladivostok-for-summit-with-Putin/3062266.html; and Scott Snyder, "Where Does the Russia-North Korea Relationship Stand?," Council on Foreign Relations, April 29, 2019, https://www.cfr.org/in-brief/where-does-russia-north-korea-relationship-stand.

132. Wikipedia, "Kim-Xi Meetings," last modified February 7, 2025, 01:32 (UTC), https://en.wikipedia.org/wiki/Kim–Xi_meetings#:~:text=Xi%20Jinping%20was%20met%20at,of%20the%20Korean%20People%27s%20Army; Justin McCurry, "Xi Jinping and Kim Jong-un Reboot Alliance with Talks and Mausoleum Visit," *Guardian* (London), June 20,

2019, https://www.theguardian.com/world/2019/jun/20/xi-jinping-north
-korea-kim-jong-un-nuclear-trump-talks-g20; and Russell Goldman, "The
Unspoken Agenda at the Xi-Kim Meeting? Could Be Messaging Trump,"
New York Times, June 19, 2019, https://www.nytimes.com/2019/06/19/world
/asia/kim-xi-summit.html.

133. Pia Deshpande, "Trump Touts 'Beautiful Letter' from Kim Jong Un," *Politico*, June 11, 2019, https://www.politico.com/story/2019/06/11/trump
-touts-beautiful-letter-from-kim-jong-un-1360138; and Letter from Kim
Jong Un to Donald Trump, June 10, 2019, in Hanmi Club, "Full English
Transcript of Letters: Letter 2018. 4.1.–2019.8.5" [in Korean], *KORUS Journal* 10 (September 2022): 84–132, https://www.rfa.org/korean/in_focus
/kjuletters-09302022162829.html/d2b8b7fcd504-ae40c815c740-ce5cc11c
-c601c5b4bcf8-1.pdf.

134. Letter from Kim Jong Un to Donald Trump, June 10, 2019.

135. Letter from Donald Trump to Kim Jong Un, June 12, 2019, in Hanmi
Club, "Full English Transcript of Letters: Letter 2018. 4.1.–2019.8.5."

136. Dagyum Ji, "Kim Jong Un Received 'Excellent' Letter' from U.S. President,
State Media," *NK News*, June 23, 2019, https://www.nknews.org/2019/06
/kim-jong-un-received-excellent-letter-from-the-u-s-president-state
-media-says/; and Choe Sang-Hun, "North Korea Says Kim Jong Un Received 'Excellent Letter' from Trump," *New York Times*, June 22, 2019,
https://www.nytimes.com/2019/06/22/world/asia/north-korea-letter.
html.

137. "Trump Says He Sent North Korean Leader 'Very Friendly Letter,'" Voice
of America, June 24, 2019, https://www.voanews.com/a/usa_trump-says-he
-sent-north-korean-leader-very-friendly-letter/6170528.html; and letter
from Donald Trump to Kim Jong Un, June 12, 2019.

Chapter Nineteen. "I want to pour the concrete myself"

1. Interview with North Korea experts, July 12, 2021.
2. Interview with North Korea experts, July 12, 2021.
3. Interview with North Korea experts, July 12, 2021.
4. Interview with former U.S. official, December 9, 2021.
5. John Bolton, *The Room Where It Happened: A White House Memoir* (New
York: Simon and Schuster, 2020), 338–339.
6. Bolton, *The Room Where It Happened*, 338–339.
7. Choe Sang-Hun, "Trump Supports Food Aid for North Korea, South Says,"
New York Times, May 7, 2019, https://www.nytimes.com/2019/05/07/world
/asia/trump-north-korea-food-aid.html.
8. Interview with former U.S. official, October 5, 2021.
9. Interview with former U.S. official, October 15, 2021; and interview with
former U.S. official, September 13, 2021.
10. Interview with former U.S. official, October 15, 2021.

11. Interview with former U.S. official, October 15, 2021; U.S. Department of the Treasury, "Treasury Designates Two Shipping Companies for Attempted Evasion of North Korea Sanctions," March 21, 2019, https://home.treasury .gov/news/press-releases/sm632; and Andrew Restuccia and Caitlin Oprysko, "Trump Surprises His Own Aides by Reversing North Korea Sanctions," *Politico*, March 22, 2019, https://www.politico.com/story/2019 /03/22/trump-north-korea-sanctions-remove-1232586.

12. Interview with former U.S. official, July 23, 2021.

13. Bolton, *The Room Where It Happened*, 334.

14. Interview with former U.S. official, October 15, 2021.

15. Bolton, *The Room Where It Happened*, 344–345; interview with former senior U.S. official, January 5, 2022; and Associated Press, "Trump Breaks with Abe, Says Not Bothered by NK Missile Tests," *Politico*, May 27, 2019, https:// www.politico.com/story/2019/05/27/donald-trump-japan-trip-shinzo-abe -press-conference-1345031.

16. Michael D. Shear, Eric Schmitt, Michael Crowley, and Maggie Haberman, "Strikes on Iran Approved by Trump, Then Abruptly Pulled Back," *New York Times*, June 20, 2019, https://www.nytimes.com/2019/06/20/world /middleeast/iran-us-drone.html; Mark Landler, Maggie Haberman, and Eric Schmitt, "Trump Tells Pentagon Chief He Does Not Want War with Iran," *New York Times*, May 16, 2019, https://www.nytimes.com/2019/05 /16/world/middleeast/iran-war-donald-trump.html; Peter Bienert, "Bolton Keeps Trying to Goad Iran into War," *The Atlantic*, June 20, 2019, https:// www.theatlantic.com/ideas/archive/2019/06/bolton-keeps-trying-goad-iran -war/592108/; Peter Baker and Maggie Haberman, "Trump Undercuts Bolton on North Korea and Iran," *New York Times*, May 28, 2019, https:// www.nytimes.com/2019/05/28/us/politics/trump-john-bolton-north-korea -iran.html; Maureen Dowd, "Will Trump Be the Sage One?," *New York Times*, May 18, 2019, https://www.nytimes.com/2019/05/18/opinion/sunday /trump-bolton-war.html; and Bolton, *The Room Where It Happened*, 415.

17. "Pompeo Says U.S. Ready Right Now to Resume Talks with North Korea," Associated Press, June 23, 2019, https://apnews.com/united-states -government-d2df23772e7546949542dce595e91390.

18. "An Interview with Steve Biegun," produced by *NK News*, podcast, July 14, 2021, https://www.nknews.org/category/north-korea-news-podcast/latest /an-interview-with-stephen-biegun-nknews-podcast-ep-191/902590/; and interview with senior U.S. official, July 13, 2021.

19. Bolton, *The Room Where It Happened*, 346.

20. Interview with former U.S. official, July 12, 2021.

21. Interview with former U.S. official, July 23, 2021; and interview with former U.S. official, July 31, 2021.

22. "An Interview with Steve Biegun."

23. Jared Kushner, *Breaking History: A White House Memoir* (New York: Broad-side Books, 2022), chap. 34, Kindle.

24. Kushner, *Breaking History*, chap. 34.
25. Interview with former U.S. official, July 31, 2021; Aaron Kidd and Kim Gamel, "In Surprise Tweet, Trump Invites North Korean Leader to DMZ Meet-and-Greet," *Stars and Stripes*, June 28, 2019, https://www.stripes.com /theaters/asia_pacific/in-surprise-tweet-trump-invites-north-korean -leader-to-dmz-meet-and-greet-1.588113.
26. Interview with former U.S. official, July 31, 2021; Kidd and Gamel, "Trump Invites North Korean Leader"; and Bolton, *The Room Where It Happened*, 352.
27. Interview with former senior U.S. official, January 5, 2021; and interview with former U.S. official, July 31, 2021.
28. Interview with former senior U.S. official, July 8, 2021.
29. Interview with former U.S. official, July 23, 2021.
30. Interview with former U.S. official, July 31, 2021.
31. "An Interview with Steve Biegun."
32. "An Interview with Steve Biegun."
33. Interview with former U.S. official, December 9, 2021; "An Interview with Steve Biegun"; interview with senior U.S. official, July 13, 2021; and interview with former U.S. official, July 31, 2021.
34. Interview with former U.S. official, December 9, 2021; and "An Interview with Steve Biegun."
35. Interview with former U.S. official, December 9, 2021; and "An Interview with Steve Biegun."
36. "An Interview with Steve Biegun."
37. "An Interview with Steve Biegun"; and interview with U.S. official, July 31, 2021.
38. "An Interview with Steve Biegun"; and interview with former U.S. official, July 31, 2021.
39. Interview with former U.S. official, July 31, 2021.
40. Interview with former U.S. official, July 31, 2021.
41. Interview with former U.S. official, July 31, 2021.
42. Interview with former U.S. official, July 31, 2021; and Seung-hyok Noh, "US President Trump's DMZ Visit, Heated Coverage on the Unification Bridge" [in Korean], Yonhap News Agency, June 30, 2019, https://www .yna.co.kr/view/AKR20190630043000060.
43. Interview with former U.S. official, July 31, 2021.
44. Interview with former U.S. official, October 12, 2022; and interview with former U.S. officer, October 12, 2022.
45. Joanne Lee, "Trump-Kim Panmunjom Summit in June 2019," unpublished research note, citing Fox News, January 19, 2021; "Tucker: History Made at the Korean Demilitarized Zone," Fox News, July 2, 2019, video, https:// www.youtube.com/watch?v=pEVfpTvIl18; and interview with former U.S. official, October 12, 2022.
46. Interview with former U.S. official, July 31, 2021; and Kushner, *Breaking History*, chap. 34.

47. "FULL COVERAGE: Moon, Kim, Trump Hold Historic Three-Way Talks on South Korean Soil," Arirang News, June 30, 2019, video, https://www.youtube.com/watch?v=kJzUWdTxck8.

48. "Moon, Kim, Trump Hold Historic Three-Way Talks"; and National Institute for Unification Education, "Introducing Panmunjom," September 2019, https://www.uniedu.go.kr/uniedu/atchfile/down/F000061658.pdf.

49. "Tucker: History Made at the Korean Demilitarized Zone."

50. "Special Report: Trump Meets North Korea's Kim Jong Un in the DMZ," NBC News, July 1, 2019, video, https://www.youtube.com/watch?v=MltgcggG4dk.

51. M. Williams, "KCTV Report on Kim-Trump Panmunjom Meeting," July 2, 2019, video, https://www.youtube.com/watch?v=pEVfpTvI118.

52. Wikipedia, "2019 Koreas—United States DMZ Summit," last modified February 7, 2025, 03:10 (UTC), https://en.wikipedia.org/wiki/2019_Koreas-United_States_DMZ_Summit.

53. Bob Woodward, *Rage* (New York: Simon and Schuster, 2020), 183.

54. "Special Report."

55. "Special Report."

56. "Special Report."

57. "Special Report."

58. "Special Report."

59. "Special Report."

60. "Special Report."

61. "Moon, Kim, Trump Hold Historic Three-way Talks."

62. "Moon, Kim, Trump Hold Historic Three-Way Talks"; and Peter Baker and Michael Crowley, "Trump Steps into North Korea and Agrees with Kim Jong Un to Resume Talks," *New York Times*, June 30, 2019, https://www.nytimes.com/2019/06/30/world/asia/trump-north-korea-dmz.html.

63. "Moon, Kim, Trump Hold Historic Three-Way Talks."

64. "Moon, Kim, Trump Hold Historic Three-Way Talks."

65. Interview with former U.S. official, July 31, 2021; and Moon Jae-in, *From the Periphery to the Center: Moon Jae In Memoirs of Foreign Affairs and Security* [in Korean] (Paju, South Korea: Kimyoungsa, 2024), 336.

66. Williams, "KCTV Report."

67. Williams, "KCTV Report."

68. Williams, "KCTV Report."

69. Williams, "KCTV Report."

70. Jim Costa, "Stephanie Grisham Bruised in 'An All Out Brawl' with North Koreans," CNN, https://www.cnn.com/2019/06/30/politics/stephanie-grisham-north-korea-scuffle/index.html; and interview with former U.S. officer, October 12, 2022.

71. Williams, "KCTV Report."

72. "US-North Korea: Trump and Kim Agree to Restart Talks in Historic Meeting," BBC, June 30, 2019, https://www.bbc.com/news/world-asia-48814975.

73. Interview with former U.S. official, July 31, 2021.

74. Interview with former senior U.S. official, January 5, 2022.

75. Interview with former U.S. official, July 23, 2021.

76. Interview with former U.S. official, July 23, 2021; interview with senior US official, July 13, 2021; and interview with senior U.S. official, January 5, 2022.

77. Interview with former U.S. official, July 31, 2021; interview with senior U.S. official, July 13, 2021; and interview with senior U.S. official, January 5, 2022.

78. Interview with former U.S. official, July 31, 2021; interview with senior U.S. official, July 13, 2021; and interview with senior U.S. official, January 5, 2022.

79. Interview with former U.S. official, July 31, 2021; interview with senior U.S. official, July 13, 2021; and interview with senior U.S. official, January 5, 2022.

80. Interview with former U.S. official, July 31, 2021; and interview with senior U.S. official, July 13, 2021.

81. Interview with former U.S. official, July 31, 2021; and interview with senior U.S. official, July 13, 2021.

82. Interview with senior U.S. official, January 5, 2022.

83. Interview with senior U.S. official, January 5, 2022.

84. Interview with senior U.S. official, January 5, 2022.

85. Interview with former U.S. official, July 31, 2021.

86. Williams, "KCTV Report"; and interview with senior U.S. official, July 13, 2021.

87. Interview with senior U.S. official, July 13, 2021.

88. Steve George, Jessie Yueng, James Griffiths, Kevin Iptak, and Joshua Berlinger, "DMZ: Donald Trump Steps into North Korea with Kim Jong Un," CNN, June 30, 2019, https://www.cnn.com/politics/live-news/trump-dmz-kim-live-intl-hnk#h_7c89c85737f16f7da758bcc1319c8b87; "Transcript: Trump and Kim Jong Un Meet at DMZ; Donald Trump Gives Hopeful Statement after Talks with South and North Korean Leaders," CNN, June 30, 2019, https://transcripts.cnn.com/show/cnr/date/2019-06-30/segment/21.

89. U.S. Department of State, Office of the Spokesperson, "Secretary of State Michael R. Pompeo Remarks to the Press," June 30, 2019; Leo Byrne, "Working Level Talks with North Korea to Resume in mid-July: Pompeo," *NK News*, June 30, 2019, https://www.nknews.org/2019/06/working-level-talks-with-north-korea-to-resume-in-mid-july-pompeo/; Yonette Joseph, "4 Takeaways from the Trump-Kim Meeting at the DMZ," *New York Times*, June 30, 2019, https://www.nytimes.com/2019/06/30/world/asia/trump-kim-north-korea-meeting.html; Matthew Keeler and Kim Gamel, "President Wraps Up South Korea Visit by Thanking Troops and Those Who Support

Them," *Stars and Stripes,* June 30, 2019, https://www.stripes.com/news
/2019-06-30/president-wraps-up-south-korea-visit-by-thanking-troops
-and-those-who-support-them-1479040.html1; and AFP and Associated
Press, "Pyongyang Calls Trump's DMZ Meeting with Kim 'Historic' and
an 'Amazing Event' after He Became the First Serving US President to Set
Foot in North Korea," *Daily Mail,* July 1, 2019, https://www.dailymail.co
.uk/news/article-7199273/North-Korea-hails-historic-Kim-Trump-summit
.html.

90. Interview with former U.S. official, July 31, 2021; and interview with former senior U.S. official, July 13, 2021.

91. Andrew Jeong and Timothy W. Martin, "Pyongyang Complains Loudly
about Quieter U.S.-South Korean Exercises," *Wall Street Journal,* August 20,
2019, https://www.wsj.com/articles/pyongyang-complains-loudly-about
-quieter-u-s-south-korean-exercises-11566300257; and interview with former senior U.S. official, January 5, 2021.

92. Sasha Ingber, "Irate over Military Exercises, North Korea Threatens to Resume Nuclear, Missile Tests," NPR, July 16, 2019, https://www.npr.org/2019
/07/16/742129952/irate-over-military-exercises-north-korea-threatens-to
-resume-nuclear-missile-tests; and Ankit Panda, "US-North Korea Dol-
drums Return after Third Trump-Kim Summit," *The Diplomat,* July 17,
2019, https://thediplomat.com/2019/07/us-north-korea-doldrums-return
-after-third-trump-kim-summit/.

93. Scott Neuman, "North Korea Conducts Missile Tests While Bolton Meets
with Officials in Seoul," NPR, July 25, 2019, https://www.npr.org/2019/07
/25/745144254/north-korea-conducts-missile-tests-while-bolton-meets
-with-officials-in-seoul; "North Korea Launches Two Short-Range Ballistic Missiles, South Korea says," CNN, July 30, 2019, https://www.cnn.com
/2019/07/30/asia/north-korea-launches-july-30-intl/index.html; and Ministry of Foreign Affairs of the Democratic People's Republic of Korea,
"Supreme Leader Kim Jong Un Guides Power Demonstration Fire of
New-Type Tactical Guided Weapon," July 26, 2019, http://www.mfa.gov
.kp/en/power-demonstration-fire-of-new-type-tactical-guided-weapon/.

94. Vivian Salama and Andrew Jeong, "North Korean Missile Tests Break U.N.
Rules, Trump Says—But Not His Agreement with Kim," *Wall Street Journal,* August 2, 2019, https://www.wsj.com/articles/north-korean-missile
-tests-break-u-n-rules-trump-saysbut-not-his-agreement-with-kim
-11564771187.

95. Letter from Kim Jong Un to Donald Trump, August 5, 2019, in Hanmi
Club, "Full English Transcript of Letters: Letter 2018. 4.1.–2019.8.5" [in
Korean], *KORUS Journal* 10 (September 2022): 84–132, https://www.rfa.org
/korean/in_focus/kjuletters-09302022162829.html/d2b8b7fcd504
-ae40c815c740-ce5cc11c-c601c5b4bcf8-1.pdf; and Robert L. Carlin, "The
Real Lessons of the Trump-Kim Love Letters," *Foreign Policy,* August 13,

2021, https://foreignpolicy.com/2021/08/13/north-korea-trump-kim-jong-un-love-letters-diplomacy-nuclear-talks.

96. Letter from Kim Jong Un to Donald Trump, August 5, 2019.
97. Letter from Kim Jong Un to Donald Trump, August 5, 2019.
98. Letter from Kim Jong Un to Donald Trump, August 5, 2019.
99. Letter from Kim Jong Un to Donald Trump, August 5, 2019.
100. Letter from Kim Jong Un to Donald Trump, August 5, 2019.
101. Letter from Kim Jong Un to Donald Trump, August 5, 2019.
102. Letter from Kim Jong Un to Donald Trump, August 5, 2019.
103. Interview with former senior Blue House official, June 4, 2023; interview with former U.S. official, July 23, 2021; and Bolton, *The Room Where It Happened*, 355.
104. Bolton, *The Room Where It Happened*, 352–354.
105. Bolton, *The Room Where It Happened*, 354; and interview with senior U.S. official, July 13, 2021.
106. Bolton, *The Room Where It Happened*, 355–360.
107. Bolton, *The Room Where It Happened*, 360.
108. Song Sang-ho, "Trump Calls Allied Exercise 'Unnecessary,' 'Total Waste of Money,'" Yonhap News Agency, August 26, 2019, https//en.yna.co.kr/view/AEN20190826001700325.
109. Interview with reporter, July 6, 2021; and Mike Pompeo, *Never Give an Inch: Fighting for the America I Love* (New York: Broadside Books, 2023), chap. 4, Kindle.
110. Carlin, "The Real Lessons of Diplomacy."
111. Author's notes, "Meeting with Steve Biegun," September 17, 2019.
112. Author's notes, "Meeting with Steve Biegun," September 17, 2019.
113. Author's notes, "Meeting with Steve Biegun," September 17, 2019.
114. Author's notes, "Meeting with Steve Biegun," September 17, 2019.
115. Lee Haye-ah, "Pompeo Cites N. Korea's 'Rogue Behavior' as Talks Stall," Yonhap News Agency, August 28, 2019, https://en.yna.co.kr/view/AEN20190828000351325; and Leo Byrne, "North Korea Has 'Sovereign Right to Defend Itself': Pompeo," *NK News*, September 6, 2019, https://www.nknews.org/2019/09/north-korea-has-sovereign-right-to-defend-itself-pompeo.
116. Associated Press, "North Korea Berates Pompeo, Says Hopes for Talks Fading," *Politico*, August 31, 2019, https://www.politico.com/story/2019/08/31/north-korea-pompeo-talks-1479251.
117. U.S. Embassy and Consulate in the Republic of Korea, "Remarks by Special Representative for North Korea Stephen E. Biegun at the University of Michigan," Weiser Diplomacy Center, September 6, 2019; and Lee Je-hun, "Will N. Korea Respond to Biegun's Persuasion and Pressure?," *Hankyoreh*, September 9, 2019, https://english.hani.co.kr/arti/english_edition/e_northkorea/909067.html.

118. Lee Haye-ah, "N. Korea Offers to Hold Talks with U.S. in Late Sept.," Yonhap News Agency, September 10, 2019, https://en.yna.co.kr/view/AEN20190909010953325; and Timothy W. Martin and Andrew Jeong, "North Korea Offers to Restart Nuclear Talks with U.S.," *Wall Street Journal*, September 9, 2019, https://www.wsj.com/articles/north-korea-fires-two-unidentified-projectiles-11568073493.

119. Oliver Hotham, "Trump Says 'New Method' Possible in U.S. talks with North Korea," *NK News*, September 19, 2019, https://www.nknews.org/2019/09/trump-says-new-method-possible-in-u-s-talks-with-north-korea/; and Foster Klug, "Trump Says Fourth Meeting with Kim Jong Un Could Happen Soon," Associated Press, September 23, 2019, https://www.militarytimes.com/news/pentagon-congress/2019/09/23/trump-says-fourth-meeting-with-kim-jong-un-could-happen-soon/.

120. "N.K. Chief Negotiator Welcomes Trump's 'New Method,' Voices Optimism over Talks," Yonhap News Agency, September 20, 2019, https://en.yna.co.kr/view/AEN20190920008951325.

121. Simon Denyer and Min Joo Kim, "North Korea Tests Missile Soon after Announcing Resumption of Nuclear Talks with U.S.," *Washington Post*, October 1, 2019, https://www.washingtonpost.com/world/asia_pacific/north-korea-and-united-states-to-resume-nuclear-talks-saturday/2019/10/01/92d52f6e-e42f-11e9-a6e8-8759c5c7f608_story.html; and Andrew Jeong and Dasl Yoon, "U.S. and North Korea to Resume Nuclear Talks, Pyongyang Says," *Wall Street Journal*, October 1, 2019, https://www.wsj.com/articles/u-s-and-north-korea-to-resume-nuclear-talks-pyongyang-says-11569927143.

122. Claire Carponen, "Stockholm's Lidingo Is an Affluent Island Suburb near the City's Downtown," *Mansion Global*, July 11, 2020, https://www.mansionglobal.com/articles/stockholms-lidingo-is-an-affluent-island-suburb-near-the-citys-downtown-217398; and photos of Villa Elfvik Strand, https://www.villaelfvikstrand.se/lokalen.

123. "Pompeo Says Hopes for Progress in Talks with North Korea," Reuters, October 5, 2019, https://www.reuters.com/article/us-northkorea-usa-pompeo/pompeo-says-hopes-for-progress-in-talks-with-north-korea-idUSKCN1WK0A1/.

124. Briefing by senior U.S. official, November 1, 2019.

125. Interview with U.S. official, July 31, 2021.

126. Interview with senior U.S. official, July 13, 2021; "An Interview with Steve Biegun"; and interview with senior U.S. official, January 5, 2022.

127. Interview with U.S. official, July 31, 2021; interview with U.S. official, January 2, 2022; and briefing by senior U.S. official, November 1, 2019.

128. Interview with U.S. official, July 31, 2021; and interview with U.S. official January 2, 2022.

129. Joanne Lee, "Description of Stockholm Talks in October 2019," unpublished research note, February 3, 2022; and Heather Donald, "North Korea

and US Resume Nuclear Talks in Conference Center on Outskirts of Stockholm," *Euronews,* October 5, 2019, https://www.euronews.com/2019 /10/05/north-korea-and-us-resume-nuclear-talks-in-conference-centre -on-outskirts-of-stockholm.

130. Agence France-Presse, "North Korean, US Official at Nuclear Talks after Latest Missile Test," *Jordan Times,* October 5, 2019, https://jordantimes.com /news/world/north-korean-us-officials-nuclear-talks-after-latest-missile -test; and briefing by senior U.S. official, November 1, 2019.

131. Interview with U.S. official, October 15, 2021.

132. "An Interview with Steve Biegun."

133. "An Interview with Steve Biegun."

134. Interview with senior U.S. official, July 13, 2021.

135. Briefing by senior U.S. official, November 1, 2019.

136. Briefing by senior U.S. official, November 1, 2019; and interview with U.S. official, July 31, 2021.

137. Interview with U.S. official, July 31, 2021.

138. Interview with U.S. official, July 31, 2021; and briefing by senior U.S. official, November 1, 2019.

139. Interview with U.S. official, July 31, 2021.

140. Briefing by senior U.S. official, November 1, 2019.

141. Briefing by senior U.S. official, November 1, 2019.

142. "An Interview with Steve Biegun"; and briefing by senior U.S. official, November 1, 2019.

143. Briefing by senior U.S. official, November 1, 2019.

144. Interview with senior U.S. official, July 13, 2021; and briefing by senior U.S. official, November 1, 2019.

145. "An Interview with Steve Biegun."

146. "An Interview with Steve Biegun"; and briefing by senior U.S. official, November 1, 2019.

147. David E. Sanger, "U.S. Nuclear Talks with North Korea Break Down in Hours," *New York Times,* October 5, 2019, https://www.nytimes.com/2019 /10/05/us/politics/trump-north-korea-nuclear.html; and Hyung-Jin Kim, "North Korea: No More Talks until US Ends 'Hostile Policy,'" Associated Press, October 6, 2019, https://apnews.com/general-news-2348fb048cc34 bc1a8265e0ce3033c6f.

148. Lee Je-hun and Noh Ji-won, "N. Korea Releases Statement Regarding Breakdown in Working-Level Talks with US," *Hankyoreh,* October 17, 2019, https:/English.hani.co.kr/arti/English_edition/e_northkorea/912317.html; and CBS News/Associated Press, "North Korea Says U.S. Must Prove 'Will' to Negotiate as 'Sickening' Nuclear Talks Fail," CBS News, October 7, 2019, https://www.cbsnews.com/news/north-korea-us-nuclear-talks-sickening -stockholm-meeting-fails-donald-trump-motivations-2019-10-07/.

149. "US Denies North Korean Nuclear Talks Failed," BBC, October 5, 2019, https://www.bbc.co.uk/news/world-asia-49947836.

150. "North Korea Says U.S. Must Prove 'Will.'"

151. Briefing by senior U.S. official, November 1, 2019.

152. Timothy W. Martin and Dasl Yoon, "Kim Jong Un, Astride a Pale Horse, Urges Self-Reliance in Face of U.S. Sanctions," *Wall Street Journal*, October 16, 2019, https://www.wsj.com/articles/kim-jong-un-astride-a-pale-horse-urges-self-reliance-in-face-of-u-s-sanctions-11571209808; Josh Smith, "'Defiant Message' as North Korea's Kim Rides White Horse on Sacred Mountain," Reuters, October 15, 2019, https://www.reuters.com/article/us-northkorea-kimjongun/defiant-message-us-north-korea-kim-rides-white-horse-on-scared-mountain-idUSKBN1WWV08G; and Alex Ward, "The Serious Message behind Kim Jong Un's Silly Horse Photos," *Vox*, https://www.vox.com/2019/10/16/20917212/kim-jong-un-horse-photos-snow-paektu.

153. Choe Sang-Hun, "Kim Jong-un Visits Sacred Mountain on Horseback, Analysts Watch His Next Move," *New York Times*, December 4, 2019, https://www.nytimes.com/2019/12/04/world/asia/kim-jong-un-white-horse.html.

154. Anthony Kuhn, "North Korea's Kim Jong Un Says He Is No Longer Bound by Nuclear Missile Moratorium," NPR, December 31, 2019, https://www.npr.org/2019/12/31/792793583/north-koreas-kim-jong-un-says-he-is-no-longer-bound-by-nuclear-missile-moratorium.

Chapter Twenty. "Not only a return to strategic patience, but a lot darker"

1. Briefing by U.S. official, December 8, 2019.

2. "DPRK Receives Letter from US President: Senior Official," Xinhua, March 22, 2020, https://www.xinhuanet.com/english/2020-03/22/c_13890 4222.htm.

3. William Gallo, "Trump Says He'd Meet with Kim Jong Un Again," Voice of America, July 8, 2020, https://www.voanews.com/a/usa_trump-says-hed-meet-kim-jong-un-again/6192408.html.

4. Interview with former congressional staffer, March 2, 2024; and Joanne Lee, "Joe Biden's Remarks on North Korea, 1973-Present," Stimson Center, private research note, October 26, 2023.

5. Interview with former congressional staffer, March 2, 2024; and Lee, "Joe Biden's Remarks on North Korea."

6. Interview with former congressional staffer, March 2, 2024; and Lee, "Joe Biden's remarks on North Korea."

7. Stephen Silver, "Joe Biden Calls North Korea's Kim Jong Un a 'Thug' During Presidential Debate," *National Interest*, October 20, 2020, https://nationalinterest.org/blog/korea-watch/joe-biden-calls-north-koreas-kim-jong-un-thug-during-presidential-debate-171193.

8. Franklin Foer, *The Last Politician: Inside Joe Biden's White House and the Struggle for America's Future* (New York: Penguin Press, 2023), 133.

9. Interview with former ROK official, March 24, 2024.

10. Interview with former ROK official, March 24, 2024.

11. "Statement of First Vice Foreign Minister of DPRK," Korean Central News Agency, March 18, 2021, https://kcna.co.jp/item/2021/202103/news18/20210318-03ee.html.

12. Chad O'Carroll, "New North Korea Envoy to Be Part Time Only," *NK News*, May 25, 2021, https://www.nknews.org/2021/05/new-north-korea-envoy-to-be-aprt-time-only/.

13. Interview with former ROK official, March 24, 2024.

14. Robert Einhorn, "The Rollout of the Biden Administration's North Korea Policy Leaves Unanswered Questions," Brookings Institution, May 4, 2021, https://www.brookings.edu/articles/the-rollout-of-the-biden-administrations-north-korea-policy-review-leaves-unanswered-questions/; Hyun-wook Kim, "A Korean Perspective on the Biden Administration's North Korea Policy," Stimson Center, February 28, 2022, https://www.stimson.org/2022/a-korean-perspective-on-the-biden-administrations-north-korea-policy/; and Elisabeth Suh, "Biden's North Korea Policy: Neither Ambitious Nor Adequate," German Council on Foreign Relations, October 1, 2021, https://dgap.org/en/research/publications/bidens-north-korea-policy.

15. Robert Carlin and Siegfried Hecker, "North Korea's Decision to Develop Fully as a Nuclear Weapons State," in *Strategic Empathy: Examining Pattern Breaks to Better Understand Adversaries' Acquisition, Threat and Use of Strategic Weapons*, James Martin Center for Nonproliferation Studies, September 2023, 85–118, https://nonproliferation.org/wp-content/uploads/2023/11/Strategic-Empathy-Report Sep23.pdf.

16. Kurt M. Campbell and Jake Sullivan, "Competition without Catastrophe," *Foreign Affairs*, August 1, 2019, https://www.foreignaffairs.com/china/competition-with-china-catastrophe-sullivan-campbell.

17. David E. Sanger and Andrew E. Kramer, "Putin Warns Biden of 'Complete Rupture' of U.S.-Russia Relationship over Ukraine," *New York Times*, December 30, 2021, https://www.nytimes.com/2021/12/30/us/politics/biden-putin-ukraine-call.html.

18. Steve Holland and David Brunnstrom, "Exclusive: US Says China and Russia Have Leverage to Stop North Korea Nuclear Test," Reuters, November 3, 2022, https://www.reuters.com/world/exclusive-us-says-china-russia-have-leverage-stop-north-korea-nuclear-test-2022-11-03/.

19. Interview with former ROK official, March 24, 2024.

20. Don Oberdorfer and Robert Carlin, "North Korea's Decision," in *The Two Koreas: A Contemporary History* (New York: Basic Books, 2013), xvii.

21. Ernest R. May, *Lessons of the Past: The Use and Misuse of History in American Foreign Policy* (New York: Oxford University Press, 1973).

22. Stephen M. Walt, *The Hell of Good Intentions: America's Foreign Policy Elite and the Decline of U.S. Primacy* (New York: Farrar, Straus and Giroux, 2018), 13.

23. Walt, *The Hell of Good Intentions*, 13.

24. "We're an empire now and when we act, we create our own reality," *The Atlantic*, Daily Dish, April 23, 2009, https://www.theatlantic.com/daily-dish /archive/2009/04/were-an-empire-now-and-when-we-act-we-create-our -own-reality/202751/.

25. "The War in Gaza and the International Context with Aaron David Miller and Stephen Walt," Williams College, video, April 25, 2024, video, https:// www.youtube.com/watch?v=fusypoWb5TA.

26. Dr. William J. Perry, *Review of United States Policy Toward North Korea: Findings and Recommendations*, Office of the North Korea Policy Coordinator, U.S. Department of State, unclassified report, Washington, DC, October 12, 1999, https://www.ncnk.org/sites/default/files/Perry_Report.pdf.

27. Nicholas D. Kristof, "Talking to Evil," *New York Times*, August 13, 2006, https://www.nytimes.com/2006/08/13/opinion/13kristof.html.

28. Stephen Walt, "Appeasement Is Underrated," *Foreign Policy*, April 29, 2024, https://foreignpolicy.com/2024/04/29/appeasement-is-underrated/.

29. Steve Coll, *The Achilles Trap* (New York: Penguin Press, 2024).

30. Robert S. Hinck and Sean Cullen, "Decoding the Adversary: Strategic Empathy in an Era of Great Power Competition," *AETHER: Journal of Strategic Airpower and Spacepower* 3 (Spring 2024): 82.

31. *Options for Strengthening ROK Nuclear Assurance*, RAND/Asan Institute for Policy Studies Joint Report, RAND Corporation, August 2023, https://www .rand.org/content/dam/rand/pubs/research_reports/RRA2600/RRA2612-1 /RAND_RRA2612–1.pdf; David Albright, *North Korean Nuclear Weapons Arsenal: New Estimates of its Size and Configuration*, Institute for Science and International Security Report, April 10, 2023; and Associated Press, "Kim Jong Un Orders 'Exponential' Expansion of North Korea's Nuclear Arsenal," NBC News, https://www.nbcnews.com/news/north-korea/north-korea -boost-nuclear-warhead-production-exponentially-leader-says-rcna63849.

32. Sue Mi Terry, "The New North Korean Nuclear Threat," *Foreign Affairs*, January 19, 2023, https://www.foreignaffairs.com/north-korea/new-north -korean-threat.

33. John Bolton, "Kim Jong Un Drops the Mask," *Wall Street Journal*, January 24, 2024, https://www.wsj.com/articles/kim-jong-un-drops-the-mask -north-korea-nuclear-threat-biden-administration-war-a7357bae.

34. Clint Work, "Navigating South Korea's Plan For Preemption," *War on the Rocks*, June 9, 2023, https://warontherocks.com/2023/06/south-koreas-plan -for-preemption/; Seukhoon Paul Choi, "As World Order Shifts, So Does South Korean Security Policy," *Arms Control Today*, July/August 2023, https://www.armscontrol.org/act/2023-07/features/world-order-shifts-so -does-south-korean-security-policy; and Jessie Yeung and Gawon Bae,

"South Korea Showcases Missiles, Drones and Tanks in Rare Military Parade," CNN, September 26, 2023, https://www.cnn.com/2023/09/26/asia/south-korea-seoul-military-parade-intl-hnk/index.html.

35. Mari Yamaguchi, "Japan Signs Agreement to Purchase 400 Tomahawk Missiles as US Envoy Lauds Its Defense Buildup," Associated Press, January 18, 2024, https://apnews.com/article/japan-us-tomahawk-missile-defense-obcabfc4a87bf1a16beceec1b0c426fb; Mari Yamaguchi, "Japan Cabinet Oks Record Military Record Budget to Speed Up Strike Capability, Eases Lethal Arms Export Ban," Associated Press, December 22, 2023, https://apnews.com/article/japan-military-budget-us-china-missile-5e1e2c4089ob3ca8ea682c2dc91f9553#:~:text=The%207.95%20trillion%2Dyen%20(%24,the%20approval%20by%20the%20parliament; Takeo Akiba, "Ahead of State Visit, an 'Epic Shift' in Japan's Defense Posture," *Washington Post*, April 7, 2024, https://www.washingtonpost.com/opinions/2024/04/07/japan-kishida-china-ukraine-akiba/; and Brad Lendon, "Japan to Develop Long-Range Missiles as Tensions with China Rise," CNN, April 12, 2023, https://www.cnn.com/2023/04/12/asia/japan-hypersonic-missiles-intl-hnk-ml/index.html.

36. Choe Sang-Hun, "In a First, South Korea Declares Nuclear Weapons a Policy Option," *New York Times*, January 12, 2023, https://www.nytimes.com/2023/01/12/world/asia/south-korea-nuclear-weapons.html; and Kim Tong-hyung, "South Korean President Reiterates That Seoul Will Not Seek Its Own Nuclear Deterrent," *The Diplomat*, February 8, 2024, https://thediplomat.com/2024/02/south-korean-president-reiterates-that-seoul-will-not-seek-its-own-nuclear-deterrent/#:~:text=Security%20%7C%20East%20Asia-,South%20Korean%20President%20Reiterates%20That%20Seoul%20Will%20Not%20Seek%20Its,the%20country's%20trade%2Ddependent%20economy.

37. Tom O'Connor, "How Biden Could End the Korean War and Avoid a Nuclear Conflict," *Newsweek*, July 26, 2023, https://www.newsweek.com/how-biden-could-end-korean-war-avoid-nuclear-conflict-1814189.

38. Michael J. Zagurek Jr., "A Hypothetical Attack on Seoul and Tokyo: The Human Cost of War on the Korean Peninsula," *38 North*, October 4, 2017, https://www.38north.org/2017/10/mzagurek100417/.

39. Steven Mintz, "Teaching What Didn't Happen: How to Use Counterfactual Thinking Constructively," *Inside Higher Education*, October 17, 2022, http://www.insidehighered.com/blogs/higher-ed-gamma/teaching-what-didn't-happen.

40. Interview with former Blue House advisor, April 7, 2024.

41. Nike Ching, "VOA Interview: US Says North Korea Shipped 10,000 Containers of Munitions to Russia," Voice of America, March 18, 2024, https://www.voanews.com/a/voa-interview-us-says-nkorea-shipped-10-000-containers-of-munitions-to-russia/7533342.html.

Epilogue

1. Sheila Kim and Mithil Aggarwal, "Trump Calls North Korea a 'Nuclear Power,' Drawing a Rebuke from Seoul," NBC News, January 21, 2025, https://www.nbcnews.com/news/world/trump-calls-north-korea-nuclear -power-drawing-rebuke-seoul-rcna188490; "Donald Trump Says He Plans to Reach Out to North Korea's Kim Jong Un," Al Jazeera, January 24, 2025, https://www.aljazeera.com/news/2025/1/24/donald-trump-says-he-plans -to-reach-out-to-north-koreas-kim-jong-un; and Choe Sang-Hun, "Trump Hints at New Talks with Kim Jong Un. It Might Be Harder This Time," *New York Times*, https://www.nytimes.com/2025/01/24/world/asia/trump -north-korea-nuclear-talks.html.

2. "Marco Rubio Confirmation Hearing," Rev, January 15, 2025, https://www .rev.com/transcripts/marco-rubio-confirmation-hearing.

3. Yonhap, "Rubio Says He'll Explore Ways to Lower Risks of 'Inadvertent' Inter-Korean War," *Korea Times*, January 16, 2025, https://www.koreatimes .co.kr/www/nation/2025/03/103_390500.html.

4. Peter Nicholas, "'A Diplomatic Mess:' Trump's Special Envoys Set to Cause Diplomatic Confusion," NBC News, January 17, 2025, https://www .nbcnews.com/politics/donald-trump/trump-special-envoys-confusion -rcna186448.

5. Vipal Monga, Santiago Pérez, and Gavin Bade, "How Talks to Avert Tariffs on Mexico and Canada Fell Apart," *Wall Street Journal*, March 6, 2025, https://www.wsj.com/world/americas/trump-tariff-negotiations-canada -mexico-0933a272?st=mVYCen&reflink=desktopwebshare_permalink.

6. Yoonjung Seo, Larry Register, and Heather Chen, "North Korea Declares Itself a Nuclear Weapons State, in an 'Irreversible Move,'" CNN, September 9, 2022, https://www.cnn.com/2022/09/09/asia/north-korea-kim-nuclear -weapons-state-law-intl-hnk/index.html.

7. Jeffrey Lewis, "It's Time to Accept That North Korea Has Nuclear Weapons," *New York Times*, October 13, 2022, https://www.nytimes.com/2022/10 /13/opinion/international-world/north-korea-us-nuclear.html.

8. Bartosz Glowacki and Aaron Mehta, "A Nuclear Poland: Logistics, Political Challenges ahead of Potential Warsaw Deal," *Breaking Defense*, March 13, 2025, https://breakingdefense.com/2025/03/a-nuclear-poland-logistics -political-challenges-ahead-of-potential-warsaw-deal/.

9. Timothy W. Martin and Dasl Yoon, "South Korea's Acting President Is Betting on Keeping U.S. Ties Strong," *Wall Street Journal*, March 12, 2025, https://www.wsj.com/world/asia/south-koreas-acting-president-is-betting -on-keeping-u-s-ties-strong-55ae2faf.

10. "World's Largest Single Rare Earth Deposit Discovered, in North Korea," *AustralianMining*, December 6, 2013, https://www.australianmining.com.au /worlds-largest-single-rare-earth-deposit-discovered-in-north-korea/.

11. Gracalin Baskaran and Meredith Schwarz, "Breaking Down the U.S.-Ukraine Minerals Deal," *CSIS Critical Questions*, February 27, 2025, https://www.csis.org/analysis/breaking-down-us-ukraine-minerals-deal.

12. Martin and Yoon, "South Korea's Acting President."

13. Richard Sokolsky and Daniel R. DePetris, "Imagining a New U.S.-South Korean Security Architecture," *38North*, November 15, 2018, https://www.38north.org/2018/11/rsokolskyddepetris111518/.

14. Sokolsky and DePetris, "Imagining."

15. Farah Stockman, "Trump's Foreign Policy May be Crude, but It's Realist," *New York Times*, March 7, 2025, https://www.nytimes.com/2025/03/07/opinion/us-foreign-policy-realism.html.

Index

The letter p *following a page number denotes a photograph.*